Angels, Angels, Everywhere

Angels, Angels, Everywhere

G. Don Gilmore

The Pilgrim Press
New York

Biblical quotations, unless otherwise indicated, are from the *Revised
Standard Version of the Bible*, copyright 1946, 1952 and © 1971 by the
Division of Christian Education, National Council of Churches, and
are used by permission. Scripture references identified JB are from
The Jerusalem Bible, copyright © 1966 by Darton, Longman & Todd
Ltd. and Doubleday and Company, Inc., and are used by permission
of the publisher. Scripture references identified KJV are from the *King
James Version* of the Bible. Other permissions granted have been
acknowledged in Notes.

Library of Congress Cataloging in Publication Data

Gilmore, G. Don.
  Angels, angels, everywhere.

  1. Angels. I. Title.
BL477.G54   291.2'15   81-8525
ISBN 0-8298-0477-3   AACR2
ISBN 0-8298-0479-X (pbk.)

The Pilgrim Press, 132 West 31 Street, New York, New York 10001

In memory of
"Joyfully yours"
Robert Bruce Pierce

CONTENTS

PREFACE

One Sunday morning during an after-church coffee hour, a woman who had a penchant for asking difficult questions inquired, "What is the heavenly host?" To put it mildly, she caught me off stride. There I was between someone's description of a recent golf match and another's detailed account of a baby's projectile vomiting. "What was that?" I asked. Once again she repeated her question, "What is the heavenly host?"

The heavenly host had something to do with angels, I knew, but more than that I did not know. In fact, had the identical question been asked in the quiet of my study, I would have been no better prepared to answer. The heavenly host was something that I should have known about. I certainly had read about it often enough in the scriptures, sung of it in hymns, and come across it in various religious contexts. But what was it?

That is how my angel research began—just digging around trying to find out about angels in general and the heavenly host in particular. I became a frequent visitor in various university libraries, trying to come up with more information on angels and becoming increasingly frustrated by the limited amount of material available.

I had no difficulty finding a plethora of angel stories, or chronicles (as I call them). In fact, when the word got around about my angel research, I had no trouble assembling a considerable file entitled "Experiences with

Angels." Friends near and far were generous in their contributions to the collection. As the number of chronicles grew, however, it was like unearthing artifacts at an archaeological dig: Individually they were impressive, but what was the relationship of the pieces to one another? How did the pieces fit together? I was soon to learn that there are no living experts in this field.

In response to a friend's suggestion, I wrote to a number of prominent religious leaders representing various faiths around the world and asked them to send me their favorite story about angels and any background material they might have on the subject. A sampling of the return mail follows.

The editor of a leading Christian journal declared, "I have no interest in the subject."

The senior minister of one of the largest churches in America confessed, "For the life of me I cannot think of one angel story that I have ever heard, not counting the ones in the Bible."

A renowned scholar lamented, "I think the whole idea is Roman Catholic [x!*!@!]. I only wish there were angels; then they could be called on for work, etc. But I have never encountered anything like them in any of my travels."

A university professor who has a doctorate in Jewish mysticism replied that he had been working on an angel book for several years and had completed only twenty pages. He let me know in no uncertain terms that he wasn't about to give out free information to someone who had not paid research dues.

The gifted leader of a world healing organization wrote, "So sorry! I have no real stories to tell you about angels or clairvoyant experiences. I am always aware of the presence of angels. They throng our services and accompany us when we pray."

One of the most influential religious leaders of our time

wrote, "Your request for something on angels brought me up short. I suddenly realized that I have done nothing in this field! In the modern scientific age, we have shrunk our conceptual world to our perceptual experience and since angels do not sing for us over our hillsides, we find that they are not 'on our map.'"

Not all my mail was that unproductive. A few respondents had wonderful angel stories and information to share, but overall the response among the religious leaders was apologetically negative. The reason may have less to do with whether there are angels and more to do with the way angels are perceived. I believe that angels are forms, images, and expressions through which the essences and energy forces of God can be transmitted and that, since there are an infinite number of these forms, the greatest service anyone can pay the angelic host is never consciously to limit the ways angels might appear to us. With that in mind, consider "The Face at the Window," which follows.

The Face at the Window

ichard's background was checkered. For three years he had a baseball scholarship at the state university, but in his senior year it was canceled because he had become—to use his own words—"a rummy drunk who did not attend classes." Despite his continuing problem with alcohol, Richard was such a fantastic prospect for the big leagues that the St. Louis Cardinals maintained their interest until he dropped out of college. He finally joined the army, mostly out of a need to get away from everything, but the military experience only added to his problem. After a year of army life he was into drugs as well. His life was in chaos.

Then Richard met and fell in love with Lil. She was his exact opposite. Her values were totally different from his. Her interest in God and the spiritual life was something Richard found at first amusing, then irritating, particularly when shortly after they were married Lil began looking for a church to attend. Although Richard protested mightily, he reluctantly accompanied Lil to our church one Sunday morning. Two nights later I was in his living room talking baseball and God. He picked up fast on my lack of formality when it came to "spiritual" things. Soon we were talking naturally about the power of the Spirit. I've never seen anyone so hungry to know just how one goes about getting in touch with God.

When Richard began attending the sharing group at our church, he was always concerned that the discussion be on a practical basis. He wanted to apply to his daily activities what was being revealed of God's guidance in and through the group. The results were amazing.

3

One rainy afternoon a few months later, I was sitting in my study looking out at the woods behind our church when I saw a strange sight. Out of the tangled underbrush came a man, who walked toward the church with his head tilted slightly up, smiling, oblivious to the rain. Thunder rumbled, but he was unperturbed. As he neared my window, I saw that it was Richard, wringing wet in a business suit, but seemingly in another world. I yelled through the downpour, "Are you all right?" "Yes," he shouted back, "I've found God." Then he was gone.

My secretary, who had grown accustomed to seeing strange people coming and going from my study, referred to this one as "the crazy man who came out of the woods." Perhaps he was crazy, but his life was so full of discovery that it was a joy to talk with him—and I did so often.

I was once involved in a difficult counseling situation with a woman (I'll call her Mrs. James) who was having severe problems in her marriage. Her husband refused to get a job, insisting instead that she be the breadwinner, but when her paycheck did not cover all the household expenses, he ridiculed and physically abused her. She described Mr. James as a man possessed. After the electric company turned off the power, he had climbed up the utility pole and reinstated the electricity; when the telephone was removed, he tapped a neighbor's line to restore service; when the water was shut off, he found a way to turn it back on.

One day Mrs. James came to me in tears, saying that her husband was on a rampage and she was afraid he might kill her. "He has a rifle," she added, "and it's loaded." She had just lost her job. My first thought was to accompany her home and try to reason with Mr. James, but she was afraid that would only increase his anger, and he might shoot me. Then I thought of Richard, who was at the time in commission sales in our city, and I said to the woman that I wished a certain friend of mine was here to

4

pray with us. Looking toward the door of my study, I saw Richard standing there. He said, "Did you want something?" I was stunned. How did he know I had been thinking about him? Although to Richard and Mrs. James there was nothing unusual about his sudden arrival, to me it was an uncanny coincidence.

Although it is not my practice to break the confidentiality of counseling sessions, I felt strongly that it was important to brief Richard on Mrs. James's problems. Then the three of us tried to come up with a way to help Mr. James. The only thing we could see to do was confront the man, so we decided to accompany Mrs. James to her home and meet her husband face-to-face.

I was still hoping that the meeting could be avoided even as we approached the house. It was a warm, clear Saturday afternoon in April. The subdivision in which the house was located was humming with activity. People were working in their yards, preparing flower beds, breaking ground for vegetable planting. Several children were playing on the sidewalk and in the street. I carefully steered the car around the youngsters and into the James's driveway. As we sat there quietly for a few moments, I tried to gather my courage to face the ordeal and suggested that we ask God to bless our undertaking. I don't remember the words I used. In fact, I'm not sure that any words were spoken. It was mostly a listening-in prayer.

Then for some reason I opened my eyes and looked out through the windshield. There before me, peering through Richard's side of the window, was the face of a child, the most striking little girl I have ever seen. She had reddish hair, freckles, and a smile I still remember despite the passing of years. The longer I looked at her, the less the present circumstances seemed to matter. In fact, it was like getting a second wind in a race or taking a sip of ice-cold lemonade on a hot day. The beauty she radiated lifted my spirits. Then I noted also in her face a

5

look of extraordinary wisdom, as if she knew everything that was worth knowing.

I didn't want to take my eyes off this child. She was all there was to see. I completely forgot about the woman next to me and her violent husband. Nothing mattered except the baffling, all-knowing look from the young-old child face. I sat immobilized, probably not as long as it seemed, then turned to look at Richard. Apparently he had seen the child too, for when he turned toward me, for just an instant, his face was just like hers—confident and knowing, serene and compassionate.

Mrs. James was still sitting quietly, eyes closed, hands clasped tightly in her lap. It was time to interrupt her prayers. I put my hand on her arm and said with surprising ease, "Let's go in and see your husband."

The three of us entered the house and found Mr. James spread out in his easy chair, his rifle propped up next to him. He was the most threatening-looking person I've ever seen, and he spoke to us menacingly.

Somehow, almost miraculously, Richard and I were able to engage the man in some semblance of conversation. In fact, after we talked for a while he seemed to become more human. I could see that he had been taking out on his wife past hurts and frustration. It became apparent that he desperately needed a friend, someone who would just listen to him, who would not accuse him or threaten him or abandon him. We heard his life's story, including things that must have been bottled up for years.

As Mr. James came to the end of his story, Richard began to share his own life story and how he had discovered the power of the Spirit with some help from his church friends. Looking at Mr. James directly, he said, "Look, if a drunk like me, who felt the whole world was against him, could have been pulled out of the garbage heap, you can too! Would you let me pick you up tomorrow morning and take you to a sharing group at church?

6

Would you let me help you find a job? Could I come back some evening and watch a game on television with you?

As we left, Mr. James was actually smiling. He even accompanied us to the door. It all seemed so unreal to me. Things had fallen into place too quickly, too easily. Had there been an intervening force at work unbeknown to us?

As Richard and I pulled out of the driveway, I casually mentioned that little girl I had seen before we entered the house. I said, "You know, she was almost like a sign, or a blessing on what was going to happen." Richard said that the beauty of her face seemed almost unworldly. We looked at each other, and the same word came out of our mouths at the same time, "*Angel.*"

After that, our sentences began to run together. We jabbered like kids. "Do you suppose?" "Could it be?" "What if it really happened?" "I mean, to us." "I mean, here at this place." "Could we have seen one?" "It had all gone so smoothly." "We could have gotten blown away. Instead we were really able to communicate with this man and help him."

Had we encountered something more than a curious neighbor child with a fascinating face? We simply had to find out. We decided to canvass the entire neighborhood and try to locate the little red-haired girl with freckled face. But—much to our joy—no one had any recollection of a child fitting the description we gave.

I believe that what Richard and I saw that afternoon was an angel form. But the form had been assembled by our common creative imaging. Both of us had daughters about the same age as the child we saw. And there was an angel-conditioning process in our sharing group at church. We expected to be involved in angelic experiences. So the angel form was the vehicle for the energy, and that is what gave us the strength and courage to meet Mr. James.

7

Incidentally, within a week, Mr. James came to a men's sharing group at our church. Richard helped him find work, and he began to show up occasionally for worship services. The Jameses were also able to work out some of their marriage problems.

Some may have other theories about what we experienced, but for our part it was an angel presence. A college professor friend of mine—who is a nice guy and very orderly in his thinking—attempted to explain the angel-sighting in rational terms. He pointed out that if people cut themselves off from sensory input like the mystics did—go on a retreat, experience absolute silence, or stare at an object for a long period of time, focus on that and that alone—they may eventually see what they believe to be an angel or some other visionary presence. He explained, "When nurses leave the hospital after working a double shift and go into a chapel to pray, they are liable to think they are seeing angels, when actually they are experiencing an imbalance in their blood level from sleep deprivation. On other occasions people often see angels, or even Jesus, at the time they are dying, because of inadequate oxygen supply to the brain. Turn up the oxygen and the angel is gone."

I appreciate the professor's concern, and his theory is very interesting, but I was not in silence that afternoon, nor was I staring at a fixed object. I was not suffering from lack of sleep—in fact, I was wide awake—and there was an adequate supply of oxygen in the car. I can only deduce from the available data that the angel experience cannot be discounted by rational explanation. Something else happened that afternoon that requires a new assumption of truth.

I hated to tell my professor friend all this. His thesis was so plausible. I'm not sure that he'll ever understand. But I hope he will read this book and spend some time going through the angel chronicles in chapter 4.

2

The Nature of
Angel Forms

A high percentage of the mail received in response to my request for stories of experiences with angels contained the emphatic proclamation that angels are messengers. It was ironic to read claims of total ignorance on the subject of angels alongside this traditional, almost arbitrary, definition.

The word angel is derived from the Greek term *angelos*, which comes from the Hebrew expression *mal'akh*, usually translated as the concrete noun "messenger." But the traditional definition weakens under the weight of a scholarly examination of angel history. From the earliest times, angels were not considered single-purpose beings. The idea of an angel as a messenger suggests but one form, like the advertising image of the retail florist association: The Greek god Mercury, the messenger of the heavens, resplendent with wings on his hat and ankles, is dispatched to deliver a bouquet of flowers to someone as swiftly as possible. On the other end of the spectrum of angel definitions is that of the author of Hebrews: "The truth is they [angels] are all spirits . . . [Heb. 1:14, JB]."

Originally there were no stereotypes of angels. Angels were seen as performing a number of functions. They may have taken the form of messengers, but not all did the same thing. At this point let me define angels as those *forms, images, or expresssions through which the essences and energy forces of God can be transmitted.* More succinctly, an angel is a form through which a specific essence or energy force can be transmitted for a specific purpose. The image or form of an angel is a creation of

11

inspired imagination that is built up in group consciousness over the years by those who have visualized angels in a particular way. For example, from the earliest times Jewish, Christian, and Muslim angels (excluding archangels) were not relegated to a single category, like messengers; rather, they were described, among other things, as *choirs of singers, a military presence, members of a heavenly court, guardians, helpers, sustainers, protectors, and judges.* Today about the only angel category available is that of a winged cherub people refer to as a messenger.

As vivid as some of these angel images may have been centuries ago, the process of building up angel forms today has all but disappeared. It's not that the essence or energy force of what we call angels has ceased to exist, it's just that the multiple expressions through which the angels previously worked have diminished, due to a shortfall of energy supplies from those who no longer believe in, have faith in, or even think about them. But the angel essences or energy forces do exist, and desire to supply people with extra resources in their daily activities; what is lacking is people's willingness to re-vision their role in contemporary life. In other words, angel images need to be updated and multiplied.

Perhaps no one has done more research on the subject of angels than Gustav Davidson. In his *A Dictionary of Angels* he describes a memorable moment during his angel research.

At this stage of the quest I was literally bedeviled by angels. They stalked and leagured me by night and day. . . . I remember one occasion—it was winter and getting dark—returning from a neighbor's farm. I had cut across an unfamiliar field. Suddenly a nightmarish shape loomed up in front of me, barring my progress. After a paralyzing moment I managed to fight my way past the phantom. The next morning I could not be sure (no more than Jacob was, when he wrestled with his dark antagonist at Penniel) whether I had encountered a ghost, an angel, a demon, or God.

Without committing myself religiously, I could conceive of the possibility of there being, in dimensions and worlds other than our own, powers and intelligences outside our present apprehension, and in this sense angels are not to be ruled out as a part of reality—always remember that we create what we believe. Indeed, I am prepared to say if enough of us believe in angels, the angels exist.[1]

Such is the testimony of one who has probably given more attention to this field of inquiry than anyone in recent times. Davidson's book is a solid collection of personal enthusiasm focused on the reconstruction of damaged forms. It is in every way a labor of love. Unfortunately, he was alone in most of his labors. His colleagues were few. To the contemporary mind, his work was mostly a curiosity, and certainly not a reality.

Those in previous generations who were the builders of the angel forms may well be today the enthusiasts for Unidentified Flying Objects. UFOs and attendant phenomena have unquestionably galvanized the imaging energies of people all over the world, much as angels did several hundred years ago. Biologist-writer and UFO expert Ivan Sanderson suggested that UFOs come not from another planet but from another set of dimensions—another whole universe! That, Sanderson concluded, is why we have not been able to catch one.[2] So when the UFO forms travel into our space operating according to another set of laws, people see them differently, but the imaging power of the beholder always determines what is seen.

The building up of angel image forms takes time and

patience and extra effort. Concentration is the labor of perception. Elizabeth Barrett Browning put it well:

> Earth's crammed with heaven
> And every common bush afire with God
> But only he who sees takes off his shoes ...
> The rest sit around and pluck blackberries.

It goes without saying that blackberry-pickers outnumber those who would be observers of the angels.

Angel forms have not become extinct. Each Christmas they are superficial appendages to all the activities of the season. There is nothing more pathetic than the flippant way angels are treated during Yuletide. It appears to be a commercial conspiracy to denigrate angels to the form of silvery pasteboard effigies crammed into the background of a window display in a downtown department store. Little wonder that trolls and fairies have superseded the angels in the public mind. I'm afraid that if there were no Christmas carols the nativity angels and their mission would be forgotten.

Even the last bastion of angel cultivation, the Roman Catholic Church, which for centuries advocated all-out devotion to the angels, seems to have lost enthusiasm for angels. A Roman Catholic friend told me that as a child she felt surrounded by the presence of the angels, because of the influence of the church, but that "It is not so today—certainly not with my kids. Perhaps when the statues were removed from our church and the curtain of mystery was drawn aside, the angels went too."

Angel forms dramatize the fact that we are not alone, that we are surrounded by a loving concern. The book of Hebrews describes it as "so great a cloud of witnesses [Heb. 12:1]." The author may not have been referring to angels, but the analogy seems appropriate. From creative consciousness, the All-in-All, God the Creator, has come pouring out a vibratory force of love and concern that can be personified in angel forms without taking anything away from the direct relationship people enjoy with God.

Let me share a recent angel experience. One cloudy Saturday afternoon I stretched out on our sun deck and drifted into that twilight zone between sleep and being awake. Gradually I felt a warmth on my face and down across my body. It was as though something was gently holding me, soothing me. With eyes still closed, I saw an angel form hovering nearby, projecting renewing energy into my tired body. My angel was a joyous presence whose touch was like the balm of Gilead. I would never have demeaned my celestial guest by envisioning it clothed in the customary angel apparel. The angel in my theater was a unique presence, not a traditional image; my visitor was warm like the summer wind blowing in from the heights of a love that knows me better than I know myself. When I opened my eyes at last, I saw the logical explanation for my angel phenomenon. The sun had come out from behind the clouds. One may rightly argue that angel experience is more than being warmed on a sun deck, and I would agree. But people no longer need to depend on angel forms that have no relevance in their lives. We can be what the French call "the realiz- ers," who pick and choose from the traditional or create new angel forms to channel the essences and energy forces of God.

This was certainly the way of Jesus. At the time of his arrest on the Mount of Olives, he turned to one compan- ion who had just drawn a sword, chopped off a servant's ear, and was ready to take on anyone who would harm Jesus. "Do you think," said Jesus, "that I cannot appeal to my Father, and he will at once send me more than twelve legions of angels [Matt. 26:53]?" Thus Jesus deliberately

15

created a unique form with which to identify the unseen resources. It may indeed have been an individual expression, but he called it like he saw it.

No matter how objective or legalistic people try to be on the subject of angels, in the last analysis angel forms exist in the eyes of the beholder. This does not mean that the components of God's love—those essences and energy forces—are simply products of the imagination. In fact, people have nothing to do with their creation or their activity. But the forms, those images through which the Spirit flows, must be constructed by people in their minds. It is a matter of what they see (or visualize) is what they get (in expression).

There is enormous subjectivity when it comes to angel experiences. A friend warned me, "Be careful about those crazy poets with their extravagant words. Beware of people like John Milton and his angel ecstasy—carrying on about 'that glorious force, that light ineffable, that fair beaming blaze of majesty.' The man is beside himself." Those words came from a man who likes everything precooked, preplanned and nailed down. He leaves no room for the spontaneous, the unrehearsed, or serendipity. He is like one of those people who attended a conference where the popular Indian medicine man Rolling Thunder was to speak. They came early with notebooks, tape recorders, and cameras and got good seats up front. When Rolling Thunder arrived, he asked that the chairs be pushed back and that the would-be audience make a circle. Then, instead of giving the customary lecture, he announced, "I'm going to teach you to dance." The teaching was the dance in which all participated and made their own unique discoveries. He closed with the words "All things are manifestations of your belief system. If you let go of your fixed realities, your limitations, your fears, your doubts, magic can enter your life."

That day Rolling Thunder was helping create a myth.

The dance was a story that involved everyone present. It was a metaphor addressed to times in which we live. It was a symbol of what the growing life should be. When Rolling Thunder chose the dance over the lecture, his myth-making was no less appropriate to the situation. The genius of the myth-makers of history has been that they choose the forms of expression consistent with their own inner leading. Those who say that myths are illusionary or irrational do not understand what myth really is. Myths are the products of creative imagination, which the dictionary defines as "the power to represent the real more fully and truly than it appears to the senses and in its ideal and universal character."[3]

Angel forms are the result of myth-building; they provide a story, metaphor, or symbol through which the essences and energy forces of God may be expressed. According to William Irwin Thompson, myth in this sense is "an imaginative description of reality in which the known is related to the unknown through a system of correspondences."[4]

Primitive peoples mythologized what they observed in the processes of nature. That is how the legends of angelic activities associated with the moon, sun, stars, and weather came about. The stories may have been fanciful, but in order for people to live with the inexorable processes, personalizing of the phenomenon was necessary. And this ancient method of humanizing the elements (e.g., angel of the sun, angel of the moon, angel of the winds) helped them become aware that there was something out there like the beneficial care of God in nature.

Author A. Clutton-Brock told of being in the Maritime Alps one June and discovering a spring in the shade of a sweet chestnut tree on the southern slope of a mountain.

Then I knew suddenly how southern people had come by their myth of the water-nymph. Standing myself in the

17

blazing sunlight, I almost saw a water-nymph among the waters of that shade. Water nymphs had always seemed to me frigid, unreal fancies; but now the spring, in its shadowed beauty and contrast with the parched heat of the mountain side, became alive, became almost a person. It was not the legend of the water-nymph that brought her to my mind, it was the life and beauty of the stream that almost brought her to my eyes. The stream seemed so clearly to be occupied with a lovely, friendly business of its own that I almost saw a lovely friendly creature doing it.[5]

Although Clutton-Brock denies it, the legend of the water nymph probably influenced him, at least subconsciously. That legend, added to the beauty of the scene activated by certain energy forces flowing through his water-nymph image, produced an exciting moment that might later have been saluted as no more than a pleasant sensual experience, a picturesque setting or just a nice trout stream to recall.

In the stories of people's encounters with angels, the experience is always colored by the personality of the beholder, and that is as it should be. The personal dimension has everything to do with the angel shapes. In fact, one's own myth-making and development of a variety of personal angel forms will make possible a connection with a wide range of spiritual energies needed in life. So the more angel imagings one can create and experience, the better.

One noon hour I sat with a surgeon friend at the Seattle-Tacoma airport, watching an incredible display of auric light and color blending into a focused configuration over Mount Rainier. My friend is very scientifically oriented, so he was attempting at first to place what we were seeing into some generic classification or category. But nothing fit. There we sat, watching the bewildering, intoxicating happening, not knowing what it was but exhilarated by what was going on out there. It did indeed draw us out of our routine selves and make that day, as he put it, "glittering and glistening with possibility." Much later, I began to realize that what we had been watching was what some experts on the subject call the aura of a mountain angel. Whatever name you give it, for our part it lifted us quite angel-like while we waited for our flight.

It is unfortunate that today angel-less religion is more often the rule than the exception. People caught up in a world of mechanical processes and boring routine feel empty and lonely. They are at the mercy of impersonal forces that by their very nature separate human beings from a recognition of who and what they are and, even more important, all that they have going for them. Religion ought to be a vehicle for freeing people today from their emptiness and loneliness, but the erosion of interest in angels, which is a by-product of denying the higher dimensions of imagination, delivers people into a state of incompleteness. Loren Eiseley described this condition as the losing struggle between "Yam, the old sea dragon of the original Biblical darkness, and, arrayed against him, some wisp of dancing light."[6]

Not many people would prefer the darkness to an angel-like "wisp of dancing light," but there is little question that the wisps have been dismissed and people have elected to muddle through on their own. Yet we are haunted by an urge as deep as life itself, an urge that has driven our species from prehistoric times. We are at heart searchers for the transcendent who actually refuse to believe in or employ the agents of the transcendent, those angel-like "wisps of dancing light."

Christians might want to inform me in no uncertain terms that Jesus has filled all their emptiness, loneliness, and incompleteness in life. But note that even Jesus was not without spiritual allies: a personal company of angels. Following his experience with the tempter, the Greek text reads: "Then the devil left him, and, look! angels came and began to minister to him [Matt. 4:11]." This particular angel form appears to come from the Greek *diakoneo*, which has to do with "minister." This special sort of angelic ministry combines comfort, refreshment, sympathetic sharing, and just being there. And in the Garden of Gethsemane, Jesus was again supplied with another form of angel activity. Following his agonizing prayer that he be delivered from death, "there appeared to him an angel from heaven, strengthening him [Luke 22:43]." Here we have the image of an angel steadying Jesus' nerves and helping restore his depleted energy reserves.

Other angel images in Jesus' life include his "twelve legions of angels," which were apparently constantly vigilant with swords drawn ready for battle. At Jesus' birth a heavenly host was heard singing over shepherds' fields: "Glory to God in the highest, and on earth peace among men with whom he is pleased [Luke 2:14]!" Angels also played a significant role in Jesus' resurrection drama. They appeared to the women who had come to visit the tomb on that first Easter, saying, "Do not be amazed; you seek Jesus of Nazareth, who was crucified. He has risen, he is not here; see the place where they laid him [Mark 16:6]."

What rings out from all these angel experiences is the incredible affirmation that angels await us in even the most unlikely places. There is a diversity of angel forms to be celebrated, and there is an element of surprise to be realized, but unless people revive their childlike wonder and imagination, they may never experience such things. The educational system tends to put the lid on the creativity and imaginativeness that we as children possess naturally. But the great educator John Dewey said, "Every great advance in science has issued from a new audacity of imagination."

Most creative people understand that because the universe extends far beyond the power of their senses, it is through the use of their imaginations that they can perceive the realities of the unseen and draw them into expression. Thomas Edison complained that once he had been able to work peacefully and productively in his laboratory in Menlo Park, New Jersey, but that after he became famous he found it difficult to make new discoveries. Professors from nearby Princeton University kept dropping by and warning him that he couldn't do this or he couldn't do that, that what he was doing was against this law or that. All this nagging negativism inhibited the great inventor to the point that he stopped trying to come up with something new. He turned off the channels of his creative imagination, which was the source of his inspiration and productivity.

J.B. Priestley worried about the way Christianity has attempted from early times to become legitimate in the eyes of the secular world by clinging to the premise of "stubborn fact." He lamented the effort of some church people who, lacking creative imagination, had attempted to make the miracles and marvels of the faith conform to a historical precedent rather than allow them to remain mysterious truths set in mythful forms. Alluding to a point made by Carl Jung, he wrote, "A culture first shaped and colored by Christianity has reached us perilously lacking in the fructifying mythic element which thousands of generations ... found necessary for their imaginative lives. We are still myth-making, but in a negative inferior way."[7] It may not be that bad, but it is at least a legitimate concern of those who wish to see a revival of angel interest and a resurgence of creating contemporary angel forms. Angel images should be given the same sort of marvelously innovative expression that artists have given the image of Jesus in recent times. Jesus' face has been painted to reveal dozens of expressions with which people can identify and use to connect with his spirit. Why can't the same thing be done with the angels?

In some quarters, angel myth-making in art is catching on. A most creative piece of angel art appeared in an advertisement in an unlikely place. Not in a theological journal or a church newsletter or a devotional guide, but in the magazine *Runner's World!*[8] The advertisement read: "The Isaiah 40:31 Poster—Catch the Vision." The year was 712 B.C., when the prophet Isaiah caught the vision inspired by God. It revealed the promise for the ultimate restoration of humankind. Now, centuries later, the vision takes on new life as it is reported in the award-winning painting by artist Daniel Moore. The painting shows a man running along a tree-lined road at early dawn. The blue sky overhead is filled with fleecy clouds that give him the appearance of being borne off the ground by angel wings.

3

The Origin
and Development
of Angel Forms

The First Angels

Three thousand years before Christ the countries of Assyria and Babylonia not only shared boundaries on the Tigris and Euphrates rivers, they were both of Semitic ancestry. Most scholars maintain that the Semites were an aggressive, tenacious, adaptive people with a flare for genius. Their earliest power struggle, however, was with a race known as the Sumerians, who lived in ancient Babylonia. In marked contrast to the intensely combative Semites, the Sumerians were placid, stay-at-home types, certainly no military match for the Semites, although they did put up a gallant struggle. Eventually the Sumerians were overwhelmed by the Semites, but their contribution to the latter was extremely significant. While the Semites were obviously the greater warriors, the Sumerians had the more influential and enduring religion, which the Semites adopted. In fact, the fusion of the Semite and Sumerian races produced the phenomenon of the Semite warrior genius spreading the religious ideas of the Sumerians through their military conquests.

Perhaps the most appropriate symbol of the Sumerian religion was the flowering plant. For the Sumerians, everything had life in it and was composed of energy, motion, and force. They believed that each person had a built-in energy source, a zi, that survived after death. The Sumerians had an elaborate system of gods and ghosts, some of whom were adopted as Semite gods. One historian has written:

Some spirits of the old order became the servants and messengers of the gods charged with errands between the divinities themselves or between god and [humankind]. Here, as far as I can make out at least, is the earliest form of that belief in angels which has had so telling an influence upon religion, poetry, and arts and satisfied so instinctive a need of the devout.[1]

In their military adventures, the Semites would not only make off with the spoils of conquest, but also lay claim to the gods of their enemies, whom they reduced to the role of servants to their gods. As Atkins points out, there were "profound distinctions of character and office" among these servant or messenger spirits, which suggest ranks or divisions as we have in most angel groupings. In addition, the Semite-Sumerian-Babylonians believed that some of their attendant spirits were involved in combat with spirits of demonic character.[2] This may be the earliest reference to warfare between the hosts of good and evil, and it predates expression of similar combat found in the Zoroastrian, Jewish, Christian, and Muslim faiths.

Before the Semites prevailed against the Sumerians in Babylonia, the old Sumerian capital city of the same region was Ur, from which the Hebrew patriarch Abraham emerged. Archaeologists working near Ur have excavated some fascinating artifacts having to do with Sumerian religion. One engraved stone found at Ur shows a winged figure descending from heaven to pour the water of life from an overflowing jar into a cup held by the king. Some scholars believe this to be the earliest representation of an angel.[3]

Most authorities agree that the divinities of the Semites (some, as we have seen, borrowed from the Sumerians) were initially personifications of the great forces of nature—the sun, moon, stars, sky, storms, water. But nowhere is this personification of deity more intimately perceived than in the home of a typical Sumerian family. Each home had a secondary god, who was believed to mediate between the family and the higher forces and to be able to take the form of a human being. This idea is identical to the primitive Jewish idea of spiritual essence becoming incarnate in human form. In the early Old Testament record, the "angel of the Lord," a symbol for God, was known to take a human appearance, as was the case when the three angels lunched with Abraham under the oaks at Mamre (see Gen. 18). And the idea of God and/or the angel of the Lord incarnating when least expected is not lost in the New Testament. In the book of Hebrews there is an admonition to neighborliness with an incredible twist: "Do not neglect to show hospitality to strangers, for thereby some have entertained angels unawares [Heb. 13:2]." Little wonder that early Christians were alive with excitement. Not only were they anticipating the return of Jesus, but they never knew but what an angel essence might emerge through the exercise of common hospitality.

The angel forms of Babylonia eventually were painted on temple walls and palace entryways as great winged creatures whose essence was either attending in worship or providing protection. Atkins suggests that these winged images later evolved into the forms of cherubim and seraphim, who are spoken of as being constantly in attendance on the Most High and cover their faces with wings and sing, "Holy, holy, holy is the Lord of hosts; the whole earth is full of his glory [Isa. 6:3]." Atkins concludes, "In the last period of mature Chaldean speculation, they [the early angel forms] became aspects—or perhaps, incarnations—of creative power, the successive thoughts of the creator realizing themselves in the successive acts of creation."[4] This is what is meant by the assertion that the essences and energy forces of God's creative power seek forms through which they can make their presence known. It is worth emphasizing that angel forms are universal presences and *not* the exclusive property of any religious group. Angels are to be found among the Zoroastrians, the Jews, the Christians, and the Muslims, and like presences can be discerned in other religions as well, but the origins go back to a much earlier time.

At this point I want to trace the development of angel forms as they have emerged in representative religious groupings. The order of presentation is historically sequential and shows trends and modifications in terms of growth and refinement.

The Egyptian Angels

The Semites (with the Sumerian addition), who contributed so much to the religious thinking in various lands, are to be found in Egypt as well. But something else at work in Egypt rivaled the influence of the Semitic religion. From prehistoric times Egypt had been collecting divinities by the hundreds. According to Egyptologist E.A. Wallis Budge, "the predynastic and prehistoric dwellers of Egypt believed that the earth, and the underworld, and the air, and the sky were peopled with countless beings, visible and invisible, which were held to be friendly or unfriendly to man according as to the operations of nature, which they were supposed to direct, were favorable or unfavorable to him."[5]

The most important religious book of the Egyptians was the Book of the Dead, which identifies by name five hundred gods and goddesses. Later, Egyptian theologians would catalog twelve hundred such deities, which included various spirits and local gods as well. Among the swarms of beneficial spirits was a group known as the Hunmamit, who were thought to aid humanity by "watching over the safety of the sun."[6] The Hunmamit appear to be the Egyptian version of angel beings. The Hunmamit were described by some as effluences, or rays of the sun, that could be compared with angel choirs, like the cherubim of Oriental angelology.

In dealing with all these beings, the most important instrument the Egyptians had was magic. In fact, in Egypt, religion and magic were virtually the same thing. Magic (which includes the use of amulets, talismans, magic name formulas, and words of power) was employed to overcome the power of the demons and accelerate the work of the friendly spirits. This ritualizing process drew out of their group obscurities most of the would-be angels or demons, which in due course were given names to match their activities.

The Zoroastrian Angels

One branch of the Aryan migration—those light-skinned long-haired warriors and shepherds from Europe—entered the ancient Persian area at least as early as 2500 B.C. The religion of these people, although difficult to trace, was unquestionably nature worship with emphasis on the influence of the sun and stars. Around 660 B.C., there emerged from this blurred and sketchy Persian background a man who, after making contact with specific angel forms, had revealed to him the one true god, Ahura Mazda, and who was subsequently empowered to transform the religious history of his people. But this man's teachings were destined to reach far beyond that of his own people. His influence would profoundly affect the religious thinking of the three major religious groups—the Hebrews, the Christians, and the Muslims.

Tradition credits this man, Zoroaster (or Zarathustra, his name in the sacred books), as having authored a sort of bible or priest's book known as the Avesta, a book containing a collection of twenty-one nasks (volumes) covering a variety of topics such as religion, philosophy, ethics, meditation, and science. The nasks are divided into three major groups known as the gathas (devotional hymns), the hadha mansarik (general commentary), and the datik (pertaining to the law).

When he was twenty years old, Zoroaster left his family (father, mother, and wife) and wandered off across the Persian countryside on a spiritual pilgrimage to help the oppressed, whose sufferings caused him great anguish, but even more to seek liberation from the barren religious practices and ideas of his ancestors. The pilgrimage eventually took him into a mountain wilderness, where he lived for seven years in self-imposed silence.

At the age of thirty, Zoroaster had a vision that totally changed his life. A figure nine times larger than a human being appeared to him, which he later identified as the archangel Vohu Manah (Good Thought). Apparently this angel form had such a purifying and inspiring effect on Zoroaster that he was able to step out of his physical body and enter the presence of God, whom he named Ahura Mazda, or Wise Lord. Incidentally, Ahura Mazda is also referred to as the Lord of Light and is visualized as presiding over a court of attending angels who reflect his radiance.

Ahura Mazda then instructed Zoroaster in certain doctrines and duties of the true religion and dispatched him as a prophet. Over the next eight years Zoroaster was met by each of the six principal archangels, who gave him further teaching to help him in his mission. The archangels are known as Amesha Spentas (Immortal Holy Ones), and they are both male and female. They include Vohu Manah (Good Thought), the guardian of cattle; Asha (Right), the guardian of fire; Khshathra (Dominion), the guardian of metals; Armaiti (Piety), the female guardian of soil; Haurvatat (Prosperity), the female guardian of waters; and Ameretat (Immortality), the female guardian of vegetation.[7]

The archangels are not beings separate from Ahura Mazda but projections of his good thought, his righteousness, his dominion, his piety, his prosperity, and his immortality. Again, these expressions include male and female polarity. John Noss has concluded that the archangels are "gifts of Ahura Mazda to man and also forces and facts in their own right."[8] Indeed, the archangel forms do personalize the forces and facts, making them more than just abstractions.

Next in rank to the Amesha Spentas (the archangels) are the Yazatas (Adorable Ones), which are the Zoroastrian angels. According to a celebrated high priest of the Parsis, "they are numbered by the hundreds and by the thousands, by the tens of thousands and by hundreds of thousands, nay even more,"[9] but only forty are mentioned in the Avesta. Once again, Ahura Mazda is not separated from his angels, for "Ahura Mazda himself is a Yazata, even as he is an Amesha Spenta."[10] The angels are said to preside over both spiritual and material phenomena, and as with the archangels, there are both males and females. Celestial Yazatas are personified in such terms as divine wisdom, rectitude, victory, felicity, charity, peace, spells, health, riches, and cattle. Material Yazatas have to do with light, wind, fire, water, earth, and so on.[11] So the Zoroastrians were aware that God was involved in all their activities by means of a particular virtue or phenomenon personified by an angel form.

Besides the archangels and angels, there is a third form of Zoroastrian angels known as the Fravashis, which most scholars insist are an adaptation from Greek influence. The Fravashis are guardian spirits that accompany each person throughout his or her lifetime and act as conscience, guide, and protector, assisting one to live a moral life and protecting that person from evil. The Fravashi is one's truest and best friend and is described in the Avesta as a strong and watchful warrior who wears armor and carries weapons.[12] The strength, swiftness, and healing power of these angels are said to be without equal.

There is evidence, however, that in some instances Zoroaster was not above taking an old nature god and converting it to an angel form to reveal more fully the infinite variety of Ahura Mazda's being. Actually, he was simply building on what was available in order to communicate more effectively the many splendored Lord of Light he had experienced, and there is really nothing new about this kind of accommodation in the history of most religions.

After a dismal beginning in the attempt to spread his new faith, legend has it that Zoroaster was able to prove the truth of his teaching by curing a horse belonging to King Vishtaspa (king of Persia). Whatever the reason, when the king was converted he became a patron to Zoroaster. In fact, Zoroastrian teachings soon became the religion of the realm; the king was squarely behind it, not to mention his sword.

Much of the theology of Zoroaster is colored by his experience with King Vishtaspa and the palace court. In fact, Ahura Mazda bears a marked resemblance to a large-scale Persian king. He is pictured as the transcendental sovereign of the universe with a court of advisers, messengers, officials, and intermediaries, all far removed from the vicissitudes of human existence and evil.

But evil is certainly not ignored in the Zoroastrian metaphysics. While Ahura Mazda (or Ormazd, as he is sometimes called) is all-powerful, he is not without an adversary. The teachings of Zoroaster do not allow for a god who created both good and evil; therefore the creation of evil was independent from the creation of Ahura Mazda. Ahriman (Lord of Darkness) is of primeval origin and is perpetually antagonistic to Ahura Mazda. The Zoroastrian dualism is profound. Darkness is darkness; Light is light. One is always opposed to the other. These opposites of goodness and evil contend not symbolically but in actuality.

In this struggle the Lord of Darkness with his army of demons and evil spirits is pitted against Ahura Mazda and his galaxy of archangels and angels. Zoroastrians take this battle seriously. The warfare is focused on the personal problems that assail the human family, sometimes bringing unexplainable grief and suffering, setbacks and afflictions.

But the end of the contest between good and evil is never in doubt. Eventually Ahriman (Lord of Darkness) will bow his knee to Ahura Mazda. The reason for this eventual capitulation is that while Ahriman may be co-equal with Ahura Mazda, he is not coeternal. He will eventually be defeated and forced to retreat into everlasting nothingness.

The angel forms of the Zoroastrians were an integral part of their lives. These forms were built up over a long period of time and were an ever-present reality in the world of the Persian people. Everyone who came in contact with them was profoundly influenced.

The Jewish Angels

The earliest attitudes of the Jews to angel forms is best described by the psalmist who in visualizing the power of

God wrote, " ... Who makest the winds thy messengers, fire and flame thy ministers [Ps. 104:4]." Along with the Babylonians, Egyptians, Persians, Greeks, and others, the ancient Jews believed that God's spirit took form in such natural phenomena as sun, moon, stars, rain, snow, lightning, wind, thunder, cold, heat, dark, and light. The verse just cited indicates that the wind could be a messenger (angel) and the fire could be a minister (angel). To be sure, the angel concept matured as the religious perceptions of the Jews evolved, but in the beginning, even for the Jews, the angels were probably revisions of nature spirits.

The Preexilic Angels

The first angel forms of Jewish history should be designated as preexilic, that is, of a time prior to an exile of some fifty-nine years. This exile, or captivity, began in 597 B.C., when a large contingent of Jewish people were removed from their Palestinian homes and marched off to Babylonia following King Nebuchadnezzar's conquest of Judah. In 538 B.C., however, Cyrus of Persia conquered the Babylonians and began releasing Jews to return to Jerusalem and rebuild their temple.

Angels appear first in Jewish history in the cherubim identified in Genesis, and their chief function is to guard—not, it is worth noting, to be little cupid messengers. The scripture reads, "He drove out the man; and at the end of the garden of Eden he placed the cherubim, and a flaming sword which turned every way, to guard the way to the tree of life [Gen. 3:24]." Concerning the cherubim, George Barton classifies them as nature-spirits, pointing out, "There is reason to believe that these beings were personified winds. They find a counterpart in the winged figures of the Assyrian sculptures which are often pictured in the (windlike) act of fertilizing the sacred palm tree."[13] And in the book of Psalms there is the statement "[God] rode on a cherub, and flew [Ps. 18:10]." So an angel form has been built up to personify a force—in this case, the wind.

Another preexilic angel form was the seraphim, which is mentioned in scripture only once, in Isaiah 6:2-6. (Note, however, that the Hebrew word *saraph*, which is almost "seraphim," is translated in the book of Numbers as "fiery serpent" [Num. 21:8]). According to Isaiah's account, seraphim have six wings and guard the throne of God. It was a seraphim that brought a burning coal from the altar fire and touched the mouth of Isaiah at the time of that prophet's extraordinary experience of Jerusalem. According to Gustav Davidson, they "unceasingly intone the Trisagion (holy, holy, holy)." Seraphim are regarded as angels of love, light, and fire. They are compared to the battling fiery sun god Horus of ancient Egypt; both are winged, both protect, and both are associated with fire.

The other significant angel form of preexilic times is the "angel of the Lord" or the "angel of God." Barton argues persuasively that the angel of the Lord is not an angel at all, according to the usual definition of the term, but is in fact Yahweh (God) who is dealing directly with creation in human form.

Genesis 32 tells of Jacob wrestling with an angel, but the angel is called "a man." In Exodus 3 the angel of the Lord appears to Moses in "a flame of fire out of the midst of a bush," but then we read, "God [humanlike] called to him out of the bush." In Joshua 5 a man appears before Joshua with drawn sword and reveals that he is commander of the army of the Lord and has come to help. Naturally, Joshua worships him as God. And in Judges 6 the godlike angel of the Lord appears to Gideon and is seen under the oak at Ophrah like a man. Once more, in

Judges 13 the wife of Manoah had a visit from the angel of the Lord, whom she described as "a man of God" who had the "countenance of the angel of God."

The idea of God, or more accurately an essence activity of God, taking the shape of a human being to do a particular angel work should not be all that startling. In fact, if the book of Genesis is correct in its declaration that "God created man in his own image, in the image of God he created him; male and female he created them [Gen. 1:27]," it would appear that humankind has been prepared from the beginning to be perfect forms through which the essences and energy forces of God could be transmitted. There is no form more ideal for that purpose than the human form, and considering the diversity possible, the idea is all the more exciting.

Maimonides, the great Jewish scholar of the twelfth century A.D., called attention to the tradition of the Jews in this regard, noting that some prophets saw angels in human form, for example, in Genesis 18:2, "[Abraham] lifted up his eyes and [saw] three men . . . in front of him." Maimonides added, "In Bereshit Rabba (Chapter 1) the following remark occurs: 'To Abraham whose prophetic power was great, the angels appeared in the form of men; to Lot, whose power was weak, they appeared as angels.'" He concludes, "Consider how clearly they say that the term angel signifies nothing but a certain action, and that every appearance of an angel is part of a prophetic vision, depending on the capacity of the person that perceives."[14] Maimonides would probably agree that *imaginative* capacity would be an even better way to put it, for he also said, "Man's imagination faculty is also called angel." When one examines the root of the word imagination, one comes back to *image* again, a form through which the essences and energy forces of God can be made manifest.

To speak of angels as human beings and yet at the same time spirits can be seen as a contradiction. But angels are essences, energy forces—all spirit. They do not come with physical bodies, but they can take on forms that have been built up or established consciously or that are a legacy in the subconscious.

Other angels of preexilic times appear in a variety of forms, each of which is special. The theory that a force acts in only one way is expressed in Bereshit Rabba (chap. 1): "One angel does not perform two things, and two angels do not perform one thing; this is exactly the property of all forces."

The Postexilic Angels

When the Jews went home to Jerusalem after their release by Cyrus of Persia, they did not return with the same mind-set they left with. Their religion had always been the center of their lives, but it had undergone great changes resulting from close association with the teachings of Zoroaster during the Exile. Profound changes in the way the Jews regarded angels can be observed in the canonical Old Testament, the accepted, authoritative scriptures of the Jews.

Another set of Jewish scriptural writings affected by Zoroastrianism is referred to as "apocalyptic," meaning to uncover or disclose. The purpose of these writings was to provide faithful Jews with spiritual reinforcement so they could endure the catastrophic historical events that had been and no doubt would be forthcoming.

The basic theme of the apocalyptic writings is that the present age of trial and struggle would soon come to a decisive close and that the archfiend and all the demons would wage a last-ditch stand against the forces of good. A final battle would result in the literal end of the world, consuming the world in fire so as to purify it from its previous evils. Only the righteous would be saved. One can understand why such literature came into existence. The Jews had experienced all kinds of cultural and religious shocks in the wake of their military defeats, the destruction of the holy temple (the most important symbol of their faith), captivity in a foreign land, exposure to the transforming power of Babylonian-Persian religion, the slow process of rebuilding the temple, the hostility of their neighbors, and so on. Little wonder that the Persian idea of a showdown between the forces of light and the forces of darkness seemed to them an appropriately dramatic vindication.

The apocalyptic writings are resplendent in lush angelologies that describe angel warfare against evil beings. The origin of this way of thinking is pure Zoroastrianism. The twelve-thousand-year dualistic struggle between the forces of Ahriman (Lord of Darkness) and Ahura Mazda was simply taken out of a Persian setting and put in a Hebrew one. It would be unfair to suggest that the apocalyptic material became an essential part of orthodox Jewish theology. In a sense, it was a kind of "pop" religion to many rabbis. While certain (mostly Persian) ideas about angels, demons, the resurrection, the future life, the cosmic setting as a triple-decker universe, and the relationship of God to the world were to some extent read back into the Jewish scriptures, there is reason to believe that most of the rabbinic writers ignored the apocalyptic literature. But this literature still affected the religious thinking of the people, whatever the rabbis may have thought of it.

While Jewish leaders were cool toward the apocalyptic message, the early leaders of Christianity embraced it. In fact, Jesus was seen as the supernatural "son of man" mentioned in the apocalyptic section of the Old Testament book of Daniel. In the Babylonian-Persian setting, Daniel prophesied,

And as I looked, the beast was slain, and its body destroyed and given over to be burned with fire. As for the rest of the beasts, their dominion was taken away ... and behold, with the clouds [probably angels] of heaven there came one like a son of man.... And to him was given dominion and glory and kingdom, that all peoples, nations, and languages should serve him; his dominion is an everlasting dominion, which shall not pass away [Dan. 7:11-14].

For early Christians living through persecution that tested their faith in an ultimate sense, the figure of the "son of man" coming on the clouds (angels) to take eternal dominion over the burning and evil earth was just what they needed to help them get through the trying times.

The best-known apocalyptic writings are found in the Old Testament book of Daniel and the New Testament book of Revelation. Other lesser-known books, sometimes called pseudepigrapha (because their authorship is uncertain), include: Ethiopian Enoch and Slavonian Enoch, Syriac Baruch IV, Ezra, Apocalypse of Peter, Ascension of Isaiah. There are also semi-apocalypses such as Assumption of Moses, the Book of Jubilees, and the Shepherd of Hermes. Most of these books are the testimony of visionaries that was received by special revelation through angel forms.

Other noncanonical Old Testament writings considered by some to be scripture are found in the Apocrypha (which means hidden or secret). These books, so rich in angel lore, are found in the Greek (Septuagint) Bible and in the Latin Vulgate. They are: 1 Esdras, 2 Esdras, Tobit, Ezra, Additions to Esther, Wisdom of Solomon, Ecclesiasticus or Wisdom of Jesus the Son of Sirach, Baruch (with the Letter of Jeremiah), Song of the Three Children, Susanna, Bel and the Dragon, Prayer of Manasseh, 1 Maccabees, and 2 Maccabees.

It might be helpful now to trace the major Jewish angel forms found in the postexilic canonical scriptures, the apocalyptic writings, and the Apocrypha with an eye to the Zoroastrian influences.

The Military Ranks of the Postexilic Jewish Angels

The book of Daniel is well known for its apocalyptic message. There the nations of the world are each watched over by an archangel or prince, and this strongly suggests that the angels are divided into militarylike ranks. There are the princes of Persia (Daniel 10:13), Greece (Daniel 10:20), and Israel, who happens to be Michael (Daniel 10:21). Daniel is the first canonical book to give the name of an archangel. Not only is Michael mentioned, but the archangel Gabriel is also given top billing (Daniel 8:16), and all in military orchestration. This is similar to the Zoroastrian organization of soldierlike angels of light who will contend against their counterparts of darkness.

The books of Enoch are resplendent with angel stories. The patriarch Enoch lived 365 years and "walked with God" (Genesis 5), and the two books of Enoch record his journeys across the earth and through the seven heavens. He became an initiate to all the mysteries of earth and heaven and he describes these initiations. The first book of Enoch was of composite authorship and written in Aramaic between the third and first centuries B.C., the second was no doubt composed in Egypt during the first fifty years A.D.

Enoch's angels are very militarylike, and they are numbered and ranked in great detail: "In the year 500, in the seventh month, on the fourteenth day of the month ... I saw how a mightily quaking made the heaven of heavens to quake, and the host of the Most High, and the angels, a thousand thousands and ten thousand times ten thousand ... [Enoch 60:1]."[15] On another occasion, he speaks of the angels as numbering "thousands and ten thousands of angels without number [Enoch 71:13]."[16] The angels are grouped and ranked in various orders with certain duties under the archangels:

> And these are the names of the holy angels who watch. Uriel, one of the holy angels, who is over the world and over Tartarus. Raphael, one of the holy angels, who is over the spirits of men. Raguel, one of the holy angels who takes vengeance on the world of the luminaries. Michael, one of the holy angels, to wit, he that is set over the spirits, who sin in the spirit. Gabriel, one of the holy angels, who is over Paradise and the serpents and the Cherubim. Remiel, one of the holy angels, whom God set over those who rise [Enoch 20:1-8].[17]

This ranking is characteristic of the Zoroastrian idea that the angel forces have specific responsibilities, like soldiers in an army.

In 2 Baruch the central figure is the historical companion of Jeremiah (see Jeremiah 36:4-32). There's no question that Baruch believes the hosts of angels are gathered for military purposes. He visualizes them as divided into the ranks of an army: "And all the armies of the angels, who (are now held fast by My word, lest they should appear, and) are held fast by a command, that they may stand in their places til their advent comes [2 Bar. 51:11-12]."[18] This sounds much like the psalmist's description of a category of angels engaged in warfare against the forces of darkness: "He let loose on them his fierce anger, wrath, indignation, and distress, a company of destroying angels [Ps. 78:49]." In Baruch, however, all the angels are organized for spiritual warfare.

Another apocalyptic writing, the Testament of Levi, reads: "And in the second (speaking of the heavens) are the hosts of the armies which are ordained for the day of judgment, to work vengeance on the spirits of deceit and of Beliar [Test. Levi 3:3]."[19]

The Jewish Angels and Satan

During the Babylonian exile the Jews discovered the adversary role of Satan and Satan's demons. Prior to the writing of the book of Job (an exile writing), Satan had been a bit player in the cosmic drama. The term devil does not even appear in the Old Testament; devils occurs four times. Outside the book of Job, Satan is mentioned five times; in the book of Job, Satan is mentioned fourteen times. It seems that, prior to the Babylonian exile, evil was explained as something personally induced. Jeremiah says that people are evil because "they did not obey or incline their ear, but walked in their own counsels and the stubbornness of their evil hearts, and went backward and not forward [Jer. 7:24]."

Thus, during and after the exposure to Persian religion, the Jews had a scapegoat to explain why they had undergone so much suffering both individually and as a nation. Before that time the only explanation was that they had brought it on themselves. The book of Job identifies the true architect of evil as the external force Satan (literally, adversary). Indeed, Job sees Satan as sharing a place in God's organization, because the "adversary" must answer to God as a member of the council of angels. This approach is unlike the Zoroastrian idea that the Lord of Darkness is totally opposite to or separate from God.

The Angel of Instruction

The instructing angel form is prominent in the book of Tobit, which was composed by an Egyptian Jew named

Tobias around 200 B.C. and adapted and circulated among the early Christians. The story has to do with the archangel Raphael helping Tobias to overcome certain problems in marrying a girl named Sarah. At first Tobias is understandably fearful about marrying this girl, because seven other husbands had been chosen for the young woman and all had subsequently died in her bridal chamber, victims of a jealous demon. Tobias laments:

> Now I am the only man my father has, and I am afraid that if I go in I will die as those before me did, for a demon is in love with her, and he harms no one except those who approach her. So now I fear that I may die and bring the lives of my father and mother to the grave in sorrow on my account. And they have no other son to bury them.

But the instructing angel says to him:

> Do you not remember the words with which your father commanded you to take a wife from among your own people? Now listen to me, brother, for she will become your wife; and do not worry about the demon, for this very night she will be given to you in marriage. When you enter the bridal chamber, you shall take live ashes of incense and lay upon them some of the heart and liver of the fish so as to make a smoke. Then the demon will smell it and flee away, and will never again return. And when you approach her, rise up, both of you, and cry out to the merciful God, and he will save you and have mercy on you. Do not be afraid, for she was destined for you from eternity [Tob. 6:14–17].

End of instruction.

Another semipopular work that uses the name of the biblical character Ezra is the second book of Esdras, where the author is instructed about future events by an angel who seems to be the pure essence of God in the form of an angel:

> The angel who had been sent to me on the former nights was sent to me again, and he said to me, "Rise, Ezra, and listen to the words that I have come to speak to you.... Therefore, Ezra, empty things are for the empty, and full things are for the full. For behold, the time will come, when the signs which I have foretold to you will come to pass, that the city which now is not seen shall appear, and the land which now is hidden shall be disclosed. And every one who has been delivered from the evils that I have foretold shall see my wonders" [2 Esd. 7:1-2, 25-27].

Precedent for the instructing angel is explicitly stated in the book of Jubilees: "For in his days the angels of the Lord descended on the earth, those who are named the watchers, that they should instruct the children of men [Book of Jubilees 4:15]."[20]

Angels as Intercessors

Another angel form in postexilic times was that of intercessor between humans and God. The fatherly, close-at-hand image of God of preexilic times had become a Persianlike potentate removed to a celestial palace on high; therefore an intercessor was needed. Whereas angels had often been imaged as messengers from God to human beings, now they were seen as taking messages to God.

> And the second voice I heard blessing the Elect One and the elect ones who hang upon the Lord of Spirits. And the third voice I heard pray and intercede for those who dwell on the earth and supplicate in the name of the Lord of Spirits [Enoch 40:4-6].[21]

In those days the holy ones who dwell above in the heavens shall unite with one voice and supplicate and pray and praise [Enoch 47:2].[22]

In (the heavens next to) it are the archangels who minister and make propitiation to the Lord for all the sins of ignorance of the righteous [Test. Levi 3:5].[23]

The Fallen Angels

In the two books of Enoch the fallen angels are prominently displayed, and an attempt is made to get at their origin. The book of Genesis states that "the sons of God [angels] came in to the daughters of men, and they bore children to them [Gen. 6:4]." George Barton has written: "Persian dualism had sufficiently influenced their [the Jews'] thoughts, so that matter was to them corrupt" and "That angels should come to the earth and have connection with human wives implied, they thought, a previous rebellion and sin on the part of the angels."[24] Enoch supplies a list of these fallen angels as well as a graphic picture of their punishment, which reads like another page from the Zoroastrian text.

And I asked the angel of peace who went with me, saying: "For whom are these chains being prepared?" And he said unto me: "These are being prepared for the hosts of Azazel [who is one of the chiefs of the two hundred fallen angels] so that they may take them and cast them into the abyss of complete condemnation, and they shall cover their jaws with rough stones as the Lord of Spirits commanded. And Michael, and Gabriel, and Raphael, and Phanuel shall take hold of them on that great day, and cast them on that day into the burning furnace, that the Lord of Spirits may take vengeance" [Enoch 54:4-6].[25]

In the Testaments of the Twelve Patriarchs there is another approach to the demons. The evil spirits are just personifications of "the evil propensities of [human-kind]—jealousy, lust, pride, chicanery, injustice, rapacity, etc." Each of these attributes was given the name of a demon.

In sum, during and after the Babylonian exile the angelology of the Jews was greatly modified as a result of Zoroastrian influence. Yahweh had become a wholly transcendent being, and the angel forms were related to God as go-betweens of various types. Gradually the angel forms also became personified, with names to match the essences and energy forces they channeled. And angels became more numerous; in fact, they were eventually counted in ranks and divisions, suggesting a military hierarchy. Finally there was a rebellion among the angels, and many were said to have fallen. According to the Jews, the fallen angels became demons against which the righteous must forever contend.

The Christian Angels

There is little question that the angel forms adopted from the Zoroastrians by the Jews are on the whole much like those found in Christianity.

The Heavenly Hosts

The first encounter with Christian angel forms is with that of a host or an army. When the angels appeared to the shepherds and proclaimed the birth of Jesus they came as a "host," which suggests a military presence: "And suddenly there was with the angel a multitude of the heavenly host praising God and saying, 'Glory to God in the highest, and on earth peace among men with whom he is pleased [Luke 2:13-14]!'" And in the Garden of Gethsemane, Jesus acknowledged that it was within his power to command several detachments of angels—as many as "twelve legions of angels" (Matthew 26:53).

This idea of an angel militia corresponds to the record in the postexilic canonical books of Job and Daniel and to sections of Psalms—all of which speak of the host of angels as an army: "He makes peace in his high heaven. Is there any number to his armies? [Job 25:2-3]" or "a company of destroying angels [Ps. 78:49]." Daniel in one of his visions speaks of a horn growing great "even to the host of heaven (Daniel 8:10)."

In the postexilic noncanonical book of Enoch, the writer has a fantastic vision of angel hosts. As he hears God summoning the hosts of heaven, for judgment (Enoch 61:10), he speaks of being in the company of those hosts rather than in companionship with sinners (Enoch 104:7), which sounds very disciplined and military-like. These imaginative forms developed in Persia. In one of the Zoroastrian Avesta writings, the Fravashi (the guardian angel forms) are described as "good, strong, beneficent"; they are well-armed, comprise many battalions, are dressed in "garments of light," and will "kill thousands of demons."[26]

A Court and Council of Angel Forces

The New Testament contains the image form of angels comprising a heavenly court surrounding the throne of God. A similar scene is depicted by the Jewish exile and postexilic writers. In the book of Revelation, which comes

47

closest to reading like a noncanonical apocalyptic or apocryphal book, there is a faithful reflection of the Zoroastrian "heavenly mansions": "Then I looked, and I heard around the throne and the living creatures and the elders the voice of many angels, numbering myriads of myriads and thousands of thousands [Rev. 5:11]." The description continues, "Salvation belongs to our God who sits upon the throne, and to the Lamb! And all the angels stood round the throne . . . [Rev. 7:10-11]."

The postexilic canonical books likewise report a council of angels in the heavens. In the book of Job, there is reference to the "sons of God" (a synonym for a gathering of angels): "Now there was a day when the sons of God came to present themselves before the Lord . . . [Job 1:6]." The same is repeated in Job 2:1. The psalmist reports on a similar angel conclave: "Let the heavens praise thy wonders, O Lord, thy faithfulness in the assembly of the holy ones! . . . Who among the heavenly beings is like the Lord, a God feared in the council of the holy ones [Ps. 89:5-7]." The noncanonical book of Enoch describes the council:

> And there I saw another vision, the dwelling-places of the Holy, And resting-places of the righteous. Here mine eyes saw their dwellings with His righteous angels, And their resting-places with the holy. And they petitioned and interceded and prayed for the children of men, And righteousness flowed before them as water. [Enoch 39:4-5][27]

The idea of God holding a council has precedent in Zoroastrianism. In the gathas and some of the yasts, there are frequent references to Ahura Mazda conferring, holding assemblies, and negotiating with his heavenly subordinates. At one point Ahura Mazda asks Zoroaster to tell others how much the Fravashis have helped him. Ahura Mazda is not above working out deals with his archangels and angels for reciprocal help. He openly asks for help. It is interesting that Ahura Mazda rallies support through solicitation rather than by decree.

Ranks of Angel Forms

The angel forms of Christians were eventually divided into seven ranks. The book of Revelation mentions "the seven spirits who are before [God's] throne [Rev. 1:4]." The seven spirits are mentioned again and identified as angels: "Then I saw the seven angels who stand before God [Rev. 8:2]." These forms are obviously archangels. The idea of seven archangels is grounded first in the Zoroastrian angelology, then in the postexilic Jewish idea expressed in Enoch. Remember, Enoch listed six as: Uriel, Raphael, Raguel, Michael, Gabriel, Remiel (Enoch 20:1-8).

Around the year 500 A.D., Dionysius the Areopagite, who many believe was converted by Paul in Athens (Acts 17:34), was the first to delineate an order of angels. He listed seven, plus the two closest to God. This list included the seraphim (purifying and enlightened powers), cherubim (power of knowing), thrones (simplicity from purification), dominions (aspiring to true lordship), authorities or virtues (powerful assimilations of the will of God), powers (orderly authorities), principalities (princely powers), archangels and angels (beings of light who reveal the divine mysteries).[28]

Once more we see the roots of these angel forms in substrata of Zoroastrianism. Under the influence of the astrological and astronomical framework of the seven known planets, the early Zoroastrians identified seven archangels or Amesha Spentas: Spenta Mainyu (Holy Spirit), Vohu Manah (Good Thought), Asha (Right), Armaiti (Piety), Khshathra (Dominion), Haurvatat (Prosperity),

49

and Ameretat (Immortality). Each represents a particular form to channel a spiritual essence or energy force.

Guardian Angel Forms

Guardian angel forms are recognized in the New Testament. With the help of an angel, Peter was released from the jail in Jerusalem. He returned to the home of Mary the mother of John, where many of the church had gathered for prayer on his behalf. When he appeared at the door, no one believed it could possibly be Peter. Rather, they said, "It is his angel [Acts 12:15]," which no doubt refers to his guardian angel.

In Matthew, Jesus explains to his disciples that the "little ones" (meaning children) are forever protected because "in heaven their angels always behold the face of my Father [Matt. 18:10]." "Little ones" or "children" could mean a person's spiritual nature, and heaven could be a dimension of enlightenment. Nevertheless, the angel seems to personify guardianship.

Among the earliest Christian writings, known as the collection of the apostolic fathers, none was more revered than that of Hermas. This Roman Christian claimed that he received his messages from Christ, who came to him in the guise of a shepherd. Concerning guardian angels, he wrote:

> Hear now in regard to faith. There are two angels with a man—one of righteousness, and the other of iniquity. . . . The angel of righteousness is gentle and modest, meek and peaceful. When, therefore, he ascends into your heart, forthwith he talks to you of righteousness, purity, chastity, contentment, and of every righteous deed and glorious virtue. . . . Trust him, then, and his works, "Look now at the works of the angel of iniquity. First he is wrath-

ful and bitter, and foolish, and his works are evil and ruin the servants of God."[29]

This writing is early, and it is provocative. Hermas did not get his ideas about angels from any of the other New Testament writers. His concept of a personal guardian angel and a personal angel of wickedness profoundly influenced Christian thought for many years to come. Two of the best-known and most acclaimed church fathers, Origen and Clement, eventually adopted Hermas' theory on personal angels with slight modification. Origen seemed fully persuaded that there is a guardian angel and an evil angel.[30] Clement of Alexandria seems somewhat less enthusiastic, granting that angels are distributed over the nations and cities and that some may be assigned to individuals.[31]

Seeking the roots of guardian angel forms, one finds in Psalms "For he will give his angels charge of you to guard you in all your ways [Ps. 91:11]." In the postexilic book Tobit, which is said to have influenced the church's thinking about guardian angels more than any other, there is the angel that accompanied Tobias (guardianlike) on his journey to the house of Sarah (Tob. 5ff.). Another postexilic writing, the Books of Adam and Eve, has a specific reference to two angels that are obviously guardians: "God the Lord gave us two angels to guard us [Adam and Eve 33:1–2]."[32] The suggestion of angel forms traveling in pairs seems to reflect an idea in the old Ras Shamra texts of Canaanite times (ca. 1350 B.C.) discovered along the coast of northern Sumeria in A.D. 1729. In that record there is an allusion to divine messengers traveling in pairs which was based on the ancient practice of dispatching two couriers, in case one should meet with an accident.[33]

The guardian angel to which the Jewish and Christian writers both refer once more seems to have its origin in Zoroastrianism. The guardian spirit known as the Fravashi seems to be the prototype for the idea of a guardian angel. Gustav Davidson reassured me that the Fravashis are really angel forms when he wrote, "Fravashi—in Zoroastrianism, the celestial prototypes of all creative beings, the guardian angels of the believers."[34]

The idea behind the Zoroastrian Fravashi is that the spirit is an essence or energy force that cares for the faithful, putting the wind to the back of those who struggle and filling them with the breath of victory, power, and healing. Zoroastrians believe that all people are accompanied by a Fravashi throughout their lifetime. These guardian angels represent the perfecting essence in a person. The role of the Fravashi is not unlike that of the etheric double, or *Ka*, of ancient Egypt. When a person dies, the guardian angel, or Fravashi, moves back to the celestial realm.

The Fravashis are great helpers, but when they are neglected the angel of good can become an angel of evil; they can become dreadful when offended or vexed.

The Wings of Angel Forms

Angels of the New Testament are said to have the power of flight, which implies the use of wings. In the book of Revelation, John declares, "Then I saw another angel flying in midheaven, with an eternal gospel to proclaim ... [Rev. 14:6]." In the Gospel of John, Jesus says, "Truly, truly, I say to you, you will see heaven opened, and the angels of God ascending and descending upon the Son of man [John 1:51]." The Gospel of Luke says, "In the sixth month the angel Gabriel was sent from God to a city of Galilee named Nazareth [Luke 1:26]." In Daniel 9:21, Gabriel is said to have come "in swift flight." One source says the literal Hebrew meaning of those words is "in winged flight."[35] Another documentation of angels with wings comes from Ezekiel. The vision described in Ezekiel 1 mentions wings a number of times. A ninth-century carved ivory cherub fits as Ezekiel's description. The angel's human face is crowned with a contemporary hairstyle. The head is set on the body of a Babylonian-style lion that has wings stretching upward from the back.[36] The postexilic book of Enoch refers to the flying angels: "And I saw in those days how long cords were given to the angels, and they took to themselves wings and flew [Enoch 61:1]."[37]

When it comes to winged angel forms, Zoroastrian roots can again be found. In the yasts, the Fravashis are pictured as "well-winged birds or the well-shot arrow as it flies."[38]

The Radiance of Angel Forms

It was said of the angel who appeared to the women at Jesus' tomb on Easter Day, "His appearance was like lightning, and his raiment white as snow [Matt. 28:3]." The radiance of the nativity angels was described by Luke: "An angel of the Lord appeared to them, and the glory of the Lord shone around them [Luke 2:9]." In the book of Revelation, John reports: "After this I saw another angel coming down from heaven, having great authority; and the earth was made bright with his splendor . . . [Rev. 18:1]."

The precedent for radiant angel forms is found in the Jewish sources. Ezekiel testified, "In the midst of the living creatures there was something that looked like burning coals of fire, like torches moving to and fro among the living creatures; and the fire was bright, and out of the fire went forth lightning [Ezek. 1:13]." And Daniel describes a shining angel: "His body was like beryl, his face like the appearance of lightning, his eyes like flaming torches, his arms and legs like the gleam of burnished bronze [Dan. 10:6]." The Zoroastrians also saw the angels clothed in radiance. Repeatedly the angels of the elements are praised for their beauty and spoken of as white, shining beautiful, and powerful, with garments of light.

Angel Choirs

Another popular Christian angel form is that of a choir singing praises around the heavenly throne of God, for example, the nativity angels serenaded the shepherds near Bethlehem: "And suddenly there was with the angel a multitude of the heavenly host praising God and saying, 'Glory to God in the highest . . .' [Luke 2:13]." In the book of Revelation we read: "Day and night they never cease to sing [before the throne], 'Holy, holy, holy, is the Lord God Almighty, who was and is and is to come' [Rev. 4:8]!"

The New Testament choirs are replicas of previous Jewish angel choirs in which the seraphim sing to one another: "Holy, holy, holy is the Lord of hosts; the whole earth is full of his glory [Isa. 6:3]." The author of the book of Enoch elaborated: "Those who sleep not [meaning the angels] bless Thee: they stand before Thy glory and bless, praise, and extol, saying: 'Holy, holy, holy, is the Lord of Spirits: He filleth the earth with spirits' [Enoch 39:12]."[39]

And once more Zoroastrian roots are found where angel choirs also sing in heavenly places. Heaven is referred to as a "home of song" where the angels continually sing praises which is an offering to Ahura.

The Angels of Judgment

In the New Testament, Jesus speaks plainly concerning angels that make judgment: "And I tell you, every one who acknowledges me before men, the Son of man also will acknowledge before the angels of God; but he who denies me before men will be denied before the angels of God [Luke 12:8-9]." Angels making judgment are also found in the book of Enoch: "I swear unto you, that in heaven the angels remember you for good before the glory of the Great One: and your names are written before the glory of the Great One. Be hopeful; for aforetime ye were put to shame through ill and affliction: but now ye shall shine as the light of heaven [Enoch 104:1-3]."[40]

In the Zoroastrian Vistap Yast there is a similar angel form, that of a judging angel who inquires about the life led by someone who has just died. The angel is very specific about the deceased's state of consciousness upon leaving the decaying world.

The Distinctive Angel Forms of the Early Church

The case for the similarities among the Zoroastrian, Jewish, and Christian angel forms has been building. So far, it would appear that the Zoroastrian angel forms influenced all the other forms. But the New Testament is not without its own contribution concerning angels. While Jesus acknowledged the importance of angel forms, he never suggests that angels should be asked for favors or that they should be worshiped—which is certainly the case in Zoroastrianism and to a degree in Judaism. In addition, Jesus seems to ignore the orders of angels, saying that God knows people's needs (Matt. 6:32) and instructing us, "Pray to your Father who is in secret [Matt. 6:6]." In other words, Jesus seems to advocate going straight to the source, which may be a reaction to excessive reliance on angels. Perhaps he wanted to curb the embellishments and extravagant ideas about angels. If people begin celebrating the forms and worshiping the image, then they are forgetting what is behind it all in the first place.

Many Christians believe that angels are not necessary when there are Jesus, the Holy Spirit, the law and the prophets. Paul believed in angels because he knew the power of their forms, but he was troubled by the excessive hold that these forms had on people, to the exclusion of their devotion to Jesus. To overcome this, he devised a chain of command so that no angel form would be outside the authority of Jesus and asserted, "All things were created through him [Jesus] and for him [Col. 1:16]." Paul then says, "Do not be taken in by people who like groveling to angels and worshiping them; people like that are always going on about some vision they had, inflating themselves to a false importance with their worldly outlook [Col. 2:18, JB]." Paul does not deny the fact that there are angel forms, he just wants to be clear about who is commander in chief of the angels. And Paul warns that nothing should come between the Christian and God, not even angels: "For I am sure that neither death, nor life, nor *angels*, nor principalities, nor things present, nor things to come, nor powers, nor height, nor depth, nor anything else in all creation, will be able to separate us from the love of God in Christ Jesus our Lord [Rom. 8:38–39]." Paul also said, "Do you not know that we are to judge angels? [1 Cor. 6:3]." In this way he shows his concern about the effect interest in, devotion to, and worship of angels would have on a person's relationship with God in Christ. Because there was to be no competition in that area, a Christian's relationship with the angel forms was to be very much under discipline.

Despite Paul's warnings, the early church did become preoccupied with angels. Nearly all the church fathers wrote about their belief in and devotion to the angels: Clement of Rome, Hermas, Justin, Athenagoras, Irenaeus, Clement of Alexandria, Origen, Gregory of Nyssa, Tertullian, Ambrose, Jerome, Augustine. But many of these writings seem to be not so much a spontaneous explanation of what is believed as a response to the challenge of some other belief or set of beliefs about angels. The very faith-belief structure of the early church was being severely tested by a movement within the church known as gnosticism, which many leaders in the church referred to as a heresy.

Gnostic ("those who know") was a label applied to many sects in the church which held a set of theological ideas that emphasized the role of angels. One Gnostic belief as it applied to angels was the practice of magical evocation. This magic was not a sleight of hand but rather the exercise of calling on the great angel forms of the cosmos in terms of their peculiar responsibilities. The Gnostics believed that God created the universe through a series of emanations or revelations of diverse divine attributes. Each sphere or stage of revelation was given a name, a distinctive energy, and an angel form that could be called on for help. Attached to this was an elaborate ritualistic system. The origin of evocation to the various angel powers representing the spheres was most likely Babylonia. In those days the Sumerian priests surveying the movement of certain stars representing the spheres or levels of power began to correlate and predict events in their lives in association with the movement of the planets.[41]

The most influential pre-Christian group of Gnostics were the Jewish Essenes, one of the three major religious orders of the Jews. They could be referred to as the survivors, or more accurately the would-be survivors, for they had survived the Babylonian captivity and even the conquest of the Greeks under Alexander the Great. Following Alexander's death, the Essenes survived the struggle of power among the generals.

The Essenes numbered about four thousand and lived

in towns and villages throughout the Palestinian area. They were determined that Judaism survive any conquest or military occupation. To that end, many of them retreated to a desolate desert encampment now known as Qumran near the Dead Sea. There they lived under holy rule and guarded the written scriptures of their faith. One of their disciplines was "to communicate their doctrine to no one in any other manner than that in which he had received them himself . . . and then he would equally perceive the books belonging to the sect and the names of the angels."[42]

The Essenes' emphasis on knowing the names of the angels was derived from the Zoroastrians and was a radical departure from the traditional view held by most Jews or Jewish orders at that time. In orthodox Judaism only two angel names were known—Michael and Gabriel—but among the Essenes there were many angel names, and the reason has to do with the system of evocation to the planetary spheres. It is likely that the Essenes used angels' names for magical purposes as shown by the fact that they were celebrated as healers and as exorcists of demons.[43] And at that time, if a person knew the name of a spiritual being such knowledge was said to give a magical power over that spirit.[44] We can assume that the Essenes used angel names to activate the spirit activity in the cosmos that would affect events on earth. The Gnostics of the early Christian church were considerably influenced by these Essene practices, and that in turn made an impact on the beginnings of Christianity.

Immediately following Jesus' death and resurrection, little heed was paid to the ideas of the various Gnostic sects. Jesus' followers were too caught up in their expectation of a second coming to be concerned about angel speculation. But toward the end of the first century, when Jesus did not return in power, the Christian church lacked a sense of direction. It had become a polyglot of religious traditions, including everyone from the gentiles whose religious background was primarily of the mystery religions to those whose immediate grandparents had been taught by Jesus.

By the second and third centuries, as the Christian faith emptied out into the non-Jewish world, people of Gnostic persuasion were becoming Christians. Gnostics such as Marcion, Saturninus, Theodotus, Valentinus, and Manes joined the church. Unquestionably these Gnostic Christians made a substantial contribution to the spread of the faith, particularly in the gentile lands where the religious mysteries abounded. The expression "mysteries" has to do with certain rites for initiation into secret knowledge. Francis Legge writes: "There seems to be doubt that the earlier Gnostics [Christian Gnostics] continued to attend the mysteries of the Chthonian deities in Greece and of their Oriental analogues Osiris, Attis, Adanes, and the likes elsewhere, while professing to place upon what they saw a Christian interpretation."[45]

Had there not been a Gnostic-Christian interpretive bridge, it would have been nearly impossible to win the gentile world to the Christian church. The early church was both challenged and profoundly influenced by the Gnostic sects. For example, the Christian sacraments of baptism and communion carry Gnostic symbols. Baptism was once a simple Jewish-Christian rite, but after the Gnostic addition it became an elaborate series of initiations. The communion service was at one time no more than a love feast, but after the Gnostic input it became a service invested with magic and mystery.

Magic was in the air when the Gnostics gathered for Christian worship, and in the midst of the magic was angel worship and devotion. Angels were thought to attend these worship services, and evoking angels for special favors was a common practice. A cherished bit of ritual from the contemporary communion service is a reminder of the Gnostic presence in Christianity: "Therefore with angels and archangels, and with all the company of heaven, we laud and magnify thy glorious Name; evermore praising thee and saying: Holy, holy, holy, Lord God of hosts. . . ."[46]

Eventually the Gnostic presence all but disappeared, through the efforts of the holy Roman emperor Constantine the Great. As much as anything else, the Gnostics simply joined the Catholic church, which took them in and learned from them. Perhaps this is why the Roman Catholic Church has been the center of angel interest and speculation down through the centuries. Some of the most inspiring words on the Catholic approach to angels were written by Anscar Vonier: Yet it would probably not have pleased the *i*-dotting, *t*-crossing master theologian of the Roman Catholic Church—the venerable angel doctor himself, Thomas Aquinas. Vonier wrote:

> As we are now, in our mortal state, we cannot think in purely spiritual elements, we must have the aid of our fantasy, and the richest imagination will be the one to conjure the most gratifying visions of heavenly messengers. But we ought to know that the reality is very different, incomparably different indeed, and immensely more beautiful; we ought not to feel sad if we are told that our vision of angels, if we have such, do not represent the heavenly visitant in his native existence but that he appears to us in the borrowed garb of imaginative impressions.[47]

Magnificent in its challenge, this statement urges the use of imagination when thinking about the angels. This is not to say, however, that the angel form is less valid because it is a product of an imaginative spirit. Rather, the idea of angel speculation is put in its proper perspective. People are invited to speculate on, to envision, to dream about angels as they choose, but they are at best imaging inadequately, compared to all the essence waves and energy forces available to them.

Despite all this open-endedness on the subject of angels, the Roman Catholic church did begin to organize several theorems concerning angelic existence:

(1) Angels have a beginning, but they cannot perish; they remain everlastingly the same; (2) Angels are not subject to the laws of time, but have a duration measure of their own; (3) Angels are completely superior to space, so that they could never be subject to its laws; (4) Angelic power on the material world is exerted directly through the will; (5) Angel life has two faculties only—intellect and will; (6) In the spirit of nature, an angel cannot err, either in intellect or will; (7) An angel never goes back on a decision once taken; (8) The angelic mind starts with fullness of knowledge, and it is not, like the human mind, subject to gradual development; (9) An angel may directly influence another created intellect, but it cannot act directly on another created will; (10) Angels have free will; they are capable of love and hatred; (11) Angels know material things and individual things; (12) Angels do not know the future; they do not know the secret thoughts of other rational creatures; they do not know the mysteries of grace, unless such things be revealed freely, either by God or by the other rational creatures.[48]

Angel Forms of Later Church History

Following the Protestant Reformation, the emerging antipapists, while paying lip service to angels, contributed little to the development and propagation of angel forms. While Thomas Aquinas and other Roman Catholic theologians may have been obsessed with nailing down every aspect of angel life, so as to pull the rug out from under the impious speculators, among the Protestants there was no interest in constructing abstract angel theories. For instance, Martin Luther regarded Dionysius' angel speculation in his Celestial Hierarchy to be a "hodge podge" over which the superstitious have "cudgeled their brains."[49] I can find Luther becoming a bit speculative about angels in only one instance: "The angels are very close to us and protect us and other creatures of God at his command. To be able to protect us they have long arms, and so they can easily chase Satan away when he tries to harm us."[50] "Long arms" seems to be Luther's slip toward speculation.

Although Protestants did acknowledge angels, they minimized their role, which had been so greatly celebrated and venerated among Roman Catholics. As a result, Protestant angels are low-profile, loosely defined entities. John Calvin, a leading sixteenth-century Protestant leader, was typical of Protestants when he put the angels in their place:

> If we would be duly wise, we must leave those empty speculations which idle men have taught apart from God's Word concerning the nature, orders, and numbers of angels.[51]

> How preposterous, then, it is for us to be led away from God by the angels, who have been established to testify that his help is all the closer to us! But they do lead us away unless they lead us by the hand straight to him, that we may look upon him, call upon him, and proclaim him as our soul keeper.[52]

Protestant theology deemphasizes angels for fear of detracting from belief in God. But the time of the Enlightenment reinforced the Protestant inclination to give angels a low profile. At the time of the Protestant Reformation, early in the sixteenth century, primitive religious concepts were being challenged not by those who were outside the Christian faith but by scientists and philosophers, most of whom were Christians. Developments in scientific theory and method increased knowledge about the world in which we live, to the disadvantage of old theories such as angels holding the universe together and functioning as powers of the sun, moon, stars, and weather.

A Polish cathedral canon and physician named Copernicus (1473-1543) declared that the earth was not the center of the universe but one of several angel-less planets revolving around the sun. His theory was reinforced by Johannes Kepler (1571-1630), who was a Christian minister and who accepted the theory of Copernicus and provided a mathematical rationale for his ideas. Then came Galileo (1564-1642), who was educated in a monastery and who gave more substance to Copernicus' theory by the use of a telescope, surveying the angel-less starry skies and opening up the field of astronomy. Francis Bacon (1561-1626) developed the procedures of natural science, stressing the observation of facts, not angel forces, as the basis for forming conclusions. Then came Thomas Hobbes (1588-1679), son of an Anglican clergyman, whose philosophy based knowledge on what is learned in natural science, not from angel speculation. René Descartes (1596-1650), a devout Roman Catholic, argued that one's senses give the true insight about the world in which we live. John Locke (1632-1704), a Christian, stressed the certainty and the adequacy of human knowledge, not angel knowledge. Sir Isaac Newton (1642-1727), an extremely religious man, made several contributions in the field of mathematics, formulating his law of gravity and motion, which canceled out the mechanistic intervention of angels.

Many others made significant contributions to the enlarging humanity's scientific horizons. The flowering of natural science resulted in bringing the human family a sense of knowledge and mastery of their own environment. But however they are read, these early Christian scientists actually wrecked the old metaphysical superstructures and challenged their church to grow beyond its primitive concepts. For example, when one has a scientific background, it is difficult to take seriously the primitive notion of a three-decker universe, with God and the angels upstairs in the heavenly places, and the devil and the demons downstairs in the basement of hell, when these spaces are all related to the positioning of the earth with other planets and their movement around the sun. So in the estimate of the new scientists the planet earth was but a functioning portion of a precisely working cosmic system subject to immutable physical laws. Any suggestion that angels were flitting around in the machinery making it go or holding it together would have appeared ridiculous.

At the close of the seventeenth century, intellectual Christians had become convinced that they should deemphasize angels, and they simply abandoned them as a serious object of thought and study. But questions remained: What do we do with the angels? Are angels to be given space in worship? Are there really personal guardians? Does the Dionysian order of angels make any sense when angels are no longer necessary to describe the workings of God's universe?

By the eighteenth century, angels were generally viewed with a combination of indifference, amusement, and contempt. There were, however, a few exceptions. Emanuel Swedenborg (1688–1772), son of a Lutheran bishop, and a handful of others not only endorsed the angels but in some cases attempted to return them to a place of veneration. Early in his career, Swedenborg was considered one of the geniuses of his time as an inventor, innovator, and prolific writer on scientific topics. Then he entered a new dimension, which he referred to as the world of the spirit, where he was allowed to enter and witness the workings of the heavenly world. There he was an observer of angelic activity. In his book *Heaven and Its Wonders and Hell*, Swedenborg meticulously describes the heavenly scene, paying close attention to the functioning of angels much as one would describe scientific theory. He wrote: "That the garments of angels do not merely appear as garments, but are real garments, is evident from the fact that angels both see them and feel them, that they care for those that are not in use, and put them on again when they need them. That they are clothed with a variety of garments I have seen many times."[53] The idea of garments in heaven is unusual, but perhaps the diversity of forms continues even there. John Wesley (1703–91), the great Methodist leader and a strong believer in angels, once said of Swedenborg, "He is one of the most ingenious, lively, entertaining madmen that ever set pen to paper."[54]

Swedenborg's spiritual child was the great poet and painter William Blake (1757–1827), whose images of spiritual beings have been called fantastic beyond imagination. Blake used Swedenborg as a source of inspiration, but did not copy his way of thinking. In fact, Blake's angels are grand superforms that make Swedenborg's angels, by comparison, functionaries on a smaller scale. To Blake, the angel was a form that symbolized the world of the spirit. His angels are known for their innocence and childlikeness, but mostly they are wild and wonderful hyperbolic expressions:

Once I saw a devil in a flame of fire who arose before an angel that sat on a cloud, and the devil uttered these words: "The worship of God is: honoring his gifts in other men, each according to his genius, and loving the greatest men best: those who envy or calumniate great men hate

65

God; for there is no other God." The angel hearing this became almost blue; but mastering himself he grew yellow, and at last white, pink and smiling, and then replied: "Thou idolater! Is not God one and is not he visible in Jesus Christ?"[55]

Christian Angel Forms in Art

The development of Christian art is a commentary on the evolution, or lack of it, in angel-consciousness on the part of both artist and audience. What follows is an overview of angels in Christian art across the centuries, with emphasis on the way angels have been presented in various settings.

In the fourth-century Church of Santa Pudenziana, a mosaic behind the cross depicts four living creatures of angelic dimension, all of which are winged. In the fifth-century Church of Santa Maria Maggiore, Rome, angels look like men with long hair and billowing robes. A typical form dated at either the fifth or the sixth century is an angel on the leaf of an ivory diptych in the British museum. It is pictured wrapped in something like drapery material, with close-cropped hair, a childlike face, and again more masculine than feminine features. In the Church of San Vitale in Ravenna, Italy, dating to the year 747, we see Christ enthroned in heaven and attended by two archangels, who are wearing long robes with large dark wings. Their hair is long, and they look masculine.

In the thirteenth-century Reims Cathedral in France, there is a work of art showing souls of the chosen being brought to Abraham by angels. The angels look very feminine, with togalike robes and small wings. Smiling angels are seen to the left of the porch of the Reims Cathedral; they are gowned and have small wings and very feminine smiles. The fresco in the Arena Chapel in Padua, Italy, is

The *Lamentations* by Giotto (1266-1367), which shows angels looking like cupids, or chubby children, flitting about wearing halos.

The *Annunciation*, a painting by Masolino (1383-1447), hangs in the National Gallery in Washington, D.C. In this work the archangel Gabriel looks like a woman dressed in a robe with a wild print. He has a large halo, his hair is curled tightly in place, and he has medium-sized wings. In a painting by Titian (1477-1576), *The Assumption of the Virgin*, the angels look like rotund children wearing flowing gowns. In *The Madonna and Child with Angels* by Hans Menley (1430-95), which hangs in the National Gallery of Art, the angels look like small china dolls with harps and small wings and robes. The angels of artist Raphael (1483-1520), particularly those in his *Sistine Madonna*, look like little children. In *Mass of St. Gregory* by Albrecht Dürer (1471-1528), an angel with curly hair and lacy wings is seen coming out of the clouds in a long, trailing nightgown. In *Tobias and the Angel* by Filippino (1459-1504), the angels are quite feminine and wear lacy gowns with soft fleecy wings and long curly hair. Tintoretto (1518-94) in his *The Last Supper* has angels swarming in the heights in a cloudlike gathering. In *The Virgin with the Saints*, by El Greco (1541-1614), the angels appear with bare arms, sleeves rolled up against a background of clouds. Their faces are like those of thirteen-year-old girls, and their hands are folded in prayerlike supplication.

Rembrandt (1606-69) in his *The Annunciation* has the masculine angel Gabriel with long wings solicitously bending over Mary, and in his *The Vision of Daniel* he has the angel tenderly bending over Daniel. Rembrandt's angels have human-like proportions, but more important, they seem to be concerned, caring beings. *The Burial of Moses* by William Blake (1757-1827) portrays the angels as feminine, with elongated wings, curly hair, long gowns,

67

and very busy. Paul Gustave Doré (1833–83) in his *Elijah Nourished by an Angel* depicts a tall angel with prominent wings who is quite feminine and has beautiful long hair.

In this overview of angels depicted in works of art over the centuries, we note sameness of angel forms. Angels are shown wearing billowing sheets and having curly hair, wings of various sizes, and stylized faces. There are exceptions, however. Rembrandt's angels seem more like compassionate human forms. And the sculpture at the Coventry Cathedral in England entitled *St. Michael the Archangel and Satan,* by Jacob Epstein (1880–1959), shows an angel who is muscular and short-haired. Although he does have the typical wings, there is such dynamic power in this form that it holds one's attention for quite a while. The change in image is refreshing.

If the sameness of angel forms reflects the church's attitude toward angels, no wonder they have become extinct. In general, angel forms are incredibly dull. There is no imagination in visualizing the power and diversity of angel forms. In fact, had the angel forms through the years been presented to the contemporary mind in more innovative, adaptive modes, and had they been portrayed in a variety of shapes, there would be no such thing as angel obscurity.

A certain theologian once deplored the sad state of department-store angels, who are reduced to wearing the same old silver gown with furry wings, halos askew, making them more objects of pity than veneration. He complained about the lack of power in the sacred symbols. But how can a window dresser be blamed, when Christian art provides so little with which to work? Maybe the call should go out for artists to use more imagination and deal with angel forms equal to the science of our day. Yes, science—not theology. Think of the possibilities presented by angel forms channeling the energy of Max Planck's quantum theory, revealing that people live in the midst of a universal stream of unlimited energy. Or what if an artist could represent the angel forms of the electro-magnetic forces of the bloodstream, or show the angel-like movement of the neutrinos, those subatomic particles that continually pass through people's bodies without their being aware of it. This might make a difference in terms of the reality expressed in angel forms. The point is that there is a need for diversity in angel forms, whereby people develop their own individual image forms through which the angel essences may flow.

The Angels of Islam

Most angel lore is a product of something that went before—sometimes it is a synthesis, sometimes an appropriation, sometimes a creative expression, but in almost every case it is derived from a former expression. At the beginning of the seventh century A.D., Judaism had been driven out of Palestine and was wandering around in foreign lands. Although they were far from home, the Jews did maintain their faith and religious influence in the world. Judaism was well known to Muhammad (A.D. 570–632), founder of Islam. Arabs learned about the religion of the Jews through commerce, and Jewish teaching centers were scattered throughout the various cities in Arab lands.

In the time of Muhammad, Christianity was in total disarray. Doctrinal controversies among the Greek Christians had split the church into factions, and the church had a leadership problem. The would-be leaders were either on retreat in the desert or behaving like fanatics. But the big problem for Christians attempting to mission-ize the Arabian land was that the Arabs, being Semites, did not take kindly to turning the other cheek—a major tenet in the religion of Jesus. In fact, the gospel of peace was an outrage to the Arabs, particularly when they were without personal example, which was most of the time.

The religion of Muhammad was seeded by both the Jews and the Christians. The extent of this cross-pollination can be seen in his first experiences with visions and voices and the encounter with the angel Gabriel. The result was an exciting, new, and different expression of what had gone before. Withdrawing to the mountains outside Mecca, Muhammad entered an austere loneliness to be instructed. "His favorite spot was a cave in the declivities at the foot of Mount Hira, a lofty conical hill two or three miles north of Mecca. Thither he would retire for days at a time; and his faithful wife sometimes accompanied him."[56] Subsequently, he brought his visions and voices to the streets of Mecca, where he chanted revelations that were later collected in a volume that became known as the Book of the Voice of God and is today the Qur'an. The Qur'an is a compendium of many religious traditions. William St. Clair Tisdall says the elements of the Qur'an came from five major sources: Ancient Arab and Jewish beliefs and practices, the Sabeans, Christianity and Christian apocryphal books, and Zoroastrianism.[57]

In the beginning Muhammad regarded the scriptures of other major religious traditions as having equal merit, but later he changed his mind and asserted the supremacy of the Qur'an. Still, he never doubted the authority of the other scriptures.

People guided in the way of Islam recognize three agents: (1) Muhammad (God's messenger); (2) the Qur'an (God's revelation); (3) angels (constant attendance). Arabs prior to the time of Muhammad knew about angels and demons. Muhammad himself learned about archangels, ministering angels, and fallen angels from Jewish and

Christian sources. But there are also traces of more ancient beliefs concerning angel forms in the Muslim angelology.

The Ranks of Muslim Angel Forms

Angels, or angel chiefs (a typical Arab form) as they are often called, are: (1) Gabriel, the chief of the chiefs, the angel of revelation. Muhammad even saw him as the Holy Spirit. Gabriel is often referred to as "the faithful spirit," "the spirit of holiness," or "the spirit of faith and truth" (Sura [in the Qur'an] 26:193).[58] (2) Michael is the angel of providence (Sura 2:98),[59] well known among the Jews, the Christians, and the Zoroastrians. (3) Israfil, the angel of the trumpet who will awaken the dead, is known as "the burning one," the angel of resurrection and song. (4) Azrael is the angel of death (Sura 32:11),[60] who writes the name of every person in a book of life at birth and erases it at death.

This sampling of angel forms combines the traditions of the Christians (Gabriel and Michael), Judaism (Gabriel and Michael), Zoroastrianism (Gabriel), and old Arabic religion (archangels as chiefs), with the unique Muslim expression of new names for the old functions of an angel using a trumpet to awaken the dead and the role played by the angel of death.

The ministering angels include Ridwan (Good Will), the angel placed at the entrance to paradise; Malik, the ruler of hell or the terrible angel who guards hell; Munnkar and Nakir, the angels who question the dead, who are said to be blue-eyed, black angels who ask to examine the souls of the recently deceased.

There are also recording angels, throne-bearers, and cherubim, who very Muslim-like do not hide their faces as they surround the throne of God. There are also hosts of ministering angels.

Then we come to the fallen angels, which include the devil, who is called either Iblis (Sura 15:32),[61] a contraction of Diabolos, or Shaitin (the Zoroastrian name for Satan). Besides Iblis, other fallen angels are Harut and Marut and the host of Iblis. In Persian lore, Harut was an angel of highest rank, one of the Zoroastrian Amesha Spentas, who was instructed with the secret name of God but fell in love with a mortal woman. In so doing he gave away the secret name and was punished by being confined head-down in a pit in Babylon (Sura 2:102).[62] The ancient lore of the Muslim states that both Marut and Harut were instructed in the same secret lore, both fell in love with the same woman, both are confined in the same pit.

The lesser spirits include fairies and jinns. Fairies are much like children, enjoying their play without causing anyone trouble. The jinns are primarily demonic, yet they can be good. They were created "from the fire of a scorching wind [Sura 15:27]"[63] and are known to possess people; in fact, the insane are said to be jinn-possessed. Tradition has it that the jinns were once angels of high estate equal to any of the angels, but because they refused to carry out a heavenly order along with their leader, Iblis, they were thrown out of heaven. They are regarded as halfway between angels and human beings (Sura 15).[64]

No paraphrase of the Qur'an will suffice to describe the activity of the angels, so what follows are some angel descriptions directly from the Muslim holy book.

Creation of the Angels, Wings and All

> Praise be to God,
> Who created (out of nothing)

> The heavens and the earth,
> Who made the angels
> Messengers with wings—
> Two or three or four (pairs):
> He adds to Creation
> As He pleases: for God
> Has power over all things
> —Sura 35:1[65]

The commentary on this passage by A. Yusuf Ali is interesting: "The grosser ideas which [people] have of angels must be dismissed from our minds. They are beings expressive of qualities or powers, which may be typified by wings."[66] Although we have encountered angel wings in other traditions, no one has explained their meaning any more perceptively than this Muslim, whose text, translation, and commentary on the Qur'an is a joy to read. Keep in mind the fact that angels are forms through which the "qualities or powers" of God are flowing.

Guardian Angels

> It was we who
> Created man, and
> We know
> What dark suggestions his soul
> Makes to him: for we
> Are nearer to him
> Than (his) jugular vein.
>
> Behold, two (guardian angels)
> Appointed to learn (his doings)
> Learn (and note them)
> One sitting on the right
> And one on the left.

Not a word does he
Utter but there is
A sentinal by him
Ready (to note it). . . .
—Sura 50:16–18[67]

Yusuf Ali suggests that the guardian angel on the right
records a person's good deeds, and the one on the left
notes the bad deeds. The play between these two angels
is that the righthand angel "bears witness" and the left-
hand angel "drives." That is, while the left side is being
driven by the evil deed, the right is bearing witness to the
good. Yusuf Ali is seeing the angel forms as those through
which the energies of God can be channeled in a balanced way.

There is a Muslim teaching that four angels are always
protecting people, two during the day and two at night.
Some have speculated about the presence of a fifth angel,
who remains with a person constantly. The day angel and
the night angel change places at dawn and sunset. These
are dangerous hours, because the jinns who hover about
may use the change of guard as an opportunity to slip into
a person's life and cause trouble. Therefore, to escape the
danger of the jinns the believer must be sure to pray at
dawn and again at sunset, while the angel exchange is
taking place,[68] for those are the times other spiritual energies must be tapped for help.

Angel Forms at the Throne of God

As in the case of other religious beliefs, the throne of
God is the scene of much angelic activity:

And thou wilt see
The angels surrounding

74

The Throne (Divine)
On all sides, singing glory
And Praise to their Lord.
—Sura 39:75[69]

A major tenet of Islam is belief in the hierarchy of angels. This belief requires a sensitivity to a world beyond our own, a spiritual realm beyond that of our senses which is filled with essences and energy forces about which we have no real understanding. One of the great faculties of human perception is the imaginative spirit, which glimpses the unseen reality of the spirit and then develops symbols with which to facilitate the spirit. For the Muslim, the Qur'an is filled with these symbols.

4

Angel Chronicles

The angel stories that follow have been chosen for their diverse ways of expressing angel forms. Some are contemporary, a few are traditional in that they are well known, but each has its own individuality.

This collection is intended to inspire readers to come alive to the possibility of developing their own angel forms through which the essences and energy forces of God can flow into their lives.

Angels, Angels, Everywhere

Wherever we go, the angels travel with us. I go to the cemetery where my loved ones are buried. The winter snow has covered the land. The sycamore has been stripped of its leaves. Huddled in my winter coat, I stand and pray above their eternal sleep. And I am at peace. There is an angel who guards the graves of those we love.

I get off the bus in a strange city late at night. The streets are empty. The buildings are dark. I must try to find a room at a cheap hotel. I carry my suitcase through the desolation and the emptiness and the loneliness, under the melancholy streetlights, through shadows. But I am at peace. There is an angel who shares my wilderness, who stands in the deserted corner, who walks through the frightening city with me.

The weather's hot. I'm worried about my job. I can't sleep. I bring all my troubles home from the office. I get out of bed and walk through the dark rooms. I go to the kitchen and get a drink of water. I go out on the porch and sit in the rattan chair. I try to be quiet so I won't wake up my family. I take a deep breath. There is an angel who sits with me through the sleepless night, who shares the solitude and the discovery I begin to make about who I am and what really matters in my life. We talk about eternal things. I am at peace.

I visit the mental hospital with my friend, the parish priest, and we walk through the wards where young [people] are staring through the dusty windows at dusty sparrows far beyond in the dusty sky. One young man is weaving the sunbeams with his long, white, nervous hands. One young man is playing patty-cake into the empty air.

Oh, such a sad world. Such sorrow and grief! I pray that all this grief shall pass away! I pray that these young [people] will rise some day in glory from the gray confusion, from the labyrinth of their thoughts.

But even here—in the hospital, in the prison, in the asylum, in the dark places—the angels appear. The angels are bearing gifts to the broken minds and the broken bodies and the broken lives. The angels are bearing grace and light and surcease. They are combing the tangled hair. They are holding the nervous hands. They are washing the distorted face.

We were having a wonderful party, and all the children were home, and we were celebrating John's birthday, and Mother had baked a special white cake and we were looking at all the photographs we'd taken on the summer vacation up in Maine. Then we suddenly all stopped and grew very quiet, and Mother said she thought she heard something out on the back porch and she thought maybe somebody was out there trying to get into our house, and I said I'd go out on the porch to see if there was anybody there.

So I went through the kitchen and out on the back porch, and I saw that the screen door was unlocked and I opened it and stuck my head outside and called into the twilight, "Is there anybody here? Is somebody wanting into our house? You're welcome to the party! Come on in! It's John's birthday!"

(Then I began to see the angels. They were everywhere!

They were entering the house with treasures in their hands—the treasures of Compassion and Understanding and Charity and Kindness and Endurance and Thoughtfulness and Faith and Peacefulness—treasures for John that he could use in his continuing growth, in the building of his life, in his continuing realization of beauty and joy.)

Then I went on back into the house and into the bright parlor, and John was starting to open his gifts, and Mother asked, "Well, was there anybody out there trying to get in?"

I laughed. "Oh, yes. It was a whole bunch of angels! I felt them rush by me into the house! They've come to celebrate!" And I took her into my arms and gave her a kiss. And I kissed John too. And all the children.

Protective Company

Dr. Smiley Blanton sent me a letter in which he described something that happened some years ago in a town in the South. At a town meeting of some kind, the local Episcopal clergyman opposed a political boss by the name of Sam, with the result that a proposal of Sam's was defeated. Sam didn't like this, and he announced publicly that he was going to kill the minister. Friends came to the minister and said, "We had better walk home with you, because it is a lonely walk and Sam will do what he said. You have to pass that dark woodlot."

"I don't want anybody with me," the minister answered. "I can handle Sam. The Lord will be with me. I was in the right. Besides, if Sam kills me, what then? He just kills my body." And he walked home alone, right through the dark woodlot, and nothing happened to him.

A few years later Sam, on his deathbed, sent for this same minister. "Reverend, I meant to kill you that night," he said. "I was in the wood with a club, all ready to knock your brains out."

"Sam, why didn't you do it?" the minister asked.

"What do you mean, why didn't I do it? Who were those two big men with you?"

"There were no big men with me," the minister replied.

From Norman Vincent Peale, *Life Can Always Be Yours* (Pawling, N.Y.: Foundation for Christian Living, 1960), p. 8. Reprinted by permission.

"Oh, yes, there were," Sam said. "I saw them."

The Bible mentions guardian angels, you know. It may be that the Bible in picturesque language is telling us of forces which one day our descendants will discover scientifically and know much more about.

The Six Angels
of Ballardville

It was a glorious spring morning and we were walking, Marion and I, through the newly budded birches and maples near Ballardville, Massachusetts.

The little path was spongy to our steps, and we held hands with the sheer delight of the day and the sheer delight of life as we strolled near a lovely brook. It was May, and because it was the examination reading period for students at Smith College, we were able to get away for a few days to visit Marion's parents.

We frequently took walks in the country, and we especially loved the spring after a hard New England winter, for it is then that the fields and the woods are radiant and calm yet show new life bursting from the earth. This day we were especially happy and peaceful; we chatted sporadically, with great gaps of satisfying silence between our sentences.

Then from behind us we heard the murmur of muted voices in the distance, and I said to Marion, "We have company in the woods this morning."

Marion nodded and turned to look. We saw nothing,

Selection from *A Life After Death* by S. Ralph Harlow, copyright © 1961 by S. Ralph Harlow and Evan Hill. Reprinted by permission of Doubleday & Company, Inc.

but the voices were coming nearer—at a faster pace than we were walking, and we knew that the strangers would soon overtake us. Then we perceived that the sounds were not only behind us but above us, and we looked up.

How can I describe what we felt? Is it possible to tell of the surge of exaltation that ran through us? Is it possible to record this phenomenon in objective accuracy and yet be credible?

For about ten feet above us, and slightly to our left, was a floating group of spirits—of angels—of glorious, beautiful creatures that glowed with spiritual beauty. We stopped and stared as they passed above us.

There were six of them, young beautiful women dressed in flowing white garments and engaged in earnest conversation. If they were aware of our existence, they gave no indication of it. Their faces were perfectly clear to us, and one woman, slightly older than the rest, was especially beautiful. Her dark hair was pulled back in what today we would call a ponytail, and although I cannot say it was bound at the back of her head, it appeared to be. She was talking intently to a younger spirit, whose back was toward us and who looked up into the face of the woman who was talking.

Neither Marion nor I could understand their words, although their voices were clearly heard. The sound was somewhat like hearing but being unable to understand a group of people talking outside a house with all the windows and doors shut.

They seemed to float past us, and their graceful motion seemed natural—as gentle and peaceful as the morning itself. As they passed, their conversation grew fainter and fainter until it faded out entirely, and we stood transfixed on the spot, still holding hands and still with the vision before our eyes.

It would be understatement to say that we were

astounded. Then we looked at each other, each wondering if the other had also seen.

"Come," I said, and I led her to a fallen birch. We sat and I said, "Now, Marion, what did you see? Tell me exactly, in precise detail. And tell me what you heard."

She knew my intent—to test my own eyes and ears, to see if I had been the victim of hallucination or imagination. And her reply was identical in every respect to what my own senses had reported to me. When she had finished she answered my unasked question.

"It seems to me," she said calmly, "that for those split seconds the veil between our world and the spirit world was lifted and for some reason, unknown to us, we were permitted to see and to hear what generally our physical eyes and ears are unable to sense."

Under normal circumstances, but probably only in subjects other than this one, I am considered a faithful, reliable witness. Attorneys have solicited my testimony, and I have testified in the courts, regarded by judge and jury as dependable and honest. And I record this story with the same faithfulness and respect for truth and accuracy as I would tell it on the witness stand. But even as I record it, I know how incredible it sounds.

The Angels
at Ravensbruck

I t was an unusual prayer, both in content and in location. "Lord, cause now thine angels to surround me; and let them not be transparent today, for the guards must not see me."

When Corrie ten Boom and her sister Betsie arrived as Dutch prisoners at the dreaded Ravensbruck prison camp, all possessions, including clothing, were to be taken from them by the Nazi guards.

Relating the horrible indignities and privations they suffered, she writes: "Together we entered the terrifying building. At a table were women who took away all our possessions. Everyone had to undress completely and then go to a room where her hair was clipped short.

"I asked a guard, who was busy checking the possessions of the new arrivals, if I might use the toilet. She pointed to a door to the showers. . . . Betsie stayed close beside me all the time. Suddenly I had an inspiration. 'Quick, take off your woolen underwear' I whispered to her. I rolled it up with mine and laid the bundle in a corner with my little Bible. The spot was alive with cockroaches, but I didn't worry about that. I felt wonderfully relieved and happy. 'The Lord is busy answering our

From *All About Angels* by C. Leslie Miller. © Copyright 1973 by Regal Books, Ventura, CA 93003.

prayers, Betsie,' I whispered. 'We shall not have to make the sacrifice of all our clothes.'

"We hurried back to the row of women waiting to be undressed. A little later, after we had our showers and put on our shirts and shabby dresses, I hid the roll of underwear and my Bible under my dress. It did bulge out obviously through my dress, but I prayed, 'Lord, cause now thine angels to surround me; and let them not be transparent today, for the guards must not see me.' I felt perfectly at ease. Calmly I passed the guards. Everyone was checked, from the front, the sides, the back. Not a bulge escaped the eyes of the guard. The woman just in front of me had hidden a woolen vest under her dress; it was taken from her. They let me pass, for they did not see me. Betsie, right behind me, was searched.

"But outside awaited another danger. On each side of the door were women who looked everyone over for a second time. They felt over the body of each one who passed. I knew they would not see me, for the angels were still surrounding me. I was not even surprised when they passed me by; but within me rose the jubilant cry, 'O Lord, if thou dost so answer prayer, I can face even Ravensbruck unafraid.'"

Jacob Atabet
and the Angel
at the Game

I t had been coming out gradually, though I had trouble believing it: He was a 49er football fan more committed than most. For ten years he had been a season-ticket holder! As the 1970 season developed, and it became apparent that the 49ers might win the first division championship in their entire history, the fate of the team became a regular theme of our talks. In October we started to go to the games, and by November we were waiting outside the locker rooms for glimpses of the 49er stars. There was always a crowd there, mainly children and teenage boys, with a few defective-looking adults around the edges, waiting to follow the players as they muscled their way to the cars.

"Hey, Brodie, I want to see you about a book," I yelled one Sunday afternoon, and the quarterback looked slightly bewildered. "Yeah," he drawled, his features sagging into an expression of weary self-restraint. "You a writer?"

A dozen children were staring up at me as I shouldered

my way through the crowd. "I'm a publisher," I gasped. "Here's my card." He gave me a skeptical look. "What kind of books do you publish?" he asked.

I glanced at [Jacob] Atabet. He was smiling encouragement. "Philosophy and religion," I said. "You could do one on the mystical side of football."

"Wha'?" He looked startled. "The what side?" The kids around him were jostling for position, and one of them was elbowing past me. "The mystical side," I shouted. "The spiritual, uncanny . . . " But my voice was drowned in the shouts.

"Write the 49er office," he yelled, and disappeared.

Atabet was shaking his head with approval. "Did you get an autograph?" he asked.

"No," I said. "But I almost touched him."

But we weren't the only ones who were driven in this strange kind of way. Toward the end of the season, after a crucial game with Atlanta, the crowd near the dressing room entrance was bigger than ever. In the very middle of it stood a group I recognized. They were pushing in close to the heroes with just as much ardor as we ever did. John Levy, our mutual friend, Mike Murphy of Esalen, George Leonard, the West Coast editor for *Look* magazine, John Clancy, a San Francisco attorney, and David Meggyesey, the former Cardinal linebacker who had written a scathing attack on pro football, were all shouldering their way toward the players.

Leonard seemed to be leading them. At six-foot-five, he towered over the children and newsboys. Now all five of them seemed desperate for a place near the quarterback.

"Hey, George," I yelled. "What're you doing?" But before I could reach him the entire group was crowding toward Brodie. Meggyesey looked guilty, and I could understand why. His book had contained an indictment of fan behavior like this. When he saw me he blushed. Clancy was shouting some strange incantation, and Levy provided protection, it seemed, from the police and stadium guards. Suddenly Leonard was next to the quarterback, peering over his shoulder. Was he whispering into his ear?

"Hey, George," I yelled, but it was clear that he was totally distracted. What a strange addiction, I thought, first Atabet and now this unlikely group.

Brodie was striding toward his car with three or four boys at his elbows. The group of five kept pace, then crowded in toward the bumpers. Leonard, it appeared, was studying Brodie's handwriting or his method of signing cards. He cocked his head from side to side to get a better view. I thought back to our first game that year, to that look in Atabet's eyes. Now Leonard and the rest were caught in it too. Even Meggyesey, with his widely publicized criticism of behavior like this, was watching the quarterback with rapt attention.

As Brodie pulled away, the entire group stared after him, five abandoned figures at the edge of the empty lot, looking just a little forlorn. I rejoined Atabet, and we followed them to a bar across the street. It was a dark and dingy place, full of beefy red-faced types who must have been drunk before the game was over. At first I couldn't see the group, but then I heard Leonard. He was standing on a chair, towering some three or four feet above the crowd, his silver hair alive in the light of beer signs. He was shouting something I couldn't hear from the door—it might've been a 49er cheer. When I got closer I could finally make it out. "The Superbowl is the Supermind!" he shouted. His group yelled it back, drawing belligerent looks from the people around them. One red-faced, bull-necked man asked them what it meant, and Clancy told him the meaning of it would soon become clear. I could see that the crowd around them was hostile and curious at once, as if there might be some truth in the strange incantation.

It was said that the Indian saint Ramakrishna could see the lineaments of God through every event in his life. That is the way I had to understand Atabet's love of professional football. During that same Atlanta game, with the 49ers trailing in the final quarter, he had seen "a kind of angel" appear above the field. It was an entity, he said, about the size of "a two-story house."

I asked him where to look.

"There." He jabbed his hand past the ear of the person in front of me. "Just above the Atlanta line." Sunlight was slanting in above the rim of the stadium, and there was a luminous haze on the field. It had to be the diffraction of light. "No. No. Not that." He shook my arm. "I mean right in the middle of it there!"

"In the middle of that haze?" I whispered. The rough-looking man sitting next to me was eyeing us suspiciously. He had worn a yellow hard hat all through the game as if he expected a fight. Atabet was getting excited. "Right in the middle of it!" He shook me. "Now see the flames?"

By squinting, I could see jets of golden light shooting up my eyelashes, but nothing that looked like an angel. I shook my head as the teams lined up. "It's moving down the field," he murmured. "Something's going to happen . . . " And as he said it Brodie threw a pass to a back who began to run toward the goal. Atabet grabbed my shoulder. "See it?" he cried, and stood up with the crowd. "See the thing moving?" The back made a beautiful move past the last Atlanta defender and crossed the goal untouched. "I saw it," he cried. "I saw it!"

"We all did," growled the man in the hard hat. "You think you're so hot because you saw it?"

But Atabet didn't hear him. "It's moving up fast," he whispered. "Look up there."

By leaning back I could see something all right. Was it a strand of sunlight and mist? Then a fogbank appeared, and suddenly the stadium turned gray. "If it's an angel, would it move around in space?" I whispered, turning my back on the glowering face beside me. "Doesn't it go back to some other plane?"

"Not if it gets into action here," he said with total conviction. "It's amazing. I've never seen such a big one."

Had the game gotten to him? The 49ers had to win it to win the division championship, something they had never done before. Everyone in the stadium had their own way of dealing with the terrible suspense. "If it's an angel, it must be a big one," I said.

"That's right," he muttered. "It's a big one."

"The supramental descent has begun!" Leonard said to the crowd. I glanced back at Jacob. Would he see that Leonard was making a joke?

He was standing near the bar, with a look of jaunty savoir faire. The handsome Basque had appeared. A look of irony had replaced the idiot sense of wonder.

"Hey, Jake!" I yelled. "Tell them about the angel." A beer had prompted the remark, along with Leonard's infectious spirit. But he only gave me a hooded look of mischief and turned in the other direction. "What's that you're saying?" I yelled up to Leonard. "What's that about the Superbowl?"

"If the 49ers win this year," he said with a voice that everyone in the place could hear, "the Superbowl becomes the Supermind!" Then he stepped down from the chair, and our conversation was lost in the confusion around us. Several faces followed him dumbly, as if he had spoken a truth they dimly sensed. I never got a chance to explore the possible connections, however, for the next time I saw him he wasn't sure what had led to his proclamation. But Atabet had no doubts. "One of them saw it," he said as we left, "even though they're joking." He turned and looked at me gravely. "Second sight," he said. "It had to be Murphy or Clancy."

Was he serious? By now I had come to believe that

94

angels were calling for names, even in places like this. But an angel descending onto the field? I could only comprehend it by seeing that his passion for transfiguration had overwhelmed him in the heat of the game. I had seen other hints of madness like this among people who were usually pillars of reason. Who could forget the bank president who ran out on the field to tackle a Chicago running back in 1968? Or the physics professor at Stanford who called a press conference to present his reasons for the 49ers' lack of defensive ability? So I decided to humor him. That diffracted light was a field in the sky for projection. You could see anything in it you wanted.

But on Monday the *Chronicle* reported three or four UFO sightings in the Bay Area. UFOs could be some people's way of fitting their visions into an acceptable framework, he said. The thing above the stadium had been "a cone of light with flames at the top," a form that might resemble a flying saucer.

"Need-determined perception?" I asked. It was a phrase he had used against me.

"All right," he said glumly. "See if I tell you about them any more. I've been to hundreds of games and I've never seen anything like it."

"But the fact that you're not painting, and all that stuff building up inside you."

"What stuff?" he said. "You mean to say I don't know the difference?"

"Well, do you?"

Instead of getting angry, he smiled and started to swear. "Well, you smart-assed, overeducated son of a bitch. After all we've been through."

"I think it was inevitable that you'd see something like that at a game," I said. "You're as crazy out there as any fan I've ever seen."

He smiled in spite of himself. "Crazy?" he said. "You think I'm crazy?"

"I've wondered why you don't try out for the team."

"All right." He sighed. "I won't talk about it any more. At least to you. Ah, well." He tossed back his head. "Let them have their simple world. But angel, we know, we know." He spread his arms wide. "Angel, speak!"

Just as he said it, a foghorn sounded. It was the lowest, most flatulent one I'd heard in years.

"Jesus!" I said. "Is that the kind of thing it is?" It sounded again, even lower than before, as if it were blowing out gas that had gathered for centuries.

"Angel!" he cried. "Now I know that you care!"

The Enigma of
the Angel Soldiers

The mystifying Spectral Armies of Mons were seen a few weeks after the German invasion of Belgium in 1914. As the rescuing British Expeditionary Force tried to stop the Kaiser's army, they were cut to pieces. The British, with 70,000 exhausted men, tried vainly to hold 160,000 Germans in check. Heavily shelled, drunk from lack of sleep, they staggered 150 miles in eleven days through the dust and heat of the Belgian plains.

On the night of August 24, 1914, strange things began to happen all along the front. One retreating British company heard the onrushing Uhlan cavalry bearing down on them. But when they turned to face the horsemen they saw unexpected reinforcements. Two officers later testified, "Suddenly, to our wonder, we saw between us and the enemy a whole troop of angels!"

The German horses were terrified. They wheeled, reared, and stampeded, despite everything the Uhlans could do to control them. In the confusion the British soldiers reached safety.

Other soldier-angels were reported by a major who told

From Harrison Brooke, "The Enigma of the Phantom Soldiers," *Beyond Reality*, no. 35 (January/February 1979), pp. 27, 54. Reprinted by permission.

how he and thirty of his troops were cut off in a trench. He told them, "Look here, we must either stay and be caught like rats in a trap, or make a sortie against the Boche. We haven't much of a chance, but personally, I don't want to be caught here!" His [troops] agreed and, rising as one with the shout "Saint George for England!" they rushed into the open toward the German positions.

As they dashed forward with fixed bayonets, the major became aware of another company—a larger group with arrows and longbows—trotting alongside them. They were, in fact, leading them against the enemy's line. Later, the major interrogated a German prisoner of war who asked, "Who was your leader on the gray-white horse? He was such an easy target . . . but we couldn't hit him!"

Lieutenant Colonel F. E. Seldon told how his cavalry was worn out from an all-night march, groggy from lack of sleep. But Seldon insisted that his mental facilities were unimpaired when, for twenty minutes, he and some of his mounted officers observed a squadron of spectral cavalry riding along beside them.

The Doctor and What Seems to Have Been the Appearance of an Angel

There was a strange sequence of dreams and other experiences which were not dreams, in the usual sense. They were more like visits, for I was taken to the same place night after night as I slept. There was one focal dream which was surrounded by other dreams that came and went and did not seem vitally important.

One of these minor dreams occurred only occasionally. In this dream, I would climb high places, only to discover my way blocked at the top. I might be climbing the steep side of a precipitous cliff, to find on reaching the top that a huge projection of rock was jutting out above my head and there would be no way to get past it on the right or on the left. That may have been the reflection of my subconscious urge to reach a goal. I mention it merely to contrast it with the central, dominant picture, which was quite different. There was no dreamlike quality about the visitation. It was always clear, plausible, and satisfying.

The place was always the same. It was a narrow monastery garden. The stone walls were covered with ivy.

From pp. 6–11 in *Everyman's Mission* by Rebecca Beard. Copyright 1952 by Harper & Row, Publishers, Inc. Reprinted by permission.

There was a white marble bench in the center with heavy sodded grass on both sides. An old stone building, that I sensed was a church or a chapel, was at the left. Behind me an open space led out upon a promontory overlooking a vast expanse of country. At the right, opposite the church, was a solid wooden door, heavily latched and reinforced by iron strips. During all the time I visited the garden, that door was never opened, and I was never curious about what lay beyond it.

The figure in the garden was always the same. I would not be able to say whether it was a man or a woman, but I had the sense of masculinity, perfectly balanced by the noblest strains of femininity. The robes were flowing, but I never saw anything of the figure above the chest. I was always conscious of the left hand. It was very expressive. On the fourth finger was a beautiful ring, which I knew to be a scarab, although up to that time I do not remember ever having seen one.

In this garden, all the questions and doubts were discussed. There may have been other individuals present. Sometimes, I had a vague feeling there were other students about, although I did not see anyone to recognize or even to outline. But I heard discussions and I heard answers. I came back in the morning with the answers. Gradually, as I grew in the practice of silence, I heard these conversations very clearly. Sometimes they were etched so vividly in my consciousness that I would tell them to my husband almost word for word. At times they were so real, I would say to him, "Did we hear or read an answer to the question that was puzzling us yesterday?" He would say, "No, I heard nothing." Then I would know I had heard it Otherwhere, not here.

There came a night when the teacher took me through the open space at the back of the garden. We walked to a very high place where we could look over the whole world, or so it seemed to me. Here I was told many things. It was here I lost all sense of separate national feeling. I became one with every country in the world. I became one with every nationality. It was more than a surface sensation, for I can honestly say that today I have absolutely no feeling of difference with the Negro, with the Chinese, with the Japanese, or with any other foreign people.

It was a gradual process of growth and search. I kept no record. I made few notes. About the end of the second year, my visits to the monastery garden ended. One night in the monastery garden the figure walked to the door that had never been opened. The hand with the ring was placed flat upon the door as it was slowly pushed open. There was no beckoning or other sign, yet I knew I was to go through that door and that I would never go back. My period of instruction was over.

I stepped outside into a place of sheer beauty. Before me was a garden filled with blossoming plants and shrubs, with walks, hedges, fountains, and pools. The perfume of it I sometimes catch in high moments of ministry as it seems to breathe through the room like a rare incense. I knew I was ready to move out into a larger experience. I did not know where or how, but the time had come. I realized my entire life would have to be reoriented and reorganized, and I knew the experience would be beautiful and rewarding.

Through some former discipline, Wally my husband evidently had come to the same point of development at which I had arrived. Most naturally, our new expression had to do with healing, since our work for years had been with those who presented physical problems. It was the burden of our desire to help others by alleviating suffering.

Sometimes we say of people that they have the gift of

101

healing in their hands. Perhaps it would be more exact to say that their complete relinquishment makes them more open channels for the healing flow of God's power to move through them. So we went forward to healing work beside the beds of pain, Wally laying his hands upon those who were ill while we both prayed.

As we stepped out into this new world of service, there were three times when I was consciously aware of One whom I knew to be greater than the figure who had taught me in the garden. The first time, I was at Unity Farm visiting a dear friend who was staying for the summer in the small house called the Arches that had been built for Myrtle Fillmore during her lifetime and where she had lived and worked. Early one morning, at my usual hour, I went out on the porch for meditation. The dawn was just breaking through a pearl-gray rosy mist. I prayed that morning for guidance. I prayed that we might rise above all sense of sex and work with men and women as children of God. As I prayed, out of the gray mist a deeper gray figure walked upon the cement porch past me, turning to smile at me. I felt the warmth of [God's] love in that smile, and I knew that my prayer was answered. A deep sense of peace and thankfulness came over me.

The second time I saw the figure, I recognized that it was the Master. Wally and I were at the bedside of a woman who was desperately ill. When we arrived, her heart was beating erratically, and her body was so cold as to be almost cyanotic. I knew she was very close to death. As we stood by the bed, I said, "Master, if there be reason why this child of yours should live, or if there be something she needs to do before she goes on, come into this room and speak the word of life."

The light increased to a radiance all about us, filling the room, as the figure moved forward to the foot of the bed and then was gone. The room remained illumined for a

102

long time as we both knelt in thanksgiving. The patient began to breathe more easily, the color crept back into her lips, and she fell into a natural sleep. We knew she was healed and would live.

To the astonishment of all who had been attending her, she got up in a few days and announced that she was going to make a trip to Chicago. We learned later that she had a daughter living there from whom she had been estranged for fifteen years. It was quite evident this separation had been on her conscience, for she went to Chicago and made peace with her daughter. A few weeks later, after she came home, she passed away quietly in her sleep without illness or evidence of pain.

The third time I was conscious of the Presence I was in the meeting room in our home where we held Quaker meeting each Sunday morning. There were long periods of silence in those meetings. I was not alone now, for my silence was now augmented by the love, the prayer, and the faith of other devoted people. One Sunday morning a woman who had lost her husband only a short time before came to the meeting for the first time. She was an agnostic, as had been her husband. Having no faith upon which to lean, she was utterly lost after he was taken away. She came that morning, looking pathetically lost. She took a place in the meeting room, and we were silent. During the time of that silent period, without opening my eyes, I was aware of the Master standing in the doorway, this time very tall, coming up almost to the ceiling. He seemed to be speaking to the sorrowing wife as though he were saying, "Be of good cheer."

After the meeting I spoke to her. "A very wonderful thing happened here this morning, a great assurance to you to be of good cheer."

"Yes," she answered softly. "I know." Then looking up at me she asked, "Did you see anything?"

"Yes, I did," I told her.

"Where did you see him?" she asked again, in a hushed voice. She was deeply moved.

"Over by the door leading into the meeting room," I answered, pointing to the entrance door from the ante-room. She did not ask me what I had seen. She went on as though I knew.

"My husband stood there and spoke to me, telling me I was to have no more question, no more doubt, no more grief, and that everything was all right."

She had seen one figure; I had seen another. Evidently both were there, and we each heard or felt the same message of good cheer and comfort.

The Nurse and
the Angels

I t is not only doctors and nurses who minister to the sick and suffering. Angels also minister to them. This too was revealed to me while I was at the hospital.

By the light of a shaded lamp, I was writing one night at a table in the middle of the ward, of which I was in charge as night nurse. The few other lights that were burning were turned low. Glancing up from the paper on which I was writing, I saw a figure moving about at one end of the long and dimly lighted room. I thought that it was some patient who had gotten out of her bed, but when I approached I perceived that it was not a patient, but an angel. The figure was tall and slender, the features were those of a woman of middle age.

I had become too familiar by this time with the sudden appearance of these radiant visitors from another world to be alarmed or startled by it, however unexpected, and I stood still and watched her. She went to three or four beds, pausing for a brief space at each one of them and laying her right hand on the heads of the patients occupying them.

After this, as long as I remained at the hospital, scarcely

From Joy Snell, *The Ministry of Angels Here and Beyond* (New York: Citadel Press, 1959), pp. 51–56. Reprinted by permission.

a day passed that I did not see this angel ministering to the sick. But it was when I was on night duty that I saw her oftenest, for it is in the dark hours, and especially during those that precede dawn, that the life forces of those who are battling with disease sink lowest and they stand most in need of whatever will stimulate their vitality and ease their pain. That this angel was endowed with some power, by means of which she could at times materially benefit the sick, was made so abundantly evident soon after I had first seen her that I came to call her in my thoughts the healing angel.

Thankful I was always, but especially at night, when I was usually the only nurse in the ward, to see her flitting among the patients and here and there laying her hand on the forehead of some sufferer, for I knew that the recipient of that ministry, though absolutely unconscious of it, would be benefited by it. Often, after such a treatment, has a patient said to me on awaking, "Oh, nurse, I feel so much better this morning. I have had such a refreshing sleep."

Occasionally patients who, I knew, had received the ministry of the healing angel would tell me that they had had beautiful dreams in which they had heard entrancing music. I wondered sometimes if they had heard. But none of them apparently ever saw, as I did, the angel who had wrought the change in them for which they were so grateful.

Her healing powers were not exercised on patients only when they were asleep. I have seen her more than once lay her hand on the forehead of a patient who was suffering such acute pain that it provoked moans and groans. And a little later, relieved of the pain, the patient would sink into a calm sleep, to awaken greatly improved. Frequently, after the healing angel had paid a visit to one of my patients, I have found that the pulse had become more regular and the temperature nearer normal.

Oftentimes the healing angel helped me when I was attending a patient, sometimes guiding my hand; at other times, incredible as it may seem, she actually assisted me to raise or shift some heavy and helpless victim of disease or accident.

Apart from those other angels of whom I have written, the healing angel was not the only one I saw among the patients in the hospital. Others came and went occasionally, much as did human visitors, except that their coming and going was different—a sudden appearing and a sudden disappearing. But the healing angel was the only one of whom I am able to affirm positively, because it was proved to me repeatedly, that she brought healing to the patients to whom she ministered.

A young woman who had been run over by a heavy vehicle and terribly injured internally afforded the most convincing proof that came under my notice of the efficacy of the healing angel's ministrations. She was placed in a ward in which I was on night duty. After making a thorough examination of her, the doctor in charge had pronounced her case hopeless.

She had been in the ward only a short time, and I was standing by her bed, wondering what I could do to alleviate her sufferings, which were great, and thinking how sad it was that her two little children should soon be deprived of a mother's love and care, when the bright angel appeared at the head of the bed with uplifted hand, pointing upward. Brief, as always, was her stay, but it caused my despondency to give way to hope, although it still seemed to me that nothing short of a miracle could keep life in that dreadfully shattered body.

About an hour later I was applying cool, damp cloths to her forehead when I saw the healing angel at the opposite side of the bed. She put forth her right hand and laid it for a moment on the hand with which I was holding the cloth against the suffer's brow. There was something very soothing in her touch, and so gentle was it, I might say that I "sensed" it rather than felt it. As she withdrew her hand, she raised her head and looked into my eyes. It was not a beautiful face that confronted me, judged by the ordinary standards of beauty, but there was stamped upon it a sweetness and tenderness that was far more attractive than mere beauty.

"Be of good cheer," she said. "She will recover."

It was the first time the healing angel had spoken to me, but often afterward when she was ministering to my patients she spoke to me words of similar hopeful import.

That night she came several times to the woman's bedside, each time laying her right hand on the patient's brow, but up to the time that I went off duty, at nine o'clock in the morning, there had been no perceptible change in the patient's condition. The following night the healing angel again paid several visits to the sufferer, and she had some refreshing sleep, but when the doctor saw her before I went off duty again, he was still convinced that her case was hopeless.

While he was talking to me about it the healing angel appeared, standing very near us. Though as plainly visible to me as was the doctor himself, I knew that he could not see her. As he again expressed the opinion that the woman could not recover, the angel gave me a sweet smile of reassurance. Emboldened by it, I said to the doctor, "The case does look hopeless as far as we can see, but still I believe that she will recover."

"Nonsense, nurse," he replied. "It is impossible that she should pull through after such terrible injuries as she has received. But we shall of course do everything that it is possible to do for her."

That night there occurred a quite perceptible improvement in her condition, and her temperature, which had been very high, was lowered.

"Yes, she does seem a little better," said the doctor in

the morning. "But it can only be a temporary improvement."

Night after night the healing angel continued to minister to her, and some weeks after she had been admitted to the hospital she was able to return to her home. She was not as strong and sound as she had been before the accident—I don't know that she ever recovered to that extent—but she was able to attend to her household duties and give her children the love and care they needed. It was regarded in the hospital as a wonderful recovery.

"I never thought to see her on her feet again," said the doctor who had repeatedly pronounced her case utterly hopeless. "I look upon her recovery as simply miraculous."

The Angels at Death

These are excerpts from a letter written by Mrs. Wortley, wife of the Rev. Canon E. J. Wortley of Jamaica, British West Indies, to her daughter on September 18, 1928:

... Your dad had a wonderful deathbed. He was ill exactly ten weeks; at first he had a slight stroke, as I told you. ... On the Friday before he died he was in one of his sweetest moods, quite clear in his mind. We were having our usual talk, and he was praying that his sufferings would soon be over; we talked of the people he hoped to see, and I reminded him of Archbishop Nuttall and one or two of our East Indian friends who had died. And he said "Oh, joy unspeakable! I had not thought of seeing them in paradise."

Then later, he suddenly said to me, "Aunt Janie has come with the angels." And after a few moments, he said it again in the calmest, most natural way. Then he stretched his arm across the bed and seemed to shake hands all up the side of the bed. So I said, "What are you doing?" to which he said, "Shaking hands with the angels." Then he turned to me as I stood next to him, and touching me gently he said, "Just move a little. You are blocking the way of one of the angels." And in a most reproving voice, he said, "You may not know the angels, but I know them all." . . .

Later on that day, he said, "Oh, my, and do I have to have another night of torment . . . ?" So I said, "Of course not. How could you when the angels have come . . . ?" But he said quietly, "They have gone." I told him, "Oh, never mind. So long as they have been here, you may be sure they came to clear the atmosphere and put a stop to all the devil's work, and you will have no more suffering." Well, he had a good night, and next day he continued comfortable. At midday on Saturday he began again to talk with the angels.

He said, "Angels, angels, are you the same angels who came before?" Twice over he said it, and then, "Two archangels. . . . Two archangels. . . ." And he went on talking, beginning every sentence "The angels . . ." but finishing in such an indistinct voice that we could not hear what he said, until we heard, "Angels, angels. Ready? Ready?" And he settled himself, lying flat on his back with his arms up in such a way, trying to ease up, that you could imagine you saw the angels bending over him to take him up. . . .

And the letter goes on to tell of his lying peacefully until he died, finally in a coma. One of the other stories mentioned is quite similar in feeling. The third tells of being awakened before dawn to a vision of two shining beings who stood waiting beside a window. As she watched, puzzled, the woman saw her mother appear, and together the three persons glided by the bed, close enough to touch, and disappeared, leaving the room electrified and glowing with light. The woman lay rejoicing that her mother, who had been sick, was now so well and filled with health. At that moment she heard the telephone, and listened to her husband take the message that her mother had died a few moments before.

111

God Will Send Angels

If it is true that we each have a guardian angel, then mine has been seen three times that I know of— each time by a different person.

My mother, Minnie Metcalf Miller, said that when I was three weeks old, and very tiny because I was premature, she was awakened in the night by a beautiful young girl bending over her.

Mother somehow understood from this beautiful visitor that her new baby, asleep in the next room, needed her. Mother said she seemed to understand that she would be facing a long ordeal, so she dressed carefully and went in to me. She found me blue in the face and struggling for breath.

There followed a long battle with pneumonia in which Mother did not have her clothes off for several nights. She said the beautiful girl was there beside her every minute of the fight with death.

A kind neighbor also saw the beautiful girl and asked my mother, "Who is the beautiful lady staying with you since the baby has been so sick? I see her come out on the front porch sometimes."

The beautiful lady disappeared when I was completely out of danger.

Years later, in 1934, she returned to rescue me again. I now had small children of my own and had just gotten a divorce. I had been told by my doctor that I must have a

From Hope Price, "He Will Send Angels," *Fate*, May 1961, pp. 55–56. Reprinted by permission from *Fate* Magazine.

serious operation, and an intensely religious woman named Lude was doing my housework. She was to stay with the three young children while I went to the hospital.

However, Lude seemed dissatisfied with conditions in our house, as she was used to working in wealthy households with other servants. One afternoon, as Lude entered the room with a vacuum cleaner, a cat, who was calling on my cat, jumped through the window, breaking the glass. This was the last straw for Lude. She gave notice rather sulkily, saying she would leave in the morning as she simply couldn't stay on.

I wondered what I would do! I couldn't leave three little children alone in the house while I was in the hospital. I finally decided I would have to call the doctor the next morning and tell him I could not have the operation.

However, early next morning Lude entered my room fairly beaming with good humor. She was wearing her white uniform.

"Breakfast is ready," she smiled.

"Why, Lude. How nice of you to get breakfast before you go," I said.

"Mrs. Price," Lude replied, "I've changed my mind. I'm not going. I had a vision last night. A beautiful young girl, an angel, came flying in to my bedside through that window the cat broke. She was all in shining white and surrounded with light. It lit up my whole room. She asked me not to leave you because you need me. I'm going to stay just as long as you need me."

So I went to the hospital comforted by the thought that the children were safely watched over by Lude.

In each case the angel was seen by a kind person with a good deal of spiritual understanding. They were the kind of persons able to see angels, obviously.

The lovely angel seems to appear when I need her most. I hope she always will. Perhaps some day I will see her myself.

113

Angel Triumph

I saw coming toward us a ghost who carried something on his shoulder. Like all the ghosts, he was unsubstantial, but they differed from one another as smokes differ. Some had been whitish; this one was dark and oily. What sat on his shoulder was a little red lizard, and it was twitching its tail like a whip and whispering things in his ear. As we caught sight of him, he turned his head to the reptile with a snarl of impatience. "Shut up, I tell you!" he said. It wagged its tail and continued to whisper to him. He ceased snarling and presently began to smile. Then he turned and started to limp westward, away from the mountains.

"Off so soon?" said a voice.

The speaker was more or less human in shape but larger than a person, and so bright that I could hardly look at him. His presence smote on my eyes and on my body too (for there was heat coming from him as well as light), like the morning sun at the beginning of a tyrannous summer day.

"Yes. I'm off," said the ghost. "Thanks for all your hospitality. But it's no good, you see. I told this little chap"—here he indicated the lizard—"that he'd have to be quiet if he came—which he insisted on doing. Of course, his

From C.S. Lewis, *The Great Divorce* (New York: Macmillan, 1952), pp. 99–105. Reprinted by permission of Macmillan Publishing Company and Collins Publishers (London).

stuff won't do here; I realize that. But he won't stop. I shall just have to go home."

"Would you like me to make him quiet?" said the flaming spirit—an angel, as I now understood.

"Of course, I would," said the ghost.

"Then I will kill him," said the angel, taking a step forward.

"Oh—ah—look out! You're burning me. Keep away," said the ghost, retreating.

"Don't you want him killed?"

"You didn't say anything about killing him at first. I hardly meant to bother you with anything so drastic as that."

"It's the only way," said the angel, whose burning hands were now very close to the lizard. "Shall I kill it?"

"Well, that's a further question. I'm quite open to consider it, but it's a new point, isn't it? I mean, for the moment I was only thinking about silencing it, because up here—well—it's so damned embarrassing."

"May I kill it?"

"Well, there's time to discuss that later."

"There is no time. May I kill it?"

"Please, I never meant to be such a nuisance. Please—really—don't bother. Look! It's gone to sleep of its own accord. I'm sure it'll be all right now. Thanks ever so much."

"May I kill it?"

"Honestly, I don't think there's the slightest necessity for that. I'm sure I shall be able to keep it in order now. I think the gradual process would be far better than killing it."

"The gradual process is of no use at all."

"Don't you think so? Well, I'll think over what you've said very carefully. I honestly will. In fact, I'd let you kill it now, but as a matter of fact I'm not feeling frightfully well today. It would be silly to do it now. I'd need to be in good health for the operation. Some other day perhaps."

"There is no other day. All days are present now."

"Get back! You're burning me. How can I tell you to kill it? You'd kill me if you did."

"It is not so."

"Why, you're hurting me now."

"I never said it wouldn't hurt you. I said it wouldn't kill you."

"Oh, I know. You think I'm a coward. But it isn't that. Really it isn't. I say! Let me run back by tonight's bus and get an opinion from my own doctor. I'll come again the first moment I can."

"This moment contains all moments."

"Why are you torturing me? You are jeering at me. How can I let you tear me to pieces? If you wanted to help me, why didn't you kill the damned thing without asking me— before I knew? It would be all over by now if you had."

"I cannot kill it against your will. It is impossible. Have I your permission?"

The angel's hands were almost closed on the lizard, but not quite. Then the lizard began chattering to the ghost so loudly that even I could hear what it was saying.

"Be careful," it said. "He can do what he says. He can kill me. One fatal word from you and he will! Then you'll be without me for ever and ever. It's not natural. How could you live? You'd be only a sort of ghost, not a real [person] as you are now. He doesn't understand. He's only a cold, bloodless, abstract thing. It may be natural for him, but it isn't for us. Yes, yes. I know there are no real pleasures now, only dreams. But aren't they better than nothing? And I'll be so good. I admit I've sometimes gone too far in the past, but I promise I won't do it again. I'll give you nothing but really nice dreams—all sweet and fresh and almost innocent. You might say, quite innocent. . . ."

"Have I your permission?" said the angel to the ghost.

116

"I know it will kill me."

"It won't. But supposing it did?"

"You're right. It would be better to be dead than to live with this creature."

"Then I may?"

"Damn and blast you! Go on, can't you? Get it over. Do what you like," bellowed the ghost, but he ended, whimpering, "God help me. God help me."

Next moment the ghost gave a scream of agony such as I never heard on earth. The burning one closed his crimson grip on the reptile, twisted it, while it bit and writhed, and then flung it, broken-backed, on the turf.

"Ow! That'd done for me," gasped the ghost, reeling backward.

For a moment I could make out nothing distinctly. Then I saw, between me and the nearest bush, unmistakably solid but growing every moment solider, the upper arm and the shoulder of a man. Then, brighter still and stronger, the legs and hands. The neck and golden head materialized while I watched, and if my attention had not wavered I should have seen the actual completing of a man—an immense man, naked, not much smaller than the angel. What distracted me was the fact that at the same moment something seemed to be happening to the lizard. At first I thought the operation had failed. So far from dying, the creature was still struggling and even growing bigger as it struggled. And as it grew it changed. Its hinder parts grew rounder. The tail, still flickering, became a tail of hair that flickered between huge and glossy buttocks. Suddenly I started back, rubbing my eyes. What stood before me was the greatest stallion I have ever seen, silvery white but with mane and tail of gold. It was smooth and shining, rippled with swells of flesh and muscle, whinnying and stamping with its hoofs. At each stamp the land shook and the trees dindled.

The new-made man turned and clapped the new

horse's neck. It nosed his bright body. Horse and master breathed each into the other's nostrils. The man turned from it, flung himself at the feet of the burning one and embraced them. When he rose I thought his face shone with tears, but it may have been only the liquid love and brightness (one cannot distinguish them in that country) which flowed from him. I had not long to think about it. In joyous haste the young man leaped upon the horse's back. Turning in his seat he waved a farewell, then nudged the stallion with his heels. They were off before I well knew what was happening. There was riding if you like! I came out as quickly as I could from among the bushes to follow them with my eyes, but already they were only like a shooting star far off on the green plain and soon among the foothills of the mountains. Then, still like a star, I saw them winding up, scaling what seemed impossible steeps, and quicker every moment, till near the dim brow of the landscape, so high that I must strain my neck to see them, they vanished, bright themselves, into the rose-brightness of that everlasting morning.

While I still watched, I noticed that the whole plain and forest were shaking with a sound which in our world would be too large to hear, but there I could take it with joy. I knew it was not the solid people who were singing. It was the voice of that earth, those woods and those waters. A strange archaic, inorganic voice that came from all directions at once. The nature or archnature of that land rejoiced to have been once more ridden, and therefore consummated, in the person of the horse.

St. Francis
and the Seraphim

The days drew on to the feast of the Holy Cross, September 14, kept holy by all Christians in remembrance of the day when the true cross had been won back from the Persian conqueror who had taken it away from Jerusalem. It was a day especially sacred for Francis because of what the cross meant to him and because it was the patronal festival of the crusaders. The day had for him now a personal sadness. He had with longing offered himself to die a martyr's death on the crusade, that he might have some share in the suffering and death of his Lord, and at that time his offering had not been accepted.

One night during these days, Leo came to the bridge and called aloud, "Domine labia mea aperies," but for the first time there was no answer. He had been forbidden to cross the bridge if Francis did not answer him, but he was so afraid that his father might be now seriously ill that he disobeyed him and crossed the bridge. The cell was empty, but he went farther on into the wood beyond, for the moon was bright and he could see the way. Then he heard Francis speaking, and coming nearer he saw him

From *My God and My All* by Elizabeth Goudge. Copyright 1959 by Coward, McCann & Geoghegan, Inc. Reprinted by permission of Coward, McCann & Geoghegan, Inc. and of David Higham Associates, Ltd. (London).

kneeling in prayer and heard the words that he said: "Who art thou, my dearest Lord? And who am I, a most vile worm and thy most unprofitable servant?" That was all his prayer, and he spoke the same words over and over again. Then it seemed to Leo that a light came from heaven and rested upon Francis, and though he himself could hear no words, he believed that they were spoken, and three times over he saw Francis take his hands from his breast and stretch them up to the light. Then the splendor was withdrawn, and in joy, knowing that all was well with Francis, Leo turned, hoping to creep away unseen. But the fallen beech leaves rustled under his feet, and Francis looked around and saw him and commanded him to stay where he was. Leo stood still, and he trembled, for he had disobeyed and he was afraid Francis would be angry with him.

Francis came toward Leo, but his eyes were now so dim that though the wood was bright with moonlight he did not know who it was who stood there, and he said, "Who art thou?" Leo said, "Father, I am brother Leo," and kneeling at Francis' feet he asked for forgiveness. Francis knew the anxious love that had prompted the disobedience, and he was not angry, but gentle and tender, and when he knew that Leo had heard his words, and seen the light and the lifting of his hands, he tried to tell him of what he had experienced in prayer. He said he had been kneeling in contemplation and he had beheld, as he was able to endure it, the goodness of God, and then he had seen the fearful abyss of his own vileness and out of the deep he had cried out, "Who art thou, my dearest Lord? And who am I?" And then the voice that had spoken to him so often spoke again from out of the light that rested upon him, asking him for three gifts, and he was distressed because he had nothing to give. He possessed nothing except his cord and tunic, and even they had been given him by God. Then the voice said, "Search in thy bosom," and putting his hands to his breast he found a golden ball there, and a second and a third, and he lifted them up to God, thanking [God that by divine mercy he now] had something that he might offer. At first he did not understand what he was offering, and then he realized that the three golden balls were poverty, chastity, and obedience. And he knew too that though God had come very close to him, [God] would come nearer still, and that it would be soon.

After they had talked together, Francis and Leo went to the little oratory, and Francis knelt before the altar and prayed that he might know something of the will of God concerning him, so that he might be able to conform himself the more perfectly to that blessed will. Then he signed himself with the sign of the cross, and turning to Leo he asked him to open the book of the Gospels and read to him the first passage upon which his eyes fell. Leo took the book and opened it, bending in the dim candlelight to see the page, and Francis, kneeling before the altar, heard him read of the crucifixion of his Lord. Twice more Leo opened the book, and twice more it opened at the story of the passion. Then Francis knew that his offering had been accepted. He was to share the suffering of Christ.

On the morning of the feast of the Holy Cross, just before dawn, he was kneeling at the entrance to his cell, his face toward the east, where soon now the light would break. Near to him was a rock which must many times have reminded him of the rock of the agony beside which [Jesus] had prayed in the Garden of Gethsemane. He was praying now, and the words of his prayer were these: "O Lord Jesus Christ, two graces do I ask of thee before I die; the first, that in my lifetime I may feel, as far as possible, both in my soul and body, that pain which thou, sweet Lord, didst endure in the hour of thy most bitter passion; the second, that I may feel in my heart as much as possible of that excess of love by which thou, O Son of God, was inflamed to suffer so cruel a passion for us sinners." He continued for a long time in this prayer and passed from it to deep contemplation, wherein the eyes of his soul beheld the passion of Christ and his infinite love. Perhaps the eyes of his body, closed in prayer, were yet aware of the glory of the dawn, and his ears of the singing of the birds in the woods below him, as the light grew. He looked up and saw the sky filled with fiery and resplendent wings and in the midst of the glory a figure. Two wings were spread above the head, two were outstretched in flight and two covered the body. It seemed to Francis that the seraph was coming from heaven to earth, drawing near with rapid flight, and he was much afraid. Then the fear changed to joy and grief and wonder, for he saw that the seraph came to him as one crucified, with arms outstretched and feet conjoined. This was his Lord, looking upon him with gracious aspect and immortal love, so near to him now that he could see the infinite beauty of the suffering face, so near at last that the pierced feet rested upon the rock. Then it seemed to him that the seraph smote him in body and soul, so that he was in great agony and yet in great joy, and afterward was so close to him that they spoke together. This moment of union seemed to Francis to lift him out of time into eternity.

Then he was alone, yet not alone, for the burning love in his heart was the same love that had come from the height of heaven down to the depth of [human] need, his joy was Christ's joy in redemption, and his pain Christ's pain. Every prayer of his life had been answered. He had fulfilled the will of God as perfectly as a [person] may, his offering of himself had been accepted, and he was wholly Christ's. In token thereof, the seal of the cross that had been set upon his immortal soul years ago was now upon his mortal body also. He bore in hands and feet and side the wounds of Christ.

The Vision of
St. Teresa of Avila

You can't exaggerate or describe the way in which God wounds the soul and the extreme pain this wound produces, for it causes the soul to forget itself. Yet this pain is so delightful that there is no other pleasure in life that gives greater happiness. The soul would always want, as I said, to be dying of this sickness.

This pain and glory joined together left me confused. I couldn't understand how such a combination was possible. Oh, what it is to see a wounded soul! I say that this reality should be understood in such a way that the soul is said to be wounded for a very sublime reason and there be clear awareness that the soul did not cause this love, but that seemingly a spark from the very great love the Lord has for it suddenly fell upon it, making it burn all over. . . .

At other times the pain becomes so severe that the soul can do neither penance nor anything else, for the whole body is paralyzed. One is unable to stir with either the feet or the arms. Rather, if one is standing, one sits down,

From *The Collected Works of St. Teresa of Avila, Volume One* translated by Kieran Kavanaugh and Otilio Rodriquez, Copyright © 1976 by Washington Province of Discalced Carmelites, Inc. ICS Publications, 2131 Lincoln Road, N.E., Washington, D.C. 20002, U.S.A. Reprinted by permission.

like a person being carried from one place to another, unable even to breathe. The soul lets out some sighs—not great ones—because it can do no more; they are felt within.

The Lord wanted me while in this state to see sometimes the following vision: I saw close to me toward my left side an angel in bodily form. I don't usually see angels in bodily form except on rare occasions; although many times angels appear to me, but without my seeing them, as in the intellectual vision I spoke about before. This time, though, the Lord desired that I see the vision in the following way: The angel was not large but small; he was very beautiful, and his face was so aflame that he seemed to be one of those very sublime angels that appear to be all afire. They must belong to those they call the cherubim, for they didn't tell me their names. But I see clearly that in heaven there is so much difference between some angels and others and between these latter and still others that I wouldn't know how to explain it. I saw in his hands a large golden dart, and at the end of the iron tip there appeared to be a little fire. It seemed to me this angel plunged the dart several times into my heart and that it reached deep within me. When he drew it out, I thought he was carrying off with him the deepest part of me, and he left me all on fire with great love of God. The pain was so great that it made me moan, and the sweetness this greatest pain caused me was so superabundant that there is no desire capable of taking it away, nor is the soul content with less than God. The pain is not bodily but spiritual, although the body doesn't fail to share in some of it, and even a great deal. The loving exchange that takes place between the soul and God is so sweet that I beg [God] to give a taste of this love to anyone who thinks I am lying.

On the days this lasted I went about as though stupefied. I desired neither to see nor to speak, but to clasp my suffering close to me, for to me it was greater glory than all creation.

Sometimes it happened—when the Lord desired—that these raptures were so great that even though I was among people I couldn't resist them. To my deep affliction they began to be made public. After I experience them, I don't feel this suffering so strongly; rather I experience what ... is very different in many respects and more valuable. But when this pain I'm now speaking of begins, it seems the Lord carries the soul away and places it in ecstasy. Thus there is no room for pain or suffering, because joy soon enters in.

May [God] be blessed forever, who grants so many favors to one who responds so poorly to gifts as great as these.

The Voices and Visions of Joan of Arc

Before giving the account of her visions and auditions which Joan presented to her judges, it is necessary to say that no critic, however skeptical, consistently doubts her veracity. To the last day of her life, though her faith in the heavenly origin of her experiences was shaken for an hour, she declared that the phenomena, whatever else they might be, were objective, as we say, that they had an external cause, were not illusions, but manifestations of beings other than herself. As M. Anatole France declares, "She had visions. These were neither feigned nor produced by trickery (*contrefaites*). She really believed that she heard voices which spoke to her and came from no human lips. ... I have raised no doubts as to the sincerity of Joan. No one can suspect her of falsehood."

Her own account of their origin, as given to her judges, ran thus: "When I was thirteen years old (or about thirteen) I had a voice from God, to help me in my conduct. And the first time I was in great fear. It came, that voice, about midday, in summertime, in my father's garden. I had not"—clearly in answer to a question—"fasted on the previous day. I heard the voice from the right side toward the church, and I rarely hear it without seeing a light. The light is on the side from which the voice comes."

From Andrew Lang, *The Maid of France* (New York: Longman, Green, 1908), pp. 42–47.

It has been supposed that the light always came from the side, and from the same side, whence it is argued, Joan was perhaps hysterical, being subject to unilateral hallucinations. But she told her judges, in answer to a question about an appearance, that "there was much light from every side" (*ab omni parte*), "as was fitting" (*et quod hoc bene decet*).

She was asked how she could see a light that on one occasion was not in front of her, a foolish question to which she did not reply. Her first emotions were those of fear and of doubt as to what these things should signify. She conceived, however, that they marked her as one set apart: "The first time that I heard the voice, I vowed to keep my maidenhood so long as God pleased. Her judges, had they known the superstition of the Scottish witches— "in our covens (assemblies) we could do nothing without our maiden"—might have twisted even this provisional vow of virginity into a proof of her witchcraft.

She believed that the voice was of God and, after hearing it thrice, knew it for the voice of an angel. The voice was for her soul's health. How did she know that? "Because it told her to be good and go often to church, and said that she must go into France." It is not apparent here that this command to go into France was not given from the first. There is no proof that it came later, after a period of mere religious and moral counsel. There is no warrant for the literary hypothesis that the voices long confined themselves to pious advice, till some priest, hearing from her of the visions, induced the voices to urge her to ride in the van of the army. On the other hand, when she set out for France in 1429, she told Jean de Novelonpont that during four or five years (since 1424 or 1425) the voices had pressed her mission upon her. The voices had uttered their monitions since she was twelve or thirteen years old.

The phenomena occurred twice or thrice a week. She

would not say, yet, in what form the voice came. She then told how she could not stay where she was after the voice bade her raise the siege of Orleans (begun in October, 1428), and was interrogated on other points.

One examiner, Beaupere, was anxious to connect her experiences, casually, with her fasting in Lent and with the sound of church bells. She certainly appears to have been apt to hear them during the ringing of church bells, whose music, says Coleridge, fell on his ears. . . .

The sounds of bells were not essential to her hearing of the voices; that, we shall see, is certain. She said that the voices, on certain occasions, were those of St. Catherine and St. Margaret. "Their heads were crowned with fair crowns, richly and preciously. To speak of this I have leave from the Lord. If you doubt, send to Poitiers, where I was examined before" (March–April 1429).

This is puzzling. She certainly appears to have described her visions, so far, to the commission at Poitiers. If so, the doctors kept their own counsel, for there is not a hint of the appearances, or even of the names of the saints, in any known evidence before her trial in 1431. The "Book of Poitiers," to which she often referred, as we show later, was not produced. Nothing is known about it, and it was not referred to in the trial of 1450-56. Clearly some person was interested in causing the concealment or destruction of this record, and that someone was not the maid. The president of the board of examiners was the archbishop of Reims, who later disparaged the maid.

Joan distinguished the saints by their naming each other by their method of salutation. They had been with her for seven years (in 1431; therefore, since 1424). She would give no details. She had forgotten which of the . . . saints appeared first, but it was recorded in the "Book of Poitiers." Before the two saints came, the archangel Michael had appeared and promised their arrival. Angels were in his company. "I saw them with my bodily eyes, as clearly as I see you. And when they departed I used to weep and wish that they would take me with them." She would not, she never would, describe the dress and aspect of St. Michael. That she "knew him by his arms," is a statement never made by her; and though a passage from her evidence is quoted to that effect, it does not contain a word on the subject. The voices of the saints were beautiful, gentle, and sweet. She "does not know" if they have arms. She had embraced the saints, and had touched St. Catherine with her ring, and had placed chaplets by their images in churches. The judges could get no more from her.

The saints appealed to all her senses; they were fragrant. She saw, heard, and touched them. Probably they appeared to her in the guise which they bore in paintings and works of sculpture; probably she saw St. Michael armed, and bearing the balances. She would not tell. We do not know why she should not have replied on these points, but she "had not permission." If she had answered that she beheld the saints as they appear in Catholic art, one does not see how such an answer could add to her peril. What trap did she consciously or subconsciously suspect in these questions? Did she foresee that, if she described the saints as they were rendered in art, the judges would say, "But the costume of the fourth century, when your saints lived on earth, was not that of the fifteenth! You have invented your story, or been deceived by fiends!" They cunningly asked her if she had her angels painted. "Yes, as they are painted in churches"; so she parried the thrust. "Do you see them so?" "I refuse to answer further."

One thing is clear. Joan made no conscious choice of saints. She did not know who these shining figures were till they informed her. It is curious that while she, like St. Catherine, was to contend for her life with hostile learned clerks and doctors, and while (in the words of an English

129

biography of St. Catherine, written when Joan was in bondage) "the Archangel Michael came to comfort" the captive saint, while in prison at Rouen, Joan never did see St. Michael. Her visions were not modeled on the lines of the contemporary legends of St. Michael and St. Catherine.

It was apparently after the arrival of her visions that Joan became sedulously devout, for which one witness, who was some twelve years older than she, confessed that he and other young men laughed at her. Since St. Remy was, as we saw, the patron of Domremy, and since the legend of the sacred oil brought for him and used in consecrating the kings of France at Reims was well known everywhere, it was natural that Joan should conceive the coronation of the dauphin to be part of the duty laid on her by her saints.

For her part, Joan resisted during three or four years the commands of her voices, from 1424 to the spring of 1428. When they bade her go to Robert de Baudricourt, who would give her an armed escort into France, to raise the siege of Orleans (begun in October, 1428), she replied, "I am a poor girl, who cannot ride or be a leader in war."

The evidence is that Joan was not more staid than other little girls, until 1424 or 1425, when her visions began; that she then became more devout than other young people; and that she resisted, on the score of her sex, youth, poverty, and ignorance, the summons of her voices, for three or four years, namely, until the spring of 1428.

An attempt at suggesting a more or less plausible way of envisaging the practical experiences of Joan will be given later. Meanwhile it is to be remembered that, for years, the monitions which reached her from the voices appeared to herself, even during the visions, as wild as they would have appeared to most skeptical neighbors. She retained (she says) her normal common sense, even when in the presence of her saints, in what we might reckon an abnormal condition. This fact differentiates her from the genuine subjects of trance, who are wholly wrapped up in their visions. Joan can only be called *une extatique* by critics ignorant of the technical meaning of "ecstasy." "In ecstasy, thought and self-consciousness cease.... In ecstasy [seers] no longer distinguish [themselves] from what [they] see."

On the other hand, hypnotized subjects often retain the normal elements of their character, resisting or trying to resist suggestions from the operator that they should do things contrary to their normal nature. But nobody has yet advanced the hypothesis that Joan was frequently hypnotized by her curé and by a succession of other piously fraudulent priests!

We have, perhaps, only one description, by an eyewitness, of Joan at the moment of receiving a saintly message. The witness is her confessor, Pasquerel, who stood by her when, in answer to her letter to Glasdale, tied to an arrow and shot across the gap in the bridge at Orleans, she was insulted and called "the harlot of the Armagnac." She wept, she prayed, she was consoled, "because she had news from her Lord." Thus it is clear that her voices came to her on occasions when she was not alone in a wood or alone listening to church bells and interpreting into audible words the rustling of the leaves or the music of the chimes. A lonely wood or the sound of bells offered propitious conditions for hearing the voices; the clamor of a crowd of church [people] in court was unpropitious; and in these circumstances the utterances of the voices were but indistinctly audible. These are the facts, and nothing indicates that Joan, when she heard the voices, was noticeably "dissociated" or in any manifestly abnormal condition. Nor is it true that she was "perpetually hallucinated" and, "as a rule" (*le plus souvent*), "in no condition to discern between truth and falsehood," as has been alleged.

131

Martin of Tours:
The Roman Soldier Saint
and His Angelic Experience

By now he was an officer. He had the rank of circuitor, which gave him the right to double rations, to one or two horses, and to an orderly. Sulpicius Severus mentions this serving man; his duty was to fight by his master's side, and apart from that to see to his lodging and his meals, to look after his horse and equipment; he was usually a slave. One scandalous fact sheds light upon the way Martin treated him. He simply reversed the roles; he served his servant. His biographer tells us that he often took his servant's shoes and cleaned them himself. One imagines that the garrison was amused; anyhow, it is clear that Martin had not changed. In a state of life in which so many are ruined, in which the exercise of authority develops harshness, unless the spirit of justice and charity bridles pride and keeps the feeling of power from swelling too far, in which relaxed morals offer compensation for army discipline, in which too often the only cure for boredom is in drunkenness and debauch, in which the grossest vices rub shoulders with the highest virtues, Martin had kept his virtues intact, had cultivated them patiently, perfected them, kept them steadily directed toward his first vocation. It is not enough to say that he remained a good soldier and a better Christian; soldiers and Christians alike could take him for a model. In a harsh age, still heavily marked by the brutality in which it was born, Martin drew, may well have been the first to draw, the ground plan for the Christian soldier.

Certainly they must have laughed at him at the beginning. The young officer who did not drink, left women alone, ate the poorest food and gave away all but the minimum, who devoted his leisure time to prayer, reading, and visiting the sick, who cleaned his orderly's boots, passed for more than slightly mad. But he disarmed all who mocked him by his serenity, his patience, and his friendliness; he showed them genuine affection, and in the end his comrades were constrained to return it. They guessed that a secret of great pride lay within the soul of this curious creature and was the motive of his most eccentric actions; they began to respect his folly and ended by reverencing him. It seems likely enough that he converted some of them—probably his tribune and his orderly, both of whom later entered God's service. Yet grasp that while the young man multiplied actions worthy of a saint, he had not even received baptism as yet, and the sin of our first parents, impressed upon his nature, still acted as an obstacle to the superabundance of grace.

It was in this period that the celebrated episode took the place of the sharing of his cloak. He was in garrison at Amiens. By all probability he must have remained there several years. His minor rank as circuitor obliged him, it seems, to ride out frequently by day and night on inspection of posts established in the town and in the country around. In the course of the winter that overlapped [the years] 338 and 339—"more severe than usual," so severe

133

indeed that "many people were frozen to death"—the younger lancer of Sabaria was returning from a night round, stiff with the cold, all the more so because he had already distributed his undergarments to various poor [people]. He was wearing only the icy steel of his armor and the great white cloak reinforced at the top with lambskin. As he arrived at one of the gates of the city, he met a poor wretch all huddled together, with his teeth chattering, completely naked. In the hurry and bustle of the morning, with a great number of people going out to their fields or in to their business, nobody yet had shown the least trace of an effective compassion. In any event, what could they have done? One does not normally go about with spare garments to cover the nakedness of beggars. Nor would it occur to anyone to strip . . . for them. It did occur to Martin. He realized in an instant, Sulpicius Severus tells us, [that] this beggar, this ultimate in beggars, the image of absolute denudation, was reserved especially for him. Upon the moment, he drew his sword, stripped off his cloak, and cut it down the middle—the lovely white cloak that all the girls ran after. He gave one half to the beggar—the warmer half, one presumes, with the wool lining—and draped himself in the other half.

It is hard to imagine the look of him in the torn rag, his limbs blue with the cold showing between the joints of his armor. The deed was met with blank incomprehension, but his equipment was a howling success. Yet not everybody laughed. "Many more sensible," adds Sulpicius Severus, "reproached themselves, lamenting that they had not done likewise, since they had more garments than he and could have clothed the beggar without going naked themselves." Martin hurried off to escape the praise and the sarcasm alike; one imagines his return to his quarters. But at least he did not incur punishment for destruction of military property; the equipment belonged to the officer.

Observe that what he did was a symbol of specifically evangelical sharing, like the breaking of bread. He had acted under the impulse of a superior power, at once lavish and prudent. He did not know the value of his act save after a dream or a vision with which we are told he was favored during the night that followed.

As he slept, Martin saw Christ standing before him, wearing the half cloak with which he had covered the beggar. Strange voices whispered in his ear: "Look, Martin! Look at the Lord. Don't you notice something?" They were the voices of the multitude of angels who thronged about his visitor. Then our Lord in a voice of glory cried out to him, "Martin, still a catechumen, covered me with this cloak."

Martin then, without being aware of it, had satisfied the Master's desire written in the Gospel: "Whatever you shall do for the least of your brethren, it will be as if you did it for me."

"Still a catechumen," our Lord had said—in praise or in mild reproach? Both, probably. However late it may have been usual to give baptism, Martin would certainly have been able to receive it by then. Yet it was not indifference or any slackening of desire which had kept him from it, but rather the difficulty of finding the leisure to prepare himself for it during his service and the impossibility of getting leave—a leave which he could have given over to preparation. Still more, as I think, it was through excess of humility. Martin judged himself not yet worthy. The extraordinary favor of which he had just been the object recalled him to a right view and removed his last scruples. "He flew to baptism," says his biographer, and emerged reborn. It was almost certainly on the night of Easter in the year 339. He was twenty-two.

The Night the Christmas Angels Sang

The greatest story in the world begins as quietly as a single snowflake drifting down into a silent forest at midnight. It begins in the home of a young girl named Mary who lived almost two thousand years ago in the town of Nazareth in the province of Galilee.

There is much that we don't know about this extraordinary event. We don't know at what time of day or night it happened. We don't know what Mary was doing; perhaps she was saying her prayers. We don't even know what Mary looked like, although ever since the greatest artists in the world have been trying to guess.

What we do know is that at one unique instant in time, so unique that it divided every other event into "before" and "after," God sent [a] messenger, the angel Gabriel, to speak to Mary: "And the angel came in unto her, and said, 'Hail, thou that art highly favoured, the Lord is with thee. . . .'"

What was the reaction of this gentle young girl, still in her teens, no doubt, perhaps her early teens? Astonishment, certainly; awe and a twinge of alarm perhaps . . .

From Norman Vincent Peale, *The Night the Angels Sang* (Pawling, N.Y.: Foundation for Christian Living, 1973), pp. 3-12. Reprinted by permission. The biblical quotations are from Luke 1—2, KJV.

surely an angel is different in manner and appearance from [a mortal].

The angel knew that she must be startled, so he tried to reassure her; "Fear not, Mary: for thou hast found favour with God." He went on to tell her that she would bear a son and name him Jesus, which means "the Lord is salvation" or "the Lord will save." This child, the angel said, would be called "the Son of the Highest," and his kingdom would have no end.

Now the astonishment in Mary's mind became perplexity. She did not doubt the truth of the angel's words, but she knew a baby had to have a father as well as a mother. She loved a young carpenter named Joseph, but no wedding ceremony had taken place. How then could this thing that the angel was predicting come about? She hesitated, then put her question into words: "How," she asked timidly, "shall this be?"

The angel must have seemed to her like a towering flame as he replied. "The Holy Ghost shall come upon thee," he told her, "and the power of the Highest shall overshadow thee." What a stupendous thing for a young girl to be told with no preparation, no warning! Only a pure and trusting heart could bear to comtemplate it. But Mary had such a heart. She must have felt deep joy flood through her as she bowed her head in humble acceptance. "Behold," she murmured, "the handmaid of the Lord; be it unto me according to thy word.

This was not Gabriel's only appearance during this miraculous year. Luke tells us that six months earlier the angel had also appeared to the husband of Mary's kinswoman Elizabeth and had predicted that she too would bear a remarkable son. Later he would be known as John the Baptist. Thus we know that John, six months older than Jesus, was also his [relative] on his mother's side.

Luke tells the story of Gabriel's appearance to Zacharias, husband of Elizabeth, in considerable detail. Zacharias and his wife were godly people who had lived a blameless life, but they had never had children. Now both were old. Elizabeth had lost all hope of ever having a baby. When the angel appeared to Zacharias as he was offering incense on the altar in the temple and told him that his wife would have a son, Zacharias could not believe it. "I'm an old man," he said, "and my wife is well advanced in years. How, then, can this be?"

The angel assured him that the prediction would come true. He added that because Zacharias had doubted, he would lose the power of speech and remain dumb until after the promised event had happened. This punishment was instantaneous. When Zacharias came out of the temple, he could not speak a word, and this affliction prevailed until after Elizabeth's child was born.

It continued until the time came to name the new baby. Elizabeth said that she wanted the child to be named John, and this puzzled her friends. "None of your relatives has that name," they said. "Why don't you name him Zacharias, after his father?" They made signs to Zacharias, trying to find out his preference in the matter. The old man asked for a writing tablet. When it was brought, he wrote down what the angel had told him: "His name is John." Immediately, says the Bible, he was able to speak freely. "And the child grew, and waxed strong in spirit, and was in the deserts till the day of his shewing unto Israel."

Meanwhile, Mary, the gentle virgin of Nazareth, had had to tell her fiancé, Joseph the carpenter, that she was with child. How did he react to this almost unbelievable story? Matthew's Gospel says that at first he was inclined to break off their engagement. He wanted to do this quietly, so that Mary would not be made "a public example." But then, in a dream, an angel told Joseph not to hesitate to marry Mary, because the child she was carrying had indeed been conceived by the Holy Spirit. And Joseph too was obedient to the voice of the angel, knowing that it was also the voice of God.

In those days the Roman emperor, Caesar Augustus, ruled most of the known world. His legions, feared and hated, enforced the *Pax Romana*—the Roman peace—everywhere. Now the emperor ordered a census taken throughout all his vast conquered territories. [All people were] ordered to return to [their] native city to be counted. As a descendant of David, Joseph had to return to Bethlehem, the town where David himself had been born a thousand years earlier. He made the journey from Nazareth, taking with him "Mary his espoused wife, being great with child."

Everyone knows the immortal story of how the weary travelers found shelter in a stable because there was no room for them at the inn. Some say this stable was actually a cave where domestic animals were kept. In that humble place, with no help, no attendants other than her husband, Mary "brought forth her firstborn son, and wrapped him in swaddling clothes, and laid him in a manger."

Ever since that luminous night, marvelous stories have clustered around it. Best loved, perhaps, is Luke's account of the "shepherds abiding in the field, keeping watch over their flock by night." Even the dullest imagination is thrilled by his description of a sky full of angels singing what was really the first Christmas carol, a promise of peace on earth that all [people] hope will be fulfilled some day.

Imagine the feeling of those shepherds, simple, honest [people], as standing there under the stars they heard the most heavenly music that ever fell upon mortal ears. No wonder they "came with haste," to "see this thing which is come to pass, which the Lord hath made known unto us." Countless artists have tried to depict the scene, the roughly clad [shepherds] kneeling beside the manger, their faces alight with adoration. In a way, those shepherds represent what all of us feel at Christmastime: wonder and reverence mixed with gratitude and joy, the indescribable blend of emotions that for lack of better words we call the Christmas spirit.

The Angels Are Present at Zoroaster's Call to Preach

One of the most significant features of the earliest Avestan scriptures is the frequent glimpses of Zoroaster in the role of agricultural missionary to a seminomadic people. He confesses himself that his call came through "the wail of the kine."

Like Moses, he protested his unfitness. Who was he to plead the cause of the cattle, who were suffering in the unsettled conditions of tribal warfare? With a sort of primitive humor, he said that the kine themselves would object to "a lord who is a powerless, feeble, pusillanimous man." But like Moses, too, he became a great leader who steadied and welded wandering tribes into a powerful established nation through the influence of a new religion. He seems to have planned definitely during his wilderness sojourn this creative, controlled evolution of his people. It was part of his divine call to service.

Zoroaster's call, however, was not primarily to scientific and economic work. There was a genuine religious experience, a mystic exaltation of spirit, a veritable vision of God.

But first the devil came.

At the door of his mountain cave the prophet wrestled with his own despairs in an emotional conflict so fiercely fought that evil seemed present in person. He was oppressed by the fact that superstition and primitive fear darkened the lives of his people; he was also troubled at the Turanian raids, which made life a misery for them. Like Buddha a century later in India, he felt deeply the problem of human suffering, but his solution of the enigma was different.

In the inspiration of a moment, he identified all these troubles and sufferings as the work of a malignant spirit, the Prince of Lies, the Demon of Doubt and Despair.

"I will not give in," he agonized. "This great demon of darkness will be conquered by the god of light.

"I will go forth and preach to my people, tell them that their old gods of fear and superstition are but agents of the great Lie Demon, Angra Mainyu, and tell them that the Turanians raiding our poor cattle are also sent by this evil one. But I will also proclaim that the time is coming when Angra Mainyu will be completely vanquished by Ahura Mazda, the supreme god of light and truth."

As he made this high resolve, his spirit felt purged, and there came to him great peace and exaltation of soul. Pure of heart, he saw God in a wonderful vision, which ranks in Zoroastrianism with Christianity's vision of John on Patmos.

This theophany is described in elaborate detail by later writers, for they recognized its importance in the life of their leader. They dated their chronology from this great moment, with rather more insight than most calendar-makers. By their reckoning, the thirty-first year of King Vishtaspa became the first Year of the Religion (1 A.R.). At dawn on the fifteenth day of the month Artavahisto (May 5, 630 B.C.), the revelation came.

The story goes that at daybreak Zoroaster stood upon the bank of the third channel of the sacred river Daitya. As he lifted some of the holy water, he suddenly saw a figure coming to him from the south bearing a shining staff. It was the archangel Vohu Manah, nine times as large as a [person]. He bade the enrapt Zoroaster lay aside his body and follow him to the audience room of the great Ahura Mazda and his holy angels.

In the presence of God and the angels, Zoroaster first noticed that he himself cast no shadow. He laid this to the exceeding brightness of the angels. The unusual nature of his surroundings evidently affected his scientific acumen. Otherwise he would have recalled that his material body was still down by the riverside, making its only permissible shadow there. Still forgetting that he was incorporeal, "he went forward and sat down in the seat of the enquirers" and was taught the cardinal principles of the "true religion." Mysterious signs and secrets were shown him which miraculously forecast coming events in the history of Zoroastrianism. Then he returned to earth, assumed his body, and following his instructions from Ahura Mazda, preached for two years to the religious leaders of his country.

What was the actual experience which came to Zoroaster by the riverbank that May dawn after his night of wrestling with the devil? It is impossible for any mystic to describe his own trance temperately and accurately. There seem to be, however, two common elements in these calls which come to prophets. They all speak of a great light or flame, and they are all commissioned to preach. Paul on the Damascus road or Moses by the burning bush or Zoroaster by the bank of the Daitya—brothers all.

It was the brightness of God's presence which most intrigued Zoroaster. Ahura Mazda means Lord of Wisdom, but wisdom and truth and light seem to have been almost interchangeable in the prophet's vocabulary, and light and fire came to play a very important part in Zoroastrianism. Parsees today deny that they worship fire, and it is true that they have been remarkably free from idolatry all through their history, but they certainly do give fire the central place in their ceremonies.

Out of this vision came a great contribution by Zoroaster to the evolution of religion, namely, the firm belief that some great day the Lord of Truth and Light would triumph over the Lord of Evil and Darkness. This millennial hope has since brought inspiration to [people] of many races and creeds.

Angel-like Forces
Attend the Birth
of Buddha Gautama

When Dipankara with all his followers had passed by, Sumedha examined the "ten perfections" indispensable to Buddhahood and determined to practice them in his future births. So it came to pass, until in the last of these births, the Bodhisatta was reborn as Prince Vessantara, who exhibited the Perfection of Supernatural Generosity and in due time passed away and dwelt in the Heaven of Delight. When the time had come for the Bodhisatta to return to earth for the last time, the deities of the ten thousand world-systems assembled together and, approaching the Bodhisatta in the Heaven of Delight, said, "Now has the moment come, O Blessed One, for thy Buddhahood; now has the time, O Blessed One, arrived!" Then the Bodhisatta considered the time, the continent, the district, the tribe, and the mother, and having determined these he assented saying, "The time has come, O Blessed One, for me to become a Buddha." And even as he was walking there in the Grove of Gladness, he departed thence and was con-

From Ananda K. Coomaraswamy, *Buddha and the Gospel of Buddhism* (New York: Harper & Row, 1964), pp. 12–14. Reprinted by permission.

ceived in the womb of the lady Maha Maya. The manner of the conception is explained as follows. At the time of the midsummer festival in Kapilavatthu, Maha Maya, the lady of Suddhodana, lay on her couch and dreamed a dream. She dreamt that the Four Guardians of the Quarters lifted her up and bore her away to the Himalayas, and there she was bathed in the Anotatta Lake and lay down to rest on a heavenly couch within a golden mansion on Silver Hill. Then the Bodhisatta, who had become a beautiful white elephant, bearing in his trunk a white lotus flower, approached from the north and seemed to touch her right side and to enter her womb. The next day, when she awoke, she related the dream to her lord, and it was interpreted by the Brahmans as follows: that the lady had conceived a man child who, should he adopt the life of a householder, would become a universal monarch; but if he adopted the religious life he would become a Buddha, removing from the world the veils of ignorance and sin.

It should be told also that at the moment of the incarnation the heavens and the earth showed signs, the dumb spoke, the lame walked, all [people] began to speak kindly, musical instruments played of themselves, the earth was covered with lotus flowers, lotuses descended from the sky, and every tree put forth its flowers. From the moment of the incarnation, moreover, four devas guarded the Bodhisatta and his mother, to shield them from all harm. The mother was not weary, and she could perceive the child in her womb as plainly as one may see the thread in a transparent gem. The lady Maha Maya carried the Bodhisatta thus for ten lunar months; at the end of that time she expressed a wish to visit her family in Devadaha, and she set out on the journey. On the way from Kapilavatthu to Devadaha there is a pleasure grove of Sal trees belonging to the people of both cities, and at the time of the queen's journey it was filled with fruits and flowers. Here the queen desired to rest, and she was carried to the greatest of the Sal trees and stood beneath it. As she raised her hand to take hold of one of its branches, she knew her time had come, and so standing and holding the branch of the Sal tree she was delivered. Four Brahma devas received the child in a golden net and showed it to the mother, saying, "Rejoice, O lady! A great son is born to thee." The child stood upright, took seven strides, and cried, "I am supreme in the world. This is my last birth. Henceforth there shall be no more birth for me!"

The Angels and Muhammad

The learned possess a great number of versions on this subject, but the best of all interpretations is that of the lord, *Rais*, the wise Abu Ali Sina, who declares: So said the prophet of God, Muhammad the selected (peace be upon him), "One night I slept in the house of my father's sister.* It was a night of thunder and lightning; no animal uttered a sound; no bird was singing; no [one] was awake; and I slept not, but was suspended between sleep and waking. The secret meaning of this might have been that it was a long while before I became desirous of understanding the divine truth. Under the shield of the night, [people] enjoy greater freedom, as the occupations of the body and the dependence of the senses are broken. A sudden night fell then, and I was still between sleep and waking, that is, between reason and sensuality. I fell into the sea of knowledge; and it was a night with thunder and lightning, that is, the seven upper

From M. Walter Dume, *The Dabistan* (New York, 1901), pp. 398–400.
*Muhammad was sleeping in the house of Omm Hani, the daughter of Abu Thaleb, in the sanctuary of the Kaba, when Jabriil awakened him; the angel called Mikail to bring him a cup full of water from the sacred well Zemzem. Jabriil cleft Muhammad's breast, drew his heart out, washed it, and, with three cups from the sacred fountain, infused into him faith, knowledge, and wisdom. He then conducted him out of the sanctuary to a place between Safa and Merva, where he made the prophet bestride Borak, which, as the angel said, was mounted by Abraham.

agents prevailed, so that the power of human courage and the power of imagination sank from their operation, and inactivity manifested its ascendancy over activity. And lo! Jabriil came down in a beautiful form, with much pomp, splendor, and magnificence, so that the house became illuminated; that is, the power of the Holy Spirit came upon me in the form of the command and made such an impression upon me that all the powers of the rational soul were renewed and enlightened by it. And what the prophet said in the description of Jabriil, 'to have seen him whiter than snow, with a lovely face, black hair, and on his forehead the inscription "There is no God but one God"; the light of his eyes charming, the eyebrows fine, having seventy thousand curls twisted of red rubies, and six hundred thousand pearls of fine water,' that is, he possessed so many beauties in the eyes of pure reason that if an impression of these beauties was made upon a sense, it was able to perceive those which have been described, and the purport of the words 'There is no God but one God' appeared in a determined light, that is, he whose eyes fall upon his perfections is removed from the darkness of infidelity and doubt and worldly connection; and in such a manner he feels himself fortified in the certitude of the Creator, and attains such a degree of virtue, that hereafter, upon whatsoever creature he looks, his faith in God's unity will be enhanced by it. And such were the charms of the angel that if one possessed seventy thousand curls he would not attain to his beauty; and such was his rapidity that thou wouldst have said, He was flying with six hundred wings and arms, so that his progress knew neither space nor time.

"What he said came upon me, and he took me to his bosom and gave me kisses between the eyes and said, 'O thou sleeper, how long sleepest thou? Rise!' That is, when the power of holiness came upon me it caressed me, opened the road of its revelation, and exalted me; a certain delight which I cannot describe diffused itself in my heart and transported me to devotion. The angel then continued, 'How long sleepest thou?' that is, 'Why indulgest thou in the delusions of falsehood? Thou art attached to the world, and as long as thou remainest in it, and before thou awakest, knowledge cannot be obtained; but I, from compassion toward thee, shall be thy guide on the road. Rise.' I trembled at his words and from fear jumped up from my place; that is, from timid respect for him no reflection remained in my heart and mind. He further said, 'Be calm, I am thy brother, Jabriil'; thus, by his kindness and revelation my terror was appeased. But he unfolded more of his mysteries, so that fear returned upon me. I then said, 'O brother, I feel the hand of an enemy.' He replied, 'I shall not deliver thee into the hand of an enemy.' I asked, 'Into whose?' He answered, 'Rise and be glad and keep thy heart within thyself'; that is, 'Preserve thy memory clear and show obedience to me, until I shall have removed the difficulties before thee.' And as he spoke I became entranced and transported, and I proceeded on the footsteps of Jabriil; that is, I forsook the sensual world, and by the aid of natural reason I followed the footsteps of holy grace."

Joseph Smith's Story on the Origin of the Book of Mormon

A Voice Speaks from the Dust

Three and one-half years elapsed after Joseph's vision in the grove at Palmyra before he again had a like experience—a like experience in that it came in the same manner, by obedience to the same spiritual law, the law of prayer. Often the boy wondered why the heavens had remained silent for so long, why the Lord had not made clear [the divine] purpose in regard to him. Now, on the evening of the twenty-first of September 1823, Joseph came to the realization that the reason for that silence was within himself. The Savior, while living in the flesh upon the earth, had instructed his followers, "Ask, and it shall be given you; seek, and ye shall find; knock, and it shall be opened unto you: For every one that asketh receiveth; and he that seeketh findeth; and to him that knocketh, it shall be opened." [Matt. 7:7ff., KJV] For three and one-half years he had failed to properly knock at the door of God.

From William E. Berrett, *The Restored Church* (Salt Lake City: Deseret Book Co., 1977), pp. 22–24. Reprinted by permission.

He had done so once, and the promise had not failed—he would do so again. To quote his own story:

"After I had retired to my bed for the night, I betook myself to prayer and supplication to Almighty God for forgiveness of all my sins and follies, and also for a manifestation to me, that I might know of my state and standing before [God]; for I had full confidence in obtaining a divine manifestation, as I had previously done. While I was in the act of calling upon God, I discovered a light appearing in my room, which continued to increase until the room was lighter than at noonday, when immediately a personage appeared at my bedside, standing in the air, for his feet did not touch the floor. He had on a loose robe of most exquisite whiteness. It was a whiteness beyond anything earthly I had ever seen; nor do I believe that any earthly thing could be made to appear so exceedingly white and brilliant. His hands were naked, and his arms also, a little above the wrist; so also were his feet naked, as were his legs a little above the ankles. His head and neck were also bare. I could discover that he had no other clothing on but this robe, as it was open, so that I could see into his bosom. Not only was his robe exceedingly white, but his whole person was glorious beyond description, and his countenance truly bright lightning. The room was exceedingly light, but not so very bright as immediately around his person.

"When I first looked upon him, I was afraid; but the fear soon left me. He called me by name, and said unto me that he was a messenger sent from the presence of God to me and that his name was Moroni; that God had a work for me to do; and that my name should be had for good and evil among all nations, kindreds, and tongues, or that it should be both good and evil spoken among all people. He said there was a book deposited, written upon gold plates, giving an account of the former inhabitants of this continent, and the sources from which they sprang.

152

He also said that the fullness of the everlasting gospel was contained in it, as delivered by the Savior to the ancient inhabitants; also that there were two stones in silver bows—and these stones, fastened to a breastplate, constituted what is called the Urim and Thummim—deposited with the plates; and the possession and use of these stones were what constituted 'seers' in ancient or former times; and that God had prepared them for the purpose of translating the book.

"After telling me these things, he commenced quoting the prophecies of the Old Testament. He first quoted part of the third chapter of Malachi, and he quoted the fourth or last chapter of the same prophecy, though with a little variation from the way it reads in our Bibles. Instead of quoting the first verse as it reads in our books, he quoted it thus: 'For behold the day cometh that shall burn as an oven, and all the proud, yea, and all that do wickedly shall burn as stubble; for they that come shall burn them, saith the Lord of Hosts, that is shall leave them neither root nor branch.'

"And again, he quoted the fifth verse thus: 'Behold, I will reveal unto you the Priesthood, by the hand of Elijah the prophet, before the coming of the great and dreadful day of the Lord.'

"He also quoted the next verse differently: 'And he shall plant in the hearts of the children the promises made to the fathers, and the hearts of the children shall turn to their fathers; if it were not so, the whole earth would be utterly wasted at his coming.'

"In addition to these, he quoted the eleventh chapter of Isaiah, saying that it was about to be fulfilled. He quoted also the third chapter of Acts, twenty-second and twenty-third verses, precisely as they stand in our New Testament. He said that that Prophet was Christ; but the day had not yet come when 'they who would not hear his voice should be cut off from among the people,' but soon

153

would come. He also quoted the second chapter of Joel, from the twenty-eighth verse to the last. He also said that this was not yet fulfilled, but was soon to be. And he further stated that the fullness of the Gentiles was soon to come in. He quoted many other passages of scripture, and offered many explanations which cannot be mentioned here.

"Again he told me that when I got those plates of which he had spoken—for the time that they should be obtained was not yet fulfilled—I should not show them to any person; neither the breastplate with the Urim and Thummim; only to those to whom I should be commanded to show them; if I did I should be destroyed. While he was conversing with me about the plates, the vision was opened to my mind that I could see the place where the plates were deposited, and that so clearly and distinctly that I knew the place again when I visited it.

"After this communication, I saw the light in the room begin to gather immediately around the person of him who had been speaking to me, and it continued to do so, until the room was again left dark, except just around me, when instantly I saw, as it were, a conduit open right up into heaven, and he ascended until he entirely disappeared and the room was left as it had been before this heavenly light had made its appearance. I lay musing on the singularity of the scene and marveling greatly at what had been told to me by this extraordinary messenger; when, in the midst of my meditation, I suddenly discovered that my room was again beginning to get lighted, and in an instant, as it were, the same heavenly messenger was again by my bedside. He commenced, and again related the very same things which he had done at the first visit, without the least variation; which having done, he informed me of great judgments which were coming upon the earth, with great desolations by famine, sword, and pestilence; and that these grievous judgments would

154

come on the earth in this generation. Having related these things, he again ascended as he had done before.

"By this time, so deep were the impressions made on my mind that sleep had fled from my eyes, and I lay overwhelmed in astonishment at what I had both seen and heard. But what was my surprise when again I beheld the same messenger at my bedside, and heard him rehearse or repeat over again to me the same things as before; and added a caution to me, telling me that Satan would try to tempt me (in consequence of the indigent circumstances of my father's family) to get the plates for the purpose of getting rich. This he forbade me, saying that I must have no other object in view in getting the plates but to glorify God, and must not be influenced by any other motive than that of building his kingdom; otherwise I could not get them. After this third visit, he ascended into heaven as before, and I was again left to ponder on the strangeness of what I had just experienced, when almost immediately after the heavenly messenger had ascended from me the third time, the cock crowed, and I found that day was approaching, so that our interviews must have occupied the whole of that night.

"I shortly after arose from my bed and as usual went to the necessary labors of the day; but in attempting to work as at other times, I found my strength so exhausted as to render me entirely unable. My father, who was laboring along with me, discovered something to be wrong with me, and told me to go home. I started with the intention of going to the house; but, in attempting to cross the fence out of the field where we were, my strength entirely failed me, and I fell helpless on the ground and for a time was quite unconscious of anything. The first thing that I can recollect was a voice speaking unto me, calling me by name. I looked up and beheld the same messenger standing over my head, surrounded by light as before. He then again related to me all that he had related to me the previous night, and commanded me to go to my father and tell him of the vision and commandments which I had received. I obeyed, and returned to my father in the field, and rehearsed the whole matter to him. He replied to me that it was of God, and told me to go and do as commanded by the messenger. I left the field, and went to the place where the messenger had told me the plates were deposited; and owing to the distinctness of the vision which I had had concerning it, I knew the place the instant that I arrived there."

The Hill Cumorah

If one travels today on New York State Highway 21, from Palmyra south toward Manchester, [one] will pass directly by the most impressive monument in the northern part of that state. If the journey be made at night, the sight is doubly impressive—for then one sees from a distance a veritable pillar of light ascending from the open plain. On closer approach the phenomenon becomes an illuminated monument on the very apex of a hill that rises some one hundred and fifty feet above the surrounding country. Surmounting the huge granite shaft is a representation of the angel Moroni. Six great floodlights play upon the unusual work of art. The hill at the base of the beautiful monument lies to the east of the highway, its north end rising abruptly from the surrounding plain and sloping gradually to the level terrain on the south. This is the hill Cumorah, known locally as "Mormon Hill."

Angel at Work

For nearly two decades people have come from all over the country to the summit of the hill overlooking the Ohio River in Covington, Kentucky to see a perfect replica of the "garden tomb" in Jerusalem. As you know, if you've been to Jerusalem, there are actually two tombs where people say that Jesus was buried. One is the venerated place under the enclosure of the Church of the Holy Sepulcher within the old city of Jerusalem. The other is a place outside the city wall known as Gordon's Calvary.* This, from an archaeological point of view, is more likely the tomb where Jesus was placed, simply because of its close proximity to a skull-faced mound that appears to have been a crucifixion site in early times. Today, it is a Muslim cemetery.

The scripture reference to the place where Jesus was crucified is called Golgotha, meaning "place of the skull." The Gospel of John reads, "Now in the place where he was crucified there was a garden, and in the garden a new tomb where no one had ever been laid [John 19:41]."

Archaeologists uncovered a garden and a tomb just adjacent to the skull-faced mound outside the city wall. Out of two hundred tombs excavated in that area, this

From the author's file.
*General Gordon was a British officer who was one of the first to see the skull-shaped mound while standing on the city wall of Jerusalem near the Damascus Gate.

tomb is the only one that has a ledge on which to roll a huge stone, as would have been the case with the tomb of Jesus, and a small opening for light as suggested in the scriptural story, enabling one to look in on Easter Day and see that Jesus was no longer there. Furthermore, this is a new tomb in which none of the crypts had yet been finished. So pilgrims visiting Jerusalem can visit both tombs, although the guides tend to go much more often to the Church of the Holy Sepulcher than to the garden tomb of Gordon's Calvary outside the city wall.

Several years ago a man by the name of Maurice Coers, minister of the Immanuel Baptist Church in Covington, Kentucky, visited the Holy Land and like many others made his pilgrimage to both tombs. He was so taken with the garden tomb, however, that not only did he believe it to be the authentic burial place of Jesus, but he began thinking of a way to reproduce it back home in Covington, Kentucky—which may seem like a wild idea but this man thought big.

One can appreciate how he felt. There is something very impressive about that place, particularly early in the morning when no one is around. People can go there and sit before the tomb that many believe to be the actual place where Jesus was laid and let that special atmosphere wash over them. I recall sitting there one morning and suddenly noting the deep groove in the step-in opening of the tomb. Someone later explained that people have come there for centuries and when they enter the tomb they first step in at the same place and that constant pressure on the stone has etched an opening the size of a foot. This would indicate that this place had been recognized for what it is across the centuries. This historical point undergirded my spiritual feelings about the place.

Coers envisioned the construction of a tomb modeled as exactly as possible after the one in which Jesus was placed following his crucifixion. He told me that the model in Covington must be perfect, so that anyone coming to the tomb in America would be stirred almost as deeply as visiting the original in Jerusalem. He plunged ahead with his project, which certainly was ambitious—perhaps too much so. In 1956 the Immanuel Baptist Church purchased a hillside that appeared to be perfect for construction of the garden tomb replica and a first-century carpenter shop, museum, chapel, and bookstore. A fund-raising campaign was launched. Church people sometimes look askance at such grand projects, wondering if the minister is merely looking for attention, but this was certainly not Coers's intent. He was not a man in search of a reputation—he only wanted to share with others the experience he had enjoyed in Jerusalem.

There was enthusiastic support for this project in the city of Covington, and many people—several of whom were not members of Coers's church—made generous contributions. Within a few months the underwriting was completed. Construction began, and hopes ran high that the project would be finished within a year. But winter freezes began to undermine all that they were attempting to do. The hillside on which the project was constructed began to give way, causing expensive landscaping, walkways, and patio, right up to the tomb entrance, to begin a downhill slide. It was discovered later that buried in the hillside were hidden springs that reacted violently to extreme changes in temperature, thus causing the landslides.

The only solution to the problem seemed to be pouring several tons of concrete on the hillside in an effort to secure it from further slippage. This effort proved to be expensive and plunged the church into further debt, causing many of the congregation to grumble. It was a trying time for Coers and his wife, Vernice, and all the other loyal associates. During the winter of 1959, more freezes and thaws occurred than usual, and despite the pressure of the reinforcing concrete, the landslide began again. Ironically, by now the hillside had been named "The Garden of Hope."

Floundering with problems beyond their resources, the church wrote to various engineering firms, seeking professional help. Several prominent engineers came to appraise the situation, and each in turn viewed the project as doomed to destruction. Gloom set in on the little group who had tried desperately to make this project a reality. They prayed persistently, but facing the inevitability of the problem, their prayers became less and less believing.

Then one day a man arrived at Maurice Coers's office and stated that he had heard of the church's plight and felt that he could be of help. He spoke with such conviction and authority that Coers received him with open arms. He claimed to have had experience with railroad construction, particularly in the mountainous regions of the West, and he insisted that the Garden of Hope presented a simple problem compared with some of his other projects.

Everyone who came in contact with this man was inspired by the confidence with which he approached the task. He seemed to know exactly what he was doing. Therefore the official board of the church was quick to give approval for him to get to work as soon as possible. The man believed that what was needed was a retaining wall patterned after the ones used in railroad construction in precipitous mountain areas. His thesis seemed reasonable. So funds were solicited, a bank loan was floated, materials were purchased, and a construction crew was hired. Good weather prevailed over the next few weeks, and the job was completed ahead of schedule. The wall was now in place. It looked formidable, but the question was—would it hold? Soon the winter weather arrived, with an onslaught of cold rarely seen in that part of the country. The cold was bad enough, but during the winter there were unsettled periods when a freeze and thaw was a daily routine. The wall could not have been tested any more severely. It held! Not a foot of earth moved, despite the elements.

There was great rejoicing among the garden enthusiasts during the early spring of 1960. No group could have been more appreciative for the work of one person. He was heralded across the community. For several weeks the church board waited patiently to receive a bill from the man, but none arrived. They figured he was waiting to see if the wall would hold, before submitting a bill for his services—but still, nothing was forthcoming. It was decided that a committee should be dispatched to the man's apartment and to thank him personally and ask how much they owed him. But on arrival they found that he had checked out several weeks before and had left no forwarding address.

The group was baffled. They had every intention of paying the man. But more than anything else, they wanted to thank him for the marvelous way he had headed up a superhuman task. They decided to check out the one reference he had submitted as having been associated with a certain engineering firm in the South, but the person making the call reported that no such firm existed. Further investigation revealed that the man had no standing in any engineering fraternity, nor was he listed among the certified engineers in the United States. The questions uppermost in everyone's mind were "Who was the man? Where had he come from and where had he gone?"

It could scarcely be stated that he had deceived them, because every day engineers from around that part of the country would stop, examine the wall, and repeat what almost became a litany, "This is a gem of a structure. The man in charge of this job is a genius. It's one of a kind. We would like to have that engineer on one of our projects."

But the man was gone, and what was more, he was

never heard from again. He had disappeared as mysteriously as he had arrived. But his masterful work is still on the hillside for everyone to see. I have the feeling that the Garden of Hope was rescued by an angel who slipped into our dimension, took on a bodily form, did his work and left. Maurice Coers shared the same idea.

The Garden Tomb was officially opened on Easter of 1960, but the guiding spirit of the project died just prior to the momentous event. I remember standing with him on a bright Sunday afternoon a few weeks before the tomb was to open to the public and just before his death. We talked about the mysterious stranger who had intervened to save the project. We agreed, unquestionably, that he was an angel. There were tears in Maurice's eyes as he spoke of "that heavenly deliverance."

Today the Garden of Hope is in splendid condition and is operating efficiently for thousands of people to make their pilgrimage. The chapel is used for weddings, churches and schools throughout the area periodically deposit students on special field trips, and it is used for worship services and seminars.

I once went there alone and walked down by the retaining wall. Something about that wall was different from any wall I'd ever seen. In the late afternoon sun it reflected a color totally different from anything around it. While the tomb and the other buildings were shadowed in the twilight colors—predominantly reds and blues— the wall gleamed golden and held that color until almost dark. It seemed appropriate; angels do love the golden light.

AFTERWORD

I am not really comfortable with what many angel absolutists have to say. Their defense of angel existence is in most cases arbitrary. Quoting the Bible or a church tradition concerning angels does not quite say it all, for as we have seen, the Bible says much about angels that is borrowed from other religions, and various traditions in this regard are less than consistent. I am not impressed by all this reach for authority. When people tell me about personal angel experiences and there is authenticity in their words, I feel a beautiful blending of the unique and common. While the general pattern of the story may be like thousands of others, the personal application is totally fresh, like old truths run through a new form. It is their experience, and they call it angel-like because an angel seems an appropriate symbol with which to communicate such an event.

Angel forms, however people approach them, must be loosely defined. Angel extinction in our time is the direct result of overloading one or two categories, for instance, thinking of all angels as messengers. Alas, many people don't take kindly to this point of view. Recently, a man told me that he thought my approach to angels too nebulous, that he preferred the more traditional way of thinking. The only problem with the traditional way is that it is nonthinking, and that makes for a dilemma. Angels have long been lost in their traditional role, because, generally speaking, people just do not think about them anymore. It has reached the point where someone nonchalantly hanging a white satin doll with gossamer wings and a bent halo on a Christmas tree is thought to be doing honor to the angels. In light of all this wretched lack of creative angel thought, I much prefer the so-called nebulous approach with all its fantastic possibilities. At least I know the essences and energy forces are there, and that it is up to me to give them form.

Most people think of angels as a phenomenon that manifested itself long ago and maybe a few times since, "but couldn't happen now." However, I would argue that the angel phenomenon—like most other phenomena—is not something that is fixed and final forever. It is constantly changing (at least it should be) and is subject to an evolving human consciousness. Can you imagine Moses, hearing God speak out of the burning bush, responding, "I've never read where God communicates out of a burning bush, therefore this can't be happening." Or Elijah, hearing God speak in a still small voice, denying the experience by saying, "Tradition says that God speaks only in earthquake, wind, and fire, never in a still small voice." Or Paul, after being toppled from his horse by the blinding light of Christ's presence on the Damascus road, saying, "Since there is no precedent for someone being unseated from a horse by the light of Christ, therefore it cannot be true." God appears to be constantly experimenting with creation, so flexibility should be the rule for our attitude with regard to spiritual phenomena.

Angel essences and energy forces, when taking a shape, are always more than what they appear to be. If a particular essence appears to one person in one angel experience, this does not exhaust the possibility of another person entertaining another angel form that will be just as effective in channeling still another essence. In all cases, the angel form is just a conduit to experience. It is only an appearance, and that is all that it is—just an appearance. The tragedy occurs when a religion is made out of a form or vehicle. That is to put up a sacrosanct wall around what appears to be. In an appearance an essence is poured into an image, enlivening it to the extent that it manifests a deceptive finality. But what gives it the quality of reality is not the appearance but the essence that was poured into it in the first place. This is what Immanuel Kant meant when he spoke of phenomena as being the product of "things in themselves" acting upon us as sensations that we synthesize into forms, categories, and ideas. The things in themselves he called the noumena, which is what makes for the phenomena.

The noumena energy seeks to express itself in a form. The essence connecting with an angel shape or phenomenon is fulfilling itself for the moment. But the angel shape is always an appearance and should not be conceptualized as once and forever. By the way, I discovered an alternative definition of the Hebrew word *mal'akh* (angel), which is translated "messenger." It can also be legitimately translated as an abstract noun message. The essence is the message of the messenger, but the essence is always more than any one category.

Angel-consciousness requires an open, childlike imagination that by its very nature is celebrative. Angel-consciousness can be triggered by any number of natural phenomena, such as a beautiful scene, lovely weather, the sight of the sea, sexual love involving the total person, seeing one's first child, exercise and movement, great art, inspiring music, engrossing literature, gaining scientific knowledge, being able to express something in vivid images in order to open up a flow of energy that puts one into the moving stream of unlimited energy.

Angel-consciousness is a product of expectant and creative imaging. Yet as we move through a study of angel forms in various religious traditions, we see how much alike many of them are. I won't say, nor have I been saying that Jews, Christians and Muslims are lacking in creative imagination. It is just that the angel stories told within the foregoing religious traditions have a way of conforming to a particular patterned package.

Imagination is a person's imaging power, but it is inseparable from the conscious and subconscious processes. To imagine is to bring into consciousness certain symbols with which to express the play between the inner and the outer. Imagination is not a superficial, off-the-wall self-deception. Imagination is the richest part of human consciousness, by which people develop forms that can be actualized in spirit. An illustration of this came one afternoon when visiting a man with whom I have little in common theologically yet have shared a good relationship with in every other way. I regard him as a friend. On this occasion, as we sat in his living room, he pulled out a list of special questions that he had been wanting to ask me for a long time. I knew he wanted to draw me into a religious argument, and, feeling trapped, I resented being put in this position. I could see no point in having a confrontation with someone I liked very much over nothing more than a few points of ancient doctrine.

As he read the first question on his list, the phone rang. I welcomed the reprieve, and during the next few moments asked God to transform this situation somehow. I found my attention drawn to a wall painting directly over the place where my friend had been sitting. It was a seascape with dramatic clouds hovering over the water. Suddenly in the midst of those clouds I saw a face. No question about it—it was there—a face so full of joy and love that it startled me. I glanced away, then looked back to see if it had been an illusion, but it was still there. An angel face? I don't know. What would an angel be doing in a painting, unless my imagination had created this particular form to channel the answer to my prayer.

When the man returned from his phone conversation, I began telling him of my appreciation for him as a friend—how much he meant to me, how much I valued the inspiration of his presence in my life, and so on. He responded in kind, and we talked on about the positive aspects of our relationship. We even got around to discussing projects that we could be mutually involved in. During this positive conversation, I watched him put his list away, and he's never mentioned it since.

It is interesting in these angel-less days how important television news has become. Morning, noon, and evening newscasts have taken on the shape of devotional moments when the powers from on high in Washington, D.C. and in New York speak to us. The Muslims may bow five times a day toward Mecca, but we do the same with our daily newscasts that fill up our waking hours. People tell me they "just live from one news break to the next." It would seem in most instances that the more explicitly awful the news, the better. In this regard, imagination has become the instrument of the negative and the agent of catastrophe. Imagination in that sense has gone wild—not with creativity, but with despair. When the imagination is rightly employed with the most positive images, including angel forms, we can draw forth the truly creative, powerful, transforming essences to do the work of renewal.

Using his imagination in this fashion, William Blake looked out on the world and saw the angels at work in the natural phenomena. They gave him a lift for his daily living.

I assert for myself that I do not behold the outward creation, and that it is to me a hindrance and not action. "What," it will be questioned, "when the sun rises do you not see a round disc of fire something like a guinea?" Oh!

167

no, no! I see an innumerable company of the heavenly hosts crying, "Holy, holy, holy, is the Lord God Almighty!" I question not my corporeal eye any more than I would question a window concerning a sight. I look through it, and not with it.[1]

The testimony of the mystics has always been that we should learn to see through the appearance level and trust ourselves more fully to the visionary. Frederick Prescott, who taught at Cornell University and from whose book the William Blake quote came, was not a psychologist but an English teacher, yet he wrote from a psychological perspective. Prescott maintained that sources of inspiration are the products not of the surface mind but of the deep mind of the human race. He spoke of individual consciousness as an island whose base is submerged in common with all the other islands of a particular group. He insisted that there is a deep common reservoir from which we all draw.

This is particularly true with the angels. Angel-consciousness is probably more native than people realize. It is not, as this study has shown, a product of superficial thought. There is a background or a history to angel experience, a hidden depth—call it mythical, human-race consciousness, whatever—but from the secret chambers in the human memory bank there is a record of people's experiences with the angels that can and should be translated into contemporary terms.

For instance, when sophisticated, well-educated Christians speak and/or write about angels, they virtually ignore Zoroastrian, Jewish, and Islamic angel forms as less authentic than Christian angel forms. Then there are some who do not believe angels exist in the first place, although most feel uneasy about coming right out and declaring that this angel business is a bunch of nonsense simply because Jesus believed in angels. The problem is

168

in translation. Christians may not be able to feel a sense of reality about Jesus' angel forms—and for that matter those of Zoroastrianism, the Jews, or the Muslims— because their cultural images are different. For instance, when Jesus spoke of "twelve legions of angels [Matt. 26:53]" he was using a form common to his culture. In general, Christians do not relate well to twelve legions of angels; they have little appreciation of what that means. Nevertheless, the Oriental mind of Jesus is part of our deep mind-consciousness, yet the ancient forms beg for new forms of expression. If only we could be as inquisitive and creative about spiritual matters as we are about technological ones. W. E. Orchard, the English clergyman, once commented, "If I saw someone walking on the water I would not say, 'You must be divine,' and let it go at that. I would say, 'Excuse me, sir, would you mind showing me how you did that?'" This should be the inquisitive spirit of angel adventure.

APPENDIX:
DEVELOPING AN
ANGEL-CONSCIOUSNESS

The angel-consciousness is something that can be developed. The question is, how to do it. How does one make an angel contact? More comprehensively, how do you develop an angel-consciousness?

Priming the Pump of the Consciousness

Developing angel-consciousness is not unlike conditioning oneself for athletic participation. It is the process of stretching the muscles of the creative imagination to facilitate a flow of power. It requires time and attention. Most of all, it requires a thoroughgoing preparation. Angel forms of the past were not produced out of haphazard, sloppy thought. They were developed gradually in creative consciousness. In constructing contemporary angel forms, people project their own qualities into the building process, but this does not mean they are less in touch with others who were doing the same thing centuries ago.

The angel-consciousness is triggered by a variety of stimuli. William Blake spoke of his contact with angels as being ignited by the sights, sounds, and smells of nature.

At the seashore he would say, "Heaven opens here and on all sides her golden gate." So these physical things become the props of perfection. Blake made a powerful point on this score: "If the doors of perception were cleansed, everything would appear to man as it is, infinite." So let the doors represent the total apparatus for developing angel-consciousness. When the doors of our perception are muddied or obscured by superficial use, we are the losers, for we will not realize what is there for us to experience. That strange little quote about "entertaining angels unawares" is an engaging idea.

For some of the items that seem essential to developing angel-consciousness, let us turn to Evelyn Underhill, who rarely mentions angels as such but who speaks masterfully about growing in spiritual consciousness. She writes,

> The condition of all valid seeing and hearing, upon every plane of consciousness, lies not in the sharpening of the senses, but in a peculiar attitude of the whole personality: in a self-forgetting attentiveness, a profound concentration, a self-merging, which operates a real communion between the seer and the seen—in a word, in contemplation.[1]

In the Chronicles, one will probably not find any angel experience that was the result of an exclusive formula or creative plan. The angel phenomenon is too oblique to use in drawing up a master blueprint for everyone to emulate. But there is something that might be suggested as a general approach. Evelyn Underhill understatedly offers an exercise in consciousness-developing that is extremely important:

> The object of our contemplation may be almost anything. . . . [For our purpose, think of an angel.] Willfully yet tranquilly refuse the messages which countless other

aspects of the world are sending; and so concentrate your whole attention on this one act of loving sight that all other objects are excluded from the consciousness field. Do not think, but as it were pour out your personality towards it: let your soul be in your eyes. Almost at once, this new method of perception will reveal unsuspected qualities in the external world. First, you will perceive about you a strange and deepening quietness; a slowing down of our feverish mental time. Next, you will become aware of a heightened significance, an intensified existence in the thing at which you look. As you with all your consciousness, lean out towards it, an answering current will meet yours. It seems as though the barrier between its life and your own, between subject and object has melted away. You are merged with it, in an act of true communion: and you know the secret of its being deeply and unforgettably, yet in a way which you can never hope to express.[2]

Evelyn Underhill often speaks about journeying toward the center—which is God—on the conviction that "angels and archangels are with us."[3] Their energies are certainly with us, but they are not recognized until people give them a symbol, or image body, through which they might operate.

There is one possibility that makes more sense the longer it is pondered. Could it be that the highest and best angel form is not external to us but one's own best and truest self? Dion Fortune once wrote,

The Holy Guardian Angel, be it remembered, is really our own high self. It is the prime characteristic of the high mode of mentation that is considered neither in voices nor visions, but is pure consciousness; it is an intensification of awareness, and from this quickening of the mind comes a peculiar power of insight and penetration which is of the nature of hyper-developed intuition. The higher consciousness is never psychic, but always intuitive.[4]

173

In consideration of this auxiliary presence that might be referred to as a holy guardian angel, the following illustrations may be provocative. The famous naturalist John Muir once described his attempt to scale Mount Ritter in the High Sierras. As expected, the climb turned out to be a succession of terrifying moments, one of which he reported in some detail.

> Cold sweat broke out. My senses filled as with smoke. I was alone, cut off from all affinity. Would I fall to the glacier below? Well, no matter. . . . Then . . . I became possessed of a *new sense*, my quivering nerves taken over by *my other self* . . . became inflexible, my eyes preternaturally clear, and every rift, flow, niche and tablet in the cliff ahead was seen through a microscope.[5]

The phenomenon of discovering or awakening to a "new sense" or being taken over by one's "other self" is immensely intriguing—for reasons that go beyond clearing the eyes and steadying the nerves. Something in this episode reaches beyond the categories of easy identification. There is something that might force one to ponder the possibility of a hidden entity, coexistent with each person, that belongs to the givenness of life—an auxiliary presence like the Zoroastrian Fravashi—that one knows and yet does not know.

Still, I must confess to a practical turn of mind. I am not impressed with someone coming down from a mountain and telling me how great it was on top, even if it is the eminent John Muir. What I want to know is, what exactly is this "new sense" or "other self"? How does it work?

Muir is not unique in his realization. Others, both ancient and contemporary, sacred and secular, have alluded to another self operating as a spiritual resource within the boundaries of their being. The innovative tennis instructor Tim Gallwey has written in his *The Inner*

174

Game of Tennis of two distinct personal components that he labeled "Self One" and "Self Two." Self One is the external, natural, ego-dominated presence that may pick up a tennis racket and after an interval of practice hit a few volleys over the net with sporadic success. But Self Two, the inner presence, with its built-in ability to pick up subtle vibrational clues—like merely watching someone else perform—is then able to play the game of tennis with amazing competence if given the opportunity to act through Self One.

Michael Murphy, acclaimed explorer of consciousness, writer, and co-founder of Esalen Institute, in his book *Golf in the Kingdom*, delineates the function of the inner body as separate from the outer body:

> The inner body is somehow enclosed or placed within our ordinary physical frame. But here the terms can be misleading. For as Shivas [his teacher] described it and as I have experienced it, the inner body is not bound to the physical frame it inhabits. It is far more elastic and free, more like a flame than a rock. . . . It is a center to operate from, an indubitable something, to be sure, but it waivers and dances like a living flame. . . . Like true gravity, the inner body stands outside our ordinary Western view of things. It is real in a way conventional Western psychology will never admit—until psychologists enter these realms themselves.[6]

Add to the Outer Self, Self One, the inner body—intuition, genius, sixth sense, ESP, psychic power, inner knowing—and you might have more angel forms to use in your creative work.

The angel-consciousness is a product of careful preparation. Generally speaking, one must develop in this area quietly and purposefully for a long period of time. One needs a slow, integrated discipline of trial and error in

175

order to create adequate forms through which divine energy can move. But the molds must be constructed carefully.

The question comes down to what resources and helps are available for making these constructions. Here are a few suggestions.

A Space

It is best to have a special place for your program of spiritual growth. Few people have developed in the art of cultivating angel forms without a private space to work. You might clear out the corner of a room, then select some religious symbols to appoint your "special place," things that suggests higher aspiration: a picture of Jesus, a rose, a cup, a shepherd's staff, a candle, prayer beads, incense, scriptures, statuary, a few helpful devotional books. These devotional objects should be thought of as reenforcing your focus for the great work. They are background aids to angel-imaging. Devotional places vary with the people who use them. For some it would be appropriate to be outdoors, under a tree, beside a stream, looking up at a mountain, in a forest. For others a roof over the head is a much better arrangement.

One cannot overlook the possibility of having a church as your special seeking place. It makes no difference which denomination you choose. The only problem with most churches today, including the Roman Catholic Church, is that they must often remain closed part of the day and always at night, due to the high incidence of burglary and vandalism. But churches do have the distinct advantage of a most stimulating environment for inner-seeking. In general, church architecture is dedicated to elevating the consciousness all the way from the stimulus of colorful stained-glass windows to the aspirational cross in the nave. Adam Smith in his book *Powers of Mind* reported that some transcendental meditators in a large city were having difficulty finding a good place to meditate. The only place they discovered that maintained a respect for silence, other than the public library, was—you guessed it—a church! Many have developed their angel-consciousness in church.

Special Music

I realize that music appreciation is extremely subjective, but music can be a magnetic conductor of certain high spiritual vibrations capable of transforming a given environmental atmosphere into an angel-building mood. For your deeper spiritual adventure, highly recommended are Bach's Cantata no. 140, which includes the exquisite chorales "Sleepers Awake!" "Raise Your Voices!" and "Glory Now to Thee Be Given!" This cantata has been called "one of the most spacious melodies in existence." Also suggested is Bach's Cantata no. 147, with its famous chorale "Jesu, Joy of Man's Desiring." In the same vein, you will enjoy the supreme experience of Bach's Mass in B Minor or his chorale from Cantata no. 179, "Now Thank We All Our God." Then there are the classic selections—*St. Matthews' Passion* and *St. John's Passion.*

It is difficult to list a few when there are so many. You should have a good recording of Handel's *Messiah* as well, for the thrills and chills of the Hallelujah Chorus on a regular basis are heartily recommended. I have little trouble believing Handel when he wrote at the time he was composing the *Messiah,* "I did think I did see all heaven before me, and the Great God Himself," which I'm sure included the angels. But Bach or Handel have no monopoly on the special music. Beethoven, Tchaikovsky,

Haydn, and so on and so on can do it too. Great classical music has the quality of universal aspiration. Much of it is full of angel essence that is shaped in the sound that carries it.

Angel Art

The angel-consciousness is an image collection of variously shaped symbols that become agencies of transferring essences and energy forces whose forms have special meaning for our personal lives. At one time or another, most people who are serious about developing angel-consciousness will read the legendary stories of the great archangels Michael, Raphael, Gabriel, and Auriel. There is a fair amount of literature concerning these extraordinary beings. One approach is to immerse yourself as much as possible in their particular zone of activity.

For instance, in the literature concerning the archangel Raphael, the main attribute of his being is that of healing, intellect, curiosity, and instruction in the sciences. His symbol is a sword or an arrow that has been well sharpened. Raphael is a being of adventure who carries a golden vial of balm. He is young, dynamically alive, and his colors are associated with spring and the dawn. Instead of reading more or just meditating on your reading, paint Raphael—not as a work for public display, but to get down on paper a concrete impression of this angel for your own image-building. Paint Raphael in pale blue with soft greens and tints of a darker blue. You need not paint him in any precise way, but more as an impressionistic sketch

The archangel Michael is personified in church history as the midday angel clad in armor. He represents the right, the creative, that which should be done. He is master of the energy of balance. His element is fire, purification, perfection. You might paint Michael with colors of deep green, vivid blues, golden and rose red.

Those who write about angels refer to the archangel Gabriel as the potency of God whose energy is associated with procreation and resurrection. Love is his great force factor. Gabriel is of the late afternoon who is a peaceful vibration. His element is fluidlike activity. Try painting Gabriel in the autumn colors: tans, browns, and dark greens.

The file on the archangel Auriel is that of the angel of night. He is associated with the earth. In winter he is seen as the creative force in the ebb period. At this time the seed is in the earth and all is dark. When our vibrations are slowed, he helps us contemplate the future. You might think of Auriel in the darkest colors, such as black, brown, and gray.

I encourage you to paint your own archangels. Too many words have been written about angels, and not enough has been done in terms of the intuitive artistic effort in which you take pencil or paint to paper and actually give a form to your feelings. Who cares what your artistic talent is. Probably no one will see this work but you. One thing though: You will be amazed how often you will make contact with the energy essence of the angel form you are painting. Art is not something that you do just with hand and eye. Art is an integrating action that combines the whole being into an absorbing single-pointed work.

Helen Smith Shoemaker told about a woman who had been trained as a sculptress but who married a minister and for several years was too busy with parish life and raising a family to get back to her sculpturing. But the day arrived when she felt the Holy Spirit urging her in this direction.

So, in excited obedience, I picked up my modeling tools again. I have sculpted the four archangels. It is a beautiful and mysterious use of a gift that was given in my youth and is being given back to me so that I can praise God with it in my old age. I have asked myself why I have been led to sculpt angels.

It began in Pittsburgh when our bishop came to celebrate the Eucharist in our church one Sunday morning. When he said the beautiful, spine-tingling phrase in the Sanctus of the Episcopal communion service—with angels and archangels and all the company of heaven, we laud and praise thy glorious name—he paused at the words "angels and archangels" and, for the first time in my Christian pilgrimage, I became aware that here, near us, were mysterious winged beings of great power about whom I knew little.[7]

It was as she saw it in the angel forms at her disposal. Whether this picture is yours or not, it might be an interesting experience to paint, draw, or sculpt your own impression of an archangel and, in so doing, invoke a remarkable experience.

Purchase some art materials—paints, brushes, canvas, pencils, pastel chalk, charcoal, whatever it takes to get you into drawing or painting your impressions of the angel forms. Again, do not worry about artistic talent. The important thing is subjective involvement. It makes little difference whether or not you can perform as a gifted artist, but please, no paint-by-number works, even of angels. Do it yourself! The idea is that you are doing this as a devotional act, and when the composition is finished it will have special meaning to you. I recall the hours I spent working on my painting of the archangels. I was so absorbed in the work that I slipped easily into a higher consciousness of that to which I had given form.

The Literature

Collecting angel literature can be frustrating because there has been so little of real value produced on this subject. Check out the Notes in this book and dig into some of those sources. Read again the Chronicles in this book carefully, and don't forget the angel stories in the Old and New Testaments. Also, you might get a copy of the Holy Qur'an, and the Avesta of the Zoroastrians. All these sources can give you marvelous angel stories and insights that will help you develop your consciousness of them. There are, of course, general spiritual or devotional books that may or may not mention angels but that heighten the spiritual consciousness. I would suggest Jacob Boehme, *The Way to Christ*, trans. John J. Stoudt (Westport, Conn.: Greenwood Press, 1979), reprint of 1947 ed.; Glenn Clark, *I Will Lift up Mine Eyes* (New York: Harper & Row, 1937); *The Collected Works of St. Teresa of Avila* (Washington, D.C.: I.C.S. Publications, Institute of Carmelite Studies, 1976); Jean Nicholas Grou, *How to Pray* (Greenwood, S.C.: Attic Press, 1964), reprint of 1955 ed.; E. Herman, *Creative Prayer* (Greenwood, S.C.: Attic Press); Ernest Holmes, *Pray and Prosper* (Los Angeles, CA: DeVorss & Co.); *The Journal of John Wesley*, ed. Percy L. Parker (Chicago: Moody Press, 1974); Thomas Kelly, *Testament of Devotion* (New York: Harper & Row, 1941); Frank Laubach, *Letters by a Modern Mystic* (Old Tappan, N.J.: Fleming H. Revell Co.); William Law, *A Serious Call to a Devout and Holy Life*, ed. John Meister, et al. (Philadelphia: Westminster Press, 1968); *St. John of the Cross*; Agnes Sanford, *The Healing Light* (Watchung, N.J.: Logos International, 1972); Douglas Steere, *On Beginnings from Within & on Listening to One Another* (New York: Harper & Row); George Stewart and George Shaw, *Lower Levels of Prayer* (Nashville, TN: Abingdon Press); Howard Thurman, *Deep Is the Hunger* (Richmond, Ind.: Friends United Press, 1973); Evelyn Underhill, *Mysticism* (Totowa, N.J.: Rowman & Littlefield, 1977); Olive Wyon, *The School of Prayer* (New York: Macmillan, Inc.).

Consciousness-conditioning

Another help in obtaining an angel-consciousness can be the use of "motivational slogans." Place inspirational slogans in strategic places around the home for constant confrontation. These slogans can be put on a mirror, on the door of the refrigerator, on a dressing table, on a desk—wherever they will be seen as you move through the day. Appropriate conditioners might include:

I am surrounded by God's busy angels, in the realm of the Spirit. God and God's helpers are never far away, but "closer than breathing and nearer than hands or feet."

> The Light of God surrounds me;
> The Love of God enfolds me;
> The Power of God protects me;
> The Host of God's angels watch over me;
> Wherever I am, God is!

I am not afraid any more. Twelve legions of angels are at my disposal. Underneath are the everlasting arms, and I abide in the love of God.

Write these affirmations in bold letters and speak them aloud to further impress the outer mind. You might write your own conditioning expressions, but do not leave out the angels.

NOTES

2. The Nature of Angel Forms

1. Gustav Davidson, *A Dictionary of Angels* (New York: Free Press, 1971), pp. ix, xii. Reprinted with permission of Macmillan Publishing Co., Inc. Copyright © 1967 by Gustav Davidson.

This is a first-rate study of angels and a sourcebook for developing one's own angel forms.

2. Bryce Bond, "Ivan Sanderson on U.F.O.'s and the Unexplained," *Argosy*, UFO Special Annual Edition, 1977, p. 63.

This extraordinary interview covers a wide range of material relating to UFOs. The late Sanderson was one of the most informed people on this subject.

3. *Webster's New Collegiate Dictionary* (Springfield, Mass.: G.&C. Merriam Co., 1958).

4. From p. 137 in *At the Edge of History* by William Irwin Thompson. Copyright © 1971 by William Irwin Thompson. Reprinted by permission of Harper & Row, Publishers, Inc.

Thompson does not claim to be a prophet, but he does know what is going on and he communicates masterfully.

5. A. Clutton-Brock, *The Spirit: God and His Relationship to Man* (London: Macmillan, 1935), p. 282.

Few writers can communicate their sense of the "personal" in the beauty of nature as this writer. He keeps raising the question of why we misunderstand myths and talk so much nonsense about them.

6. Loren Eiseley, *The Unexpected Universe* (New York: Harcourt Brace Jovanovich, 1969), p. 76. Used by permission.

Eiseley was a naturalist, but also one of the most perceptive writers ever. Anyone would be deeply touched in spirit as well as enlightened in mind by Eiseley's work.

7. J. B. Priestley, *Man and Time* (New York: Dell, 1968). p. 144.
Priestley's section on the problems of Christianity's acceptance of and dependence on history and the rejection of myth is stimulating reading.
8. *Runner's World*, May 1979, p. 7.

3. The Origin and Development of Angel Forms

1. From pp. 70-71 in *Procession of the Gods* by Gaius Glenn Atkins. Copyright 1936, 1930 by Harper & Row, Publishers, Inc. Reprinted by permission of Harper & Row, Publishers, Inc.
This is one of the classics on comparative religion. It combines great scholarship with poetic prose.
2. Ibid., p. 71.
3. From *Man and Angels* by Theodora Ward (New York: Viking Press, 1969), p. 10. Copyright © 1969 by Theodora Ward. Used by permission.
Of all the angel books of the last decade, this is the best, with the exception of Gustav Davidson's work.
4. Atkins, *Procession of the Gods*, op. cit., p. 71.
5. E. A. Wallis Budge, *Egyptian Magic* (New York: Dover, 1971), p. viii. Used by permission of Dover Publications, Inc.
6. James Hastings, *Encyclopaedia of Religion and Ethics*, vol. 4 (New York: Charles Scribner's Sons, 1959), p. 585.
Anyone who would study angels should read this volume, the best work anywhere on the subject of spirits and demons.
7. John B. Noss, *Man's Religions* Third Edition (New York: Macmillan, 1963), p. 480. Copyright © 1963 by Macmillan Publishing Co., Inc. Used by permission.
8. Ibid., p. 472.
9. Maneckji Dhalla, *History of Zoroastrianism* (Bombay: K. R. Cama Oriental Institute, 1963), p. 173.
10. Ibid.
11. Ibid.
12. Charles Dudley Warner, ed., *Library of the World's Best Literature*, vol. 3, trans. J. Darmesteter (New York: J.A. Hill Co., 1902), p. 1096.
13. George Barton in Hastings, *Encyclopaedia*, op. cit., vol. 4, p. 594.
14. Moses Maimonides, *The Guide for the Perplexed* (New York: Dover, 1956), p. 162. Used by permission of Dover Publications, Inc.

Maimonides presents an incredible store of Jewish wisdom, blending philosophy, religion, and scientific thought as well as anyone ever has.

15. From *The Apocrypha and Pseudepigrapha of the Old Testament* edited by R.H. Charles, vol. 2 (1913), p. 223. Reprinted by permission of Oxford University Press.

16. Ibid., p. 237.

17. Ibid., p. 201.

18. Ibid., p. 509.

19. Ibid., p. 305.

20. Ibid., p. 18.

21. Ibid., p. 211.

22. Ibid., p. 214.

23. Ibid., p. 306.

24. George Barton in Hastings, *Encyclopaedia*, op. cit., vol. 4, p. 600.

25. Charles, *The Apocrypha and Pseudepigrapha of the Old Testament*, op. cit., vol. II, p. 220.

26. Farvardin Yast 13:45–47 in Warner, ed., *Library*, vol. 3, p. 1096.

27. Charles, *The Apocrypha and Pseudepigrapha of the Old Testament*, op. cit., vol. II, p. 210.

28. Dionysius the Areopagite, *Mystical Theology and the Celestial Hierarchies* (Surrey, Eng.: Shrine of Wisdom), pp. 42, 46, 51, 54. Used by permission.

29. James Donaldson and Alexander Roberts, eds., *The Anti-Nicene Fathers*, vol. 2 (Grand Rapids: Eerdmans, 1956), p. 27. Used by permission of William B. Eerdmans Publishing Company.

30. Ibid., vol. 4, p. 332.

31. Ibid., vol. 2, p. 517.

32. Charles, *The Apocrypha and Pseudepigrapha of the Old Testament*, op. cit., vol. II, p. 142.

33. *The Interpreter's Dictionary of the Bible*, 4 vol. (Nashville: Abingdon Press, 1962), vol. A–D, p. 129.

34. Davidson, *A Dictionary of Angels*, op. cit., p. 112. Reprinted with permission of Macmillan Publishing Co., Inc. Copyright © 1967 by Gustav Davidson.

35. *Interpreter's Dictionary*, vol. A–D, p. 133.

36. Taken from *The Book of Jewish Knowledge* by Nathan Ausubal (New York: Crown, 1964), p. 4. Used by permission of Crown Publishers, Inc.

37. Charles, *The Apocrypha and Pseudepigrapha of the Old Testament*, op. cit., vol. II, p. 225.

38. Yasna 47:27–29, in Warner, ed., *Library*, vol. 3, p. 1095.

39. Charles, *The Apocrypha and Pseudepigrapha of the Old Testament*, op. cit., vol. II, p. 211.

40. Ibid., p. 276.

41. Francis Legge, *Forerunners and Rivals of Christianity*, book 1 (New Hyde Park: University Books), p. 113. Used by permission.

Few historians write as well as Francis Legge. He tells the story of Christianity, as someone said, "without fear of favor."

42. Ibid., p. 153.

43. Ibid., p. 158.

44. Ibid.

45. Ibid., book 2, p. 21.

46. *Pilgrim Hymnal* (New York: The Pilgrim Press, 1958), p. 496. Copyright © 1958 by The Pilgrim Press.

47. George D. Smith, ed., *The Teaching of the Catholic Church*, vol. 1 (New York: Macmillan, 1950), pp. 258–59.

This book contains a remarkable statement on the use of imagination with regard to the angels.

48. Ibid., p. 259.

49. Helmut T. Lehman, ed., *Luther's Works*, vol. 2 (Philadelphia: Fortress Press, 1965), p. 109. Used by permission.

50. Ibid., vol. 54, p. 172.

51. *Calvin: Institutes of the Christian Religion*, ed. John T. McNeill, Library of Christian Classics, vol. 20 (Philadelphia: Westminster Press, 1960), p. 164.

52. Ibid., vol. 22, p. 172.

53. Emanuel Swedenborg, *Heaven and Its Wonders and Hell* (New York: Swedenborg Foundation, 1952), p. 133. Used by permission.

54. *The Journal of John Wesley* by John Wesley (Chicago: Moody Press, 1951), p. 309. Copyright 1951 Moody Press, Moody Bible Institute of Chicago. Used by permission.

55. *The Portable Blake*, ed. Alfred Kazin (New York: Viking Press, 1955), p. 263.

56. William Muir, *The Caliphate: Its Rise, Decline and Fall* (London: Religious Tract Society, 1892), p. 35.

57. In Atkins, *Procession of the Gods*, op. cit., p. 441.

The Sabeans were Gnostics who lived in Yemen about 700 or 800 B.C. They worshiped the planets, the stars, the moon, the sun, and Venus.

58. Abdullah Yusuf Ali, *The Holy Koran* (Washington, D.C.: American International Printing Co., 1946) p. 969.

59. Ibid., p. 44.

60. Ibid., p. 1094.

61. Ibid., p. 643.
62. Ibid., pp. 44–45.
63. Ibid., p. 642.
64. Ibid., p. 643.
65. Ibid., p. 1152.
66. Ibid.
67. Ibid., pp. 1412, 1413.
68. Hastings, *Encyclopaedia*, vol. 4, p. 617.
69. Ali, *The Holy Koran*, op. cit., p. 1259.

Afterword

1. Quoted in Frederick Clarke Prescott, *The Poetic Mind* (Ithaca: Cornell University Press, 1959), p. 139. Copyright © 1922 by the Macmillan Company.

Appendix: Developing an Angel-consciousness

1. Evelyn Underhill, *Mysticism* (New York: Meridian Books, 1955), p. 300. Used by permission of E. P. Dutton Publishers.
2. Ibid., pp. 301–2.
3. Ibid., p. 304.
4. Dion Fortune, *The Mystical Qabalah* (London: Ernest Benn, 1970), p. 197. Used by permission.
5. Linnie Marsh Wolfe, *Son of the Wilderness* (New York: Knopf, 1964), p. 162. Used by permission.
6. Michael Murphy, *Golf in the Kingdom* (New York: Dell, 1972), pp. 139–40. Copyright © 1972 by Michael Murphy. Used by permission of Viking Penguin, Inc.
7. From *The Exploding Mystery of Prayer* by Helen Smith Shoemaker. Copyright © 1978 by The Seabury Press, Inc. Used by permission.

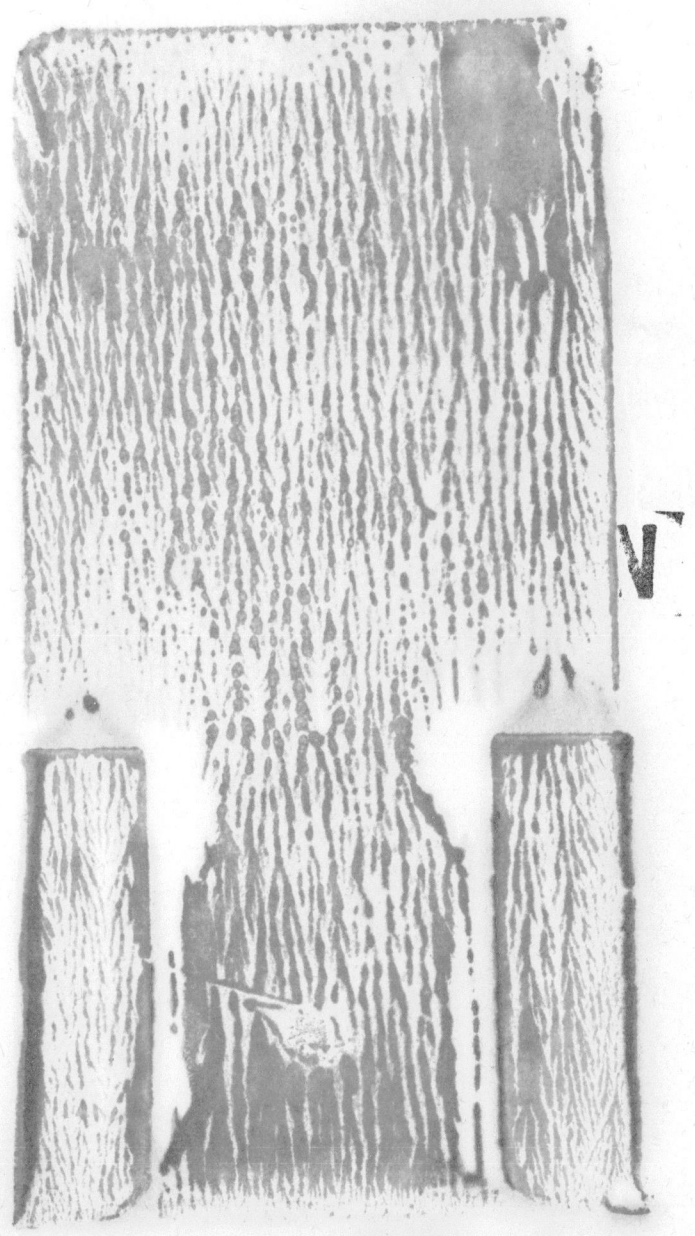

APPLICATION CONSIDERATIONS
FOR LINEAR INTEGRATED CIRCUITS

CONTRIBUTORS

A. A. AHMED, *Radio Corp. of America, Somerville, New Jersey*

W. F. ALLEN, Jr., *Philco-Ford Corporation, Blue Bell, Pennsylvania*

JERRY AVERY, *Texas Instruments Incorporated, Dallas, Texas*

LEONARD BROWN, *Signetics Corporation, Santa Clara, California*

DAVID CAMPBELL, *Fairchild Semiconductor, Mountain View, California*

JERRY EIMBINDER, *EEE Magazine, New York, New York*

MICHAEL ENGLISH, *Fairchild Semiconductor, Mountain View, California*

HARRY GILL, *Raytheon Semiconductor, Mountain View, California*

ALFREDO GOMEZ, *Computer Components, Palm Beach Gardens, Florida*

L. H. HOKE, Jr., *Philco-Ford Corporation, Blue Bell, Pennsylvania*

HEINRICH KRABBE, *Zeltex, Concord, California*

DAVID LONG, *Fairchild Semiconductor, Mountain View, California*

PETER H. MACK, *Sprague Electric Company, North Adams, Massachusetts*

HANS W. MAMIE, *Transitron Electronic Corporation, Wakefield, Massachusetts*

A. C. MARKKULA, Jr., *Fairchild Semiconductor, Mountain View, California*

NORMAN S. PALAZZINI, *Sprague Electric Company, North Adams, Massachusetts*

ED RENSCHLER, *Motorola Semiconductor Products, Phoenix, Arizona*

WILLIAM ROUTH, *National Semiconductor, Santa Clara, California*

RICHARD L. SANQUINI, *Radio Corp. of America, Somerville, New Jersey*

RALPH SEYMOUR, *Signetics Corporation, Santa Clara, California*

RAY STATA, *Analog Devices, Cambridge, Massachusetts*

DOUGLAS R. SULLIVAN, *Transitron Electronic Corporation, Wakefield, Massachusetts*

BRENT WELLING, *Motorola Semiconductor Products, Phoenix, Arizona*

ROBERT J. WIDLAR, *National Semiconductor, Santa Clara, California*

APPLICATION CONSIDERATIONS FOR LINEAR INTEGRATED CIRCUITS

JERRY EIMBINDER, *Editor*

Wiley-Interscience, a Division of John Wiley & Sons

New York · London · Sydney · Toronto

Library of Congress Catalog Card Number: 71-111352

SBN   471   234400

Printed in the United States of America

Preface

This book is intended for the working engineer and the authors have assumed that the reader is familiar with linear integrated circuits.

The novice and student may stumble over some of the terminology as a result, but, with a little supplementary reading, they too should be able to follow the discussions. They may, however, be disappointed if they are looking for basic treatment of semiconductor physics (carrier phenomena, surface properties, diffusion profiles, etc.). There are other sources for this information.

This does not mean that every paragraph in this book is devoted directly to designing circuits or systems with linear integrated circuits. In fact the first two chapters deal with other areas. But both of these areas are of prime concern to the engineer designing systems or equipment with linear integrated circuits.

The factors to consider in selecting a linear integrated circuit are covered in Chapter 1. Here 10 general rules are presented to help the integrated-circuit user sift out the one best integrated circuit for his application from all those that are available.

"Specmanship" is the art of making your product appear better on a data sheet than competitive products look on their data sheets. Sometimes this can be done by omission as well as by listing performance figures under unrealistic operating conditions. The pitfalls that lie in wait for readers of operational-amplifier data sheets are covered in Chapter 2.

To illustrate the capabilities of operational-amplifier integrated circuits, a variety of applications are discussed in Chapter 3. The applications fall into five groups: simple amplifiers, operational amplifiers, transducer amplifiers, wave shapers and generators, and power supplies. Many of the circuits use integrated circuits having internal compensation thus eliminating the need for frequency-stabilization components. Key design considerations for each circuit are mentioned.

The next two chapters, Chapters 4 and 5, explore the functioning and the application of the fully (internally) compensated operational-amplifier integrated circuit. Both chapters delve into circuits of the 741 type.

To help the circuit designer determine the high-frequency performance obtainable from an amplifier, several formulas are given in Chapter 6. Two packaged wideband inverter operational amplifiers are used in illustrative examples to demonstrate the use of the formulas.

Sometimes full-fledged operational amplifiers are not needed to solve a design problem. In two of the six integrated-circuit applications discussed in Chapter 7, differential-amplifier integrated circuits are employed to satisfy the application's requirements.

Several applications for the wideband monolithic amplifier are looked at in Chapter 8. The key characteristics required for a good wideband amplifier are also covered.

The application of linear integrated circuits to frequency-modulation detector applications is analyzed in Chapter 9, using the Foster-Seeley discriminator as a starting point. Advantages and disadvantages of various approaches to solid-state discriminator circuitry are covered. In Chapter 10 more discussion is presented of FM-detector circuitry and designing with a wideband limiter/detector integrated circuit is thoroughly analyzed.

Diffusing two identical operational amplifiers into a single chip has several advantages, as is pointed out in Chapter 11. The 739 is used as the basis for the discussion.

The analog multiplier integrated circuit is a recent development, and for this reason some attention is paid to the theory behind its operation in Chapter 12. Basic applications, however, are covered to demonstrate how it can be used.

A quick look at a basic integrated-circuit multiplexer built with metal-oxide-semiconductor (MOS) switches is taken in Chapter 13.

Voltage regulators are the center of attention in Chapters 14 through 17. Various commercially available voltage-regulator integrated circuits are investigated and their use is demonstrated.

The use of line-driver and line-receiver integrated circuits in digital systems is covered in Chapter 18. and comparators are examined in Chapter 19.

General considerations for applying various linear integrated circuits are presented in Chapter 20.

Jerry Eimbinder

New York, New York
December 1969

Contents

Chapter 3.

APPLICATIONS FOR OPERATIONAL AMPLIFIERS 19

by William Routh

Chapter 4.

**APPLICATIONS FOR FULLY COMPENSATED OPERATIONAL
    AMPLIFIERS** 42

by Michael English

x   *Contents*

Chapter 8.

THE VERSATILE WIDEBAND IC AMPLIFIER 82

by Brent Welling

Chapter 9.

APPLYING INTEGRATED CIRCUITS TO FM-DETECTOR
    APPLICATIONS 97

by W. F. Allen, Jr., and L. H. Hoke, Jr.

Chapter 16.

POSITIVE VOLTAGE REGULATORS 235

by Robert J. Widlar

Chapter 17.

NEGATIVE VOLTAGE REGULATORS 251

by Robert J. Widlar

Chapter 18.

A HIGH-SPEED DATA TRANSMISSION SYSTEM 273

by Jerry Avery

Chapter 19.

DESIGNING WITH INTEGRATED COMPARATORS 288

by Alfredo Gomez

Chapter 20.

**PRACTICAL CONSIDERATIONS IN THE DESIGN OF SYSTEMS USING
LINEAR INTEGRATED CIRCUITS** 296

by A. C. Markkula, Jr.

APPLICATION CONSIDERATIONS FOR LINEAR INTEGRATED CIRCUITS

1

Factors To Consider in Selecting a Linear Integrated Circuit

by Jerry Eimbinder

EEE Magazine, New York

In choosing a linear integrated circuit (particularly if it is an operational-amplifier IC), finding one that meets your requirements can be only half the job[1]. Often there will be many ICs available that you can use. In this case narrowing down to the one IC best suited for your application can be a truly difficult task.

First of all, the specifications on the data sheet are not the whole story. Factors often not readily obtainable from the data sheet that can affect your choice include reliability, availability, acceptability of the package, compatibility of the IC with the system supply requirements, ability to withstand the application's environmental stresses, and degree to which the device is accident-proof.

Then, of course, there is price. Prices are rarely, if ever, present on data sheets. But if the device you are considering is subjected to a lot of tests that you do not need, it is a good bet that you will do better with regard to price if you look somewhere else. The same is true if the package is metal and you can get by with plastic or if the allowable operating temperature range exceeds your requirements.

The rules presented in the following paragraphs can help in selecting that one IC that is right for your application. They are, of course, general rules, but, applied in conjunction with a little common sense, they can be very helpful.

1.1 RULE 1: DO NOT OVERSPECIFY

Decide which specifications are critical and which are not. If you are building a voltage regulator with operational-amplifier ICs and there is a large differential voltage during turn-on, you will have to consider this as a very critical parameter. If you are working with a very-high-gain, high-source impedance amplifier, you will want to consider offset current more critical than offset voltage. If you specify both very tightly, you will send up the cost of the amplifier needlessly.

There are many parameters that can be given for an operational-amplifier IC (e.g., input offset voltage and current, input bias current, input impedance, input common-mode range, slew rate, common-mode and power-supply rejection, bandwidth, output drive capability, open-loop gain, drift, noise, and dissipation). Certainly, the parameters that are optimized will vary from IC type to IC type. How the parameters are optimized will depend on the markets at which the IC's manufacturer is aiming[2].

There is usually enough compromise involved in designing a linear IC so that it can fit a variety of applications. Siegel, however, warns that some of the miscellaneous applications suggested on a manufacturer's data sheet, although technically feasible, may be financially ludicrous[3]. Gifford indicates which parameters are the key ones for various applications and suggests typical values in Chapter 1 of *Designing with Linear Integrated Circuits* [4].

1.2 RULE 2: CHECK THE SAFETY FEATURES

Besides selecting which specifications you want and which you do not need, you may have to do some choosing regarding safety factors, too. Therefore as part of your elimination procedure you will want to check the safety features. One question that should be asked is: Can this IC get me into trouble? Problems that will arise under fault conditions should be considered. Will the output become seriously distorted? Will the IC be destroyed? Some ICs are more goof-proof than others, and this is a factor not to be taken lightly.

For example, operational-amplifier ICs can be bought with or without output short-circuit protection and input overvoltage protection. Since the emitter-to-base junctions of input transistors are sensitive to damage by large applied voltages, some form of input protection may be desirable.

Ungrounded soldering irons, excessive input signals, and static discharges are all apt to challenge the input of the IC.

1.3   RULE 3: WEIGH COST AGAINST PERFORMANCE

Of course, when you add any features, even ones concerned with safety, you must consider how they will affect the overall cost — not just the immediate cost of the chip. Reducing the cost of building or maintaining the system, however, should justify adding to the chip cost.

Cost, understandably, keeps getting into the picture during the evaluation of an IC. Throughout the elimination process you must continually weigh cost against performance. From the standpoint of economics a designer today should be looking at operational-amplifier ICs that require little or no compensation. The prices of resistors and capacitors are bottoming out; to save money in the future these components will have to be eliminated by incorporating them into the chip. On the other hand, if it is planned to use a fully compensated operational-amplifier IC right now, it is better to avoid limitations with regard to frequency.

Judging cost is complicated by the fact that determining the overall system cost involves guesswork. Nevertheless it should not be too difficult to decide, for example, whether using a dual operational-amplifier IC instead of two separate units or a high-gain amplifier instead of two low-gain amplifiers are economical moves. Sometimes, as in the case of the dual operational-amplifier IC, the close temperature tracking of two circuits on one chip is especially desirable, and the weighing becomes more complex.

Reducing the "can count" (the number of packages used) is generally a good idea from a reliability standpoint, but the designer should make sure that this does not adversely affect flexibility and performance.

1.4   RULE 4: CONSIDER FREQUENCY COMPENSATION

The frequency compensation that will be required differs widely among commercially available operational-amplifier ICs. At one time, in fact, opponents of operational-amplifier ICs cited the need for frequency-compensation networks as the prime reason for not using operational-amplifier ICs.

The discrete components required for frequency compensation do add to the space requirements and the assembly cost. Various arrangements used for commercially available operational-amplifier ICs can require from zero to seven components [5], depending on the IC and the application. Certainly, it is of key importance for the designer to consider frequency compensation. He should look at the operational-amplifier IC and attempt to determine how prone it is to oscillation if the supply is not exactly bypassed properly. The IC should be evaluated to see whether oscillation will occur with varying capacitive loads and how probable it is that stray capacitance around the circuit will send it into oscillation.

Too much bandwidth in an amplifier can work against you. Extra capacitors may be needed across the feedback resistors to prevent oscillation.

1.5   RULE 5: COMPARE THE SPECIFICATIONS OF VARIOUS VENDORS

It is essential to understand the nature of the input signal and to spell out what the worst-case conditions will be in terms of voltage swing, noise, supply variations, and so on. If this is done, you are in a good position to compare the specifications of various vendors. In working with the data sheets of IC manufacturers care should be exercised in checking to see if the test conditions of both manufacturers are the same for a particular characteristic.

For example, in comparing offset voltages determine whether the source impedances specified by both manufacturers are the same. In looking at slew rate make sure that both manufacturers are making their measurements at the same gain.

Operational-amplifier specifications are evolved from nonlinear characteristics, and, as Stata warns[6], it is not surprising if the circuit does not "play the first time around."

It is common practice for a semiconductor-device manufacturer to give specifications for his product under favorable operating conditions. Therefore the user must also attempt to relate the data-sheet information to his own application.

Widlar points out[7] that it is difficult to get the whole story on any IC from a data sheet. He notes that the IC must also be designed so that its operation does not become erratic under certain conditions.

He also points out that it is not difficult to design an IC which will satisfy the requirements of a specific application and which can be manufactured with reasonable yield. The real trick, he says, is to design an IC that can be used in hundreds of different applications without complaints from the users.

Examples of IC assets that may not show up on the data sheet, cited by Widlar, include continuous short-circuit protection, capability not to latch up or perform erratically when the inputs are driven outside their operating range, ease in determining correct compensation, and reliability.

1.6 RULE 6: CHECK THE PRODUCT'S HISTORY

Many people think that IC manufacturers leave reliability information out of their data sheets for these two reasons: IC reliability does not vary much from manufacturer to manufacturer, and customers will not put much stock in the IC makers' figures. Actually the real reason for the absence of this information from the specification sheet is rather simple: the IC makers just do not have it when they publish the sheet.

Specification sheets are prepared shortly before ICs are announced, and there is insufficient time to run lifetest programs. Even after new ICs come out, the IC manufacturers are constantly modifying their masks and processing procedures to improve yields or performance. For example, the manufacturer may reduce the size of an individual die to increase the number of dies per wafer. Conversely, he may find that there is some interaction between active elements because the transistors on the chip are too close together. Possibly he may want to reduce the length of extra long metal interconnection patterns.

How then do you judge the reliability of competitive ICs? Some engineers believe that there is a relationship between noise and reliability. This has been disputed, however, and discounted by several top semiconductor-device authorities, including National Semiconductor's Bob Widlar.

There is a good possibility that you will not have enough time to run your own lifetests, and, even if you do, the manufacturer may change the device six times during the course of your test program. Instead you will be better off if you check the product's history. Find out if there are other applications similar to yours in which the same device has been used with success. For that matter, see how successful the manufacturer has been with products of this type. Is this his first attempt at it or does he have a long history of developing such devices?

Some designers refuse to use any IC that is not available from several sources. Whereas this policy will usually keep you out of trouble if your main source of supply dries up, it has one drawback. It could be a year or two before you can take advantage of advancements in the state of the art[8].

If a new IC looks good and you decide to use it, you are gambling that either it is so good that other companies will add it to their lines or the original supplier can be depended on to continue supplying it. One American washing-machine manufacturer guarantees to make every part used in his products available for 35 years. There are no such guarantees in the semiconductor business.

Some IC manufacturers will hold units in bonded stock for possible future purchase; however, a higher price per unit is usually paid as a premium. Depending on the terms of the contract, the customer may wind up paying for the whole inventory even if he does not use it[8].

1.7 RULE 7: DETERMINE WHETHER THE IC LENDS ITSELF TO MASS PRODUCTION

If that new IC really looks good and it can put you one step ahead of your competition, then see whether the circuit lends itself to mass production. This is not easy to determine, but if the circuit is very complex, the chip is large, and the vendor has had delivery problems in the past, you may have reason to be nervous.

You might keep in mind that the more complex the chip, the greater the cost, and, quite possibly, the lower the yield. This does not mean that you should shy away from complex chips; but if the chip is crammed with a wide variety of tight-tolerance, difficult-to-make components, look out.

1.8 RULE 8: CONSIDER THE PROBABILITY OF WIDE ACCEPTANCE OF THE IC

At this point of your evaluation you could also consider the probability of wide acceptance of the IC. If the volume will not be significant, obviously the cost is not going to drop measurably in the future. However, if the IC is versatile, the chances of its being second sourced are much improved.

The prices of newly announced ICs are based primarily on developmental costs, anticipated yield, and projected sales volume. However, even the best guesswork by an IC manufacturer cannot accurately determine what his competition is going to do. If a number of his competitors jump in, the price will go down.

1.9 RULE 9: CHECK FOR APPLICABLE LITERATURE

One factor, sometimes overlooked, is evaluating your own capability to work with a product. First of all, is your knowledge of the product adequate for you to design it into your application? In this area it is important to check for availability of application literature published by the IC manufacturer. This will not only help you engineer the product into your circuit it will also give you a good indication of how much the IC maker knows about the use of his own product.

The applications literature on linear ICs fortunately has been extensive. However, because of the rapid progress of the IC industry, some of the material that has been published suggests design solutions that are no longer economically feasible. Care should be exercised in using older literature on linear ICs as design criteria.

1.10 RULE 10: EVALUATE THE TESTING ASPECTS

Finally, if you can understand and design with the IC, can the rest of your company handle it? Will special assembly rigs have to be built to accommodate the package? Undoubtedly you will have to evaluate the testing aspects. With IC manufacturers going to more and more complex chips, incoming inspection and testing are becoming more involved.

Questions that arise concerning inspection are: Does the plant have the facilities to check out the devices thoroughly? Can existing test equipment be modified and used or must new equipment be obtained? The IC user will have to test the devices when they arrive and also to determine how they will be tested in completed systems by field maintenance personnel [9].

Every application has its own unique problems, but, regardless of the specific problems being encountered, the 10 general rules mentioned in this chapter should not be overlooked. By applying them, deciding which operational-amplifier IC to use should become an easier task.

REFERENCES

[1] Eimbinder, Jerry, "Selecting the Right Linear IC for Your Application," *EEE*, November 1968, pp. 48–52.

[2] Gifford, Jack, "The Performance/Economics/Marketplace Inter-Relationships," Wescon Proceedings, Session 1, 1967, pp. 22–29.

[3] Siegel, Murray, "Murray Siegel of Fairchild Speaks out on IC User Beefs," *EEE*, October 1967, pp. 86–89.

[4] Eimbinder, Jerry, Editor, *Designing with Linear Integrated Circuits,* John Wiley and Sons, New York, 1969, pp. 1–12.

[5] Widlar, Robert J., "Monolithic Op Amp with Simplified Frequency Compensation," *EEE,* July 1967, pp. 58–63.

[6] Stata, Ray, "Ray Stata of Analog Devices Speaks out on What's Wrong with Op-Amp Specs," *EEE*, July 1968, pp. 44–50.

[7] Widlar, Robert J., "Bob Widlar of National Semiconductor Speaks out on What Makes a Good IC," *EEE*, August 1968, pp. 80–85.

[8] Eimbinder, Jerry, "Is a Single Source Safe," *EEE*, August 1968, pp. 96–97.

[9] Eimbinder, Jerry, Editor, *Linear Integrated Circuits: Theory and Applications*, John Wiley and Sons, New York, 1968, pp. 93–110.

2

Interpreting Operational-Amplifier Specifications

by Ray Stata

Analog Devices, Cambridge, Massachusetts

Operational amplifiers are complicated. They have many specifications, and most are only approximations of what is happening in the black box. Most parameters, such as voltage drift, current drift and open-loop gain, are nonlinear functions of temperature; others, such as common-mode rejection and common-mode impedance, are nonlinear functions of input voltage. Almost all parameters depend on supply voltages. Therefore, when you use a single number to specify a parameter, you must qualify the conditions of the measurements. Comprehensive graphs would be necessary to define performance completely.

Confronted with 50 more or less mysterious numbers, most engineers tend to select an operational amplifier in terms of familiar values and to forget about the rest. An engineer who wants to replace a sensitive relay with a low-cost amplifier might simply concern himself with the output-current rating and neglect such factors as drift or gain.

2.1 THE LACK OF STANDARDS

Then there is the lack of standards for operational-amplifier specifications. Though various efforts have been made to unify terms throughout industry, this has not yet been done, so manufacturers have loopholes for specsmanship.

Along with real, honest-to-goodness specsmanship, we find inadvertent errors of omission. The holes in the specification or usually the lack of additional information is not revealed until the engineer has assembled umpteen amplifiers into his product and the whole batch is waiting to be shipped.

In one case a customer purchased a differential amplifier with a $5 \mu V/°C$ drift specification. The data sheet said that this number meant maximum voltage drift. What the sheet neglected to say was that the specifications hold only for steady-state temperature conditions. What happened during thermal transients was another kettle of fish that no numbers covered.

Though we were able to show that this point had been covered in an early application note, we certainly had not referred to it in specification sheets for any amplifiers. Actually we did not know how to specify this mode of operation quantitatively; and some competitors had omitted the point.

Now let us take a closer look at some of the major specifications and see how these problems come up.

2.2. VOLTAGE DRIFT

It sometimes helps to go back to first principles. We all know that a transistor's base-emitter voltage varies at roughly $2400 \mu V/°C$. This variation develops an output, or offset, exactly as though a true input of corresponding magnitude were driving the transistor. The use of differential pairs enables the net voltage offset to be drastically reduced because the transistors can be matched so that their offsets track within a few microvolts over the temperature range. This is how the amplifier comes to have a drift specification of $5 \mu V/°C$ instead of $2400 \mu V/°C$; the transistors track within $5 \mu V$ for every $2400 \mu V$ of base-emitter drift; that is, for every 1°C rise.

However, there is a flaw here. What happens if the base-emitter junctions are not at the same temperature? The specification states a figure for maximum drift, but this is really a tracking specification for base-emitter junctions at the same temperature.

2.3 THERMAL CONSIDERATIONS

Obviously thermal gradients caused by adjacent heat-dissipating components can make nonsense of such specifications by making one junction hotter than the other. It takes only 0.1°C differential between the two junctions to develop $2400/10 = 240 \mu V$ offset. To say the least, this is a substantial offset for an operational amplifier with a maximum drift specification of 5 μV/°C.

In fact offsets are caused not only by such obvious temperature-gradient sources as adjacent heat-dissipating elements and room-air drafts but also by changes in the amplifier's own load current. Altering the out-out current from 2 to 20 mA produces an internal temperature transient that develops an offset resulting from unequal heating of the input transistor pair until temperature equilibrium is reestablishèd. And when the amplifier has settled to its new output level, the input signal will invariably set the load current back to 2 mA, starting the problem all over again.

Offsets resulting from warmup and changes in operating conditions can be particularly annoying when an instrument or system is being adjusted. It takes only finger heat on one side of a differential amplifier to produce a distinctly measurable offset error. How does one put performance specifications on such nebulous factors?

One way to sidestep the temperature-gradient error is to avoid the differential amplifier. A chopper-stabilized amplifier automatically corrects for transient offsets of this kind. Its error-sensing circuit is independent of mismatches between the transistors. Sometimes, however, the chopper unit is not a wise choice. Apart from being twice as big and costly as a differential amplifier, the chopper-stabilized unit has only a single input terminal. (The other terminal is "used up" in the stabilizing circuit.) A single-ended amplifier cannot easily be used in noninverting or differential circuits. So what you gain in one area you lose in another.

Fortunately some differential amplifiers are inherently less susceptible to temperature gradients. Single-chip dual-transistor front-end circuits cut down thermal inertia and reduce physical spacing between base-emitter junctions of each differential pair. Monolithic IC operational amplifiers are generally good on this score because of the small spacing between junctions.

Consequently temperature transients never pull the two junctions more than a few hundredths of a degree apart. Such amplifiers offer a meaningful steady-state maximum voltage drift of about 1 μV/°C, with a short-lived and worst-case offset of about 75 μV for 40°C thermal shock.

Although an amplifier with a dual-transistor input exhibits a considerable improvement in offset stability, there is no way of discerning this fact in comparing the usual published offset-drift specifications. A user can get some idea of comparative thermal-gradient performance by making thermal shock tests, like dropping the amplifier into an oil bath 40°C above ambient. The response will be like that shown in Figure 2.1.

We have raised one problem and then beaten it down. But are there not other problems that only specsmanship has solved thus far?

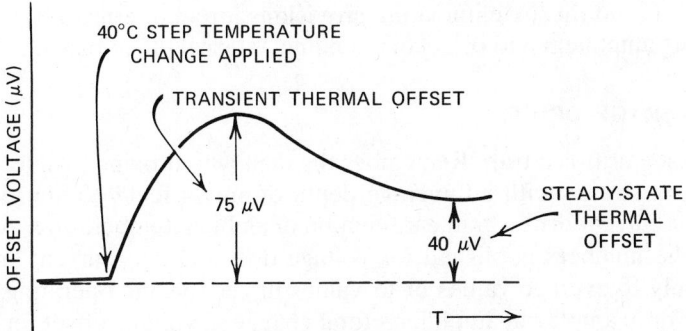

Figure 2.1. Offset voltage characteristic after subjecting amplifier to oil bath at a temperature 40°C above ambient.

2.4 ZEROING CAN HIDE SECOND-ORDER DEFECTS

What happens when you adjust an amplifier's offset potentiometer to zero its output at the selected working temperature? Not surprisingly, there is more to the process than meets the eye. And it is not always easy to tie up the sources of error in neat, crisp numbers.

The offset potentiometer is frequently a variable resistor in series with a collector load resistor. The amplifier's output is zeroed by altering collector current to change voltage balance between the two front-end transistors.

So what? Well, it turns out that there is a second-order effect that causes interaction between the actual value of collector current and the rate at which the transistor's base-emitter voltage drifts with temperature. Adjust the collector current in one transistor of a matched differential pair, and it no longer tracks the other as temperature varies. True, the adjustment modifies the base-emitter drift by only 0.7 μV/°C for each 250-μV change in emitter-base voltage or initial offset voltage.

However, such differences can swamp the carefully designed tracking specifications of today's state-of-the-art differential amplifiers. For example, some chopperless differential amplifiers have better than 1 μV/°C maximum voltage drift. To zero an initial offset voltage of 1 mV with the internal balance potentiometer in one of these amplifiers would introduce a change in temperature drift of 2.8 μV/°C, and that really creates problems.

Some manufacturers neglect to point out the second-order effects caused by trimmer adjustments, but, as operational-amplifier specifications improve, these effects can no longer be ignored. One must really know the condition of the balance resistor to specify voltage drift uniquely.

We get around this by eliminating provisions for an internal offset trim on low-drift amplifiers and by recommending external offset biasing circuits.

2.5   AVERAGE DRIFT

Average drift is a trap. Remember the man who drowned while wading through a stream with an average depth of only 4 feet? Neither voltage drift nor current drift is a linear function of ambient temperature. Accordingly, the numbers published for voltage drift and bias-current drift can refer only to average values or to values under specific operating conditions. For example, an amplifier's total change in voltage offset for a temperature excursion from −25 to +85°C might be 2200 μV (referred to the input). The average drift rate over this interval works out to 2200 μV/110°C, or 20 μV/°C. But examination of the actual drift curve shows that the drift rate at the extremes of temperature can exceed the specified average drift rate by a substantial amount (see Figure 2.2).

There is a special problem when the drift curve changes slope — a real live possibility. Here the average slope calculated by subtracting end points is entirely meaningless. Nonetheless some manufacturers have taken advantage of this golden opportunity for specsmanship (see Figure 2.3).

Perhaps trickier to interpret than the voltage-drift figures are the nonlinear errors caused by exponential variation of bias currents in field-effect-transistor (FET) and varactor-bridge amplifiers. Usually the bias current at a given temperature is specified and the specification reader is reminded that the bias current doubles for approximately 10°C temperature rise, as illustrated in Figure 2.4.

If a value of bias-current drift is given, it is usually quoted at room temperature, where the slope of the bias-current-versus-temperature curve (i.e., drift) is shallowest. But at 85°C the bias current and drift slope will

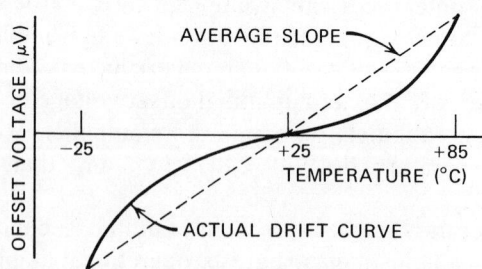

Figure 2.2.   Curves illustrating that average drift values can conceal the presence of larger actual drift values.

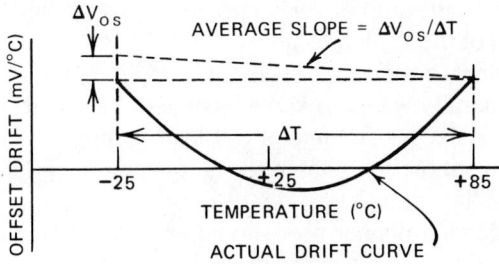

Figure 2.3. Curve illustrating that average slope calculated by subtracting end points can be meaningless.

be 64 times worse than that at room temperature, making the FET amplifier a worse choice for high-temperature applications than some bipolar transistor types. This is not really a question of specsmanship, but it certainly requires that the user know his way around a specification sheet.

2.6 OUTPUT

An amplifier output rating of ± 10 V, ± 20 mA implies that the user can drive a 500 Ω load at the full signal swing of 10 V, 20 mA. For discrete-component operational amplifiers this is usually what such specifications mean. But some IC manufacturers have a different interpretation. "Sure you can get 10 V output; certainly it will develop 20 mA," they say, but they often forget to add, "so long as you don't ask for them simultaneously." In fact it is not unusual for an IC amplifier labeled as having a

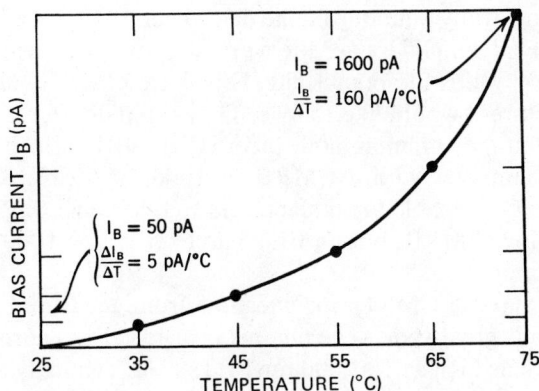

Figure 2.4. Bias current as a function of temperature.

± 10 V, ± 5 mA output to have a maximum power rating of only a fraction of the product of the *VI* figures given.

If an engineer needs an operational amplifier with a relatively high output, he generally wants to know what gain he is getting at that current level. If 20 mA is the amplifier's full-load rating, it would be nice and simple if the manufacturer stated the amplifier's open-loop dc gain at this full load. Not all manufacturers do.

The operational-amplifier user should know his amplifier's rolloff curve in order to build a circuit with adequate gain stability over the working frequency range. The manufacturer may be perfectly justified in departing from the conventional 6 dB/octave frequency compensation to achieve desirable features like fast settling time, high slew rate, fast overload recovery, or increased gain stability over a wide range of frequencies.

But to obtain these improved features generally requires fast rolloff characteristics and therefore a tendency toward oscillation. The key to preventing instability, of course, is knowing that you have this kind of amplifier. You can then use one or more well-known circuit techniques to tame the oscillations.

The great crime occurs when manufacturers use fast rolloff compensation to obtain improved published specifications without giving an open-loop response curve or some other indication of what is going on.

2.7 COMMON-MODE SPECIFICATIONS

To many engineers the common-mode rejection ratio (CMRR) of an amplifier is a rather mysterious number that they would like to forget. Many operational-amplifier manufacturers feel the same way. In fact, if a particular amplifier has a poor common-mode specification, some manufacturers thoughtfully omit it from the data sheet.

Low-cost FET amplifiers are the worst culprits, with typical common-mode rejection ratios of about 1000. This is exactly the kind of number that manufacturers would like to lose. They often do. For a noninverting amplifier circuit the common-mode error is 1/CMRR, which works out to 0.1% for an amplifier with a CMRR of 1000, or 60 dB. Recently new circuit tricks have enabled manufacturers to overcome this fundamental limitation of low CMRR, but an FET amplifier with a 1000,000 CMRR tends to cost more than $100.

Picking a typical CMRR specification from measured operational-amplifier data is great sport. The numbers vary over an enormous range — from 500:1 to as high as 100,000 for FETs — all seemingly at random. A reasonable way for a manufacturer to select a typical common-mode figure for his data sheet is to pick a value that is met by 70 or 80% of all units of that particular type. Some manufacturers, with considerable ingenuity, average all the test numbers to find a "typical" value. Tweaking up a few samples to get a 100,000 CMRR can do great things for averages of this kind and can, of course, lead to very respectable-looking common-mode rejection figures.

As with drift, an amplifier's common-mode-rejection performance can vary with operating conditions, notably with the value of common-mode input voltage, as we can see in Figure 2.5. This leaves room for some really fancy footwork. For example, some well-known FET types boast a common-mode voltage range of ± 10 V. But the common-mode rejection figures are specified for a ± 5-V common-mode range. It is possible for the CMRR to degrade by as much as a factor of 10 when the applied common-mode voltage is raised from 5 to 10 V (see Figure 2.5).

Another difficulty with CMRR is that, since it is a nonlinear function of input common-mode voltage, a single specification number can at best give an average value over the test-voltage range. For small input-signal variation about some large common-mode voltage, the specified "average" CMRR gives little indication of the actual errors to be expected as a result of the steeper error slope at high voltages.

2.8 FULL-POWER RESPONSE

We all know that an amplifier rated at, say, 10-MHz unity-gain bandwidth does not give full output-voltage swing at this frequency. In-

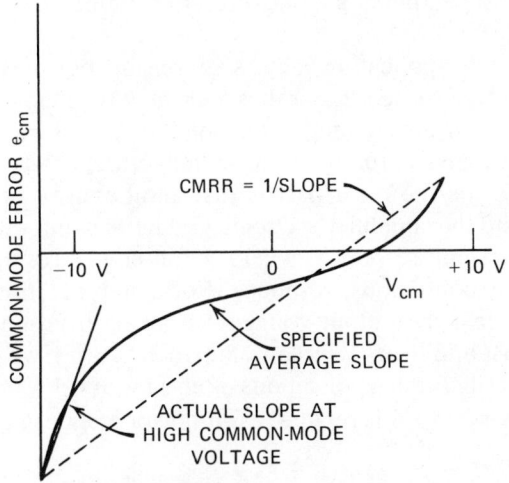

Figure 2.5. Common-mode rejection ratio is a nonlinear function; a single specification number at best gives only an average value over the test-voltage range.

variably distortion caused by internal slew-rate limiting induces the manufacturer to specify the maximum full-power frequency several decades lower.

Generally an amplifier with a 10-MHz unity-gain bandwidth would have a full-power response of about 1 MHz or perhaps as low as 100 kHz. At the "small signal" unity-gain bandwidth the achievable output-voltage swing is usually related to the swing at the full-power bandwidth by the ratio of the full-power response f_p to the unity-gain bandwidth f_t. Thus, for example, you get only a 100-mV swing from a 10-V amplifier at unity-gain bandwidth for an amplifier with an f_p of 100 kHz and an f_t of 10 MHz.

One large problem with full-power-response specifications is that no one really says what he means by the published minimum number. For one thing full-power response has nothing to do with amplitude versus frequency as the term "response" normally implies. Instead it is a measure of output distortion caused by slew-rate limiting.

However, there can be a monstrous difference, depending on whether 1 or 10% is set as the acceptable distortion level. We have evaluated some amplifiers whose output looks like a triangle at the specified full-power response. Where do you draw the line on the acceptable distortion level?

Distortion is only one consideration in setting the criteria for the full-power-response specification. A subtle, but very often more important, side effect is dc offset error resulting from rectification. Feedback signals developed by an asymmetrical, distorted output will not counterbalance the input signal at the amplifier's summing junction. Thus the error signal is rectified by the amplifier's input stage, generating an undesirable offset voltage.

How can such application factors be reasonably prevented? Should each data sheet be turned into a thesis, or may the manufacturer assume that his customers are already aware of the difficulties awaiting them? There is no easy answer for either the manufacturer or the customer.

Slewing rate for the most part is just another way of looking at the rate limiting of the amplifier's circuitry. The slewing-rate specification applies to transient response, whereas full-power response applies to steady-state, or continuous, response. For a step-function input slewing rate tells how fast the output voltage can swing from one voltage level to another. Fast amplifiers will slew at up to 300 V/μs, whereas amplifiers designed primarily for dc applications often slew at 0.1 V/μs or less.

Maximum slew rate S is related to full-power response f_p by

$$S = 2f_p E_o. \tag{2.1}$$

As the voltage swing is reduced below the peak output E_o, the operating frequency can be proportionately increased beyond f_p without exceeding

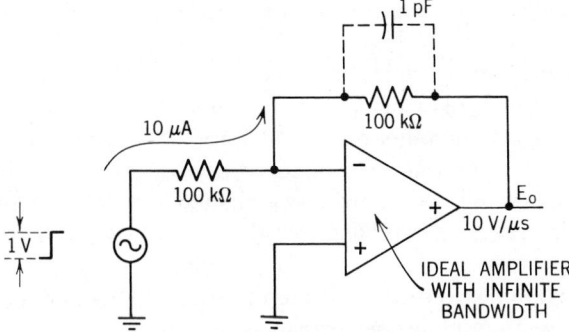

Figure 2.6. In the circuit shown regardless of the operational amplifier's speed the slew rate is limited by the 1 pF of stray capacitance. As a result the slew rate is limited to 10 V/μs.

the slewing rate. For many amplifiers the slewing rate may differ in the inverting and noninverting configurations – a fact that is not always apparent from published specifications. Moreover there is almost always a difference in slewing rate between fall time and rise time, and between positive and negative output signals. Opportunities for specsmanship arise here since many possible slopes can be measured.

A recurrent complaint by customers is that an amplifier does not meet its slewing-rate specification. Closer inquiry typically shows that the customer is trying to obtain a 100-V/μs slew rate with a circuit like the one in Figure 2.6.

The problem here is that the inevitable 1 pF of stray capacitance must be charged by the 10-μA signal current. This limits the output slew rate to 10 V/μs regardless of how fast the operational amplifier may be. With an input impedance of 10 kΩ or less, the customer would obtain the desired 100-V/μs slewing rate. In other words, you cannot get fast response from an inverting amplifier when using high input impedance because of the slugging effect of stray capacitance.

2.9 SETTLING TIME

Settling time is a parameter of increasing interest. This specification defines the time required for the output to settle to within a given percentage of final value in response to a step-function input. Common accuracies of interest are settling time to 0.1 and 0.01%. Heretofore engineers have been forced to use slewing rate and unity-gain bandwidth as rough indicators of relative settling-time performance when comparing or choosing amplifiers, since no other data are given. As it turns out, these two specifications have little bearing on settling time, particularly to 0.01%.

Manufacturers now realize this and are beginning to publish settling-time figures. The hooker here is that settling time is really a closed-loop parameter (whereas all other operational-amplifier specifications are open-loop parameters), and therefore depends on the closed-loop configuration and gain. Fortunately, even when published for only one gain, usually unity gain, it serves as a realistic yardstick for comparing amplifier performance.

The few examples shown illustrate the tremendous difficulties in specifying operational-amplifier performance and the many pitfalls confronting the user. In the long run the user and manufacturer are on the same side in seeking unambiguous communications.

There is one further point that can be most important of all. An engineer should breadboard his critical circuits instead of relying totally on paper designs.

3

Applications for Operational Amplifiers

by William Routh

National Semiconductor, Santa Clara, California

The operational amplifier is a useful device because it can be used in a feedback loop whose feedback properties determine the feed-forward characteristics of the amplifier and loop combination. To suit it for this use the ideal operational amplifier would have infinite input impedance, zero output impedance, infinite gain, and an open-loop 3-dB-down point at infinite frequency rolling off at 6 dB/octave. Unfortunately the cost of such an amplifier would also be infinite.

Intensive development of the operational amplifier, particularly in integrated form, has resulted in circuits that are quite good approximations of the ideal for finite cost. Quantity prices for the best contemporary integrated amplifiers are low compared with transistor prices of 5 years ago. The low cost and high performance provided by IC operational amplifiers permit their being designed into equipment and system functions where it would be impractical to use discrete components. An example is a low-frequency function generator that may use 15 to 20 operational amplifiers in generation, wave shaping, triggering, and phase-locking.

The availability of the low-cost integrated operational amplifier makes it mandatory that systems and equipment engineers be familiar with operational-amplifier theory[1–4]. This chapter presents amplifier applications ranging from a simple unity-gain buffer to relatively complex generator and wave-shaping circuits, all taking advantage of the operational amplifier's characteristics.

The discussion is shaded toward the practical; amplifier parameters are discussed as they affect circuit performance, and application restrictions are outlined.

The applications that are covered are arranged in order of increasing complexity in five categories: simple amplifiers, operational circuits, transducer amplifiers, wave shapers and generators, and power supplies. The integrated amplifiers shown in the circuit diagrams are for the most part internally compensated so that frequency-stabilization components are not used; however, as the discussion will show, other amplifiers may be used with stabilization components in many of these circuits to achieve greater operating speeds.

3.1 THE INVERTING AMPLIFIER

The basic operational-amplifier circuit is shown in Figure 3.1. This circuit, as the name implies, inverts. It offers a closed-loop gain of R_2/R_1 provided that this ratio is small compared with the amplifier open-loop gain. The input impedance is equal to R_1; the closed-loop bandwidth is equal to the unity-gain frequency divided by 1 plus the closed-loop gain.

The main considerations to keep in mind when using this circuit are (a) R_3 should be chosen to be equal to the parallel combination of R_1 and R_2 (to minimize the offset-voltage error resulting from bias current), and (b) there will be an offset voltage at the amplifier output equal to the closed-loop gain times the offset voltage at the amplifier input.

Offset voltage at the input of an operational amplifier is composed of two components; in specifying the amplifier these components are identified as input offset voltage and input offset current. The input offset voltage is fixed for a particular amplifier; however, the contribution resulting from input offset current is dependent on the circuit configuration used. For minimum offset voltage at the amplifier input without circuit adjustment

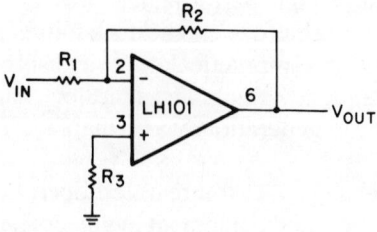

Figure 3.1.   Inverting amplifier. Output voltage V_{OUT} is equal to $-(R_2/R_1)V_{IN}$. For minimum error resulting from input bias current, $R_3 = R_1/R_2$.

the source resistance for both inputs should be equal. In this case the maximum offset voltage would be the algebraic sum of the amplifier offset voltage and the voltage drop across the source resistance resulting from offset current. Amplifier offset voltage is the predominant error term for low source resistances, and offset current produces the main error for high source resistances.

In high source-resistance applications offset voltage at the amplifier output may be set by adjusting the value of R_3 and using the variation in voltage drop across it as an input-offset-voltage trim.

Offset voltage at the amplifier output is not as important in ac-coupled applications. Here the only consideration is that any offset voltage at the output reduces the peak-to-peak linear output swing of the amplifier.

The gain-frequency characteristic of the amplifier and its feedback network can team up to cause oscillation. If this condition is to be avoided, the phase shift through the amplifier and feedback network must never exceed 180° for any frequency where the gain of the amplifier and its feedback network is greater than unity. In practical applications the phase shift should not approach 180° since this is a situation of conditional stability. Obviously the most critical case occurs when the attenuation of the feedback network is zero.

Amplifiers that are not internally compensated may be used to achieve increased performance in circuits in which feedback network attenuation is high. As an example, the LM101 (operational-amplifier IC) may be operated at unity gain in the inverting amplifier circuit with a 15-pF compensating capacitor since the feedback network has an attenuation of 6 dB; this IC, however, requires 30 pF in the noninverting unity-gain connection in which the feedback network has zero attenuation. Since amplifier slew rate is dependent on compensation, the LM101 slew rate in the inverting unity-gain connection will be twice that for the noninverting connection, and the inverting gain-of-ten connection will yield 10 times the slew rate of the noninverting unity-gain connection. The compensation tradeoff for a particular connection is stability versus bandwidth; larger values of compensation capacitor yield greater stability and lower bandwidth and vice versa.

The preceding discussion of offset voltage, bias current, and stability applies to most amplifier applications and is referenced in later sections. A detailed treatment has been given by Paynter[4].

3.2 THE NONINVERTING AMPLIFIER

A high-input-impedance noninverting circuit is shown in Figure 3.2. This circuit gives a closed-loop gain equal to the ratio of the sum of R_1

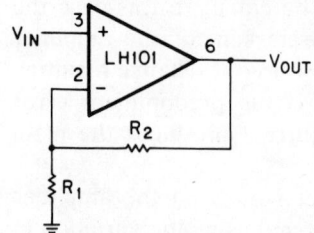

Figure 3.2. Noninverting amplifier. Output voltage V_{OUT} is equal to $[(R_1 + R_2)/R_1]V_{IN}$. For minimum error resulting from input bias current, $R_1/R_2 = R_{SOURCE}$.

and R_2 to R_1, and a closed-loop 3-dB bandwidth equal to the amplifier unity-gain frequency divided by the closed-loop gain.

The primary differences between this circuit arrangement and the inverting circuit are (a) the output is not inverted (b) the input impedance is very high and is equal to the differential input impedance multiplied by loop gain (open-loop gain/closed-loop gain). In dc-coupled applications the input impedance is not as important as the input current and the voltage drop across the source resistance.

Precautions to be observed are the same for this amplifier as for the inverting amplifier with one exception. The amplifier output will go into saturation if the input is allowed to float. This may be important if the amplifier must be switched from source to source. The compensation tradeoff discussed for the inverting amplifier is also valid for this connection.

3.3   THE UNITY-GAIN BUFFER

The unity-gain buffer is shown in Figure 3.3. The circuit gives the highest input impedance of any operational-amplifier circuit. Input impedance is equal to the differential input impedance multiplied by the open-loop gain, in parallel with common-mode input impedance. The gain error of this circuit is equal to the reciprocal of the amplifier open-loop gain or to the common-mode rejection, whichever is less.

Input impedance is a misleading concept in a dc-coupled unity-gain buffer. Bias current for the amplifier will be supplied by the source resistance and will cause an error at the ampiifier input because of its voltage drop across the source resistance. Since this is the case, a low-

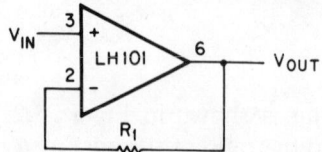

Figure 3.3. Unity-gain buffer. Output voltage V_{OUT} is equal to V_{IN}. For minimum error resulting from input bias current, $R_1 = R_{SOURCE}$.

bias-current amplifier such as the LH102[5] should be chosen as a unity-gain buffer when working from high source resistances. Bias-current-compensation techniques have been covered by Widlar[6].

Three important considerations in the use of this circuit are (a) the amplifier must be compensated for unity-gain operation, (b) the output swing of the amplifier may be limited by the amplifier common-mode range, and (c) some amplifiers exhibit a latch-up mode when the amplifier common-mode range is exceeded. The LH101, if used in this circuit, eliminates these problems; for faster operation the LM102 may be chosen.

3.4 THE SUMMING AMPLIFIER

The summing amplifier, a special case of the inverting amplifier, is shown in Figure 3.4. The circuit gives an inverted output that is equal to the weighted algebraic sum of all three inputs. The gain of this circuit for any input is equal to the ratio of the appropriate input resistor to the feed-back resistor R_4. Amplifier bandwidth may be calculated as in the inverting amplifier shown in Figure 3.1 by assuming the input resistor to be the parallel combination of R_1, R_2, and R_3. Precautions to be observed are the same as for the inverting amplifier. If an uncompensated amplifier is used, compensation is calculated on the basis of bandwidth, as discussed in the section describing the simple inverting amplifier.

The advantage provided by this circuit is that no interaction occurs between inputs, and thus operations such as summing and weighted averaging are implemented very easily.

3.5 THE DIFFERENCE AMPLIFIER

The difference amplifier is the complement of the summing amplifier; it allows the subtraction of two voltages or, as a special case, the cancellation of a signal common to the two inputs. This circuit is shown in Figure 3.5 and is useful as a computational amplifier in making a differential to single-ended conversion or in rejecting a common-mode signal.

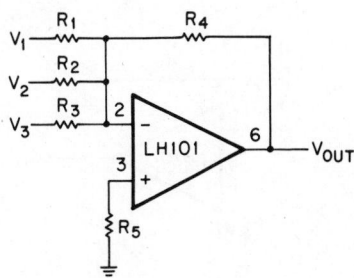

Figure 3.4. Summing amplifier. Output voltage V_{OUT} is equal to $-R_4[(V_1/R_1)+(V_2/R_2)+(V_3/R_3)]$.

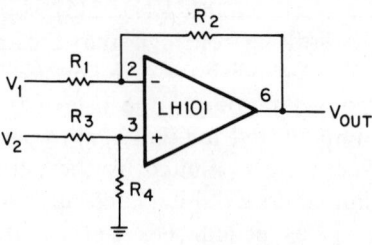

Figure 3.5. Difference amplifier. Output voltage V_{OUT} is equal to $[(R_1+R_2)/(R_3+R_4)]\times$ $[(R_4/R_1)V_2] - (R_2/R_1)V_1$. For $R_1 = R_3$ and $R_2 = R_4$, $V_{OUT} = (R_2/R_1)(V_2-V_1)$. For minimum error resulting from input bias current, $R_1/R_2 = R_3/R_4$.

Circuit bandwidth may be calculated in the same manner as for the inverting amplifier, but input impedance is somewhat more complicated. Input impedance for the two inputs is not necessarily equal; inverting input impedance is the same as for the inverting amplifier of Figure 3.1, and the noninverting input impedance is the sum of R_3 and R_4. Gain for either input is the ratio of R_2 to R_1 for the special case of a differential input single-ended output where $R_1 = R_3$ and $R_2 = R_4$. The general expression for gain is given in the figure. Compensation should be chosen on the basis of amplifier bandwidth.

Care must be exercised in applying this circuit since input impedances are not equal for minimum bias-current error.

3.6 DIFFERENTIATOR

The differentiator is shown in Figure 3.6 and, as the name implies, is used to perform the mathematical operation of differentiation. The form shown in the circuit is not the practical form; it is a true differentiator and is extremely susceptible to high-frequency noise since ac gain increases at the rate of 6 dB/octave. In addition the feedback network of the differentiator, R_1C_1, is an RC low-pass filter that contributes a 90° phase shift to

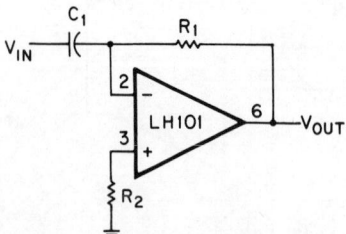

Figure 3.6. Differentiator. Output voltage V_{OUT} is equal to $-R_1C_2[d/dt(V_{IN})]$. For minimum error resulting from input bias current, $R_1 = R_2$.

the loop and may cause stability problems even with an amplifier that is compensated for unity gain.

A practical differentiator is shown in Figure 3.7. Here both the stability and noise problems are corrected by the addition of two components, R_1 and C_2. The elements R_2 and C_2 form a 6-dB/octave high-frequency roll-off in the feedback network and R_1 and C_1 form a 6-dB/octave rolloff network in the input network for a total high-frequency rolloff of 12 dB/octave to reduce the effect of high-frequency input and amplifier noise. In addition lead networks are formed by R_1 and C_1 and by R_2 and C_2 in the feedback loop, which, if placed below the amplifier unity-gain frequency, provide a 90° phase lead to compensate the 90° phase lag of R_2 and C_1 and prevent loop instability. A gain–frequency plot is shown in Figure 3.8 for clarity.

3.7 INTEGRATOR

An integrator is shown in Figure 3.9. This circuit performs the mathematical operation of integration. It is essentially a low-pass filter with a frequency response decreasing at 6 dB/octave. An amplitude-frequency plot for the circuit is shown in Figure 3.10.

The circuit must be provided with an external method of establishing initial conditions as shown in the figure by switch S_1. When S_1 is in position 1, the amplifier is connected for unity gain and capacitor C_1 is discharged, setting an initial condition of zero volts. When S_1 is in position 2, the amplifier is connected as an integrator and its output will change in accordance with a constant multiplied by the time integral of the input voltage.

Precautions to be observed with this circuit are: the amplifier used must in all cases be stabilized for unity-gain operation and R_2 must equal R_1 for minimum error resulting from bias current.

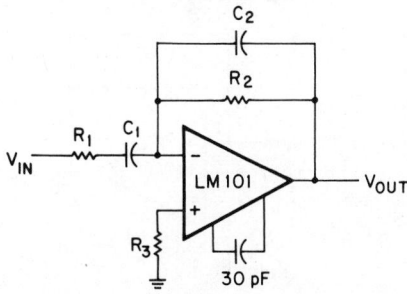

Figure 3.7. Practical differentiator. Corner frequency $f_c = \frac{1}{2}\pi R_2 C_1$; $f_h = \frac{1}{2}\pi R_1 C_2$; $f_c \ll f_h \ll f_{\text{unity-gain}}$.

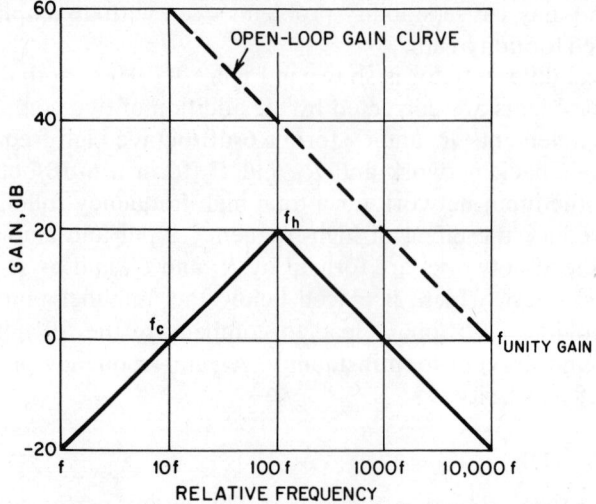

Figure 3.8.   Differentiator frequency response.

3.8   SIMPLE LOW-PASS FILTER

A simple low-pass filter is shown in Figure 3.11. This circuit has a 6 dB/octave rolloff after reaching a closed-loop 3-dB point defined by f_c. Gain below this corner frequency (A_e) is defined by the ratio of R_3 to R_1. The circuit may be considered as an ac integrator at frequencies well above f_c; however, the time-domain response is that of a single RC rather than an integral.

The value of R_2 should be chosen so that it is equal to the parallel combination of R_1 and R_3, thus minimizing errors resulting from bias current.

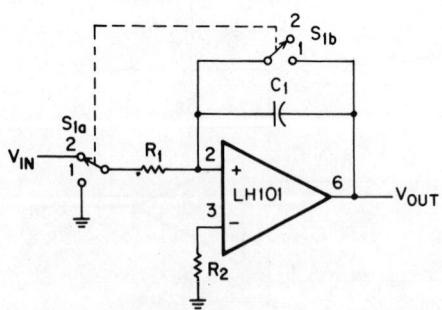

Figure 3.9.   Integrator. Output voltage $V_{\text{OUT}} = -(1/R_1 C_1) \int_{t_1}^{t_2} V_{\text{IN}} \, dt$; $f_c = \frac{1}{2}\pi R_1 C_1$. For minimum offset error resulting from input bias current, $R_1 = R_2$.

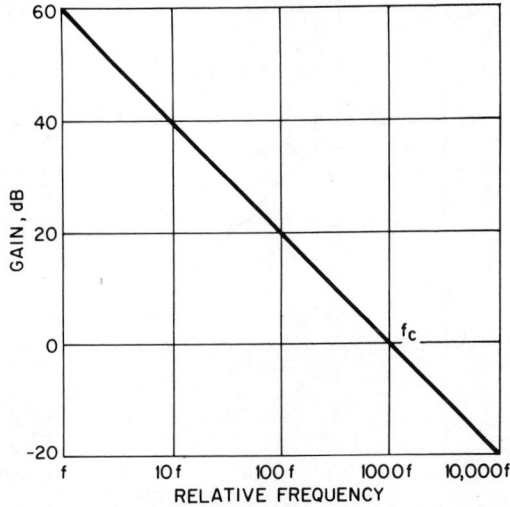

Figure 3.10. Amplitude-frequency plot for the integrator circuit.

Either the amplifier should be compensated for unity gain or an internally compensated amplifier should be used.

A gain–frequency plot of the circuit response is shown in Figure 3.12 to illustrate the difference between this circuit and the true integrator.

3.9   THE CURRENT-TO-VOLTAGE CONVERTER

Current may be measured in two ways with an operational amplifier. The current may be converted into a voltage by using a resistor and then amplified or the current may be injected directly into a summing node. Converting into voltage is undesirable for two reasons: first, an impedance

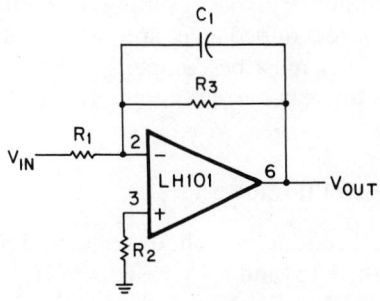

Figure 3.11.   Simple low-pass filter: $f_e = \frac{1}{2}\pi R_1 C_1$; $f_c = \frac{1}{2}\pi R_3 C_1$; $A_e = R_3/R_1$.

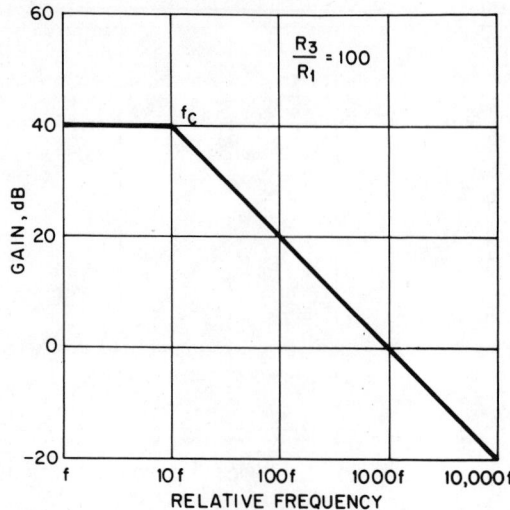

Figure 3.12.   Gain-frequency plot for low-pass filter.

is inserted into the measuring line and causes an error; second, amplifier offset voltage is also amplified, with a subsequent loss in accuracy. The use of a current-to-voltage transducer avoids both of these problems.

The current-to-voltage transducer is shown in Figure 3.13. The input current is fed directly into the summing node, and the amplifier output voltage changes to extract the same current from the summing node through R_1. The scale factor of this circuit is R_1 volts per ampere. The only conversion error in this circuit is I_{bias}, which is summed algebraically with I_{IN}.

This basic circuit is useful for many applications other than current measurement. For example, it can be employed as a photocell amplifier.

The only design constraints that come into play are that scale factors must be chosen to minimize errors resulting from bias current, and, since voltage gain and source impedance are often indeterminate (as with photocells), the amplifier must be compensated for unity-gain operation. Valuable techniques for bias-current compensation have been covered by Widlar[6].

3.10   PHOTOCELL AMPLIFIERS

Amplifiers for photoconductive, photodiode, and photovoltaic cells are shown in Figures 3.14, 3.15, and 3.16, respectively.

The voltages of all photogenerators have some dependence on both speed and linearity. It is obvious that the current through a photoconduc-

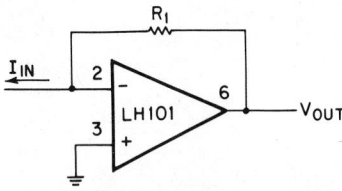

Figure 3.13. Current-to-voltage converter. Output voltage V_{OUT} is equal to $I_{IN} R_1$.

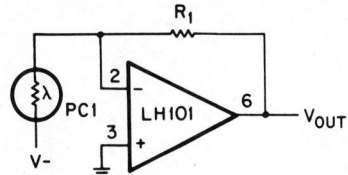

Figure 3.14. Photoconductive-cell amplifier.

tive cell will not display strict proportionality to incident light if the cell terminal voltage is allowed to vary with cell conductance. Somewhat less obvious is the fact that photodiode leakage and photovoltaic-cell internal losses are also functions of terminal voltage. The current-to-voltage converter neatly sidesteps gross linearity problems by fixing a constant terminal voltage, zero in the case of photovoltaic cells and a fixed bias voltage in the case of photoconductors or photodiodes.

Photodetector speed is optimized by operating into a fixed, low load impedance. Currently available photovoltaic detectors show response times in the microsecond range at zero load impedance. Photoconductor speeds are slow, but faster speeds can be obtained at low load resistances.

The feedback resistance R_1 is dependent on cell sensitivity and should be chosen for either maximum dynamic range or for a desired scale factor. The value of R_2 is elective: in the case of photovoltaic cells or of photodiodes it should equal R_1; in the case of photoconductive cells it should be chosen to minimize bias-current error over the operating range.

3.11 PRECISION CURRENT SOURCE

A precision current source is shown in Figures 3.17 and 3.18. The configurations depict sink or source for conventional current, respectively.

Caution must be exercised in applying these circuits. The voltage compliance of the source extends from BV_{CER} of the external transistor to

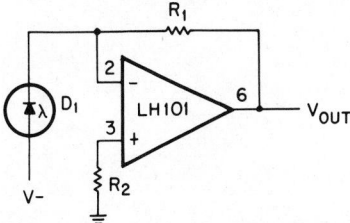

Figure 3.15. Photodiode amplifier. Output voltage V_{OUT} is equal to $R_1 I_D$.

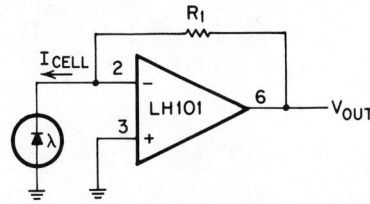

Figure 3.16. Photovoltaic-cell amplifier. Output voltage is equal to $I_{CELL} R_1$.

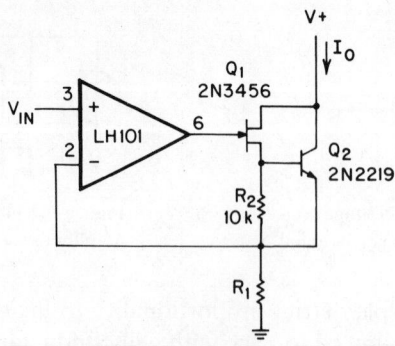

Figure 3.17.   Precision current sink: $I_o = V_{IN}/R_1$; $V_{IN} \geqslant 0$ V.

approximately 1 V more negative than V_{IN}. The compliance of the current sink is the same in the positive direction.

The impedance of these current generators is essentially infinite for small currents, and the generator outputs are accurate so long as V_{IN} is much greater than V_{OS} and I_o is much greater than I_{bias}.

The sink and source illustrated in Figures 3.17 and 3.18 use a field-effect transistor to drive a bipolar output transistor. It is possible to use a Darlington connection in place of the FET-bipolar combination in cases where the output current is high and the base current of the Darlington input would not cause a significant error.

The amplifiers used must be compensated for unity gain, and additional compensation may be required depending on load reactance and external transistor parameters.

3.12   ADJUSTABLE VOLTAGE REFERENCES

Adjustable voltage-reference circuits are shown in Figures 3.19 and 3.20. The two circuits have different areas of application. The basic difference between the two is that the circuit in Figure 3.19 illustrates a voltage

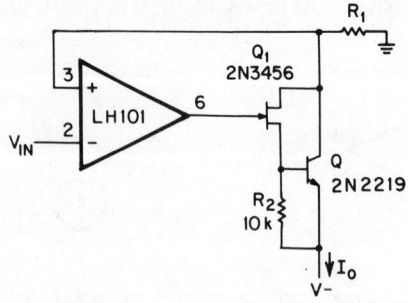

Figure 3.18.   Precision current source: $I_o = V_{IN}/R_1$; $V_{IN} \leqslant 0$ V.

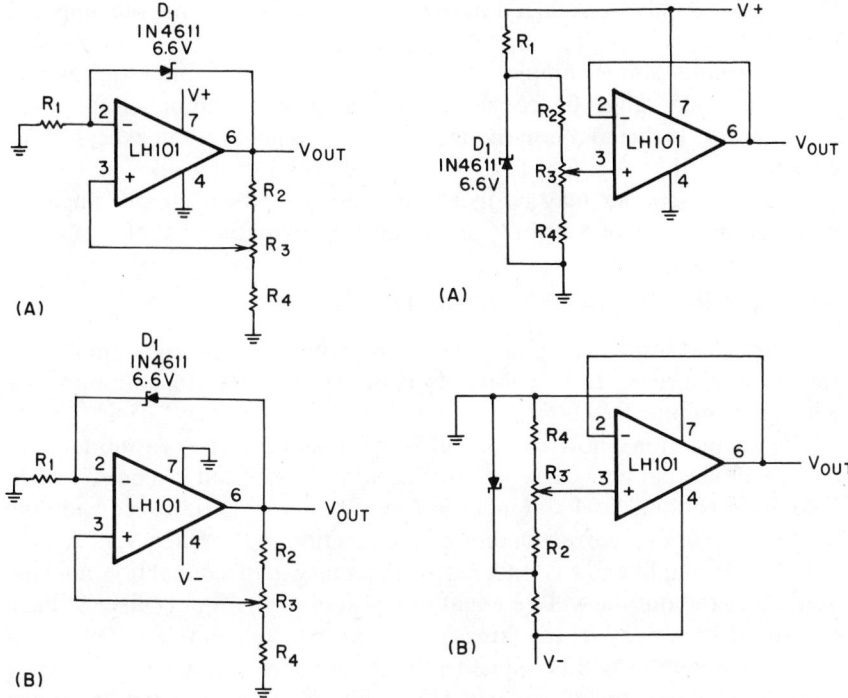

Figure 3.19. Voltage references: (*a*) positive; (*b*) negative. Voltage source provides a voltage greater than the reference-diode voltage.

Figure 3.20. Voltage references: (*a*) positive; (*b*) negative. Voltage source provides a voltage less than the reference-diode voltage.

source that provides a voltage greater than the reference diode, whereas the circuit in Figure 3.20 represents a voltage source that provides a voltage lower than the reference diode. The figures show both positive and negative voltage sources.

High-precision extended-temperature applications of the circuit in Figure 3.19 require that the range of adjustment of V_{OUT} be restricted. When this is done, R_1 may be chosen to provide optimum zener current for a minimum zener temperature coefficient. Since I_Z is not a function of V^+, the reference temperature coefficient will be independent of V^+.

The circuit of Figure 3.20 is suited for high-precision extended-temperature service if V^+ is reasonably constant since I_Z is dependent on V^+. The values of R_1, R_2, R_3, and R_4 are chosen to provide the proper I_Z for minimum temperature coefficient and to minimize errors due to I_{bias}.

The circuits shown should both be compensated for unity-gain operation or, if large capacitive loads are expected, should be overcompensated.

Output noise may be reduced in both circuits by bypassing the amplifier input.

The circuits shown employ a single power supply; this requires that common-mode range be considered in choosing an amplifier for these applications. If the common-mode range requirements are in excess of the capability of the amplifier, two power supplies may be used. The LH101 operational amplifier may be used with a single power supply since the common-mode range is from V^+ to within approximately 2 V of V^-.

3.13   THE RESET STABILIZED AMPLIFIER

The reset stabilized amplifier, a form of chopper-stabilized amplifier, is shown in Figure 3.21. The amplifier is operated in the closed-loop mode with a gain of one.

The connection shown is useful in eliminating errors resulting from offset voltage and bias current. The output of this circuit is a pulse whose amplitude is equal to V_{IN}. Operation may be understood by considering the two conditions corresponding to the position of S_1. When S_1 is in position 2, the amplifier is connected in the unity-gain connection and the voltage at the output will be equal to the sum of the input offset voltage and the drop across R_2 resulting from input bias current. The voltage at the inverting input will be equal to the input offset voltage. Capacitor C_1 will charge to the sum of the input offset voltage and V_{IN} through R_1. When C_1 is charged, no current flows through the source resistance and R_1, so there is no error resulting from the input resistance.

The switch S_1 is then changed to position 1. The voltage stored on C_1 is inserted between the output and inverting input of the amplifier and the output of the amplifier changes by V_{IN} to maintain the amplifier input at the input offset voltage. The output then changes from $(V_{OS} + I_{bias}R_2)$ to

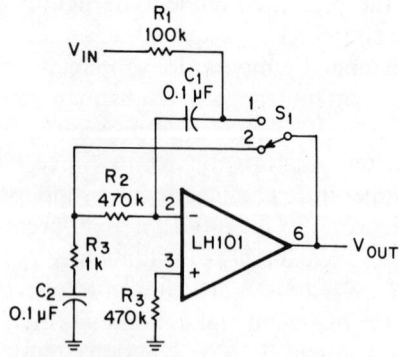

Figure 3.21.   Reset stabilized amplifier.

$V_{IN} + (V_{OS} + I_{bias}R_2)$ as S_1 is switched from position 2 to position 1. Amplifier bias current is supplied through R_2 from the output of the amplifier when S_1 is in position 2 or from C_2 when S_1 is in position 1. Resistor R_3 serves to reduce the offset at the amplifier output if the amplifier must have maximum linear range or if it is desired to dc couple the amplifier.

An additional advantage provided by this connection is that the input resistance approaches infinity as the capacitor C_1 approaches full charge, thus eliminating errors resulting from loading of the source resistance. The time spent in position 2 should be sufficiently long with respect to the charging time of C_1 to permit maximum accuracy.

The amplifier used must be compensated for unity-gain operation, and it may be necessary to overcompensate because of the phase shift across R_2 resulting from C_1 and the amplifier input capacitance. Since this connection is usually used at very low switching speeds, slew rate is not normally a practical consideration, and overcompensation does not reduce accuracy.

3.14 ANALOG MULTIPLIER

A simple analog multiplier is shown in Figure 3.22. This circuit circumvents many of the problems associated with the log-antilog circuit and provides three-quadrant analog multiplication that is relatively temperature insensitive and not subject to the bias-current errors that plague most multipliers.

The circuit operation may be understood by considering A_2 as a controlled-gain amplifier amplifying V_2, with the gain dependent on the ratio of R_5 to the resistance of PC_2 and by considering A_1 as a control amplifier

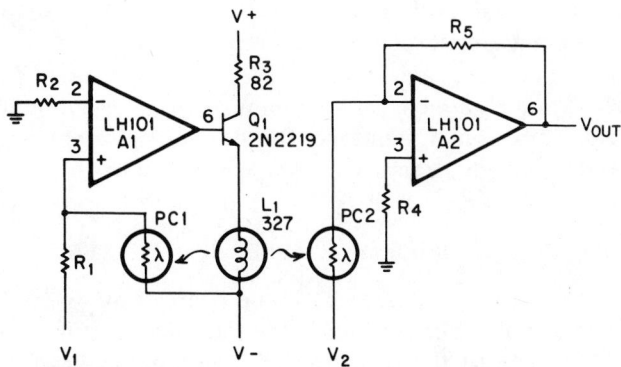

Figure 3.22. Analog multiplier. Output voltage V_{OUT} is equal to $V_1V_2/10$; $V_1 \geqslant 0$ V; $R_5 = R_1(V^-/10)$.

that establishes the resistance of PC_2 as a function of V_1. In this way it is seen that V_{OUT} is a function of both V_1 and V_2.

The control amplifier A_1 provides drive for the lamp L_1. When an input voltage V_1 is present, L_1 is driven by A_1 until the current to the summing junction from the negative supply through PC_1 is equal to the current to the summing junction from V_1 through R_1. Since the negative supply voltage is fixed, this forces the resistance of PC_1 to a value proportional to R_1 and to the ratio of V_1 to V^-. The lamp L_1 also illuminates PC_2 and, if the photoconductors are matched, causes PC_2 to have a resistance equal to PC_1.

The controlled gain amplifier A_2 acts as an inverting amplifier with a gain that is equal to the ratio of R_5 to the resistance of PC_2. If R_5 is chosen equal to the product of R_1 and V^-, then V_{OUT} becomes simply the product of V_1 and V_2. Resistor R_5 may be scaled in powers of 10 to provide any required output scale factor.

The cells PC_1 and PC_2 should be matched for best tracking over temperature since the temperature coefficient of resistance is related to the resistance match of cells with the same geometry. Small mismatches may be compensated by varying the value of R_5 as a scale-factor adjustment. The photoconductive cells should receive equal illumination from L_1; this can be accomplished by mounting the cells in holes in an aluminum block and placing the lamp midway between them. This mounting method provides controlled spacing and also provides a thermal bridge between the two cells to reduce differences in cell temperature. This technique may be extended to use FETs or other devices to meet special resistance or environment requirements.

The circuit as shown provides an inverting output whose magnitude is equal to one-tenth the product of the two analog inputs. Input V_1 is restricted to positive values, but V_2 may assume either positive or negative values. This circuit is restricted to low-frequency operation by the lamp time constant.

Resistors R_2 and R_4 are chosen to minimize errors resulting from input offset current as previously mentioned for the photocell amplifier. Resistor R_3 is included to reduce the inrush current when L_1 starts to turn on.

3.15   FULL-WAVE RECTIFIER AND AVERAGING FILTER

The circuit shown in Figure 3.23 is the heart of an average-reading, rms-calibrated ac voltmeter. As shown, the circuit is a rectifier and averaging filter. If C_2 is deleted, the averaging function is removed and the circuit becomes a precision full-wave rectifier; deletion of C_1 provides an absolute-value generator.

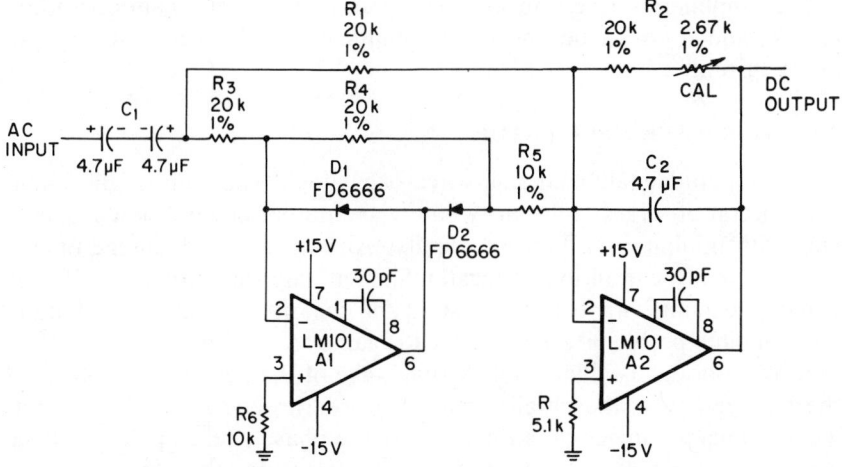

Figure 3.23. Full-wave rectifier and averaging filter.

The circuit operation may be understood by following the signal path first for negative then for positive inputs. For negative signals the output of amplifier A_1 is clamped to $+0.7\,\text{V}$ by D_1 and disconnected from the summing point of A_2 by D_2. Then A_2 functions as a simple unity-gain inverter, with input resistor R_1 and feedback resistor R_2 giving a positive-going output.

For positive inputs A_1 operates as a normal amplifier connected to the A_2 summing point through resistor R_5. Amplifier A_1 then acts as a simple unity-gain inverter with input resistor R_3 and feedback resistor R_5. The gain accuracy of A_1 is not affected by D_2 since it is inside the feedback loop. Positive current enters the A_2 summing point through resistor R_1, and negative current is drawn from the A_2 summing point through resistor R_5. Since the voltages across R_1 and R_5 are equal and opposite, and R_5 is one-half the value of R_1, the net input current at the A_2 summing point is equal to, and opposite from, the current through R_1, and amplifier A_2 operates as a summing inverter with unity gain, again giving a positive output.

The circuit becomes an averaging filter when C_2 is connected across R_2. The operation of A_2 is then similar to the simple low-pass filter previously described. The time constant R_2C_2 should be chosen so that it is much larger than the maximum period of the input voltage that is to be averaged.

Capacitor C_1 may be deleted if the circuit is to be used as an absolute-value generator. When this is done, the circuit output will be the positive absolute value of the input voltage.

The amplifiers chosen must be compensated for unity-gain operation, and R_6 and R_7 must be chosen to minimize output errors due to input offset current.

3.16 SINE-WAVE OSCILLATOR

An amplitude-stabilized sine-wave oscillator is shown in Figure 3.24. This circuit provides high-purity sine-wave output down to low frequencies with minimum circuit complexity. An important advantage of this circuit is that the traditional tungsten-filament-lamp amplitude regulator is eliminated along with its time-constant and linearity problems. In addition, the reliability problems associated with a lamp are eliminated.

A Wien-bridge oscillator takes advantage of the fact that the phase of the voltage across the parallel branch of a series and a parallel RC network connected in series is the same as the phase of the applied voltage across the two networks at one particular frequency and that the phase lags with increasing frequency and leads with decreasing frequency. When this network – the Wien bridge – is used as a positive-feedback element around an amplifier, oscillation occurs at the frequency at which the phase shift is zero. Additional negative feedback is provided to set the loop gain to unity at the oscillation frequency, to stabilize the frequency of oscillation, and to reduce harmonic distortion.

The circuit presented here faithfully follows the classic form except for its negative-feedback stabilization scheme. In the circuit, negative peaks in excess of −8.25 V cause D_1 and D_2 to conduct, charging C_4. The charge stored in C_4 provides bias to Q_1, which determines the amplifier gain.

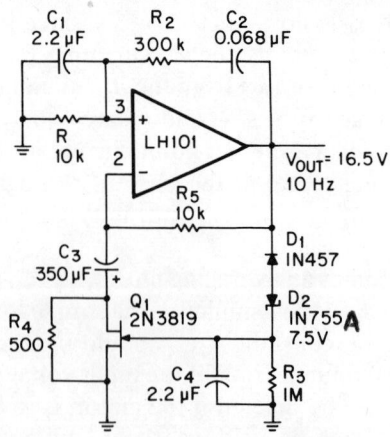

Figure 3.24. Wien-bridge sine-wave oscillator.

There is a low frequency rolloff capacitor C_3 in the feedback network that prevents offset voltage and offset-current errors from being multiplied by amplifier gain.

Distortion is determined by the amplifier open-loop gain and by the response time of the negative-feedback loop filter, R_5 and C_4. A tradeoff is necessary in determining amplitude-stabilization time constant and oscillator distortion. Resistor R_4 is chosen to adjust the negative-feedback loop so that the FET is operated at a small negative gate bias. The circuit shown provides optimum values for a general-purpose oscillator.

3.17 TRIANGLE-WAVE GENERATOR

A constant-amplitude triangular-wave generator is shown in Figure 3.25. This circuit provides a variable-frequency triangular wave whose amplitude is independent of frequency.

The generator contains an integrator that functions as a ramp generator, and a threshold detector with hysteresis which is the reset circuit. The integrator has been described earlier in this chapter. The threshold detector is similar to a Schmit trigger in that it is a latch circuit with a large dead zone. This function is implemented by using positive feedback around an operational amplifier. When the amplifier output is in either the positive or negative saturated state, the positive-feedback network provides a voltage at the noninverting input that is determined by the attenuation of the feedback loop and the saturation voltage of the amplifier. To cause the amplifier to change states, the voltage at the input of the amplifier must change polarity by an amount larger than the amplifier input offset voltage.

When this occurs, the amplifier saturates in the opposite direction and remains in that state until the voltage at its input again reverses. The complete operation of the circuit may be grasped by examining its operation with the output of the threshold detector in the positive state. The

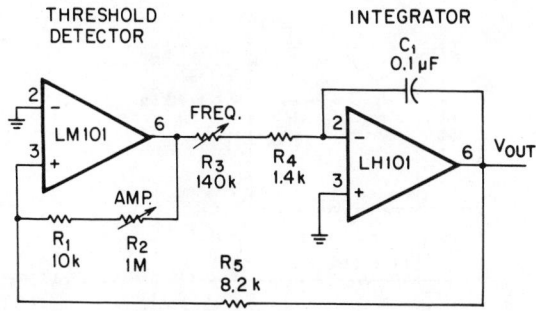

Figure 3.25. Constant-amplitude triangular-wave generator.

detector positive saturation voltage is applied to the integrator summing junction through the combination R_3 and R_4, causing a current I^+ to flow. The integrator then generates a negative-going ramp with a rate of I^+/C_1 volts per second until its output equals the negative trip point of the threshold detector. The threshold detector then changes to the negative output state and supplies a negative current I^- at the integrator summing point. The integrator now generates a positive-going ramp with a rate of I^-/C_1 volts per second until its output equals the positive trip point of the threshold detector, where the detector again changes output state and the cycle repeats.

The triangular-wave frequency is determined by R_3, R_4, and C_1, and by the positive and negative saturation voltages of the amplifier A_1. The amplitude is determined by the ratio of R_5 to the combination of R_1 and R_2 and the threshold-detector saturation voltages. The positive and negative ramp rates are equal, and positive and negative peaks are equal if the detector has equal positive and negative saturation voltages. The output waveform may be offset with respect to ground if the inverting input of the threshold detector A_1 is offset with respect to ground.

The generator may be made independent of temperature and supply voltage if the detector is clamped with matched zener diodes, as shown in Figure 3.26.

The integrator should be compensated for unity gain, and the detector may be compensated if power-supply impedance causes oscillation during its transition time. The current into the integrator should be large with respect to I_{bias} for maximum symmetry, and offset voltage should be small with respect to peak V_{OUT}.

3.18   TRACKING REGULATED POWER SUPPLY

A tracking regulated power supply is shown in Figure 3.27. This supply is very suitable for powering an operational-amplifier system since posi-

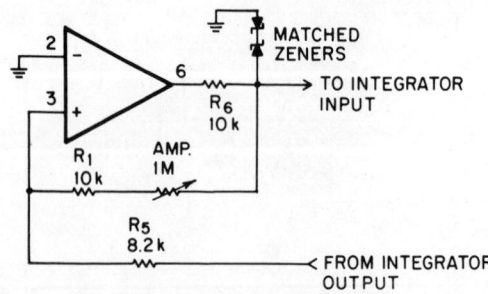

Figure 3.26.   Threshold detector with regulated output.

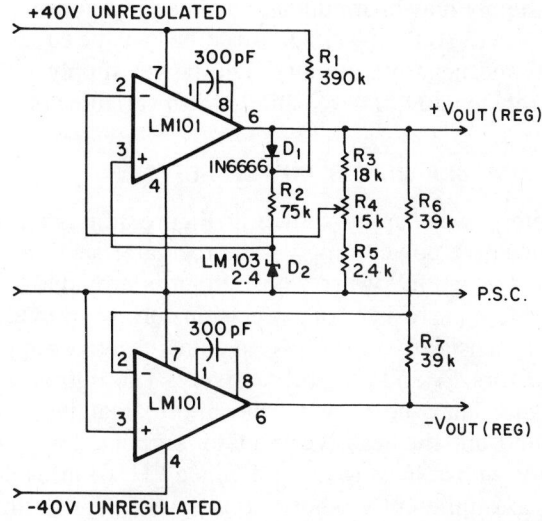

+40V UNREGULATED

-40V UNREGULATED

Figure 3.27. Tracking regulated power supply. Output voltage V_{OUT} is variable from ± 5 to ± 35 V. Negative output tracks positive output to within the ratio of R_6 to R_7.

tive and negative voltages track, thus eliminating common-mode signals originating in the supply voltage. In addition, only one voltage reference and a minimum number of passive components are required.

The operation of the power supply may be understood by first considering the positive regulator. The positive regulator compares the voltage at the wiper of R_4 with the voltage reference D_2. The difference between these two voltages is the input voltage for the amplifier, and, since R_3, R_4, and R_5 form a negative-feedback loop, the amplifier output voltage changes in such a way as to minimize this difference. The voltage-reference current is supplied from the amplifier output to increase the power-supply-line regulation. This allows the regulator to operate from supplies with large ripple voltages. Regulating the reference current in this way requires a separate source of current for supply startup. Resistor R_1 and diode D_1 provide the startup current. Diode D_1 decouples the reference string from the amplifier output during startup, and R_1 supplies the startup current from the unregulated positive supply. After startup, the low amplifier output impedance reduces reference-current variations because of the current through R_1.

The negative regulator is simply a unity-gain inverter with input resistor R_6 and feedback resistor R_7.

The amplifiers must be compensated for unity-gain operation.

The power supply may be modulated by injecting current into the wiper of R_4. In this case the output-voltage variations will be equal and opposite at the positive and negative outputs. The power-supply voltage may be controlled by replacing D_1, D_2, R_1, and R_2 with variable voltage reference.

3.19 PROGRAMMABLE BENCH POWER SUPPLY

The complete power supply shown in Figure 3.28 is a programmable positive and negative power supply. The regulator section of the supply comprises two voltage followers whose input is provided by the voltage drop across a reference resistor of a precision current source.

Programming sensitivity of the positive and negative supply is 1 V per 1000 Ω or resistors R_6 and R_{12}, respectively. The output voltage of the positive regulator may be varied from approximately 2 to 38 V with respect to ground, and the negative regulator output voltage may be varied from −38 to 0 V with respect to ground. Since LH101 amplifiers are used, the supplies are inherently short-circuit-proof. This current-limiting feature also serves to protect a test circuit if this supply is used in integrated-circuit testing.

Internally compensated amplifiers may be used in this application if the expected capacitive loading is small. If large capacitive loads are expected, an externally compensated amplifier should be used, and the amplifier

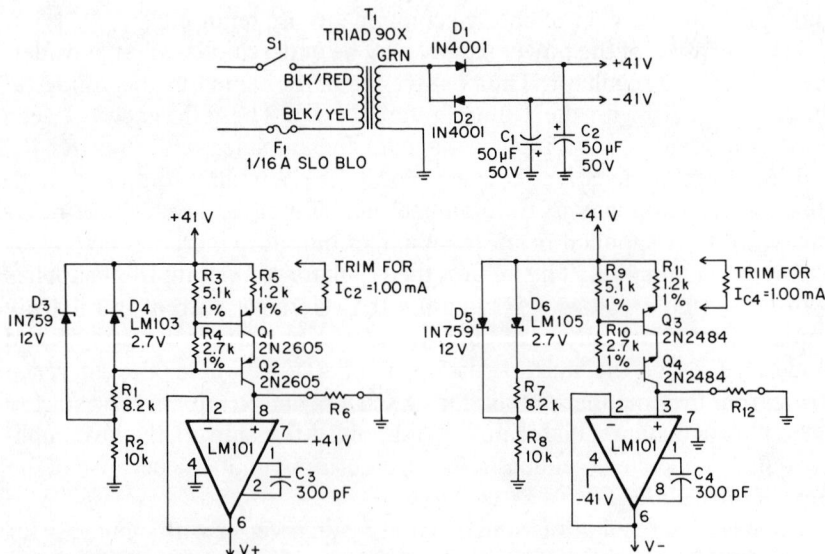

Figure 3.28. Programmable positive and negative power supply for testing ICs.

should be overcompensated for additional stability. Power-supply noise may be reduced by bypassing the amplifier inputs to ground with capacitors in the range of 0.1 to 1.0 μF.

3.20 CONCLUSIONS

The foregoing circuits illustrate the versatility of the integrated operational amplifier and provide a guide to a number of useful applications. The precautions mentioned cover the more common pitfalls encountered in amplifier use.

REFERENCES

[1] Williams, Tapley, and Clark, "D.C. Amplifier Stabilized for Zero and Gain," *AIEE Transactions*, **67**, 1948.

[2] Su, K. L., *Active Network Synthesis*, McGraw-Hill, New York, 1965.

[3] Jackson, A. S., *Analog Computation*, McGraw-Hill, New York, 1960.

[4] Paynter, H. M., Editor, *A Palimpsest on the Electronic Analog Art*, George A. Philbrick Researches, Inc., Boston.

[5] Widlar, R. J., "A Fast Integrated Voltage Follower with Low Input Current," *Microelectronics*, **1**, No. 7, June 1968.

[6] Widlar, R. J., "Drift Compensation Techniques for Integrated D.C. Amplifiers," *EDN*, June 10, 1968, pp. 24–29.

4

Applications for Fully Compensated Operational Amplifiers

by Michael English

Fairchild Semiconductor, Mountain View, California

Fully compensated operational-amplifier ICs, available since 1968, have changed some of the design rules for IC users. This chapter covers some of the more important considerations that come into play when incorporating these ICs into equipment.

4.1 VOLTAGE REGULATOR

The voltage follower is frequently used as a buffer amplifier to reduce voltage error caused by source loading and to isolate high-impedance sources from following circuitry. A circuit diagram for the follower is shown in Figure 4.1. The gain of this circuit is essentially unity. The output duplicates, or follows, the input voltage; hence the name "voltage follower."

The voltage follower is a "worst case" for stable operation since maximum feedback is applied. Normally external components are required to reduce the gain below unity at high frequencies and prevent oscillation. A fully compensated operational-amplifier IC of course does not require external stabilizing components since it has an internal monolithic compensation network.

Voltage followers are also subject to "latch-up," which may occur if the · input common-mode voltage limit is exceeded. If the input transistor at

42

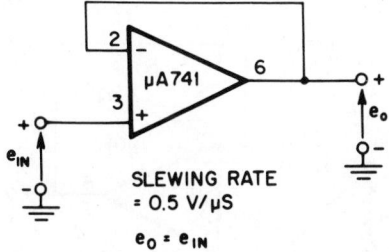

Figure 4.1. Unity-gain voltage-follower arrangement.

the inverting input saturates, then the input to this transistor is fed directly to its collector circuit through the collector-base junction. Thus the inverting input becomes noninverting if the common mode limit is exceeded. This results in positive feedback holding the IC in saturation.

The input stage of a fully compensated operational-amplifier IC should be designed to prevent latch-up. If it is, no external protective circuitry will be required. The μA741, for example, couples this protection with a larger common-mode range than most monolithic operational amplifiers and is therefore capable of larger output voltage excursions. The worst-case common-mode range of the μA741 is typically ± 12 V, thus allowing voltage-follower output swings up to ± 12 V.

The accuracy of a voltage follower is determined by the open-loop gain of the operational amplifier and by its common-mode rejection ratio. The expression for the accuracy is

$$\frac{e_o}{e_{IN}} = \frac{1 + (1/\text{CMRR})}{1 + (1/A_{OL})}, \tag{4.1}$$

where the common-mode rejection ratio in decibels is given by $\text{CMRR}_{dB} = 20 \log_{10} \text{CMRR}$. Using typical figures from the μA741 data sheet, $A_{OL} = 75,000$, CMRR = 90 dB; the dc accuracy of the voltage follower turns out to be better than 0.003%.

4.2 INTEGRATOR

The integrator, shown in Figure 4.2, provides an output that is proportional to the time integral of the input signal. The gain function for the integrator is given by

$$e_o = -\frac{1}{R_1 C_1} \int e_{IN} \, dt. \tag{4.2}$$

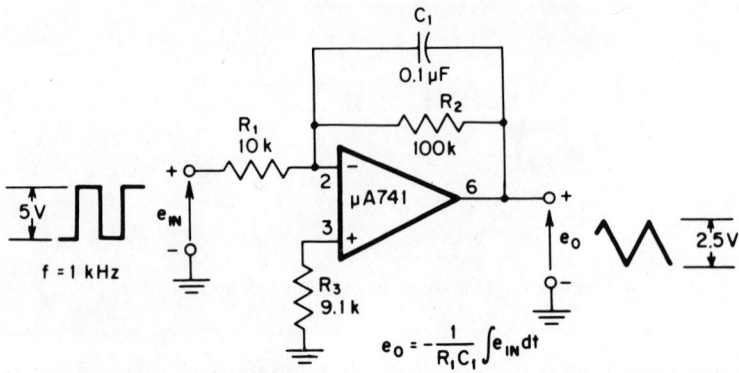

Figure 4.2. Integrator circuit provides an output that is proportional to the time integral of the input signal.

R_1 and C_1 are labeled in the figure. As an example, consider the response of the integrator to a symmetrical square-wave input signal with an average value of 0 V. If the input has a peak amplitude of A volts, the peak-to-peak output can be calculated by integrating over one-half the input period, giving

$$|e_o \ (p\text{-}p)| = \frac{1}{R_1 C_1} \int_0^{T/2} A \, dt = \frac{A}{R_1 C_1}\left(\frac{T}{2}\right). \tag{4.3}$$

The waveshape will be triangular and will correspond to the integral of the square wave. For the component values shown in Figure 4.2 and assuming $A = 5$ V and $T = 1$ ms, (4.3) yields

$$e_o \ (p\text{-}p) = \left(\frac{5}{10^{-3}}\right)\left(\frac{10^{-3}}{2}\right) = 2.5 \text{ V} \quad (p\text{-}p).$$

Resistor R_2 is included to provide dc stabilization for the integrator. It limits the low-frequency gain of the amplifier and minimizes drift. The minimum frequency at which the circuit will perform as an integrator is given by

$$f = \frac{1}{2R_1 C_1} \text{ Hz.} \tag{4.4}$$

For best linearity the frequency of the input signal should be at least 10 times the frequency calculated by using (4.2). The linearity of the circuit illustrated is better than 1% with an input frequency of 1 kHz.

Although it is not immediately obvious, the integrator, if it is to operate reliably, requires both large common-mode and differential-mode input-voltage ranges. There are several ways in which the input-voltage limits may be inadvertently exceeded. The most obvious is that transients occurring at the output of the amplifier may be coupled back to the input by the integrating capacitor C_1. Thus either common-mode or differential voltage limits may be exceeded.

Another less obvious problem can occur when the amplifier is driven from fast-rising or fast-falling input signals, such as square waves. Because the output of the amplifier cannot respond to an input instantaneously during the short interval before the output reacts, the summing point at pin 2 of the amplifier may not be held at ground potential. If the input-signal change is large enough, the voltage at the summing point can exceed the safe limits for the amplifier. Fully compensated operational-amplifier ICs with large differential input-voltage ranges obviously offer greater protection against this occurring. The range for the μA741 is ± 30 V.

4.3 DIFFERENTIATOR

The differentiator circuit of Figure 4.3 provides an output proportional to the derivative of the input signal. The gain function of the differentiator is given by

$$e_o = -R_1 C_1 \frac{de_1}{dt}. \tag{4.5}$$

Since the differentiator performs the reverse of the integrator function, a triangular input will produce a square-wave output. For a 2.5-V peak-to-peak triangle wave with a period of 1 ms we have, for the circuit illustrated,

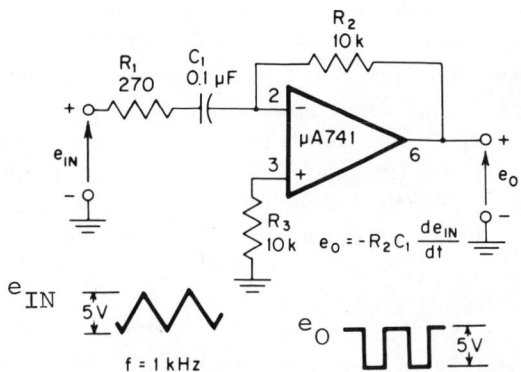

Figure 4.3. Differentiator circuit provides an output that is proportional to the derivative of the input signal.

$$\frac{de}{dt} = \frac{2.5}{0.5} = 5 \text{ V/ms} = 5 \text{ kV/s},$$
$$e_o = -(10^4)(0.1 \times 10^{-6})(5 \times 10^3)$$
$$= 5.$$

The resistor R_1 is needed to limit the high-frequency gain of the differentiator. This makes the circuit less susceptible to high-frequency noise and ensures dynamic stability. The corner frequency at which gain limiting comes into effect is given by

$$f = \frac{1}{2R_1C_1}. \tag{4.6}$$

This frequency should be at least 10 times the highest input frequency for accurate operation. A maximum value for the corner frequency is determined by stability criteria. In general it should be no larger than the geometric mean between $\frac{1}{2}(R_2C_1)$ and the gain-bandwidth product of the operational amplifier. Since the μA741 has a gain-bandwidth product of approximately 1 MHz, its limit for f is given by

$$f < \left(\frac{1 \times 10^6}{2R_2C_1}\right)^{1/2}. \tag{4.7}$$

The differentiator is subject to damage from fast-rising input signals as is the integrator and, as has been discussed, the circuit is also susceptible to high-frequency instability. The wide range of input voltages and the built-in frequency compensation of the μA741 are particularly important when the amplifier is used as a differentiator.

4.4 VOLTAGE-REGULATOR REFERENCE AMPLIFIER

Operational amplifiers are frequently used as reference amplifiers in voltage-regulated power supplies. A typical circuit with variable output voltage is shown in Figure 4.4. The purpose of the amplifier is to isolate the voltage reference, a zener diode in Figure 4.4, from changes in loading at the supply output. This results in lower supply output impedance and hence improved load regulation. Also, because of the high gain at the μA741, the voltage applied to the inverting input of the amplifier from the output-voltage divider is always maintained within a few millivolts of the reference.

Thus the output voltage may be varied by changing the divider. The 800-kΩ input impedance of the μA741 keeps loading of the reference zener to a minimum. The output impedance of the circuit shown is less than 0.1 Ω, and the line regulation is approximately 0.4% for input voltages varying from 20 to 30 V.

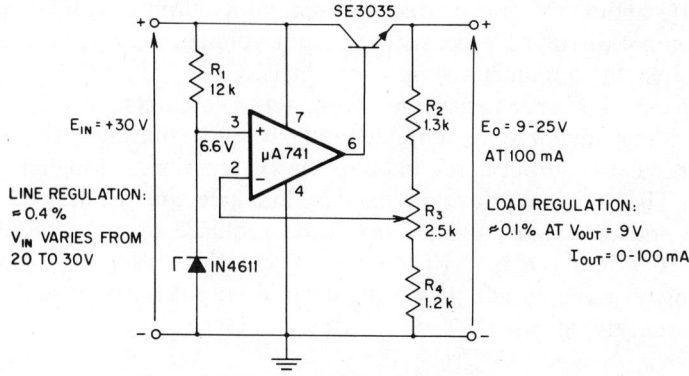

Figure 4.4.   Variable-voltage regulated power supply.

4.5   HIGH-VOLTAGE REGULATED POWER SUPPLY

The μA741, with proper biasing, can be used to control regulated-power-supply voltages many times its normal operating voltage. Figure 4.5 shows a 100-V regulated power supply using the μA741 as the control amplifier.

Zener diodes D_1 through D_3 supply proper operating voltages to the IC. The diodes reference the amplifier voltages to the power-supply output so that the bias levels can follow the output voltage over a wide range of adjustment. The zener diode D_1 keeps the positive supply terminal voltage

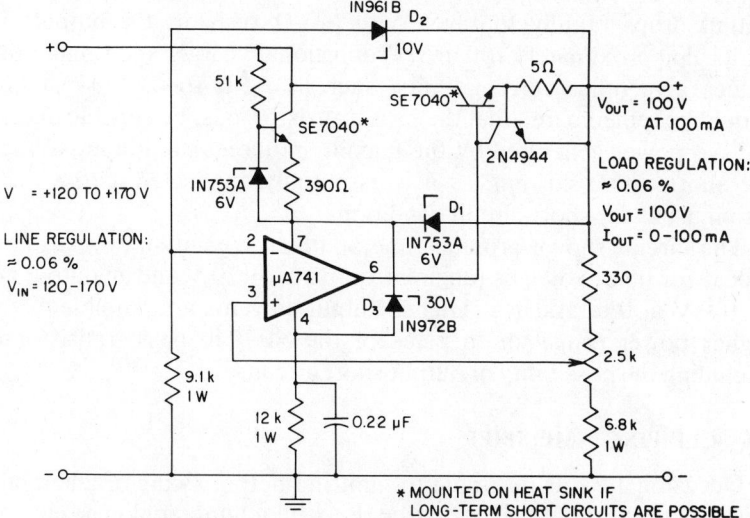

Figure 4.5.   High-voltage regulated power supply.

of the IC about 6 V greater than the regulator output; D_2 holds the inverting input about 10 V below the output voltage; D_3 maintains a 30 V drop across the amplifier's supply terminals. One of the SE7040 transistors, biased by a zener-resistor network, acts as a current source, supplying operating current to the amplifier and part of the biasing network.

The regulator output is fed back to the IC amplifier through a voltage divider. The division ratio is obtained by first selecting the desired output voltage and calculating the division ratio required to make the divider output 10 V less (D_2 is a 10-V zener diode) than the output from the regulator. For the circuit shown the desired output is 100 V and D_2 is a 10-V diode, giving

$$e_o\left(\frac{R}{R_{\text{tot}}}\right) = e_o - V_{D2},$$

$$100\left(\frac{R}{R_{\text{tot}}}\right) = 100 - 10,$$

$$\left(\frac{R}{R_{\text{tot}}}\right) = 0.9 = \text{division ratio.}$$

The regulator is protected against short circuits by the 2N944 transistor and the 5-Ω resistor in series with the output. As the output current increases, the voltage drop across the 5-Ω resistor increases, turning on the 2N4944. The transistor thus shunts base current away from the SE7040 pass transistor. If output current is further increased, the voltage output drops rapidly to zero. With a 5-Ω resistor, the output current limits at approximately 100 mA. Proportionally larger and smaller resistor values give other current limits, such as 2.5 Ω for a 200-mA limit. It should be remembered that the pass transistor must be capable of dissipating the power generated by the maximum unregulated input voltage and the short-circuit current, as it is essentially connected across the input terminals under short-circuit conditions.

The circuit shown provides line and load regulation of approximately 0.06% for input voltages ranging from 120 to 170 V and an output voltage of 100 V at 0 to 100 mA. Higher output currents are possible by using a higher power transistor in place of the SE7040 pass transistor or by excluding the possibility of output short circuits.

4.6   CLIPPING AMPLIFIER

Occasionally it is desirable to limit the output swing of an amplifier to within specific limits. This can be done by adding nonlinear elements to the feedback network, as shown in Figure 4.6.

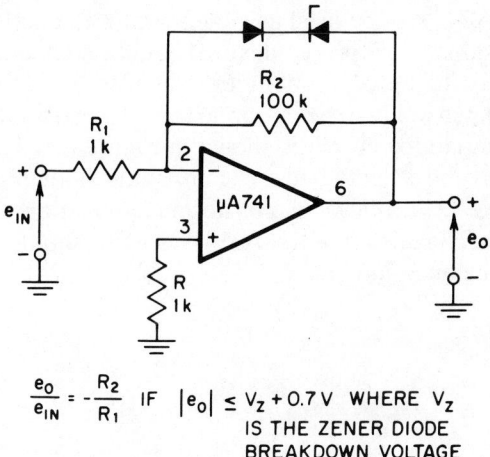

$$\frac{e_0}{e_{IN}} = -\frac{R_2}{R_1} \quad \text{IF} \quad |e_0| \leq V_Z + 0.7\,\text{V} \quad \text{WHERE } V_Z$$
IS THE ZENER DIODE
BREAKDOWN VOLTAGE

Figure 4.6.   Clipping amplifier circuit.

The zener diodes quickly reduce the gain of the amplifier if the output tries to exceed the limits set by the zener voltages. When the zeners are not conducting, the gain is determined by the feedback resistors R_1 and R_2.

It is often overlooked that an amplifier used as a clipper must be frequency compensated for a gain of unity. This is because the gain of the circuit passes through unity as the zener diodes begin their clipping action. The μA741 poses no problems in this respect because it is internally compensated for unity gain.

4.7   COMPARATOR

Many control functions require that a comparison be made between two voltages and that an output be supplied indicating which of the two is

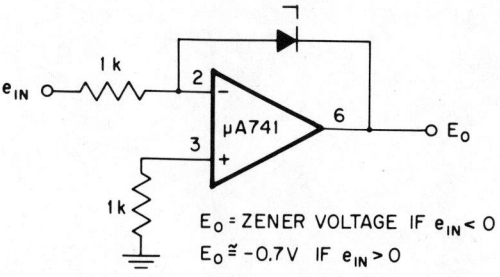

$E_0 = $ ZENER VOLTAGE IF $e_{IN} < 0$
$E_0 \cong -0.7\,\text{V}$ IF $e_{IN} > 0$

Figure 4.7.   Comparator circuit.

greater. The μA741 can be used as a comparator in many applications in which high speed is not a prerequisite. It cannot compete with comparators designed for high-speed operation, such as μA710 types, because the internal compensation network limits the response time.

A typical comparator circuit is shown in Figure 4.7. The zener bounding voltage may be selected to be compatible with high-level Diode-Transistor Logic DTL micrologic or normal compatible Current-Sinking Logic CCSL logic levels, or with MOS device thresholds, or the amplifier can be used in the open-loop mode.

5

Understanding Fully Compensated
IC Operational Amplifiers

by Harry Gill

Raytheon Semiconductor, Mountain View, California

The present generation of monolithic operational amplifiers includes fully frequency-compensated ICs that are short-circuit-proof, may be easily balanced, and are not prone to go into oscillation when used with capacitive loads.

The design concept on which today's fully compensated operational-amplifier ICs is based was first applied in 1967 by National Semiconductor in its LM101. The key to this approach is the employment of current sources as collector loads (see Figure 5.1). Previously, in the first-generation, 709-type monolithic operational amplifiers resistive collector loads had been used (see Figure 5.2). Operational-amplifier ICs that use the current-source-as-collector-load technique include the RM4101, shown in Figure 5.3 and the 741, shown in Figure 5.4. The 741 is the internally compensated version of the 101.

The 709 has a typical open-loop voltage gain of 45,000; its total diffused resistance is 171 kΩ. The 741 has a typical open-loop voltage gain of 125,000; its total diffused resistance is 56 kΩ, and it includes short-circuit protection as well as a 30-pF MOS frequency-compensating capacitor that eliminates any need for external hardware. The die sizes of both the 709 and 741 are identical at 55 mils square.

The 709 has three gain stages, and most of the 171 kΩ of diffused resis-

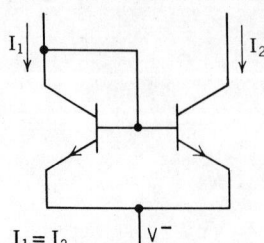

Figure 5.1. Current-source collector load first used in LM101.

tance is in the ac-signal path, whereas only 12 kΩ of the 56 kΩ of the 741 is in the ac-signal path. Liberal use of lateral *pnp* transistors is made in the 741 and 4101, but their use is restricted to areas in which their inherently poor frequency characteristics will not hamper the amplifier's frequency response.

5.1 THE INPUT STAGE

In the second-generation (741, 4101) operational-amplifier ICs the input transistors Q_1 and Q_2 in effect are emitter followers that drive the emitters of Q_3 and Q_4 differentially (see Figure 5.5). Since Q_3 and Q_4 are

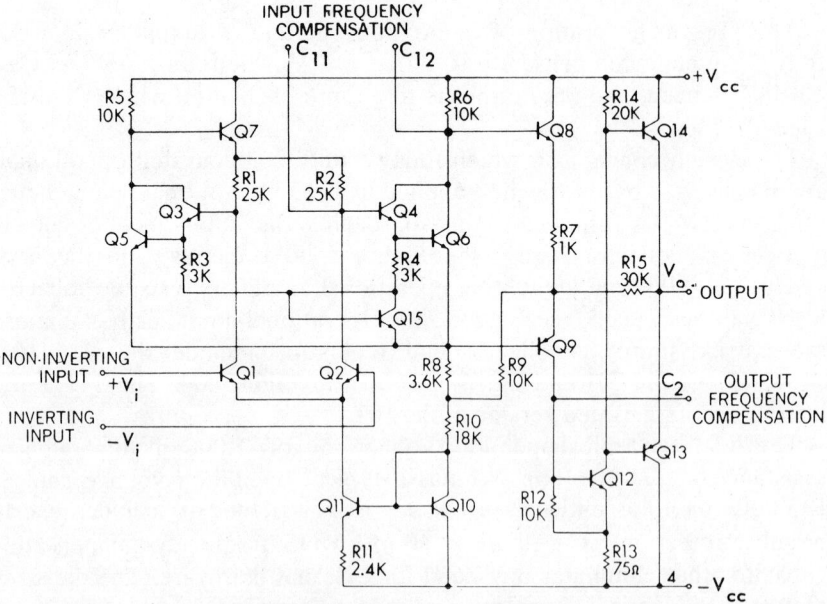

Figure 5.2.   Operational amplifiers of the 709 type use resistive collector loads.

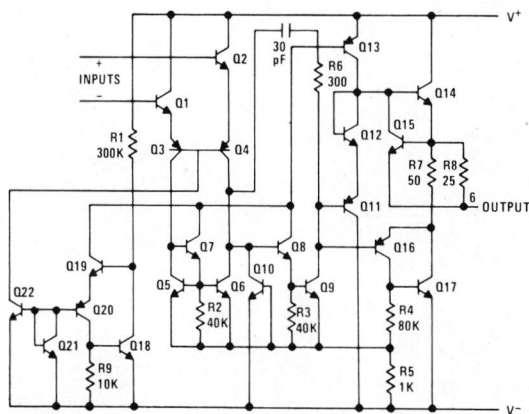

Figure 5.3.   Complete circuit diagram for the LM4101, a type operational-amplifier IC.

lateral *pnp* transistors, they are used as common-base amplifiers; this permits their poor frequency characteristics to be circumvented. Transistors Q_5 and Q_6 are a current source and provide the load for Q_4. A not-so-obvious advantage of this configuration is that it allows the full differential current gain to appear single ended at the collector of Q_4. Should I_4 increase, I_3 will decrease by the same amount, and this decrease will produce a similar decrease in I_6 ($I_4 = I_6$ in the balanced condition). The net effect will be an output current equal to $I_4 - I_6$. Since I_6 is always equal to I_3, the output current will be $I_4 - I_3$.

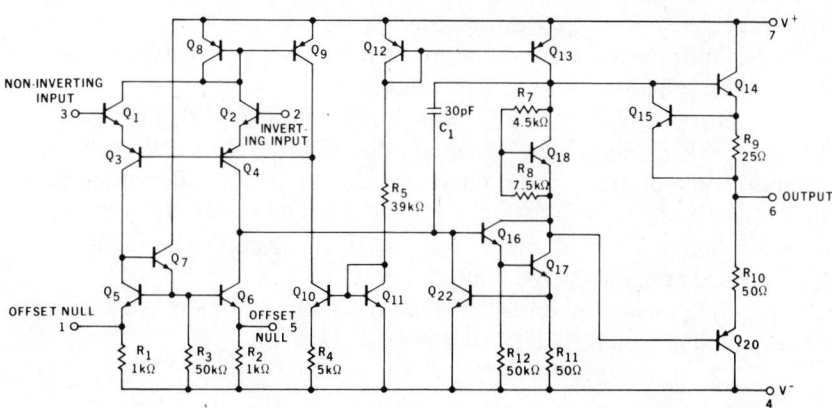

Figure 5.4.   The 741, like the 101, uses the current-source-as-collector-load approach. The 741 includes a 30-pF capacitor, which eliminates the need for external compensating elements.

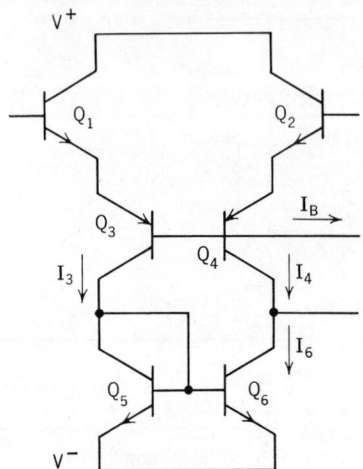

Figure 5.5. Input stage for 101 and 741 type operational-amplifier ICs.

Several advantages are obtained by using this unlikely looking circuit. These are the following:

1. The necessary level shifting is accomplished differentially in the first stage by using transistors in a configuration that minimizes the effect of their poor frequency characteristics.

2. An extremely high output impedance (2 MΩ) is provided for driving the second stage, and a node is available at which frequency compensation can be accomplished easily.

3. High voltage gain is achieved since the collector of Q_4 sees only the input impedance of the second stage as a load.

4. The ac input impedance is doubled because of the two additional base-emitter junctions between the input pairs.

5. Because of the uniformly doped epitaxial base of the lateral *pnp* transistor, BV_{CBO} equals BV_{EBO}, at a value of 80 to 90 V. With this type of input configuration, a circuit designer can use a differential input-voltage range equal to the supply voltage, without destroying the device. If conventional *pnp* transistors were used in place of the laterals, the input-voltage range would be limited to ±14 V.

6. The output is conveniently located so that a simple *npn* common-emitter amplifier can be used as the second stage.

5.2 THE SECOND STAGE

The second stage, or driver (Figure 5.6), is a standard Darlington-configured *npn* common-emitter amplifier with a *pnp* current source as

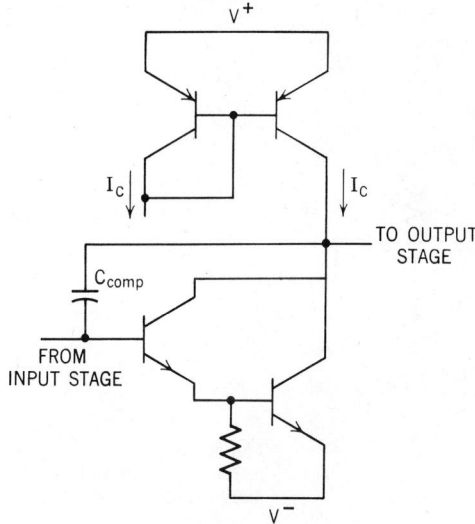

Figure 5.6. Driver stage used in 741 ICs.

the collector load impedance. The compensation capacitor is usually applied around this stage to obtain a constant 6 dB/octave rolloff out to unity gain. The advantages of placing the feedback here are that a very high impedance (1 MΩ) is seen at the input and high current gain (2×10^4) is available from this stage. In this manner a relatively small (30 pF) capacitor can limit the open-loop bandwidth of the amplifier to 7 Hz.

5.3 THE OUTPUT STAGE

The output (Figure 5.7) is usually taken from a complementary emitter follower operated near or at class B operation. A small amount of standby current (100 μA) is maintained through the output pair to eliminate cross-over distortion. The main advantage of this output configuration is the large amount of output current available in the positive and negative direction. However, to get this current gain we need another *pnp* transistor. There are two methods of obtaining a *pnp* transistor at the output:

1. Use a vertical or substrate *pnp* that has a *p* base diffusion as the emitter, the *n* epitaxial layer as the base, and the *p* substrate as the collector. This method can be applied only when the collector is connected directly to the most negative voltage in the circuit. However, this device leaves much to be desired as a transistor. Its current gain is usually

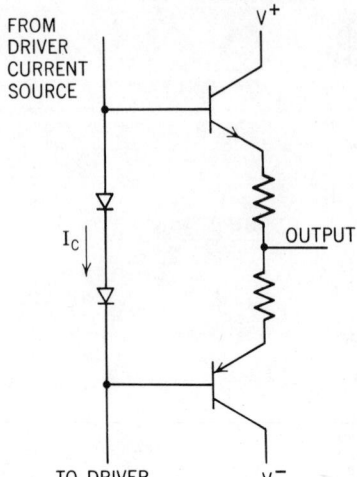

FROM
DRIVER
CURRENT
SOURCE

V^+

I_C

OUTPUT

TO DRIVER V^-

Figure 5.7. Complementary output stage can provide considerable positive or negative output current.

low because of the wide base width, and the gain falls off rapidly above 1 mA collector current.

2. Connect a lateral *pnp* and a standard *npn* transistor together, as shown in Figure 5.8. This configuration provides an equivalent *pnp* current gain equal to the product of the *pnp* and *npn* current gains. The beta cutoff frequency for this device will be the same as for the *pnp* transistor alone.

The standby current for the output stage is usually developed by inserting either a resistor or diffused junctions (diodes, base-emitter junctions) between the bases of the output pair transistors and in series with the driver's collector load. The use of resistors is usually not desirable because of poor thermal matching as compared with diodes. Active diodes ($V_{CB} = 0$) or transistors are generally used to develop the necessary turnon voltage required for the proper standby current.

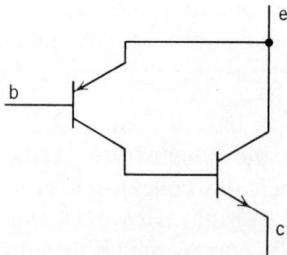

e

b

c

Figure 5.8. Use of a lateral *pnp* transistor in conjunction with a vertical *npn* device provides an equivalent *pnp* current gain that is equal to the product of the *pnp* and *npn* current gains.

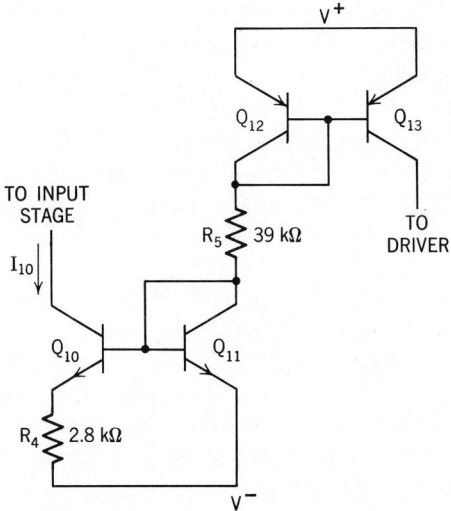

Figure 5.9. Bias supply arrangement for the 741 IC.

5.4 BIASING CIRCUITS

Second-generation operational amplifiers are not restricted to a narrow range of supply voltages. Most amplifiers can be operated successfully over a 5:1 supply-voltage range. This gives the user great flexibility in designing circuits. Again, the reason is the simple current source shown in Figure 5.1. For a given input current the output current will be maintained for output voltages from near saturation to BV_{CEO}; the output impedance will equal h_{oe}.

Biasing of operational amplifiers can be accomplished in several ways. The simplest method is used in the 741 (Figure 5.9). Here the main bias supply is simply a resistor (R_5) with one reference diode connected at each end and current sources Q_{11} and Q_{13} connected to the diodes. The current that flows through R_5 equals the collector current of Q_{13}. The current through Q_{10} is less than the current through R_5 because of the addition of R_4 to the emitter of Q_{10}. Its value can be determined by calculating the ratio of the current through R_5 to the current required through Q_{10}. Since $V_{BE}/\Delta I_C = 18$ mV/octave (60 mV/decade), the voltage across R_4 can be determined, and this allows the determination of R_4 ($R_4 = \Delta V_{BE}/I_e Q_{10}$). The Q_{10} collector current will change relatively little with large changes in R_5 current because of the logarithmic relationship of the currents.

A more sophisticated circuit is used in the 4101 (Figure 5.10). In this circuit a constant collector current is maintained through Q_{19} while the supply voltage is varied over a wide range. A relatively constant current through Q_{19} is obtained because the V_{BE} of Q_{18} changes by only 18 mV/ octave of the collector current. For a 4:1 change in supply voltage the collector current of Q_{18} will also change by 4:1 (since almost all the current through R_1 becomes the collector current for Q_{18}). Since R_1 is a buried FET resistor, its value is voltage dependent, increasing with increasing voltage, so that the actual change in Q_{18} collector current will be less than the supply-voltage change.

For Q_{19} to bias Q_{18} properly it must also supply current through R_9. At an operating current of about 100 μA the V_{BE} of Q_{18} will be approximately 600 mV, and the current through R_9 will be 60 μA. Thus, when the V_{BE} of Q_{18} changes 36 mV for a 4:1 (2-octave) change in supply voltage, the current Q_{19} has to supply to R_9 changes by only 6%; Q_{19} also has to supply the base current of Q_{18}, but this need is small compared to the current through R_9. Although the 300-kΩ resistor R_1 in Figure 5.10 looks as though it would require a large amount of die area, it is in fact a buried epitaxial FET used as a resistor, and it consumes less die area than the 39-kΩ resistor of Figure 5.9.

Another bias circuit that bears attention is the one required to supply the input *pnp* transistors with base drive. To maintain the proper operating current for the first stage the base drive to Q_3 and Q_4 in Figure 5.3 must change because the current gain of Q_3 and Q_4 is process and temperature dependent.

The 101 (depicted in Figure 5.3) uses the circuit shown in Figure 5.11. As mentioned in the discussion of Figure 5.10, Q_{20} has a constant emitter current supplied to it by Q_{19}. Because of the common process and temperature conditions that exist, the current gain of Q_{20} will track the current gains of Q_3 and Q_4. The base current of Q_{20} is used as the base

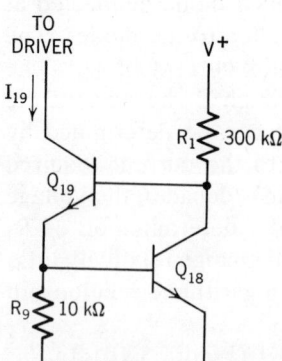

Figure 5.10. Simplified diagram representing 101 (or LM4101) bias supply.

drive for Q_3 and Q_4. This is accomplished by using Q_{21} and Q_{22} as a current source to transfer the base current of Q_{20} to the base of Q_3 and Q_4. This scheme requires that Q_{20} and Q_3, Q_4 track, and as a result this is an open-loop approach.

The 741 uses the circuit of Figure 5.12 to bias its input stage. This circuit is a closed-loop system that does not require matching or tracking of current gains (except for Q_3 and Q_4, of course). The circuit is designed so that I_{10} equals the sum of the input pair (Q_1, Q_2) collector currents. As an example, as temperature increases, less base drive (I_{34}) is required to maintain I_3 and I_4 constant; therefore, if I_9 does not change, I_3 and I_4 will increase. However, $I_3 + I_4 + I_{34}$ passes through the reference diode Q_8. As the current through Q_8 increases, it causes an equivalent increase in the collector current of Q_9. Increasing I_9 will then reduce the base drive to Q_3 and Q_4, restoring the original collector currents. Mathematically, because the collector current of Q_9 equals the collector current of Q_8, the argument can be presented as follows:

$$I_{10} = I_{34} + I_9 \text{ and } I_9 = I_3 + I_4 + I_{34}. \tag{5.1}$$

If

$$I_3 = I_4 = I_C$$

and

$$I_{34} = \frac{2I_C}{h_{fe}},$$

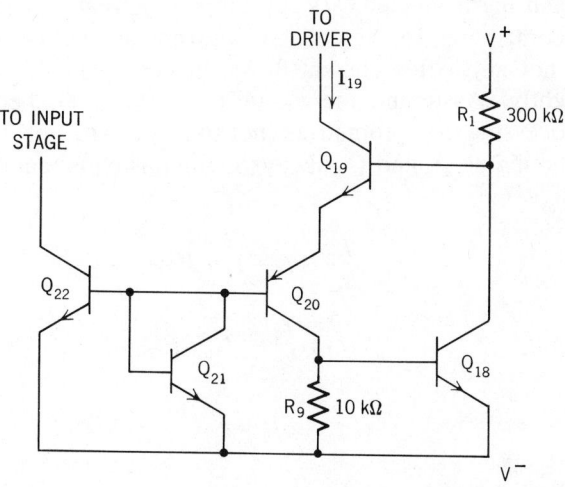

Figure 5.11. Input-pair bias supply used in the 101 IC.

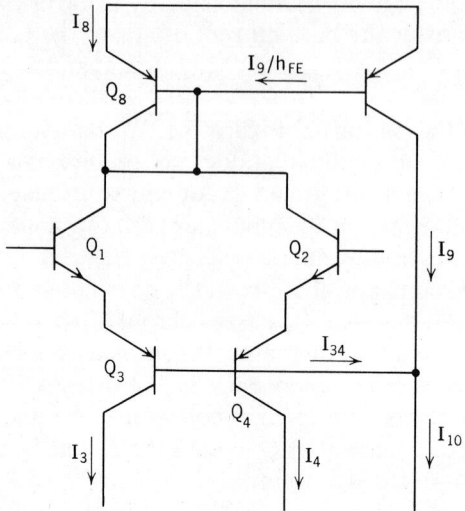

Figure 5.12.   Input-stage bias supply of the 741.

then

$$I_{10} = 2I_C\left(1 + \frac{2}{h_{fe}}\right). \tag{5.2}$$

This analysis has neglected Q_9's current gain. In reality the base current of Q_9 also contributes to the collector current of the first stage (which means that not all of this current flows through Q_8). This modifies the solution slightly. Assuming the h_{fe} of $Q_9 \simeq h_{fe}Q_3$, Q_4 because of the identical processing and geometries (not the case with the 101) and that the V_{BE} matching of Q_8 and Q_9 always maintains equal emitter currents, then

$$I_8 + \frac{I_9}{h_{fe}} = I_3 + I_4 + I_{34};$$

$$I_9 + \frac{I_9}{h_{fe}} = I_8, \tag{5.3}$$

and

$$I_{10} = I_9 + I_{34}$$

as before. Simplifying, we obtain

$$I_3 = I_4 = I_C$$

and
$$I_{34} = \frac{2I_C}{h_{fe}}.$$

Then

$$I_9\left(1 + \frac{2}{h_{fe}}\right) = 2I_C + \frac{2I_C}{h_{fe}},$$

$$I_9 = I_{10} - I_{34} = I_{10} - \frac{2I_C}{h_{fe}},$$

$$\left(I_{10} - \frac{2I_C}{h_{fe}}\right)\left(1 + \frac{2}{h_{fe}}\right) = 2I_C\left(1 + \frac{1}{h_{fe}}\right). \tag{5.4}$$

Solving for I_{10} yields

$$I_{10} = 2I_C\left(1 + \frac{2}{h_{fe}^2 + 2h_{fe}}\right). \tag{5.5}$$

For an error of $< 10\%$ in $I_{10} = 2I_C$, $h_{fe} > 3.5$. A current gain of greater than 3.5 is easily achieved with proper geometry and processing.

5.5 FREQUENCY COMPENSATION

Second-generation fully compensated operational amplifiers apply frequency compensation to one stage only, the driver. The reason the driver is selected is the high input and output impedances associated with it; the driver has high current gain and is isolated from outside influences by the input and output stages. The high input impedance and high gain of the driver stage provide the designer with the means of achieving a low rolloff frequency (6 Hz) with a relatively small (30-pF) capacitor. The capacitor is placed at a point in the circuit where a pole already exists as a result of the C_{ob} (2-pF) of the driver transistor.

The driver can be considered to be a 60-dB amplifier, with an input and output impedance of 1.4 MΩ and 90 kΩ, that is driven from a 2.5-MΩ source impedance.

The open-loop bandwidth can be obtained from the formula

$$BW_{(-3\,dB)} = \frac{1}{2\pi(1 + A_{V2})(C_{comp} + C_{ob})[(R_{01}/R_{IN2}) + R_{02}]}. \tag{5.6}$$

Applying the values of Figure 5.13 yields

$$BW_{-3\,dB} = 6\,Hz.$$

You may ask, why compensate at all? Because a second pole exists at 3 to 5 MHz where the amplifier still has 10- to 20-dB gain. By the time the gain falls to 0 dB, the amplifier's phase margin would be approaching 0. In reality a negative phase margin would exist because of substrate and various stray capacitances. Enough compensation is applied so that the gain margin is 10 to 20 dB.

5.6 DERIVATION OF GAIN

The 741 amplifier can be analyzed to indicate how this type of operational-amplifier IC derives its high gain from just two gain stages. The 741 has been chosen for analysis because of its straightforward design (refer to Figure 5.4).

Determining the DC Bias Currents. The amplifier's bias current is determined by R_5 and R_4. At ±15 V the current through R_5 is

$$I_5 = \frac{V^+ + V^- - V_{BE12} - V_{BE11}}{R_5}, \tag{5.7}$$

where $V^+ = V^- = 15$ V, $V_{BE12} = V_{BE11} = 0.6$ V, and $R_5 = 39$ kΩ. Substituting these values, we obtain $I_5 = 740\,\mu$A.

Since Q_{12} is the reference diode for the driver current source Q_{13}, and assuming the h_{FE} of Q_{13} is about 5, the collector current of Q_{13} will be approximately $I_5 - I_5/h_{FE}$, or 600 μA.

The determination of I_{10} must be arrived at graphically or by successive approximations. The designer of the circuit does not have this problem since I_{10} is known to him and his only problem is finding the value of R_4. Incidentally the actual value of R_4 is about 2800 Ω, not the 5000 Ω that appears on the schematic.

To solve for I_{10} graphically take a sheet of three-cycle semilog graph paper. Plot ΔV_{BE} 0 to 180 mV along the linear axis and I_C 1 to 1000 μA along the log axis, and draw a straight line from the point 0 mV, 1 μA to 180 mV, 1000 μA (60 mV/decade). This line represents the movement of $V_{BE} - VS - I_C$ for Q_{11}. Now plot a curve of $(\Delta V_{BE} + R_4 I_C) - VS - I_C$ for Q_{10}. For example, at $I_C = 1\,\mu$A, $V'_{BE} = \Delta V_{BE} + R_4 I_C = 0$ mV + (2.8 kΩ) × (1 μA) = 2.8 mV.   At $I_C = 10\,\mu$A, $V'_{BE} = \Delta V_{BE} + R_4 I_C = 60$ mV + (2.8 kΩ) × (10 μA) = 88 mV.

Repeat this procedure for 2, 5, 20, 50, and 100 μA. Using a french curve, connect the points calculated. Draw a line along the $I_C = 740\,\mu$A line until it meets the Q_{11} line. Draw another line perpendicular to the 740 μA line, joining it at the intersection of the Q_{11} line (about 172 mV). Continue the 172-mV line until it reaches the $Q_{10} + R_5$ line. Read the current (I_C) at the intersection (about 27 μA).

We now have established that the driver is operating at 600 μA and the input stage is operating at about 27 μA (13.5 μA each side) based on the discussion of the 741 input-stage bias scheme.

Determining the Input-Stage Gain. The gain (g_m) of the input stage is determined by its operating current and is given by the formula $g_m = I_C/V_{BE} = q\,I_C/kT$ or $I_C/26$ mV at room temperature. However, only one-fourth of the input-signal voltage (V_i) appears across either input of Q_3 or Q_4 (a total of 4 V_{BE} junctions appear across V_i). Since $V_i = 4\Delta V_{BE}$, then the output-signal current for each side is $\frac{1}{4}g_m V_i$. The circuit of Q_5, Q_6, and Q_7 translates Q_3 signal current to the output of Q_4, thus doubling the output-signal current. The output current (I_o) is $\Delta I_3 + \Delta I_4$ (from previous discussion) or $\frac{1}{2}g_m V_i$. At $I_C = 13.5\,\mu$A, $g_m = 500\,\mu$mho; therefore the output current $I_o = V_i\,250\,\mu$mho. At 13 μA for I_C, the h_{oe} of Q_4 and Q_6 is 0.2 μmho. The output impedance of the input stage is thus

$$R_{01} = \frac{1}{h_{oe4} + h_{oe7}} = 2.5 \text{ M}\Omega.$$

Driver-Stage Gain and Impedance Levels. From the facts that Q_{17} is operating at a 600-μA collector current (almost all of Q_{13}'s collector current flows through Q_{17}) and Q_{16} operates at 15 μA $(V_{BE17}/R_{12}) + I_{B17}$ and by assuming the current gains of 150 for Q_{17} and 100 for Q_{16}, input impedance can be calculated:

$$R_{IN2} = (h_{fe16} \times h_{fe17})\,(R_{11} + r_{e17}).$$

If

$$r_{e17} = \frac{26}{0.6\,(\text{mA})} = 43\,\Omega$$

and

$$R_{11} = 50\,\Omega$$

then

$$R_{IN2} = 1.40 \text{ M}\Omega.$$

$$R_{02} = \frac{1}{h_{oe17} + h_{oe13}}; \qquad R_{L2} = h_{fe14}R_L.$$

Then

where

$$R_{02} = 125 \text{ k}\Omega; \qquad R_{L2} = 300 \text{ k}\Omega,$$

$h_{oe17} = 4\,\mu$mho, $h_{oe13} = 4\,\mu$mho, $R_L = 2$ kΩ, and $h_{fe14} = 150$.

For a total collector impedance (R'_{L2}) of $R_{02}/R_{L2} = 88.5$ kΩ:

$$A_{V2} = \frac{R'_{L2}}{r_{e17} + R_{11}} = 950 = 59.6 \text{ dB}.$$

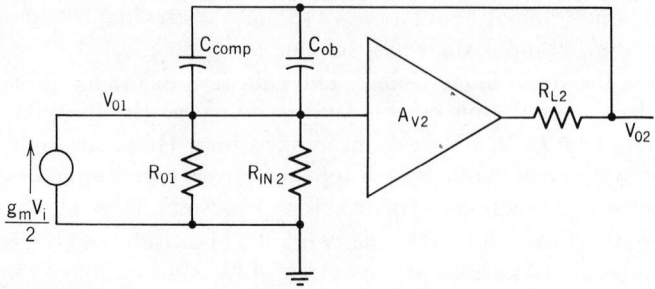

Figure 5.13. Equivalent circuit for driver stage: gm = 500 μmho, R_{01} = 2.5 MΩ, R_{IN2} = 1.4 MΩ, C_{ob} = 2 pF, C_{comp} = 30 pF, A_{V2} = 59.6 dB, R_{L2} = 88.5 kΩ.

Since the input impedance (R_{IN2}) of the driver has been found, the voltage gain (AV_1) of the input stage can be calculated:

$$V_{01} = I_o \left(\frac{R_{01}}{R_{IN2}}\right) \quad \text{and} \quad I_o = \tfrac{1}{2}g_m V_i.$$

$$A_{V1} = \frac{V_{01}}{V_i} = \tfrac{1}{2}g_m \left(\frac{R_{01}}{R_{IN2}}\right) = 225 = 46.1 \text{ dB},$$

where g_m = 500 μmho, R_{01} = 2.5 MΩ, and R_{IN2} = 1.4 MΩ. Overall amplifier gain $A_V = A_{V1} + A_{V2}$. Therefore

$$A_V = 59.6 + 46.1 = 105.7 \text{ dB } (172{,}000).$$

Calculation of Open-Loop Bandwidth.   Refer to Figure 5.13. In the discussion on frequency compensation it was shown that the bandwidth is determined by the gain and input impedance of the driver, the output impedance of the input stage, and the value of the compensation capacitor used. The bandwidth may be expressed by

$$\text{BW}(f) = \frac{1}{2\pi(A_{V2}+1)(C_{ob}+C_{comp})(R_{01}+R_{IN2})}$$

where A_{V2} = 950, C_{ob} = 2.5 pF, C_{comp} = 30 pF, R_{01} = 2.5 MΩ, and R_{IN2} = 1.4 MΩ. With the above values, BW(f) = 5.8 Hz. Knowing BW and A_V, the 0-dB gain frequency may be found as follows:

$$f(0 \text{ dB}) = \text{BW}(A_V),$$

$$= 5.8 \text{ Hz}(1.72 \times 10^5) = 1 \text{ MHz}.$$

REFERENCES

Lin, H. C., et al., "Lateral Complementary Transistor Structure for Simultaneous Fabrication of Functional Blocks," *Proc. IEEE*, December 1964, pp. 1491–1495.

6

High-Frequency Characteristics of Wideband Inverter Operational Amplifiers

by Heinrich Krabbe

Zeltex, Concord, California

Amplifier characteristics — such as frequency response, slew rate, and settling time — are often misunderstood in high-frequency applications of wideband, inverter operational amplifiers. Frequency response and slew rate are, in general, independent amplifier characteristics. They must be dealt with independently when predicting and analyzing the closed-loop response of an amplifier. For most cases amplifier limitations in wideband applications are caused by frequency response rather than slew rate.

In the following paragraphs general formulas are used to describe methods that allow the designer to predict quickly the performance of an amplifier in a given configuration.

The calculation of frequency response, open- and closed-loop transfer functions, beta, settling time, and slew-rate limits are covered. A method of improving the frequency response of amplifiers is also described.

6.1 CALCULATING FREQUENCY RESPONSE

The frequency response of an amplifier can be calculated by using a simple formula. The basic frequency response of an amplifier depends entirely on its open-loop rolloff rate (normally −6 dB/octave), its gain-bandwidth point, its input impedance, and the closed-loop gain configuration.

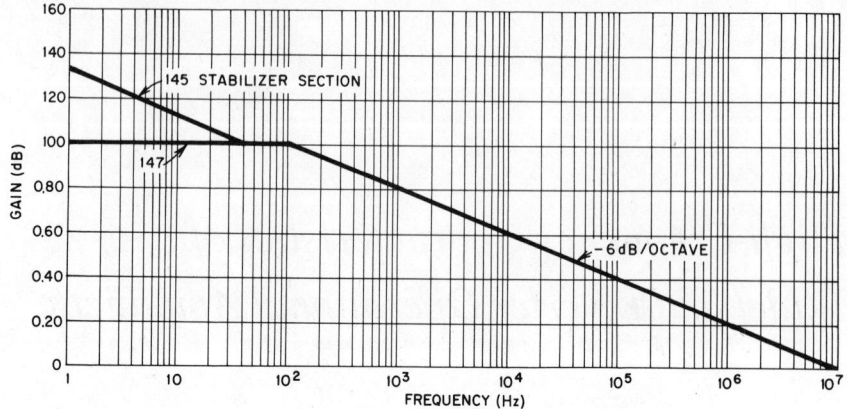

Figure 6.1.   Open-loop Bode plot for 145 and 147 operational amplifiers.

Since it is essential to know the rolloff characteristics of an amplifier in order to derive expressions for calculating frequency response, the 145 and 147 operational amplifiers made by Zeltex will be used as examples. The 145 is chopper stabilized, the 147 is not.

The high-frequency sections of both amplifiers are identical; consequently the Bode plot of each amplifier (see Figure 6.1) is identical above 30 or 40 Hz. The open-loop characteristics of the 147 may be considered to be a perfect single-order system (see Figure 6.2) for which the open-loop transfer function is

$$\frac{e_{\text{out}}}{e_{\text{in}}} = \frac{-A}{\tau S + 1}, \tag{6.1}$$

where A is the open-loop dc gain, τ is the time constant of the open-loop amplifier, and S is the Laplace operator.

The closed-loop transfer function of the simple amplifier system shown in Figure 6.3 can be expressed as

$$\frac{e_{\text{out}}}{e_{\text{in}}} = \frac{(-A)/(\tau S + 1)}{1 + (A\beta)/(\tau S + 1)} = \frac{-A}{(\tau S + 1) + A\beta}, \tag{6.2}$$

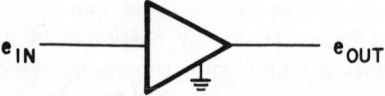

Figure 6.2.   Simple open-loop amplifier.

where β is the attenuation ratio for the feedback voltage. It can be assumed that $A\beta$ is always greater than unity since the amplifier is never operated at the open-loop dc gain in a closed-loop configuration. Thus

$$\frac{e_{\text{out}}}{e_{\text{in}}} = \left(\frac{-A}{\tau}\right)\left[\frac{1}{S+(A\beta/\tau)}\right]. \tag{6.3}$$

The Bode plot for the 145 and 147 leads to the conclusion that

$$f_c = \frac{f_{\text{GBW}}}{A} \quad \text{or} \quad \omega_c = \frac{\omega_{\text{GBW}}}{A}, \tag{6.4}$$

where f_c is the desired closed-loop corner frequency (-3-dB bandwidth). Since

$$\tau = \frac{1}{\omega_c}, \tag{6.5}$$

(6.5) can be combined with (6.4), resulting in

$$\tau = \frac{A}{\omega_{\text{GBW}}}. \tag{6.6}$$

Substituting this term into (6.3) provides

$$\frac{e_{\text{out}}}{e_{\text{in}}} = -\omega_{\text{GBW}}\left[\frac{1}{S+\beta\,(\omega_{\text{GBW}})}\right] = \frac{1}{(S/\omega_{\text{GBW}})+\beta}. \tag{6.7}$$

or

Since S is $j\omega$ (Laplace operator), (6.7) can be rewritten as

$$\frac{e_{\text{out}}}{e_{\text{in}}} = -\frac{1}{(j\omega/\omega_{\text{GBW}})+\beta}. \tag{6.8}$$

Thus the $e_{\text{out}}/e_{\text{in}}$ term represents a complex quantity of which the amplitude response is simply

$$\frac{e_{\text{out}}}{e_{\text{in}}} = -\frac{1}{[(\omega/\omega_{\text{GBW}})^2+\beta^2]^{1/2}} \tag{6.9}$$

or

$$\frac{e_{\text{out}}}{e_{\text{in}}} = -\frac{1}{[(f_x/f_{\text{GBW}})^2+\beta^2]^{1/2}}, \tag{6.10}$$

where ω is replaced by f_x, ω_{GBW} by f_{GBW}, and f_x is the variable frequency. From the preceding expression it can be seen that the -3-dB point of any closed-loop amplifier depends only on β (providing the amplifier rolls off at -6 dB/octave).

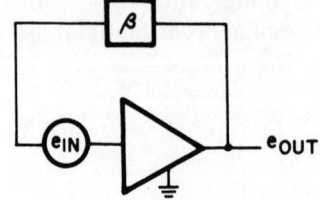

Figure 6.3.   Amplifier with feedback loop.

As long as the GBW of the amplifier is known, the -3-dB bandwidth can be calculated as follows:

$$\frac{f_{-3\,\mathrm{dB}}}{f_{\mathrm{GBW}}} = \beta \quad \text{or} \quad f_{-3\,\mathrm{dB}} = \beta f_{\mathrm{GBW}}. \tag{6.11}$$

However, β has not been completely defined. As already stated, β is the attenuation ratio for the feedback voltage. To derive β the circuit of Figure 6.4 may be used. The part of e_{out} that appears at the amplifier junction in the circuit of Figure 6.4 is

$$e_{\mathrm{out}} = \frac{R_{\mathrm{in}}/Z_{\mathrm{in}}}{R_f + (R_{\mathrm{in}}/Z_{\mathrm{in}})}. \tag{6.12}$$

Therefore

$$\beta = \frac{R_{\mathrm{in}}/Z_{\mathrm{in}}}{R_f + (R_{\mathrm{in}}/Z_{\mathrm{in}})}. \tag{6.13}$$

For the 145 and 147 amplifiers Z_{in} is expressed as R and is a fixed 10-kΩ resistor (provided the bandwidth terminal is open). For example, if $R_f = R_{\mathrm{in}} = 10\,\mathrm{k\Omega}, \beta$ is

$$\frac{5K}{10K + 5K} = \frac{1}{3}.$$

Substituting β equals $\frac{1}{3}$ in (6.11), the frequency response of the 145 and 147 is found to be

$$f_{-3\,\mathrm{dB}} = \beta f_{\mathrm{GBW}} = \tfrac{1}{3} \times 10\,\mathrm{MHz} = 3.3\,\mathrm{MHz}.$$

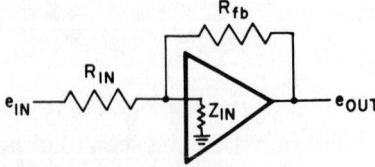

Figure 6.4.   Closed-loop amplifier showing components used in deriving β.

It should be kept in mind that excessive stray capacitance (expecially in the feedbackloop) can cause a high-frequency shunt across R_f and consequently cause a change in β.

The frequency response can be improved to approximately 5 MHz by using a 1 : 1 inverter configuration; that is, if $R_{in} = R_f = 1$, β approaches its limit of $\frac{1}{2}$ because the value of Z_{in} remains unchanged; consequently its shunting effect on R_{in} becomes less significant.

6.2 IMPROVING FREQUENCY RESPONSE

Generally, low impedances must be used to improve the high-frequency response of an amplifier. Since the 145 and 147 amplifiers have closed-loop integrator overall compensation (see Figure 6.5), an ideal way of increasing the frequency response if readily available. By shunting the resistance of Z_{in}, the input impedance is decreased and the gain-bandwidth product is increased. This increase in gain bandwidth can be employed to obtain a higher frequency response; however, R_{in} and R_f must also be decreased. The following discussion explains how the frequency response of the 145 and 147 amplifiers can be increased from 5 MHz at a closed-loop gain of 1 to 10 MHz at a closed-loop gain of 10.

In Figure 6.5, with R_{BW} shorted, the extreme gain-bandwidth of the amplifiers is obtained. Figure 6.6 shows the Bode plots of the 145 and 147 amplifiers with a bandwidth terminal shorted. The dashed line represents the interpreted response curve. As shown in Figure 6.6, the amplifiers are no longer perfect single-order systems and must be handled

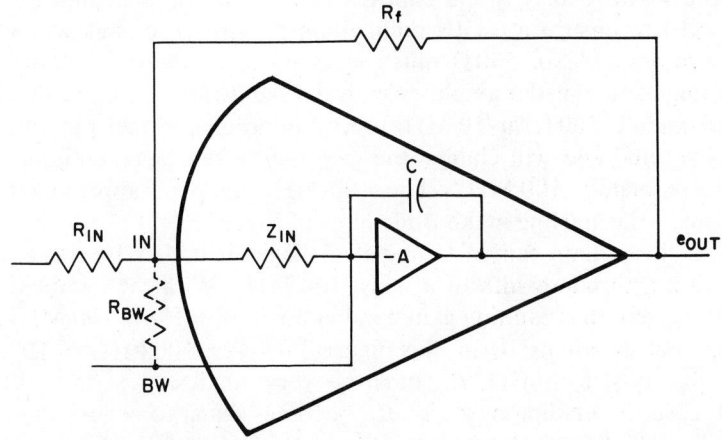

Figure 6.5.   Block diagram representing the 147 operational amplifier.

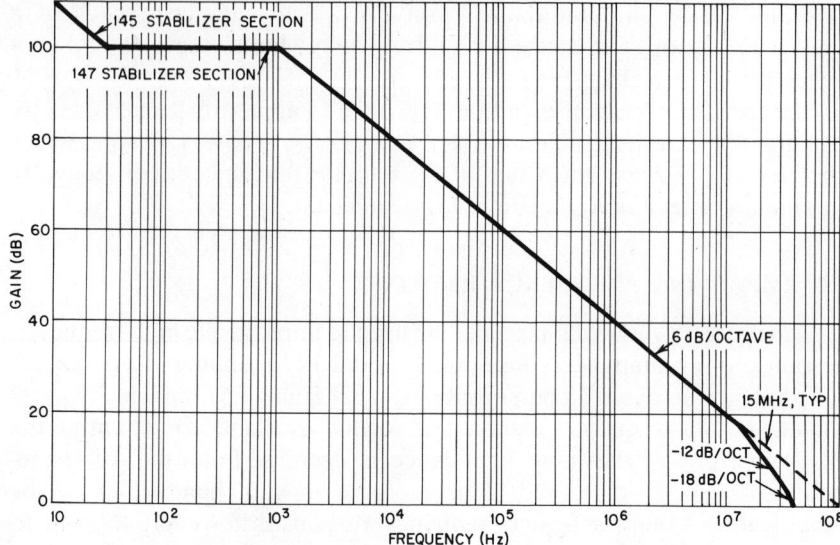

Figure 6.6.   Open-loop Bode plot showing 100 = MHz gain.

very carefully. Since the -6 dB/octave rolloff slope continues to approximately 15 MHz, it is imperative to keep the loop closure definitely under 10 MHz if a generally stable amplifier is desired. Higher frequency loop closures can be obtained whenever needed for special circuit configurations.

If the -6 dB/octave slope continues to 100 MHz, β cannot be larger than 1/10 to ensure a -3 dB point (loop-closure) at or below 10 MHz. Furthermore a Z_{in} of 500 Ω must be assumed in the β calculations (the input impedance of the amplifier with the bandwidth terminal shorted, is approximately 500 Ω at 10 MHz). Any intermediate resistor value can be substituted and will change the gain bandwidth between limits of 10 to approximately 100 MHz. The 100-MHz figure is approximated, as shown by a dashed line in the Bode plots of Figure 6.6.

For a closed-loop gain of 10 and a -3 dB point at 10 MHz it is essential to have a gain bandwidth of at least 100 MHz. With the bandwidth terminal shorted, the resulting gain bandwidth at 10 MHz is 100 MHz. This means that β equals $\frac{1}{10}$ of this figure ($\beta = \frac{1}{10} \times 100$ MHz $= 10$ MHz). With Z_{in} equal to 500 Ω, R_{in} must be very small or less than 50 Ω, in which case the loading of Z_{in} or R_{in} becomes equal to or less than 10%. Therefore R_f becomes fixed at 500 Ω and β equals approximately $\frac{1}{11}$, and the desired gain bandwidth cannot be realized. However, since most of the amplifiers have a typical gain bandwidth of at least 120 MHz, the desired bandwidth can still be obtained.

6.3 SETTLING TIME

In certain applications it is necessary to know the settling time of an amplifier. Settling time is the time-domain description of frequency response. The settling time can be easily computed to any desired accuracy if the frequency response of the closed-loop system is known, provided the amplifier is a perfect single-order system and has no internal charge-discharge nonlinearities.

Above the -3-dB point, the response of the closed-loop system must necessarily follow the open-loop response of the amplifier (-6 dB/octave). Thus the closed loop has the response of an RC integrating network or single-order system with a time constant of $\frac{1}{2}f_c$. This is approximately 50 ns in the previously calculated 3.3-MHz response. Thus, if the 10k/10k inverter configuration of the 145 or 147 is driven with a perfect-rise square wave, the output rises to 63% in 50 ns; the rise time (10 to 90%) is approximately 110 ns, or 2.2 time constants.

The closed-loop time constant ($\frac{1}{2}f_c$) is used as the basis for finding th theoretical settling time. Since an accuracy of 1% requires approximately five time constants (7 time constants for 0.1% and 10 for 0.01%), the closed-loop constant is simply multiplied by the number of constants to obtain the desired accuracy. The settling time to this accuracy may then be calculated. Care must be used in making actual measurements since settling times to 0.01% within $2\,\mu$s are very difficult to measure. The circuit shown in Figure 6.7 is recommended for measuring settling time.

The values of resistors connected to point e_e must be kept low because of the input of the oscilloscope (the oscilloscope must have a fast over-

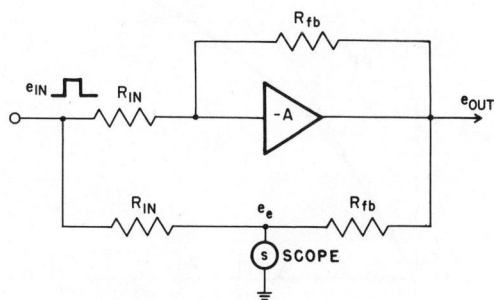

Figure 6.7. Circuit for measuring settling time.

load-recovery time). Also the input signal must be a clean, fast-rising square wave since ringing on the leading and trailing edges greatly impairs the reading. The waveform at point e_e for $R_{\text{in}} = R_f$ is a differentiated impulse representing one-half the difference between e_{in} and e_{out}. Therefore, if a 20-V peak-to-peak square wave is used on the input, the time for a 0.01% accuracy reading must be measured to the point at which the error signal at e_e is less than 1 mV.

6.4   SLEW RATE

Frequency response seldom influences or limits the slew rate. Slew-rate limitations are mainly influenced by internal phase-compensation networks, current-drive capabilities in output or driver stages, and output loading.

The maximum rate of rise of output voltage that the amplifier can sustain, regardless of the rise time of the input signal, is known as the slew rate. However, the rise time of the output voltage of fast amplifiers is usually limited by the amplifier's frequency response rather than by slew rate.

This can be proven by noting that the minimum slew rate of the 145 and 147 amplifiers is $250 \text{ V}/\mu\text{s}$; however, the maximum slew rate required for passing a 10-V peak-to-peak square wave is $200 \text{ V}/\mu\text{s}$ (using the calculated time constant of 50 ns; i.e., 10 V/50 ns). This maximum slew rate is well below the slew rate limit. Moreover, as Figure 6.8 reveals, the maximum slope is required for only a very small portion at the beginning of the slope curve. Even for a 20-V peak-to-peak signal there is no visible slew-rate limitation because the amplifier has ample recovery time over the full rise time of the waveform.

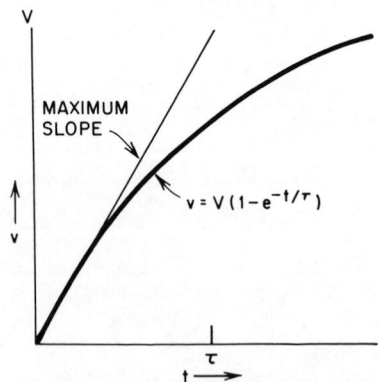

Figure 6.8.   Rise time in a single-order system.

This slew-rate limit may also be expressed in terms of maximum frequency for full output. To do this the maximum slope of a sine wave is found by differentiating the expression $v = E \sin \omega t$ with respect to t. Thus

$$\text{slew rate} = \frac{dv}{dt} = \omega E \cos \omega t, \qquad (6.14)$$

and, since the maximum slope of the sine wave occurs at $0°$,

$$\cos \omega t = 1 \qquad (6.15)$$

and

$$\frac{dv}{dt} = \omega E. \qquad (6.16)$$

Since E is the peak amplitude and is normally $10\,V$, the derivative becomes

$$\frac{dv}{dt} = 10\,\omega. \qquad (6.17)$$

With a slew rate of $250\,V/\mu s$, this provides

$$\omega = 2.5 \times 10^7$$

and

$$f = \frac{2.5 \times 10^7}{6.28} = 4\,\text{MHz},$$

which assures that a 4-MHz sine wave of 10 V (peak) can be sustained by the amplifier without distortion.

An amplifier may not meet slew-rate specifications if the output-current capability is exceeded. Care must be taken when capacitive loading is present and fast rise times are expected. The current necessary to charge a certain capacitance can be easily found by the expression

$$\frac{dv}{dt} = \frac{i}{c} \qquad (6.18)$$

$$i = c\frac{dv}{dt} \qquad (6.19)$$

6.5 LOOP GAIN VERSUS CLOSED-LOOP ACCURACY AT HIGH FREQUENCIES

At dc the loop gain of an amplifier (the portion eliminated by feedback) is the reciprocal of its given closed-loop accuracy; that is, an accuracy of 1% indicates a loop gain of 100. However this is not true at high frequencies where the open-loop gain of the amplifier rolls off at -6 dB/

octave. At high frequencies the loop gain required to obtain a specific amplitude accuracy is significantly decreased because of the 90° phase shift between the amplifier input and output. The gain equation of the single-order system may be used to determine the necessary loop-gain for a given accuracy at high frequencies (vector quantities resulting from 90° phase shift are represented by the gain equation).

For example, the loop gain required at a point where the accuracy is 1% or the total amplitude is 0.99 is determined by the gain equation:

$$\text{amplitude} = \frac{1}{[(1)^2 + (F_x/F_{3\,dB})^2]^{1/2}}. \tag{6.20}$$

Consequently the loop gain required for a 1% amplitude accuracy at high frequencies is much smaller than that required at dc. However, it must also be mentioned that for a dynamic accuracy of a given percentage the loop gain must be the same as that given for dc. Dynamic accuracy means instantaneous accuracy that includes amplitude and phase.

Solving for $F_x/F_{3\,dB}$, we obtain

$$(0.99)^2 \left[(1)^2 + \left(\frac{F_x}{F_{3\,dB}} \right) \right]^2 = 1$$

and

$$\left(\frac{F_x}{F_{3\,dB}} \right)^2 = \frac{1 - (0.99)^2}{(0.99)^2}$$

or

$$\frac{F_x}{F_{3\,dB}} = \frac{1}{7}.$$

7

Popular Linear-Integrated-Circuit Applications

by Leonard Brown and Ralph Seymour

Signetics Corporation, Santa Clara, California

Linear-integrated-circuit applications historically have been performed by using operational amplifiers in a "gain block" approach. This has led to the universal acceptance of the IC operational amplifier in just a few years, and the resulting sales volume of operational amplifiers has led to a marked reduction in the price of the devices.

Nevertheless not all applications are best suited to this approach either from an economic or a design-integrity viewpoint. As a result some of the applications discussed in this chapter do not use operational amplifiers.

7.1 LONG-TIME-CONSTANT MONOSTABLE (ONE SHOT)

The circuit shown in Figure 7.1 can provide ramp durations in the range of 0.1 to 1.0 s. If built with a 515 differential amplifier, it requires only a single 5-V power supply for both the amplifier and the control logic.

As illustrated, the 515 is connected as an integrator with a fixed input voltage set by the resistor divider chain (R_1, R_2, Z_1). The charging current available for the capacitor C is therefore set by this fixed reference voltage and the input resistor R. The slope of the ramp voltage at the output of the amplifier is thus controlled by the resistor R and the capa-

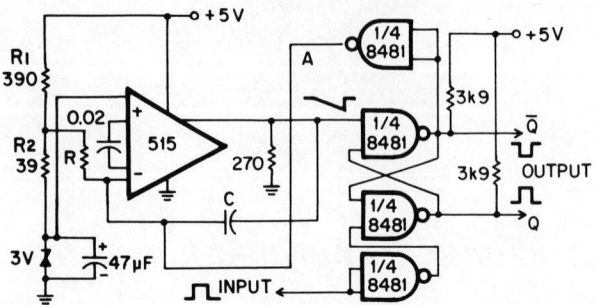

Figure 7.1. Monostable multivibrator. Time constant $T = 20RC$ (covers 0.1- to 1-s range with $C = 5\,\mu F$ for $1\,k\Omega \leqslant R \leqslant 10\,k\Omega$). Duty cycle $\leqslant 95\%$; input pulse width, $0.5\,\mu s$. Timing period starts on positive transition of input pulse.

citor C. With $C = 5.0\,\mu F$, the duration of the ramp will vary from 0.1 to 1.0 s as R is changed from 1 to 10 kΩ.

In the quiescent or stable state the $\bar{Q}$ output is high, which forces the output A low, clamping the summing junction of the amplifier around ground and causing the output of the 515 to be high. The $\bar{Q}$ output is not affected by the amplifier's "high" output because it is controlled by the "low" input from the cross-coupled Q terminal. On receiving an input pulse the flip-flop changes state and the Q output goes "high." In turn the summing junction of the amplifier is released, and the amplifier integrates the dc input voltage, causing a negative-going ramp at the in-

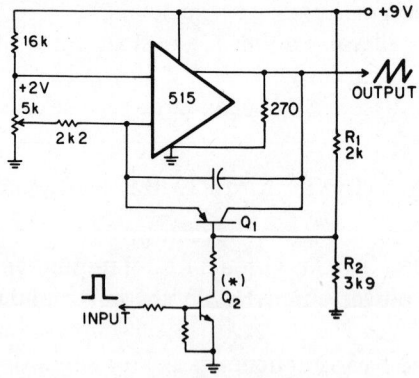

Figure 7.2. Ramp generator. For best linear operation use a low-loss-type capacitor (such as a mica type) for C. Q_1 can be a 2N2907 or a 2N3638. A 2N2222 or a 2N3642 can be used for Q_2 (Q_2 and its associated circuitry may be replaced by a DCL gate such as the $\frac{1}{4}$ 8841).

put to the cross-coupled latch. When the ramp reaches the threshold voltage of the 8481 gate, the latch changes state and resets the integrator.

In this application the equation for the timing is approximate because it includes nonlinear effects as a result of exceeding the 515 negative common-mode voltage.

7.2 RAMP GENERATOR

Operation of the 515 from a single supply is again illustrated in the circuit of Figure 7.2, which is a triggerable ramp generator. The amplifier is connected as an integrator with a fixed dc bias applied to its inputs through the input resistor divider bias chain. Transistor Q_1 is required to discharge the capacitor and hence reset the integrator and is triggered through Q_2. In the quiescent state the output sits at approximately $+6$ V as determined by the resistor chain $R_1 R_2$.

Applying a positive pulse to the input turns on Q_2 and causes the transistor Q_1 to conduct, discharging C and returning the output voltage to approximately $+2$ V, as determined by the input bias chain. At the end of the pulse the base of Q_1 returns to approximately $+6$ V and Q_1 is reverse biased. The integrating capacitor now commences to charge through the 2.2-kΩ input resistor, and the output will describe a ramp function until it is clamped by the $+6$ V of the bias chain (R_1, R_2) or is reset by a following input pulse.

The ramp timing (slope) is controlled by the 2.2-kΩ input resistor and the value of the integrating capacitor. Capacitor C may be calculated to a first-order approximation by the expression

$$C = \frac{10^{-4}}{\text{operating frequency}}. \tag{7.1}$$

7.3 AUDIO PREAMPLIFIER WITH RIAA/NAB COMPENSATION

The high open-loop gain of operational amplifiers makes them natural candidates for applications requiring precision frequency-shaped characteristics at audio frequencies. An example, illustrated in Figure 7.3, is an audio preamplifier with switched equalization networks corresponding to the RIAA and NAB compensation requirements (see Figure 7.4).

The amplifier is connected in the noninverting configuration with the frequency shaping performed in the negative-feedback loop. The low-frequency response (below 10 Hz) is controlled by R_1 and C_1. Capacitor C_1 is required to make the dc gain equal to unity to avoid having an excessive output offset voltage. Resistor R_{S1} should be selected to match the required transducer loading.

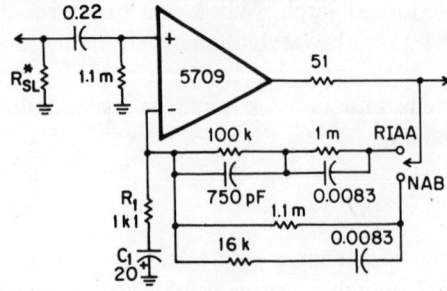

Figure 7.3. Audio preamplifier with RIAA/NAB compensation. Output noise 0.8 mV rms (with input shorted).

7.4 TONE-CONTROL CIRCUIT

The circuit in Figure 7.5 is intended for use in conjunction with the circuit of Figure 7.3 to provide the bass and treble controls of a complete audio preamplifier. The IC employed is a 516 operational amplifier with unity-gain compensation in a conventional feedback configuration.

In Figure 7.5 amplifier *A* may be a 5709 or 516. Frequency compensation such as would be used for unity-gain noninverting amplifiers must be used. The turnover frequency is 1 kHz. At 20 kHz, as can be seen from the response curve (Figure 7.6), the circuit provides 20 dB of bass boost and bass cut; at 20 kHz there is 19 dB of treble boost and 19 dB of treble cut.

7.5 CRYSTAL OSCILLATOR

An extremely useful and simple square-wave oscillator that can be crystal controlled from 1 to 10 MHz may be constructed by using only

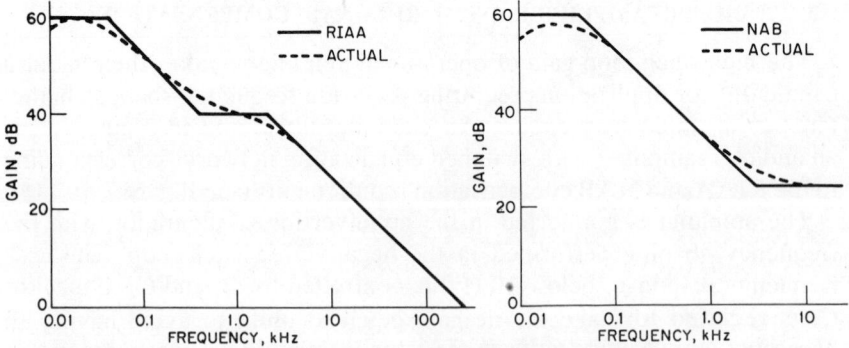

Figure 7.4. RIAA and NAB compensation.

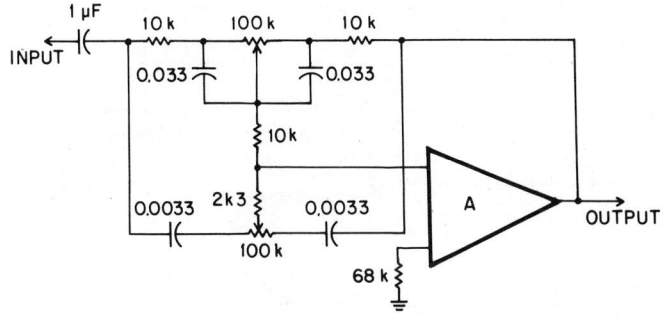

Figure 7.5. Tone-control circuit.

three capacitors and a 501 wideband amplifier. The availability of an external interstage connection (pins 3 and 4) on the IC simplifies the design and minimizes the number of external components required. The output drive may be increased by the addition of a 156 logic gate, as illustrated in Figure 7.7.

The value of *C* can be calculated from

$$C = \frac{2.12 \times 10^{-3}}{f} \text{ farads.}$$

Depending on the specific crystal type used, the output (pin 6) of the 501 may not be high enough to drive the following logic (156). If this is the case, decreasing the value of the two capacitors will increase

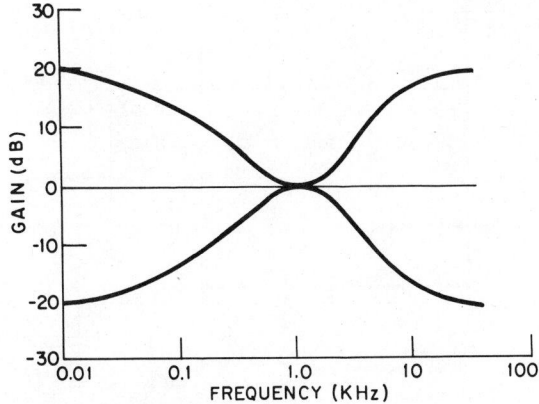

Figure 7.6. Response curve for tone-control circuit.

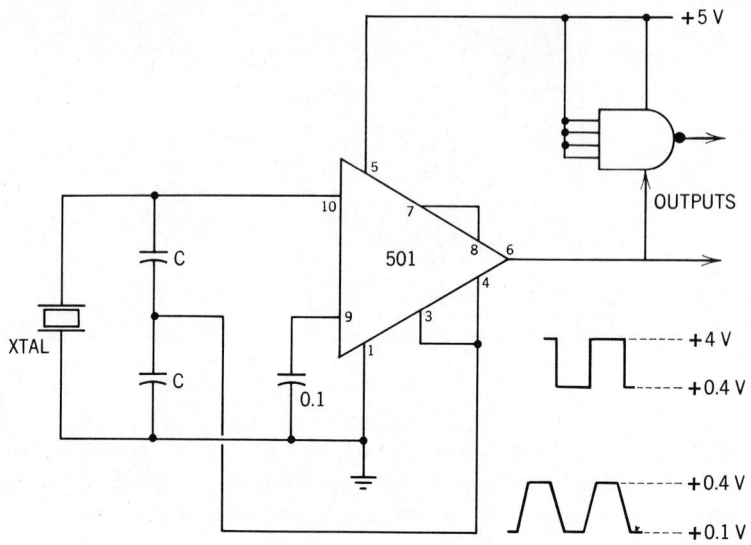

Figure 7.7. Crystal-controlled square-wave oscillator.

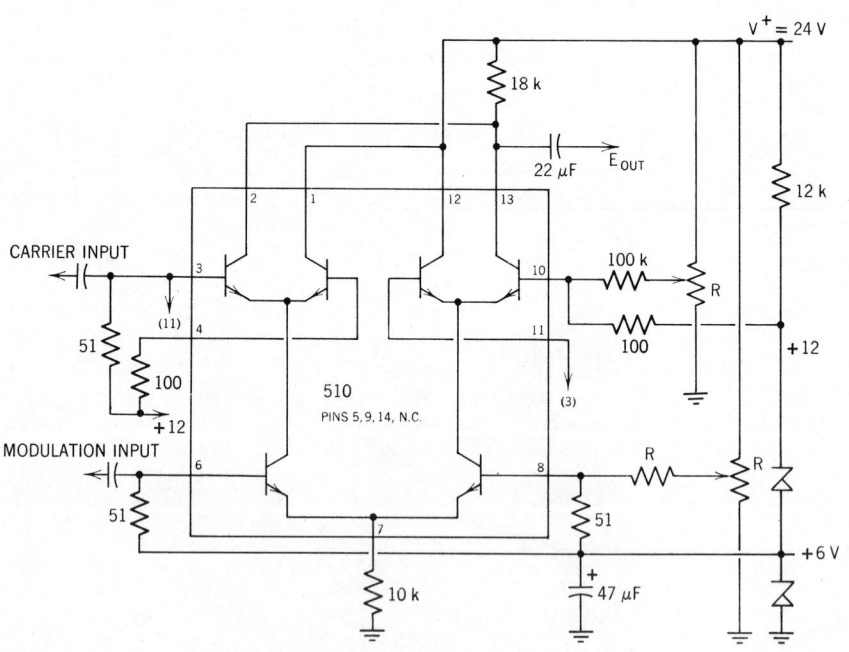

Figure 7.8. Doubly balanced modulator.

the output drive. If a 501A is used instead of a 501, modification of the pin numbers shown is necessary.

7.6 DOUBLY BALANCED MODULATOR

A doubly balanced modulator, useful in phase comparators, FM detectors, synchronous demodulators, and balanced mixers, is shown in Figure 7.8. A 510 dual differential amplifier is employed in an ac-coupled configuration.

Although the transistors display excellent matching thanks to the monolithic construction, additional circuitry is required to optimize the carrier and/or modulation balance.

For low distortion the modulation input levels should be on the order of 50 mV or less. However, if square-wave operation is satisfactory, the 510 can handle input signals of up to 5 V before the device ratings are exceeded. In the higher voltage mode of operation the load impedance should be selected to ensure that the output transistors do not saturate.

In the circuit shown in Figure 7.8 signal suppression of more than 50 dB can be achieved and an output swing of 6 V peak to peak is attainable. The frequencies of the carrier and modulating signal were 22 and 1 KHz, respectively, under test conditions. Satisfactory operation can be achieved with carrier frequency of up to 30 MHz.

8

The Versatile Wideband
IC Amplifier

by Brent Welling

Motorola, Phoenix, Arizona

For economic reasons a monolithic wideband amplifier should be designed so that it can fit into a wide variety of applications. In this chapter the use of the MC1545, a wideband amplifier, is described in such applications as a gated video switch, a preamplifier for a core-memory sense amplifier, a balanced modulator, a frequency-shift keyer, an amplitude modulator, a pulse amplifier, multiplexing circuits, and others.

8.1 CIRCUIT DESCRIPTION AND OPERATION

Before moving on to the applications, a look at the MC1545 will help to clarify the discussion of its use. The circuit diagram is shown in Figure 8.1 (pin numbers correspond to the G-suffix TO-5 package). The circuit consists basically of a constant-current-source transistor Q_7 and a switching differential amplifier, Q_5 and Q_6, which splits a constant current between two differential amplifiers, or channels, composed of transistor pairs Q_1, Q_2 and Q_3, Q_4; the amount of current depends on the voltage applied at pin 1, the gating pin. The collectors of both channels are tied together and connected to a common-load resistor (1 kΩ). By using this technique, the amount of current flowing through each of the 1 kΩ load resistors is constant and independent of which channel—Q_1, Q_2 or Q_3,

82

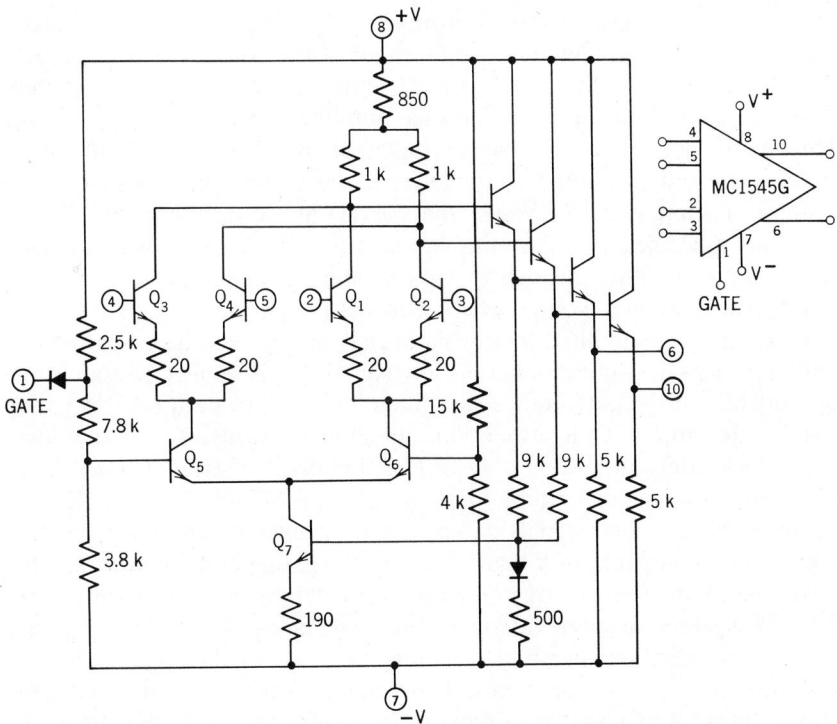

Figure 8.1. Circuit diagram for the MC1545G. Pin numbers shown are for the IC package in G-suffix TO-5 case.

Q_4— is conducting. As a result there is essentially no dc level shift at the output when one channel is turned off and the other channel is turned on. The steady-state measured change in the differential output voltage when switching from one channel to the other is typically 15 mV. The amplified signal that appears at the collectors of the input channels is transferred to the output via Darlington emitter followers to provide a low output impedance and at the same time buffer the input differential amplifiers from any capacitive loading that would tend to lessen the frequency response.

Common-mode feedback is provided from the emitter of the first emitter follower back to constant-current source Q_7 to stabilize the dc operating point of the circuit and provide excellent common-mode rejection.

Either of the two input channels can be selected as follows: bias the MC1545 so that there is sufficient positive voltage applied to the gating pin (pin 1 on the G package); or leave the gating pin open so that the voltage at the base of transistor Q_6 is more negative than the voltage at the base of transistor Q_5. As a result transistor Q_5 will be "on" and transistor Q_6 will be "off." Under this condition all of the constant current that is established in the collector of Q_7 passes through transistor Q_5 and establishes a bias current in the differential amplifier composed of Q_3 and Q_4. Hence any signal applied to these transistors is amplified and will appear differentially at the output. However, if the gating pin is connected to ground or some negative value, the voltage at the base of transistor Q_5 becomes more negative than the voltage at the base of Q_6, which causes the constant to flow through Q_6 and establishes the bias current in the differential amplifier composed of transistors Q_1 and Q_2. In this state any signal that is applied to transistors Q_1 and Q_2 will be amplified and will appear at the output, whereas any signal that is applied to transistors Q_3 and Q_4 will be gated off. The voltage required to perform this gating function at pin 1 is compatible with all standard forms of saturated logic (e.g., Resistor-Transistor-Logic RTL, Diode-Transistor Logic DTL, Transistor-Transistor Logic TTL).

Since either of two signals can be gated through the amplifier, depending on the application of a logic signal to the gating pin, applications that arise include a video matrix cross-point switch, a frequency-shift keyer for FSK systems, a gated video amplifier, a gated oscillator, a preamplifier for core-memory sensing, and a channel selector for data acquisition. In addition to these obvious uses, there are a number of other possible applications, including the amplitude modulator and the balanced modulator.

Figure 8.2 shows a plot of voltage gain versus frequency for temperatures of -55, 25, and $125°C$. These curves indicate that the MC1545 is a good wideband device and can serve as a pulse amplifier. In addition to its wide bandwidth, the MC1545 is dc coupled and can provide a differential output when a signal and its complement are required as inputs to

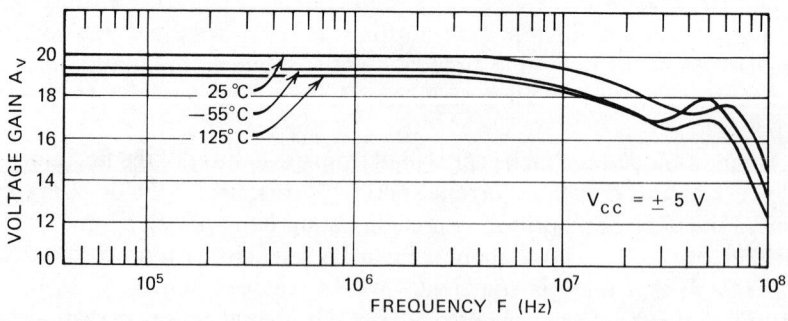

Figure 8.2. Plots of single-ended voltage gain versus frequency at $V_{cc} = \pm 5$ V.

drive logic functions. Rise time, fall time, and propagation delay are typically 6 ns for this device, which makes it compatible with modern, second-generation logic systems.

As was explained earlier, the amount of attenuation that is given to an input signal when the amplifier is gated "off" is a function of the dc voltage at the gating pin. A curve showing this attenuation versus gate voltage is given in Figure 8.3. As would be expected, the amount the input signal is attenuated is a function of the input frequency. This characteristic is shown in Figure 8.4. The curve indicates that above 30 kHz the amplifier begins to show a certain amount of capacitive feedthrough, resulting primarily from the physical closeness of the pins; performance could be improved by the use of proper shielding between pins. However, even at an input frequency of 10 MHz, a channel separation of better than 60 dB can be achieved.

Another important parameter of a wideband amplifier is common-mode rejection, which again is a definite function of frequency. This is shown in Figure 8.5, which demonstrates the reduction that occurs in common-mode-rejection capability for the MC1545 as frequency increases.

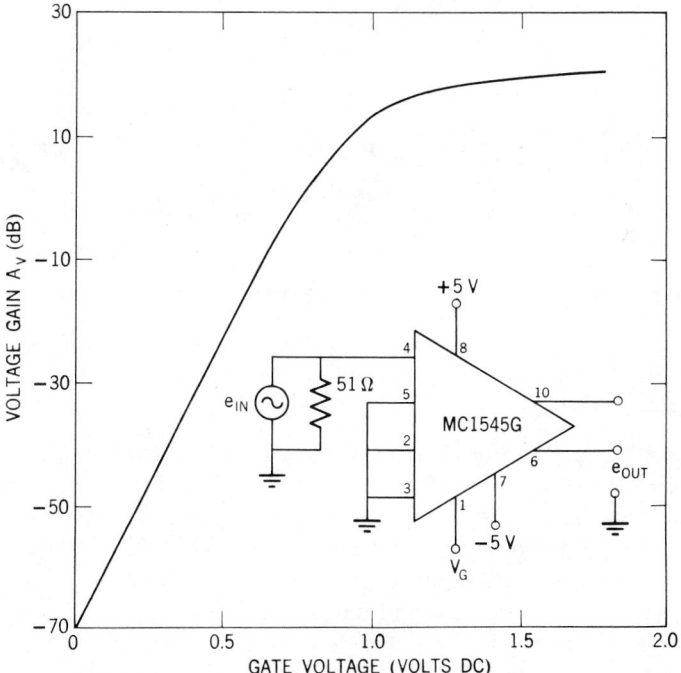

Figure 8.3.   Voltage gain as a function of gate voltage.

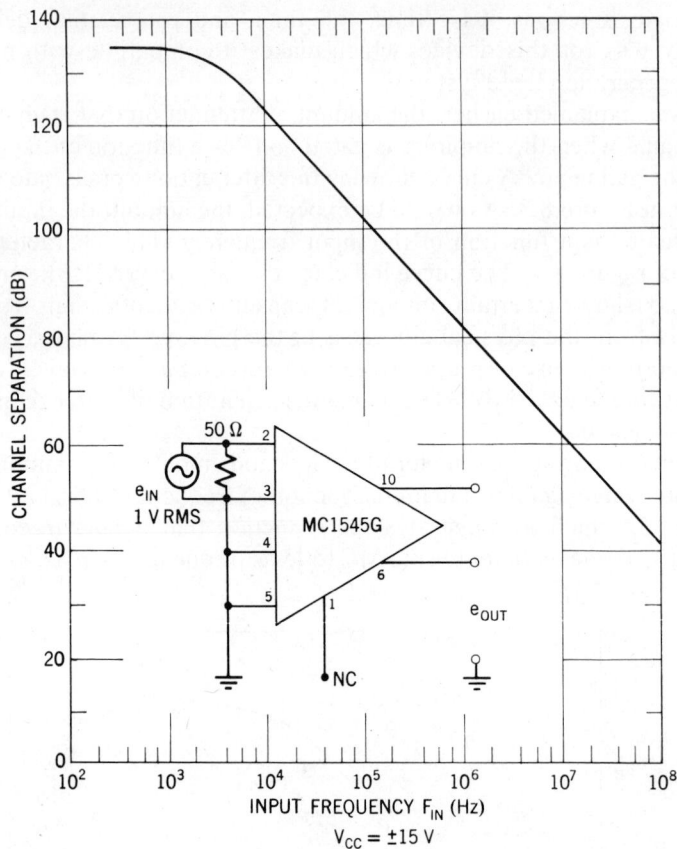

Figure 8.4. Channel separation versus input frequency. Channel separation $\stackrel{\Delta}{=} 20 \log A_V - 20 \log (e_o/e_{in})$.

8.2   VIDEO SWITCH

Figure 8.6 shows the MC1545G connected as a gated analog switch. The number of external components required for this type of application is very small. In this particular case only one resistor is required.

In this application a signal (analog or digital) is applied to the amplifier at pin 4. With the logic signal at pin 1 at a logic 1 state (positive voltage), the input signal is amplified and passed through the amplifier. However, if the logic signal at pin 1 is at a logic 0 state, the amplifier is turned "off" and no signal will pass through the device. If it were required that the opposite logic levels pass or block the signal, the input signal can just as

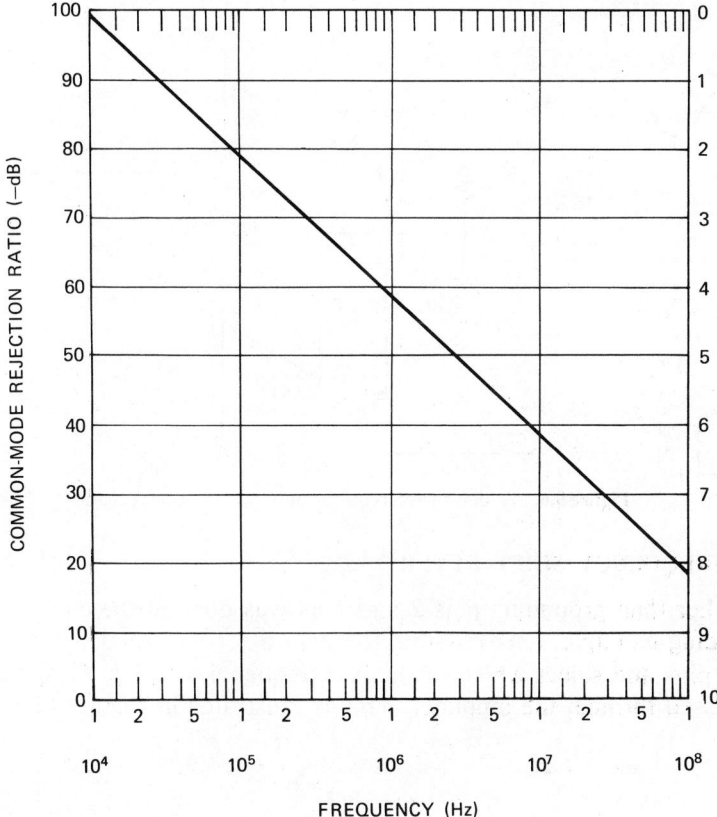

Figure 8.5. Common-mode rejection versus frequency.

easily be applied to pin 2 or 3 with pins 4 and 5 grounded. In this case a high logic level would block transmission, and a low logic level would pass the signal.

Hence the use of inverters is not necessary. If "channel select time" is considered to be the time delay from the 50% point of the gate pulse to the 50% point of the full output swing, it is approximately 20 ns. During the time that the gating logic is in the low state, the circuit that gates the MC1545 must sink a maximum of 2.5 mA, which most forms of saturated logic can do easily. When the gating logic is in the high state, the circuit that gates the MC1545 must source only the leakage current of a reverse-biased diode, which is $2 \mu A$ maximum. These requirements are quite similar to the input requirements of a standard DTL or TTL logic gate.

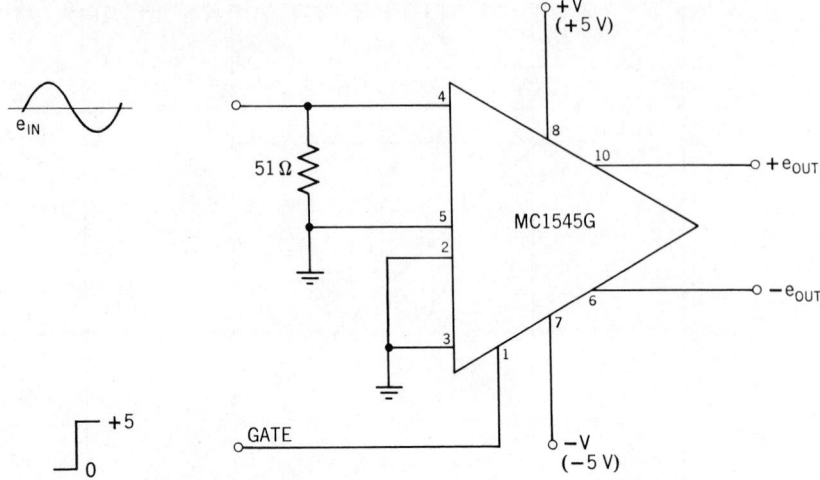

Figure 8.6.   Video switch requires only one external resistor.

8.3   FREQUENCY SHIFT KEYER

Rather than grounding pins 2 and 3 as was done in the circuit of the preceding example, it is possible to apply a second frequency to these input pins and select which of the two frequencies, either F_1 or F_2, will be passed through the amplifier. This is illustrated in Figure 8.7. In the

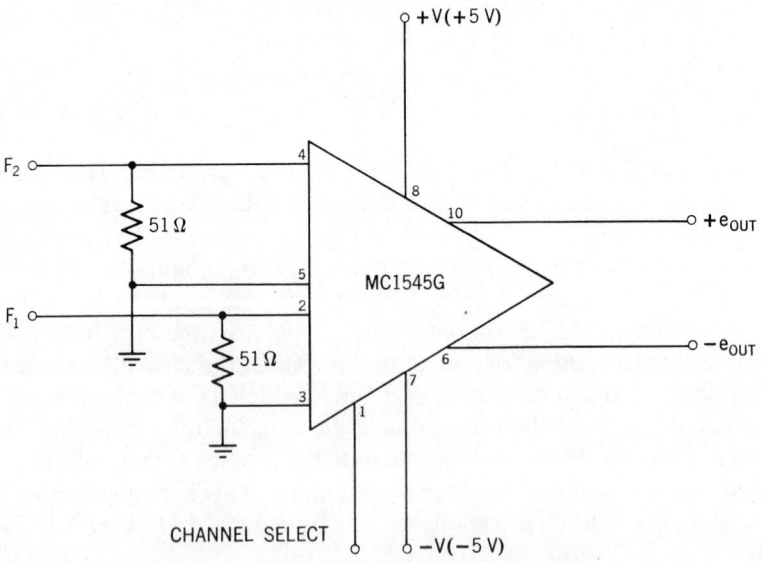

Figure 8.7.   Multiplexer (frequency-shift keyer).

circuit shown frequency F_2 will be passed when the voltage at pin 1 is greater than $+1.5$ V, and F_1 will be passed when the voltage at pin 1 is approximately 0 V.

The MC1545 can be used as a gated sense amplifier-preamplifier in core-memory systems. If it is able to strobe independent of the system's read signal, the sense amplifier can be gated "on" after the large common-mode pulse has passed, to sense the low-voltage-level differential signal stored in the core. This reduces the sense-amplifier recovery time from microseconds to nanoseconds, since the channel select propagation delay time is on the order of 20 ns.

In addition to this preamplifier application, another use can be made of this design by paralleling and cascading a number of MC1545 units to form a "one-of-N" data selector for data processing. A simple example of this is shown graphically in Figure 8.8.

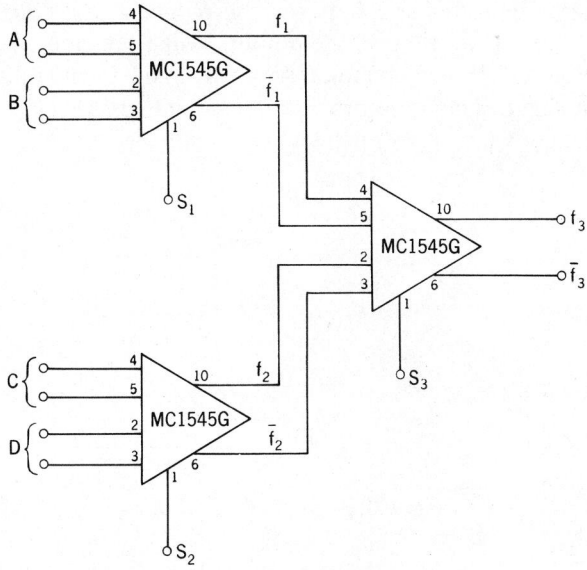

Figure 8.8. One-out-of-four data selector.

Input-Output Truth Table

S_3	S_2	S_1	f_3
0	0	X	D
0	1	X	C
1	X	0	B
1	X	1	A

Note. Saturated positive logic levels are assumed.
X = don't-care condition.

8.4 WIDEBAND DIFFERENTIAL AMPLIFIER WITH AUTOMATIC GAIN CONTROL

The gate characteristics of the MC1545, shown in Figure 8.3, also make it useful as an automatic gain control (AGC) amplifier. With a dc voltage applied to the gate pin, as much as 100 dB of AGC can be obtained. Since there is essentially no dc level shift with AGC, the output waveform will collapse symmetrically about zero with little or no distortion. The circuit configuration is shown in Figure 8.9.

8.5 AMPLITUDE MODULATOR

Figure 8.10 shows the gate characteristics of the MC1545 with gain plotted on a linear scale. By biasing the gate at approximately 1.025 V (point B) and impressing an audio signal on the bias, the gain of the channel varies quite linearly between the points A and C on the curve, giving very little distortion on the output. Using the gate characteristics shown in Figure 8.10, the up modulation (M_U) and downmodulation (M_D) may be calculated. The waveform is depicted in Figure 8.11.

The up and down modulation factors are defined as

$$M_U = \frac{E_{max} - E}{E} \qquad (8.1)$$

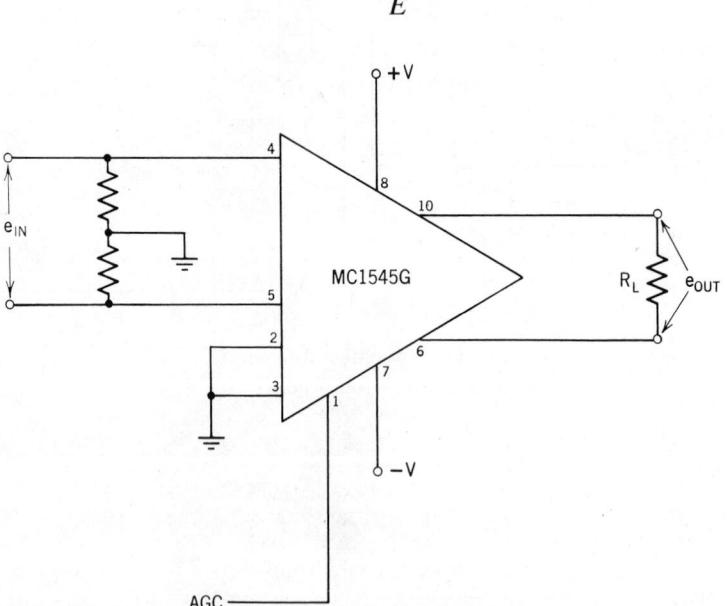

Figure 8.9.   Wideband amplifier with AGC.

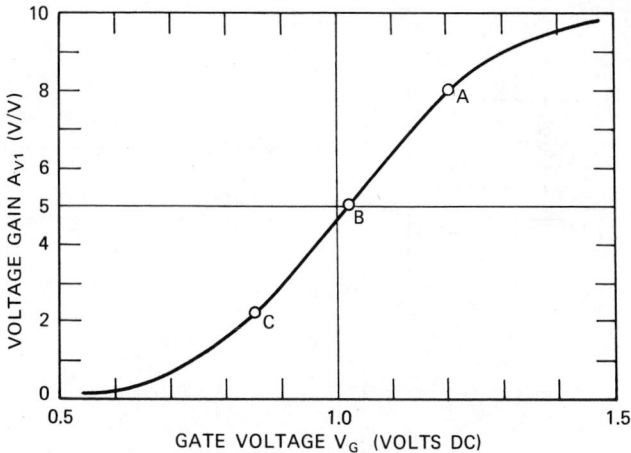

Figure 8.10. Voltage gain versus gate voltage $V_{CC} = \pm 5\,\text{V}$. Gain of amplitude-modulator circuit varies linearly between points A and C.

$$M_D = \frac{E - E_{\min}}{E} \qquad (8.2)$$

where E = peak amplitude of the unmodulated carrier, $E_{\max}$ = maximum amplitude attained by the modulated carrier envelope, and $E_{\min}$ = minimum amplitude of the modulated carrier envelope.

Constraining the gate voltage to vary around the point B with a maximum occurring at point A and a minimum at point C, and letting the rf carrier input be e_{IN}, (see Figure 8.12), then

$$e_{\text{OUT}} = e_{\text{IN}} A_{V_1}. \qquad (8.3)$$

Thus the values of E, $E_{\max}$, and $E_{\min}$ are

$$E = e_{\text{IN}}(A_{V_1})_B, \qquad (8.4)$$

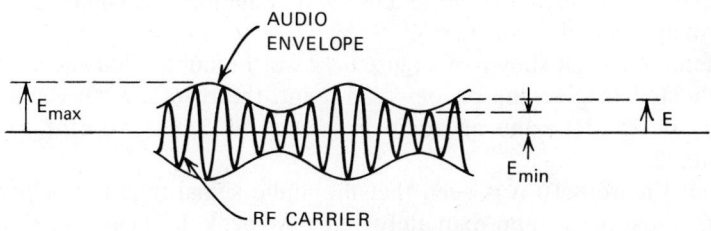

Figure 8.11. Amplitude-modulated waveform.

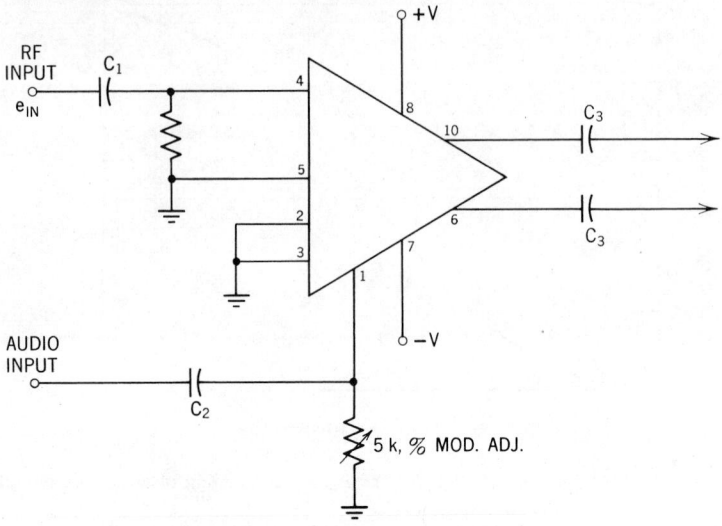

Figure 8.12.   Amplitude modulator.

$$E_{max} = e_{IN}(A_{V_1})_A,$$ (8.5)

$$E_{min} = e_{IN}(A_{V_1})_C.$$ (8.6)

Substituting in (8.1) and (8.2) provides

$$M_U = \frac{(A_{V_1})_A - (A_{V_1})_B}{(A_{V_1})_B},$$ (8.7)

$$M_D = \frac{(A_{V_1})_B - (A_{V_1})_C}{(A_{V_1})_B}$$ (8.8)

Next, inserting the values of $(A_{V_1})_A$, $(A_{V_1})_B$, and $(A_{V_1})_C$, from Figure 8.10 into (8.7) and (8.8), $M_U = 0.58$; $M_D = 0.54$.

These are the values of up and down modulation that can be expected without appreciable distortion.

When the circuit shown in Figure 8.12 was breadboarded and the resistor adjusted to give the proper bias point, the results for a carrier frequency of 25 MHz and an audio frequency of 5 kHz were $M_U = 0.54$; $M_D = 0.52$.

From Figure 8.10 it is seen that the audio signal required to perform this modulation is approximately 350 mV peak to peak. The output waveform for this circuit shows that the distortion is very low.

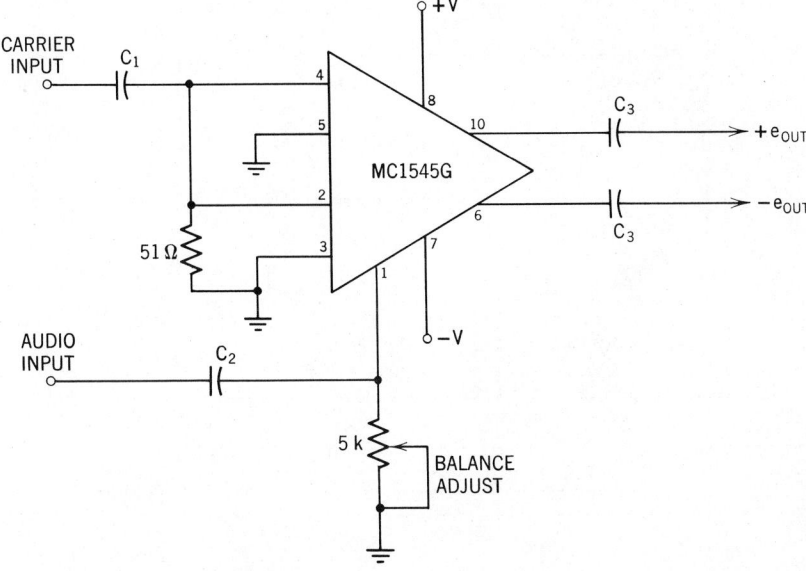

Figure 8.13. Balanced modulator. Operation of this circuit is similar to that of the amplitude modulator except that the input differential amplifiers are connected with their collectors cross-coupled.

8.6 BALANCED MODULATOR

The MC1545 can be connected as shown in Figure 8.13 to function as a balanced modulator. The circuit operation here is quite similar to the operation previously discussed for the amplitude modulator except that the input differential amplifiers have been connected with their collectors cross-coupled. This is easily seen in Figure 8.14, in which the input stage has been redrawn to reflect its actual operation. If the carrier level is sufficient to switch completely the top differential-amplifier pairs, the circuit will function as indicated by the approximately equivalent circuit in Figure 8.14. Here the modulation signal is alternately switched between differential amplifiers at the carrier rate. The result is that the modulation input signal is multiplied by a symmetrical switching function that shifts the spectrum of the modulation input and places it symmetrically about the odd harmonics of the carrier. This is demonstrated in Figure 8.15.

Mathematically the switching function can be expressed as

$$S(t) = 2 \sum_{n=1}^{\infty} A_n \cos n\omega_c t, \tag{8.9}$$

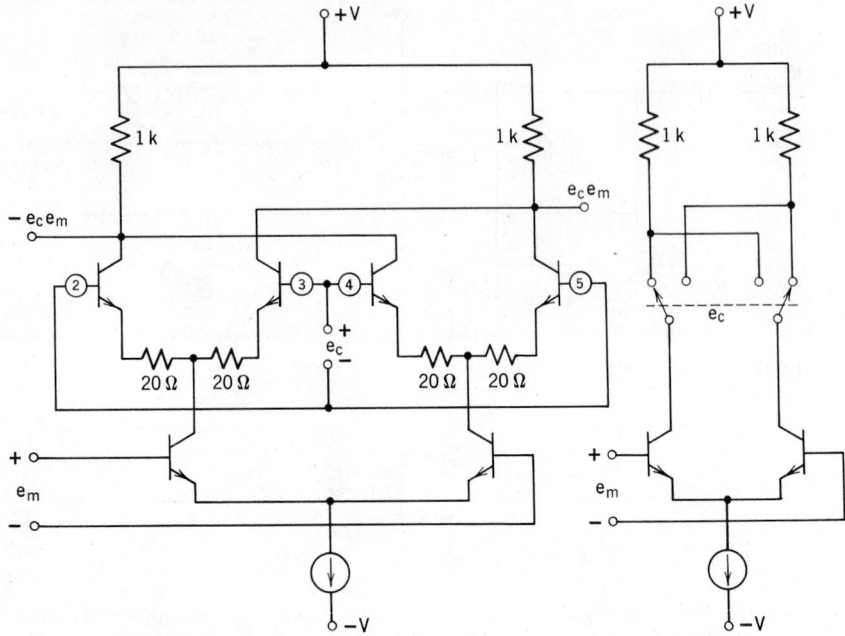

Figure 8.14.   Balanced-modulator model and approximate equivalent.

where

$$A_n = \left[\frac{\sin (n\pi/2)}{n\pi/2} \right].\qquad(8.10)$$

Only the odd harmonics are present since $\sin (n\pi/2) = 0$, for even values of n. If the input modulation is given by

$$e_m = E_m \cos \omega_m t,\qquad(8.11)$$

the output will be given by

$$e_{\text{OUT}} = 2 E_m \sum_{n=1}^{\infty} A_n \cos n\omega_c t \cos \omega_m t.\qquad(8.12)$$

By use of the following trigonometric identity,

$$\cos A \cos B = \tfrac{1}{2}[\cos (A+B) + \cos (A-B)],\qquad(8.13)$$

the final result is expressed in the desired form:

$$e_{\text{OUT}} = E_m \sum_{n=1} A_n[\cos(n\omega_c + \omega_m)t + \cos(n\omega_c - \omega_m)t]. \qquad (8.14)$$

Hence the output is composed of only the sum and difference frequencies (sidebands), and the carrier is suppressed. When the circuit of Figure 8.13 was evaluated, the carrier rejection that could be achieved was 62 dB with $f_c = 15$ kHz and $f_m = 3$ kHz; 47 dB with $f_c = 455$ kHz and $f_m = 10$ kHz; and 36 dB with $f_c = 30$ MHz and $f_m = 10$ kHz.

8.7 PULSE AMPLIFIER

Pulse amplifiers are used in many applications, such as pulse-radar intermediate-frequency circuitry, pulse-width modulation, and pulse-amplitude-modulation systems.

Integrated circuits like the MC1545 are a good choice for pulse-amplifier applications because of their large bandwidth (see Figure

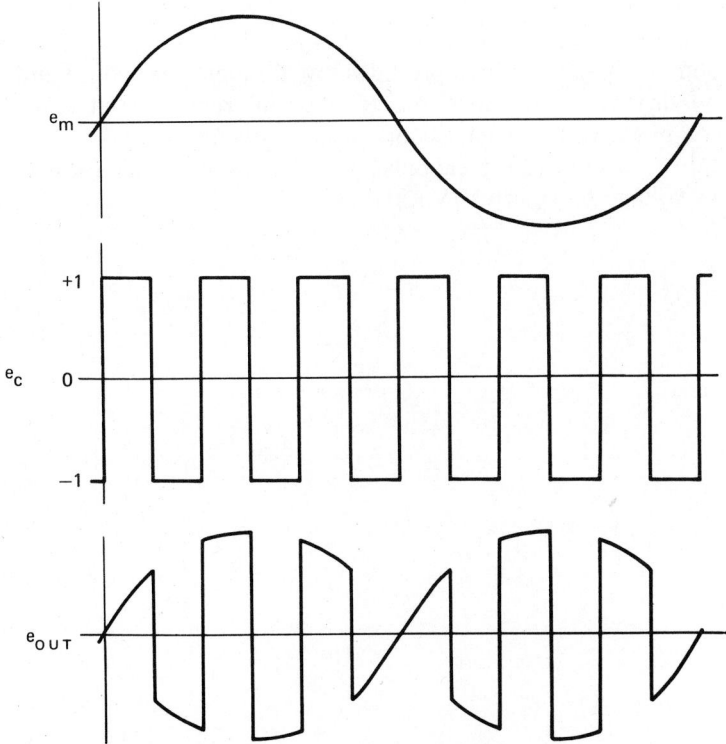

Figure 8.15. Balanced-modulator waveforms; e_c is the switching function $S(t)$.

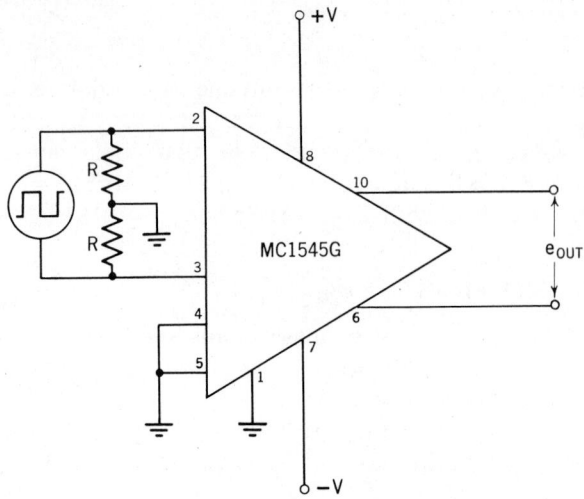

Figure 8.16.   Pulse amplifier.

8.2), and dc coupling (which provides low-frequency response and there-fore no droop). Also, since the IC has differential input and output, common-mode signals, such as noise, are greatly attenuated.

Figure 8.16 shows a typical pulse-amplifier connection for the MC1545 giving a voltage gain of 10 V/V (20 dB).

9

Applying Integrated Circuits to FM-Detector Applications

by W. F. Allen, Jr., and L. H. Hoke, Jr.

Philco-Ford Corporation, Blue Bell, Pennsylvania

Economic considerations made it mandatory that integrated circuits be high-volume production items. For this reason linear-circuit activity to date has been dominated by operational amplifiers, comparators, and, more recently, voltage regulators. Numerous other types of linear circuits have been developed, but, because of the widely differing requirements of linear applications, none of these circuits has enjoyed the volume required for the manufacturer to sell it profitably at a low price.

Another circuit that has the potential of becoming a high-volume item is the limiter-detector portion of an FM receiver; commercial television and FM receivers, as well as military FM receivers, can use the circuit.

As has been the case in the implementation of other circuits in IC form, careful analysis of the application and environment is necessary to determine the particular detector that is to be used. Discrete-component FM detectors have relied extensively on specially designed transformers for their operation. In consumer-products applications where size is not a consideration this approach is acceptable. In military applications where miniaturization is essential more suitable circuits are available that take advantage of the low cost of active components.

Because the economic factors involved in selecting ICs are rapidly changing, selection of the right IC for a particular application is no easy matter; a number of circuits are discussed in this chapter so that designers can weigh the variables that relate to their particular application.

9.1 INTEGRATED-CIRCUIT CONSIDERATIONS

When inductive elements are used in conjunction with ICs, care must be exercised to ensure against the generation of induced voltages more negative than the substrate.

A liability of *pn* isolated ICs is the device-substrate parasitic capacitance associated with diffused transistors, diodes, and resistors. In the frequency range of interest this parasitic capacitance is not usually a problem except in certain applications that require precise balance. The diodes that are available in *pn* isolated ICs have, in addition to parasitic capacitance, parasitic diode and transistor action, which must be taken into account. Voltage breakdown conditions must also be considered.

Three configurations used for monolithic IC diodes are shown in Figure 9.1. The simple base-emitter structure of Figure 9.1*a* has a typical forward

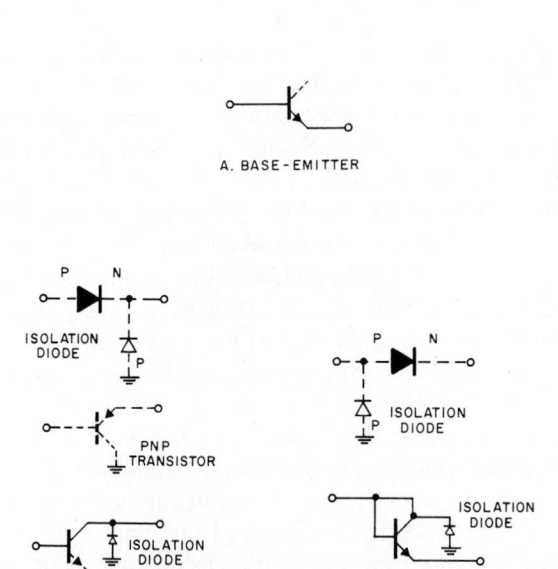

Figure 9.1. Types of monolithic diodes, their structure and associated parasitics: (*a*) base-emitter; (*b*) base-collector; (*c*) diode-connected transistor.

conduction voltage of approximately 0.7 V and a reverse breakdown voltage of about 6 V.

A second configuration, the base-collector diode shown in Figure 9.1*b*, displays a forward conduction voltage of approximately 0.7 V and reverse breakdown of 30 V or more, depending on the collector material. The isolation diode formed by the collector-substrate junction becomes a critical factor with this configuration. A negative 0.7 V on the cathode terminal (collector) of the main diode causes the parasitic isolation diode to conduct. Forward biasing of the main diode at a potential above ground converts the entire device into a grounded-collector *pnp* structure. Such a configuration has about unity beta.

A third monolithic diode configuration is shown in Figure 9.1*c*. The collector and base of a transistor are used as the anode and the emitter as the cathode. This connection displays a higher perveance than the simple base-emitter diode described earlier. Reverse breakdown of the diode-connected transistor occurs at about 6 V. The isolation diode associated with this structure conducts when the anode of the main diode goes more negative than 0.7 V with respect to the substrate. This problem is avoided by using a large negative bias on the monolithic substrate.

9.2 FOSTER-SEELEY DISCRIMINATOR

The Foster-Seeley discriminator is a popular, often-used circuit [1, 2]. A representative diagram is shown in Figure 9.2. In the interest of component reduction the high-frequency choke, which in the classical

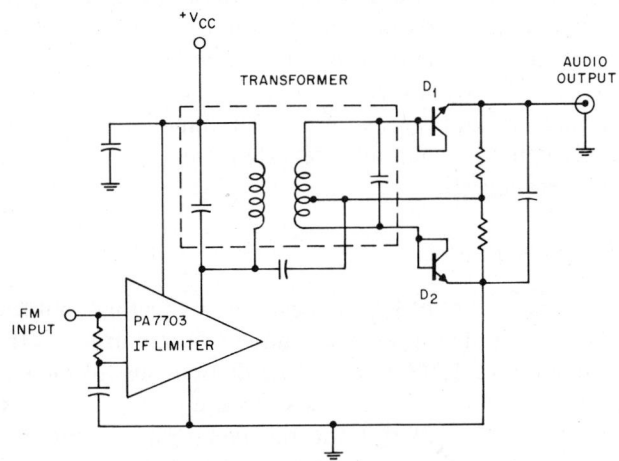

Figure 9.2.   Foster-Seeley discriminator.

design is usually included between the secondary winding center tap and the diode load resistors, has been eliminated. Consequently the primary will be loaded more heavily.

The sensitivity of the Foster-Seeley discriminator has been given by Sturley[3]:

$$S = \frac{dE}{d\Delta f} = \frac{2g_m e_g r_{D1} n_d}{f_m} \frac{Q_2(E_2/E_1)}{(1 + Q_1 Q_2 K^2)[1 + \frac{1}{4}(E_2/E_1)]^{1/2}}, \qquad (9.1)$$

where S is the static change in output voltage for a frequency offset of Δf; $g_m e_g$ is the current driven into the primary winding by the transistor preceding the discriminator r_{D1} is the resonant impedance of the primary circuit; n_d is the diode conduction efficiency; Q_1 and Q_2 are the quality factors of the primary and secondary circuits, respectively; E_1 and E_2 are the primary and secondary voltages at the midfrequency f_m; and K is the coupling coefficient. The value of K is obtained from

$$K = \frac{M}{(L_1 L_2)^{1/2}}.$$

The Foster-Seeley discriminator has several disadvantages when considering converting it to IC form. First, the double-tuned transformer is a bulky component that has no integrated equivalent. Second, the diode load resistors are limited in size to 10 to 20 kΩ, thereby causing a compromise in the discriminator design, especially for narrow-band cases. Third, the diodes that are fabricated by monolithic pn function-isolation techniques can severely reduce the sensitivity of the discrimination by virtue of their low reverse-breakdown characteristic and their parasitic elements. There are a number of variations of the Foster-Seeley discriminator, and several types of double-tuned-circuit slope-detector discriminators which, as far as integrated components are concerned, have similar characteristics.

9.3 RATIO DETECTOR

The ratio-detector circuit has several distinct features not found in the Foster-Seeley discriminator[4]. First, and most important, is the use of a stabilizing capacitor or battery across the diode loads for the suppression of amplitude-modulation components in the output. This stabilizing component can be eliminated if the receiver system contains a limiter stage just ahead of the detector, which will normally be the case in IC designs. This approach is imperative from a miniaturization viewpoint.

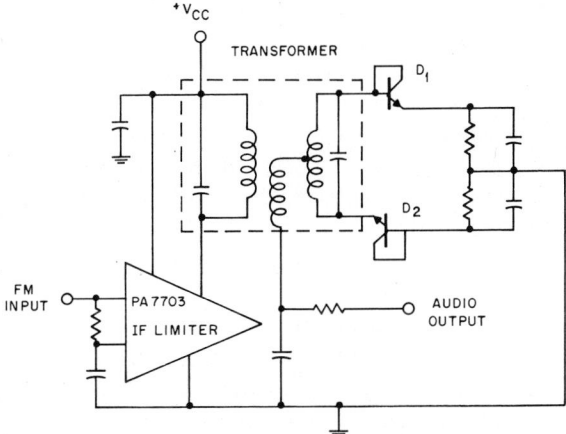

Figure 9.3.   Ratio detector.

A second modification, as can be seen by comparing Figure 9.3 with Figure 9.2, is that the diodes are reversed and the recovered audio is taken from a tertiary winding that is tightly coupled to the primary of the transformer. Diode-load-resistor values are generally selected to be much lower (about 5 to 10 kΩ) than those for the Foster-Seeley discriminator circuit. These values are easier to fabricate in monolithic integrated circuits.

The sensitivity of the ratio detector is one-half that given by the equation for the Foster-Seeley discriminator. In general, however, the design values for Qs, primary-secondary coupling, loads, and soon, will differ greatly because of the different operating conditions.

In the ratio detector, as in the discriminator circuit, special attention must be given to the monolithic design. The problems from parasitics associated with the diodes, discussed earlier, are also of concern in the ratio-detector circuit. In Figure 9.3 the anode of diode D_1 (collector-base node) must be biased at a voltage sufficiently positive with respect to the monolithic substrate to prevent the isolation diode from conducting. From a practical point this means that either a relatively large negative voltage is placed on the substrate or that the reference point for the secondary circuit is a virtual ground rather than actual ground.

A second problem associated with the reversed-diode connection is that of capacitive unbalance. The isolation-diode capacitance, in the range of several picofarads, exists between collector and ground, whereas the stray capacitance between emitter (cathode) and ground is at least an order of magnitude smaller. For diode D_1 of Figure 9.3 the parasitic capacitance is manifested from one side of the secondary winding to ground whereas for diode D_2 it is in parallel with the load filter capacitor. In monolithic circuit form this situation is easily corrected by connecting an. additional collector-isolation junction capacitor to the cathodes of both D_1 and D_2, as shown in Figure 9.4.

The substrate bias problem previously mentioned can be solved by rearranging the diodes and loads as shown in Figure 9.5. In this case the recovered output voltage is referenced to ground, thereby providing an automatic-frequency-control source. In addition, base-collector junction diodes with reverse-breakdown voltages of 30 V or more can be used, thus leading to larger secondary voltage and high sensitivity. The grounded cathode (collector diffusion) of diode D_1 has no parasitic element. The parasitic diode associated with diode D_2 is in parallel and has the same polarity as D_2, thereby contributing to the perveance. To balance this the area of diode D_1 can be increased slightly.

The performance of the ratio detector is very good, and in applications that can tolerate the transformer the circuit should be considered.

9.4 COUNTER DETECTOR

The counter-type detector demodulates an FM wave by counting the zero (or other fixed level) crossings of the wave. The demodulation is accomplished by generating a fixed-area pulse for each zero crossing and integrating the energy content of the pulses. The detection method is illustrated by the exaggerated FM wave of Figure 9.6, which shows the generated pulses corresponding to the positive-going zero crossings. The resulting pulses are integrated by an *RC* filter whose output is the recovered information. The sensitivity of the system[5] is determined as follows:

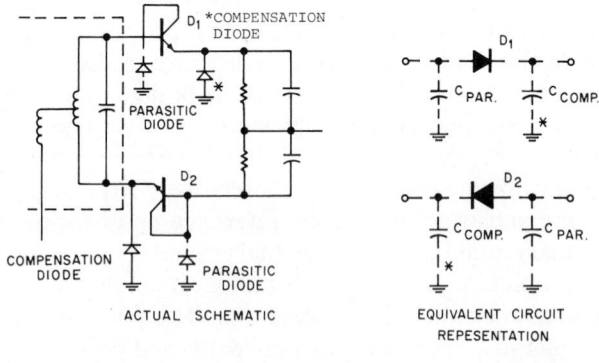

Figure 9.4. Ratio detector with diodes to compensate parasitic capacitance.

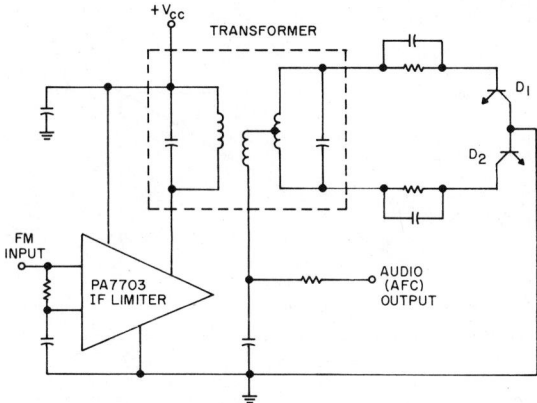

Figure 9.5. Modified ratio detector with AFC reference.

First, consider that the pulse is "on" $Y\%$ of the period of the carrier frequency. If the frequency is increased to the point where the pulse is always on, the output of the integrator is AV_{in}, where A is a constant of the integrator; V_{in} is defined in Figure 9.6. At the carrier frequency the output is YAV_{in}. As the frequency of the input decreases to zero, the output of the integrator also goes to zero. Therefore the discriminator sensitivity (%) is

$$S = \frac{YAV_{in}}{100 f_m},\tag{9.2}$$

where f_m is the carrier center frequency. The discriminator curve is shown in Figure 9.7.

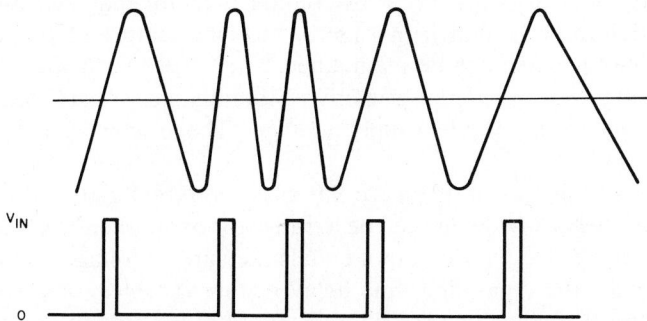

Figure 9.6. FM signal and resulting pulses for pulse-counter detector.

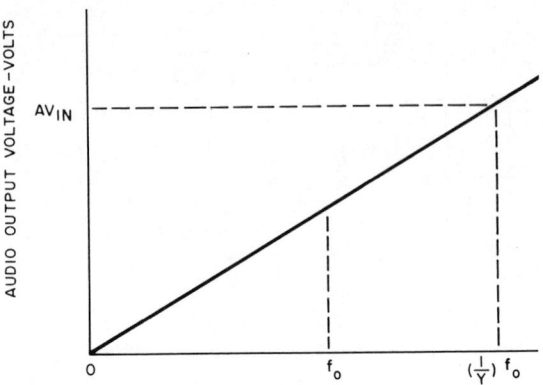

Figure 9.7.   Counter detector frequency-to-dc characteristic.

Equation 9.2 points out that the sensitivity is related inversely to the carrier frequency, and directly to the generated pulse width. Obviously sensitivity is directly related to the integrator efficiency. Equation 9.2 also shows that a system with a predetermined output frequency should be operated with the widest possible pulse consistent with the period of the highest frequency expected. At 11.5 MHz the period is 87 ns. Since an actual generated pulse will not be perfectly rectangular, it is desirable to provide a safety factor in determining the largest pulse width that can be safely used. Why conversion to a lower frequency is desirable is immediately apparent.

As an example, let $A = 1$, $Y = 50\%$, $V_{in} = 5.75$, and $f_o = 11.5$ MHz. Then $S = 0.25$ mV/kHz. Converting to 455 kHz, and using the same conditions as above, the sensitivity is improved by a factor of 25, giving a sensitivity of 6.25 mV/kHz.

A considerable number of circuits can be used as counter detectors. Blocking oscillators, delay lines, multivibrators, charge-storage devices, and saturated inductors are a few. A counter detector that uses a monostable multivibrator is shown in Figure 9.8. One feature of this circuit is that its output pulse can be maintained "on" over the majority of the period, giving the maximum sensitivity obtainable at the operating frequency and the available supply voltage. The circuit is completely integrable.

A similar circuit shown in Figure 9.9 uses a NAND gate and a delay line[6]. The time-delay device can be a transistor or another NAND gate. In this circuit a pulse whose output equals the supply voltage and whose duration equals the delay line time delay occurs for every negative excursion of the FM signal, so the filtered output represents the recovered audio signal.

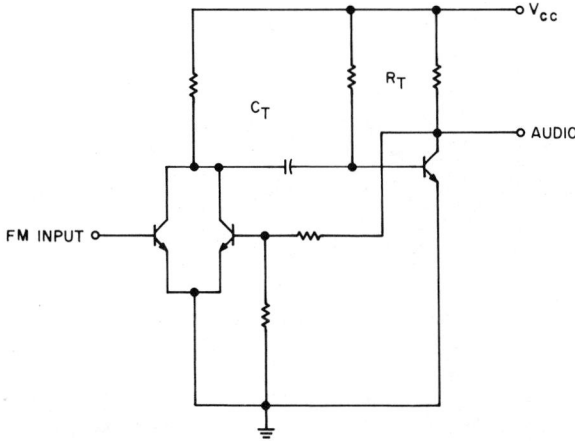

Figure 9.8.   Multivibrator counter detector.

A circuit that uses a charge-storage principle [7, 8] is shown in Figure 9.10. A type PA7703 monolithic amplifier is used as a limiter. When the limiter output stage is cut off, C charges through D_1 to V_{CC}, with the diode end of C being negative. During this time D_2 is reverse biased and does not conduct. During that part of the cycle when the collector potential of the limiter swings toward its lowest value, capacitor C discharges through diode D_2 in series with its load R_0; thus one current pulse flows through the load R_0 of diode D_2 for each cycle of operation.

The total charge acquired by capacitor C during each cycle is $C(V_{CC} - V_D)$. The portion of this total charge that passes through diode Q_2 and R_0 once each cycle is equal to $C(V_{CC} - V_{C\min} - 2V_D)$, where $V_{C\min}$ is the most negative excursion of the limiter output. As long as V_{CC} and $V_{C\min}$ remain constant, and the time constants of the charge and discharge circuits are sufficiently small compared with the period of the input signal, the total quantity of current that flows through R_0 in each cycle is constant, and the average value of current through R_0 is dependent on the repetition rate of the input signal.

The sensitivity of the circuit in Figure 9.10 can be computed on the basis of a discharging capacitor having a current equal to a pulse of

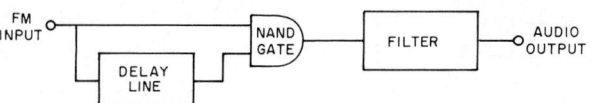

Figure 9.9.   NAND-gate counter detector.

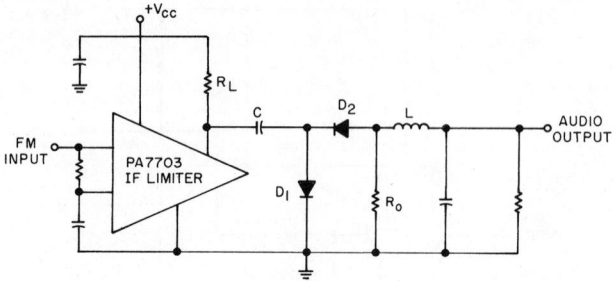

Figure 9.10.   Charge-transfer pulse-counting detector.

peak value V and a pulse duration equal to one time constant. If five time constants are allowed for the complete discharge of the capacitor and an equal amount of time for charging the capacitor, then Y in (9.2) is 10% and the sensitivity is

$$S = \frac{AV_{\text{in}}}{10f_m}, \tag{9.3}$$

where

$$V_{\text{in}} = (V_{CC} - V_{C\,\text{min}} - 2V_{BE})\left(\frac{R_o}{R_L + R_o}\right).$$

Equation 9.3 shows that the sensitivity of the charge-transfer counter detector is less than that of the previously mentioned monostable multivibrator circuit.

The counter-detector circuit has several problem areas. First, its sensitivity is a function of V_{CC} and V_D. Therefore the power supply must be well regulated.

Variations with temperature of the components, especially of the diodes, can significantly affect the circuit operation. To minimize such effects the capacitor should be charged to much greater than 0.7 V. Internal voltage regulators can be used to minimize the effects of power-supply variations. In addition, the value of capacitor C (in conjunction with other inherent circuit capacitances) is determined by the maximum permissible number of time constants in the charge and discharge circuits. A practical viewpoint is that the voltage across the capacitor should rise to greater than 99% of V_{CC} during one-half of the cycle and fall to within 99% of the minimum value during the next half cycle. This is a severe limitation on the frequency sensitivity of this circuit. Also, the af filter must be designed so that it does not bias D_2. This is the

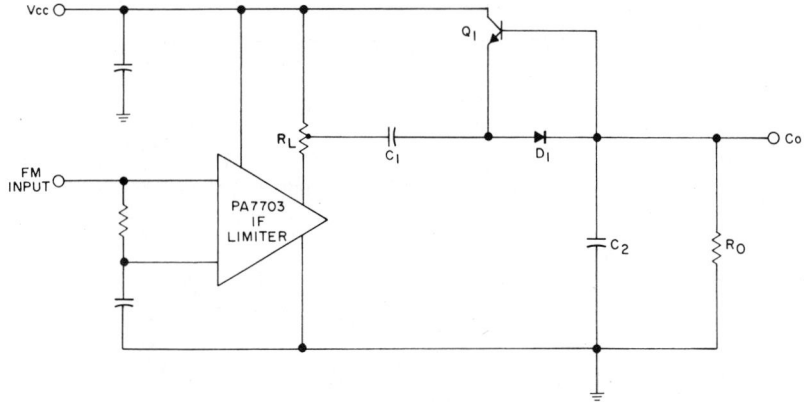

Figure 9.11.   Charge-transfer pulse-counting detector with simplified filtering.

reason for the inductor in Figure 9.10. A circuit that does not require an inductor is given in Figure 9.11.

In the circuit of Figure 9.11 transistor Q_1 has its base connected to the output and controls the amount of charge transferred by capacitor C_1, resulting in a linear detector characteristic. In addition to the previous considerations mentioned concerning the time constant of the charging path, the output filter capacitor C_2 must be much larger than C_1, and R_o must be much smaller than the reactance of C_1 at the carrier frequency. The tapped resistor at the limiter output slows the charging rate of Q_1 to prevent switching spikes.

The charge-storage detector derivation has assumed a square-wave output from the limiter. This allows the capacitor to charge fully and discharge fully. Some deviation from a square wave is tolerable since charge will alternately be stored and transferred, but a sine-wave input to the detector is intolerable, since the capacitor begins discharging the moment it is fully charged, and the frequency of the input wave then influences the amount of charge stored.

9.5 RC PHASE-SHIFT DISCRIMINATOR

The *RC* phase-shift discriminator is similar in operation to the conventional Foster-Seeley discriminator. Both circuits rely on a phase-shift network to sense the change in frequency of the FM signal: the Foster-Seeley circuit uses a double-tuned transformer for this sensing, whereas the *RC* phase-shift discriminator uses an *RC* network.

An *RC* phase-shift discriminator we have investigated is shown in Figure 9.12. This circuit can best be analyzed by considering it in three

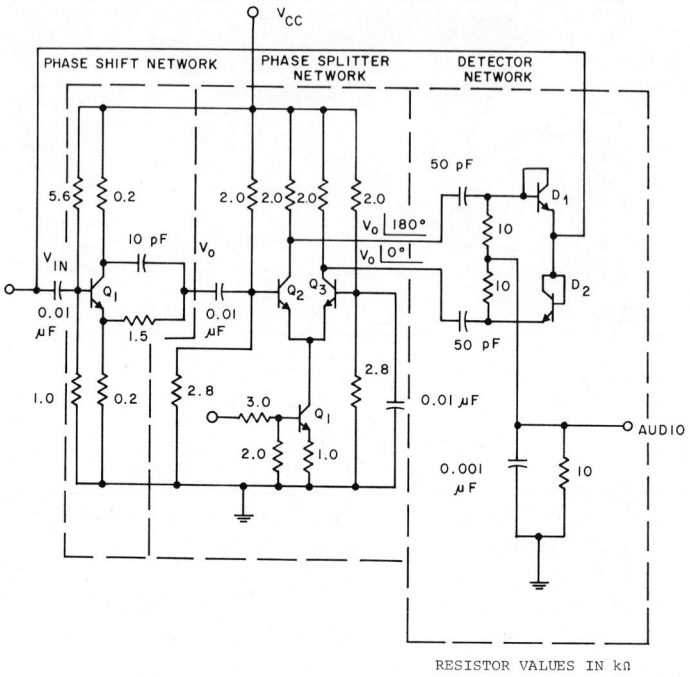

Figure 9.12. RC phase-shift discriminator.

functional parts: (a) a phase-shift network, (b) a phase-splitter network, and (c) a detector network. The output of the phase-shift network is the signal shifted in phase 90° at carrier center frequency, greater than 90° at a frequency higher than center frequency, and less than 90° at a frequency lower than center frequency. Inspection of the transfer function [9] given by

$$\frac{V_o}{V_1} = \exp\,(2j\arctan RC\omega),\tag{9.4}$$

shows that R and C must be chosen to satisfy the relation $\omega_0 = 1/RC$, where ω_0 is the carrier radian center frequency. Note that the amplitude of the transfer function is constant. The output of the phase-shift network is fed to a differential amplifier that functions as an amplifier and phase splitter, with its outputs always 180° out of phase and varying as the carrier frequency varies. The phase conditions at the output of the phase splitter are analogous to those present in a Foster-Seeley discriminator and are likewise compared to the input signal across the detector network.

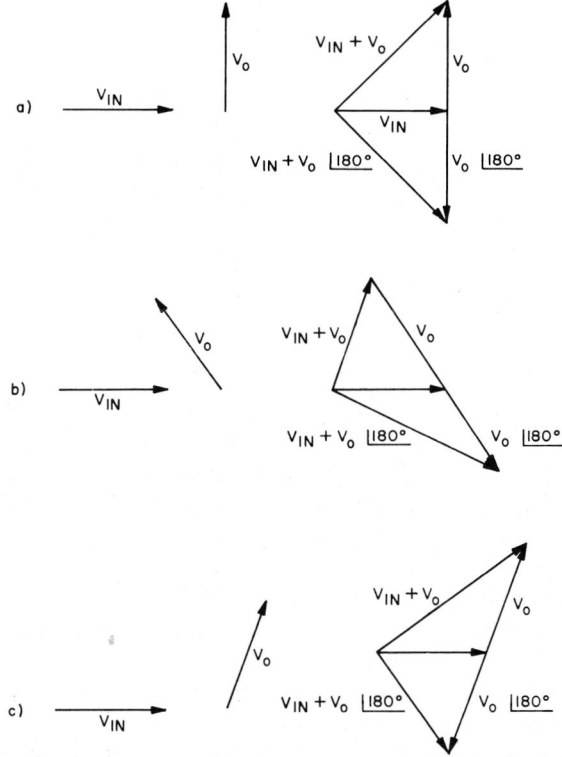

Figure 9.13. *RC* phase-shift discriminator phase relations.

The discriminator phase conditions are graphically illustrated in Figure 9.13.

Although the phase relationships in the *RC* phase-shift discriminator are similar to those in the Foster-Seeley discriminator, inspection of the transfer function shows that the resistor-capacitor phase-shift network has unity *Q* factor. Therefore low sensitivity and a large linear discriminator range would be expected. This was confirmed in a breadboard layout of the circuit of Figure 9.12, which has a sensitivity of 0.4 mV/kHz at 11.5 MHz. Because of the large peak-to-peak separation, the circuit alignment is not critical.

More elaborate phase-shift networks could be used to give higher sensitivity, but the added complexity would make the circuit more critical, probably to the point of requiring external components for tuning. Since attenuation is inherent in the phase shift of an *RC* network, an additional gain stage would be required either in the phase-shift network or in the phase splitter. This added complexity negates the advantages of the phase-shift discriminator, and the simpler circuit of Figure 9.12 appears to offer more promise in the wideband, high-deviation systems.

A different approach to *RC* FM discriminators has been given by Lemke[10], whose technique uses two distributed *RC* null networks with null frequencies situated on either side of the carrier input. The outputs from the distributed *RC* networks are then rectified and subtracted. Amplifiers are used to boost the output of the *RC* network prior to rectification. Lemke's work was done with thin-film techniques, but the principle can be extended to monolithic form. The most obvious problem is that of adjusting the center-frequency point of the discriminator curves.

9.6 QUADRATURE DETECTOR

The quadrature detector uses a phase-detecting principle to recover information from an FM signal. The incoming FM signal is applied directly to one port of a phase detector and then through a phase-sensitive network to the second port. Several types of quadrature-detector circuits have been developed[11–14], the simplest requiring but a single transistor stage. A simple circuit that illustrates quadrature-detector operation is shown in Figure 9.14. The circuit was described by Sziklai[11].

The circuit makes use of the condition that the transistor emitter-to-collector path is essentially an open circuit when the base is negative relative to the emitter, and a short circuit when the base is positive relative to the emitter. The transformer secondary is tuned to the carrier frequency. At center frequency the secondary voltage is 90° out of phase with the primary. As the signal frequency is changed, the secondary voltage lags the primary voltage by an angle smaller than 90° if the signal frequency is increased and lags by an angle greater than 90° if the frequency is decreased. Therefore the amount of time that the base is positive with respect to the emitter is directly related to the incoming signal frequency, and the voltage developed across the load varies accordingly. This detec-

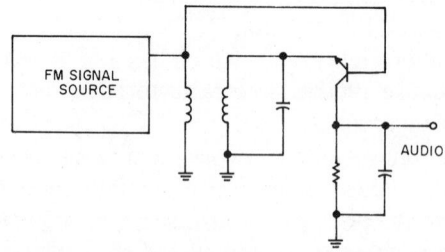

Figure 9.14.   Single-transistor quadrature detector.

tor has the advantage of simplicity. However, it has poor sensitivity and does not operate well at higher frequencies because the emitter-base junction is heavily saturated during the "on" period, causing signal distortion. For this reason the circuit is not often used. These operational deficiencies can be largely eliminated by extending the principle of operation to emitter-coupled circuits.

Before discussing quadrature detectors that use emitter-coupled transistors, we shall review the operation of a simple emitter-coupled amplifier.

In Figure 9.15, for balanced conditions, with $R_1 = R_2$, and Q_1 and Q_2 matched, the currents through the two transistors are equal under no-signal conditions. If a positive voltage of sufficient magnitude is introduced at the base of Q_1, it turns "on" and a current of amount I flows through Q_1, whereas Q_2 is turned "off." A negative voltage of the same magnitude at the base of Q_1 has the opposite effect, causing a current of magnitude I to flow through Q_2 and R_L. The resulting output voltage is also shown in Figure 9.15. The desirable feature is that the state is current limited and therefore is not driven into heavy saturation with large-amplitude signals.

The operating characteristics of the emitter-coupled pair are used to make a slightly different quadrature detector, as shown in Figure 9.16. Again, a transformer could have been used to obtain the 90° phase shift; however, a different scheme is used to achieve this function in micro-miniature form. In this circuit C_1 is made large and couples the input signal into Q_1 without phase shift. The value of C_2 is selected so that its reactance is large compared with the tuned-circuit impedance of C_3L at resonance. With this choice of values the signal frequency is shifted 90° by C_2 at resonance. There is no phase shift produced by the tuned circuit at resonance. As the FM signal deviates from the resonant frequency, the phase shift across C_2 remains a constant 90°, whereas the phase varies across the tuned circuit. This phase variation, when properly applied to an emitter-coupled amplifier, results in quadrature-detector operation. This is graphically illustrated in Figure 9.16. Examination shows that for a phase shift of "B" with respect to "A", the pulse width of the output signal will be directly proportional to the time coincidence of the negative portions of the two input signals. The output-pulse width is therefore directly related to the variation of the input signal about the carrier frequency.

The circuit of Figure 9.16 is satisfactory and in discrete-component form would probably offer the best and most economical approach to a transistor quadrature detector. There is some interaction of the two inputs at the base of Q_1; however, this can be eliminated by using an additional

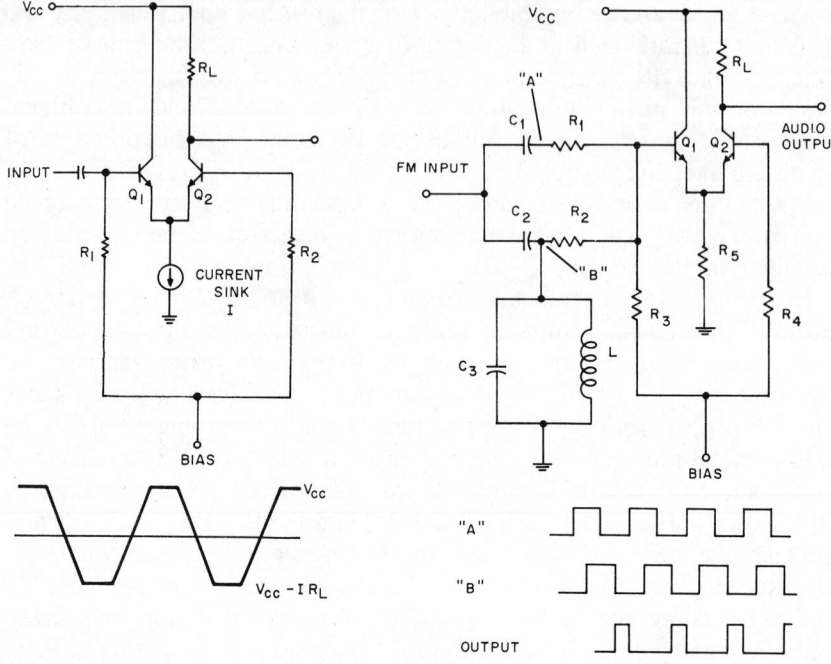

Figure 9.15. Emitter-coupled amplifier.

Figure 9.16. Emitter-coupled quadrature-detector circuit.

transistor in an emitter-coupled triplet configuration[15], as shown in Figure 9.17. The operation of this circuit is similar to the operation previously described except for the isolation of the inputs with a transistor. The isolation resistors R_1 and R_2 are made smaller in value for the circuit of Figure 9.17. Consequently there is better isolation with less signal attenuation, and the space required for the transistor on the IC chip is offset by the decreased space required by the resistors R_1 and R_2.

The sensitivity of this type of circuit for a simple tuned-circuit phase-shift network is given by

$$S = \frac{R_L I_1(\phi/360)}{\tan \phi[(f_0)/2Q]} \ \text{V/Hz},\qquad(9.5)$$

where ϕ = phase shift across tuned circuit at a particular frequency, f_0 = carrier frequency, Q = phase-shift tuned circuit Q, loaded, R_L = collector load resistor, and I_1 = total available output current.

The Q of the phase-shift network is adjusted to provide a linear phase shift over the information bandwidth, with approximately 0.32% deviation

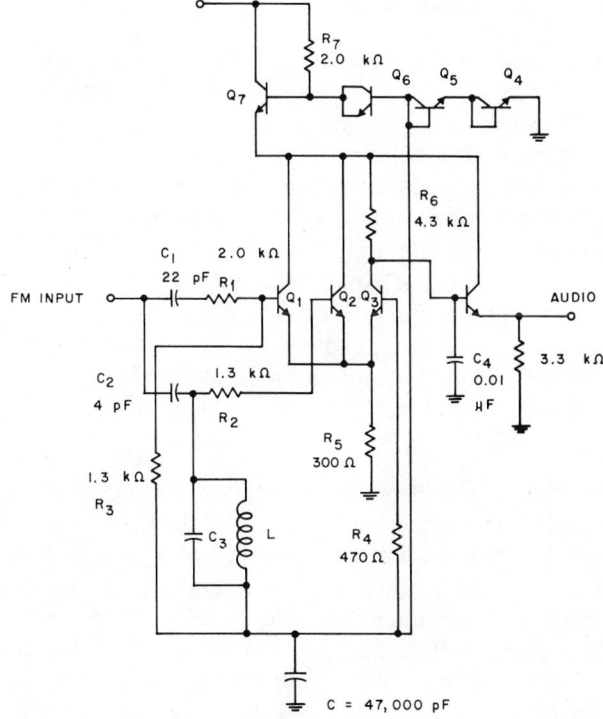

Figure 9.17. Emitter-coupled triplet quadrature detector.

from linearity occurring at 6% phase shift and 1% occurring at 10% phase shift.

With the exception of the tuned circuit C_3L, the quadrature detector can be integrated, and the integrated component values are not critical. The most important requirement for operation is that the resonant frequency of the tuned circuit not be influenced by the input-signal level or by ambient conditions. The most practical way of accomplishing this is to swamp the circuit capacitance with a large capacitor, which thereby requires a small-value inductor for resonance. For instance, if a 600-pF capacitor is used, the required inductor is approximately 0.4μH at 11.5 MHz. Compatible microminiature components with these values are available.

This type of circuit should find widespread use since all of the components are readily integrated except for the tuned circuit, which can be implemented with simple microminiature parts. In addition, the circuit has acceptable sensitivity and is easily tuned.

9.7 CRYSTAL DISCRIMINATOR

Crystal discriminators provide good performance and can be purchased to complement the crystal filter preselector of systems that use them. However the filters are voluminous and in some respects defeat the purpose of microminiaturization.

The crystal discriminator circuit of Figure 9.18 has been investigated [16]. The electrical characteristics of this circuit are excellent. The circuit requires three nonintegrable components – namely, an inductor, a variable capacitor, and a series-resonant crystal. By using ultraminiature components and thin-film techniques, this circuit has been assembled in a TO-5 package. The resistors, capacitors, and diodes are integrable and could readily be fabricated in monolithic form.

9.8 APPLICATIONS

Two examples can illustrate the application of the ratio detector and the quadrature detector. Figure 9.19 shows the diagram of the Philco-Ford CP1053, which contains a limiter, a ratio detector, and audio preamplifier. The chip measures 44 by 40 mils. The circuit was designed specifically for application in consumer television and FM receivers. Pertinent specifications are as follows: i-f gain, 76 dB at 4.5 MHz, 57 dB at 10.7 MHz; limiting threshold, $500\,\mu$V at 4.5 MHz, 1.6 mV at 10.7 MHz; recovered audio 120 mV rms at 25-kHz deviation, 360 mV rms at 75-kHz deviation; power dissipation, 80 mW.

For this application the ratio detector was selected because it provided an excellent automatic-frequency-control reference, which is necessary in high-quality FM receivers. The linearity, bandwidth, and sensitivity

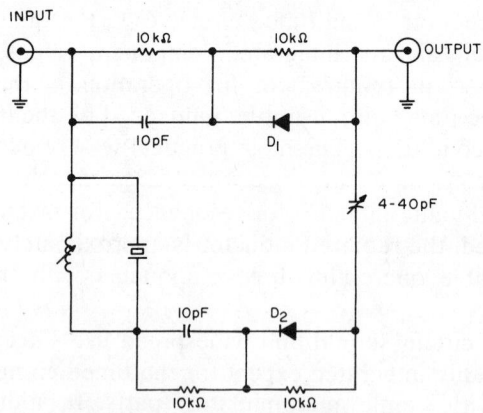

Figure 9.18.   Crystal-discriminator circuit.

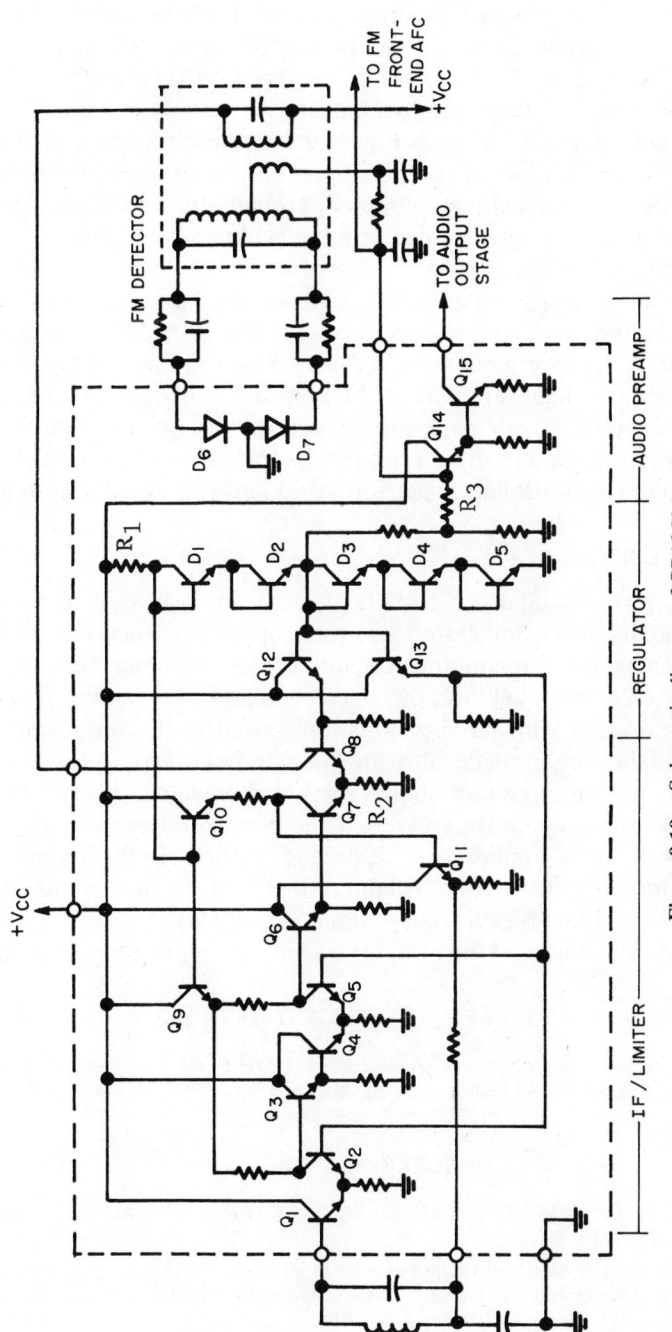

Figure 9.19. Schematic diagram of CP1053.

are comparable to those of existing systems, thereby making the conversion from current transistor practice to ICs rather straight forward. The physical size of the transformer required by this approach is not prohibitive in the consumer-product industry.

A second example is shown in Figure 9.20. This circuit was developed for a miliary application. It contains two emitter -coupled limiter stages that are internally capacitively coupled, a quadrature detector, and two balanced diodes that can alternatively be used in a ratio detector. Parasitic capacitance compensation, as shown in Figure 9.4, is included. The quadrature detector shown in Figure 9.17 was used in this case primarily because microminiaturization was a system objective. The counter and *RC* discriminators were not used because of their low sensitivity. Circuit specifications include: i-f gain at 11.5 MHz, 25 dB; recovered audio (8-kHz deviation), 80 mV peak to peak; power dissipation, 63 mW. The rather low limiter gain of this circuit results from the system partitioning, which resulted in 50-dB limiter gain on a previous circuit in the system.

9.9   CONCLUSIONS

Several FM demodulator circuits have been discussed in terms of their capability to be integrated and their operation when fabricated in *pn* junction isolated monolithic circuit form. The object has been to examine the circuit capability, the size considerations, and the economic factors associated with circuits commonly used in discrete-component designs and those that can be fabricated in monolithic form.

There is no one optimum choice for a demodulator, but satisfactory choices for many applications are available in 16 form. This was illustrated by the two applications described earlier. Both circuits have potential for high production volume. It should be further noted that systems having low i-f levels (approximately 1 MHz) can use the counter detector to advantage and thus employ a completely integrated circuit.

ACKNOWLEDGMENTS

Some of the work described was sponsored by USAECOM Contract No. DAABO 7-67-C-0406. Russell Gilson and Andrew Saldutti of USAECOM offered many valuable suggestions.

REFERENCES

[1] Freeland, E. C., "FM Receiver Design Problems," *Electronics*, **22**, No. 1, January 1949, pp. 104–110.

[2] Tellier, Joseph C., "Analysis of the Behavior of a Limiter-Discriminator FM Detector in the Presence of Impulse Noise," *Proceedings of IRE National Electronics Conference*, Vol. III, November 1947, pp. 680–696.

Note: Terminal numbers refer to leads of 14-lead metal-bottom flatpack.

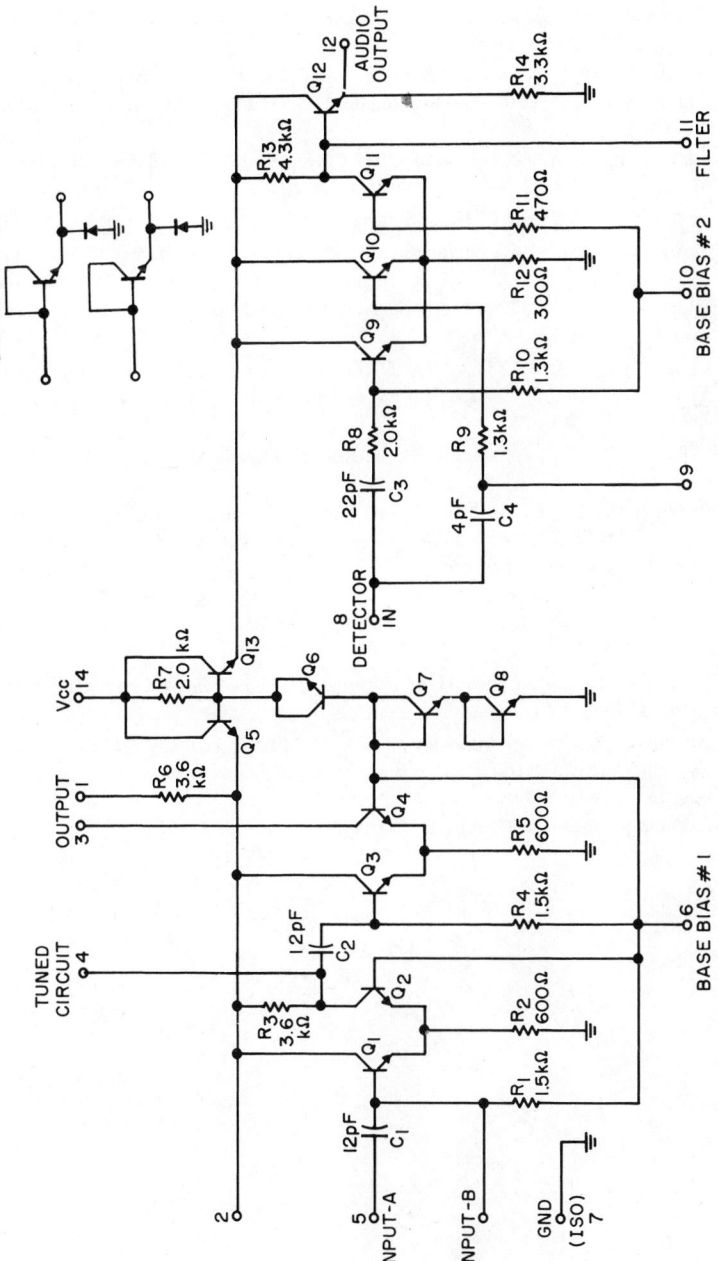

Figure 9.20. Schematic diagram of CP1058.

117

[3] Sturley, K. R., "The Phase Discriminator—Its Use as Frequency-Amplitude Converter for FM Reception," *Wireless Engineer*, February 1944, pp. 72–78.

[4] Seeley, William S., and Avins, Jack, "The Ratio Detector." *RCA Review*, **VIII**, June 1947, pp. 201–236.

[5] Allen, William F., *Linear Integrated Circuits*, Technical Report ECOM-0406-1, Contract No. DAAB07-67-0406? for the U.S. Army Command, Ft. Monmouth, N.J., November 1967, p. 8.

[6] Glasgal, Ralph A., "Solid State Ultra-Linear Wideband FM Demodulator," *Audio*, May 1964, pp. 25–32, 61.

[7] Seeley, S. W., Kimball, C. N., and Barco A., *RCA Review*, **6**, January 1942, p. 269.

[8] Scroggie, M. G., "Low Distortion FM Discriminator," *Wireless World*, April 1956, pp. 158–162.

[9] Delpech, J. F., "Audio Discriminator Measures Large Frequency Changes," *Electronics*, **39**, May 2, 1966, p. 76.

[10] Lemke, Peter B., "A Distributed RC Network Broadband FM Discriminator in Thin-Film Technique," *EEE Journal of Solid State Circuits*, **SC-2**, No. 3, September 1967.

[11] Sziklai, G. C., "Symmetrical Properties of Transistors and Their Applications," *Proceedings of IRE*, **41**, June 1953, pp. 723.

[12] Creamer, E. M., et al., "Low Cost, High Performance Transistor Television Receivers," *IEEE Transactions on Broadcast and Television Receivers*, **BTR-13**, No. 2, July 1967, pp. 108–115.

[13] Schiess, G., and Palmer, "Transistorized Sound Section for TV Receivers," *IRE Transactions on Broadcast and Television Receivers*, **BTR-4**, No. 3, June 1958, pp. 36, 37.

[14] Kiver, Milton S., *Transistors in Radio and Television*, McGraw Hill, New York, 1956, pp. 188–189.

[15] Bingham, D., "Novel Multi-Purpose LIC's Introduce New Concepts into Circuit Design," *IEEE Transactions on Broadcast and Television Receivers*, **BTR-13**, No. 2, July 1967, pp. 108–115.

[16] De Filipo, Vincent J., USAECOM, private communication.

10

FM-Detector-Limiter Integrated Circuits

by Peter H. Mack and Norman S. Palazzini

Sprague Electric Company, North Adams, Massachusetts

Integrated circuits can simplify designing the limiting and detecting functions in an FM system provided the designer accepts a few changes in philosophy. The basic considerations governing the use of an integrated approach to FM detector-limiter circuitry are covered in this chapter.

The IC to be used in the design examples is the ULN-2111A, a monolithic circuit designed primarily for application in television sound systems or FM radio receivers. The main feature of its design is a quadrature-detection scheme in which a simple single adjustment of the phase-shift network is all that is required to get satisfactory operation.

10.1 THE DETECTOR-LIMITER IC

The ULN-2111A uses a three-stage wideband limiter and a full-wave balanced coincidence detector. The circuit is shown in Figure 10.1. In discussing the circuit it is convenient to discuss the limiter, the phase-shift network and its buffering, and the FM coincidence detector.

The limiter is comprised of three identical differential-amplifier stages (1, 2, and 3 in Figure 10.1), which are direct coupled through emitter followers. The direct coupling of the three-stage limiter is possible by using an internal stabilized voltage reference (a five-diode series string), dc-level shifting between stages and overall dc negative feedback. The external capacitors C_2 and C_3 eliminate the strong negative feedback in

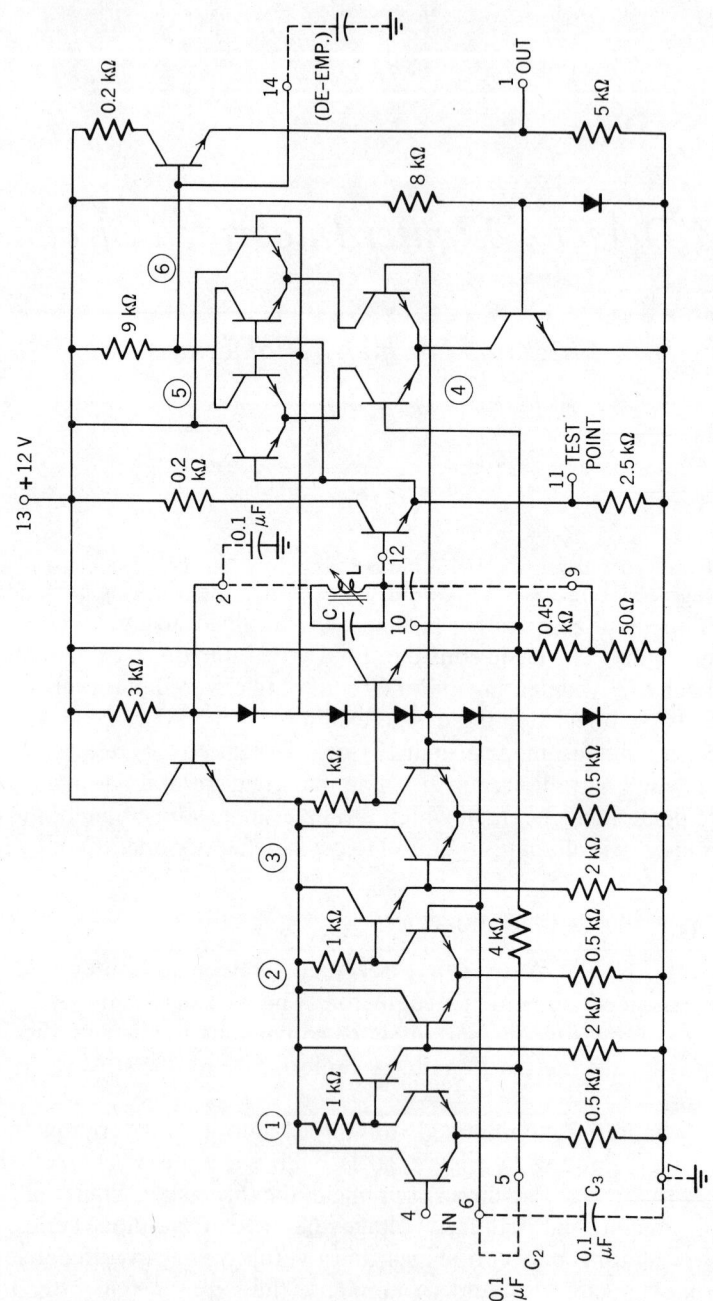

Figure 10.1. Circuit diagram for ULN-2111A IC FM detector and limiter.

the frequency band of interest (4.5 to 10 MHz) and provide dc stabilization. For flexibility in driving the different phase-shift networks two limiter outputs are made available. The full square-wave voltage output of 1.4 V peak to peak is applied directly to gate 4 of the coincidence detector. The other output provides a − 20-dB replica of the signal.

In the configuration shown in Figure 10.1 the signal from the amplifier is picked off at pin 9 and applied through a small capacitance, to a parallel-tuned circuit.

The bias reference voltage for balancing the upper detector pairs is obtained by tying one side of the tuned quadrature network to pin 2. The signal is applied to the detector at pin 12 and reaches a maximum at resonance of the tuned circuit.

In operation the tuned circuit serves to apply a varying phase-shifted signal of $\pm 90°$ as the FM carrier deviates around the designated center frequency. The detector is double balanced at lower and upper detector pairs, thus ensuring repeatability of the dc S-curve center voltage value.

The detector is also designed to operate as a full-wave detector, thus providing higher conversion efficiency.

The complete monolithic circuit is contained on a 60 by 60 mil silicon chip. The circuit consists of 19 transistors, 6 diodes, and 18 resistors. Of the 19 transistors used, 11 operate with a maximum collector-emitter supply of 2.8 V; the remaining transistors operate in the common-collector mode and therefore do not require an isolated region.

10.2   APPLICATION IN FM AND TELEVISION CIRCUITRY

The basic design philosophy behind the ULN-2111A is that the function of balance should be placed in the active rather than the passive portion of the system. The major difference between this philosophy and previous design approaches is that balance need not be adjustable, and consequently restrictions associated with the design and adjustment of balanced-coil detectors (such as the ratio detector) are greatly relieved.

In any system using a balanced discriminator the major figures of merit include audio recovery, AMR, dynamic range, and THD. Of these characteristics, only audio recovery must be adjusted to the circuit externally.

Audio recovery is affected primarily by the resonant simple *LC* network and the injection value at the detector input. To obtain a proper value for audio recovery specific characteristics of the S curve must be selected. Primarily this selection reduces to a choice of slope of the S curve giving a specified value for $\Delta V/\Delta f$, which is the basic expression of audio recovery. Two values must be chosen: (a) the peak-to-peak separation desired and (b) the peak-to-peak voltage required at the nodes of the S-curve.

The peak-to-peak separation is usually defined by the service for which the system is intended. For FM this value is 550 kHz, and for television it is 150 kHz. Once the choice is made, and the center frequency, as well as the peak-to-peak separation is known, an approximation of the circuit Q can be made, by using

$$Q = \frac{f}{f_0}, \qquad Q = \frac{f_0}{\Delta f}. \qquad (10.1)$$

For television applications the value of the circuit Q is approximately

$$Q = \frac{4.5 \times 10^6}{150 \times 10^3} = 30.$$

Although the desired circuit Q is fairly low (indicating a high-L network), it is desirable to use a high-C network. The input to the detector will introduce some variable capacitance. This can be minimized through the use of at least 100 pF as the C part of the resonant circuit. The inductor chosen along with this capacitance value will yield a network with a Q somewhat higher than desired. This should be reduced through use of a parallel resistor across the network. Figure 10.2 shows complete quadrature networks for television and FM circuitry. Optimum component values are given in the figure.

The final component required is a small decoupling capacitor placed between the network and the low amplifier output. To ensure linear detector operation the reactance of this capacitor should be substantial as compared with the impedance of the tuned circuit at resonance.

The other factor governing the audio output is the injection value at the input to the detector. The optimum value is 60 mV rms at the resonant frequency of the network. Figure 10.3 shows a normalized plot of V_{inj} versus V_f, where V_f represents a normalized output for any simple LC network. Note that the output (V_f) has a linear relationship with V_{inj} up to approximately 50 mV. Above this value the function breaks into a curve, then flattens out, indicating that the detector is in a switching mode.

Figure 10.4*a* and *b* demonstrates the detector operation in the linear (low injection) mode and the switching (high injection) mode. Note that in the linear mode a greater portion of the S-curve is linear, thus producing lower distortion than in the switching mode. For best operation the low-injection mode is recommended, with V_{inj} set as high as possible. The optimum injection value is 60 mV rms.

To complete the circuit it is necessary to select a de-emphasis capacitor and several bypass capacitors. The de-emphasis capacitor should have a

Chart of Component Values for Operation at 4.5 MHz, (Television)
and 10.7 MHz (FM)

	Component Value	
	TV (4.5 MHz)	FM (10.7 MHz)
L_2 Inductance	7–14 μH	1.5–3 μH
L_2 Nominal unloaded Q	50	50
L_2 Nominal DC resistance	50 Ω	50 Ω
C_A	3.0 pF	4.7 pF
C_B	120 pF	120 pF
R_1	20 kΩ	3.1 kΩ
Loaded network Q	30	20
C_5 and C_6	0.1 μF	0.1 μF
C_2	0.1 μF	0.1 μF
C_{de}	0.01 μF	0.01 μF

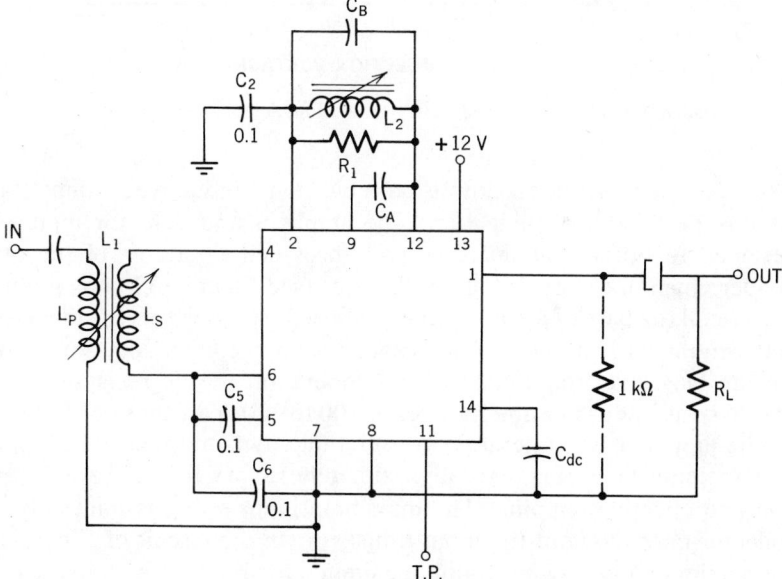

Figure 10.2.   Quadrature network for television and FM receivers.

time constant of 5 μs. Satisfactory results will be obtained with a value in
the range of 0.01 to 0.05 μF. The bypasses are not critical, and any value
from 0.05 to 0.01 μF will do. As with any bypass capacitor, the objective

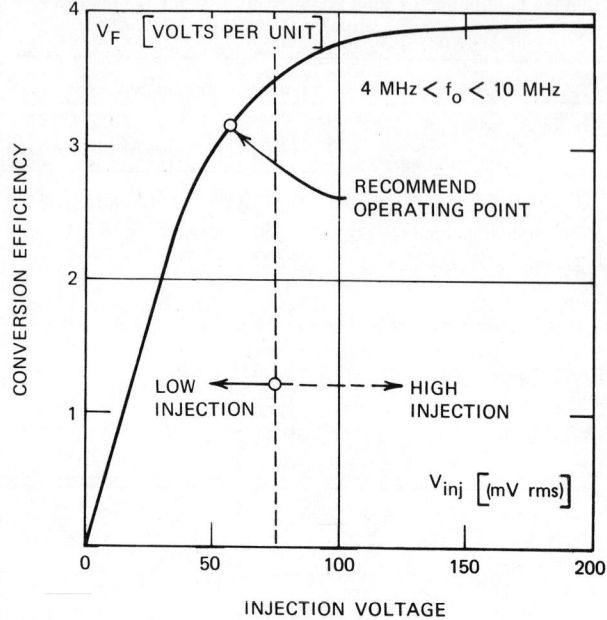

Figure 10.3.   Conversion efficiency V_F as a function of injection voltage V_{inj}.

is to keep the reactance as low as possible. A noninductive, ceramic capacitor is best in this application. The amplifier and detector inputs are designed to operate at dc bias levels provided by a part of the diode divider chain in the device. In both cases (see Figure 10.2) it is intended that a coil, or part of a transformer, be used as a low dc resistance path between the bias source and the respective input connection, thus providing the bias level required. For best operation the dc resistance value should be as low as possible. Values of 100 to 300 Ω are quite satisfactory.

The amplifier will tolerate a considerable dynamic range at the input. The minimum level of input is approximately 1.0 mV for good AMR rejection and effective clipping. The maximum input swing is limited by the collector-base diode of the input transistor. In the circuit of Figure 10.2 the maximum peak swing should be limited to about 1.5 V. The dynamic tolerable range will then be in excess of 60 dB, which is more than adequate for satisfactory performance.

The detector output loading is not critical. The source resistance is quite low (on the order of 200 Ω). To prevent clipping at the output when the ac load impedance is less than 2000 Ω, a 1000-Ω resistor should be added between the output and the ground.

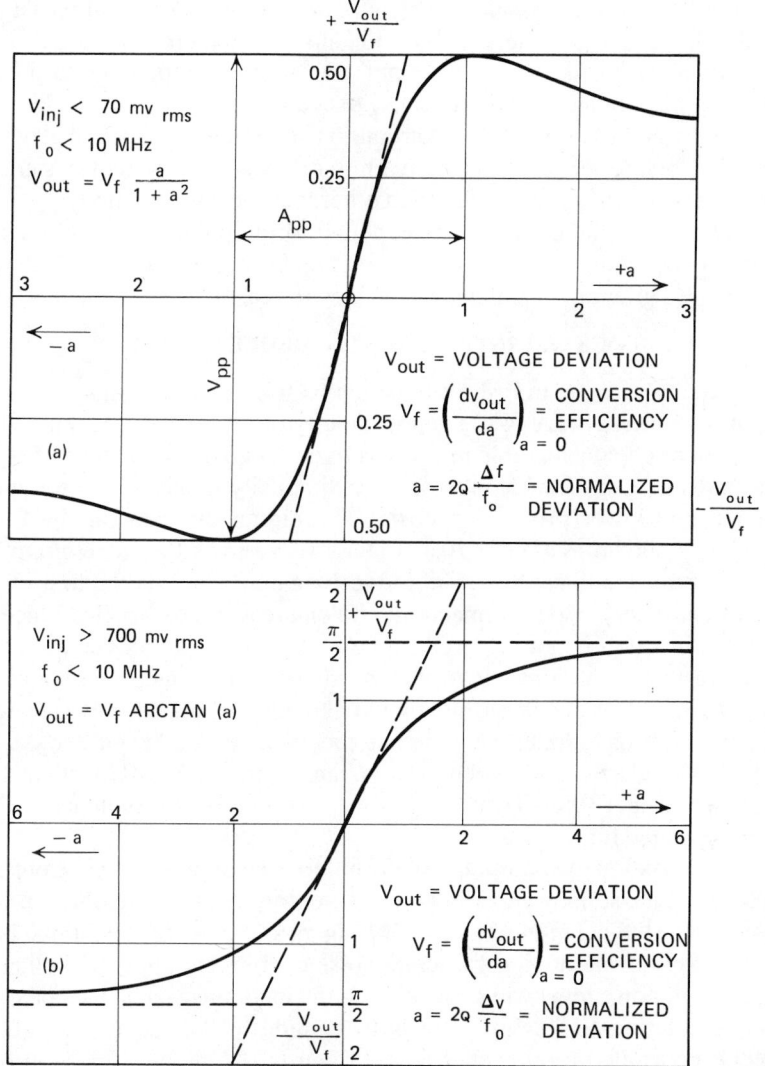

Figure 10.4. Transfer characteristics (FM) operation for (*a*) low injection voltage and (*b*) high injection voltage.

Tuning the device in a system is quite simple. Two alternatives are available: (a) tune the receiver to a strong station and then tune the quadrature coil to maximum audio output or (b) apply an FM generator to the amplifier input through a small decoupling capacitor, and tune as above.

The circuit layout should be carried out with reasonable care inasmuch as the device has an inherent high gain and wide-bandpass characteristics. It is important to separate the input and output components to prevent undesired coupling, which may cause oscillation.

The ULN-2111A is a simple circuit to use. Balance and symmetry are a function of the monolithic circuit, thus relieving the system designer of many restrictions normally found in other methods of detection.

Tuning adjustment has been simplified to the point that special equipment is not required in the field to give the desired results. Operation can be ensured after any maintenance cycle with reasonable confidence.

10.3   TWO-BLOCK FM INTERMEDIATE-FREQUENCY STRIP

An i-f strip for use in FM receiver applications can be designed by using a pair of ULN-2111A ICs. The availability of inespensive ceramic filters has generated considerable interest in fixed tuned nonadjustable i-f strips. The advantages of such i-f strips are simplicity, smaller space requirements, and lower production costs. The circuit diagram for the ULN-2111A is shown in Figure 10.1. Figure 10.5 shows the same circuit but with certain modifications to improve its gain for use as the first of two series gain blocks. The connections shown are wired externally. Since the detector section is not required in the first gain block, conversion of the detector to an additional stage of gain will increase available amplification by 10 dB. This is accomplished by unbalancing the detector by grounding pin 12 and broadbanding by reducing the collector load from 9 to 0.9 kΩ. The two blocks in series will produce a maximum of 130 dB of gain, which represents a net 100-dB gain after insertion losses of approximately 30 dB are subtracted for filtering.

Figure 10.6 shows output waveforms for signal input levels from 3 to 200 μV. The source generator is a Boonton 202H developing a low-distortion sine-wave-modulated FM signal of 75-KHz deviation. Note that at low levels of signal a white-noise component appears, indicating that a high noise level will appear when the incoming signal disappears. A simple solution to this problem is to include in the receiver a squelch switch controlled by detected noise. Figure 10.7 shows a diagram for a two-block i-f stage. The second block is hooked up as a standard quadrature detector. De-emphasis of 75 μs is supplied by a 0.001-μF capacitor at pin 14. Filtering at this point will be required even for stereo applications to prevent the strip from oscillating. For stereo, however, this capacitor may be reduced to 100 pF, which is sufficiently small to maintain satisfactory bandpass.

No provision has been made in the strip for automatic gain control. Because of the limiting action of the amplifier and the wide dynamic input

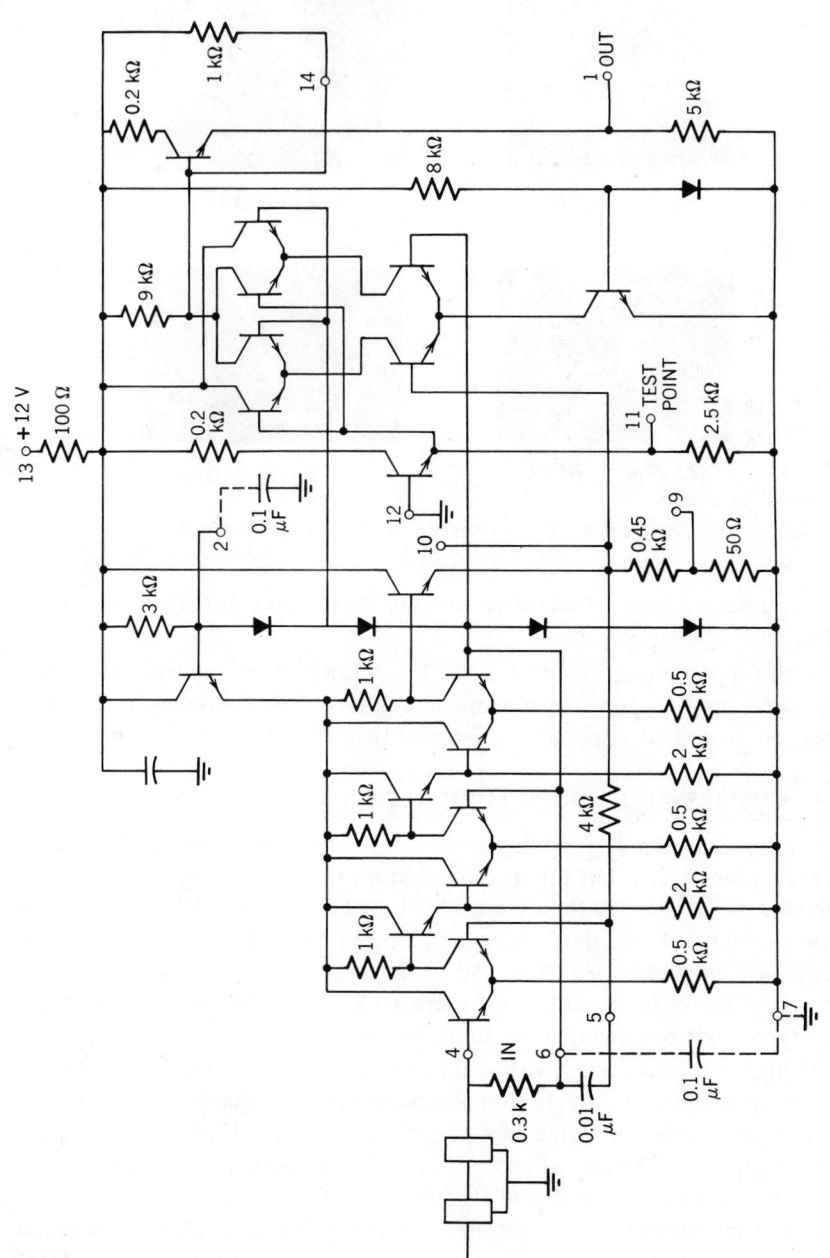

Figure 10.5. ULN2111A modified for use as wideband amplifier.

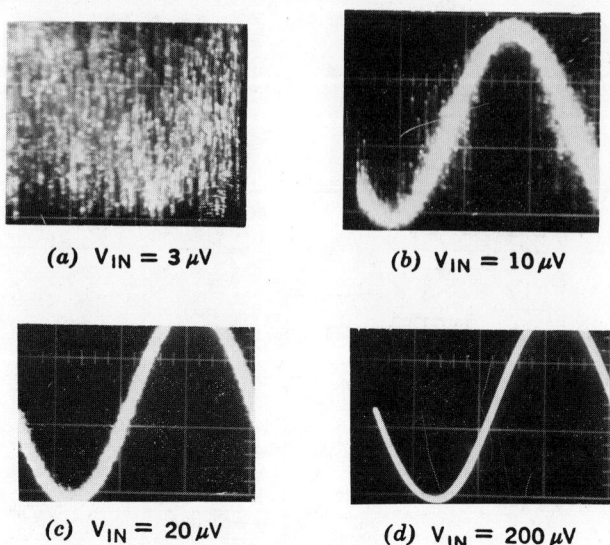

(a) V_{IN} = 3 μV   (b) V_{IN} = 10 μV

(a) $V_{IN} = 3\,\mu V$ *(b)* $V_{IN} = 10\,\mu V$

(c) $V_{IN} = 20\,\mu V$ *(d)* $V_{IN} = 200\,\mu V$

Figure 10.6.   Output waveforms for two-block i-f strip.

range of permissible signal range, no automatic gain control is required for FM-receiver service.

Other applications for the ULN-2111A range from suppressed-carrier and pulse modulation to wideband amplifiers. The following discussion treats each of these applications separately.

10.4 SUPPRESSED CARRIER MODULATION

Suppressed carrier modulation can be provided by using the ULN-2111A. The test circuit for this application is shown in Figure 10.8; the waveforms sampled at the output are shown in Figure 10.9. In the waveform in Figure 10.9a the carrier frequency is 50 kHz and the modulator frequency is 3 kHz. At this low frequency the feedback capacitor is changed to 6.8 μF, as shown in Figure 10.8. This value is necessary for a 55-dB gain to be realized in the amplifier section at low frequencies.

At higher frequencies, as shown in the waveform of Figure 10.9b, the carrier frequency is 5 MHz and the modulating frequency is 5 kHz. At these frequencies the value of C_{fb} can be 0.05 μF. A plot of frequency versus gain for different values of C_{fb} is shown in the wideband-amplifier illustrations (Figures 10.19 and 10.20).

In the circuit diagram in Figure 10.8 the modulating signal input is at pin 12. A phase-shift network is not a requirement. Instead a 50-Ω

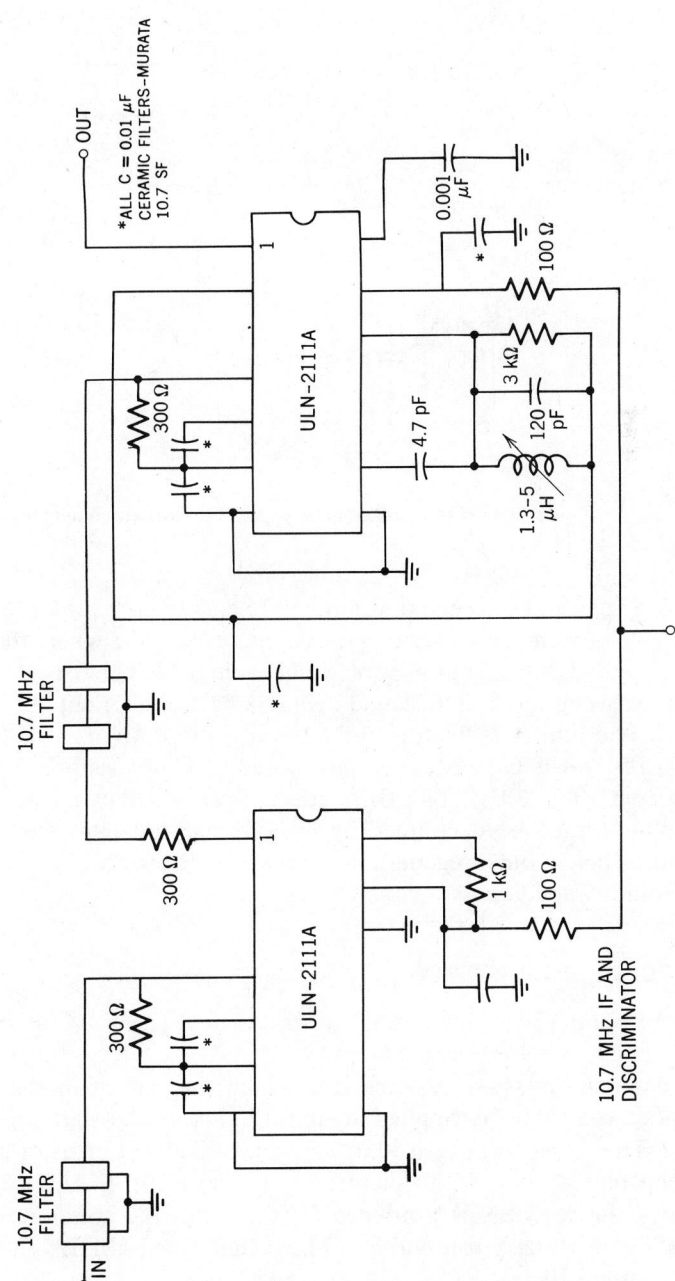

Figure 10.7. Diagram of two-block i-f strip.

129

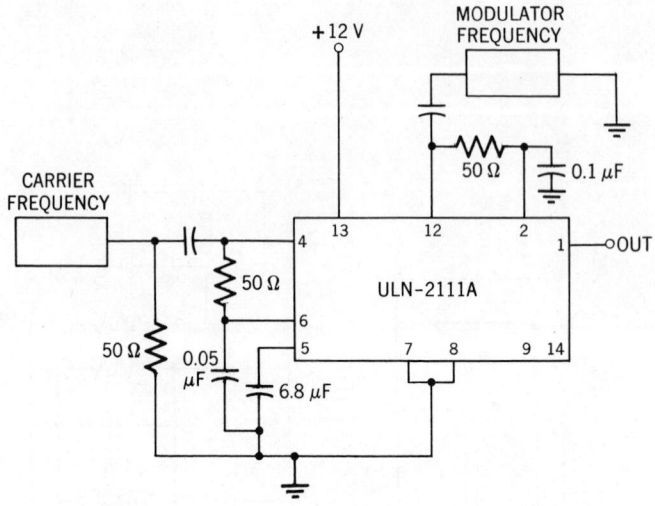

Figure 10.8.   Circuit diagram for suppressed carrier modulator.

resistor is placed between pins 2 and 12 to ensure proper bias to the input of the gate detector. By adjusting the dc bias of the gate where the modulation is applied, full carrier suppression is achieved. The 0.1-μF capacitor placed between pin 2 and ground decouples the limiter supply. Since the input to the limiter is floating and consequently requires a dc reference, a 50-Ω resistor is used between pins 4 and 6. This resistor can be of any value from 50 to 200 Ω. This dc reference is provided by the diode supply line, which must be decoupled by an external capacitor from pin 6 to ground. This avoids regeneration between bases through insufficient base-source impedance.

10.5 PULSE MODULATION

A pulse-modulation circuit is illustrated in Figure 10.10; the waveforms are given in Figure 10.11.

In data-transmission systems, for which the circuit in the figure is designed, the pulse is applied to pin 12. No phase-shift requirement exists. The value of C_{fb} is $0.05\,\mu$F, and a 3000-Ω resistor is placed between pin 14 and V_{CC} to increase the bandwidth. Figure 10.11a and b shows the waveforms produced by the following conditions: $f_1 = 20$ MHz, $f_2 = 1$ MHz, pulse width $= 20\,\mu$s; and $f_1 = 20$ MHz, $f_2 = 1$ MHz, pulse width $= 200\,\mu$s.

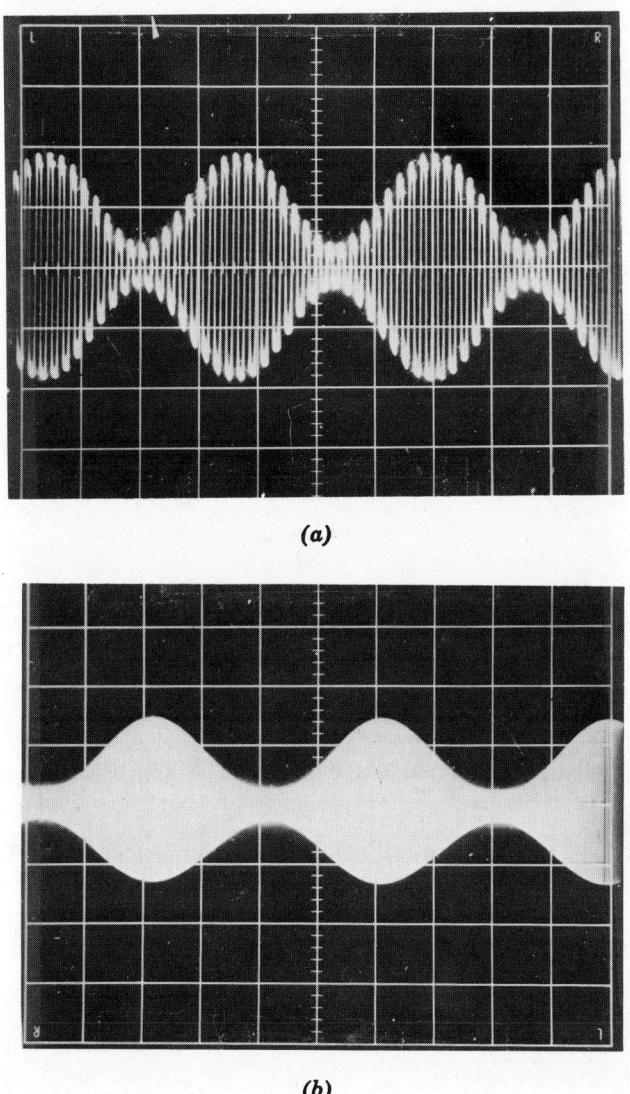

(a)

(b)

Figure 10.9. Suppressed-carrier-modulator waveforms for operation with $V_{CC} = +12$ V: (*a*) carrier frequency = 50 kHz, modulator frequency = 3 kHz; (*b*) carrier frequency = 5 MHz, modulator frequency = 5 kHz. Amplitude = 1 V/cm.

10.6 BALANCED-PRODUCT MIXER

Figures 10.12 and 10.13 show the circuit diagram and waveforms for a balanced-product mixer. Mixing between two signals at 10 and 11 MHz

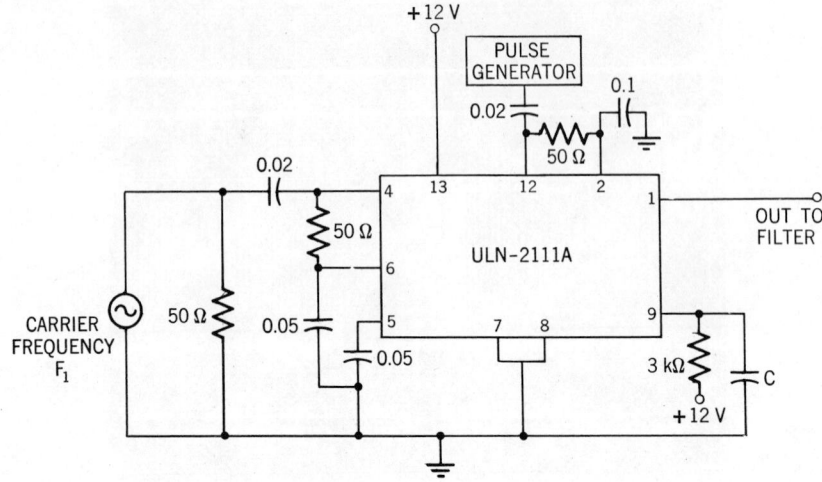

Figure 10.10. Pulse-modulator circuit diagram.

was tried with the results shown in Figures 10.13*a* and *b*. The actual video bandwidth after conversion is limited to 2.6 MHz and can be increased to 10 MHz simply by adding a 3000-Ω external resistor between pin 14 and V_{CC}.

10.7 SYNCHRONOUS AM DETECTION WITH CARRIER RECOVERY

Figure 10.14 shows the circuit diagram for the synchronous AM detector. When the carrier reference is available, the ULN-2111A can be operated directly as a synchronous detector. As such, it can recover the envelope of an AM signal either with or without the carrier, and with double or single sideband.

When the pilot carrier is absent, the envelope should be recovered by operating on the sidebands. One application is the color demodulator in color television sets. In the case of a double-sideband signal with carrier, the carrier has been recovered by simple symmetrical limiting. The modulated signal is applied to both inputs simultaneously. One channel limits the signal and provides the zero-crossing reference, while the other operates linearly and preserves the envelope.

The recovered envelope for a 90% amplitude-modulated signal of 100 mV rms at various frequencies is shown in Figure 10.15. The dips are caused by 90 and 270° phase shifts in the limiter. Photographs of the recovered envelope for different frequencies are shown in Figure

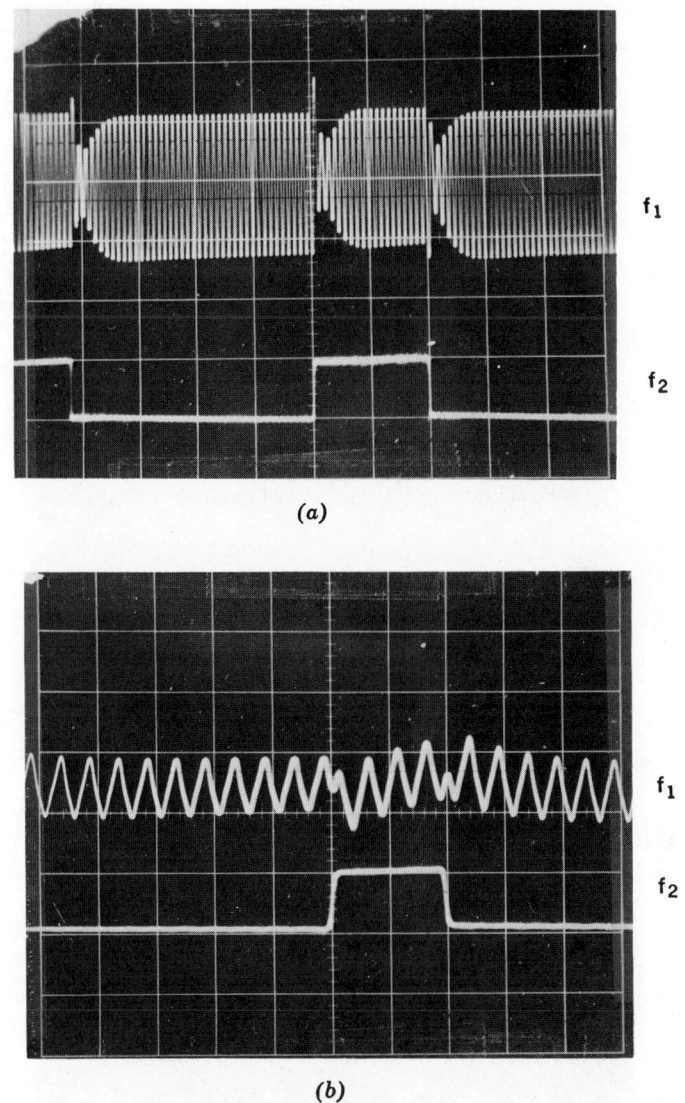

(a)

(b)

Figure 10.11.   Pulse-modulator waveforms: (a) $F_1 = 20\,\text{MHz}$ at $20\,\text{mV}$, $F_2 = 20\,\text{MHz}$ at $0.5\,\text{V}$, pulse width $= 2\,\text{ns}$; (b) $F_1 = 20\,\text{MHz}$ at $20\,\text{mV}$, $F_2 = 1\,\text{MHz}$ at $0.5\,\text{V}$, pulse width $= 200\,\text{ns}$.

10.16. This type of detector has many advantages over the envelope detector in current television receivers. For example, elimination of the

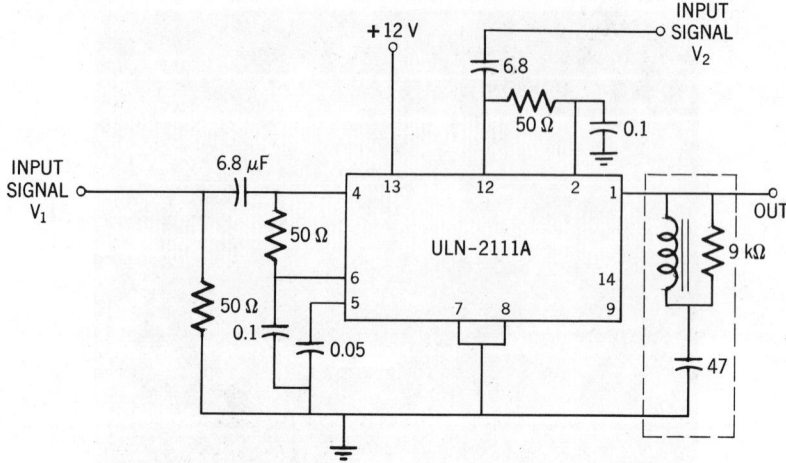

Figure 10.12.   Balanced-product-mixer circuit diagram.

distortion resulting from single-sideband transmission, elimination of sound buzz, chroma beats, and so on, are a few of the advantages of this detection system.

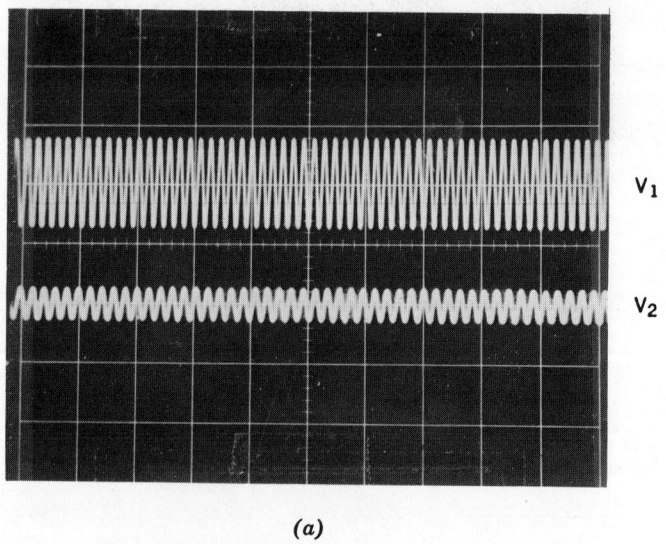

(a)

Figure 10.13.   Waveforms for balanced-product mixer: *(a)* $V_1 = 11$ MHz at 80 mV (upper waveform, $V_2 = 10$ MHz at 30 mV (lower waveform).

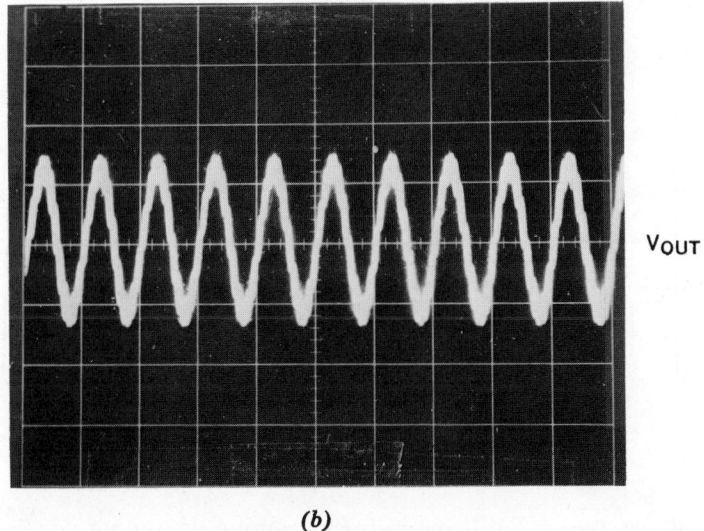

V_{OUT}

(b)

Figure 10.13 (Cont'd).   Waveforms for balanced-product mixer: (b) V_{ont} = 1 MHz. Amplitude = 1.5 V/cm.

10.8 PHASE COMPARATOR

The coincidence-gated detector is actually a phase comparator. It can be used for a variety of servo-loops with automatic phase controlling, for example, in chroma and horizontal synchronization processing. Figure

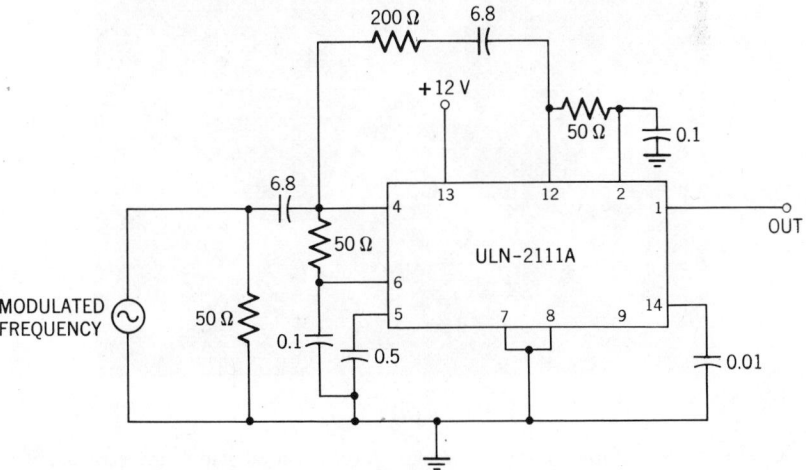

Figure 10.14.   Circuit diagram for synchronous AM detection with carrier recovery.

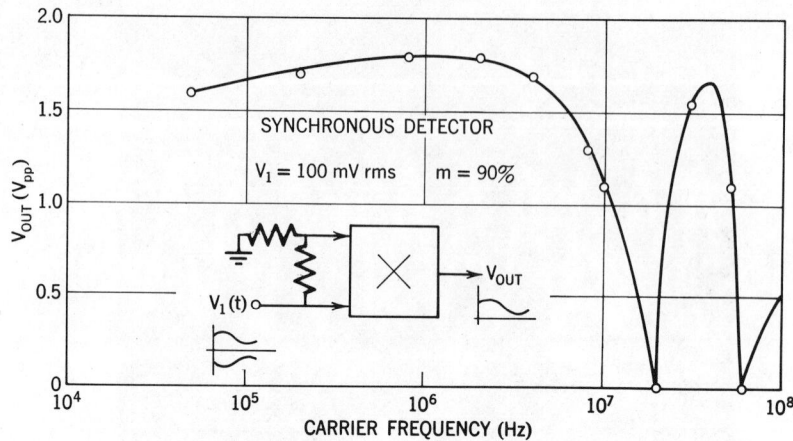

Figure 10.15.   Output voltage versus carrier frequency.

10.17 shows the circuit diagram for measuring the output voltage when E_{in_2} is phase shifted from E_{in_1}. A plot of the output voltage versus phase shift is given in Figure 10.18. The frequency employed is 4.5 MHz. The voltage input to E_{in_2} must be at least 0.2 V rms to ensure proper operation of the detector network.

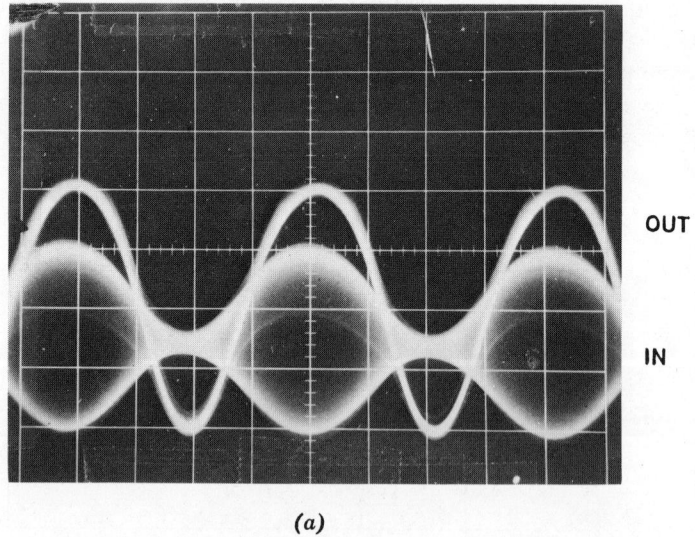

(a)

Figure 10.16.   Waveforms for synchronous AM detection with carrier recovery: *(a)* modulating frequency = 400 Hz, carrier frequency = 1 MHz, input amplitude = 600 mV$_{p\text{-}p}$, output amplitude = 2 V$_{p\text{-}p}$.

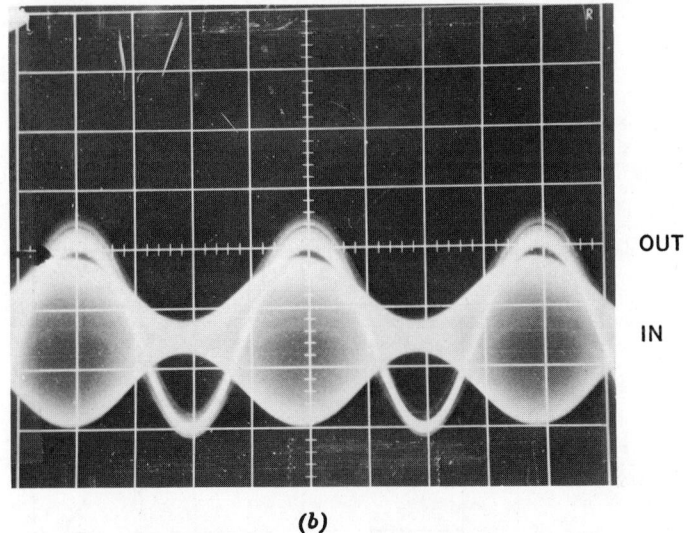

(b)

Figure 10.16 (Cont'd). Waveforms for synchronous AM detection with carrier recovery: modulating frequency = 400 Hz, carrier frequency = 4.5 MHz, same amplitudes as in (*a*).

10.9 WIDEBAND AMPLIFIER

The three-stage limiter can be used as a wideband amplifier. Figure 10.19 shows the effects of C_{fb} on gain and frequency. The circuit diagram

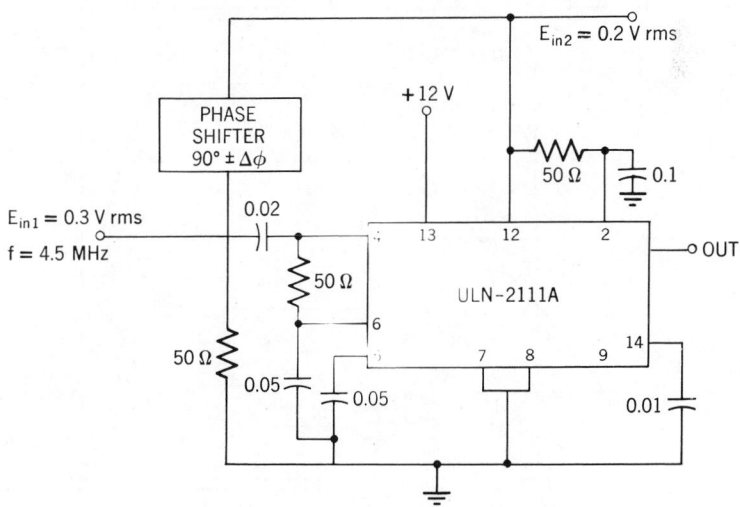

Figure 10.17. Phase-comparator circuit diagram.

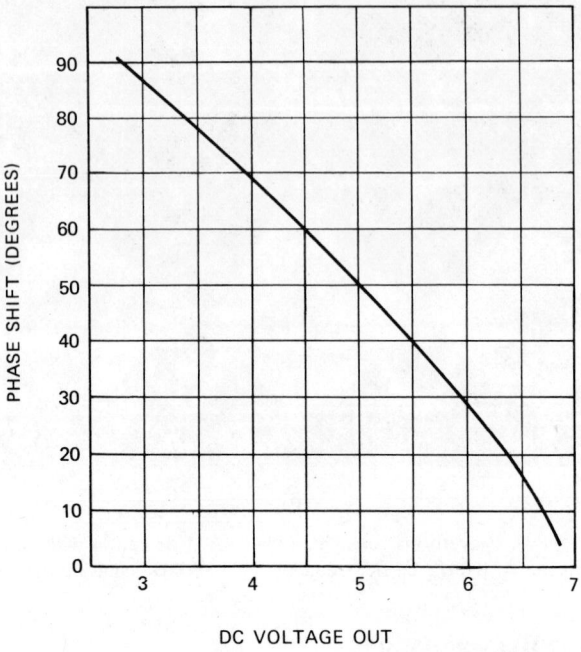

Figure 10.18. Phase shift versus output voltage for phase-comparator circuit.

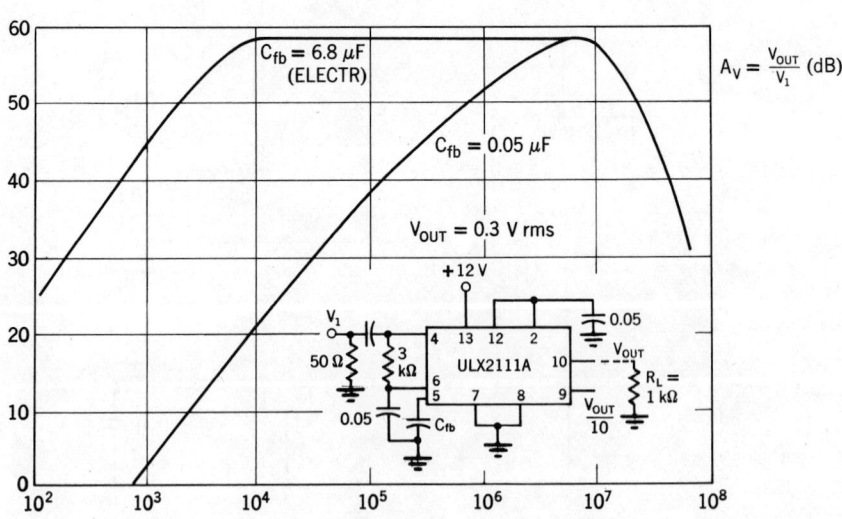

Figure 10.19. Wideband-amplifier circuit and frequency response.

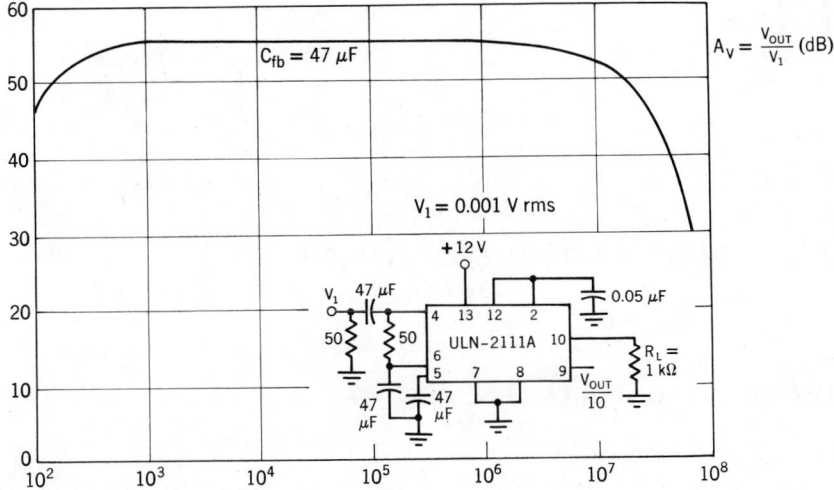

Figure 10.20. Wideband-amplifier operated with $C_{fb} = 47\ \mu\mathrm{F}$.

and curves for $C_{fb} = 0.05$ and $6.8\ \mu\mathrm{F}$ are also shown. The normal output voltage at pin 10 would be 0.3 V rms. Figure 10.20 illustrates the effects of increasing C_{fb} to $47\ \mu\mathrm{F}$. In both cases good symmetrical limiting will result.

11

The Dual Operational Amplifier

by David Long and David Campbell

Fairchild Semiconductor, Mountain View, California

The use of an IC with two identical operational amplifiers on a single chip is covered in this chapter. The IC employed to demonstrate the advantages of this design approach is the μA739, a device intended for use in low-noise industrial signal-processing equipment and in preamplifiers of consumer home-entertainment equipment.

In designing low-level amplifiers there are two major requirements: (a) the equivalent input noise of the circuit must be as low as possible and (b) the output dynamic range should be large enough to handle the variations in input-signal level encountered in a broad range of applications. If the circuit adequately meets these two conditions, the IC user can move along to look at dc circuit performance, low-frequency characteristics, power consumption, noise, short-circuit protection, amplifier isolation, and required compensation techniques.

11.1 DC CIRCUIT PERFORMANCE

Usually a dual-operational-amplifier IC consists of two identical operational amplifiers on a single chip and sharing a common bias supply. Each amplifier is a mirror image of the other. First we consider the bias circuit and one amplifier.

The amplifier shown in Figure 11.1 is the μA739. It consists of three

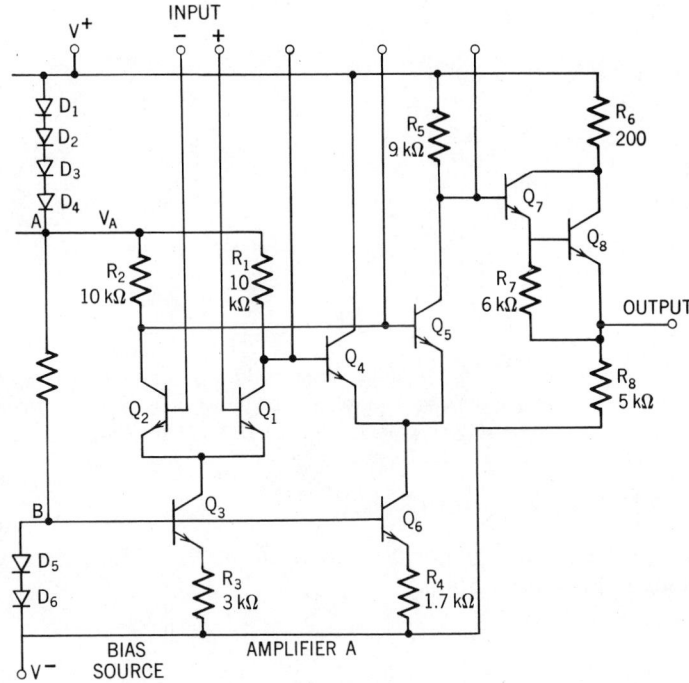

Figure 11.1a.   Amplifier *A*. One of the pair of amplifiers in the dual operational amplifier
μA739. Bias source is included with amplifier circuit.

gain stages: a differential input stage; a differential-in, single-ended-out
second stage; and a class A composite *pnp/npn* output stage.

With a 30-V supply, the output stage will saturate when the collector
of Q_5 drops 1.8 V below V^+. This requires that $200\,\mu$A flow through
R_5. A reserve current of $150\,\mu$A is made available from the current
source to provide for worst-case resistor values, the base current of Q_7
and a maximum load current of 9 mA. This ensures that the collector
potential of Q_5 cannot fall below its base potential.

Level translation is achieved in the output stage, which is composed
of the composite *pnp* combination Q_7 and Q_8. A single *pnp* device cannot
be used here since an integrated lateral *pnp* cannot provide adequate
h_{FE}. The addition of Q_8 to the circuit permits achieving the necessary
gain without changing the basic structure of the class A common-emitter
output stage. Figure 11.1*b* shows how this increase in h_{FE} is obtained.
Resistor R_7 is added to the collector load of Q_7 in order to reduce the
loop gain and phase shift in the local feedback loop of the composite
pnp device. This inclusion of R_7 also increases the slew rate.

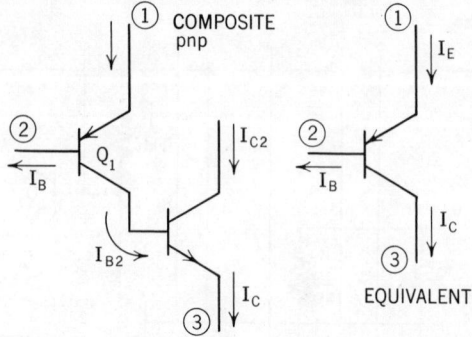

Figure 11.1b.   Composite *pnp* configuration. When the low-h_{FE} lateral *pnp* Q_1 is combined with a high-h_{FE} *npn*, a high-gain *pnp* equivalent structure results. In this circuit: $I_{B2} = I_B h_{FE1}$; $I_C = (1 + h_{FE2}) I_{B2} = I_{B2} h_{FE1}(h_{FE2}+1)$, $I_C/I_B = h_{FE1}(h_{FE2}+1) \simeq h_{FE1} h_{FE2}$.

11.2   LOW-FREQUENCY GAIN

The output-stage gain is given by the ratio of R_8 to R_6; for the circuit values shown this ratio is 5000/200, or 25.

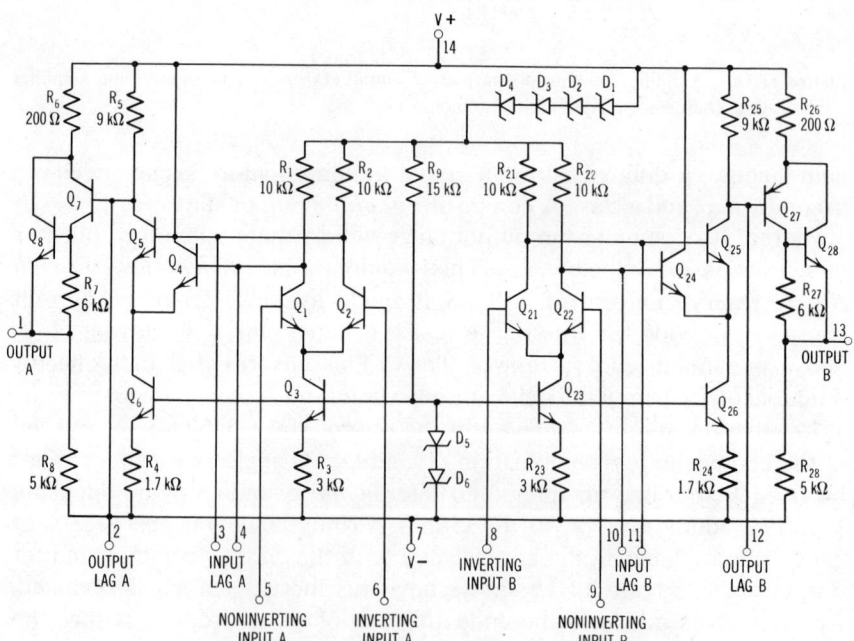

Figure 11.1c.   Circuit diagram for the μA739.

The gain of each of the first two stages is given by $g_m R_L$, where $g_m = 40\,I_E$ (in milliamperes) and R_L is the parallel combination of the load resistance and the input impedance of the next stage. For the first stage $I_E = 0.1$ mA, therefore $g_{m1} = 4.0$ mA/V. The differential input impedance of the second stage is approximately $2\beta r_{e2} \simeq 16$ kΩ. Therefore $R_L = 6.2$ kΩ, and the differential voltage gain of the first stage is 25.

The input impedance to the third stage is approximately $\beta(Q_7, Q_8) \times R_6 \simeq 40$ kΩ. The effective load on the second stage is 7.4 kΩ. The emitter current is 0.17 mA; therefore $g_{m2} = 0.7$ mA/V. The voltage gain A_{V2} of the second stage is equal to 26. Transistors Q_1 and Q_2 form a differential input pair, with Q_3 acting as a current source. Bias for the base of Q_3 is obtained from the combined V_{BE} drops of D_5 and D_6. If it is assumed for the moment that $V_{BE} = 0.6$ V for all transistors and diodes, the voltage across R_3 is 0.6 V. The current through it must therefore be 200 μA. This current divides equally between the collector loads R_1 and R_2, causing a voltage drop of 1 V across each load resistor. The collector voltages of Q_1 and Q_2 are therefore $V_A - 1$ V.

The transistor differential pair Q_4 and Q_5 is supplied by the current source Q_6, which derives its bias from the same point as Q_3. This current source supplies 350 μA.

Again, assuming perfect matching and neglecting the Early effect (basewidth modulation) the current supplied by Q_6 is divided equally between Q_4 and Q_5. If the base current of Q_7 can be neglected, the collector voltage of Q_5 will be $V^+ - 1.6$ V.

Now consider the worst-case collector-base reverse-bias voltages on Q_4 and Q_5. If a large positive differential voltage is applied to the amplifier input, the entire current from Q_3 (200 μA) will pass through Q_1, and Q_2 will be off. The collector voltages of Q_1 and Q_2 will then be

$$V_{C_1} = V_A - 2 \text{ V}, \tag{11.1}$$

and

$$V_{C_2} = V_A. \tag{11.2}$$

Q_5 will be turned fully on, since its base will be 2 V higher than the base of Q_4. Under these conditions saturation of Q_5 is prevented by the four diodes, D_1 through D_4. The highest voltage that appears on the base of Q_5 is $V^+ - 2.4$ V.

To summarize, the low-frequency gain values obtained are $A_{V1} = 25$, $A_{V2} = 26$, $A_{V3} = 25$.

The total gain from input to output is

$$A_{V0} = A_{V1} A_{V2} A_{V3} \tag{11.3}$$
$$= 25 \times 26 \times 25 = 16{,}250 \text{ or } 84 \text{ dB}.$$

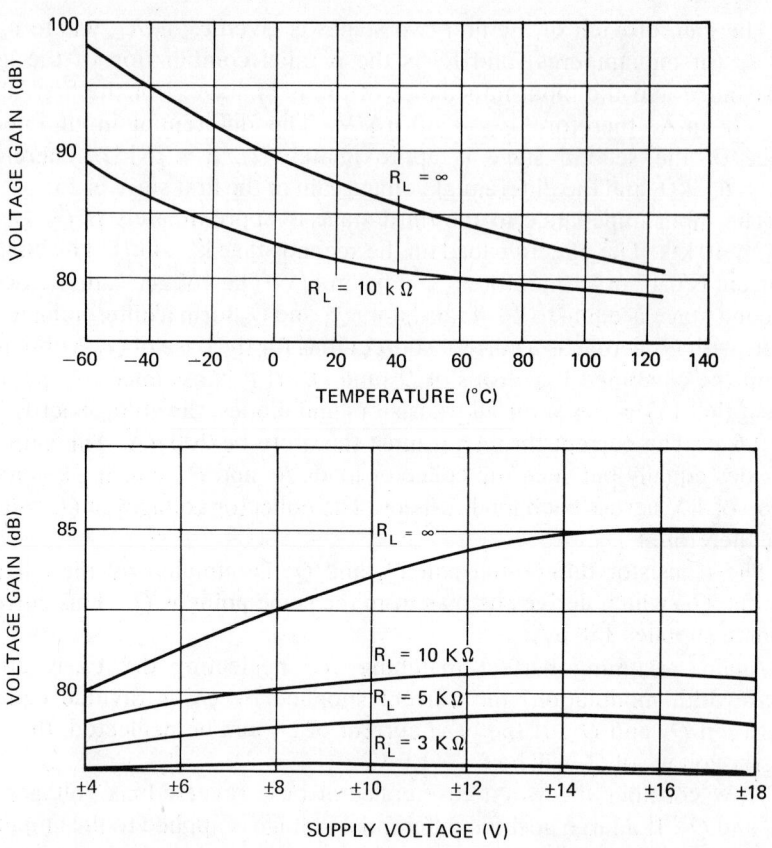

Figure 11.2. Uncompensated open-loop voltage gain: (*a*) as a function of temperature; $V_s = \pm 15$ V; $T_A = 25°$C, $f = 10$ kH$_2$. (*b*) As a function of supply voltage; $V_0 = 0.5$ V rms; $T_A = 25°$C; $f = 10$ kHz.

The total gain is relatively constant for wide variations in absolute value of the individual resistors in the circuits. In the first two stages g_m has a proportional relationship with emitter current, which in turn is inversely proportional to the resistor in the emitter of the current source. Therefore the ratio of the current-source resistor value to the collector load resistance determines the gain. The gain of the output stage is also dependent on resistor ratios.

The calculation of the full-temperature and supply-voltage dependence on gain is a long procedure and is not included here. The variation of voltage gain measured for changes in temperature and supply voltage is shown in Figure 10.2*a* and *b*.

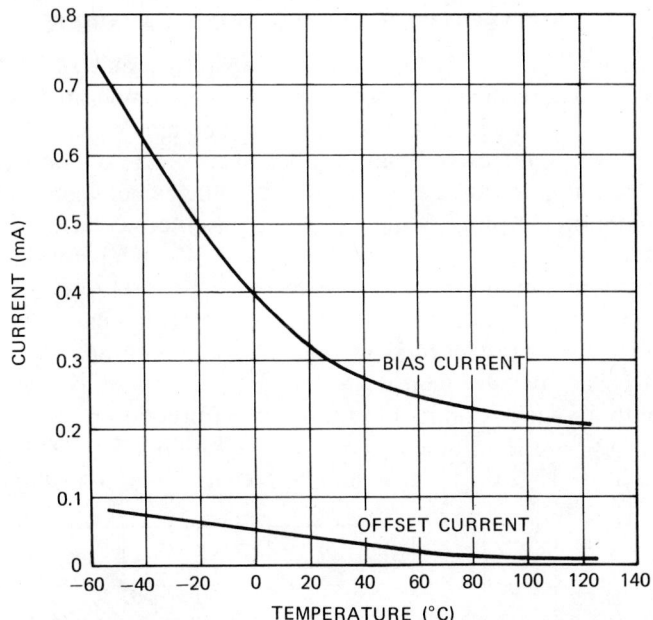

Figure 11.3. Input offset current and bias current as functions of temperature; $V_s = \pm 15$ V, $V_{IN} = 0$ V.

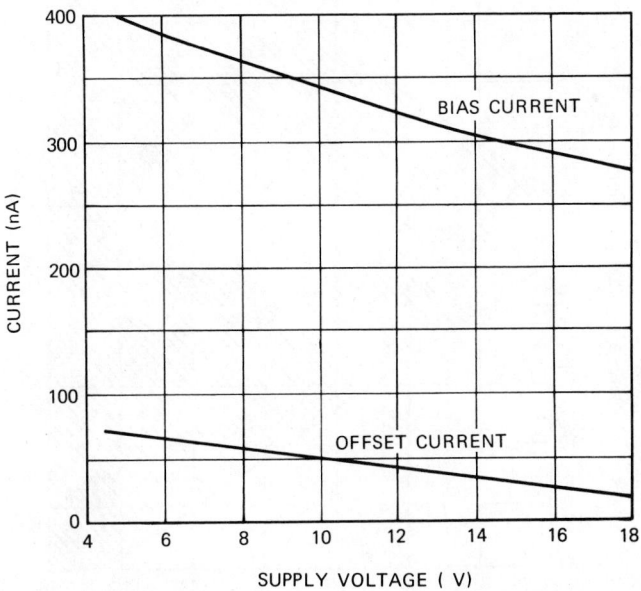

Figure 11.4. Input offset current and bias current as functions of supply voltage; $T_A = 25°C$, $V_{IN} = 0$ V.

145

11.3 BIAS STABILITY AND SIGNAL-HANDLING CAPABILITY

Offset voltage is also a function of temperature and supply voltage. How input bias current and offset current vary with temperature and supply voltage is shown in Figures 11.3 and 11.4. The bias scheme used in the μA739 IC was selected for gain stability over a wide operating range; it enables the amplifier to be used at supply voltages between 9 and 36 V. The common-mode range is limited to the base voltage at Q_3 ($2V_{BE}$) and the collector voltage of Q_1 and Q_2 ($V^+ - 4V_{BE} - 1$). Thus for operation at ±15 V the common-mode range is approximately $+11.5$ to -13.8 V. At ±4.5 V this range reduces to $+1.0$ to -2.8 V. In either case the common-mode range may be exceeded without causing latch-up. The common-mode range is shown in Figure 11.5.

The output swing is limited in the positive direction by the saturation voltage of Q_8 and the voltage across R_7 to within 2.5 V of the positive supply; that is, 12.5 V for 15-V supply. Negative output swing is limited

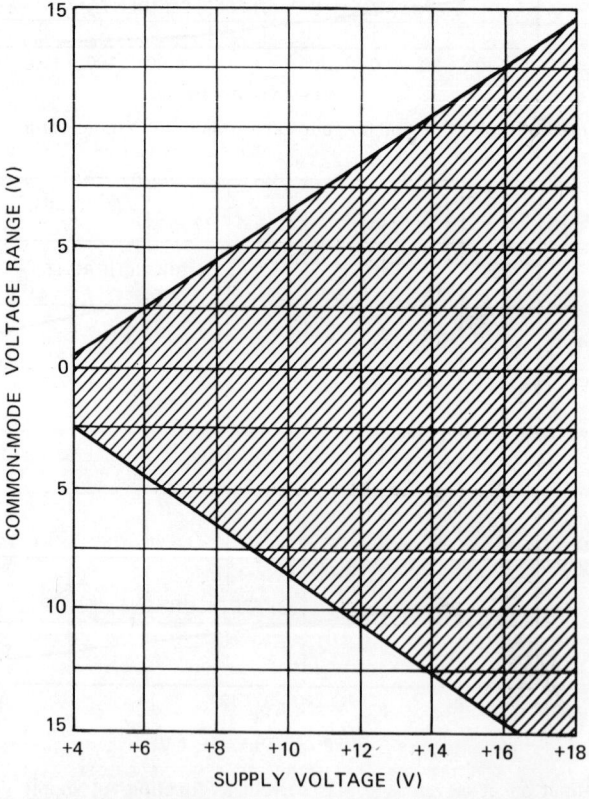

Figure 11.5. Common-mode range as a function of supply voltage; $T_A = 25°C$.

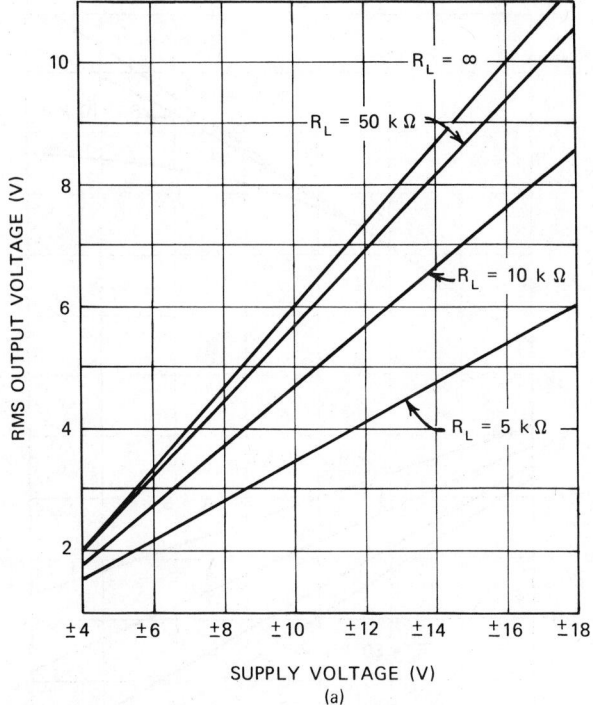

Figure 11.6a. Output-voltage capability as a function of supply voltage, R_L to ground, V_{OUT} dc $= 0$, $T_A = 25°C$, $f = 1$ kHz.

by the load on the output. The output swing is shown in Figures 11.5 and 11.6.

11.4 POWER DISSIPATION

The typical dissipation for the μA739 with a 30-V supply is 350 mW. Figure 11.7a shows the typical supply current with various loads as a function of supply voltage; Figure 11.7b depicts the variation of supply current with temperature; and Figure 11.7c gives the device dissipation under the same conditions. These specifications are for an output voltage halfway between the positive and negative supplies — the normal quiescent mode in a linear amplifier circuit. The maximum permissible dissipation for the package is 500 mW derated linearly at 7.7 mW/°C above 60°C.

11.5 SHORT-CIRCUIT PROTECTION

Short-circuit output current is limited by the available drive. Consider the case in which the output terminal is shorted to the negative supply.

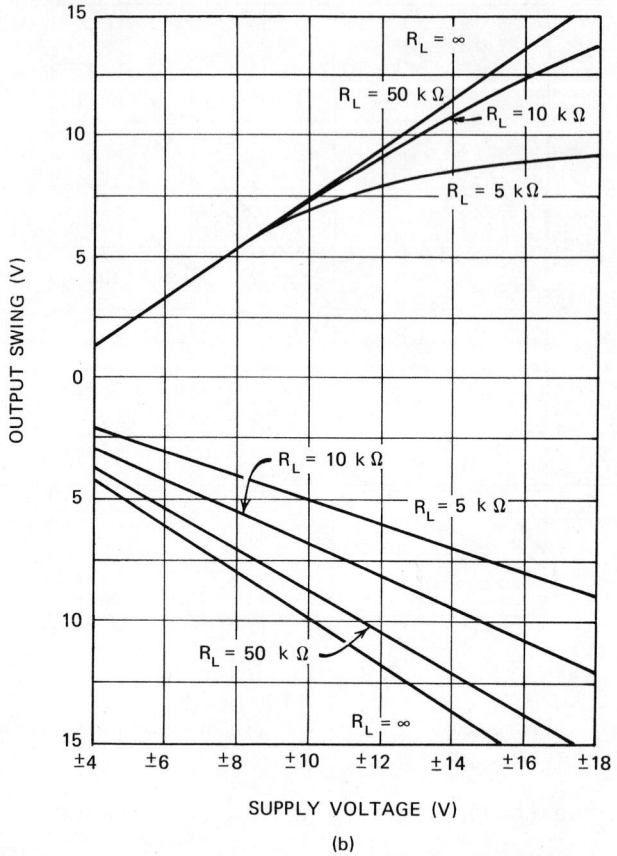

Figure 11.6b. Typical output-voltage swing as a function of supply voltage; $T_A = 25°C$, R_L to ground.

Maximum output current exists when the entire collector current of Q_6 passes through R_5. This assumes infinite h_{FE} for the output composite *pnp*, a worst case for this mode. The voltage across R_5 will be 4.1 V, and the voltage across R_6 will be 3.4 V. The maximum current through R_6 and into the short circuit is therefore 17 mA. The dissipation in Q_8 when operating from ± 15 V will be approximately 460 mW—close to the maximum for the package. A continuous short circuit would raise the temperature about 60°C.

No damage will occur to the device under these conditions with operation at normal ambient temperatures. Simultaneously shorting both outputs, however, could raise the chip temperature above the maximum allowed for the package.

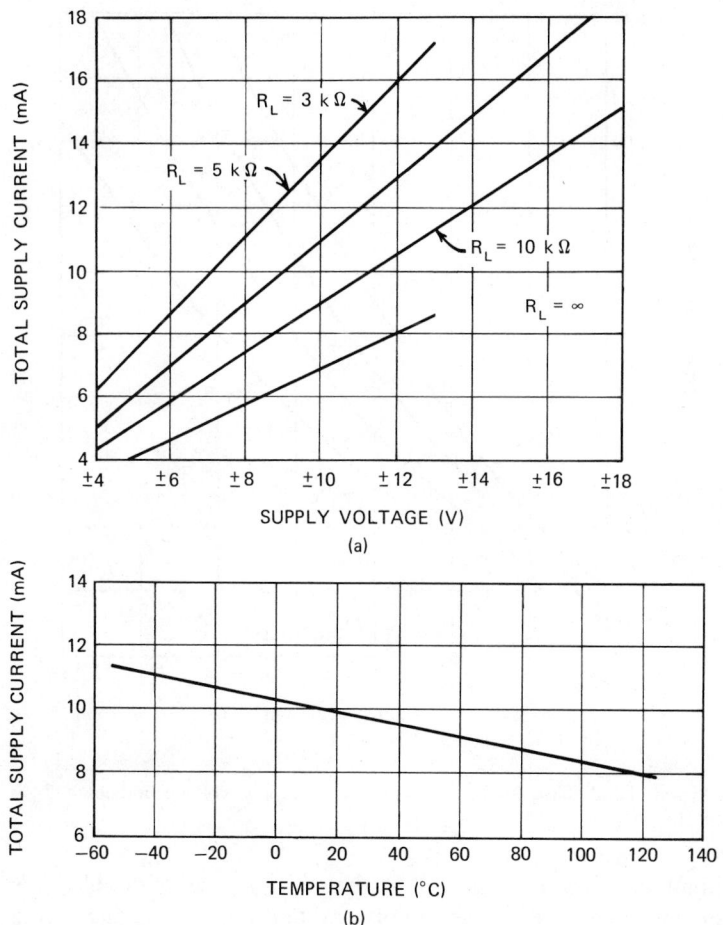

Figure 11.7. Total supply current: (*a*) as a function of supply voltage; $V_0 = 0$, $T_A = 25°C$, R_L to pin 7. (*b*) As a function of temperature; $V_s = \pm 15$ V, $V_0 = 0$, $R_L = \infty$.

11.6   CHANNEL ISOLATION

Figure 11.1*c* shows how the second channel of the μA739 is added. Any signal emanating from one channel to the bias circuit will have been attenuated by the common-mode rejection. It will then be further attenuated by the low impedances at *X* and *Y* (Figure 11.1*c*) and will appear at common-mode points in the other channel. The isolation at 1 kHz will be at least equal to the combined common-mode rejections of the two amplifiers. At very high frequencies coupling between the device leads and the

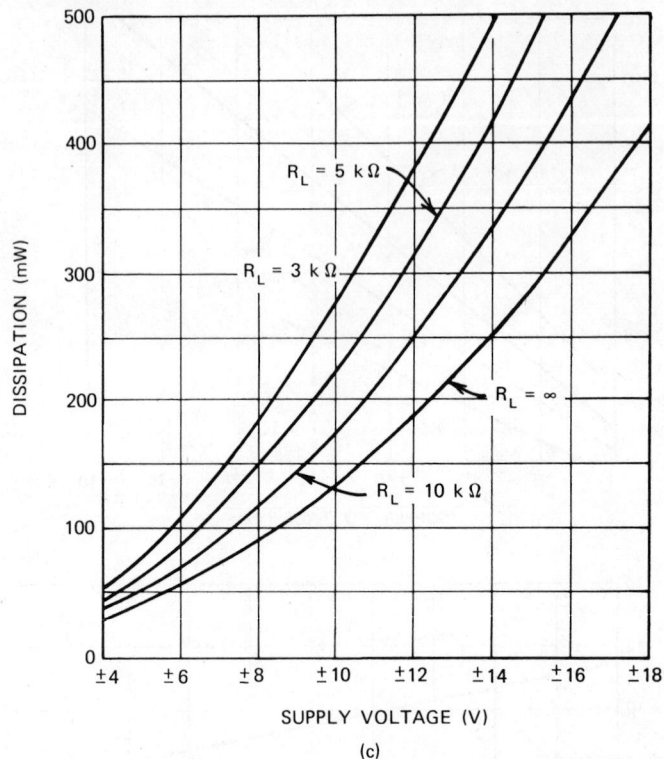

Figure 11.7c. Total dissipation as a function of supply voltage and load, $T_A = 25°C$, $V_0 = 0$, R_L to pin 7.

accompanying circuit wiring will be the major source of coupling. At low frequencies inadequate power supply and bias decoupling may reduce the isolation. Finally, at very low frequencies thermal coupling across the chip will cause some slight interaction.

These effects are illustrated in Figure 11.8. Channel isolation is so dependent on external circuit and signal conditions that it is difficult to give a precise specification for this parameter. Figure 11.8 demonstrates that the isolation is entirely adequate for most operations. Figure 11.9 shows common-mode rejection as a function of frequency.

11.7   NOISE

The choice of the input-stage collector current depends on the source impedance for which the circuit is to be optimized. High source impedances call for low collector currents in order to keep noise current

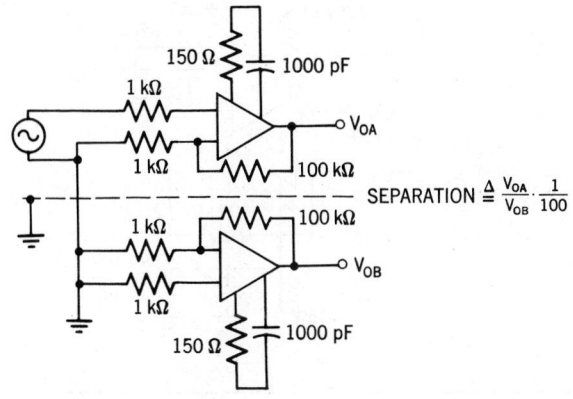

$$\text{SEPARATION} \triangleq \frac{V_{OA}}{V_{OB}} \cdot \frac{1}{100}$$

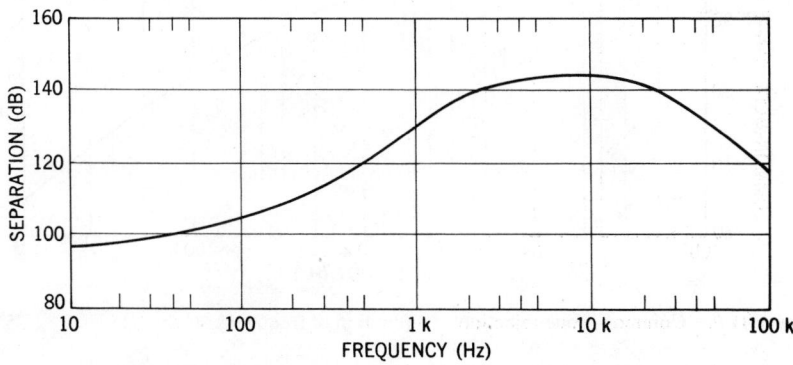

Figure 11.8. Channel separation as a function of frequency; $V_s = \pm 15$ V, $T_A = 25°C$, $R_L = \infty$.

down; low source impedances require low emitter resistances and therefore require higher collector currents to obtain low noise voltage. For best signal-to-noise ratio the noise figure is optimized for low-impedance sources (500 Ω to 5 kΩ). Spot noise voltage and current are plotted in Figure 11.10a and b, and wideband noise voltage and current are plotted in Figure 11.11a and b.

Other sources of noise are $1/f$ noise and "popcorn" noise. In particular popcorn noise (also termed "burst," or "multistate," noise) is most objectionable. This kind of noise, frequently encountered in bipolar semiconductor devices, is characterized by discrete pulses superimposed on the normal wideband noise. The amplitude of these pulses is generally constant, whereas the frequency and length are completely random. The noise is probably caused by recombination effects at the silicon-chip

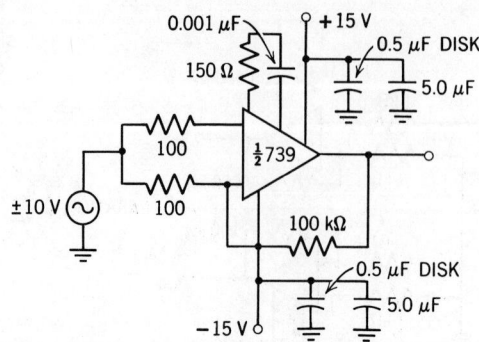

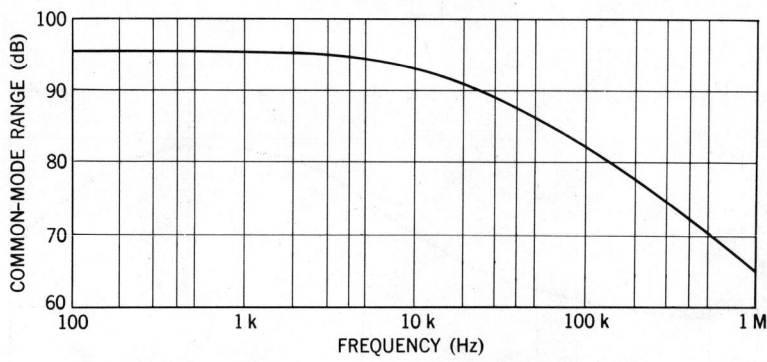

Figure 11.9. Common-mode rejection as a function of frequency; $V_{ss} = \pm 15$ V, $T_A = 25°C$, $R_L = \infty$.

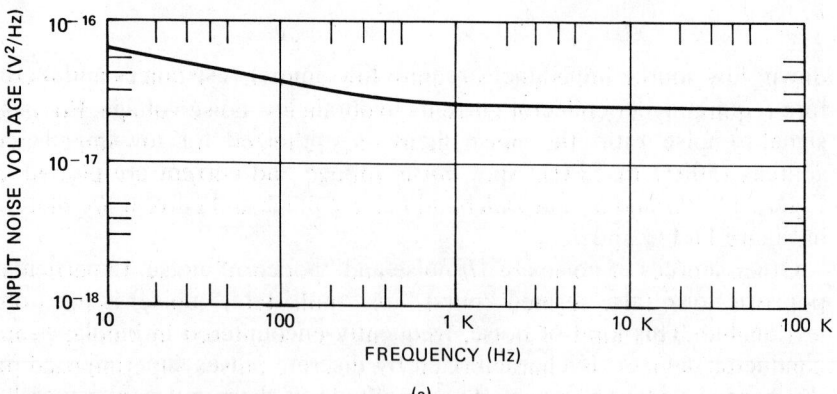

(a)

Figure 11.10a. Input noise voltage as a function of frequency; $V_{ss} = \pm 15$ V, $T_A = 25°C$, $R_s = 100 \ \Omega$.

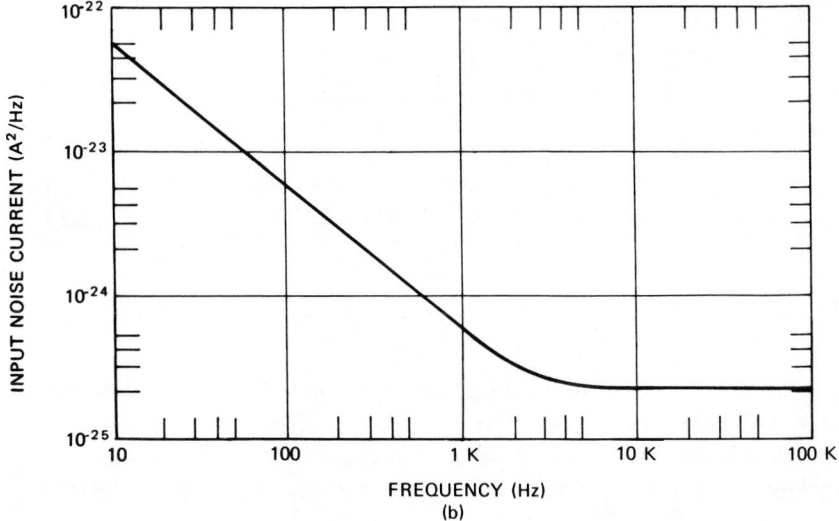

Figure 11.10*b*. Input noise current as a function of frequency; $V_{ss} = \pm 15$ V, $T_A = 25°C$, $R_s = 100$ kΩ.

surface and is most prevalent at low temperatures with high source impedances. IC processing improvements have reduced burst noise and $1/f$ noise.

11.8 COMPENSATION

Compensation of the μA739 can be customized to the individual circuit. For a given application the output-voltage swing and the closed-loop gain will determine the compensation required.

The open-loop gain and phase responses are plotted in Figure 11.12.

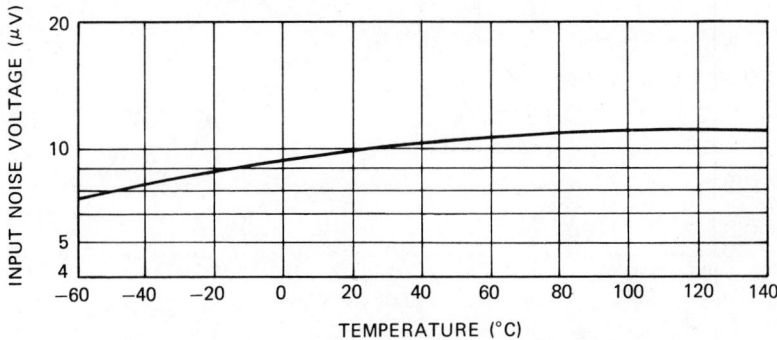

Figure 11.11*a*. Wideband noise voltage as a function of temperature, $BW = 150$ kHz, $V_{ss} = \pm 15$ V, $R_s = 130$ Ω.

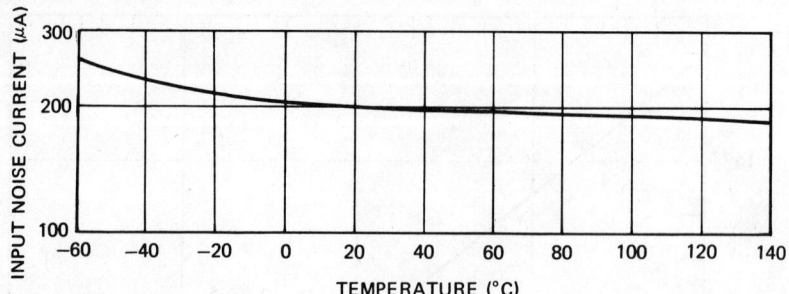

Figure 11.11*b*. Wideband noise current as a function of temperature, BW = 150 kHz, $V_{ss} = \pm 15$ V, $R_s = 100$ kΩ.

The dominant pole at 600 kHz is caused by the transit delay in the lateral *pnp*. Two other major poles at 1 and 2 MHz are caused by the phase shift at the collectors of the differential-gain stages. For very high source impedances the input capacitance will add a pole, as shown by the dashed

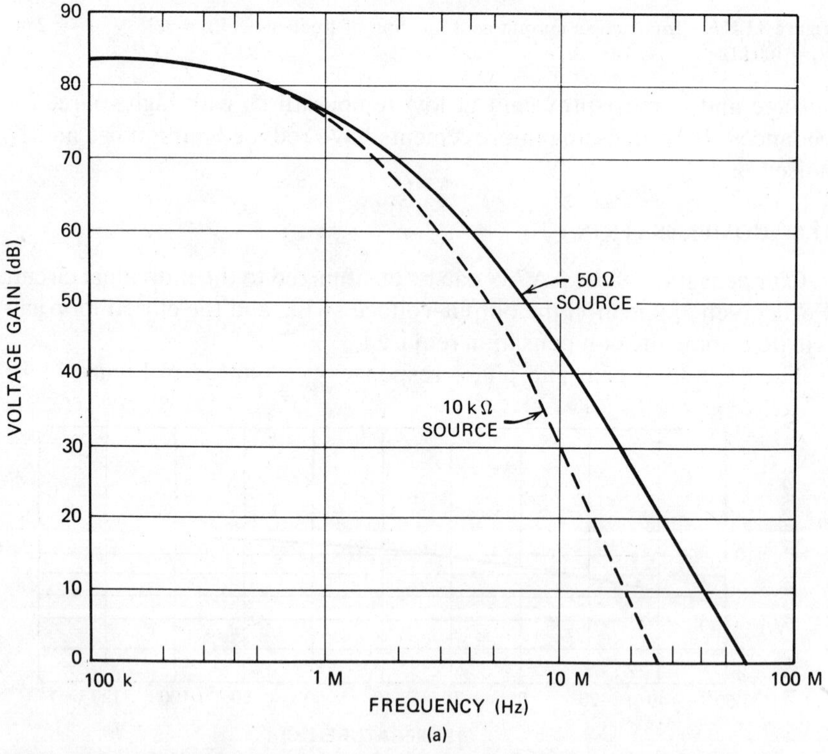

Figure 11.12*a*. Uncompensated open-loop operation: frequency response; $V_{ss} = \pm 15$V, $T_A = 25°$C.

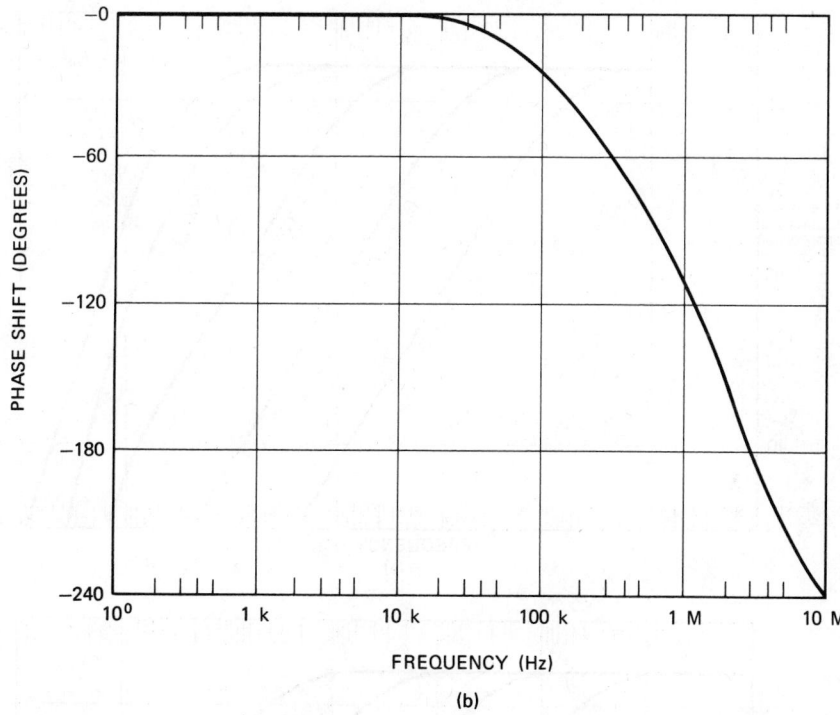

Figure 11.12*b*.   Uncompensated open-loop operation: phase shift; $V_s = \pm 15V$, $T_A = 25°C$.

line in Figure 11.12. The variation of 180° phase-shift frequency with supply voltage is shown in Figure 11.13. The compensation networks given apply over the voltage range of 8 to 30 V.

For many applications a single capacitor is sufficient to ensure stability of the circuit. Single-component compensation can be accomplished

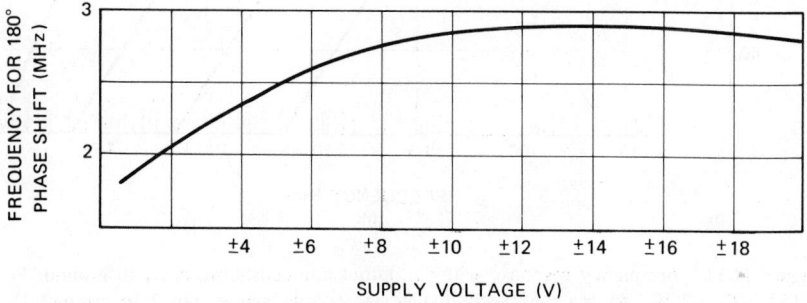

Figure 11.13.   Open-loop 180° phase-shift frequency as a function of supply voltage.

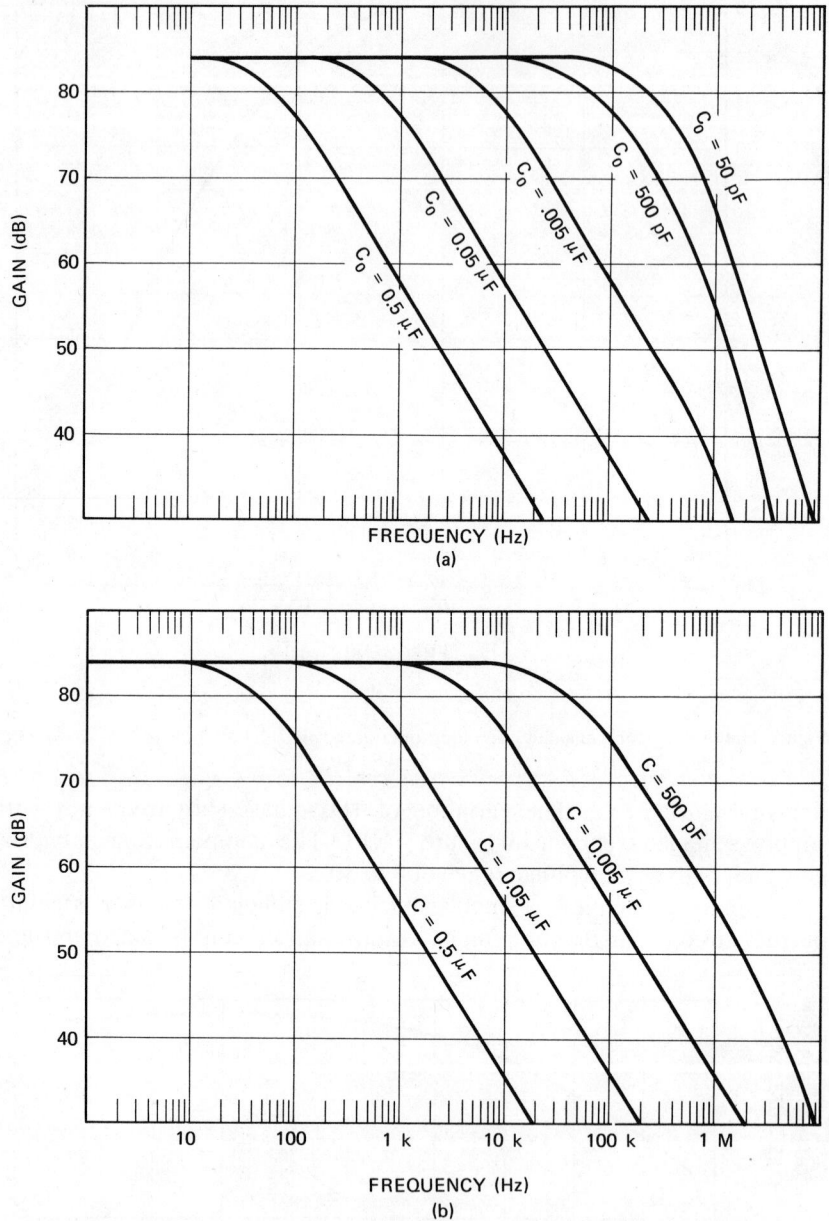

Figure 11.14. Frequency response with (a) output compensation, pin 1 to ground; $V_{ss} = \pm 15$ V, $T_A = 25°C$, $R_L = \infty$. (b) Second-stage lag compensation, pin 2 to ground; $V_{ss} = \pm 15$ V, $T_A = 25°C$, $R_L = \infty$.

156

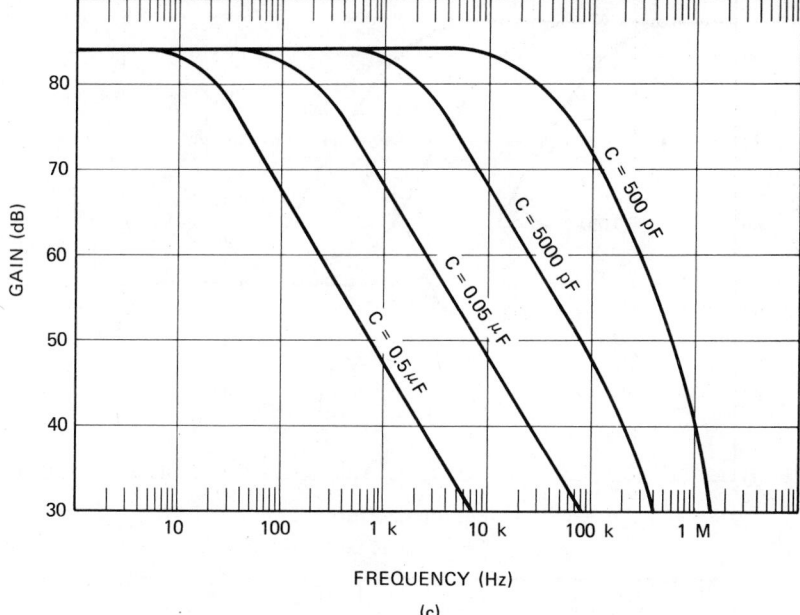

Figure 11.14c.   Input compensation, pin 3 to pin 4, $V_{ss} = \pm 15V$, $T_A = 25°$, $R_L = \infty$.

between pin 1 and ground, between pins 3 and 4, and from pin 2 to either supply or ground. If compensation is used shunting pin 2, it should be placed between pin 2 and pin 14 (V^+) rather than between pin 2 and ground. Examination of the output circuit indicates the reason for this. If the capacitor is grounded, signals on the power supply are amplified through the output stage as a common-base circuit. This degrades the amplifier sensitivity to high-frequency power-supply noise. If the capacitor is placed between pins 2 and 14, high-frequency power-supply signals become a common-mode input to the output stage. Frequency response for various capacitor values is shown in Figure 11.14a, b, and c.

Feedback compensation can be used to control the amplifier-frequency response; the capacitors can be placed between pins 1 and 2 or 2 and 3. Compensation around the output stage is similar to lag compensation from pin 2 to pin 14; the capacitor value needed is smaller, and the pole caused by the output stage is better controlled above 0.1 MHz.

Second-stage feedback compensation converts this stage to a voltage follower. An advantage of this compensation is that it produces both a pole and a zero in the forward response. The amount of attenuation inserted is equal to the second-stage gain plus 6 dB. Frequency response of the μA739 for feedback compensation is shown in Figure 11.15a and b.

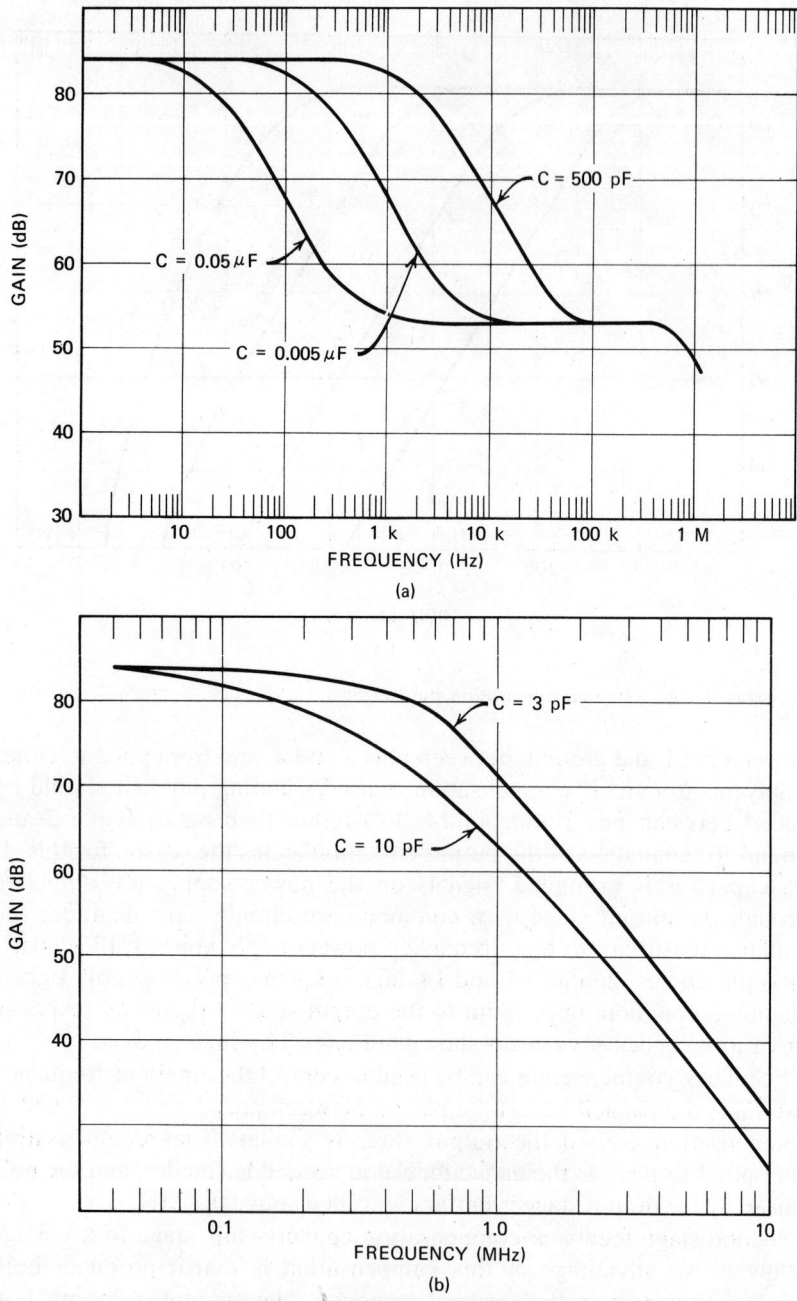

Figure 11.15. Frequency response with (*a*) second-stage feedback compensation, pin 2 to pin 3, $V_{ss} = \pm 15$ V, $T_A = 25°C$, $R_L = \infty$. (*b*) Output stage feedback, pin 1 to pin 2, $V_{ss} = \pm 15$ V, $T_A = 25°C$.

158

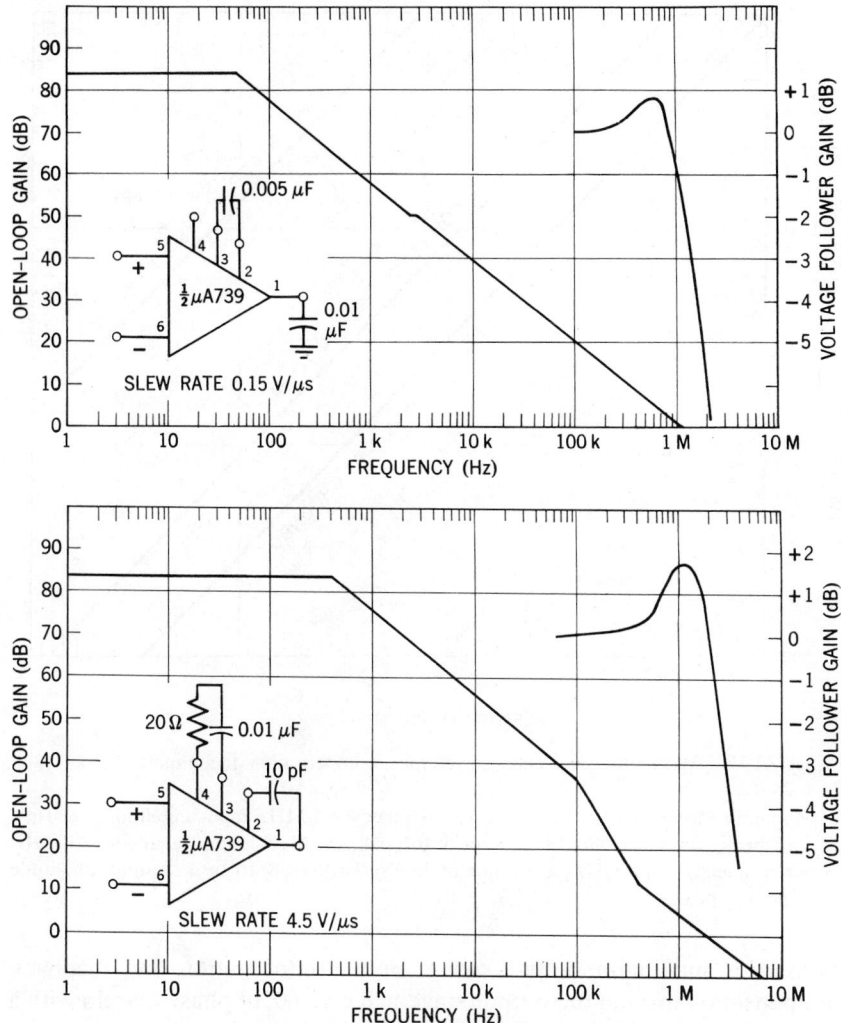

Figure 11.16. (*a*) Low slew-rate unity-gain frequency response; $V_{ss} = \pm 15$ V, $T_A = 25°C$, $R_L = \infty$. (*b*) Maximum slew-rate unity-gain frequency response, $V_{ss} = \pm 15$ V, $T_A = 25°C$, $R_L = \infty$.

Unity-gain compensation for phono preamplifiers, integrators, and most dc applications requires compensation around more than one stage for adequate phase margin. For applications in which slew rate is not a factor output compensation combined with second-stage feedback compensation (Figure 11.16*a*) can be used to keep the number of components to a mini-

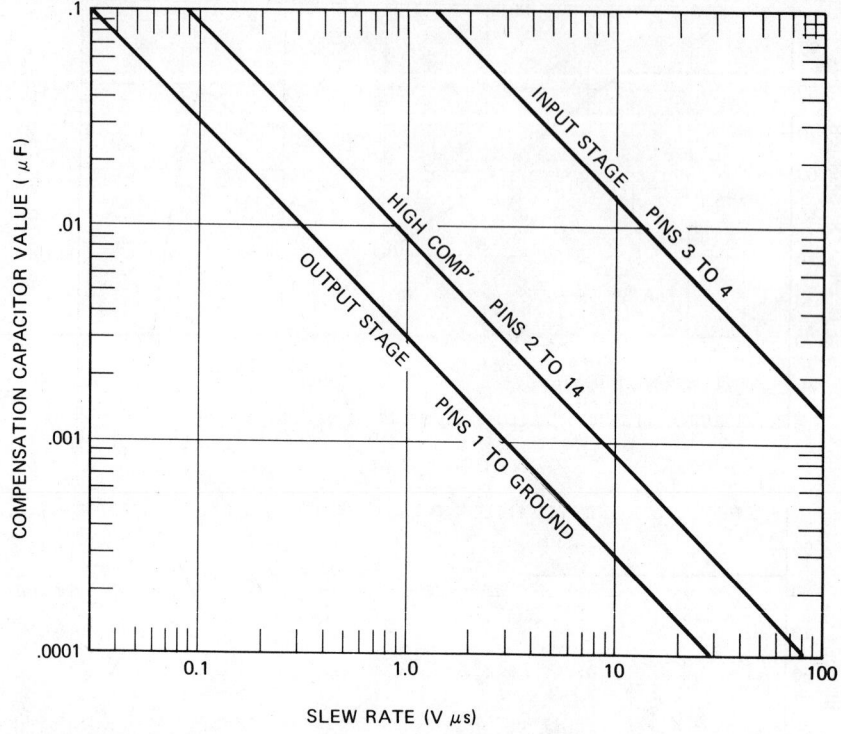

Figure 11.17. Maximum slew rate for various compensation techniques; $V_s = \pm 15$ V, $T_A = 25°C, R_L = \infty$.
(*a*) Modulating frequency = 400 Hz, carrier frequency = 1 MHz, input amplitude = 600 mV peak to peak, output amplitude = 2 V peak to peak; (*b*) Modulating frequency = 400 Hz, carrier frequency = 4.5 MHz, input amplitude = 600 mV peak to peak, output amplitude = 2 V peak to peak.

mum. For maximum output swing input compensation and feedback compensation around the output stage will give 60° of phase margin with a 3 V/μs slew rate. Phase lead must be included in the input compensation, as shown in Figure 11.16*b*.

The slew rate can be predicted for any value of capacitor. Figure 11.17

$$S = \frac{I}{C}A, \tag{11.4}$$

where I is the available current to charge the compensating capacitor, C is the capacitor value, and A is the gain from the compensating point to the output. For example, if 0.01 μF is used between pins 3 and 4 and $I = 200\,\mu$A, $A = 25.7 \times 25$, and $S = 12.8$ V/μs.

shows slew rate versus capacitance for the compensation networks indicated. The slew rate may be calculated from

11.9   OPERATING SAFEGUARDS

When connecting the μA739 in a circuit, it is important to observe proper lead orientation. If the μA739 is installed in reverse, V^+ and V^- will be interchanged, excessive currents will flow in the substrate diode, and the IC may be damaged.

When the μA739 is used, bypass capacitors should be connected from the supply terminals to ground to eliminate the effects of power-supply lead inductance. A 0.01-μF disk capacitor mounted close to the IC pin provides enough decoupling to eliminate the effects of this inductance.

12

The Linear Four-Quadrant Multiplier

by Edward L. Renschler

Motorola Semiconductor, Phoenix, Arizona

At the 1968 EEE Linear IC Clinic (March 21, 1968, New York), Jim Solomon of Motorola made two predictions. First, he forecast that 1968 would be "the year of the multiplier," and, second, he predicted that the multiplier would become the second basic analog building block (the operational amplifier was really the first basic building block for purely analog work).

With respect to his first prediction Jim Solomon spoke very wisely. 1968 was indeed a good year for packaged analog multipliers. More than a half-dozen companies introduced a four-quadrant multiplier, all with a price under $100[1]. Some vendors offered monolithic four-quadrant multipliers to take advantage of the improved reliability and temperature characteristics offered by monolithic construction.

Solomon's second prediction, that the multiplier will become the next analog building block, seems to be rapidly becoming a reality. With the price of the multiplier coming down and the number of available devices becoming larger, more and more designers are taking advantage of the capabilities offered by the multiplier. The near future should surely prove out Jim Solomon's second prediction.

This chapter first covers the development and analysis of a linear circuit, exhibiting four-quadrant multiplier properties, which is suitable for monolithic construction. After the development and analysis of the circuit has been discussed, some basic applications will be presented to demonstrate a few possible uses. Although the applications of a four-quadrant linear multiplier are virtually unlimited, it is hoped that the few applications to be covered will encourage the designer to "think multiplier".

12.1 METHODS OF ANALOG MULTIPLICATION

There are many methods by which analog multiplication can be performed[1]. The following is not intended to be a complete list; it is offered as a brief comparison of techniques.

1. Hall effect.   The principle on which the Hall-effect multiplier is based is that the voltage across a conductor is proportional to both the current through it and the strength of the magnetic field across it.

2. Magnetoresistance.   A magnetoresistance multiplier is basically a Wheatstone bridge made up of flux-sensitive resistors; the two variables to be multiplied are the current in the coil producing the flux and the voltage across the bridge.

3. Variable transconductance.   In a multiplier of the variable-transconductance type the output of a transistor amplifier depends on the signal and the magnitude of the effective emitter resistance (common-emitter configuration assumed) which can be controlled by the emitter current magnitude. Hence the output at the collector is proportional to the input signal times a function of the emitter current.

4. Quarter Square.   This technique makes use of the mathematical identity

$$XY = \tfrac{1}{4}[(X+Y)^2 - (X-Y)^2].$$

Diodes are generally used to generate the required square-law functions.

5. Pulse Height/Width.   Here an oscillator generates a train of rectangular pulses; one input modulates the height of the pulses and the other modulates the width. The area of the pulses is then proportional to the product of the two inputs.

6. Triangle Averaging.   This is a variation of the quarter-square method. Instead of the square-law functions used in the quarter-square method, quadratic functions are generated by the integration of clipped triangular waveforms.

7. Logarithmic Sum.   This is the technique by which an ordinary slide rule operates.

$$XY = \text{antilog}\,[\log X + \log Y].$$

Log and antilog functions can be easily generated by using a nonlinear element in conjunction with an operational amplifier[2].

12.2   VARIABLE TRANSCONDUCTANCE

Of these seven methods of performing analog multiplication, the third (variable transconductance) is best suited to monolithic implementation. The concept of variable transconductance is being used in the design of analog multipliers in monolithic form.

Keeping the variable-transconductance technique in mind, let us recall the classical example of analog multiplication from communication systems – that of amplitude modulation, as illustrated in Figure 12.1 in which ω_0 represents a carrier frequency and ω_s the frequency of the modulating signal. The product as shown is

$$e_0 = KE_1 \cos \omega_s t \cos \omega_0 t. \tag{12.1}$$

By using a trigonometric identity (12.1) becomes the familiar sum and difference spectra:

$$e_0 = \frac{KE_1}{2}[\cos (\omega_0 + \omega_s)t + \cos (\omega_0 - \omega_s)t]. \tag{12.2}$$

Note that only the frequency characteristics and not the amplitude of the carrier are being maintained. You may recall from communication-system theory that the carrier-signal zero crossings are often used to generate the switching function $S(t)$, as shown in Figure 12.2. Since the switching signal can be conveniently represented in Fourier series form as

$$S(t) = 2 \sum_{n=1}^{\infty} A_n \cos n\omega_0 t, \tag{12.3}$$

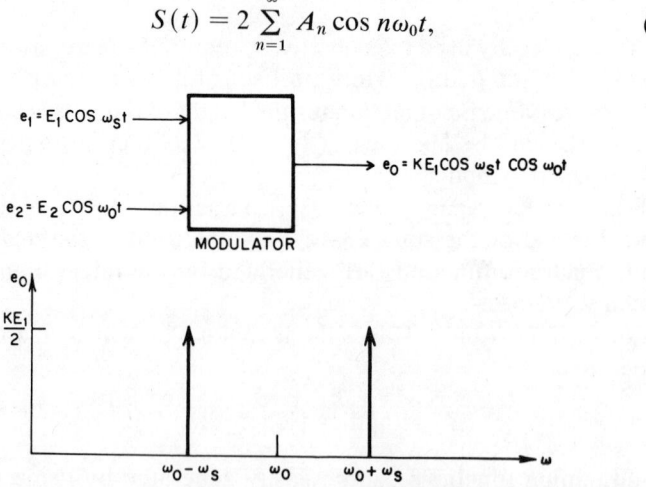

Figure 12.1.   Block diagram and frequency spectrum for balanced modulation.

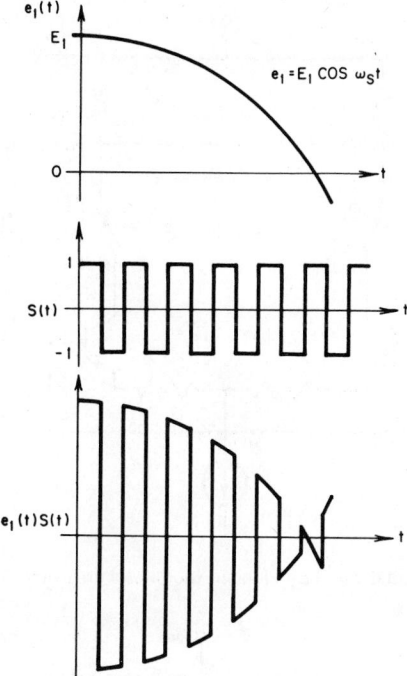

Figure 12.2. Modulated output $e_1(t)S(t)$ is generated by a switching function $S(t)$ and an input voltage $e_1(t)$.

where the Fourier coefficients are

$$A_n = \left[\frac{\sin(n\pi/2)}{(n\pi/2)} \right],$$ (12.4)

the product signal can be expressed as

$$e_0 = 2Ke_1(t)\, S(t)$$

$$= 2KE_1 \cos \omega_s t \sum_{n=1}^{\infty} A_n \cos n\omega_0 t.$$ (12.5)

The switching function introduces all of the odd harmonics of the carrier frequency with the harmonic amplitudes decreasing as the harmonic order increases, as shown by (12.3) and (12.4). A simple model of this switching function is shown in Figure 12.3, where the switching action of $S(t)$ is produced by a single-pole double-throw transistor switch controlled by $e_2(t)$. The switches use transistor current-mode gates with collectors so that full-wave balanced multiplication results between an input voltage $e_1(t)$ and the switching voltage $e_2(t)$.

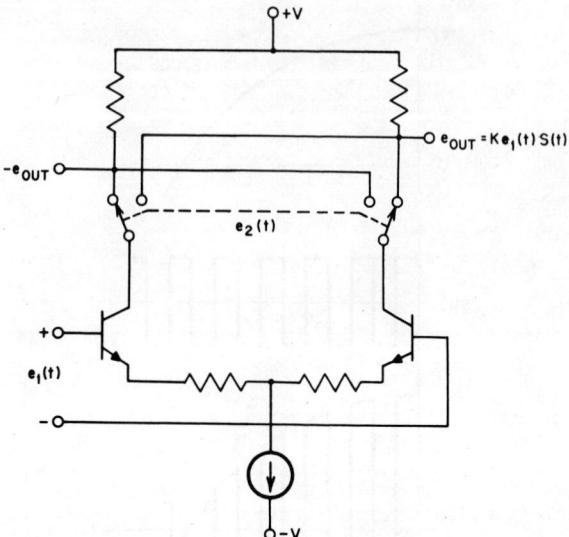

Figure 12.3. Simple model for the balanced modulator in which $S(t)$ is generated with a switch controlled by $e_2(t)$.

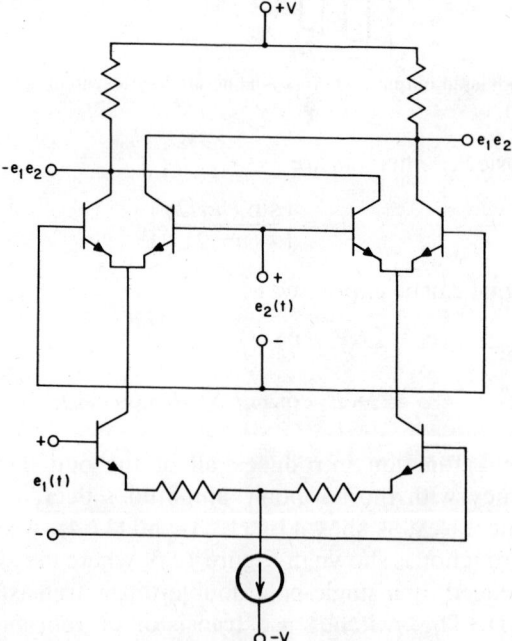

Figure 12.4. In this basic multiplier circuit, the switch of Fig. 3 has been replaced by current-mode transistor gates.

166

Figure 12.4 demonstrates the basic multiplier circuit, which accomplishes the desired modulation function. As already mentioned, the carrier signal (e_2) is best represented mathematically by the Fourier series expansion of the switching function $S(t)$, given in (12.3). In most applications an output filter is used with the multiplier to eliminate all terms in the Fourier series beyond the first. This is illustrated in Figure 12.5. After filtering, the output voltage e_0 contains only the product of the two input sinusoids, with amplitude information contained in e_1 only.

The sum and difference frequencies are seen in the expression for the output by applying a trigonometric expansion. Theoretically e_1 and e_2 appearing in the output approach zero. The closeness of the e_1 and e_2 outputs to zero is a measure of how well balanced the circuit is. In practice a rejection of 40 to 60 dB is achieved, depending on the frequency and the signal amplitude[3]. There are many applications for a multiplier of this type; however, the circuit developed thus far does not yet truly multiply $e_1(t)$ by $e_2(t)$ since amplitude information is removed from $e_2(t)$ in the generation of the switching function $S(t)$. This circuit can be modified, however, to respond linearly to both inputs, as illustrated in Figure 12.6, in which the input voltages V_x and V_y are linearly multiplied to produce the product V_xV_y at the output.

Until recently the fabrication of a circuit that could perform this multiplication and retain reasonable linearity has not been possible with other than digital techniques. The reason for this is that in order to multiply the inputs must be processed nonlinearly, and the nonlinear processing usually distorts at least one input. In the multiplier discussed here the basic configuration described earlier is used, but the e_2 input is first nonlinearly conditioned with the complement of the nonlinearity later used in multiplication. This e_2 signal conditioning is developed, as shown in Figure 12.7.

To see how the e_2 signal is preconditioned, let us look at Figure 12.7 and consider a transistor's collector response to an input base-emitter voltage.

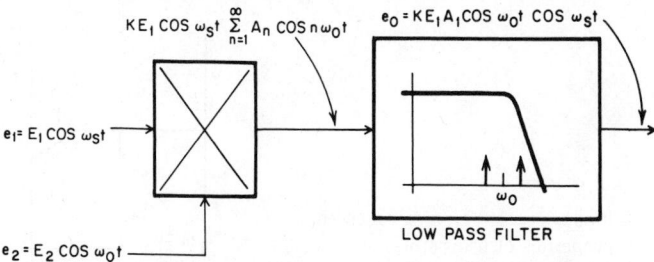

Figure 12.5. Balanced modulator. Output filter is used with the multiplier to eliminate all terms beyond the first one in the Fourier Series.

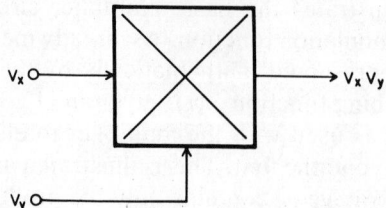

Figure 12.6.   Ideal black-box linear multiplier for which the output is the product of the two inputs.

For two identical transistors as shown an input I_1 produces an output I_2, which is approximately equal to I_1. The circuit achieves this by first converting the input current into a voltage ϕ_1, which is logarithmically related to I_1, and then converting ϕ_1 into a current I_2, which is exponentially related to ϕ_1. Two identical transistors are used so that the logarithmic operation cancels the exponential operation. Thus the output I_2 responds linearly to the input I_1. Note that I_1 is processed nonlinearly in the transistor junctions. Therefore it should be possible to multiply and obtain a linear response using the devices available with monolithic processing.

In Figure 12.8 we see a modified version of the balanced multiplier in which the e_2 input (V_y) is processed through a diode-transistor network to produce a linear response via nonlinear processing. Our original circuit of Figure 12.4 responded linearly to the e_1-input V_x, so that the output of the new circuit is now linearly dependent on both V_x and V_y.

A monolithic version of the improved multiplier circuit is shown in Figure 12.9, and this is, in fact, a schematic of the MC1595. In this

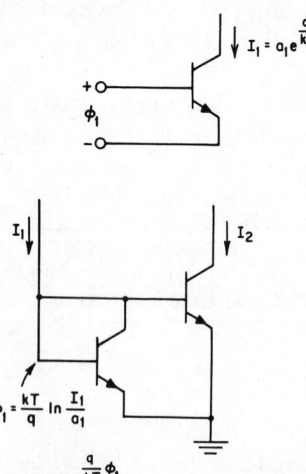

Fig. 12.7.   Multiplier preconditioning relies on the non-linear properties of transistors. Shown here are the basic Ebers-Moll transistor (top) and a pair of identical transistors (below) with B approaching infinity.

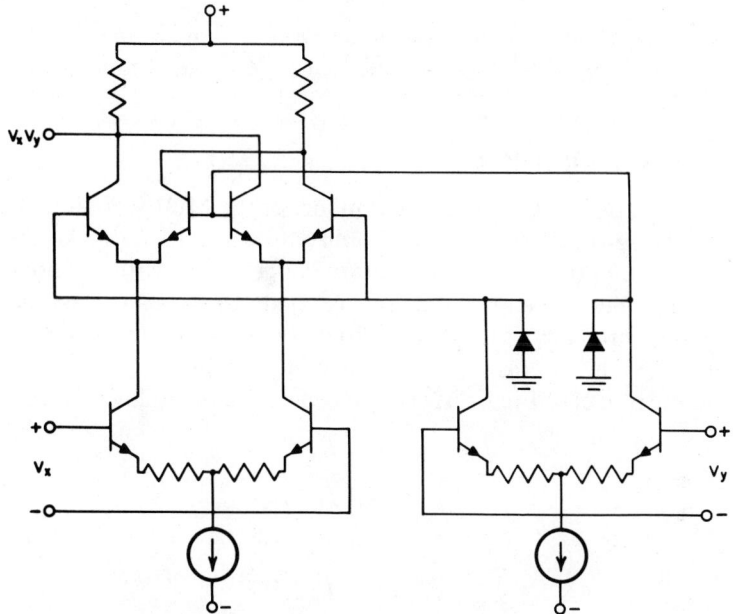

Figure 12.8. Modified version of the balanced multiplier with a diode-transistor network to process the V_y input for linear response.

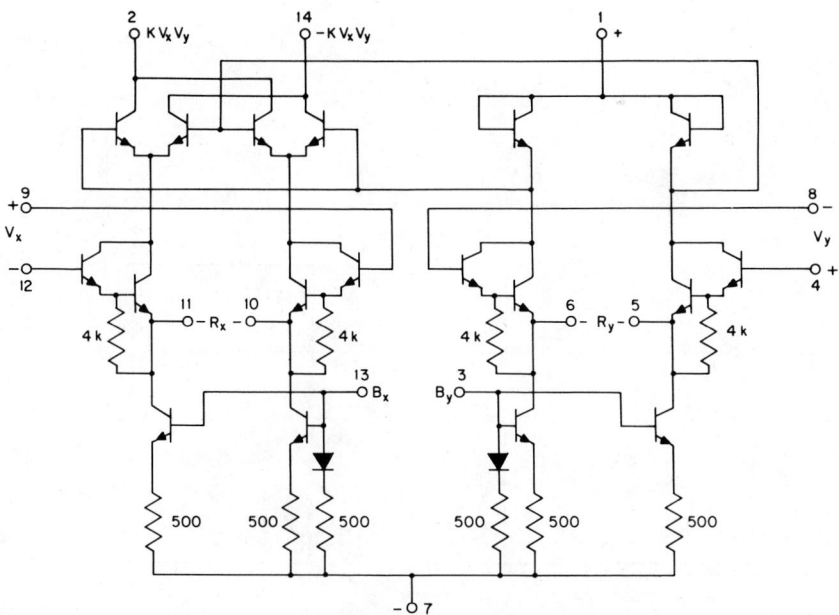

Figure 12.9. Monolithic version of the linear multiplier.

practical circuit input emitter degeneration and operating currents are adjustable by the user to accommodate a wide range of input signals and applications.

12.3   ANALYSIS OF THE IC

Figure 12.10 shows an equivalent model of the MC1595 which we will use to analyze the circuit[2]. To simplify the analysis we make the conventional assumptions: (a) devices of similar geometry within a monolithic chip are assumed to be identical and matched; (b) transistor base currents are ignored with respect to the magnitude of collector currents; therefore collector and emitter currents are assumed to be equal.

From the model of Figure 12.10, we can derive the following equations:

$$I_3 + I_y = I_6 + I_4, \tag{12.6}$$

$$I_4 - I_y = I_5 + I_7, \tag{12.7}$$

$$I_A = I_6 + I_7, \tag{12.8}$$

$$I_B = I_4 + I_5, \tag{12.9}$$

$$I_4 = \frac{I_3 + I_y}{1 + e^{(\phi_1 - \phi_2)/V_T}}, \tag{12.10}$$

$$I_5 = \frac{I_4 - I_y}{1 + e^{(\phi_2 - \phi_1)/V_T}}, \tag{12.11}$$

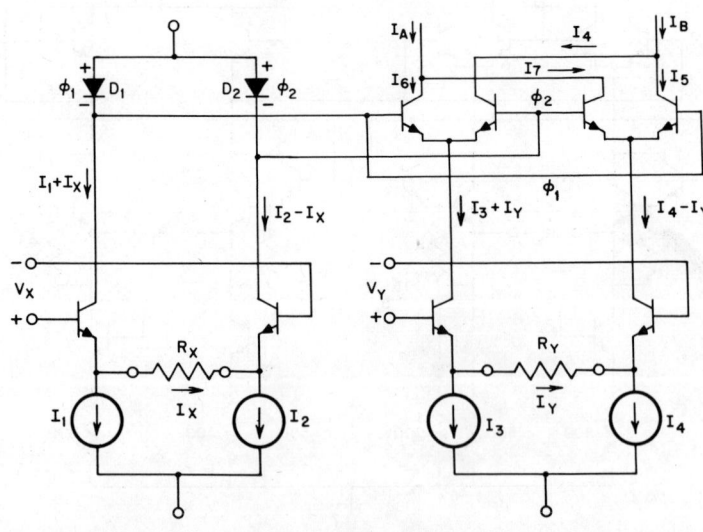

Figure 12.10.   Equivalent model of the integrated multiplier.

$$I_6 = \frac{I_3 + I_y}{1 + e^{(\phi_2 - \phi_1)/V_T}}, \tag{12.12}$$

$$I_7 = \frac{I_4 - I_y}{1 + e^{(\phi_1 - \phi_2)/V_T}}, \tag{12.13}$$

where $V_T = kT/q \approx 26$ mV at 25°C.
For simplicity let us define

$$m = \left(\frac{\phi_1 - \phi_2}{V_T}\right). \tag{12.14}$$

Then, substituting (12.10) and (12.11) into (12.9) and solving for I_B, we get

$$I_B = \frac{I_3(1 + e^{-m}) + I_4(1 + e^m) - I_y(e^m - e^{-m})}{(1 + e^m)(1 + e^{-m})} \tag{12.15}$$

and similarly with (12.12), (12.13), and (12.8), we can solve for I_A:

$$I_A = \frac{I_3(1 + e^m) + I_4(1 + e^{-m}) + I_y(e^m - e^{-m})}{(1 + e^m)(1 + e^{-m})}. \tag{12.16}$$

Now let us define a differential current as

$$\Delta I = I_A - I_B. \tag{12.17}$$

From (12.15) and (12.16) this reduces to

$$\Delta I = \frac{(e^m - e^{-m})(I_3 - I_4 + 2I_y)}{(1 + e^m)(1 + e^{-m})}. \tag{12.18}$$

For diodes D_1 and D_2 in Figure 12.10 we can write the following:

$$I_1 + I_x = a_{11}(e^{\phi_1/V_T} - 1) \approx a_{11}e^{\phi_1/V_T}, \tag{12.19}$$

$$I_2 - I_x = a_{11}(e^{\phi_2/V_T} - 1) \approx a_{11}e^{\phi_2/V_T}, \tag{12.20}$$

where the approximate equivalence is justified by assuming that the diodes are sufficiently forward biased. Further, we can see that

$$\frac{I_1 + I_x}{I_2 - I_x} = e^{(\phi_1 - \phi_2)/V_T} = e^m, \tag{12.21}$$

which, when substituted into (12.18), yields

$$\Delta I = \frac{(I_1 - I_2 + 2I_x)(I_3 - I_4 + 2I_y)}{(I_1 - I_2)}. \tag{12.22}$$

For the desired case in which $I_1 = I_2$ and $I_3 = I_4$ (which can be controlled quite well on a monolithic chip)

$$\Delta I = \frac{2I_x I_y}{I_1}. \tag{12.23}$$

The currents I_x and I_y are given by

$$I_x = \frac{V_x}{R_x + 2r_{e_1}}, \tag{12.24}$$

$$I_y = \frac{V_y}{R_y + 2r_{e_2}}, \tag{12.25}$$

where r_{e_1} and r_{e_2} are the bulk emitter resistances in the V_x and V_y differential-amplifier pairs. Therefore the output can be written as a product of the input voltages:

$$\Delta I = \frac{2V_x V_y}{I_1(R_x + 2r_{e_2})(R_y + 2r_{e_2})}. \tag{12.26}$$

From (12.26) we see that the multiplier operates in all four quadrants, giving sign and magnitude with respect to each input, linearly.

12.4 USING THE MULTIPLIER

To set up the multiplier for evaluation the following straightforward procedure is recommended.

Comparing Figure 12.10 with Figure 12.11, we note that the current source value $I_3 = I_4$ is determined by the biasing on pin 3, and the value of $I_1 = I_2$ is determined by the biasing on pin 13. Let us call these two values I_3 (for pin 3) and I_{13} (for pin 13).

If we now inset resistors R_L in the differential collectors where ΔI is felt, the output voltage is expressed as $2\Delta I R_L$, or

$$V_{out} = \frac{2V_x V_y R_L}{I_3[R_x + (2kT/qI_{13})][R_y + (2kT/qI_3)]},$$
$$= KV_x V_y \tag{12.27}$$

where $kT/q \simeq 26$ mV at 25°C.

The scale factor K can be adjusted by proper selection of I_3, R_x, and R_y, and is usually set to 1/10 so that the input and output dynamic ranges will be compatible.

As an example, let us assume that the multiplier is to give

$$V_{out} = \frac{V_x V_y}{10} \quad \text{for} \begin{cases} -10 \text{ V} \leqslant V_x \leqslant +10 \text{ V}, \\ -10 \text{ V} \leqslant V_y \leqslant +10 \text{ V}. \end{cases} \tag{12.28}$$

The value of the current sources I_3 and I_{13} can be determined by applying a known potential to pins 3 and 13, respectively. One should

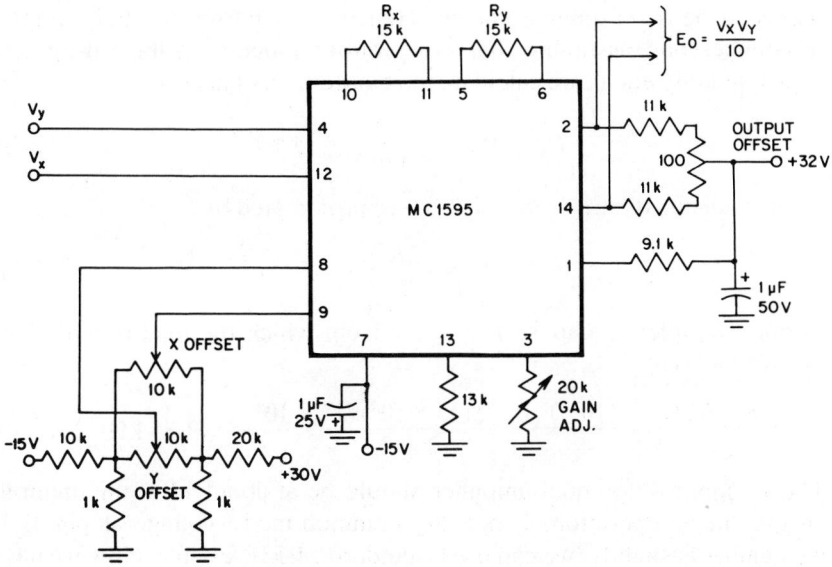

Figure 12.11. Basic test configuration.

select a value of current that will keep the chip power dissipation to an acceptable value and yet maintain operation in a good exponential portion of the diode curve. Values from 0.5 to 2.0 mA are feasible, and we assume a current of 1 mA to illustrate the operation of the device. The exact value of the current sources can be fixed once the voltage of the negative supply has been chosen. A negative supply of −15 V is selected for this mode of operation to allow a −10-V input capability and ensure linear operation in the current-source transistor, while staying within the 30-V maximum rating between any input pin and the negative supply pin (as specified in the data sheet). With $-V_{CC} = -15$ V, we set each of the current sources to 1 mA, by putting a resistor from pin 3 to ground and from pin 13 to ground. The resistor value is calculated as follows:

$$(R + 500\,\Omega)(1\text{ mA}) = (15 - 0.7)\text{ V},$$

$$R = 13.8\text{ k}\Omega. \tag{12.29}$$

Since this is not a critical adjustment, a convenient value is 13 k$\Omega \pm 5\%$, $\frac{1}{4}$ W.

Referring once again to Figure 12.10 and (12.24), (12.25), and (12.26), we see that, to be able to ignore the nonlinear effects that occur when r_e becomes significant with respect to R_E, we must ensure that neither $(I_2 - I_x)$ nor $(I_4 - I_y)$ approaches zero. A value of $\frac{1}{3}$ mA minimum current seems to be a reasonable choice. Hence, by ignoring the bulk emitter resistances and assuming that base-emitter junction voltage drops are approximately equal, we calculate the emitter resistances as

$$R_x = R_y = \frac{10 \text{ V}}{2/3 \text{ mA}} = 15 \text{ k}\Omega. \tag{12.30}$$

The gain constant K from (12.27) is approximated by

$$K = \frac{2R_L}{I_3 R_x R_y}. \tag{12.31}$$

In our example we choose $K = 1/10$, from which the load resistors are each found to be

$$R_L = \frac{K I_3 R_x R_y}{2} = \frac{(10^{-1})(10^{-3})(15 \times 10^3)(15 \times 10^3)}{2} = 11.25 \text{ k}\Omega. \tag{12.32}$$

The V_y-input differential amplifier should be at about 13-V minimum to ensure linear operation; hence the common-mode voltage at pin 1. If we change I_3 slightly, we can use a standard 11-kΩ resistor. Now we have specified everything we need except a common-mode resistor from pin 1 to the positive supply.

With a 10-V input at V_y, the voltage at pin 7 must be about 13.7 V. The 13-V collector potential appears at the bases of the cross-coupled differential pair, where the minimum collector potential for linear operation should be about 16 V. Adding to this the voltage swing seen in the load resistor R_L, the positive supply should be about 32 V. For this supply voltage we can calculate the common-mode resistor R_{CM} to give the required voltage at pin 1:

$$R_{CM} = \frac{(32 = 13.7) \text{ V}}{2 \text{ mA}} = 9.15 \text{ k }\Omega. \tag{12.33}$$

Since the collector potential is not critical, a value of 9.1 k$\Omega \pm 5\%$ is acceptable.

Figure 12.11 shows the complete test configuration, with the component values that we have calculated. One other factor that should be considered is the offset voltage at each input. Offsets can be nulled with two potentiometers, as shown in Figure 12.11. Also there will be some offset at the differential output. This can be nulled with a third potentiometer.

With the test circuit of Figure 12.11, the output of the multiplier is at a common-mode level of about 22 V. One way to avoid the common-mode problem is to ac couple the output.

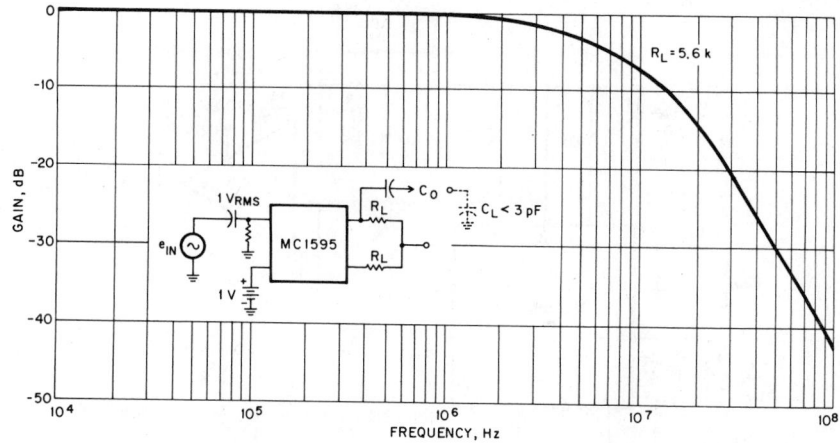

Figure 12.12.   Frequency response of the MC1595 without external amplifiers.

Figure 12.12 shows the basic frequency response of the MC1595 with ac coupling. For the bandwidth measurement one input to the multiplier was a 1-V dc signal, whereas the other input was an ac signal of 1 V rms.

As can be seen in Figure 12.12, the output is 0.1 V rms for frequencies up to 1 MHz. Response is 3 db down at 4.5 MHz and 10 dB down at about 14 MHz. Bandwidth depends on load resistance ($R_L = 5.6 \, \mathrm{k}\Omega$ for the response shown). The frequency-response curve exhibits a single-pole characteristic, with the pole located at about 4.5 MHz.

At this frequency there are 45° of phase shift. Hence the output can be expressed as

$$V_0 = V_x V_y \cos \phi, \tag{12.34}$$

where $V_x = 1.0 \, \mathrm{Vdc}$, $V_y = 1.414 \cos \omega t$, and ϕ is the relative phase shift due to rolloff. A 3° phase shift will cause the output to roll off by about 1%. This 3° phase-error bandwidth is typically specified as 700 kHz. (Phase error is the relative phase shift seen differentially at the outputs.)

As we have already seen, the configuration of Figure 12.11 gives a common-mode output of 22 V. If ac coupling is undesirable, one may wish to add a voltage translator at the multiplier output to shift the level down to a ground reference. Figure 12.13 shows one way of doing this. Here the common-mode voltage is reduced by the 10-to-1 attenuation networks, and the differential output voltage is fed into an operational amplifier that can operate nicely with 2 V common mode. The amplifier has a closed-loop gain of 10. The resulting output is still $(V_x V_y)/10$ and appears single ended about a ground reference. This circuit has the

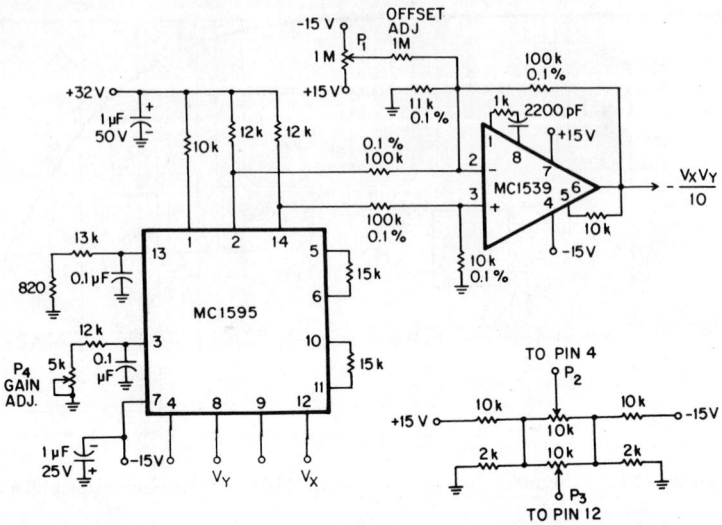

Figure 12.13. Resistive dividers and an external op amp can be added to give an output voltage referenced to ground.

advantage of being rather simple and relatively insensitive to temperature variations.

But the circuit of Figure 12.13 has some disadvantages. The finite slew rate of the operational amplifier limits the frequency response to around 50 kHz for large signal swings (± 10 V). Another disadvantage is the need for a third power supply.

An alternative configuration[4] is shown in Figure 12.14. This circuit uses discrete components to perform the level shifting. Hence it is inexpensive, simple, and can operate at higher frequencies than the operational-amplifier version. (Response of the discrete-component circuit is ultimately limited by the 7.5-kΩ resistor and stray capacitances at the output.) The circuit of Figure 12.14 has the added advantage of operating entirely from ± 15 V supplies.

But this circuit has some disadvantages too. It is somewhat temperature sensitive if the base-emitter junctions of the *npn* and the *pnp* are not matched to track with temperature. This problem can be minimized by using a complementary pair of transistors mounted in a single package (e.g., the Motorola MD6100). A second problem with the level-shifting circuit is that it has a high output impedance and poor current-drive capability. This problem can be solved by using an operational amplifier connected as a source follower, as shown in Figure 12.15.

To summarize: The circuit of Figure 12.13 is recommended for dc operation over a wide temperature range. For ac applications, in which

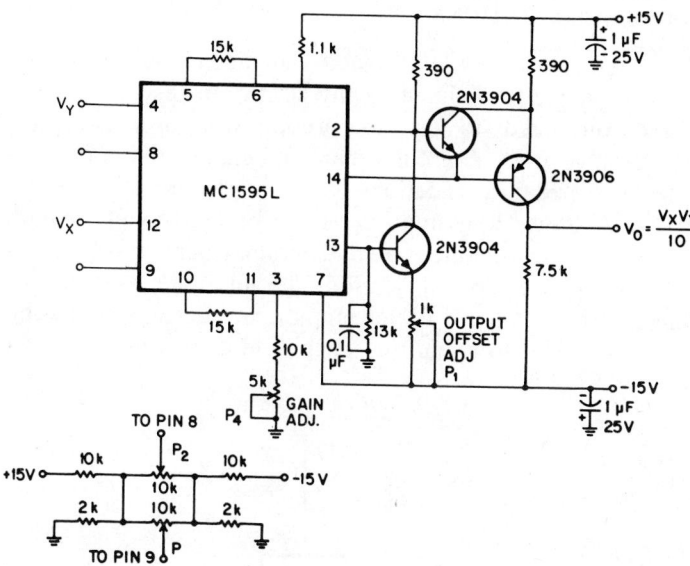

Figure 12.14.   This circuit uses discrete transistors instead of an op amp at the output, hence it offers better frequency response.

the input and output can be capacitively coupled, the circuit shown in Figure 12.14 is preferred. To achieve lower output impedance the circuit of Figure 12.14 can be modified as in Figure 12.15.

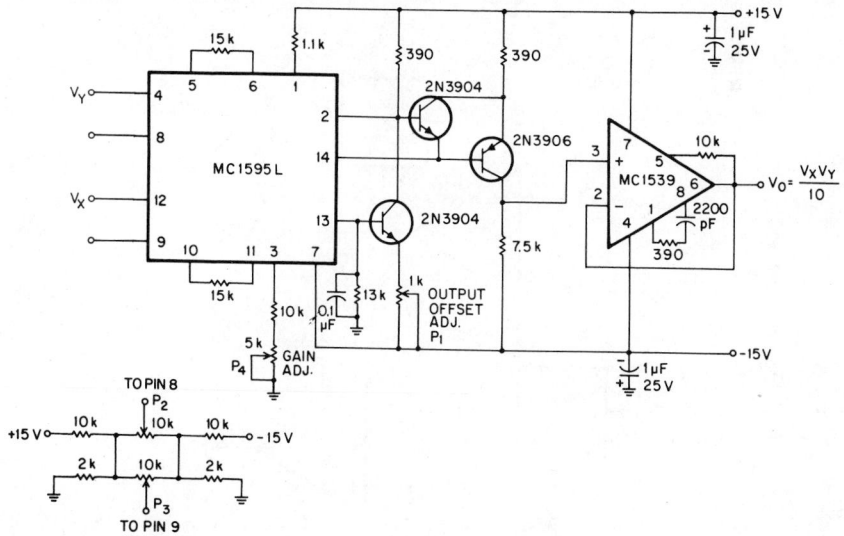

Figure 12.15.   Discrete-component level-shifting circuit with source-follower output.

12.5 SIMPLE APPLICATIONS

Possible applications for a four-quadrant linear multiplier are almost limitless. The device lends itself to any control or instrumentation problem in which one needs to form the product of two or more quantities. Here are a few very basic circuits that can be developed into more complex circuits for specific applications.

Figure 12.16 shows how multipliers can be connected for multiplication, division, finding a square root, and obtaining a mean-square value. In the divide and square-root applications the multiplier is used as a feedback element around an operational amplifier in such a way that the multiplier output is forced to equal the magnitude of the input to the circuit.

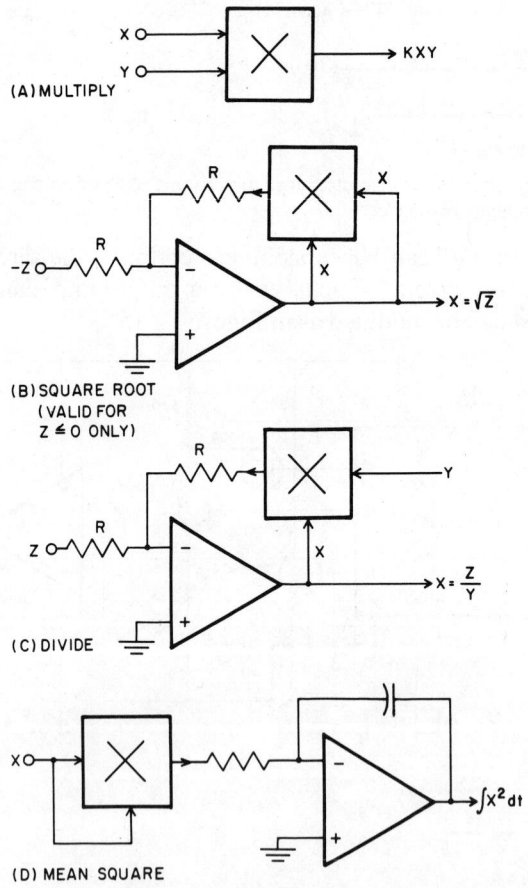

Figure 12.16. Some basic multiplier applications.

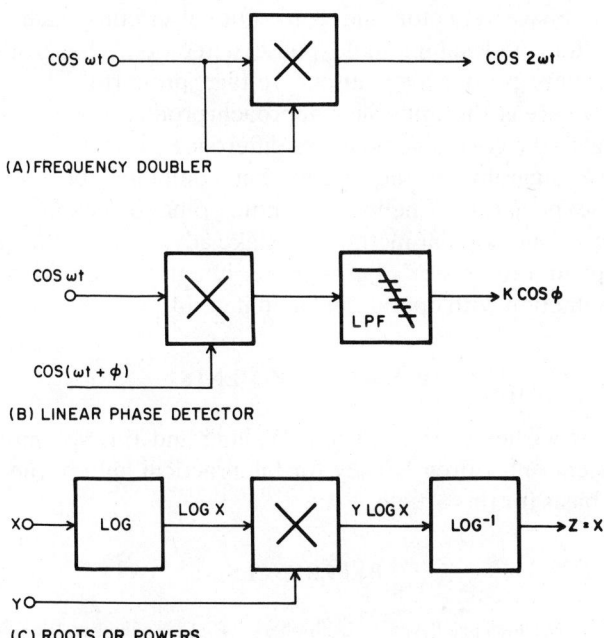

Figure 12.17. More basic applications.

Circuit accuracy will usually be somewhat worse in the divide and square-root modes than in the multiply or square modes. For a multiplication accuracy of 1% of full scale (this means that, if the maximum multiply output is ±10 V, an error of ±0.1 V is obtained regardless of input), the divide error can be several percent of full scale as the divisor decreases below a few volts.

Three additional applications are shown in block diagram form in Figure 12.17. The frequency doubler operates on the principle that

$$(\cos \omega t)^2 = \tfrac{1}{2}(1 + \cos 2\omega t). \tag{12.35}$$

The output signal contains the doubled frequency plus a dc offset component.

The linear phase detector operates on the principle that

$$K \cos \omega t \cos (\omega t + \phi) = \frac{K}{2} \cos (2\omega t + \phi) + \frac{K}{2} \cos \phi. \tag{12.36}$$

With the low-pass filter (LPF), the second harmonic is filtered out, leaving the required $\cos \phi$ signal. There is an important difference between this type of phase detector and conventional circuits such as flip-flop phase detectors and sample-hold phase detectors. These other phase-detector circuits produce an output voltage proportional to the phase difference, whereas the multiplier approach produces an output voltage proportional to the cosine of the phase difference.

The block diagram for the circuit that computes roots or power is largely self-explanatory. The log and antilog functions can be obtained in various ways. One popular method is to take advantage of the exponential relationships in a transistor's base-emitter junction when the transistor is used in conjunction with operational amplifiers [4].

ACKNOWLEDGMENTS

The author wishes to thank Brent Welling and Jim Solomon for their encouragement and Loren Kinsey for his practical help in the work that formed the basis for this article.

REFERENCES

[1] "Special Survey: Packaged Analog Multipliers," *EEE*, November 1968, Vol. 16, No. 11. pp. 80–94.
[2] *Transistor Logarithmic Conversion Using an Integrated Operational Amplifier*, Motorola Application Note AN-261, October, 1968.
[3] Solomon, J. E., "Recent Advances in Space Communications," *Linear Integrated Circuits for Space Applications Series*, Lecture 8, University of California Extension, Los Angeles, Summer, 1968.
[4] Free, M. G., *An Integrated Linear-Transconductance Analog Multiplier*, Thesis for the Degree of Master of Science in Electrical Engineering, University of Arizona, 1969.

13

Multiplexing with Complementary MOS Integrated Circuits

by R. L. Sanquini and A. A. Ahmed

Radio Corporation of America, Somerville, New Jersey

Although the p-type MOS switch is replacing the bipolar-transistor and mechanical-relay counterparts, it will in turn eventually be replaced by the complementary MOS switch because the latter device offers many performance advantages without sacrificing any of the advantages of p-type MOS switches. The advantages of complementary MOS (COS/MOS) switches include the ability to operate with control-signal amplitudes compatible with conventional forms of logic gates, micro power consumption, and minimum transients in the signal output when the channel is switched. This chapter describes a monolithic complementary MOS four-channel multiplexer, developed for switching analog or digital signals in analog-to-digital converters, telemeters, control systems, and multiple-channel data transmissions.

13.1 COS/MOS CONSTRUCTION

The cross-sectional view of the complementary switch shown in Figure 13.1 illustrates the COS/MOS construction. A p-type diffusion forms a so-called well to isolate the n-channel transistor from the p-channel transistor. With zero bias applied from gate to source, few carriers are available for conduction. As the gate-to-source voltage is increased (made

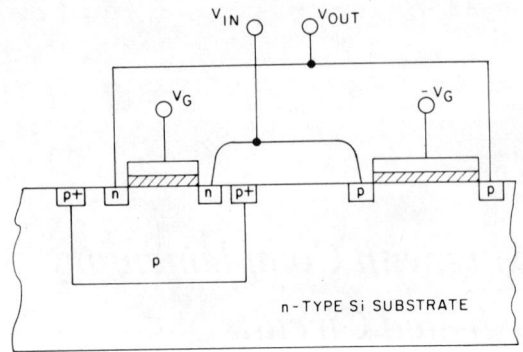

Figure 13.1.   Cross-sectional diagram of complementary MOS switch.

more positive on the *n*-channel units and more negative on the *p*-channel units), charges are induced near the silicon-oxide interface that form an ohmic path between the source and the drain, and current flow increases rapidly.

The COS/MOS process permits design of a multiplexer that operates at conventional logic voltage levels with high absolute noise immunity, good linearity, low "on" resistance, high "off" resistance, and low capacitance.

13.2 BASIC MULTIPLEXER CHANNEL

Each channel of the multiplexer consists of a simple inverter and a switch, as shown in Figure 13.2. The inverter section is shown in Figure 13.3 along with its transfer characteristics. The circuit consists of one *p*-channel and one *n*-channel MOS transistor, both sharing a common drain electrode. When the input is high $(+V)$, the *n*-channel transistor is turned on, the *p*-channel transistor is off, and the output is low. When the input is low, the *n*-channel device is turned off, the *p*-channel device is on, and the output is high.

In either state the power consumed is low (on the order of picowatts) because one of the two devices connected in series is turned off. The small static power dissipation does not change if the circuit is used to drive other insulated-gate stages because the stages draw no average gate current as a result of their extremely high input impedance $(10^{12}\,\Omega)$. During switching, when the capacitance at the output must be charged to the high level through the "on" *p*-channel transistor, some power is dissipated in the *p*-channel unit. The charge stored in the capacitor is dissipated in the *n*-channel transistor when the input becomes high. The dynamic power P required for switching is equal to $C_o V_o^2 f$, where C_o is

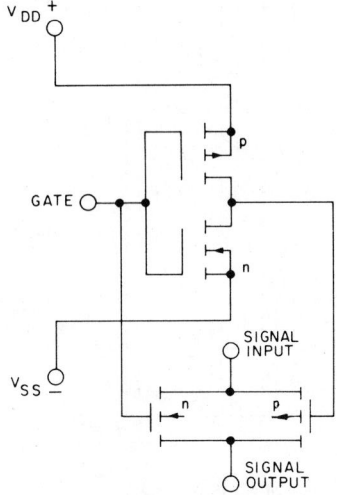

Figure 13.2. Basic multiplexer channel.

the output capacitance in farads, V_o is the supply voltage in volts, and f is the frequency in hertz.

Power dissipation as a function of frequency is shown for the inverter circuit in Figure 13.4.

13.3 *p*-CHANNEL MOS SWITCH

A review of the *p*-channel MOS switch will be helpful in evaluating the COS/MOS multiplexer. An elementary *p*-channel signal switch is shown

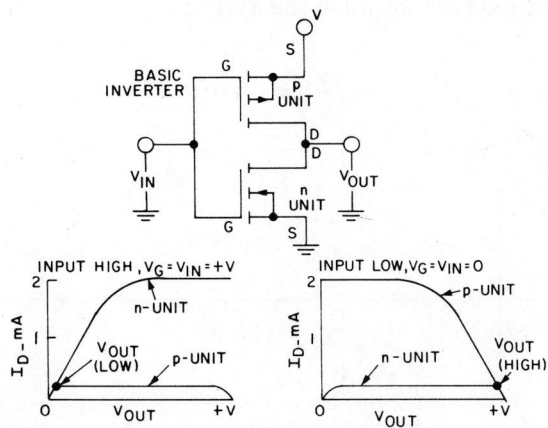

Figure 13.3. Basic MOS inverter circuit and its characteristics.

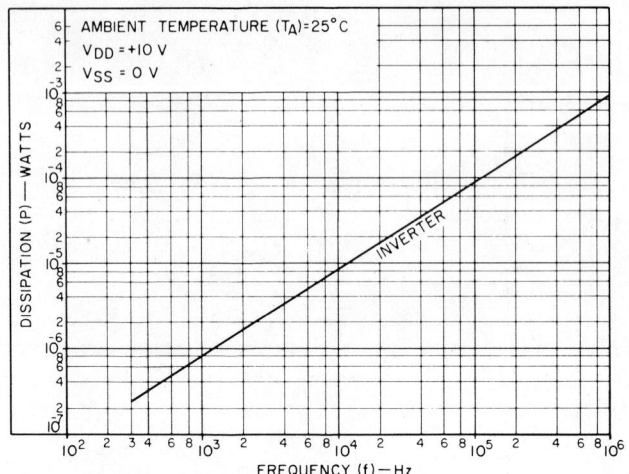

Figure 13.4.   Typical dissipation characteristics of MOS inverter.

in Figure 13.5. When V_{in} is negative, the input terminal becomes the drain, and the device is in the source-follower mode. If the gate is biased to a negative voltage ("on" condition), the channel resistance is low as long as the source remains more positive than the gate by an amount equal to the threshold voltage. This limit sets a boundary condition for the maximum permissible negative signal swing.

When the signal swing is positive, the device remains in the low-channel-resistance condition and operates in the common-source mode. With this polarity the limit is no longer set by the above mechanisms. Both regions of operation are shown in Figure 13.6.

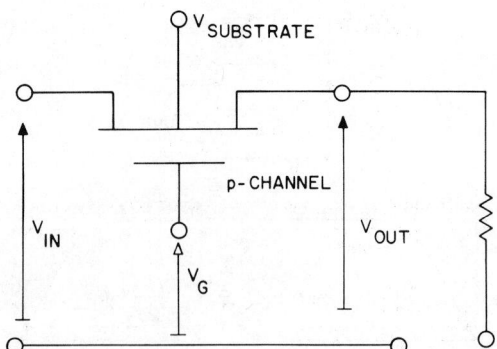

Figure 13.5.   Diagram of *p*-channel MOS switch.

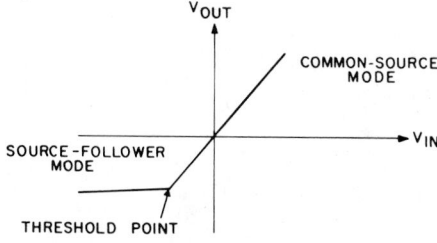

Figure 13.6. Transfer characteristic of *p*-channel switch.

In the "off" condition the gate is set to a positive voltage (on a *p*-channel device) and the channel resistance is high. In the common-source mode the device turns on again when the signal is more positive than the gating signal by an amount equal to the threshold voltage. There is another mechanism, however, by which the device may turn on, involving parasitic bipolar-transistor action with the substrate. (Generally the MOS action occurs first.)

It is clear from the preceding discussion that the signal swing is restricted in one polarity to a voltage considerably lower than that of the gating signal. It is also apparent that any abrupt change in the gating signal produces a transient in the signal path as a result of the gate-channel capacitance. These disadvantages may be largely overcome by the use of a complementary symmetrical system.

13.4 COMPLEMENTARY SWITCH

If complementary *p*- and *n*-channel units are connected in parallel and gating voltages are applied in complementary fashion, the composite characteristics shown in Figure 13.7 are obtained. In this arrangement the transfer characteristic is no longer restricted by the source-follower effect, and the signal may swing up to the gate voltage in both polarities. The "off" condition is subject to the previous limits set by the gating voltages. Because complementary gating is used, the transients in the signal circuit cancel out if the gate-to-channel capacitances in the *p*- and *n*-channel units are equal. These characteristics may be modified to some extent by practical limitations. In the central portion of the transfer characteristic it is apparent that both channels are in parallel. If the load resistance is not large compared with the channel resistances, some variation in the transmission loss may occur over the range. However, this condition is not usually encountered in practice. Another cause of slight nonlinearity in the characteristic is the effect of the substrate on the threshold level. Instead of overlapping, as shown in Figure 13.7, the

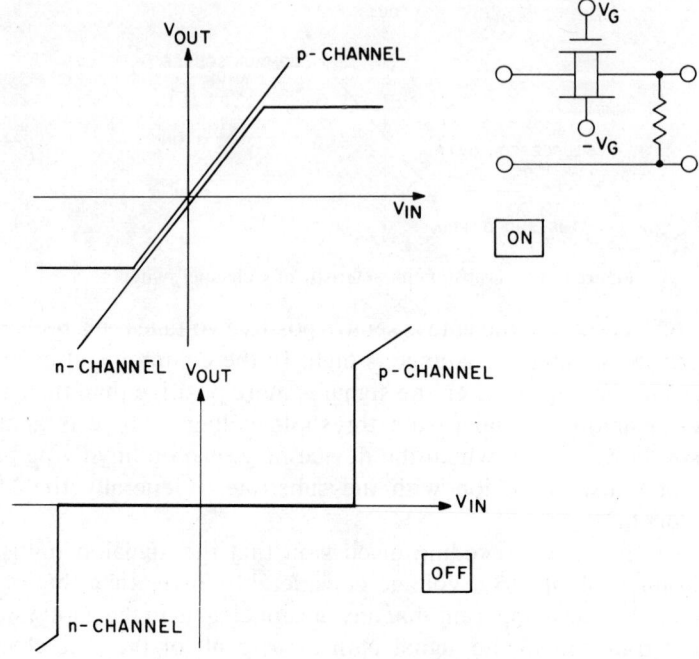

Figure 13.7. Transfer characteristic of COS/MOS switch.

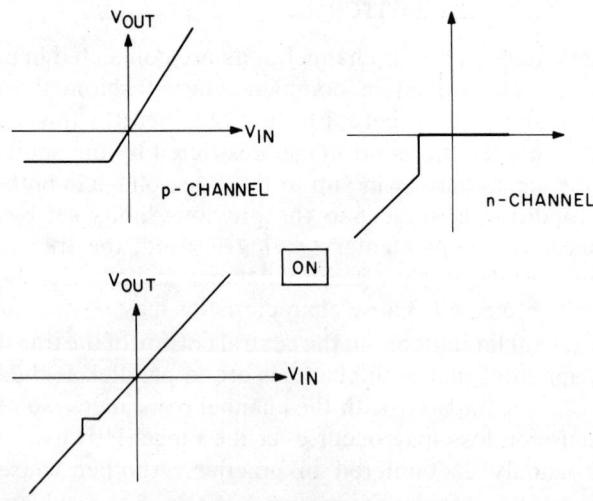

Figure 13.8. Effect of substrate potential on threshold level of COS/MOS switch.

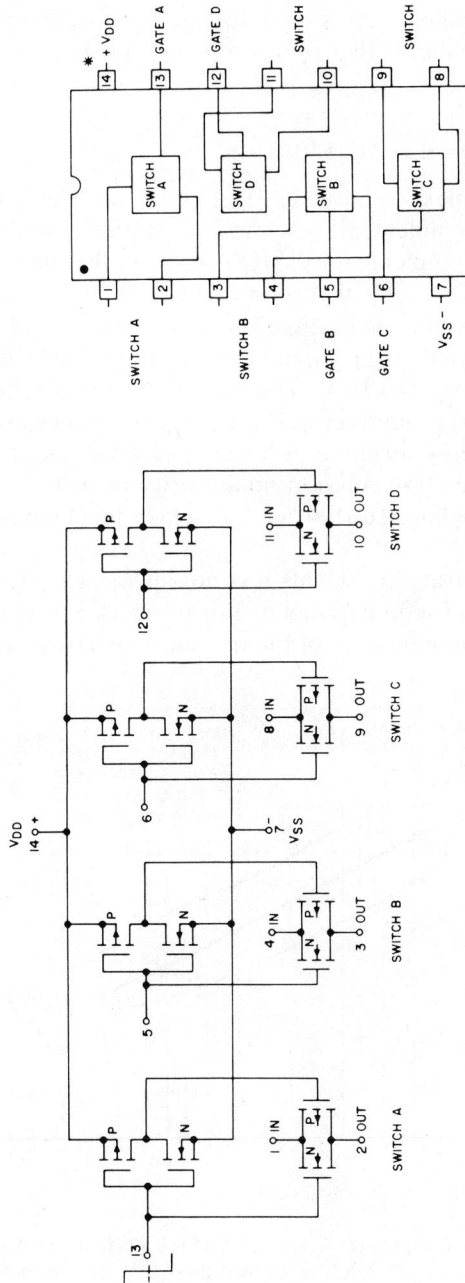

Figure 13.9. TA5460 four-channel COS/MOS multiplexer. Note: All switch *p*-channel substrates are internally connected to terminal 14. All switch *n*-channel substrates are internally connected to terminal 7.

187

characteristics may exhibit a gap, as illustrated in Figure 13.8, as a result of shifting of the threshold levels by substrate action. However, results obtained in practice indicate that this problem is not serious at the levels normally used.

13.5   PERFORMANCE CHARACTERISTICS

The TA5460 multiplexer, shown in Figure 13.9, illustrates some of the advantages of using complementary symmetry MOS in a multiplexer. As in the case of most complementary MOS devices, the quiescent power consumption is very low; typical current drain is 100 nA for all four units on the chip. Perhaps the most significant advantage over single-gate systems is that the signal-swing capability is equal to the switching logic levels, normally ±5 V or 0 to 10 V. The "on" "off" signal ratio, shown in Figure 13.10, obviously improves at lower frequencies because the feed-through is almost purely capacitive. A lower load resistance also increases this ratio but increases transmission nonlinearity as well. For example, with a 10-kΩ load audio distortion is 1%, which is adequate for many applications.

In the case of other analog signals it is not always easy to relate percentage distortion to a useful parameter. For this reason TA5460 devices are characterized for nonlinearity of the transmission characteristic. This

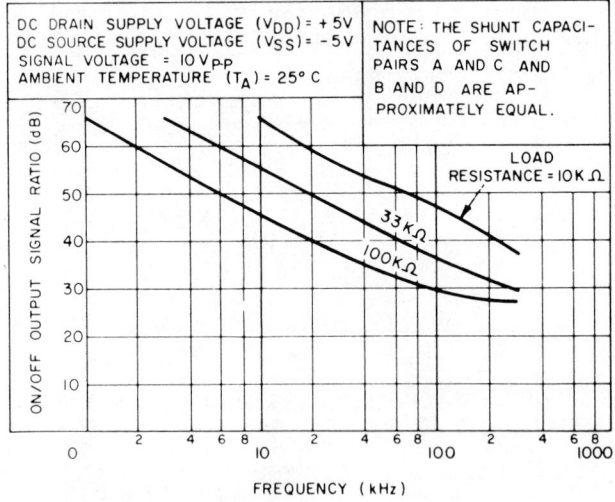

Figure 13.10.   Typical on-off output-signal ratios of TA5460 as a function of signal frequency; $V_{DD} = +5$ V, $V_{ss} = -5$ V, $T_A = 25°C$, signal voltage = 10 V (p = p). Note: The shunt capacities of switch pairs A and C and B and D are approximately equal.

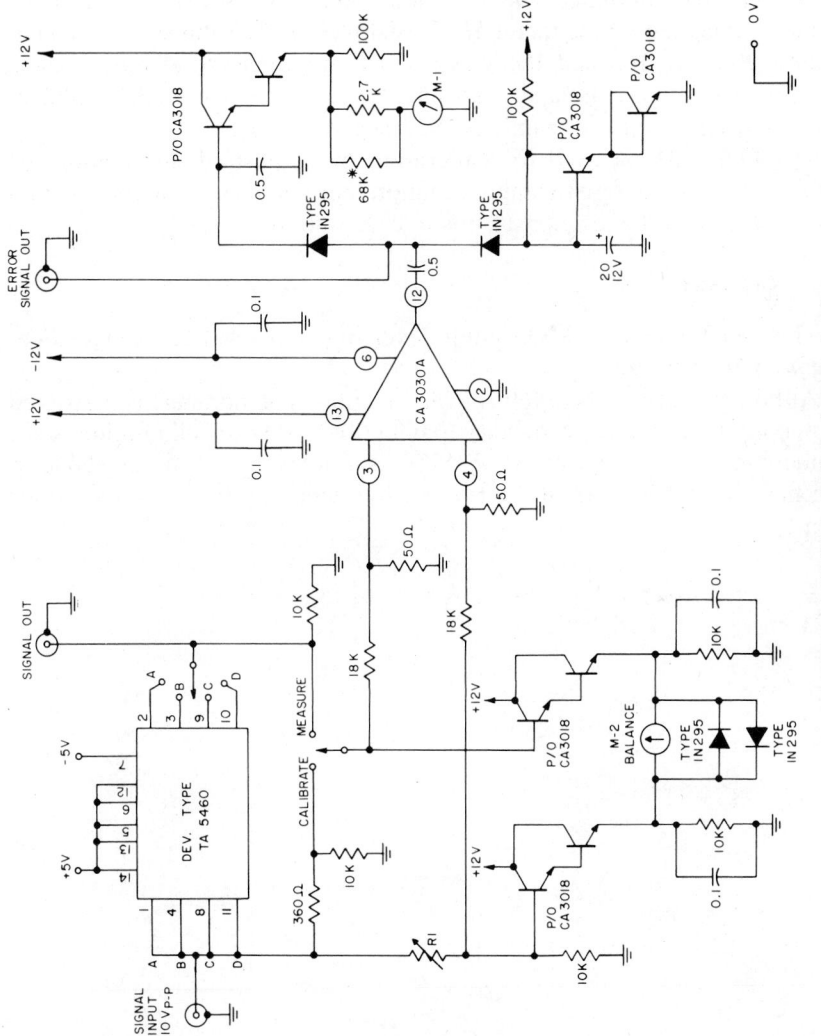

Figure 13.11. Multiplexer linearity test circuit.

nonlinearity is measured as a deviation from an optimum straight-line approximation; the test circuit used is similar to the one shown in Figure 13.11. Basically the transmitted signal is reduced to some extent in amplitude by a voltage divider and is then compared with the input signal. The resulting difference signals are amplified, and the peak negative swing is set to ground potential. The resulting wave is peak detected, and the value is indicated on the meter M_1. Resistor R_1 is then adjusted for a minimum value on M_1, and the value of the minimum total positive and negative deviation from a straight line is read on the meter. The value of R_1 used is equal to the dynamic on-channel resistance.

The meter M_2 is used for calibration or, if desired, for finding the straight-line characteristic approximation that matches the actual characteristic at zero voltage and peak positive excursion.

13.6   SUMMARY

The complementary MOS multiplexer offers several advantages over the p-channel circuit.

Although the No. TA5460 (developmental type number) is restricted in maximum frequency capability to about 0.2 MHz, this limitation is not fundamental to the design. COS/MOS multiplexers will be available in the near future that extent the present frequency by more than an order of magnitude.

14

Voltage-Regulator ICs with Foldback Current Limiting

by Douglas R. Sullivan and Hans W. Mamie

Transitron Electronic Corporation, Wakefield, Massachusetts

Damage by short-circuit power dissipation in a voltage regulator can be avoided if the IC contains an overload-protection circuit with externally programmable foldback characteristics. Foldback current limiting maximizes the output-current capability in the regulated state for a given package power-dissipation rating, while minimizing the available current to a temporarily shorted load.

14.1 DESIGN APPROACHES

There are a number of ways to design a regulator with high-current capability. A popular approach is shown in Figure 14.1. Here a voltage proportional to the output voltage is fed back to the error amplifier through the resistor divider composed of R_1 and R_2. The error amplifier output fed back to the series regulating transistors is at a magnitude that keeps the difference between the feedback voltage and the reference at a minimum, and regulation is achieved.

The principal advantage of the approach shown in Figure 14.1 is simplicity. However, there are a number of performance compromises that are associated with this circuit. These compromises are caused by the use of the resistor divider made up of R_1 and R_2, which is employed to

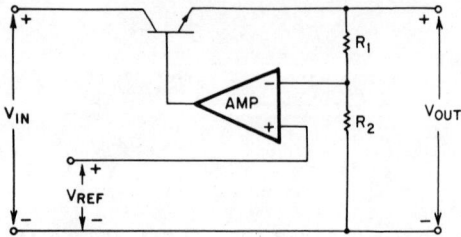

Figure 14.1.   Simple voltage regulator.

set the value of the regulator-output voltage. The loop gain of the regulator is proportional to the resistor-divider ratio, decreasing as the divider ratio is decreased. Therefore, as the desired output voltage is increased, the divider ratio, and therefore the regulator loop gain, is decreased. As the loop gain is decreased, the regulator-output impedance increases, degrading the no-load to full-load regulation characteristics. Along with this effect, one finds that the regulator's bandwidth is also degraded.

Current limiting is usually achieved by adding a resistor in series with the emitter of the output power transistor. The voltage across this resistor is fed to a control transistor, as shown in Figure 14.2. If the output current exceeds a predetermined value, which is programmable by selecting the size of the resistor, R_{SC}, the control transistor is turned on, and as a result the base current available to the output power transistor is limited or reduced. Thus output current limiting is achieved, simply, but not without a compromise in performance.

The chief compromise in using the type of current limiting shown in Figure 14.2 is increased power dissipation. Since the current-sensing resistor R_{SC} is in series with the regulator output, the minimum input-output voltage differential is increased by the current-limiting sense

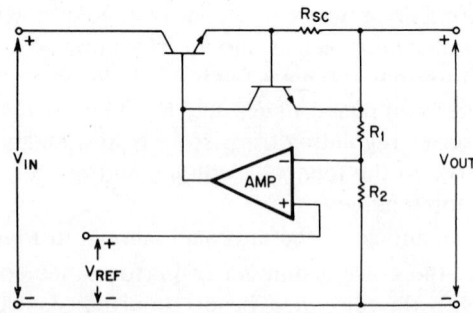

Figure 14.2.   Simple voltage regulator with current limiting.

voltage. This is at least 600 mV and can result in a total circuit-power dissipation, under regulation conditions, that is up to 25% higher than that in cases when no current limiting is employed. Another disadvantage of this design approach is that the current-sensing resistor increases the output impedance of the regulator; especially at higher output voltages where the loop gain is low because of the resistor ratio, $R_2/(R_1 + R_2)$.

An alternative approach to the regulator-circuit design is shown in Figure 14.3. Here the output error amplifier and power transistor are connected as a noninverting amplifier with a gain of 1. Variation of the output voltage setting is achieved by the addition of a reference-level-shifting amplifier whose gain, and hence the regulator-output voltage, is determined by the resistor divider composed of R_1 and R_2. Since the load on the level-shifting amplifier is constant, there is no degradation in the regulation characteristics for different output-voltage settings. The output power amplifier, on the other hand, offers maximum loop gain, minimum output impedance, and wide bandwidth, all of which are constant over the full voltage range of the amplifier.

The resistor R_{SC} in series with the collector of the output transistor is used to sense the output current of the regulator. The voltage across this resistor is fed to additional circuitry such that the base current available to the power transistor is limited and current limiting can be achieved. The addition of this resistor to the circuit does not increase the minimum input-output voltage differential. Current sources and other circuitry common to the output error amplifier account for a voltage drop from the positive supply to the base of the power transistor that far exceeds the 600 mV necessary to drive the current-limit circuitry. All that is needed to take advantage of this voltage drop is a power transistor with a low saturation resistance. Thus no increase in circuit-power dissipation is required, and none of the output parameters of the regulator is degraded by the addition of current limiting.

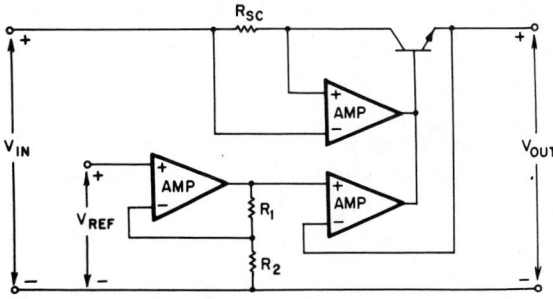

Figure 14.3.   Complex voltage regulator with current limiting.

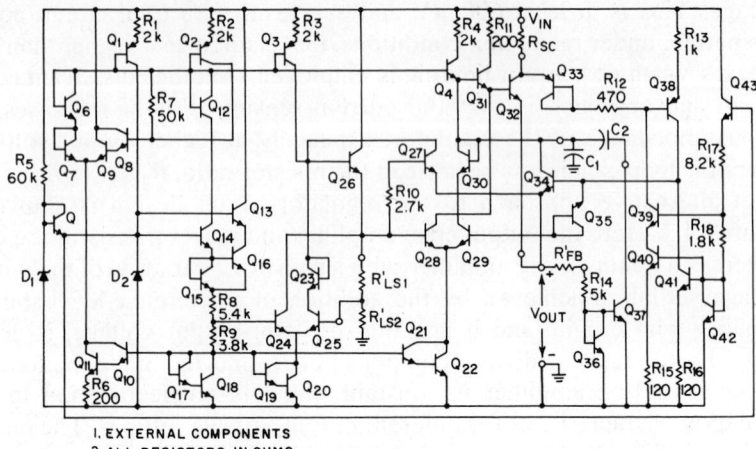

I. EXTERNAL COMPONENTS
2. ALL RESISTORS IN OHMS

Figure 14.4.   The TVR2000 is a monolithic voltage regulator with foldback current limiting.

14.2   CURRENT-LIMITING VOLTAGE REGULATOR

A complete circuit diagram of the TVR2000, a monolithic voltage regulator with foldback current limiting, is shown in Figure 14.4, and the complete functional block diagram is depicted in Figure 14.5. As can be seen in Figure 14.5, the regulator contains a temperature-compensated reference. The reference is level shifted by a noninverting amplifier whose gain is determined by an external resistor divider. The output amplifier is connected as a noninverting amplifier with a gain of 1, and output-

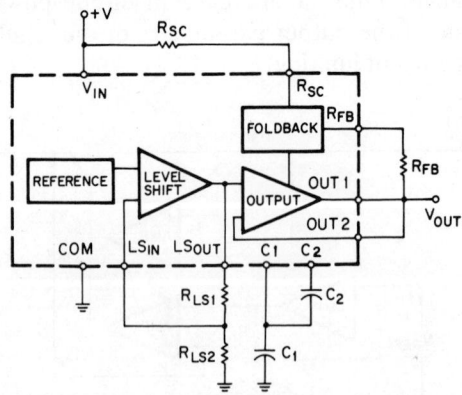

Figure 14.5.   Temperature-compensated reference is level shifted by a noninverting amplifier. Gain of amplifier is determined by external resistor divider.

current sensing for short-circuit current limiting is done on the collector side of the output power transistor. Thus the output characteristics are constant and are independent of the addition of current limiting.

The start circuit is comprised of D_1, R_5, and Q_5. Diode D_2 serves as the main reference and is temperature compensated by Q_{14}, Q_{15}, Q_{17}, Q_{18}, and R_8, and R_9. The voltage at the emitter of Q_{15} has a positive temperature coefficient because of the positive temperature coefficient of D_2 and the negative temperature coefficient of the base-emitter diodes of Q_{14} and Q_{15}. The voltage at the base of Q_{17} has a negative temperature coefficient because of the negative temperature coefficient of the base-emitter diodes of Q_{17} and Q_{18}. Resistors R_8 and R_9 are selected so that the voltage at their common point has a temperature coefficient nearly equal to zero. This voltage is the temperature-compensated reference for the regulator.

The reference diode D_2 and resistor R_8 and R_9 set the current in the matched Darlington *npn* current sources $Q_{17}Q_{18}$, $Q_{19}Q_{20}$, and $Q_{21}Q_{22}$. A current divider is formed by Q_{15} and Q_{16} which sets the current in each of the matched *pnp* current sources Q_1, Q_2, Q_3, and Q_4 at one-half of that in the matched *npn* current sources. This factor of one-half is required because two of the *pnp* current sources, Q_3 and Q_4, are used as collector loads in two differential amplifiers whose emitter current sources are $Q_{19}Q_{20}$ and $Q_{21}Q_{22}$, respectively.

Transistor Q_5 is back biased and turned off as soon as the *pnp* current source Q_1 begins furnishing current to the reference diode D_2. Since Q_1 is matched to Q_2, their collector currents are equal. Neglecting base currents, the collector current of Q_2 is equal to the emitter current of Q_{14}. As already discussed, the collector current of Q_2 is one-half that of the Darlington current source $Q_{17}Q_{18}$, which in turn is proportional to the reference voltage and the resistors R_8 and R_9. Thus the reference diode regulates its own excitation current.

Transistors Q_{24} and Q_{25} form the differential inputs for the reference-level-shifting amplifier. The current source for this differential amplifier is $Q_{19}Q_{20}$. To obtain maximum gain Q_3, a *pnp* current source, is used as the collector load for Q_{25}. Differential drive for the output transistor Q_{26} is provided by connecting its emitter as the collector load for Q_{24}. The closed-loop gain of the reference-level-shifting amplifier is determined by the external resistors R_{LS1} and R_{LS2}. Since this amplifier is connected as a noninverting amplifier, its gain is always greater than or equal to one.

Transistors Q_{28} and Q_{29} provide a balanced input for the output differential amplifier. The design of this amplifier is very similar to that of the level-shifting amplifier, the circuit consisting of a current source $Q_{21}Q_{22}$, a collector load Q_4, and a differentially driven output transistor Q_{31}. The amplifier output transistor Q_{31} and the regulator series-pass, power transistor Q_{32} are connected as a Darlington pair, providing maximum output-current capacity with minimum standby-current drain. Transistor Q_{27} is used to shut down the reference-level-shifting amplifier under regulator-output short-circuit conditions, protecting the base-emitter diodes of Q_{28} and Q_{29}. Stabilization of the output amplifier is achieved by use of the external capacitor C_1.

Current limiting is obtained by turning on the control transistor Q_{34}, diverting some of the base current intended for the Darlington pair Q_{31}-Q_{32}. Availability of base current for the control transistor Q_{34} depends on the relative magnitude of the collector current in Q_{37}, Q_{38}, and Q_{41}. Summation of currents at the base of Q_{34} yields the equation

$$I_{C38} - I_{C37} - I_{C41} = I_{B34} \simeq 0, \qquad (14.1)$$

where I_{C38} is proportional to I_{OUT}, I_{C37} is proportional to V_{OUT}, and I_{C41} is a constant equal to 0.2 mA. The final relationship describing the foldback characteristic is

$$\frac{I_{OUT}R_{SC} + (0.2 \times 10^{-3})(R_{12} + R_{SC})}{R_{12}} - \frac{V_{OUT}}{R_{FB} + R_{14}} - 0.2 \times 10^{-3} = I_{B34} \simeq 0.$$

$$(14.2)$$

Thus for $V_{OUT} = 0$ (short circuit) I_{OUT} is a function of R_{SC}, and the V_{OUT} versus I_{OUT} foldback slope is a linear function of both R_{SC} and R_{FB}. For $R_{FB} = \infty$, the foldback slope is vertical, resulting in straight current limiting without foldback. The equation for straight current limiting is the same as that for the short-circuit current. Substituting values of R_{12} and R_{13} into the foldback relationship above reduces this equation to

$$R_{SC}I_{OUT} \cong 0.1 \text{ V (short circuit)}. \qquad (14.3)$$

Stabilization of the foldback circuitry is accomplished with the external capacitor C_2.

Typical foldback characteristics with a value of R_{SC} of 5 Ω are shown in Figure 14.6. Here $P_{\max}$, the maximum circuit-power dissipation, occurs at the intersection of the foldback curve and $I_{p/2}$ where I_p is the intersection of the V_{IN} line with the desired foldback slope.

A plot of the intersection of V_{IN} and the various foldback slopes, for constant maximum power dissipation, results in the familiar hyperbolic lines. The hyperbolic lines are plotted as a function of the intersection of V_{IN} and the various foldback slopes only for the convenience of peak-power prediction. It must be remembered that this peak power actually occurs at $I_{p/2}$. For short-circuit conditions it is clear that the foldback short-circuit power is less than: (a) the peak power at $I_{p/2}$; (b) the power at

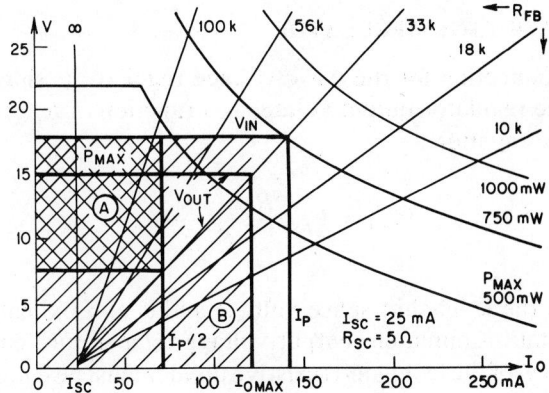

Figure 14.6. Typical foldback characteristics. Maximum circuit-power dissipation occurs at the intersection of the foldback curve and $I_p/2$.

$I_{OUT\,max}$ (regulated state); or (c) the short-circuit power if straight current limiting were employed at $I_{OUT\,max}$.

The circuit design is slanted toward a relatively large active-to-passive component ratio, as evidenced by the component count of 43 transistors, 2 diodes, and 18 resistors. Considerable advantage was derived throughout the circuit from transistor matching, which is inherent in monolithic technology. The monolithic version of the circuit resulted in a chip size of 70 by 85 mils. Important features of the IC are its power transistor with low saturation voltage at a collector current up to 200 mA, a unique lateral *pnp* transistor design, and the use of epitaxial-pinch-resistor technology. Typical electrical characteristics for the TVR2000 are included in Table 14.1.

TABLE 14.1   Characteristics

Maximum power dissipation (TO-100 case)	800 mW
Maximum output current	200 mA
Input-voltage range	8 to 40 V
Output-voltage range ($0 \leqslant I_L \leqslant$ mA)	3 to 37.8 V
Minimum input-output voltage differential ($0 \leqslant I_L \leqslant$ 100 mA)	2.2 V
Output impedance ($0 \leqslant I_L \leqslant$ 100 mA)	40 MΩ
Line regulation ($\Delta V_{IN} = 1$ V)	0.02% V_{OUT}
Level-shift sense voltage	2.8 V
Output-voltage temperature stability	0.003% per °C
Standby-current drain ($V_{IN} = 30$ V)	2.8 mA
Output noise voltage ($0 \leqslant f \leqslant$ 10 kHz)	40 μV rms

14.3 BASIC VOLTAGE REGULATOR

The interconnection for the basic voltage regulator is shown in Figure 14.5. Here the regulator-output voltage is a function of R_{LS1} and R_{LS2} and is given by the equation

$$V_{OUT} = V_{LSS} \frac{R_{LS1} + R_{LS2}}{R_{LS2}}, \tag{14.4}$$

where V_{LSS} is the level-shift sense voltage and is approximately equal to 2.8 V. To obtain a minimum output-voltage temperature coefficient the impedance level of the level-shift resistive divider must be equal to 2.25 kΩ. Therefore the following equation can be formulated:

$$\frac{R_{LS1} R_{LS2}}{R_{LS1} + R_{LS2}} = 2.25 \text{ k}\Omega. \tag{14.5}$$

14.4 FREQUENCY COMPENSATION

External capacitor C_1 stabilizes the regulator section while C_2 is used to stabilize the current-limiting circuitry. When the current-limiting option is not used, so that $R_{SC} = 0$ and the R_{FB} terminal is grounded or left open, C_2 can be eliminated. C_2 can also be eliminated for certain high-capacitance loads. However, if the regulator is to be operated over long leads or from an inductive source, an 0.1-μF decoupling capacitor may be required from the input terminal to ground. Table 14.2 summarizes the recommended values of C_1 and C_2 for various capacitive loadings of the regulator output.

TABLE 14.2 Frequency Compensation

Load Capacitance	Current Limiting	C_1 (pF)	C_2 (pF)
0	No	1000	0
$100 \text{ pF} \leqslant C_L \leqslant 100 \ \mu\text{F}$	No	2000	0
$0 \leqslant C_L \leqslant 1 \ \mu\text{F}$	Yes	5000	1000
$1 \ \mu\text{F} \leqslant C_L \leqslant 20 \ \mu\text{F}$	Yes	$\dfrac{C_L}{100}$	1000
$20 \ \mu\text{F} \leqslant C_L \leqslant 100 \ \mu\text{F}$	Yes	$0.2 \ \mu\text{F} + \dfrac{2C_L}{1000}$	1000
$1 \ \mu\text{F} \leqslant C_L \leqslant 100 \ \mu\text{F}$	Yes	$0.05 \ \mu\text{F}$	0

14.5   CURRENT LIMITING

The short-circuit current is a function of R_{SC}. The equation for the short-circuit current, including transistor beta effects, is

$$I_{OSC} = \frac{120 \text{ mV}}{R_{SC}}. \tag{14.6}$$

The slope of the current-limiting characteristic is a function of R_{SC} and R_{FB}. The slope is vertical when R_{FB} is infinite (open circuit or R_{FB} terminal grounded); when smaller values of R_{FB} are used, foldback current limiting results. The equation for the foldback slope is

$$\text{slope} = \frac{R_{SC}(R_{FB}+5 \text{ k}\Omega)}{1.35 \text{ k}\Omega}. \tag{14.7}$$

It should be noted that, when the output voltage is less than 0.7 V, the slope-control transistor Q_{37} becomes inoperative, causing the slope to be vertical just above I_{SC}. This slight nonlinearity in the foldback slope need be considered only when the ratio of the maximum output current to the short-circuit current is very large. If multivalued operation or hysteresis is to be avoided,

$$\frac{I_{SC}}{0.7 \text{ V}} \geq \frac{I_{\text{OUT max}}}{V_{\text{OUT}}}. \tag{14.8}$$

Of course, for operation over wide temperature ranges the negative 2 mV/°C temperature coefficient of the base-emitter diode of Q_{37} must also be remembered.

The minimum input-output voltage differential specification of 2.2 V applies with or without current limiting as long as the maximum voltage across R_{SC} is limited to 500 mV. This is necessary to prevent saturation of the output transistor. Therefore, for a maximum current of 100 mA, the maximum value of R_{SC} is 5 Ω, which results in a minimum short-circuit current of 24 mA; for a maximum output current of 50 mA the maximum value of R_{SC} is 10 Ω, resulting in a minimum short-circuit current of 12 mA. If larger ratios of maximum output current to minimum short-circuit current of 12 mA. If larger ratios of maximum output current to minimum short-circuit current are required, the user need only provide additional input-output voltage differential. For example, if a short-circuit current of 10 mA and a maximum input current of 100 mA were required, R_{SC} would be 12 Ω and the minimum input-output voltage differential would necessarily be increased by 700 mV to 2.9 V. Thus for ratios of maximum output current to minimum short-circuit current greater than 4:1 the additional input-output voltage differential required is given by the following equation:

$$R_{SC} I_{\text{OUT max}} - 0.5 = V_{\text{diff}} \quad \text{(additional).} \tag{14.9}$$

This equation applies only if the R_{SC}, $I_{\text{OUT max}}$ product is greater than 500 mV.

14.6 CURRENT-EXPANDED POSITIVE REGULATOR

A current-expanded positive voltage regulator is shown in Figure 14.7. In this application foldback current limiting can be employed so that both the regulator and power transistor Q_1 are protected under short-circuit conditions. All of the comments made in discussing current limiting as well as the specifications in Table 14.1 apply, with the additional requirement that the minimum input-output voltage differential be increased by the V_{BE} voltage of the power transistor. The maximum output current is limited only by the beta of the power transistor, whereas the output impedance is reduced by this same beta.

14.7 CURRENT-EXPANDED NEGATIVE REGULATOR

A negative voltage regulator is shown in Figure 14.8. Here the maximum output current is limited only by the beta and the power rating of the transistor Q_1. The regulated output voltage appearing across resistors R_1 and R_2 is determined by the following equation:

$$|V_{\text{OUT}}| = \frac{V_{LSS} (R_1 + R_2)}{R_2}. \tag{14.10}$$

In (14.10) V_{LSS} is the level-shift sense voltage and is approximately equal 2.8 V. Resistor R_{LS} should be set equal to or larger than 2 kΩ to avoid

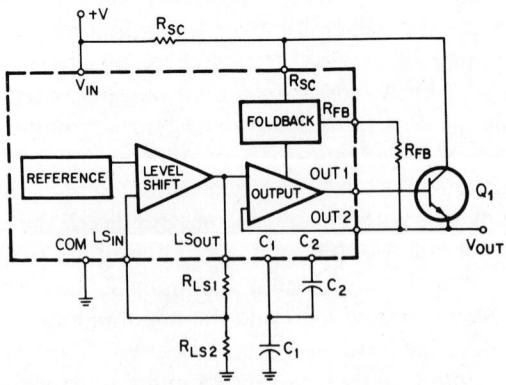

Figure 14.7. Current-expanded positive voltage regulator with foldback current limiting.

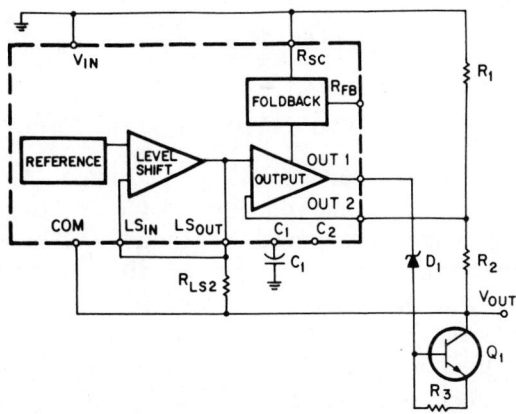

Figure 14.8.   Current-expandable negative voltage regulator.

overloading of the level-shift output, and the impedance level of the parallel combination of R_1 and R_2 should be kept low enough to supply 0.1 mA to the No. 2 output terminal. Absolute value signs are used in (14.9) and succeeding equations to avoid confusion.

The voltage at the No. 1 output terminal must follow the relationship

$$|V_{\text{OUT}\#2}| \geq |V_{\text{OUT}\#1}| \geq |V_{\text{diff}}|, \tag{14.11}$$

where V_{diff} is 2.2 V minimum and $V_{\text{OUT}\#2}$ is given by the equation

$$|V_{\text{OUT}\#2}| = |V_{\text{OUT}}| - |V_{LSS}|. \tag{14.12}$$

In order to meet the requirements set forth in (14.10) and (14.11) the following relationship can be used in selecting the zener diode:

$$|V_{\text{IN}}| + |V_{LSS}| - |V_{\text{OUT}}| - |V_{BE1}| \leq V_Z \leq |V_{\text{IN}}| - |V_{BE1}| - |V_{\text{diff}}|, \tag{14.13}$$

where $V_{LSS} = 2.8$ V, $V_{\text{diff}} = 2.2$ V minimum, and V_{BE1} is the base-emitter voltage for Q_1. If V_Z is centered between the limits established by (14.13), the allowable ripple on V_{IN} will be symmetrical [equal (+) and (−) swings], and the allowable peak-to-peak ripple will be

$$\Delta V_{\text{IN max}} = |V_{\text{OUT}}| - |V_{LSS}| - |V_{\text{diff}}|. \tag{14.14}$$

The output-voltage range is −8 to −40 V since the full regulated output appears across the regulator input to common terminals.

The minimum difference between $-V_{\text{IN}}$ and V_{OUT} is dependent on the saturation voltage of Q_1, whereas the output impedance is given by

$$Z_{\text{OUT}} = \frac{Z_{OR}(R_1 + R_2)}{\beta_1 R_2}, \tag{14.15}$$

where Z_{OR} is the output impedance of the basic regulator and β_1 is the current gain of Q_1.

14.8 CURRENT-EXPANDED NEGATIVE FLOATING REGULATOR

The negative voltage regulator shown in Figure 14.8 can be easily converted to a negative floating voltage regulator, as shown in Figure 14.9. The only extra components needed are R_4 and D_2. The voltage rating of the zener diode D_2 must be between 8 and 40 V, and R_4 must be small enough to supply (a) the regulator standby current of 4 mA, (b) the zener diode D_2 excitation current, and (c) the base current for Q_1. The output current is limited only by the beta and power rating of Q_1. All of the other considerations mentioned in the negative-voltage-regulator discussion apply here.

14.9 POSITIVE FLOATING REGULATOR

A positive floating voltage regulator is shown in Figure 14.10. In this circuit Q_1 compensates for the base-emitter diode of Q_2 so that the voltage across R_1 is equal to the voltage across the level-shifting resistors R_{LS1} and R_{LS2}. This voltage is simply the level-shifted reference voltage as measured with respect to the regulator common terminal and is given by the equation

$$V_{R1} = \frac{V_{LSS}(R_{LS1} + R_{LS2})}{R_{LS2}}, \tag{14.16}$$

where V_{LSS} is the 2.8-V level-shift sense voltage.

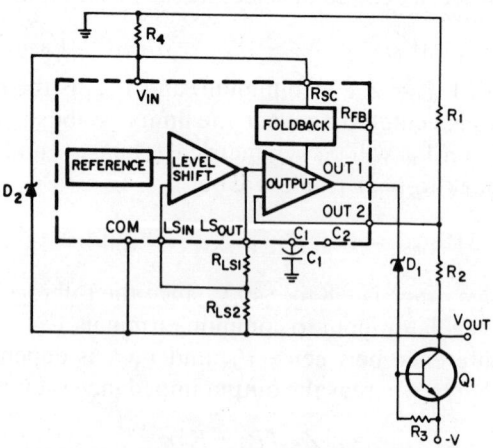

Figure 14.9. Current-expandable negative floating voltage regulator.

The current through R_2 is essentially equal to that through R_1 if the base current of Q_2 is neglected, and the voltage across R_2 plus the V_{BE} of Q_1 equals the voltage at which the common terminal of the regulator will float. Therefore the output voltage is determined by

$$V_{OUT} = \frac{V_{LSS}(R_{LS1}+R_{LS2})(R_1+R_2)}{R_{LS2}R_1}. \qquad (14.17)$$

The output-voltage range is unlimited except that the output voltage must be at least 2.2 V below the input voltage and 3 V above the voltage at the regulator common terminal. As in the basic voltage regulator, the voltage from the V_{IN} terminal to the common terminal must be between 8 and 40 V.

14.10   CURRENT-EXPANDED POSITIVE FLOATING REGULATOR

A current-expanded positive floating voltage regulator is shown in Figure 14.11. Voltage regulator No. 1 regulates the difference between $V_{OUT\#2}$ and V_{OUT}. This voltage difference is given by

$$V_{OUT\#2} - V_{OUT} = \frac{V_{LSS}(R_{LS1}+R_{LS2})}{R_{LS2}}. \qquad (14.18)$$

Voltage regulator No. 2 regulates $V_{OUT\#2}$ (to ground), which is given by the equation

$$V_{OUT\#2} = \frac{(V_{OUT}+V_{LSS})(R_{LS3}+R_{LS4})}{R_{LS4}}. \qquad (14.19)$$

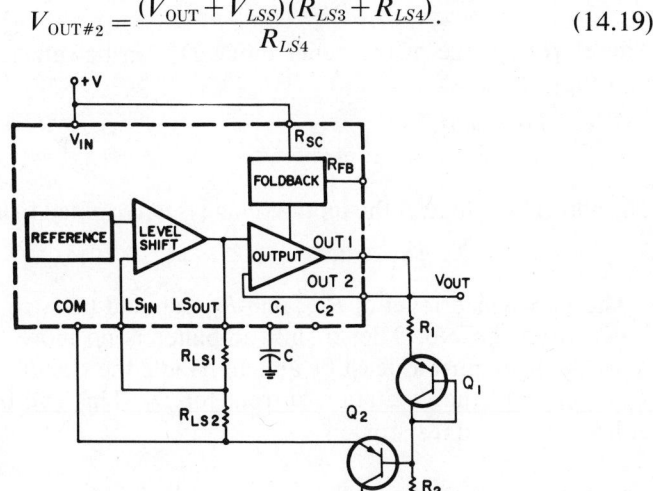

Figure 14.10.   Positive floating voltage regulator.

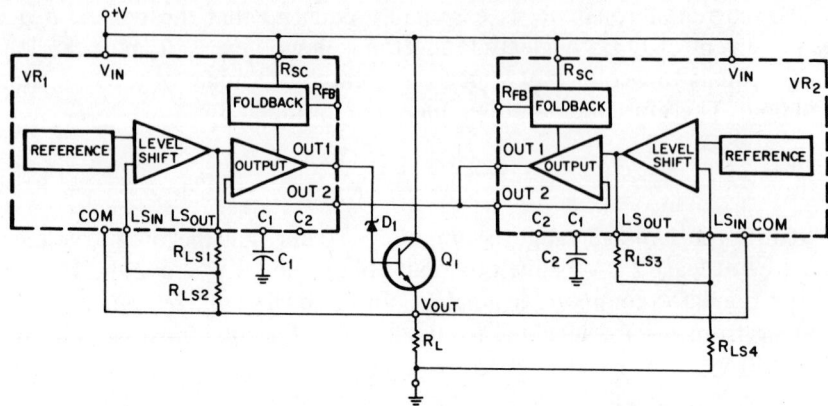

Figure 14.11.   Current-expandable positive floating voltage regulator.

Combining (14.18) and (14.19) produces the final equation for the output voltage:

$$V_{\mathrm{OUT}} = \frac{V_{LSS}R_{LS4}}{R_{LS3}}\left(\frac{R_{LS1}+R_{LS2}}{R_{LS2}} - \frac{R_{LS3}+R_{LS4}}{R_{LS4}}\right) \qquad (14.20)$$

The limits of $V_{\mathrm{OUT\#1}}$ for regulator No. 1 are given in the relationship

$$V_{\mathrm{OUT}} + \frac{V_{LSS}(R_{LS1}+R_{LS2})}{R_{LS2}} \le V_{\mathrm{OUT\#1}} \le V_{\mathrm{IN}} - V_{\mathrm{diff}}. \qquad (14.21)$$

Therefore the size of the zener diode D_1 can be selected from the relationship

$$\frac{V_{LSS}(R_{LS1}+R_{LS2})}{R_{LS2}} - V_{BE1} \le V_Z \le V_{\mathrm{IN}} - V_{\mathrm{OUT}} - V_{BE1} - V_{\mathrm{diff}}. \qquad (14.22)$$

The allowable range of the input voltage is determined from

$$V_{\mathrm{OUT}} + 8\text{ V} \le V_{\mathrm{IN}} \le V_{\mathrm{OUT}} + 40\text{ V}. \qquad (14.23)$$

The impedance level of R_{LS3} and R_{LS4} should be such that the current drawn from the No. 2 level-shift amplifier is no more than 2 mA. The minimum load must at least be able to handle the standby current of both regulators and the excitation current for D_1. This can be accomplished with a small bleed resistor.

14.11 REMOTE SHUTDOWN REGULATOR

Figure 14.12 shows a voltage regulator with foldback current limiting in an application where the output voltage can be shut down by an

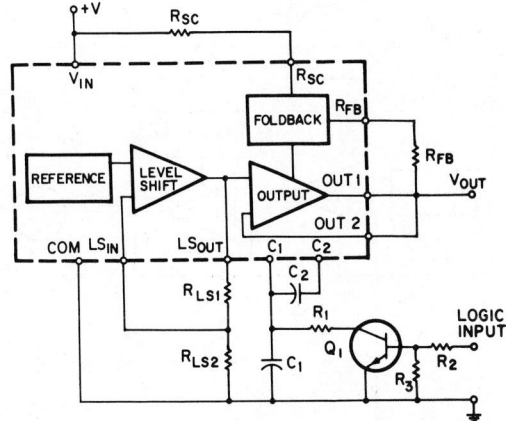

Figure 14.12. Remote shutdown voltage regulator with foldback current limiting.

external command. The output of the regulator will remain essentially at zero as long as there is a positive voltage at the logic input. Resistor R_1 is included in the circuit to limit the spike current resulting from the discharging of the capacitor C_1 and can have a value up to 1 kΩ. Resistors R_2 and R_3 should be so selected that transistor Q_1 is saturated and can support a collector current greater than 0.5 mA when the logic input is high.

14.12 EXTERNAL REFERENCE REGULATOR

In some applications it is desirable to run the voltage regulator with an external reference voltage, as shown in Figure 14.13. Connecting a number of regulators to the same external reference will produce a system in which all of the regulator-output voltages are very nearly equal (approximately 5-mV maximum difference). Since the internal reference and level-shifting-amplifier temperature coefficients are eliminated, the various regulator outputs will have very low temperature coefficients and will track well. Also thermal feedback effects resulting from changes in load currents are minimized.

The zener diode D_1 is included to protect the base-emitter diodes of the level-shift amplifier when the external reference voltage is greater than 7 V, whereas R_2 limits the current to D_1. For values of external reference voltage less than 7 V the zener diode can be eliminated and R_2 can be shorted. The required current drain from the external reference voltage is approximately 0.5 mA.

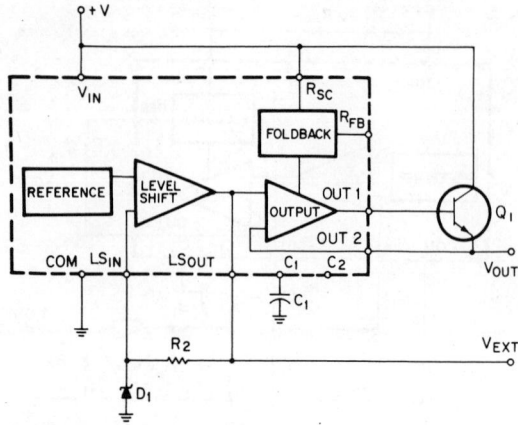

Figure 14.13. External reference regulator.

14.13 SWITCHING REGULATOR

The requirement for high output current in the presence of a large input-output voltage differential results in excess power dissipation and low efficiency. Power dissipation can be reduced and the efficiency can be increased by using a switching regulator similar to that shown in Figure 14.14. Here the output transistor Q_1 is switched on and off, under the control of the TVR2000 regulator. During the period that Q_1 is saturated energy is stored in the inductor L_1 and the capacitor C_3, as well as being supplied to the load. During the period that Q_1 is off the energy stored in L_1 and C_3 is used to energize the load, with D_1

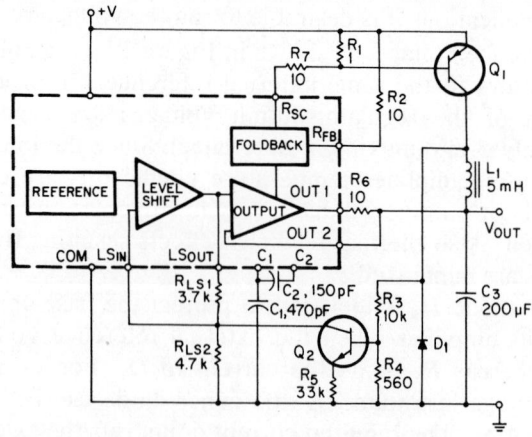

Figure 14.14. High-efficiency switching regulator.

being used as a return path for the current. Since energy is transferred to the inductor L_1 only when Q_1 is saturated, the circuit is very efficient.

In the circuit of Figure 14.14 the drive for the output transistor comes from the R_{SC} terminal of the regulator, which is the collector of the internal power transistor. The current at this terminal is switched on and off by causing a small square wave to appear at the output of the level-shift amplifier. This is accomplished by connecting the level-shift amplifier in the usual manner with R_{LS1} and R_{LS2} selected to set the desired output voltage, and using Q_1 to sink a square wave of current from the R_{LS1}, R_{LS2} common point. Since this point is the feedback point for the level-shift amplifier, its voltage is held constant at 2.8 V. Therefore the square wave of current from Q_2 must flow through R_{LS1}, causing a square wave of voltage to appear at the level-shift output terminal, which is also an input to the output amplifier, and the square-wave voltage that appears there will control the current in R_7 and therefore the transistor Q_1.

Transistor Q_2, in conjunction with R_3, R_4, and R_5, is used to determine the magnitude of the current through R_{LS1}, which should be set to produce at least a 10-mV square wave at the output of the level-shift amplifier. Connecting R_3 to the collector of Q_1 results in the proper feedback polarity for oscillation to take place. Excess storage time in the switching transistor Q_1 can be limited by carefully selecting the base current so that the overdrive is not too large. Constant overdrive for Q_1 is achieved with the internal foldback circuitry. The magnitude of the base current of Q_1, and therefore its overdrive, is determined by the selection of R_2 and R_7. The relationship for I_{B1} for various values of R_2 and R_7 is

$$I_{B1} = \frac{V_{IN}[1 \text{ k}\Omega/(R_2 + 5 \text{ k}\Omega)] + 0.2 \text{ V} - V_{BE1}}{R_7} \qquad (14.24)$$

where the 1-kΩ, 5-kΩ, and 0.2-V parameters are internal to the regulator.

Resistor R_6 is used to isolate the regulator from the heavy capacitive loading so that minimum compensation can be used. Minimizing the compensation maximizes the switching frequencies that can be obtained with good efficiency. The switching frequency is a function of L_1, C_3, V_{IN}, V_{OUT}, and ΔV_{OUT}, the output ripple. The relationships for switching frequency are given in the following equations:

$$f = \frac{1}{t_{on} + t_{off}}, \qquad (14.25)$$

$$t_{on} = \left(\frac{2L_1 C_3 \Delta V_{OUT}}{V_{IN} - V_{OUT}} \right)^{1/2}, \qquad (14.26)$$

$$t_{off} = \left(\frac{2L_1 C_3 \Delta V_{OUT}}{V_{OUT}} \right)^{1/2}. \qquad (14.27)$$

The measured characteristics for the switching regulator shown in Figure 14.14 are given in Table 14.3.

TABLE 14.3   Switching-Regulator Performance

V_{IN}	15 V
V_{OUT}	5 V
I_{load}	1 A
Efficiency	75%
$V_{LS\,OUT}$ (ripple)	30 mV peak to peak
V_{OUT} (ripple)	40 mV peak to peak
Frquency	4.5 kHz
Load regulation (no load to full load)	50 mV
Line regulation ($V_{IN} = 1V$)	7.5 mV

14.14   CONCLUSIONS

Important characteristics for a monolithic voltage regulator to have are the following:

1. Efficiency.   The 2.2-V minimum input-output voltage differential of the TVR2000 is one of the lowest available. The fact that this specification applies even with current limiting further enhances its importance. The 8-V minimum input-voltage range is also one of the lowest available, providing for high efficiency in low-voltage applications.

2. Constant Output Characteristics.   The addition to a voltage-regulator IC of a reference level-shift amplifier and the connection of the output amplifier as a unity-gain connection, result in output characteristics that are constant over the full voltage range of the regulator. Output parameters should not be degraded by current limiting.

3. Foldback Current Limiting.   Full advantage can be taken of the package power-dissipation rating if the IC allows selecting the type of current limiting best suited for the application. The current-limiting option can also be used when the regulator is expanded with an external power transistor.

4. Versatility.   The TVR2000, for example, can be used in a number of different applications, including plus or minus regulator, plus or minus floating regulator, switching regulator, or remote-shutdown regulator.

In selecting a voltage-regulator IC the user should closely examine the electrical characteristics to make sure that electrical performance is not being sacrificed for efficiency or versatility.

15

Integrated Voltage Regulators

by Edward L. Renschler

Motorola Semiconductor Products, Phoenix, Arizona

Until recently monolithic ICs have been limited mainly to applications that do not require large output powers. However, with the advance of IC technology, these old barriers are starting to come down. Motorola's new IC voltage regulators, the MC1560 and the MC1561, are a good example of the new trend. Though there have been a number of hybrid and IC voltage regulators on the market since 1967, most of these have been quite limited in both regulation performance and load-current capability (often less than 40 mA) without the use of external power transistors. The MC1560 and the MC1561, however, are among the first of a new breed of monolithic regulators offering excellent performance, self-contained high-current capability, and exceptional versatility.

Motorola's voltage regulators are available in two packages. The "G" designation indicates the 10-pin TO-5 can (case 71A), and the "R" designation refers to a new 9-pin TO-66 power package (case 614) which Motorola has introduced to the industry for power IC products. The data sheets give the physical dimensions and pin layouts of these packages.

A comparison of the data sheets for the MC1560 and the MC1561 shows that they are identical circuits, the only difference being that the MC1561 exhibits a higher voltage-breakdown characteristic than the MC1560.

Since the devices are identical, everything said about the MC1560 will apply to the MC1561; therefore only the MC1560 is detailed in this chapter. Both regulators are specified over the full military temperature range (−55 to +125°C). Also available are the industrial versions (0 to 75°C), the MC1460 and MC1461; these also are available in both the "R" and "G" packages.

A photomicrograph of the MC1560 voltage-regulator die is shown in Figure 15.1.

15.1 DESIGN FEATURES

As shown in the functional diagram of Figure 15.2, the IC regulator is composed of three main sections: (a) a zero-temperature coefficient (zero-TC) reference-voltage (V_R) generator, (b) a dc level-shifting series voltage regulator, and (c) a unity-gain output series voltage regulator.

The design of the MC1560 regulator is novel in that it eliminates the usual compromises between the ac and dc performance that must be made when only one feedback amplifier is used. These functions have been separately optimized by using a "regulator-within-a-regulator" approach [1].

Also, the unity-gain main regulator provides performance characteristics essentially independent of the dc output voltage. This feedback amplifier is frequency compensated by using a capacitor across the load. This does not restrict the frequency response of the output impedance.

The output impedance of conventional voltage regulators is actively

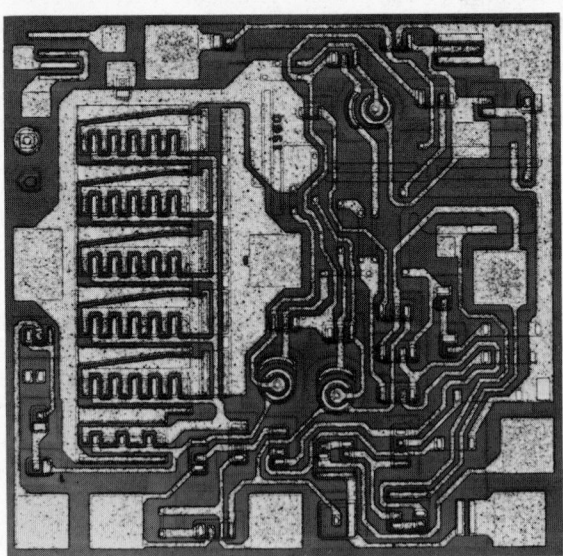

Figure 15.1.   Chip photograph.

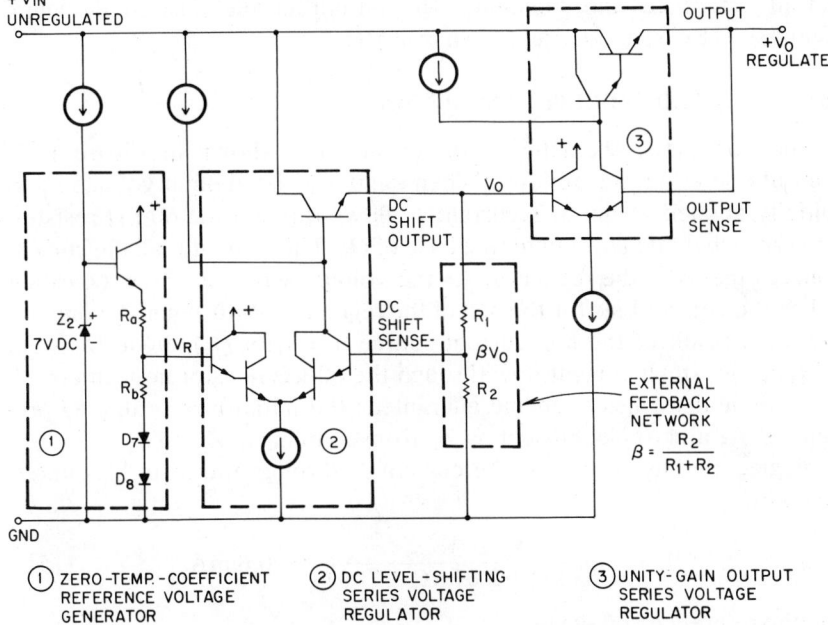

Figure 15.2. Regulator block diagram.

maintained low, typically from dc to 100 Hz or, at most, to a few kilo-
hertz. As shown in a curve on the data sheet, the output impedance of the
MC1560/61 is only 0.06 Ω at 1 MHz.

The temperature-compensated reference voltage V_R is developed on
the monolithic chip by using two resistors, R_a and R_b, to balance the
positive temperature coefficient of the zener reference diode Z_2 against
the negative temperature coefficient of a pair of forward-biased diodes,
D_7 and D_8. This voltage is used as the reference for the dc-level-shifting
series voltage regulator which acts to maintain $\beta V_0 = V_R$ as shown in
Figure 15.2. Two external resistors, R_1 and R_2, are used to establish the
output voltage as given by

$$V_0 = \left(1 + \frac{R_1}{R_2}\right) V_R \qquad (15.1)$$

and β is given by

$$\beta = \frac{R_2}{R_1 + R_2}. \qquad (15.2)$$

The output of the dc-shifting regulator is used as the reference voltage
for the unity-gain output series voltage-regulator stage.

This second regulator directly compares the output voltage with the output reference and maintains the output at the desired dc level, established by R_1 and R_2, as shown in (15.1).

15.2 DETAILED CIRCUIT DESCRIPTION

The complete schematic of the regulator is shown in Figure 15.3. Circuit operation is as follows: When the unregulated input voltage V_{IN} is initially applied to pin 3, a current I_A flows through the 60-kΩ resistor, and through diode D_1, to enter the base of Q_9. This activates all the current sources that bias the regulator. As the voltage across Z_2 rises, Q_9 establishes the correct bias for the rest of the regulator. With zener Z_2 conducting (as a result of the *pnp* current-source transistor Q_1), diode D_1 is cut off, and the small current flow through the 60-kΩ resistor now enters Z_1. This diode-disconnect scheme guarantees the initial bias setup and prevents noise and ripple, present on Z_1, from coupling to Z_2.

Neglecting base currents, the current I_1 through the main bias line is given by

$$I_1 = \frac{V_{Z_2} - 3V_{BE}}{4.63 \text{ k}\Omega + 2.67 \text{ k}\Omega + 700 \text{ }\Omega} \simeq 0.6 \text{ mA} \tag{15.3}$$

and the reference voltage is

$$V_R = V_{Z_2} - V_{BE_9} - (4.63 \text{ k}\Omega)I_1 = 7.0 \text{ V} - 0.7 \text{ V} - (4.63 \text{ k}\Omega)(0.6 \text{ mA})$$
$$= 3.5 \text{ V}. \tag{15.4}$$

Two diodes are used in the zero-TC network to achieve the added advantage that current I_1 is also temperature stabilized — even though diffused resistors are used in the IC. This zero-TC reference current establishes all current biasing in the regulator.

The *pnp/npn* composite transistors, Q_1 through Q_6, which act as constant-current sources, are also referenced to I_1. The voltage reference for these sources is set up at the collector of Q_9 by the constant current, $\alpha I_1 \simeq I_1$, drawn through the 834-Ω resistor by Q_9. This guarantees that all the current sources have zero TC, and, further, that the current sources track to prevent voltage offsets in the differential amplifier, should small temperature-induced changes exist in the zero-TC current references I_1.

The Darlington-pair transistors, Q_{14} through Q_{17}, provide a high-input-impedance differential amplifier. Reference voltage V_R at the base of Q_{14} is compared with the voltage at the base of Q_{17} (pin 8), the "dc-shift-sense" input. Under normal operation pin 6 is directly tied to pin 9, and the output-voltage-adjusting resistors, R_1 and R_2, are placed between pin 9, pin 8, and ground. Thus the output of the dc-shifting series voltage regulator is applied to the base of Q_{12} and provides the reference voltage for the output differential amplifier (Q_{12} and Q_{13}). Diode D_2 protects the

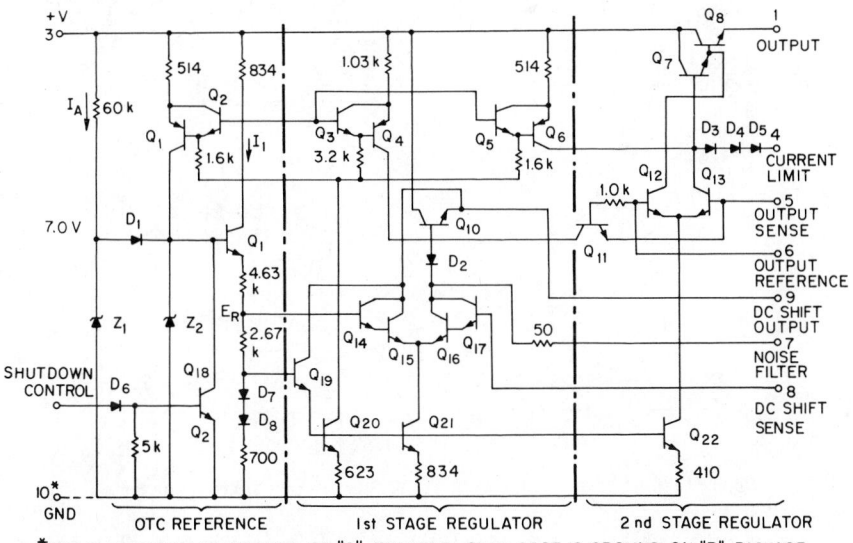

Figure 15.3. Complete circuit diagram for the voltage regulator.

regulator against the discharge of the noise-filter capacitor C_N when the regulator is shut down. Normally pin 5 (the output sense) is directly tied to the output, so that the output voltage is compared with the output reference voltage that has been applied to the base of Q_{12}. Transistor Q_{11} provides protection for the differential amplifier (Q_{12} and Q_{13}) when the output of the regulator is short circuited. Normally Q_{11} is cut off. However, when pin 5 is grounded, transistor Q_{11} conducts and prevents a reverse-bias breakdown of the base-emitter junction of transistor Q_{13}.

Transistors Q_7 and Q_8 form a Darlington series-pass output device, which is designed with large geometry to allow for high-current-handling capabilities.

Diodes D_3, D_4, and D_5 are for short-circuited or overcurrent protection. This is accomplished as shown in the circuit of Figure 15.4. The diode string is forward biased when the load current creates a drop of approximately V_{BE} across R_{SC}.

This diverts the base-current drive through the diodes and therefore limits the maximum output current. For small load currents, where the forward drop of the Darlington pair is not excessive, I_{SC} is given by

$$I_{SC} = \frac{V_{BE}}{R_{SC}} \simeq \frac{0.6 \text{ V}}{R_{SC}} \quad (25°C). \quad (15.5)$$

Diode D_6 and transistor Q_{18} of Figure 15.3 form the MC1560's "shutdown control." When the voltage at pin 2 exceeds $2V_{BE}$ above the

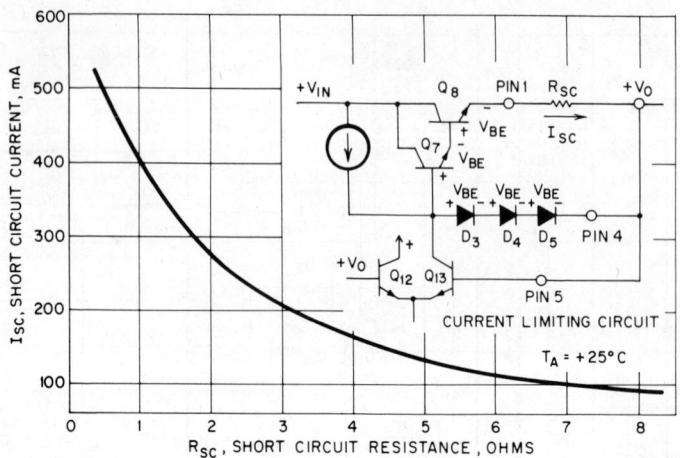

Figure 15.4.   Short-circuit current I_{SC} versus short circuit resistance R_{SC}.

potential on pin 10, D_6 is forward biased and Q_{18} conducts. The current previously flowing through zener Z_2 is shunted through Q_{18}; thus the bias is removed from the rest of the circuit and the regulator shuts down. In this shutdown mode the regulator draws only a standby current, established by $V_{IN}/60$ kΩ (i.e., 300 μA for a 20-V input). When driving pin 2, one must ensure that the drive current into pin 2 never exceeds 10 mA, its maximum rating; a current of 1 mA is adequate to guarantee shutdown.

The MC1560 and the MC1561 voltage regulators combine advanced circuit design with conventional all-diffused processing technology to provide the performance outlined in Table 15.1.

TABLE 15.1   Regulator Performance

	MC1560	MC1561
Output-voltage range	+2.5 V to +17 Vdc	+2.5 V to +37.0 Vdc
Input-voltage range	+8.5 V to +20 Vdc	+8.5 V to +40.0 Vdc
Required input-output voltage differential $(V_{IN} - V_{OUT})$	2.1 Vdc (typical)	2.1 Vdc (typical)
TC of output voltage	±0.002%/°C	±0.002%/°C
Load current (without external transistor)	R: 500 mAdc (maximum) G: 200 mAdc (maximum)	500 mAdc (maximum) 200 mAdc (maximum)
Input regulation	0.002%/V_{IN} (typical)	0.002%/V_{IN} (typical)
Output impedance (dc to 100 kHz)	0.025 Ω (typical)	0.020 Ω (typical)

15.3 SPECIFYING A MONOLITHIC VOLTAGE REGULATOR

Unfortunately there is no consistent terminology that is used by all vendors for specifying regulator parameters in data sheets. The following, however, is a list of the terms used by Motorola, together with a brief explanation for each.

Output Voltage Range. This is the range of output voltages over which the specifications apply. A particular output voltage is established by a user-selected external resistive divider network.

Output Current. Each of Motorola's monolithic voltage regulators is capable of sourcing a certain amount of current into a load without use of external transistors. The current is specified on the data sheet as a maximum and a minimum for each device. For example, the MC1561R must supply at least 1 mAdc to maintain its regulation characteristics, and, when the proper heat sink is used, it will source 500 mAdc for any output voltage from 2.5 to 37 Vdc.

Input-Output Voltage Differential. This quantity $(V_{IN} - V_{OUT})$ is the voltage required to bias the circuitry that supplies drive current to the series-pass transistor. As the input voltage drops in magnitude and approaches the output-voltage dc level, the regulator will drop out of regulation at the minimum value of this specification.

Input-Voltage Range. The input-voltage range is specified on the data sheet as a minimum and a maximum. This indicates that at least the minimum voltage must be present to bias properly the zener diode on the IC chip. The input voltage must always exceed the output voltage by at least the specified "input-output differential." For example, the MC1561 has a minimum "input-output voltage differential" $(V_{IN} - V_{OUT})$ specification of 2.1 Vdc typical and 2.7 Vdc maximum. Therefore, to get 32 V out of the MC1561, one should supply at least 34.1 V, and 34.7 V maximum may be required at the input to obtain a 32.0-V regulated voltage at the output.

15.4 REGULATION AND OUTPUT IMPEDANCE

Load Regulation. This is the percentage change in output voltage for a dc step change in load current from the minimum to the maximum specified values. Mathematically it is expressed as

$$\text{load regulation} = \frac{V_{NL} - V_{FL}}{V_{NL}} \times 100 \qquad (\% \, V_{OUT}), \qquad (15.6)$$

where V_{NL} is the output voltage with minimum load current, and V_{FL} is the output voltage when the specified full-load current is being drawn; the units are percent of V_{OUT} ($\% \, V_{OUT}$).

Output Impedance.   This quantity Z_{OUT} is a small-signal ac parameter. It indicates the regulator's ability to prevent fluctuating signal-frequency currents, drawn by one circuit load, from creating common power-supply voltage changes. If the value of Z_{OUT} is high, this can create undesirable coupling between the circuits powered by the common voltage regulator and thereby cause system oscillations.

Output impedance is measured by superimposing a known ac small-signal current on a dc biasing load current and measuring the resultant ac output voltage. The magnitude of the dc bias current should be large enough to greatly exceed the peak value of the ac current waveform, so that the voltage regulator remains active for the full ac cycle. (As most regulators only source load current, they tend to shut off, instead of absorbing or "sinking" current from the output terminals.)

The recent availability of monolithic IC voltage regulators has added new significance to output impedance and regulation specifications. With the more familiar discrete regulators, on the other hand, there usually is good correlation between Z_{OUT} and load regulation at a particular dc output voltage. For discrete regulators the preferred specification has been load regulation, because the percentage basis of this specification naturally disguises the typically poor absolute dc performance that occurs with widely used discrete-component regulator circuits that have the output-level-setting resistors directly across the load. The large attenuation of these resistors at high output voltages reduces the amount of feedback and therefore causes large output-voltage changes. These large changes in the amount of feedback cause wide variations in output impedance. Thus Z_{OUT} has not yet been adopted as the preferred parameter to specify, and hence it is an unfamiliar term to power-supply users.

With the "regulator-within-a-regulator" design of the MC1560/61 IC voltage regulators, the unity-gain output series regulator operates at a constant maximum amount of feedback, independent of V_{OUT}. Thus, for perhaps the first time, a voltage regulator has a constant Z_{OUT} and a changing percent load regulation. Now the percentage basis makes for an improved load-regulation specification. But the Z_{OUT} specification still does not tell the whole story. Later, we shall look at the effects of thermal feedback on regulator performance.

Input Regulation.   This is the percentage change in output voltage per volt change in input voltage. It is expressed as

$$\text{input regulation} = \frac{\Delta V_{OUT}}{V_{OUT} \times \Delta V_{IN}} \times 100 \qquad (\%/V_{IN}), \qquad (15.7)$$

where ΔV_{OUT} is the change in the output voltage V_{OUT} for the input change ΔV_{IN}. The units are $\%/V_{IN}$.

For completely packaged line-operated voltage regulators the term "line regulation" is usually used to show the dependence of the output voltage on the ac power "line" variations. However, since IC regulators do not operate directly off the line, the term "input regulation" is preferable.

As with load regulation, input-regulation specifications should clearly distinguish between transient regulation and dc regulation caused by thermal-feedback effects. The basic specification should be given by ac test, as the dc changes (drifts) can then be calculated separately for the particular application conditions of interest.

15.5   THERMAL CONSIDERATIONS

Unfortunately all monolithic IC regulators exhibit a phenomenon that is not encountered with discrete-component regulators. This is thermal feedback that occurs within the chip. The large changes in IC power dissipation that accompany the dc load-regulation test create changes in the junction temperature of the die. Two solutions exist for this problem:

1. Design a temperature-compensated circuit that is essentially immune to change in T_j.
2. Use a power package to keep the T_j changes small.

Motorola has adopted both solutions. The two approaches both help, because dc load regulation depends on both the change in power dissipated in the IC (and therefore $(V_{IN} - V_{OUT})$ and ΔI_L) and on the type of heat sinking used – with strong dependence on the IC package.

An example will indicate the relative values of the parameters and show how the data-sheet information can be used to estimate performance. Consider the following dc load-regulation test with

$$V_{IN} = 12 \text{ Vdc},$$
$$V_{OUT} = 5 \text{ Vdc},$$
$$\Delta I_L = 49 \text{ mA (say 1 to 50 mA)},$$
$$Z_{OUT} = 0.025 \ \Omega \text{ (typical)},$$
$$TC_{V_{OUT}} = 0.002\%/C° \text{ (typical)}.$$

In our example we compare two extreme situations, a TO-5 in free air $(T_A = 25°C)$ and a TO-66 with a good heat sink $(T_C = 25°C)$. For the TO-5 can $\theta_{jA} = 185°C/W$, and for the TO-66 package $\theta_{jC} = 7°C/W$. The change in the IC dissipation is given by

$$\Delta P_d = (V_{IN} - V_{OUT})\Delta I_L = (7 \text{ V})(49 \text{ mA}) = 343 \text{ mW}. \qquad (15.8)$$

The junction temperature change ΔT_j is given by

$$\Delta T_j = \theta_{jA}\, \Delta P_d \quad (\text{or} \quad \theta_{jC}\, \Delta P_d). \tag{15.9}$$

For the TO-5 can in free air

$$\Delta T_j = (185°\text{C/W})(0.343 \text{ W}) = 63.5°\text{C}, \tag{15.10}$$

and, assuming a linear TCV_{OUT},

$$\Delta V_{\text{OUT}} = (0.002\%/°\text{C})(63.5°\text{C}) = 0.127\% \tag{15.11}$$

simply from thermal feedback. The TO-66 package would create

$$\Delta T_j = (7°\text{C/W})(0.343 \text{ W}) = 2.4°\text{C} \tag{15.12}$$

to give

$$\Delta V_{\text{OUT}} = \left(\frac{0.002\%}{°\text{C}}\right)(2.4°\text{C}) = 0.0048\% \tag{15.13}$$

from thermal feedback. The benefits of the power package are made clear by this example. It is interesting to note also that, as a result of Z_{OUT} only, we would have expected

$$\Delta V_{\text{OUT}} = Z_{\text{OUT}}(\Delta I_L) = (0.02\,\Omega)(49 \text{ mA}),$$

which gives

$$\Delta V_{\text{OUT}} = 1.225 \text{ mV}$$

or

$$\Delta V_{\text{OUT}} = \frac{(1.225 \times 10^{-3})(10^2)}{5.0} = 0.0245\%\ V_{\text{OUT}}. \tag{15.14}$$

For the TO-66 package Z_{OUT} is the dominant effect that one would see. But with the TO-5 package thermal feedback can mask the effects of Z_{OUT}. When the data sheet gives values of Z_{OUT}, θ_{jA}, θ_{jC}, and TCV_{OUT}, the dc load regulation can be estimated for any particular case of $(V_{\text{IN}} - V_{\text{OUT}})$, ΔI_L, and thermal conditions. Because of the variability of many of these parameters in different applications, the dc load regulation as given on a data sheet does not hold for all cases and therefore should be calculated for each particular application. For those situations that require performance comparable to the dc load regulation specification, an external current-boosting transistor used with the MC1560R will give a dc ΔV_{OUT}

of -3 mV for a $+5$-V output, when operated with load currents from 10 mA to 3 A — i.e., 0.06% load regulation over an approximately 3-A ΔI_L.

Temperature Coefficient. This is the output-voltage stability with a change in operating temperature. From the MC1560 data sheet

MC1560:

$$TCV_{\text{OUT}} = \frac{\pm (V_{\text{OUT max}} - V_{\text{OUT min}})(100)}{(180°C)(V_{\text{OUT}} \text{ at } 25°C)} \left(\frac{\%}{°C}\right) \qquad (15.15)$$

MC1460:

$$TCV_{\text{OUT}} = \frac{\pm (V_{\text{OUT max}} - V_{\text{OUT min}})(100)}{(75°C)(V_{\text{OUT}} \text{ at } 25°C)}, \qquad (15.16)$$

where it is assumed that the output-voltage adjusting resistors maintain a constant ratio, independent of the temperature change. Unfortunately, as with most temperature coefficients, there is not a simple linear slope between the extreme points of temperature. The specification merely states that the actual change will fit into a rectangular area on the ΔV_{OUT} versus T_j curve, defined by the end points.

15.6   HOW TO USE THE IC REGULATOR IN PRACTICAL CIRCUITS

The basic voltage-regulator connection for the MC1560 is shown in Figure 15.5. As we have already seen, resistors R_1 and R_2 form the feedback network that sets the voltage at pin 6 and, consequently, the output voltage. Hence output voltage can be easily adjusted by varying resistor R_1.

Since pin 8 is the base of a Darlington input amplifier, the input current to pin 8 is extremely small, and R_1 and R_2 can be selected with little regard for their parallel resistance. For situations in which temperature variations are critical, resistors R_1 and R_2 should have identical temperature coefficients. Recalling that the voltage at pin 8 equals the reference voltage, we find from Figure 15.5,

$$V_R \simeq 3.5 \text{ V} = I_R R_2. \qquad (15.17)$$

If R_2 is chosen as 6.8 kΩ, then $I_R \simeq 0.5$ mA.

The output voltage can now be found from

$$V_{\text{OUT}} = V_R + I_R R_1 \qquad (15.18)$$

or

$$V_{\text{OUT}} \simeq 3.5 \text{ V} + \frac{R_1}{2} \qquad (15.19)$$

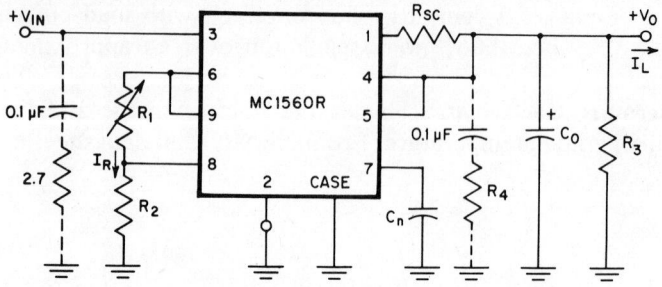

Figure 15.5.   Basic voltage regulator circuit.

for R_1 in kΩ and $R_2 = 6.8$ kΩ. Hence the output voltage is a linear function of the value of R_1. This relationship suggests a number of possible uses for the regulator – for example, as a resistively programmed test supply. An actual plot of the linear relationship between V_{OUT} and R_1 is shown in Figure 15.6.

Because the MC1560 incorporates vhf transistor devices, one should take the same precautions as for other high-frequency circuits when wiring these regulator circuits. A series RC combination of a 0.1-μF disk-ceramic capacitor and a 2.7-Ω 0.25-W composition resistor may be necessary across the input (pin 3 to ground) to damp large input-lead inductances. The connection to pin 5 should be as short as possible; or, alternatively, a 10-Ω 0.25-W composition resistor, shunted from pins 1 to 5 at the IC, can be used to remove "remote-sense" line parasitic-inductance effects.

Capacitor C_n reduces output noise by restricting the bandwidth of the first regulator stage. This attenuates zener noise at the input to this

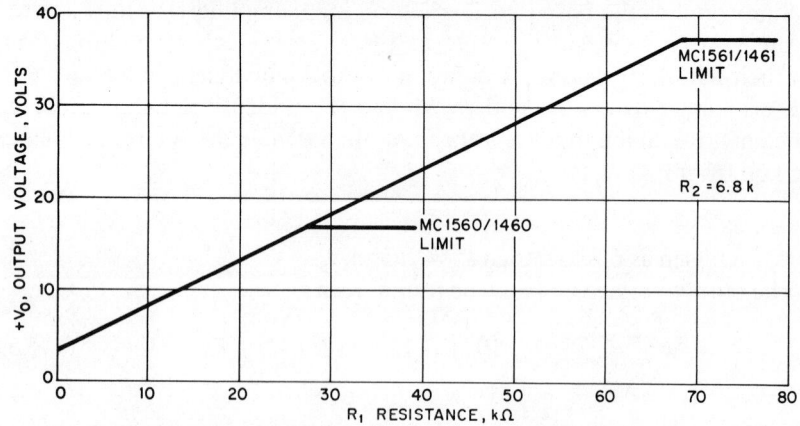

Figure 15.6.   Output voltage V_0 as a function of resistor R_1.

regulator. A 0.1-μF capacitor reduces output noise typically to less than 150 μV rms.

For the basic connection capacitor C_0 should be greater than 10 μF. For some applications, such as current boosting and voltage boosting, values of 50 μF or more may be necessary.

The fixed load resistor R_3 is chosen to draw a minimum current of 1 mA with no external load. In many cases this will not be needed as a minimum load may already exist. Resistor R_{SC} provides current limiting for short-circuit protection as previously described. From the data sheet we see that R_{SC} does not appreciably affect the output impedance.

The unregulated input voltage V_{IN} must be greater than 8.5 V for correct biasing. Also, of course, V_{IN} should exceed V_{OUT} by at least the minimum "input-output voltage differential," which is approximately 2.5 V.

15.7 SHUTDOWN TECHNIQUES

One very useful feature of the MC1560 is its built-in shutdown capability. Referring again to Figure 15.3, the shutdown terminal is pin 2. When diode D_6 and the base-emitter junction of Q_{18} are forward-biased, they shunt current from reference zener Z_2, thus turning off all reference current sources within the chip. While the regulator is shutdown the only current that can flow into pin 3 from the $+V_{IN}$ source is current I_A through the 60-kΩ resistor into Z_1 (i.e., approximately 250 μA for a 15-V input). To activate shutdown, one simply applies a potential greater than two diode drops with a current capability of 1 mA. Note that if a hard supply (i.e., 3 V) is applied directly to pin 2, the shutdown circuitry will be

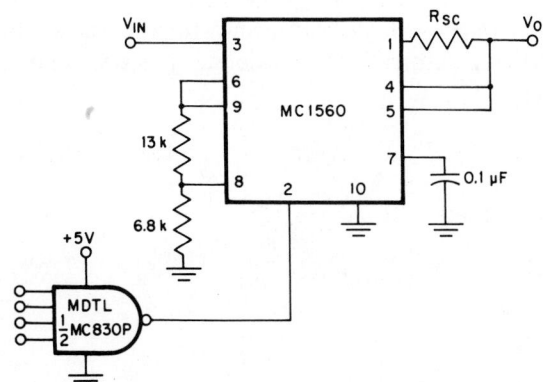

Figure 15.7. Logic-controlled shutdown.

destroyed since there is no inherent current limiting. Maximum rating for the drive curent into pin 2 is 10 mA, whereas 1 mA is adequate for shutdown.

Figure 15.7 shows how the regulator can be controlled by a logic gate. Here it is assumed that the regulator operates in its normal mode – as a positive regulator referenced to ground – and that the logic gate is of the saturating type, operating from a positive supply to ground. The high logic level should be greater than about 1.5 V and should source no more than 10 mA into pin 2.

The gate shown is of the MDTL type. MRTL and MTTL can also be used as long as the drive current is within safe limits (this is important when using MTTL, where the output stage uses an active pull-up). Typical output stages for gates in the MRTL, MDTL, and MTTL lines are shown in Figure 15.8.

15.8 THERMAL SHUTDOWN

As we have already seen, monolithic regulators have one characteristic that discrete regulators do not have – namely, thermal feedback within the die. Since regulator shutdown is initiated when the voltage at pin 2 exceeds $2V_{BE}$, the MC1560's thermal feedback allows a novel protection scheme.

The junctions of D_6 and Q_{18} are at approximately the same temperature as the output device, hence a fixed dc voltage at pin 2 can provide automatic shutdown when a predetermined junction temperature is reached, as shown in Figure 15.9. This occurs because of the normal temperature coefficient of a silicon-diode junction (-1.7 mV/°C). The zener diode provides a fixed dc voltage that can be varied by adjusting R_b. A zero-TC zener is necessary if the complete circuit will be subjected to temperature changes. The relationship for the voltage V_A, needed to shut down the regulators for a particular junction temperature T_j, is approximated by

$$V_A = 2V_{BE}(+25°C) + 2\left(\frac{\Delta V_{BE}}{\Delta T}\right)(T_j - 25°C), \qquad (15.20)$$

and, if we assume that

$$V_{BE}(+25°C) = 0.7 \text{ V} \quad \text{and} \quad \frac{\Delta V_{BE}}{\Delta T} = -\frac{1.7 \text{ mV}}{°C},$$

(15.20) becomes

$$V_A \simeq [1.4 - 3.4 \times 10^{-3}(T_j - 25°C)] \text{ volts.} \qquad (15.21)$$

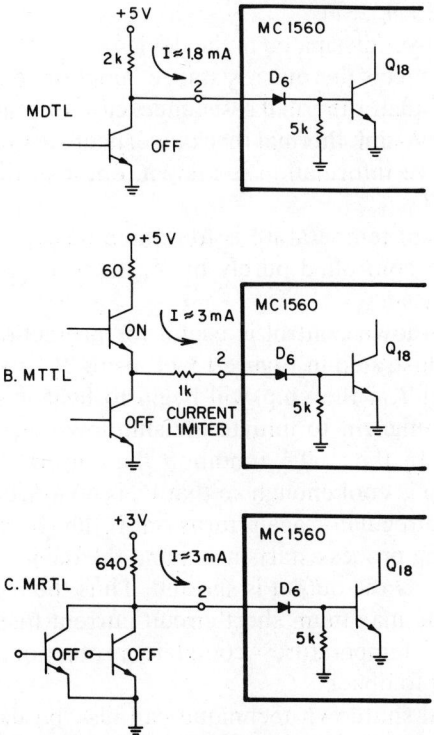

Figure 15.8. Logic-gate output circuitry for digital shutdown.

As an example, if we desire to shut down the MC1560 at $T_j = +140°C$, V_A becomes 1 V, as shown in Figure 15.9.

Since junction temperature is not easily measured, one might want to relate T_j to a more easily measured quantity, such as ambient temperature T_A. This is possible because

$$T_j = T_A + \theta_T P_D, \tag{15.22}$$

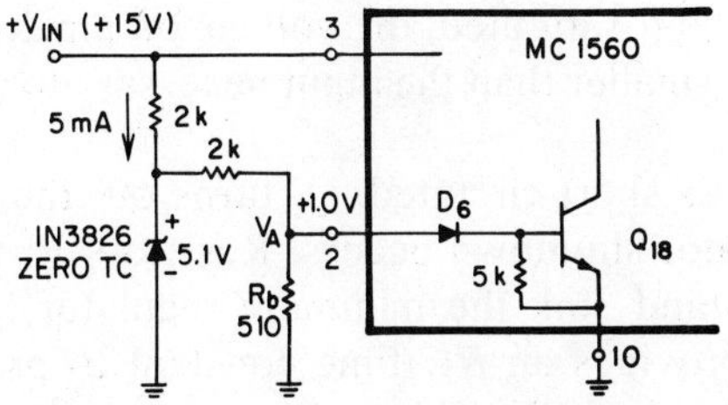

Figure 15.9. Junction-temperature (T_j) shutdown circuit.

where $\theta_T = \theta_{jc} + \theta_{cs} + \theta_{sa}$,   (15.23)

P_D = power dissipated in the device,

θ_{jc} = device's thermal resistance, junction to case,

θ_{cs} = insulator thermal resistance, case to heat sink,

θ_{sa} = heat-sink thermal resistance, heat sink to ambient.

Once the above information is known, one can then proceed to control shutdown by T_A.

If the ambient temperature is to remain nearly constant, and the shutdown is to be controlled purely by T_j, then the circuit shown in Figure 15.10 can be used.

The T_j shutdown control is useful for protection during output short circuits. As illustrated in Figure 15.11, using R_{SC} to limit the output short-circuit current I_{SC}, the chip will begin to heat with the output shorted. When V_A is sufficient to initiate the shutdown mechanism, the regulator will turn off. In the "off" condition the chip (at T_j) begins to cool off. When the chip is cool enough so that V_A is no longer adequate to keep Q_{18} turned on, the regulator again turns on. If the short still exists at the output, the heating process starts again and the device continues in a cycling mode, as long as the output is shorted. Thus the technique provides control of both the maximum short-circuit current (using R_{SC}) and the maximum junction temperature – complete protection, actually superior to that of current foldback.

The thermal-shutdown technique can also be used when one is using an external pass transistor for current boosting. This is shown in Figure 15.12. In this configuration an output short circuit heats Q_2. Transistor Q_1 monitors the heat-sink temperature and conducts for a predetermined temperature increase above T_a as set by R_2 and R_3. Resistor R_4 limits the drive current into pin 2, as in the earlier circuit.

15.9 NONTHERMAL TECHNIQUES

A fairly conventional circuit, which does not use T_j control for short-circuit shutdown, is shown in Figure 15.13. In this circuit Q_1 is normally saturated because of the base drive supplied through the resistor divider R_1 and R_2. With Q_1 saturated, the voltage on pin 2 is $V_{CE(sat)}$ of Q_1, which is considerably smaller than the input necessary to overcome the required threshold.

If the output is short-circuited, Q_1 turns off, the voltage at pin 2 rises, and thus regulator shutdown occurs. Resistors R_1 and R_2 can be chosen to saturate Q_1 and sink the minimum regulator load current of 1 mA. Capacitor C_1 provides an RC time constant to prevent shutdown when V_{IN} is initially applied. When the short circuit is removed, the regulator must be manually reset before it will return to normal operation.

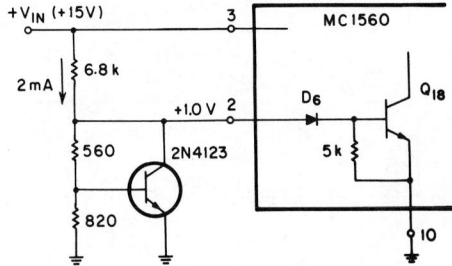

Figure 15.10. Junction-temperature shutdown using T_A reference.

For automatic restarting the circuit of Figure 15.13 can be modified as shown in Figure 15.14. When the output is shorted, Q_1 turns off, allowing the potential at the base of Q_2 to rise according to the (51-kΩ × 2 μF) RC time constant. Transistor Q_2 acts as an emitter follower for base potentials above about 0.7 V, and the voltage applied to pin 2 of the regulator is one-half the potential at the emitter of Q_2. The regulator will shut down when the base potential reaches about 3.7 V. At about 8 V the threshold of the unijunction transistor is reached and it fires—removing the charge stored in the 2-μF capacitor. If during this time the short has been removed from the regulator's output, the circuit will once again regulate normally; if not, Q_1 will remain off and the restart circuit will recycle until the short is removed. The recycling duty cycle is controlled by the RC time constant.

Should one desire to use current-foldback protection, the circuit of Figure 15.15 will achieve this. Here the circuit works as follows: The voltage across R_1 (V_{R1}) is initially set to $2V_{BE}$ ($\simeq 1.4$ V) by tailoring the values of R_1 and R_2 for the desired V_{OUT}. For Q_1 to conduct, the voltage across R_3 ($I_{OUT} \times R_3$) must equal $V_{R1} + V_{BE} \simeq 3V_{BE}$. When Q_1 conducts, the collector, connected to pin 4, robs current drive from the series-pass elements, giving the desired current foldback.

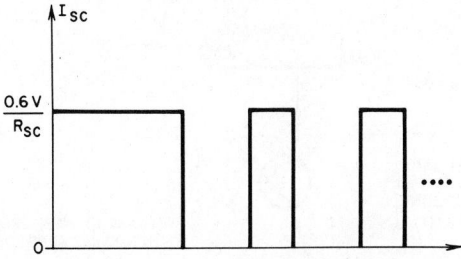

Figure 15.11. Junction-temperature shutdown action with short-circuit output.

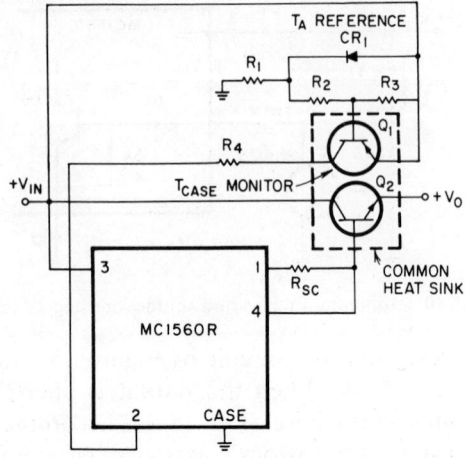

Figure 15.12.   Thermal shutdown when using external pass transistor.

One more protection scheme warrants discusssion—a circuit for out-put-overvoltage protection. Figure 15.16 shows a circuit that will shut down the regulator with an increase in V_{OUT}, and will recycle to turn the system back on.

Shutdown occurs when V_{OUT} exceeds the desired level by one V_{BE}. The voltage turns on transistor Q_1, which in turn fires the SCR, causing the output to be shorted to ground. This short circuit causes the shutdown circuitry to activate. (Q_2 turns off.) The recycling will then turn the system back on.

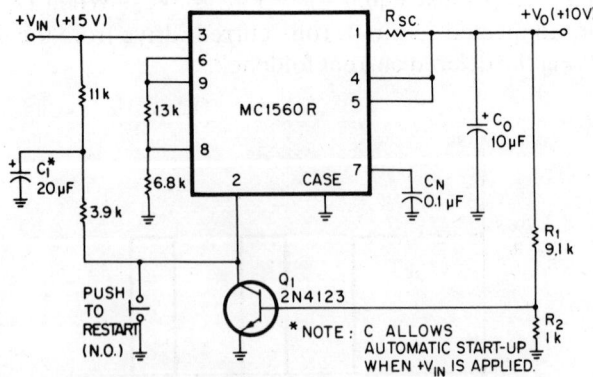

Figure 15.13.   Automatic shutdown when output is shorted (manual restart).

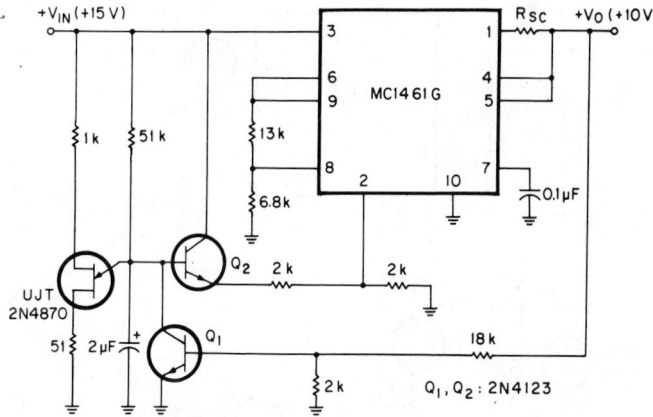

Figure 15.14. Automatic on-off sequencing circuit for short-circuit protection.

15.10 VOLTAGE BOOST

Often one needs a regulated voltage at levels above the maximum output level of the basic regulator. To achieve this one must "boost" the voltage up to the desired level and close the loop around this boosted value to obtain good output regulation.

The circuit in Figure 15.17 illustrates the voltage-boosting concept. It develops a regulated 100-V output with a current capability of about 100 mA from an unregulated 110-V source. The IC regulator is set up conventionally, to supply about 25 V from a 30-V input. A 75-V zener is connected between the 25-V output and the series-pass transistor.

The current limit is set by R_{SC} ($= 5.6 \, \Omega$) to about 100 mA, to protect the system from short circuits. Even with an output short, the 2N3738 works well within its safe area. Diode D_1 prevents the regulator from being shorted when the 100-V output is shorted. The loop is closed from the 100-V output back to pin 5, through a resistive divider. One minor disadvantage is that regulation is worsened by the four-to-one divider.

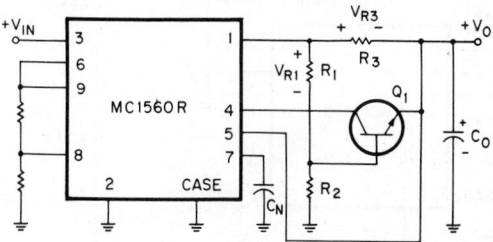

Figure 15.15. Current-foldback protection circuit.

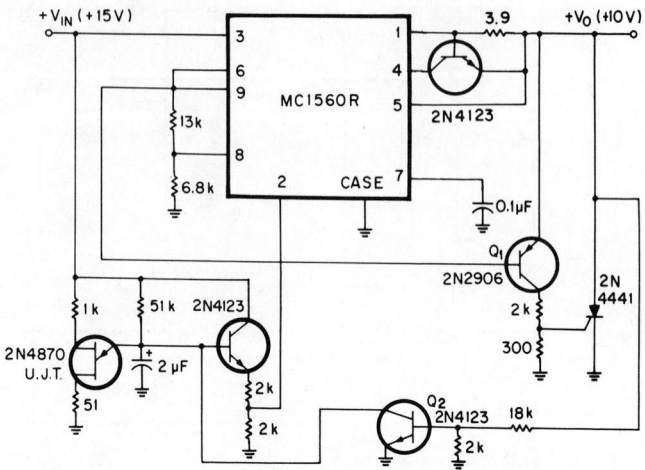

Figure 15.16. SCR "crowbar" overvoltage protection with automatic shutdown and recycling.

The 2-kΩ resistor has two functions: it pulls minimum load current from the IC regulator, and it provides a dc current path to operate the 75-V zener above its knee.

15.11 CURRENT BOOST

Despite the impressive current capability of these monolithic regulators, there is much interest in current-boost circuits. To obtain currents

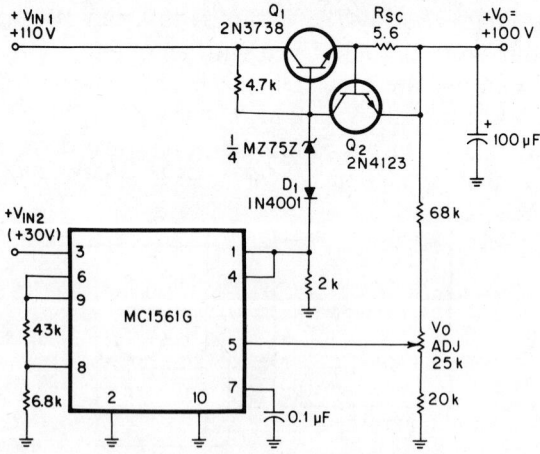

Figure 15.17. Voltage-boost circuit.

above about 500 mA, external series-pass transistors must be used. One widely accepted circuit is shown in Figure 15.18. Here a MC1560G is used in conjunction with a 2N3055 series-pass element to achieve a 5-A capability at minimal cost. In this particular circuit the output voltage is adjustable, using the potentiometer between pins 9 and 8. The output short-circuit current (I_{SC}) value is determined by R_{SC}.

With this configuration some instability may exist:

1. A low-frequency sawtooth oscillation may occur, especially under light loading. A 51-Ω resistor from pin 1 to pin 5, mounted at the pins of the MC1560G package, and a fixed load R_L solve this problem by pre-loading the regulator to about 10 mA. The resistor also kills any stray inductance in the remote sense lead.

2. A high-frequency parasitic oscillation may occur (10 to 100 MHz). The *RC* damping networks, shown from pins 3 and 5 to ground, solve this problem.

The 2N3055, a widely used low-cost device, has a minimum worst-case beta (h_{fe}) of 20 at $I_C = 4.0$ A. Therefore, assuming a worst-case condition, the MC1560G would have to supply 200 mA into the base of the 2N3055 to provide a 4-A load current. The betas are seldom near the minimum value, and thus the circuit can typically supply 5 A. If a worst-case design were required, the MC1560R would solve the problem.

A simple *pnp* current-boost circuit is shown in Figure 15.19. In this circuit a silicon *pnp* (2N4904) is used; however, a germanium power device can be substituted. Parasitic problems are less severe with this configuration, and fewer parts are needed. The 20-Ω resistor from $+V_{IN}$ to pin 3 supplies bias current to the regulator even when the *pnp* pass element is shut down. The thermal-shut-down technique of Figure 15.12 can be used here also. As shown in Figure 15.19, the circuit is set up to supply about 2 A maximum.

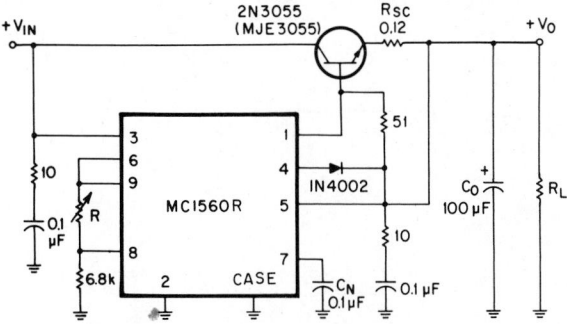

Figure 15.18. Current boost using *npn* transistor.

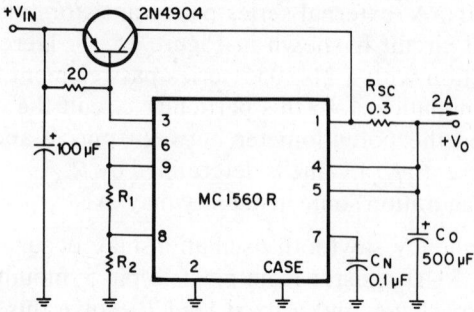

Figure 15.19. Current boost using *pnp* transistor.

A high-current 5-V regulated output can be obtained by using a *pnp-npn* boost circuit, as shown in Figure 15.20. An output level of 5 V is very popular for digital applications. In this circuit, with only three external devices (two 2N2728 *pnp*'s and one 2N5301 *npn*), well-regulated voltages with load currents up to 100 A are possible. At these current levels the V_{CE} of the pass devices should be kept to a minimum for maximum efficiency and minimum internal power dissipation. The 2N2728 transistor offers a $V_{CE(sat)}$ of 0.075 V and an h_{fe} of 20, both at the 50-A level. To source 100 A the driver transistor (2N5301-*npn*) is required to supply 5 A into the two paralleled *pnp*'s. The h_{fe} of the 2N5301 is 15 minimum at 10 A; therefore the MC1560R can easily supply the necessary drive current. The 100-Ω resistor, shown from pins 1 to 5 on the regulator, serves to preload the MC1560R. The 20-Ω resistor, from base to emitter of Q_1, preloads the driver. Resistance-capacitance damping maintains stable operation.

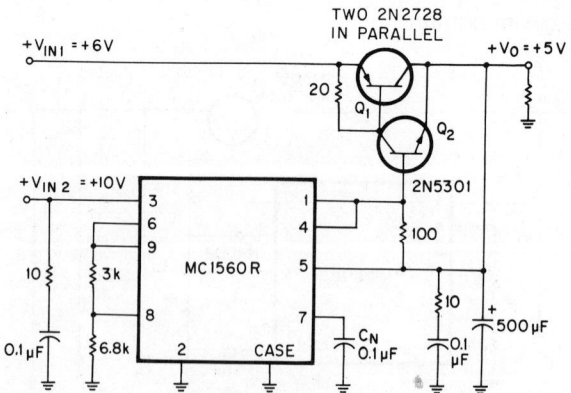

Figure 15.20. Current boost with complementary *pnp–npn* circuit.

15.12 SWITCHING REGULATOR

Figure 15.21 shows a self-oscillating switching regulator. Here the output voltage is 5 V with a 5-A load capability. For load-current changes of 50 mA to 5 A the measured output-voltage change (ΔV_{OUT}) is 50 mV. For an input-voltage change of 10 to 30 V, the ΔV_{OUT} is 22 mV. Output ripple is less than 60 mV peak to peak. Various application notes[2, 3] provide a more thorough analysis of switching regulators.

15.13 ZERO-TEMPERATURE-COEFFICIENTS REFERENCE

The excellent temperature coefficient of the MC1560-61 suggests that the device can be used as a simple reference element or as an adjustable zero-TC source. The circuit of Figure 15.22 shows how the IC regulator can be used as an adjustable zero-TC voltage source. In this circuit only the reference section of the regulator is used. Thus the output V_{REF} will source very little current, but will be adequate for applications in which it looks into a high impedance (e.g., an operational-amplifier noninverting input).

15.14 POWER-SUPPLY APPLICATIONS

The circuit of Figure 15.23 gives two different regulated potentials from one regulator package. The first output V_{OUT1} (10 V) is adjusted via a 6.8- and 13-kω divider network, as before. This 10-V output is then used as the reference for the second regulated output V_{OUT2}, which is adjusted via the 10-kω and 10-kω divider (2 : 1 to 10 V), hence V_{OUT2} = 20 V. Output V_{OUT2} is current limited by the 1.5-ω resistor at pin 1, and current boosting is needed for V_{OUT1} to allow a reasonable load capability.

Figure 15.24 shows the configuration for a ±15-V complementary

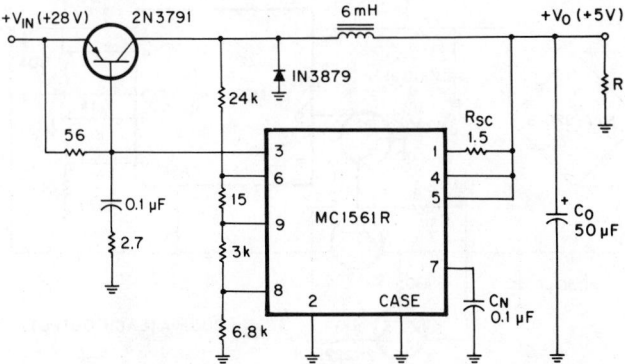

Figure 15.21.   Self-oscillating switching regulator.

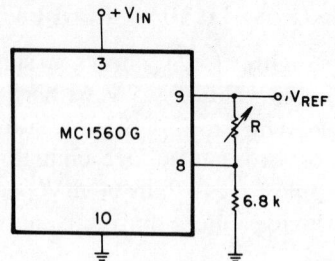

Figure 15.22. Adjustable zero −TC reference source.

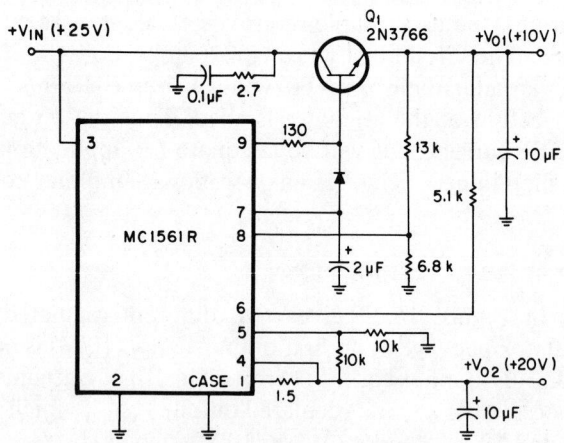

Figure 15.23. Circuit to provide two regulated output voltages.

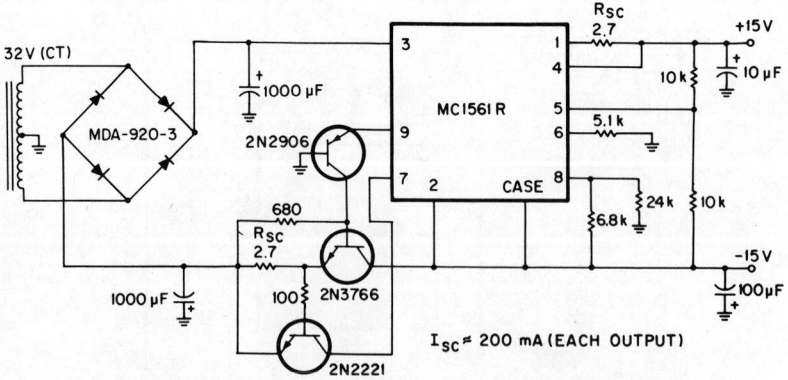

Figure 15.24. Complementary-tracking power supply with ±15-volt outputs.

232

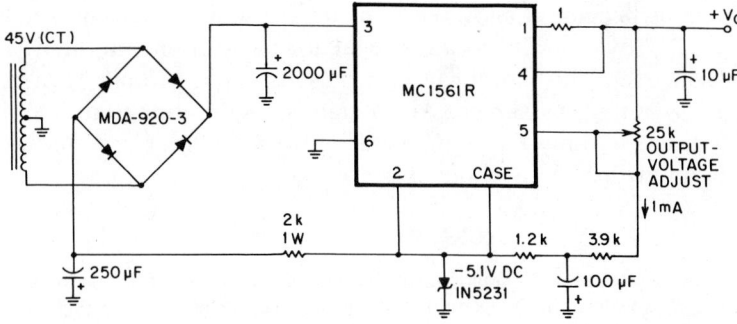

Figure 15.25.   Lab supply with output adjustable from zero to +25 volts dc.

tracking regulator. The ac-line-operated circuit is complete with a 32-V (CT) transformer and an MDA-920-3 full-wave bridge. The complete regulator will provide ±15 V with a 200-mA capability. No-load to full-load regulation is about 0.1%. The +15-V output is slaved to the −15-V output side, so its regulation can be only half as good as that of the −15-V side, because of the two-to-one resistive divider. The circuit should be of considerable interest to operational-amplifier users. This type of connection is only possible when the regulator is of the "regulator-within-a-regulator" design.

In Figure 15.25 we see a configuration for a laboratory ply that gives 0 to 25 V (adjustable), with a current limit of 0.5 A unboosted. This circuit, too, is complete with transformer and full-wave bridge.

The final application to be considered here is a digitally controlled three-terminal negative regulator, shown in Figure 15.26. This circuit

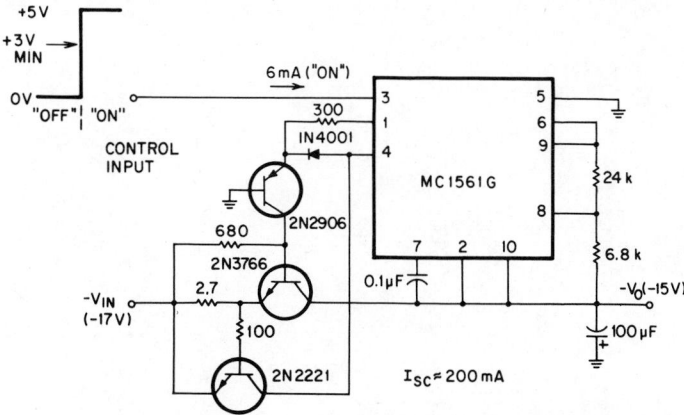

Figure 15.26.   Digital-controlled three-terminal negative regulator.

is interesting because it allows us to maintain the shutdown characteristic (that pin 2 provides with positive-regulator connections) in the negative mode also. Here the shutdown logic pulse is applied to pin 3, gating on the -15-V output, as shown. Again standard saturating (0 to 5 V) logic can be used, as only 6 mA of drive into pin 3 is required. As shown, current limit will occur at about 200 mA.

ACKNOWLEDGMENTS

The author wishes to thank Don Kesner, Marv Gienger, Don Schrock, and Mike Garden for their assistance during the preparation of this paper. Special thanks go to Tom Frederiksen for his many contributions to the voltage-regulator effort.

REFERENCES

[1] Frederiksen, T., "A Monolithic High-Power Series Voltage Regulator," *IEEE Transactions on Circuit Theory*, December, 1968.
[2] Shiner, B., *Switching Voltage Regulator Uses Discrete and Integrated-Circuit Approaches*, Motorola Application Note AN-457, February, 1969.
[3] Gienger, M., and Kesner, D., *Voltage and Current Boost Techniques Using the MC1560-61*, Motorola Application Note, AN-498, December, 1969.

16

Positive Voltage Regulators

by Robert J. Widlar

National Semiconductor, Santa Clara, California

Integrated-circuit voltage regulators are seeing rapidly increasing usage. The LM100, one of the first, has already been widely accepted. This circuit is designed for versatility and can be used as a linear, switching, shunt, or current regulator. The output voltage can be set between 2 and 30 V with a pair of external resistors, and the IC works with unregulated input voltages down to 7 V. Dissipation limitations of the IC package restrict the output current to less than 20 mA, but external transistors can be added to obtain output currents in excess of 5 A. The use of the LM100 in many applications has been described[1–3].

One complaint that has been made about the LM100 is that it does not have good enough regulation for certain applications. In addition, it becomes difficult to prove that the load regulation is satisfactory under worst-case design condition. These problems prompted development of the LM105, which is nearly identical to the LM100 except that a gain stage has been added for improved regulation. In the great majority of applications the LM105 is a plug-in replacement for the LM100.

16.1 AN IMPROVED REGULATOR

The load regulation of the LM100 is about 0.1%, no load to full load, without current limiting. When short-circuit protection is added, the regulation begins to degrade as the output current becomes greater than about one-half the limiting current. This is illustrated in Figure 16.1*a*. The LM105, on the other hand, gives 0.1% regulation up to currents closely approaching the short-circuit current. As shown in Figure 16.1*b*, this is particularly significant at high temperatures.

The current-limiting characteristics of a regulator are important for two reasons: first, it is almost mandatory that a regulator be short-circuit protected because the output is distributed to enough places for the probability of it becoming shorted to be quite high. Second, the sharpness of the limiting characteristics is not improved by the addition of external booster transistors. External transistors can increase the maximum output current, but they do not improve the load regulation at currents approaching the short-circuit current. Thus it can be seen that the LM105 provides more than 10 times better load regulation in practical power-supply designs.

Figure 16.2 shows that the LM105 also provides better line regulation than the LM100. These curves give the percentage change in output voltage for an incremental change in the unregulated input voltage. They show that the line regulation is worst for small differences between the input and output voltages. The LM105 provides about three times better regulation under worst-case conditions. Bypassing the internal reference of the regulator makes the ripple rejection of the LM105 almost a factor of 10 better than the LM100 over the entire operating range, as shown in the figure. This bypass capacitor also eliminates noise generated in the internal reference zener of the IC.

The LM105 has also benefited from the use of new IC components developed after the LM100 was designed. These have reduced the internal power consumption, so that the LM105 can be specified for input voltages

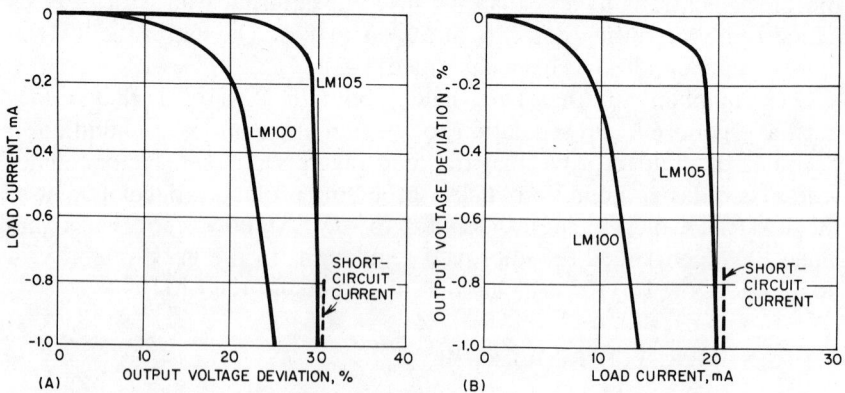

Figure 16.1. Comparison of load regulation of ICs without (LM100) and with added gain stage (LM105) for equal short-circuit currents at (*a*) $T_j = 25°C$, $R_{SC} = 10/\Omega$, and (*b*) $T_j = 125°C$, $R_{SC} = 10\ \Omega$.

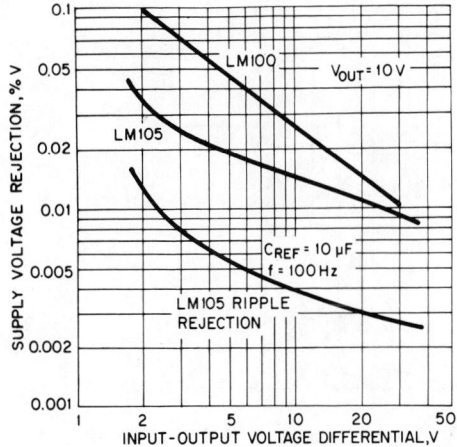

Figure 16.2. Line regulation characteristics of the LM100 and LM105.

up to 50 V and output voltages to 40 V. The minimum preload current required by the LM100 is not needed on the LM105.

16.2 CIRCUIT DESCRIPTION

The differences between the LM100 and the LM105 can be seen by comparing the schematic diagrams in Figures 16.3 and 16.4. The transistors Q_4 and Q_5 have been added to the LM105 to form a common-collec-

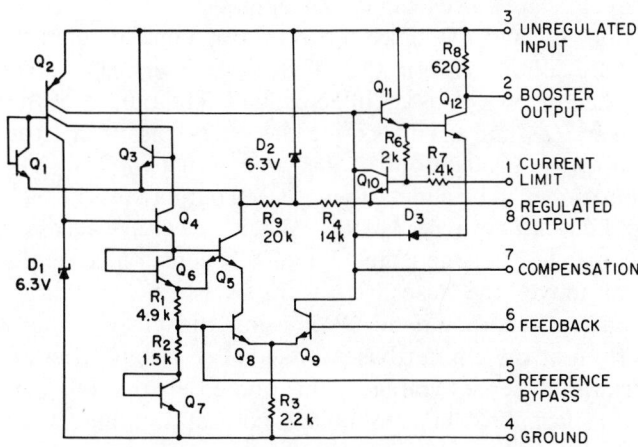

Figure 16.3. Circuit diagram of the LM100 voltage regulator.

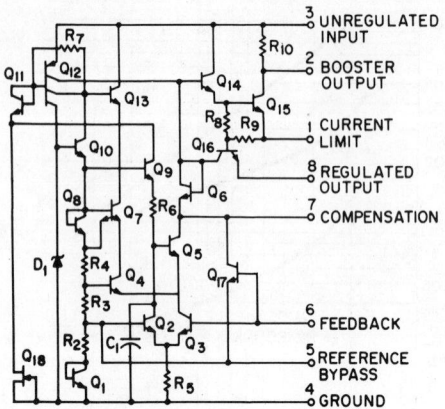

Figure 16.4.   Circuit diagram of the LM105 voltage regulator.

tor, common-base, common-emitter amplifier; a single common-emitter differential amplifier was used in the LM100.

In the LM100 generation of the reference voltage starts with zener diode D_1, which is supplied with a fixed current from one of the collectors of Q_2. This regulated voltage, which has a positive temperature coefficient, is buffered by Q_4, divided down by R_1 and R_2, and connected in series with a diode-connected transistor Q_7. The negative temperature coefficient of Q_7 cancels out the positive coefficient of the voltage across R_2, producing a temperature-compensated 1.8 V on the base of Q_8. This point is also brought outside the circuit so that an external capacitor can be added to bypass any noise from the zener diode.

Transistors Q_8 and Q_9 make up the error amplifier of the circuit. A gain of 2000 is obtained from this single stage by using a current source, another collector on Q_2, as a collector load. The output of the amplifier is buffered by Q_{11} and used to drive the series-pass transistor Q_{12}. The collector of Q_{12} is brought out so that an external *pnp* transistor, or *pnp-npn* combination, can be added for increased output current.

Current limiting is provided by Q_{10}. When the voltage across an external resistor connected between pins 1 and 8 becomes high enough to turn on Q_{10}, it removes the base drive from Q_{11} so the regulator exhibits a constant-current characteristic. Prebiasing the current-limit transistor with a portion of the emitter-base voltage of Q_{12} from R_6 and R_7 reduces the current-limit sense voltage. This increases the efficiency of the regulator, especially when fold-back current limiting is used. With foldback limiting, the voltage dropped across the current-sense resistor is about four times larger than the sense voltage.

As for the remaining details, the collector of the amplifier, Q_9, is brought out so that external collector-base capacitance can be added to frequency stabilize the circuit when it is used as a linear regulator. The resistors R_9 and R_4 are used to start up the regulator, while the rest of the circuitry establishes the proper operating levels for the current source transistor Q_2.

The reference circuitry of the LM105 is the same, except that the current through the reference divider, R_2, R_3, and R_4, has been reduced by a factor of 2 on the LM105 for reduced power consumption. In the LM105 Q_2 and Q_3 form an emitter-coupled amplifier, with Q_3 being the emitter-follower input and Q_2 the common-base output amplifier. The resistor R_6 is the collector load for this stage, which has a voltage gain of about 20. The second stage is a differential amplifier, using Q_4 and Q_5, of which Q_5 actually provides the gain. Since it has a current source as a collector load, one of the collectors of Q_{12}, the gain is quite high — about 1500. This gives a total gain in the error amplifier of about 30,000, which is 10 times higher than that for the LM100.

It is not obvious from the schematic, but the first stage (Q_2 and Q_3) and second stage (Q_4 and Q_5) of the error amplifier are closely balanced when the circuit is operating. This will be true regardless of the absolute value of components and over the operating temperature range. The only thing that affects balance is component matching, which is good in a monolithic IC, so the error amplifier has good drift characteristics over a wide temperature range.

Frequency compensation is accomplished with an external integrating capacitor around the error amplifier, as with the LM100. This scheme makes the stability insensitive to loading conditions — resistive or reactive — while giving good transient response. However, an internal capacitor C_1 is added to prevent minor-loop oscillations resulting from the increased gain.

Additional differences between the LM100 and LM105 are that a field-effect transistor Q_{18} connected as a current source, starts the regulator when power is first applied. Since this current source is connected to ground, rather than the output, the minimum load current before the regulator drops out of operation with large input-output voltage differentials is greatly reduced. This also minimizes power dissipation in the IC when the difference between the input and output voltage is at the worst-case value. With the LM105 circuit configuration, it was necessary to add Q_{17} to eliminate a latch-up mechanism that could exist with lower output-voltage settings. Without Q_{17}, this could occur when Q_3 saturated and cut off the second-stage amplifiers Q_4 and Q_5, causing the output to latch at a voltage nearly equal to that of the unregulated input.

16.3 POWER LIMITATIONS

Although it is desirable to put as much of the regulator as possible on the IC chip, there are certain basic limitations. For one, it is not a good idea to put the series-pass transistor on the chip. The power that must be dissipated in the pass transistor is too much for practical IC packages. Further, ICs must be rated at a lower maximum operating temperature than power transistors. This means that even with a power package a more massive heat sink would be required if the pass transistor were included in the IC.

Assuming that these problems could be solved, it is still not advisable to put the pass transistor on the same chip with the reference and control circuitry: changes in the unregulated input voltage or load current produce gross variations in chip temperature. These variations worsen load and line regulation because of temperature interaction with the control and reference circuitry.

To elaborate, it is reasonable to neglect the package problem since it is potentially solvable. The lower maximum operating temperatures of ICs, however, present a more basic problem. The control circuitry in an IC regulator runs at fairly low currents. As a result it is more sensitive to leakage currents and other phenomena that degrade the performance of semiconductors at high temperatures. Hence the maximum operating temperature is limited to 150°C in military-temperature-range applications. On the other hand, a power transistor operating at high currents may be run at temperatures up to 200°C, because even a 1-mA leakage current would not affect its operation in a properly designed circuit. Even if the pass transistor developed a permanent 1-mA leakage from channeling, operating under these conditions of high stress, it would not affect circuit operation. These conditions would not trouble the pass transistor, but they would most certainly cause complete failure of the control circuitry.

These problems are not eliminated in applications with a lower maximum operating temperature. Integrated circuits are sold for limited-temperature-range applications at considerably lower cost. This is based mainly on a lower maximum junction temperature. They may be rated so that they do not blow up at higher temperatures, but they are not guaranteed to operate within specifications at these temperatures. Therefore in applications with a lower maximum ambient temperature it is necessary to purchase an expensive full-temperature-range part in order to take advantage of the theoretical maximum operating temperatures of the IC.

Figure 16.5 makes the point about dissipation limitations more strongly. It gives the maximum short-circuit output current for an IC regulator in a TO-5 package, assuming a 25°C temperature rise between the chip and

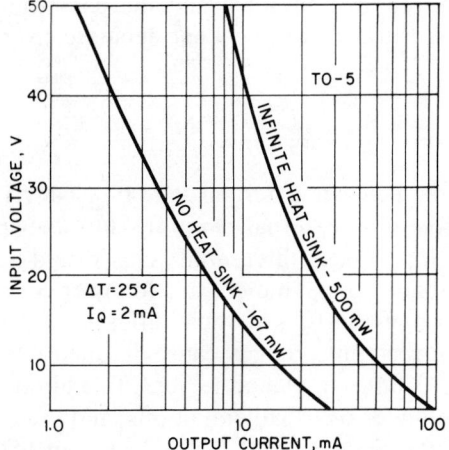

Figure 16.5. Dissipation-limited short-circuit output current for an IC regulator in a TO-5 package.

ambient and a quiescent current of 2 mA. Dual, in-line, or flat packages give results that are, at best, slightly better, but are usually worse. If the short-circuit current is not of prime concern, Figure 16.5 can also be used to give the maximum output current as a function of input-output voltage differential. However, the increased dissipation resulting from the quiescent current flowing at the maximum input voltage must be taken into account. In addition, the input-output voltage differential must be measured with the maximum expected input voltages.

The 25°C temperature rise assumed in arriving at Figure 16.5 is not at all unreasonable. With military-temperature-range parts this is valid for a maximum junction temperature of 150°C with a 125°C ambient. For low-cost parts, marketed for limited-temperature-range applications, this maximum differential appropriately derates the maximum junction temperature.

In practical designs the maximum permissible dissipation will always be to the left of the curve shown for an infinite heat sink in Figure 16.5. This curve is realized with the package immersed in circulating acetone, Freon, or mineral oil. Most heat sinks are not quite as good.

To summarize, power transistors can be run with a temperature differential, junction to ambient, three to five times as great as an integrated circuit. This means that they can dissipate much more power, even with a smaller heat sink. This, coupled with the fact that low-cost multilead power packages are not available and that there can be thermal interactions between the control circuitry and the pass transistor, strongly suggests that the pass transistors be kept separate from the integrated circuit.

16.4 USING BOOSTER TRANSISTORS

Figure 16.6 shows how an external pass transistor is added to the LM105. The addition of an external *pnp* transistor does not increase the minimum input-output voltage differential. This would happen if an *npn* transistor were used in a compound emitter-follower connection with the *npn* output transistor of the IC. A single-diffused, wide-base transistor like the 2N3740 is recommended because it causes fewer oscillation problems than double-diffused, planar devices. In addition, it seems to be less prone to failure under overload conditions, and low-cost devices are available in power packages such as the TO-66 or even TO-3.

When the maximum dissipation in the pass transistor is less than about 0.5 W, a 2N2905 may be used as a pass transistor. However, it is generally necessary to observe carefully the thermal deratings and provide some sort of heat sink.

In the circuit of Figure 16.6 the output voltage is determined by R_1 and R_2. The resistor values are selected on the basis of a feedback voltage of 1.8 V to pin 6 of the LM105. To keep thermal drift of the output voltage within specifications the parallel combination of R_1 and R_2 should be approximately 2 kΩ. However, this resistance is not critical. Variations of ±30% will not cause appreciable effects.

The 1-μF output capacitor C_2 is required to suppress oscillations in the feedback loop involving the external booster transistor Q_1 and the output transistor of the LM105. The capacitor C_1 compensates the internal regulator circuitry to make the stability independent for all loading conditions. It is not normally required if the lead length between the regulator and the output filter of the regulator is short.

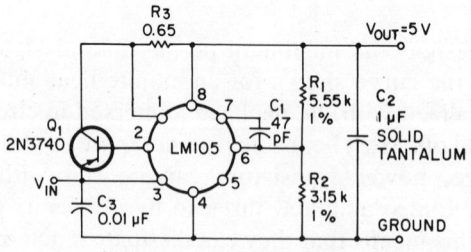

Figure 16.6. Voltage regulator with 0.2-A load current. Output voltage is determined by R_1 and R_2.

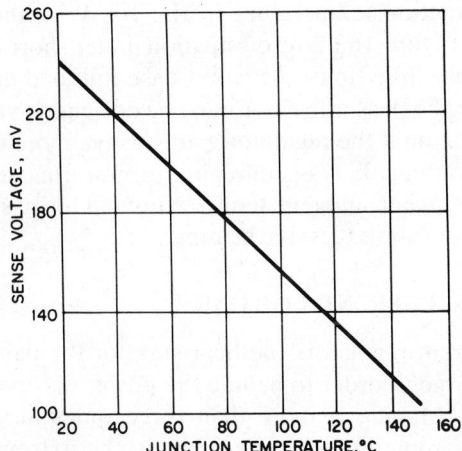

Figure 16.7. Maximum voltage drop across current-limit resistor at full load for worst-case load regulation of 0.1%, $I_0 = 12$ mA.

Current limiting is provided by R_3. The current-limit resistor should be selected so that the maximum voltage drop across it, at full-load current, is equal to the voltage given in Figure 16.7 at the maximum junction temperature of the IC. This ensures a no-load to full-load regulation of better than 0.1% under worst-case conditions.

The short-circuit output current is also determined by R_3. Figure 16.8 shows the voltage drop across this resistor, when the output is shorted, as

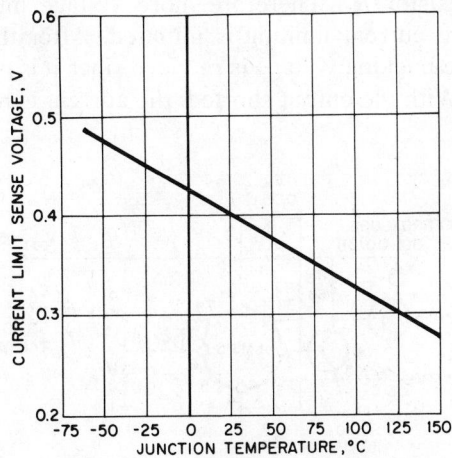

Figure 16.8. Voltage drop across current-limit resistor required to initiate current limiting.

a function of junction temperature in the IC. With the type of current limiting used in Figure 16.6, the dissipation under short-circuit conditions can be more than three times the worst-case full-load dissipation. Hence the heat sink for the pass transistor must be designed to accommodate the increased dissipation if the regulator is to survive more than momentarily with a shorted output. It is encouraging to note that the output current will decrease at higher ambient temperatures. This assists in protecting the pass transistor from excessive heating.

16.5 FOLDBACK CURRENT LIMITING

With high-current regulators the heat sink for the pass transistor must be made quite large in order to handle the power dissipated under worst-case conditions. Making it more than three times larger, to withstand short circuits, is sometimes inconvenient in the extreme. This problem can be solved with foldback current limiting, which makes the output current under overload conditions decrease below the full-load current as the output voltage is pulled down. The short-circuit current can be made but a fraction of the full-load current.

A high-current regulator using foldback limiting is shown in Figure 16.9. A second booster transistor Q_1 has been added to provide a 2-A output current without causing excessive dissipation in the LM105. The resistor across its emitter-base junction bleeds off any collector-base leakage and establishes a minimum collector current for Q_2 to make sure that the circuit will not oscillate. The foldback characteristic is produced with R_4 and R_5. The voltage across R_4 bucks out the voltage dropped across the current-sense resistor R_3. Therefore more voltage must be developed across R_3 before current limiting is initiated. After the output voltage begins to fall, the bucking voltage is reduced since it is proportional to the output voltage. With the output shorted, the current is reduced to a value

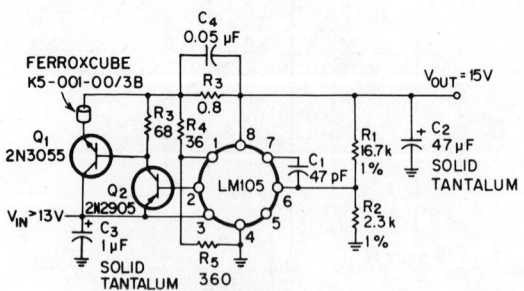

Figure 16.9.   Foldback-current limiting included in a 2-A voltage regulator.

determined by the current-limit resistor and the current-limit sense voltage of the LM105.

Figure 16.10 illustrates the limiting characteristics. The circuit regulates for load currents up to 2 A. Heavier loads will cause the output voltage to drop, thus reducing the available current. With a short on the output, the current is only 0.5 A.

In design the value of R_3 is determined from

$$R_3 = \frac{V_{\text{lim}}}{I_{SC}}, \tag{16.1}$$

where V_{lim} is the current-limit sense voltage of the LM105, given in Figure 16.8, and I_{SC} is the design value of short-circuit current. The value of R_5 is then obtained from

$$R_5 = \frac{V_{\text{OUT}} + V_{\text{sense}}}{I_{\text{bleed}} + I_{\text{bias}}}, \tag{16.2}$$

where V_{OUT} is the regulated output voltage, V_{sense} is maximum voltage across the current-limit resistor for 0.1% regulation as indicated in Figure 16.7, I_{bleed} is the preload current on the regulator output, and I_{bias} is the maximum current coming out of pin 1 of the LM105 under full-load conditions. The value of I_{bias} will be equal to 2 mA plus the worst-case base drive for the *pnp* booster transistor Q_2. It should be made at least 10 times greater than I_{bias}.

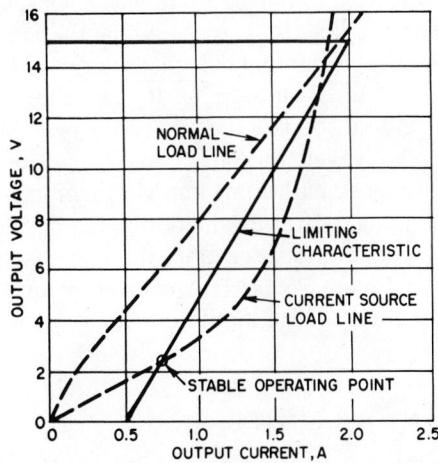

Figure 16.10.   Limiting characteristics of regulator with foldback current limiting.

Finally, R_4 is given by

$$R_4 = \frac{I_{FL}R_3 - V_{sense}}{I_{bleed} + I_{bias}}, \tag{16.3}$$

where I_{FL} is the output current of the regulator at full load.

It is recommended that a ferrite bead be strung on the emitter of the pass transistor, as shown in Figure 16.9, to suppress oscillations that may show up with certain physical configurations. It is advisable also to include C_4 across the current-limit resistor.

In some applications the power dissipated in Q_2 becomes too great for a 2N2905 under worst-case conditions. This can be true even if a heat sink is used, as it should be in almost all applications. When dissipation is a problem, the 2N2905 can be replaced with a 2N3740. With a 2N3740, the ferrite bead and C_4 are not needed because this transistor has a lower cutoff frequency.

One of the advantages of foldback limiting is that is sharpens the limiting characteristics of the IC. In addition, the maximum output current is less sensitive to variations in the current-limit sense voltage of the IC: in this circuit a 20% change in sense voltage will affect the trip current by only 5%. The temperature sensitivity of the full-load current is likewise reduced by a factor of 4, whereas the short-circuit current is not.

Even though the voltage dropped across the sense resistor is larger with foldback limiting, the minimum input-output voltage differential of the complete regulator is not increased above the 3 V specified for the LM105 as long as this drop is less than 2 V. This can be attributed to the low sense voltage of the IC by itself.

Figure 16.10 shows that foldback limiting can be used with only certain kinds of load. When the load looks predominantly like a current source, the load line can intersect the foldback characteristic at a point at which it will prevent the regulator from coming up to voltage, even without an overload. Fortunately most solid-state circuitry presents a load line that does not intersect. However, the possibility cannot be ignored, and the regulator must be designed with some knowledge of the load.

With foldback limiting, power dissipation in the pass transistor reaches a maximum at some point between full load and short-circuited output. This is illustrated in Figure 16.11. However, if the maximum dissipation is calculated with the worst-case input voltage, as it should be, the power peak is not too high.

16.6 HIGH-CURRENT REGULATOR

The output current of a regulator using the LM105 as a control element can be increased to any desired level by adding more booster transistors,

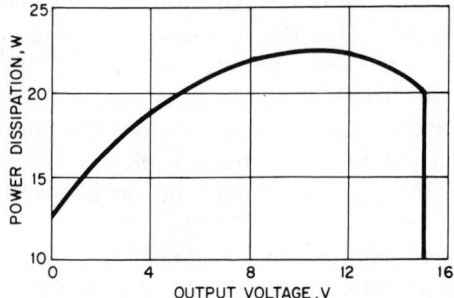

Figure 16.11. Power dissipation in series-pass transistors under overload conditions in regulator using foldback current limiting, $V_{IN} = 28$ V, $I_{FL} = 2.0$ A, $I_{SC} = 0.5$ A.

thus increasing the effective current gain of the pass transistors. A circuit for a 10-A regulator is shown in Figure 16.12. A third *npn* transistor has been included to get higher current. A low-frequency device is used for Q_3 because it seems to withstand abuse better. However, high-frequency transistors must be used to drive it. Both Q_2 and Q_3 are double-diffused transistors with good frequency response. This ensures that Q_3 will present the dominant lag in the feedback loop through the booster transistors and back around the output transistor of the LM105. This is further guaranteed by the addition of C_3.

The circuit as shown has a full-load capability of 10 A. Foldback limiting is used to give a short-circuit output current of 2.5 A. The addition of Q_3 increases the minimum input-output voltage differential by 1 to 4 V.

16.7   DOMINANT FAILURE MECHANISMS

By far the biggest reason for regulator failures is overdissipation in the series-pass transistors. This has been borne out by experience with the

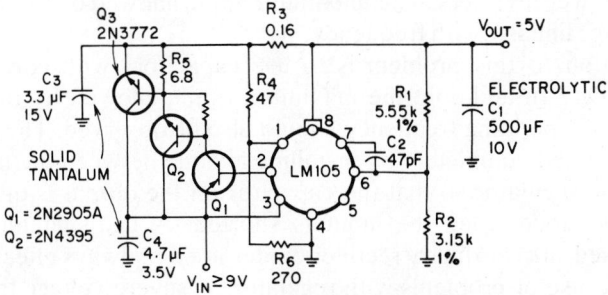

Figure 16.12.   Ten-ampere regulator with foldback current limiting.

LM100. Excessive heating in the pass transistors causes them to short out, destroying the IC. This has happened most frequently when *pnp* booster transistors in a TO-5 can, such as the 2N2905, are used. Even with a good heat sink, these transistors cannot dissipate much more than 1 W. The maximum dissipation is less in many applications. When a single *pnp* booster is used and power can be a problem, it is best to go to a transistor such as the 2N3740, in a TO-66 power package, and use a good heat sink.

Using a compound *pnp-npn* booster does not solve all problems. Even when breadboarding with transistors in TO-3 power packages, heat sinks must be used. The TO-3 package is not very good thermally without a heat sink. Dissipation in the *pnp* transistor driving the *npn* series-pass transistor cannot be ignored either. Dissipation in the driver with worst-case current gain in the pass transistor must be taken into account. In certain cases this could require that a *pnp* transistor in a power package be used to drive the *npn* pass transistor. In almost all cases a heat sink is required if a *pnp* driver transistor in a TO-5 package is selected.

With output currents above 2 to 4 A, it is good practice to replace a 2N3055 pass transistor with a 2N3772. The 2N3055 is rated for higher currents, but its current gain falls off rapidly. This is especially true at either high temperatures or low input-output voltage differentials. A 2N3772 will give substantially better performance at high currents, and it makes life much easier for the *pnp* driver.

The second biggest cause of failure has been the output filter capacitors on power inverters providing unregulated power to the regulator. If these capacitors are operated near their maximum dc voltage rating with excessive ripple across them, they will sputter; that is, they short momentarily and clear themselves. When they short, the output capacitor of the regulator is discharged back through the reverse-biased pass transistors or the control circuitry, frequently causing destruction. This phenomenon is especially prevalent when solid tantalum capacitors are used with high-frequency power inverters. The maximum ripple allowed on these capacitors decreases linearly with frequency.

The solution to this problem is to use capacitors with conservative voltage ratings. In addition, the maximum ripple allowed by the manufacturer at the operating frequency should also be observed. The problem can be eliminated completely by installing a diode between the input and output of the regulator so that the capacitor on the output is discharged through this diode when the input is shorted. A fast-switching diode should be used since ordinary rectifier diodes are not always effective.

Another cause of problems with regulators is severe voltage transients on the unregulated input. Even if these transients do not cause immediate failure in the regulator, they can feed through and destroy the load. If the load shorts out, as is frequently the case, the regulator can be destroyed by subsequent transients.

This problem can be solved by specifying all parts of the regulator to withstand the transient conditions. However, when ultimate reliability is needed, this is not a good solution. Especially since the regulator can withstand the transient, yet severely overstress the circuitry on its output by feeding the transients through. Hence a more logical recourse is to include circuitry that suppresses the transients. A method of doing this is shown in Figure 16.13. A zener diode, which can handle large peak currents, clamps the input voltage to the regulator while an inductor limits the current through the zener during the transient. The size of the inductor is determined from

$$L = \frac{\Delta V \Delta t}{I} \qquad (16.4)$$

where ΔV is the voltage by which the input transient exceeds the break-down voltage of the diode, Δt is the duration of the transient, and I is the peak current the zener can handle while still clamping the input voltage to the regulator. As shown, the suppression circuit will clamp 70-V, 4-ms transients on the unregulated supply.

16.8   CONCLUSIONS

The LM105 is an exact replacement for the LM100 in the majority of applications and provides about 10 times better regulation. There are, however, a few differences. In switching-regulator applications[2] the size of the resistor used to provide positive feedback should be doubled, since the impedance seen looking back into the reference bypass terminal is twice that of the LM100 (2 versus 1 kΩ). In addition, the minimum output voltage of the LM105 is 4.5 V, compared with 2 V for the LM100. In low-voltage regulator applications the effect of this is obvious. How-

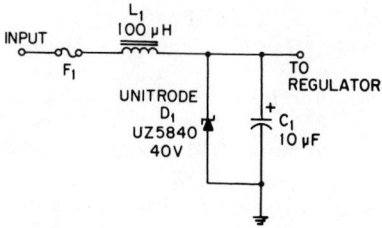

Figure 16.13.   Suppression circuitry for removal of large voltage spikes from unregulated supplies.

ever, it also imposes some limitations on current-regulator and shunt-regulator designs[3]. Lastly, clamping the compensation terminal (pin 7) within a diode drop of ground or the output terminal will not guarantee that the regulator is shut off, as it will with the LM100. This restricts the LM105 in the overload shutoff schemes[3] that can be used with the LM100.

Dissipation limitations of practical packages dictate that the output current of an IC regulator be less than 20 mA. However, external booster transistors can be added to obtain any desired output current. Even with satisfactory packages, considerably larger heat sinks would be needed if the pass transistors were put on the same chip as the reference and control circuitry, because an IC must be run at a lower maximum temperature than a power transistor. In addition, heat dissipated in the pass transistor couples into the low-level circuitry and degrades performance. All this suggests that the pass transistor should be kept separate from the IC.

Overstressing series-pass transistors has been the biggest cause of failures with IC regulators. This applies not only to the transistors within the IC but also to the external booster transistors. Hence in designing a regulator it is of the utmost importance to determine the worst-case power dissipation in all the driver and pass transistors. Devices must then be selected that can handle the power. Further, adequate heat sinks must be provided since even power transistors cannot dissipate much power by themselves.

Normally the highest power dissipation occurs when the output of the regulator is shorted. If this condition requires heat sinks that are so large as to be impractical, foldback current limiting can be used. With foldback limiting, the power dissipated under short-circuit conditions can actually be made less than the dissipation at full load.

The LM105 is designed primarily as a positive-voltage regulator. A negative regulator, the LM104, which is a functional complement to the LM105[4], has also been designed.

REFERENCES

[1] Widlar, R. J., *A Versatile, Monolithic Voltage Regulator*, National Semiconductor AN-1, February 1967.

[2] Widlar, R. J., *Designing Switching Regulators*, National Semiconductor AN-2, April 1967.

[3] Widlar, R. J., *New Uses for the LM100 Regulator*, National Semiconductor AN-8, June 1968.

[4] Widlar, R. J., *Designs for Negative Voltage Regulators*, National Semiconductor AN-21, October 1968.

17

Negative Voltage Regulators

by Robert J. Widlar

National Semiconductor, Santa Clara, California

Although positive voltage regulators can be adapted for use in applications requiring negative voltage regulation, some sacrifice in complexity, performance, and flexibility results. This can be avoided by using negative regulators, as shown in this chapter.

17.1 THE NEGATIVE REGULATOR

The negative regulator used in the circuits described in this chapter is the LM104. This IC can supply any output voltage from 0 to 40 V while operating from a single unregulated supply. The output voltage is set by a single programming resistor, and remote sensing at the load is possible. The IC regulates within 0.01% in circuits using a separate floating bias supply, in which the maximum output voltage is limited only by the breakdown of external pass transistors.

17.2 CIRCUIT OPERATION

The circuit diagram for the LM104 is shown in Figure 17.1. The basic reference for the regulator is zener diode D_1. The reference diode is supplied from a *pnp* current source Q_8, which has a fixed current gain of 2. This arrangement permits the circuit to operate with unregulated input voltages as low as 7 V, substantially increasing the efficiency of low-voltage regulators.

251

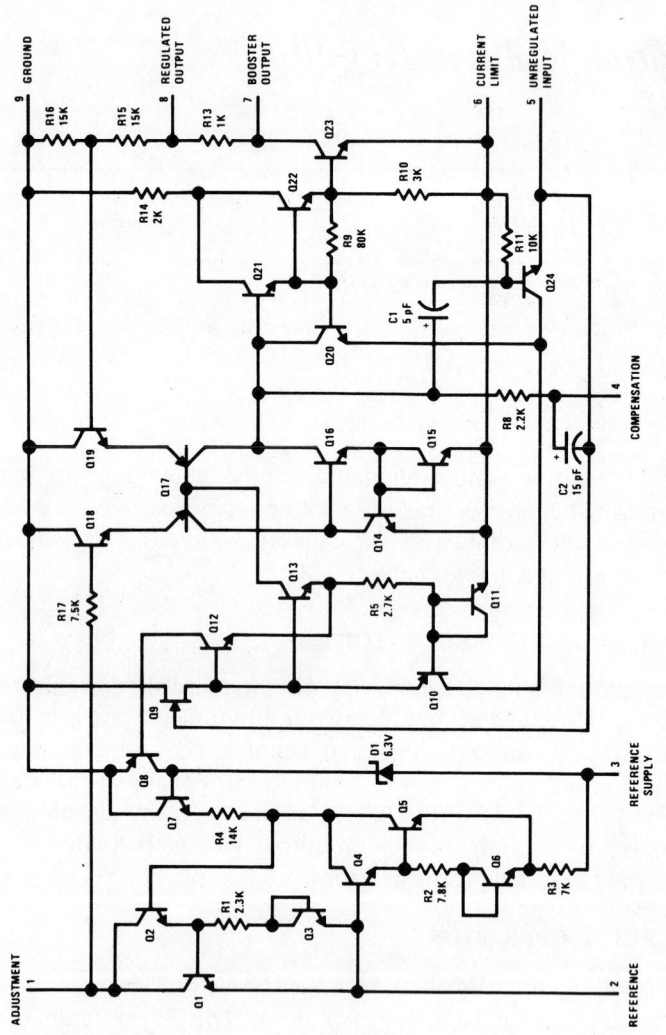

Figure 17.1. Circuit diagram for negative voltage regulator LM104.

252

The reference supply is temperature compensated by using the negative temperature coefficient of the transistor emitter-base voltages to cancel the positive coefficient of the zener diode. The design produces a nominal 2.4 V between the reference and reference-supply terminals of the IC. Connecting an external 2.4-kΩ resistor between those terminals gives a 1-mA reference current from the collectors of Q_1 and Q_2, which is independent of temperature. The reference voltage supplied to the error amplifier is developed across a second external resistor connected between the adjustment terminal and ground.

The reference-supply terminal is normally connected to the unregulated supply. However, improved line regulation can be obtained by pre-regulating the voltage on this terminal. This improvement occurs because Q_1, Q_2, and Q_7 do not see changes in input voltage. Normally it is the change in the emitter-base voltage of these transistors with changes in collector-base voltage that determines the line regulation.

When the reference-supply and unregulated-input terminals are operated from separate voltage sources, it is important to make sure that the unregulated-input terminal of the IC does not get more than 2 V more positive than the reference-supply terminal. If this happens, the collector-isolation junction of Q_6 becomes forward biased and disrupts the reference.

The error amplifier of the regulator is quite similar to the LM101 operational amplifier. Emitter-follower input transistors Q_{18} and Q_{19} drive a dual *pnp* that is operated in the common-base configuration. The current gain of these *pnp* transistors is fixed at 4 so that the base can be driven by a current source (Q_{13}). Active collector loads are used for the input stage so that a voltage gain of 2000 is obtained. The transistors Q_{21} and Q_{22} provide enough current gain to keep the internal, series-pass transistor from loading the input stage. The resistor R_{14} limits the base drive on Q_{23} when it saturates with low, unregulated-input voltages. The collector of Q_{23} is brought out separately so that an external booster transistor can be added for increased output-current capability. The resistor R_{13} establishes the minimum operating current in Q_{23} when booster transistors are used.

The error amplifier operates properly with common-mode voltages all the way up to ground. Because of this, the circuit will regulate with output voltages to 0 V.

Current limiting is provided by Q_{24}. When the voltage between the current-limit and unregulated-input terminals becomes large enough to turn on Q_{24}, it will pull Q_{10} out of saturation and remove base drive from Q_{21} through Q_{20}. This causes the series-pass transistor to exhibit a constant-current characteristic. The preload current, provided for Q_{24}

by Q_{10} before current limiting is initiated, gives a much sharper current-limit characteristic. The components C_1 and R_{11} are included in the limiting circuitry to suppress oscillations.

The error amplifier is connected to a divider on the output (R_{15} and R_{16}) to keep the reference-current generator from saturating with low input-output voltage differentials. A compensating resistor R_{17}, which is equal to the equivalent resistance of the divider, is included to minimize offset error in the error amplifier.

The major feedback loop is frequency compensated by the brute-force method of rolling off the response with a relatively large capacitor on the output. The capacitor C_2 is included in the IC to compensate for the effects of series resistance in the output capacitor. A compensation point is also brought out so that more capacitance can be added across C_2 for certain regulator configurations. The resistor R_8 improves the load-transient response, especially when compensation is added on pin 4.

The purpose of Q_9, which is a collector field-effect transistor, is to bias the current-source transistors Q_{12} and Q_{13}. It also supplies the preload current for the current-limit transistor Q_{24} through Q_{10}.

17.3   LOW-POWER REGULATOR

The circuit shown in Figure 17.2 can provide output voltages between 0 and -40 V at currents up to 25 mA. The output voltage is linearly dependent on the value of R_2, giving approximately 2 V for each 1 kΩ of resistance. The exact scale factor can be set up by trimming R_1. This should be done at the maximum output-voltage setting in order to compensate for any mismatch in the internal divider resistors of the integrated circuit.

Short-circuit protection is provided by R_3. The value of this resistor should be chosen so that the voltage drop across it is 300 mV at the

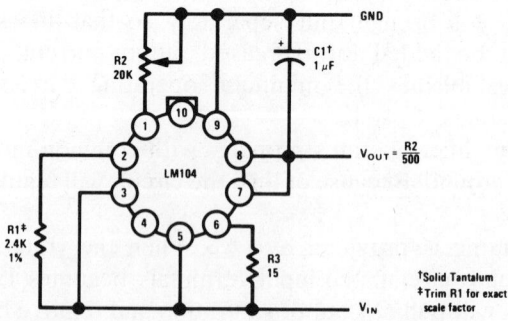

Figure 17.2.   Low-power voltage regulator can supply outputs of 0 to 40 V at current levels up to 25 mA.

maximum-load current. This ensures worst-case operation up to full load over a −55 to 125°C temperature range. With a lower maximum operating temperature the design value for this voltage can be increased linearly to 525 mV at 25°C.

For an output-voltage setting of 15 V the regulation, no load to full load, is better than 0.05%; and the line regulation is better than 0.2% for a ± 20% input-voltage variation. Noise and ripple can be greatly reduced by bypassing R_2 with a 10-μF capacitor. This will keep the ripple on the output less than 0.5 mV for a 1-V, 120-Hz ripple on the unregulated input. The capacitor also improves the line-transient response by a factor of 5.

An output capacitor of at least 1 μF is required to keep the regulator from oscillating. This should be a low-inductance capacitor, preferably of solid tantalum, installed with short leads. It is not usually necessary to bypass the input, but at least a 0.01-μF bypass is advisable when there are long leads connecting the circuit to the unregulated power source.

It is important to watch power dissipation in the integrated circuit even with load currents of 25 mA or less. The dissipation can be in excess of 1 W with large input-output voltage differentials, and this is above the rating for the device.

17.4 INCREASED OUTPUT CURRENT

When output currents above 25 mA are required or when the dissipation in the series-pass transistor can be higher than about 0.2 V, under worst-case conditions, it is advisable to add an external transistor to the LM104 to handle the power. The connection of an external booster transistor is shown in Figure 17.3. The output-current capability of the regulator is increased by the current gain of the added *pnp* transistor, but it is still necessary to watch dissipation in the external pass transistor. Excessive dissipation can burn out both the series-pass transistor and the IC.

For example, with the circuit shown in Figure 17.3, the worst-case input voltage can be 25 V. With a shorted output at 125°C, the current through the pass transistor will be 300 mA, and the dissipation in it will be 7.5 W. This clearly establishes the need for an efficient heat sink.

For lower power operation a 2N2905 with a clip-on heat sink can be used for the external pass transistor. However, when the worst-case dissipation is above 0.5 W, it is advisable to employ a power device, such as the 2N3740, with a good heat sink.

The current-limit resistor is chosen so that the voltage drop across it is 300 mV, with maximum-load current, for operation to 125°C. With

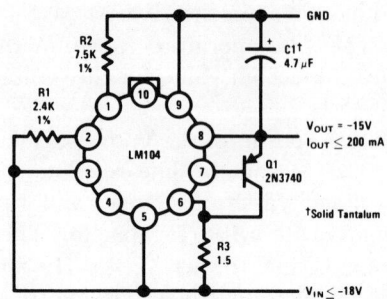

Figure 17.3.   Negative voltage regulator with external booster transistor.

lower maximum ambients this voltage drop could be increased by 2.2 mV/°C. If possible, a fast-acting fuse rated about 25% higher than the maximum-load current should be included in series with the unregulated input.

When a booster transistor is used, the minimum input-output voltage differential of the regulator will be increased by the emitter-base voltage of the added transistor. This establishes the minimum differential at 2 to 3 V, depending on the base drive required by the external transistor.

When output currents in the ampere range are needed, it is necessary to add a second booster transistor to the LM104 circuitry. This connection is shown in Figure 17.4. The output-current capability of the LM104 is increased by the product of the current gains of Q_1 and Q_2. However, it is still necessary to watch the dissipation in both the series-pass

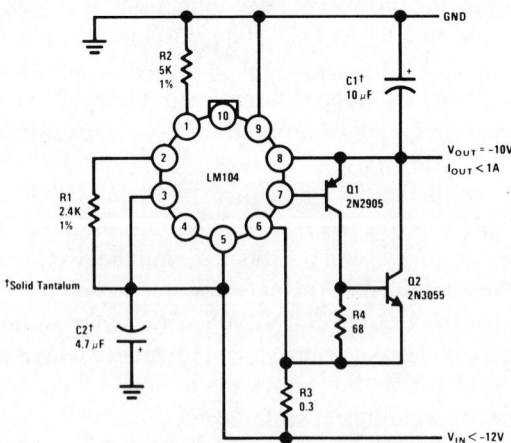

Figure 17.4.   Use of voltage regulator with two booster transistors.

transistor Q_2 and its driver Q_1. A clip-on heat sink is definitely required for Q_1, and it is advisable to replace the 2N2905 with a 2N3740, which has a good heat sink when output currents greater than 1 A are needed. A 1000-pF capacitor would also be added between pins 4 and 5 to compensate for the poorer frequency response of the 2N3740. The need for an efficient heat sink on Q_2 should be obvious.

Experience shows that a single-diffused transistor such as a 2N3055 (or a 2N3772 for higher currents) is preferred over a double-diffused, high-frequency transistor for the series-pass element. The slower single-diffused devices are less prone to secondary breakdown and oscillations in linear-regulator applications.

As with the lower current regulators, C_1 is required to frequency compensate the regulator and prevent oscillations. It is also advisable to bypass the input with C_2 if the regulator is located any distance from the output filter of the unregulated supply. The resistor across the emitter-base junction of Q_2 fixes the minimum collector current of Q_1 to minimize oscillation problems with light loads. It is still possible to experience oscillations with certain physical layouts, but these can almost always be eliminated by stringing a ferrite bead, such as a Ferroxcube K5-001-00/3B, on the emitter lead of Q_2.

The use of two booster transistors does not appreciably increase the minimum input-output voltage differential over that for a single transistor. The minimum differential will be 2 to 3 V, depending on the drive current required from the IC.

With high-current regulators remote sensing is sometimes required to eliminate the effect of line resistance between the regulator and the load. This can be accomplished by returning R_2 and pin 9 of the LM104 to the ground end of the load and connecting pin 8 directly to the high end of the load.

The low resistance values required for the current-limit resistor R_3 are sometimes not readily available. A suitable resistor can be made by using a piece of resistance wire or even a short length of Kovar lead wire from a standard TO-5 transistor.

The current-limit sense voltage can be reduced to about 400 mV by inserting a germanium diode (or a diode-connected germanium transistor) in series with pin 6 of the LM104. This diode will also compensate the sense voltage and make the short-circuit current essentially independent of temperature.

With high-current regulators it is especially important to use a low-inductance capacitor on the output. The lead length on this capacitor must also be made short. Otherwise the capacitor leads can resonate with smaller bypass capacitors (such as 0.1-μF ceramic), which may be connected to the output. These resonances can lead to oscillations. With short leads on the output capacitor the Q of the tuned circuit can be made low enough not to cause trouble.

17.5 FOLDBACK CURRENT LIMITING

High-current regulators dissipate a considerable amount of power in the series-pass transistor under full-load conditions. When the output is shorted, this dissipation can easily increase by a factor of 4. Hence, with normal current limiting, the heat sink must be designed to handle much more power than the worst-case full-load dissipation if the circuit is to survive short-circuit conditions. This can increase the bulk of the regulator substantially.

This situation can be eased considerably by using foldback current limiting. With this method of current limiting the available output current actually decreases as the maximum load on the regulator is exceeded and the output voltage falls off. The short-circuit current can be adjusted to be a fraction of the full-load current, minimizing dissipation in the pass transistor.

The circuit shown in Figure 17.5 accomplishes just this. Normally Q_3 is held in a nonconducting state by the voltage developed across R_4. However, when the voltage across the current-limit resistor R_7 increases until it equals the voltage across R_4 (about 1 V), Q_3 turns on and begins to rob base drive from the driver transistor Q_1. This causes an increase in the output current of the LM104, and it will go into current limiting at a current determined by R_5. Since the base drive to Q_1 is clamped, the output voltage will drop with heavier loads. This reduces the voltage drop

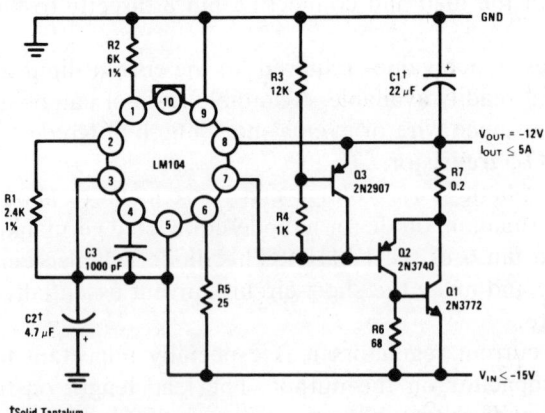

†Solid Tantalum

Figure 17.5. Circuit with foldback limiting.

across R_4 and therefore the available output current. With the output completely shorted, the current will be about one-fifth the full-load current.

During design, R_7 is chosen so that the voltage drop across it will be 1 to 2 V under full-load conditions. The resistance of R_3 should be 1000 times the output voltage. The value of R_4 is then determined from

$$R_4 \simeq \frac{R_7 R_3 I_{FL}}{V_{OUT} + 0.5 \text{ V}}, \qquad (17.1)$$

where I_{FL} is the load current at which limiting will occur.

If it is desired to reduce the ratio of full-load to short-circuit current, this can be done by connecting a resistance of 2 kΩ or more between the emitter and base of Q_3.

17.6   SYMMETRICAL POWER SUPPLIES

In many applications, such as powering operational amplifiers, there is a need for symmetrical positive and negative supply voltages. A particularly economical solution to this design problem is the circuit shown in Figure 17.6. It uses a minimum number of components, and the voltage at both outputs can be set up with ±1.5% by a single adjustment. Furthermore the output voltages will tend to track with temperature and variations in the unregulated supply.

The positive voltage is regulated by an LM105, while an LM104 regulates the negative supply. The unusual feature is that the two regulators are interconnected by R_3. This not only eliminates one precision resistor, but the reference current of the LM104 stabilizes the LM105 so that a ±10% variation in its reference voltage is only seen as a ±3% change in output voltage. This means that in many cases the output voltage of both regulators can be set up with sufficient accuracy by trimming a single resistor, R_1.

The line regulation and temperature drift of the circuit are determined primarily by the LM104, so both output voltages will tend to track. Output ripple can be reduced by a factor of about 5 to less than 2 mV/V by bypassing pin 1 of the LM104 to ground with a 10-μF capacitor. A center-tapped transformer with a bridge rectifier can be used for the unregulated power source.

17.7   ADJUSTABLE CURRENT LIMITING

In laboratory power supplies it is often necessary to adjust the limiting current of a regulator. Of course, this can be done by using a variable

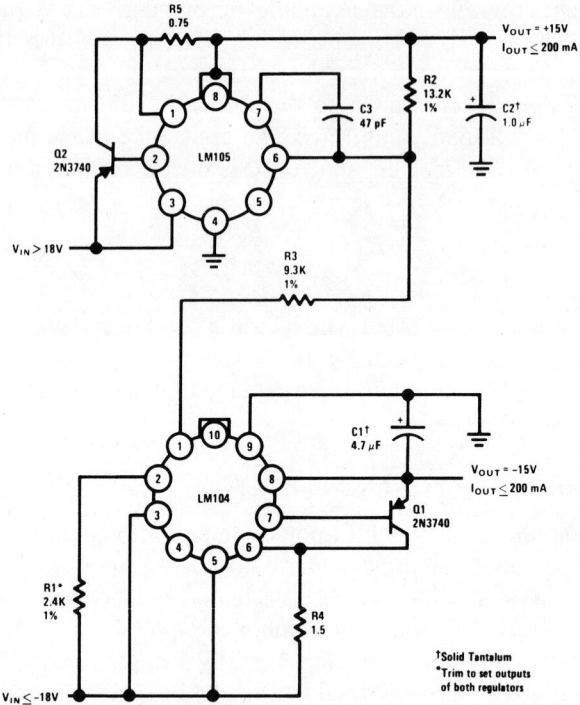

Figure 17.6. Symmetrical power supply. Positive voltage is regulated by LM105; negative-voltage regulation is handled by LM104.

resistance for the current-limit resistor. However, the current-limit resistor can easily have a value below that of commercially available potentiometers. Discrete resistance values can be switched to vary the limiting current, but this does not provide continuously variable adjustment.

The circuit shown in Figure 17.7 solves this problem and gives a linear adjustment of limiting current over a 5:1 range. A silicon diode D_1 is included to reduce the current-limit sense voltage to approximately 50 mV. Approximately 1.3 mA from the reference supply is passed through a potentiometer, R_4, to buck out the diode voltage. Therefore the effective current-limit sense voltage is nearly proportional to the resistance of R_4. The current through R_4 is fairly insensitive to changes in ambient temperature, and D_1 compensates for temperature variations in the current-limit sense voltage of the LM104. Therefore the limiting current will not be greatly affected by temperature. It is important that a potentiometer be used for R_4 and connected as shown. If a rheostat

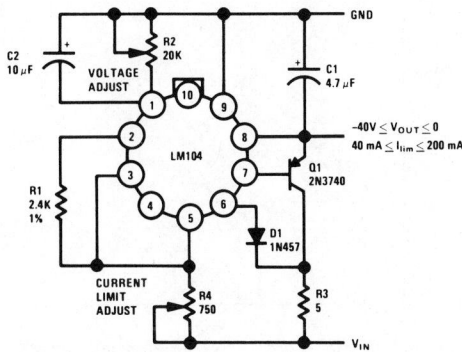

Figure 17.7. Circuit with adjustable current limiting.

connection were used, it could open during adjustment and momentarily increase the current-limit sense voltage to many times its normal value. This could destroy the series-pass transistors under short-circuit conditions.

The inclusion of R_4 will soften the current-limiting characteristics of the LM104 somewhat because it acts as an emitter-degeneration resistor for the current-limit transistor. This can be avoided by reducing the value of R_4 and developing the voltage across R_4 with additional bleed current to ground.

17.8 IMPROVING LINE REGULATION

The line regulation for voltage variations on the reference-supply terminal of the LM104 is about five times worse than it is for changes on the unregulated input. Therefore a zener-diode preregulator can be used on the reference supply to improve line regulation. This is shown in Figure 17.8.

The design of this circuit is fairly simple. It is only necessary that the minimum current through R_4 be greater than 2 mA with low input voltage. Further, the zener voltage of D_1 must be 5 V greater than one-half the maximum output voltage to keep the transistors in the reference-current source from saturating.

17.9 USING PROTECTIVE DIODES

It is a little known fact that most voltage regulators can be damaged by shorting out the unregulated-input voltage while the circuit is operating even though the output may have short-circuit protection. When the input voltage to the regulator falls instantaneously to zero, the output

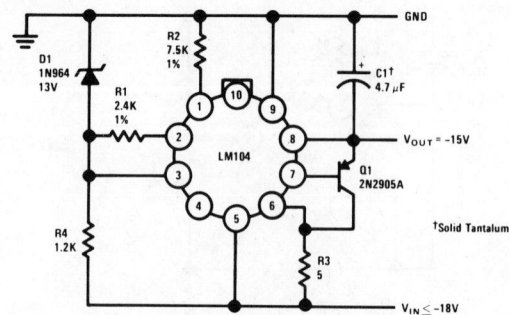

Figure 17.8.   Use of a zener diode to improve line regulation.

capacitor is still charged to the nominal output voltage. This applies voltage of the wrong polarity across the series-pass transistor and other parts of the regulator, and they try to discharge the output capacitor into the short. The resulting current surge can damage or destroy these parts.

When the LM104 is used as the control element of the regulator, the discharge path is through internal junctions forward biased by the voltage reversal. If the charge on the output capacitor is on the order of 40 V/μF, the circuit can be damaged during the discharge interval. However, the problem is seen not only with IC regulators. It also happens with discrete regulators, whose series-pass transistor usually gets blown out.

The problem can be eliminated by connecting a diode between the output and the input so that it discharges the output capacitor when the input is shorted. The diode should be capable of handling large current surges without excessive voltage drop, but it does not have to be a power diode since it does not carry current continuously. It should also be relatively fast. Ordinary rectifier diodes will not do because they look like an open circuit in the forward direction until minority carriers are injected into the intrinsic base region of the p-i-n (p, intrinsic, n) structure.

This problem is caused not only by accidental physical shorts on the input. It has shown up more than once when regulators are driven from high-frequency dc-dc converters. Tantalum capacitors are frequently used as output filters for the rectifiers. When these capacitors are operated near their maximum voltage ratings with excessive high-frequency ripple across them, they have a tendency to sputter—that is, short momentarily and clear themselves. When they short, they can blow out the regulator; but they look innocent after the smoke has cleared.

The solution to this problem is to use capacitors with conservative voltage ratings, to observe the maximum ripple ratings for the capacitor, and to include a protective diode between the input and output of the regulator to protect it in case sputtering does occur.

Heavy loads operating from the unregulated supply can also destroy a voltage regulator. When the input power is switched off, the input voltage can drop faster than the output voltage and cause a voltage reversal across the regulator, especially when the output of the regulator is lightly loaded. Inductive loads, such as a solenoid, are particularly troublesome in this respect. In addition to causing a voltage reversal between the input and the output, they can reverse the input voltage, causing additional damage.

In cases like this it is advisable to use a multiple-pole switch or relay to disconnect the regulator from the unregulated supply separate from the other loads. If this cannot be done, it is necessary to put a diode across the input of the regulator to clamp any reverse voltages, in addition to the protective diode between the input and the output.

Yet another failure mode can occur if the regulated supply drives inductive loads. When power is shut off, the inductive current can reverse the output-voltage polarity, damaging the regulator and the output capacitor. This can be cured with a clamp diode on the output. Even without inductive loads it is usually good practice to include this clamp diode to protect the regulator if its output is accidentally shorted to a negative supply.

A regulator with all these protective diodes is shown in Figure 17.9. The diode D_1 protects against output-voltage reversal, D_2 prevents a voltage reversal between the input and the output of the regulator, and D_3 prevents a reversal of the input-voltage polarity. In many cases D_3 is not needed if D_1 and D_2 are used, since these diodes will clamp the input voltage within two diode drops of ground. This is adequate if the input-voltage reversals are of short duration.

17.10 HIGH-VOLTAGE REGULATOR

In the design of commercial power supplies it is common practice to use a floating bias supply to power the control circuitry of the regulator. As shown in Figure 17.10, this connection can be used with the LM104 to regulate output voltages that are higher than the ratings of the IC. Better regulation can also be obtained because it is a simple matter to preregulate the low-current bias supply so that the IC does not see ripple or line-voltage variations and because the reduced operating voltage minimizes power dissipation and associated thermal effects from the current delivered to the booster transistor.

The bias for the LM104, which is normally obtained from a separate winding on the main power transformer, is preregulated by D_1. The value of R_4 is selected so that it can provide the 3-mA operating current for the IC as well as the base drive of the booster transistor Q_1 with full load and minimum line voltage. The booster transistor regulates the voltage from

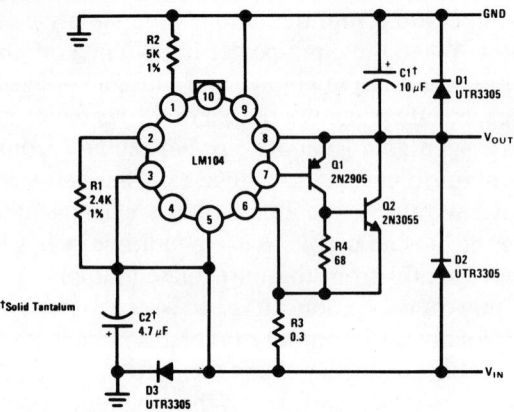

Figure 17.9.   Regulator with protective diodes.

the main supply, and its breakdown voltage will determine the maximum operating voltage of the complete regulator.

The connection of the LM104 is somewhat different from the usual: the internal divider for the error amplifier is shorted out by connecting pins 8 and 9 together. This makes the output voltage equal to the voltage drop across the adjustment resistor R_2 instead of twice this voltage, as is normally the case. The capacitors C_2 and C_3 must also be added to prevent oscillation. The value of C_3 can be increased to 4.7 μF to reduce noise on the output.

It is necessary to add Q_2 and R_5 to provide current limiting. When the output current becomes high enough to turn on Q_2, there will be an abrupt rise in the output current of the LM104 as Q_2 tries to remove base drive

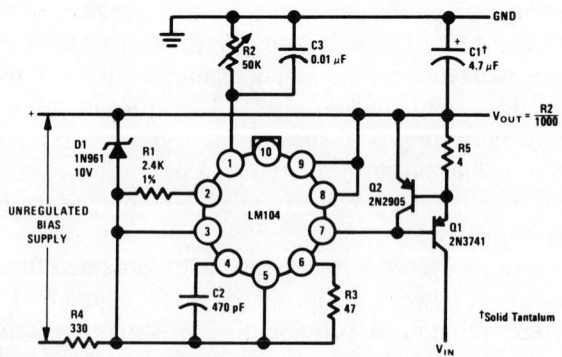

Figure 17.10.   High-voltage regulator has floating bias supply.

from the booster transistor. Any further increases in load current will cause the LM104 to limit at a current determined by R_3, and the output voltage will collapse. The value of R_3 must be selected so that the IC can deliver the base current of Q_1 at full load without limiting.

A second *npn* booster transistor can be used in a compound connection with Q_1 to increase the output current of the regulator. However, with very-high-voltage regulators the most economical solution may be to use a high-voltage *pnp* driving a vacuum tube for the series-pass element.

Remote sensing, which eliminates the effects of voltage dropped in the leads connecting the regulator to the load, can be provided by connecting R_2 to the ground end of the load and pins 8 and 9 to the high end of the load.

17.11 SWITCHING REGULATOR

Linear regulators have the advantages of fast response to load transients as well as low noise and ripple. However, since they must dissipate the difference between the unregulated-supply power and the output power, they sometimes have a low efficiency. This is not always a problem with ac line-operated equipment because the power loss is easily afforded, because the input voltage is already fairly well regulated and because losses can be minimized by adjusting transformer ratios in the power supply. In systems operating from a fixed dc input voltage, the situation is often much different. It might be necessary to regulate a 28-V input voltage down to 5 V. In this case the power loss can quickly become excessive. This is true even if efficiency is not one of the more important criteria, since high power dissipation calls for expensive power transistors and elaborate heat-sinking methods.

Switching regulators can be used to reduce dissipation greatly. Efficiencies approaching 90% can be realized even though the regulated-output voltage is only a fraction of the input voltage. With proper design transient response and ripple can also be made quite acceptable.

The circuit shown in Figure 17.11 uses the LM104 as a self-oscillating switching regulator and operates in much the same way as a linear regulator. The reference current is set up at 1 mA with R_1, and R_2 determines the output voltage in the normal fashion. The circuit is made to oscillate by applying positive feedback through R_5 to the noninverting input on the error amplifier of the LM104. When the output voltage is low, the internal pass transistor of the IC turns on and drives Q_1 into saturation. The current feedback through R_5 then increases the magnitude of the reference voltage developed across R_2. Until the output voltage comes up to twice this reference voltage, Q_1 will remain on. At this point the error amplifier

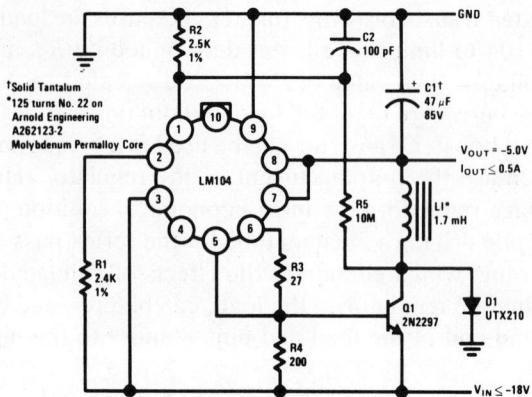

Figure 17.11.   Switching regulator circuit.

goes into linear operation, and the positive feedback makes the circuit switch off. When this happens, the reference voltage is lowered by feedback through R_5, and the circuit will stay off until the output voltage drops to where the error amplifier again goes into linear operation. Hence the circuit regulates with the output voltage oscillating about the nominal value, with a peak-to-peak ripple of around 40 mV.

The power conversion from the input voltage to a lower output voltage is obtained by the action of the switch transistor Q_1, the catch diode D_1, and the *LC* filter. The inductor is made large enough to ensure that the current through it is essentially constant throughout the switching cycle. When Q_1 turns on, the voltage on its collector will be nearly equal to the unregulated-input voltage. When it turns off, the magnetic field in L_1 begins to collapse, driving the collector voltage of Q_1 to ground, where it is clamped by D_1.

If, for example, the input voltage is 10 V and the switch transistor is driven at a 50% duty cycle, the average voltage on the collector of Q_1 will be 5 V. This waveform will be filtered by L_1 and C_1 and appear as a 5-V dc voltage on the output. Since the inductor current comes from the input while Q_1 is on, but from ground through D_1 while Q_1 is off, the average value of the input current will be half the output current. The power output will therefore equal the input power if switching losses are neglected.

In design the value of R_3 is chosen to provide sufficient base drive to Q_1 at the maximum-load current. The value of R_4 must be low enough for the bias current coming out of pin 5 of the LM104 (approximately 300 μA) not to turn on the switch transistor. The purpose of C_2 is to remove transients that can appear across R_2 and cause erratic switching. It should not be made so large that it severely integrates the waveform fed back to this point.

17.12 HIGH-CURRENT SWITCHING REGULATOR

Output currents up to 3 A can be obtained with the switching-regulator circuit shown in Figure 17.12. The circuit is identical with the one described previously, except that Q_2 has been added to increase the output-current capability by about an order of magnitude. It should be noted that the reference-supply terminal is returned to the base of Q_2 rather than the unregulated input. This is done because the LM104 will not function properly if pin 5 gets more than 2 V more positive than pin 3. The reference current, as well as the bias currents for pins 3 and 5, is supplied from the unregulated input through R_5, so its resistance must be low enough for Q_2 not to be turned on with about 2 mA flowing through it.

The line regulation of this circuit is worsened somewhat by the unregulated-input voltage being fed back into the reference for the regulator through R_6. This effect can be eliminated by connecting a 0.01-μF capacitor in series with R_6 to remove the dc component of the feedback.

There are a number of precautions that should be observed with all switching regulators, although they are more inclined to cause problems in high-current applications. For one, fast-switching diodes and transis-

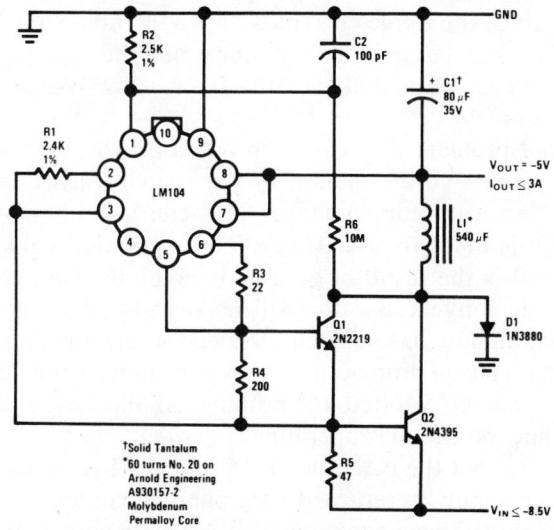

Figure 17.12. Switching regulator capable of handling output currents to 3 A.

tors must be used. If D_1 is an ordinary junction rectifier, voltages on the order of 10 V can be developed across it in the forward direction when the switch transistor turns off. This happens because low-frequency rectifiers are usually manufactured with a pin structure that presents a high forward impedance until enough minority carriers are injected into the diode base region to increase its conductance. This not only causes excessive dissipation in the diode, but the diode also presents a short circuit to the switch transistor when it first turns on, until all the charge stored in the base region of the diode is removed. Similarly a high-frequency switch transistor must be used, since excessive switching losses in low-frequency transistors, such as the 2N3055, make them overheat.

It is important that the core material used for the inductor have a soft saturation characteristic. Cores that saturate abruptly produce excessive peak currents in the switch transistor if the output current becomes high enough to run the core close to saturation. Powdered molybdenum-Permalloy cores, on the other hand, exhibit a gradual reduction in permeability with excessive current, so the only effect of output currents above the design value is a gradual increase in switching frequency.

One thing that is frequently overlooked in the design of switching circuits is the ripple rating of the filter capacitors. Excessive high-frequency ripple can cause these capacitors to fail. This is an especially important consideration for capacitors used on the unregulated input as the ripple current through them can be higher than the dc load current. The situation is eased somewhat for the filter capacitor on the output of the regulator since the ripple current is only a fraction of the load current. Nonetheless proper design usually requires that the voltage rating of this capacitor be higher than that dictated by the dc voltage across it for reliable operation.

One unusual problem that has been noted in working with switching regulators is excessive dissipation in the switch transistors caused by high emitter-base saturation voltage. This can also show up as erratic operation if Q_1 is the defective device. This saturation voltage can be as high as 5 V and is the result of poor alloying on the base contact of the transistor. A defective transistor will not usually show up on a curve tracer because the low base current needed for linear operation does not produce a large voltage drop across the poorly alloyed contact. However, a bad device can be spotted by probing on the bases of the switch transistors while the circuit is operating.

It is necessary that the catch diode D_1 and any bypass capacitance on the unregulated input be returned to ground separately from the other parts of the circuit. These components carry large current transients and can develop appreciable voltage transients across even a short length of wire. If C_1, C_2, or R_2 have any common ground impedance with the catch diode or the input bypass capacitor, the transients can appear directly on the output.

17.13   SWITCHING REGULATOR WITH CURRENT LIMITING

The switching-regulator circuits described previously are not protected from overloads or a short-circuited output. The current limiting of the LM104 is used to limit the base drive of the switch transistor, but this does not effectively protect the switch transistor from excessive current. Providing short-circuit protection is no simple problem, since it is necessary to keep the regulator operating in the switching mode when the output is shorted. Otherwise the dissipation in the switch transistor will become excessive even though the current is limited.

A circuit that provides current limiting and protects the regulator from short circuits in shown in Figure 17.13. The current through the switch transistor produces a voltage drop across R_9. When this voltage becomes large enough to turn on Q_3, current limiting is initiated. This occurs because Q_3 takes over as the control transistor and regulates the voltage on pin 8 of the LM104. This point, which is the feedback terminal of the error amplifier, is separated from the actual output of the regulator by

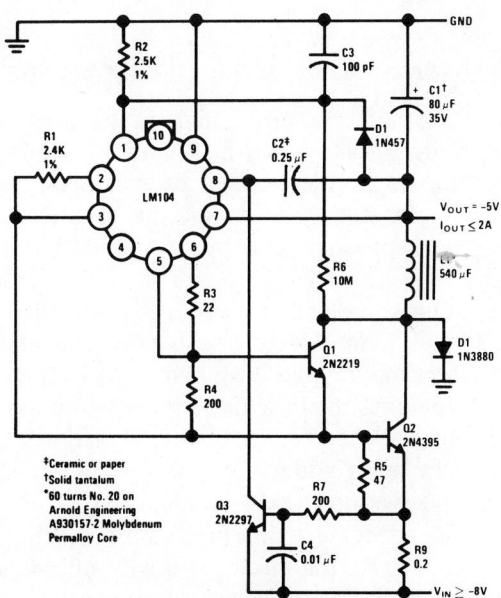

Figure 17.13.   Switching regulator with current limiting.

not shorting the regulated output and booster output terminals of the IC. Hence, with excessive output current, the circuit still operates as a switching regulator, with Q_3 regulating the voltage fed back to the error amplifier as the output voltage falls off.

A resistor, R_7, is included so that excessive base current will not be driven into the base of Q_3. Capacitor C_4 ensures that Q_3 does not turn on from the current spikes through the switch transistor caused by pulling the stored charge out of the catch diode (these are about twice the load current). This capacitor also operates in conjunction with C_2 to produce sufficient phase delay in the feedback loop for the circuit to oscillate in current limiting. However, C_4 should not be made so large that it appreciably integrates the rectangular waveform of the current through the switch transistor.

As the output voltage falls below half the design value, D_1 pulls down the reference voltage across R_2. This permits the current-limiting circuitry to keep operating when the unregulated-input voltage drops below the design value of output voltage, with a short on the output of the regulator.

A transistor with good high-current capability was chosen for Q_3 so that it does not suffer from secondary breakdown effects from the large peak currents (about 200 mA) through it. With a shorted output, these peak currents occur with the full input voltage across Q_3. The average dissipation in Q_3 is, however, low.

17.14 SWITCHING REGULATOR WITH OVERLOAD SHUTOFF

An alternative method for protecting a switching regulator from excessive output currents is shown in Figure 17.14. When the output current becomes too high, the voltage drop across the current-sense resistor R_8 fires an SCR that shuts off the regulator. The regulator remains off, dissipating practically no power, until it is reset by removing the input voltage.

In the actual circuit complementary transistors Q_3 and Q_4 replace the SCR since it is difficult to find devices with a low enough holding current (about 25 μA). When the voltage drop across R_8 becomes large enough to turn on Q_4, this removes the base drive for the output transistors of the LM104 through pin 4. When this happens, Q_3 latches Q_4, holding the regulator off until the input voltage is removed. It will then start when power is applied if the overload has been removed.

With this circuit it is necessary that the shutoff current be 1.5 times the full-load current. Otherwise the circuit will shut off when it is switched on with a full load because of the excess current required to charge the output capacitor. The shutoff current can be made closer to the full-load

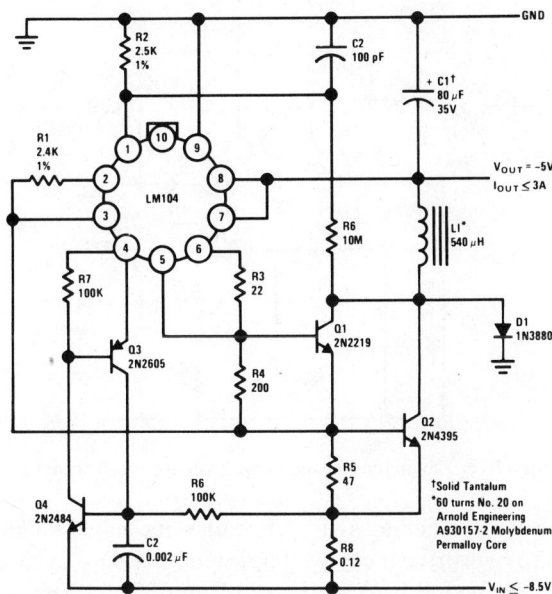

Figure 17.14.   Switching regulator with overload shutoff.

current by connecting a 10-μF capacitor across R_2, which will limit the charging current for C_1 by slowing the rise time of the output voltage when the circuit is turned on. However, this capacitor will also bypass the positive feedback from R_6 that makes the regulator oscillate. Therefore it is necessary to put a 270-Ω resistor in the ground end of the added capacitor and provide feedback to this resistor from the collector of Q_1 through a 1-MΩ resistor.

17.15 DRIVEN SWITCHING REGULATOR

When a number of switching regulators are operated from a common power source, it is desirable to synchronize their operation to distribute more uniformly the switched current waveforms in the input line. Synchronous operation can also be beneficial when a switching regulator is operated in conjunction with a power converter.

A circuit that synchronizes the switching regulator with a square-wave drive signal is shown in Figure 17.15. It differs from the switching regulators already described in that positive feedback is not used. Instead a triangular wave with a peak-to-peak amplitude of 25 mV is applied to the noninverting input of the error amplifier. The waveform is obtained by integrating the square-wave synchronizing signal. This triangular wave

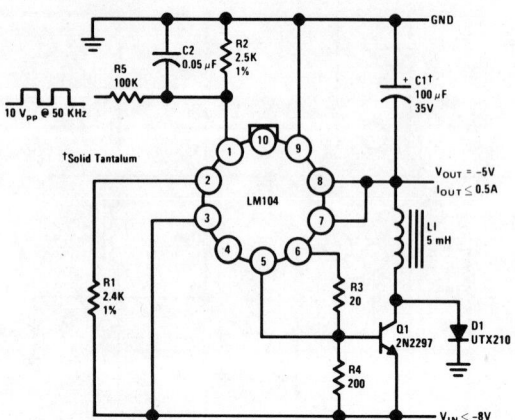

Figure 17.15.   Switching regulator with square-wave drive signal.

causes the error amplifier to switch because its gain is high enough for the waveform to overdrive it easily. The switching duty cycle is controlled by the output voltage fed back to the error amplifier. If the output voltage goes up, the duty cycle will decrease since the error amplifier will pick off a smaller portion of the triangular wave. Similarly the duty cycle will decrease if the output voltage drops. Hence the duty cycle is controlled to produce the desired output voltage.

Without a synchronous drive signal the circuit will self-oscillate at a frequency determined by L_1 and C_1. This self-oscillation frequency must be lower than the synchronous-drive frequency. Therefore more filtering is required for a driven regulator than for a self-oscillating regulator operating at the same frequency. This also means that a driven regulator will have less output ripple.

The value of C_2 is chosen so that its capacitive reactance at the drive frequency is less than one-tenth the resistance of R_2. The amplitude of the triangular wave is set at 25 mV with R_5. It is advisable to ac couple the drive signal by putting a capacitor in series with R_5 so that it does not disturb the dc reference voltage developed for the error amplifier.

18

A High-Speed Data Transmission System

by Jerry Avery

Texas Instruments, Dallas, Texas

   Digital systems often require the use of long lines for the transmission of digital information between various equipment locations within the system. These long lines are frequently located in noisy environments that can cause propagation of false information if steps are not taken to overcome the noise and its effects on data transmission. In the past this problem has been. overcome by using special line drivers and/or line receivers to interface between the transmission line and the logic circuitry (see Figure 18.1).

   Line-driver circuits translate the small logic-level swings of the processing and peripheral portions of the computer to either higher voltage levels or matched impedance (current mode) levels for transmission to other areas of the computer. Balanced lines may be used to help overcome noise problems; line receivers must reject the common mode and induced noise on the ttransmission lines and convert the signals back to forms that are compatible with the standard logic circuits of the computer.

   The following paragraphs cover the use of a compatible line driver and line receiver to overcome noise problems in a high-speed data-transmission system.

18.1   LINE-DRIVER CHARACTERISTICS

Input Characteristics. The input of the driver is TTL (transistor-transistor logic) compatible with two inputs per driver. The inputs are

273

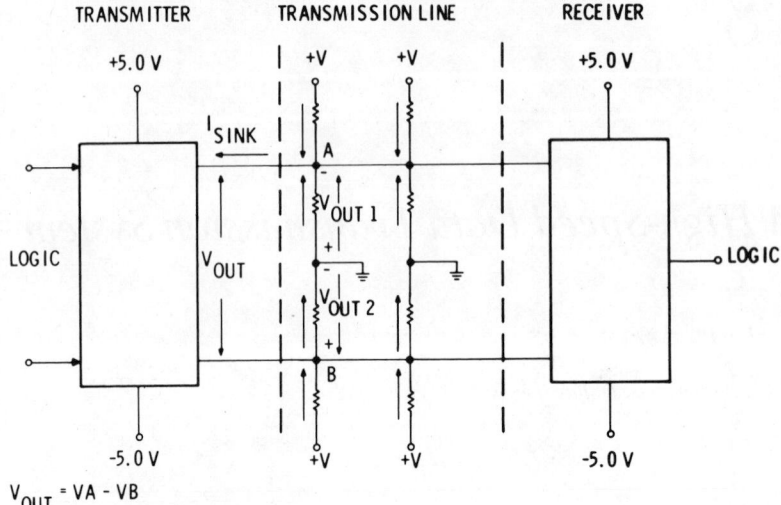

Figure 18.1. Typical data-transmission system.

designated A_1-A_2 and B_1-B_2. The switching point is between 0.4 and 2.4 V and typically at 1.4 V.

Input Requirements. The logical "1"-input voltage $[V_{IN}(1)]$ required at an input terminal to ensure a logical "1" at the in-phase output terminal is typically 1.4 V.

Typical Input DC Noise Immunity. The input gates of the driver will change states at 1.4 V. The output from a TTL gate is typically 3.3 V in the logical "1" state and 0.2 V in the logical "0" state. Therefore the driver can typically tolerate 1.9 V of negative-going noise in the "1" state and 1.2 V of positive-going noise in the "0" state before causing the input gate to false trigger.

Guaranteed Input DC Noise Immunity. Simply stating that a circuit will not false trigger is no adequate guarantee for a design engineer. The IC manufacturer must also guarantee voltage levels that allow a specific noise margin. The logic "0" input test voltage to the driver is 0.8 V; with a guaranteed maximum logical "0" of 0.4 V for the TTL circuits, the guaranteed noise margin is 400 mV.

Output Characteristics. The output is a differential amplifier capable of driving single ended or balanced. It has a high common-mode output-voltage range of +10 V to −3 V. The large drive range not only allows the gate to drive long lines but also gives it better noise margins at the receiver.

The differential output also allows the signal to be transmitted on a balanced line, so that common-noise signals induced in the two conductors of the transmission line are ignored at the receiver.

18.2 DRIVER-CIRCUIT DESCRIPTION

The SN75109 is a high-speed data transmitter designed to be used in such applications as line drivers in balanced or unbalanced applications, party-line systems, and level converters.

This monolithic dual line driver has two independent channels and common supply voltage and ground. Each line driver consists of a TTL-compatible input stage followed by a level shifter and a differential pair providing a current mode output signal.

An inhibitor input gate (TTL compatible) provided to each output stage may be used to turn off either output stage, regardless of the input signal applied. A common strobe (inhibitor input) is also available for inhibiting both channels (see Figure 18.2).

Input Stage.   The multiple-emitter transistor Q_1 is used to provide inherent switching-time advantages over other saturated logic schemes.

A low voltage at the inputs A or B will allow current to flow through the base-emitter diode of Q_1, which is in saturation (see Figure 18.3). No drive current will pass through the base collector junction until the voltage at the base of Q_2 exceeds the forward voltages across diodes D_2 and D_3 $(V_{FD2} + V_{FD3})$, for the differential stage Q_2-Q_3 operates basically as a switch. The voltage (V_C) at the base of Q_2 (point C) equals

$$V_{IN} + V_{offset}Q_1, \tag{18.1}$$

where $V_{offset} = V_{CE}$.

The input D at the base of Q_3 is referenced at $2 V_{BE}$ above ground by using the forward drop across the two diodes D_2 and D_3. Therefore, when V_D is greater than V_C, Q_3 is on and Q_2 is off, leading to

$$V_E = V_{CC1} - (R_2 + R_4)(I_S + I_B), \tag{18.2}$$

$$V_F = V_{CC1} - R_2 I_S - (R_2 + R_3) I_B, \tag{18.3}$$

where I_S is the current provided by the current source $(Q_4, D_1,$ and $R_6)$ and I_B is the current flowing into the next stage. The value of I_S can be obtained from

$$I_S = \frac{V_{CC1} - V_{FD1}}{R_6} = 1.4 \text{ mA (typical).} \tag{18.4}$$

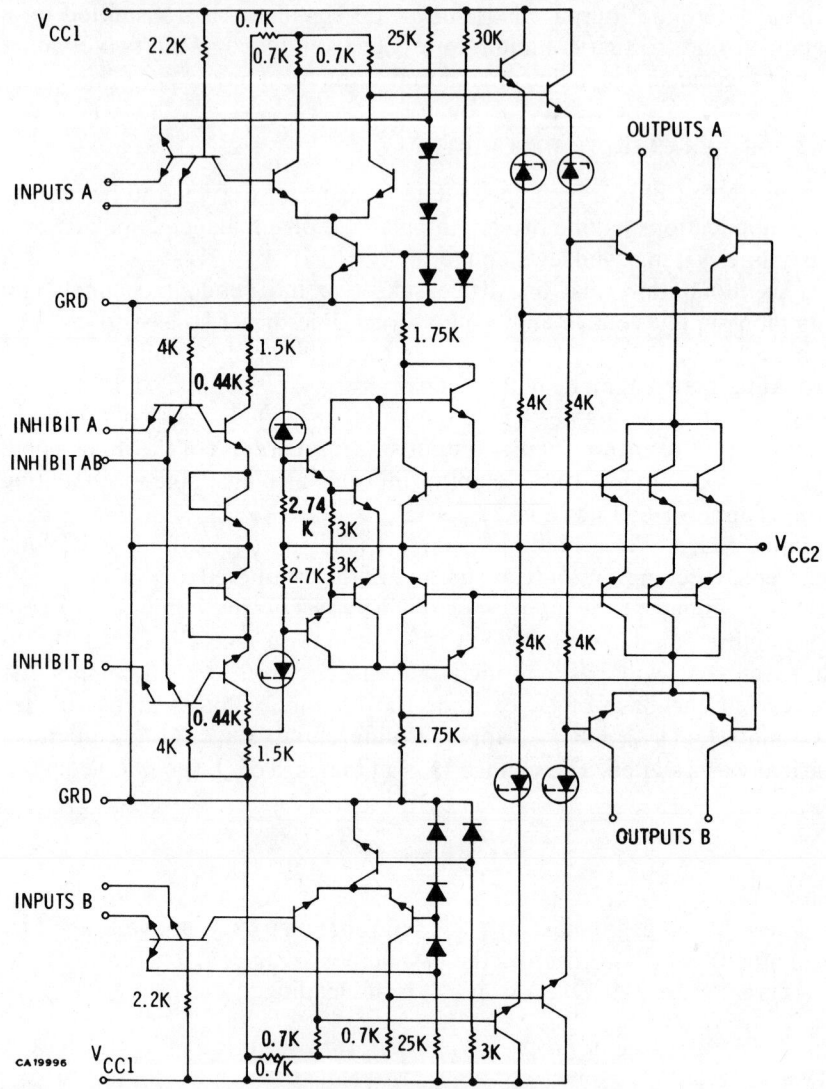

Figure 18.2. Driver inhibit stage.

The reverse situation occurs when V_C is greater than V_D. A clamp voltage at point C is provided through diodes D_2, D_3, D_4 and the offset voltage V_{CE} of Q. This voltage is given by

$$VC_{\text{clamp}} = V_{FD2} + V_{FD3} + V_{FD4} + V_{\text{offset}\,Q_1}. \tag{18.5}$$

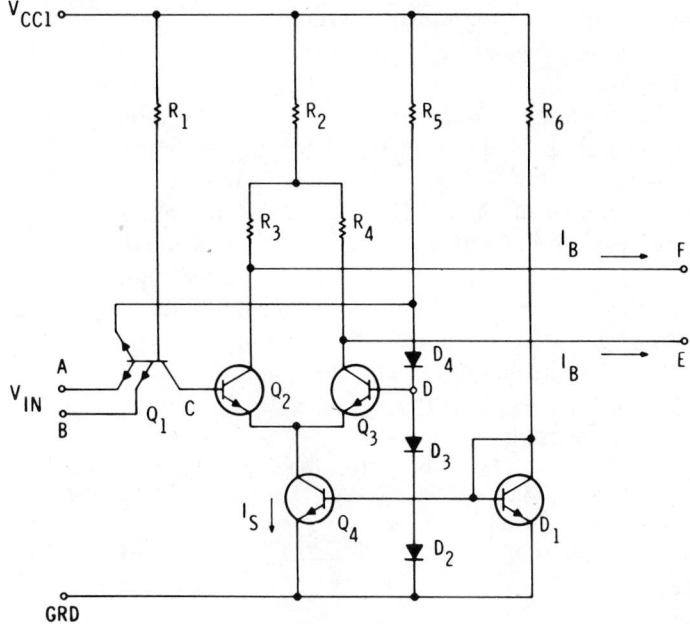

Figure 18.3. SN75107 circuit schematic.

If inputs *A* and *B* are raised to a voltage above the clamp level, the current flowing through the base-emitter junction of Q_1 (or Q_2) will decrease until these emitters are finally reverse biased. However, transistor Q_1 will not be turned off, as in a standard gate, but will remain in the saturation region since the clamping emitter tied between R_5 and D_4 is now forward biased.

Threshold-Noise Margin. As expected from the preceding analysis, the driver input has an input logic threshold-voltage level of approximately $2V_{BE}$.

Besides the logic threshold, the same noise margins that are guaranteed for series 54 are ensured at each of the driver inputs. This is accomplished by testing each logic input under standard series 54 conditions, at 2 V in the logical "1"-input condition and 0.8 V in the logical "0"-input condition. An absolute minimum of 0.4 V of noise margin is therefore guaranteed at each input, since the specific driving logic is 2.4 V minimum with a logical "1" input and 0.4 V maximum with a logical "0" input under worst-case conditions.

Input-Current Requirements. Input-current requirements reflect worst-case conditions for $T_A = -55$ to 125°C and a ΔV_{CC} of ±10%. The Q_1 base-emitter saturation during a logical "0"-input level will require no more than 3.0 mA flowing out of the emitter. Each input requires some current into it at a logical "1" level. This current is 40 μA maximum for each emitter input.

Level-Shifting Stage. Refer to Figure 18.4. The voltage levels computed at the points E and F in the preceding section are shifted down through Q_9 and Z_1, and Q_{10} and Z_2 to points G and H.

Careful matching of Q_9 and Q_{10}, Z_1 and Z_2, and R_7 and R_8 is made to provide points G and H with a nominally 1–V differential.

Output Stage. (See Figure 18.5.) The differential voltage at inputs G and H is large enough to switch completely the differential pair Q_{13} and Q_{14}. Therefore, when V_G is greater than V_H, Q_{13} is on and Q_{14} is off. Q_{13} will then sink the amount of current I_S supplied by the current source constituted by Q_{15}, Q_{16}, Q_{17}, Q_{18}, Q_{19}, and R_9. It operates as explained in the following paragraphs.

The point I is $2V_{BE}$ above V_{CC2}, forcing a current I_o through R_9 that is equal to

$$I_o = \frac{V_{CC2} - 2V_{BE}}{R_9}. \tag{18.6}$$

This current will supply the base drive for Q_{15}, Q_{16}, Q_{17}, and Q_{19} as well as the collector current for Q_{19} ($I_o - 4I_B$). Close matching of these four transistors will lead to a total I_S (sink current) of approximately $3I_o$.

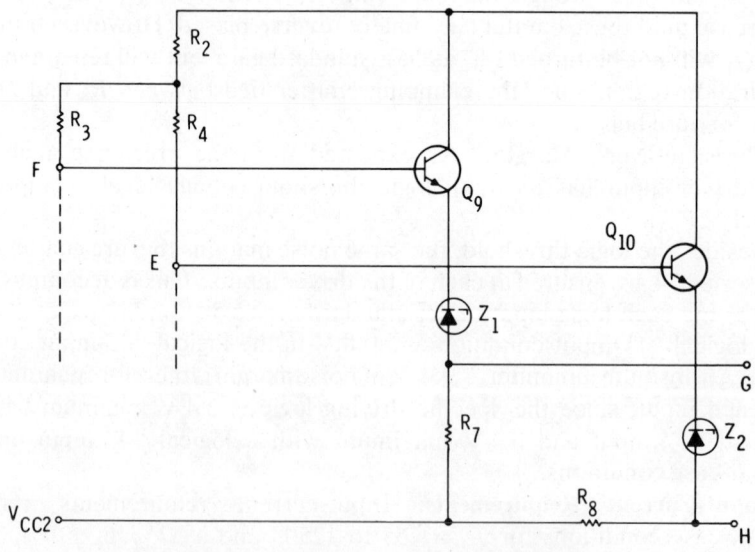

Figure 18.4. Receiver input differential stage.

OUTPUTS

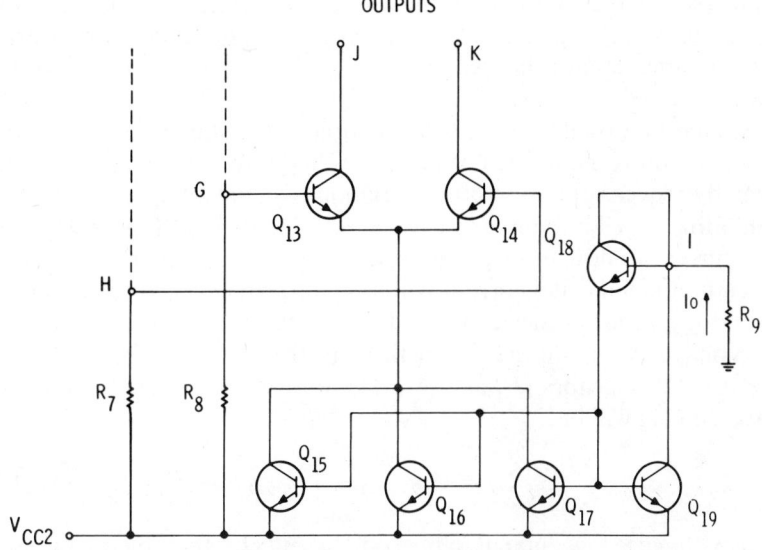

Figure 18.5.   Receiver level-shifting stage.

This structure saves about one-third of the power required by a standard current source using only one diode and one transistor. Furthermore two V_{BE} drops are required at point I for proper operation. This advantage will be demonstrated.

Inhibitor Stage.   As already stated, this stage has been designed to enable or inhibit the driver function.

Enabling.   Here also the multiple-emitter input transistor has been chosen for the reasons stated in the description of the input operation. When the strobe inputs are raised to a high voltage, the transistor Q_{25} is turned off and the Q_{23} base-drive current is supplied through the base-collector diode of Q_{25}. Q_{23} will saturate, and the current flowing through R_{12} and R_{13} will lower the voltage at point L.

This voltage will then be shifted through the zener diode Z_3, and finally the voltage V_o at the base of Q_{21} will be

$$V_0 = \frac{(R_{13}/R_{12})V_{CC1} + [1+(R_{13}/R_{12})]V_{CC2} - [1+(R_{13}/R_{12})]V_{23} + V_{CE(sat)} + V_{BE}}{1+(R_{13}/R_{12})+(R_{13}/R_{11})},$$

(18.7)

where $V_{CE(sat)}$ and V_{BE} are measured at Q_{23} and Q_{24}, respectively. This voltage V_o will be low enough to turn off transistors Q_{21} and Q_{20}, and therefore the driver output current will not be affected. Obviously worst-case conditions are reached, as far as voltage-supply values are concerned, when V_o is maximum; that is, when V_{CC1} and V_{CC2} are at their maximum values.

It should be noted that V_o is a function of resistance ratios and does not depend on resistor absolute values. Therefore resistance fluctuations caused by process or temperature variations will not affect V_o.

Inhibiting.   A low voltage at the strobe inputs (see Figure 18.6) will allow current to flow through the base-emitter junction of Q_{25}, which will then saturate, and drive current will pass through its base collector diode. Q_{23} and Q_{24} will be turned off, and the voltage at point L will be high. This voltage when shifted down through the zener diode$_{23}$ will supply drive to the transistors Q_{21} and Q_{20}. Therefore the voltage at point I with respect to V_{CC2} will be

$$V_1 = V_{CE \text{ sat } Q21} + V_{BE \, Q20}. \tag{18.8}$$

This voltage is low enough to turn off Q_{18} and Q_{19}, thereby inhibiting the driver outputs. The current supplied through R_9 will flow mainly through Q_{21} and Q_{20}.

Worst-case conditions are reached, as far as the voltage-supply values are concerned, when V_0 is minimum; that is, when V_{CC1} = minimum and V_{CC2} = minimum.

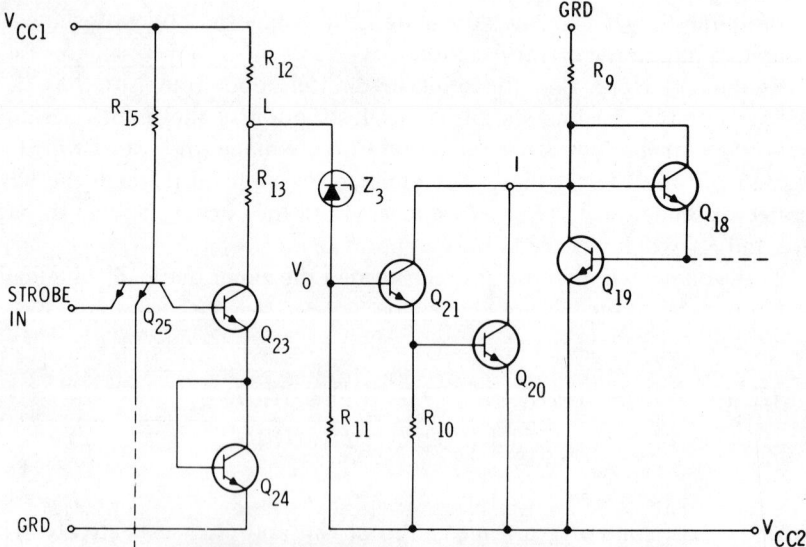

Figure 18.6.   Receiver second differential stage.

Inhibitor Threshold-Noise Margins. The inhibitor input presents a TTL gate configuration with an input logic threshold-voltage level of approximately $2 V_{BE}$. This circuit features the same noise margins as the driver inputs, and operation is guaranteed in the same manner as explained in the paragraphs on input operation.

Inhibitor Input-Current Requirements. Input-current requirements reflect worst-case conditions for $T_A = -55$ to $125°C$ and $\Delta V_{CC} = \pm 10\%$. The input of the inhibitor requires no more than 3.0 mA out of the input at a logical "0" level; therefore one load ($N = 1$) has a 3.0-mA maximum.

The input also requires current at a logical "1" level. This current is $40 \mu A$ maximum. It should be noted that the common strobe used to inhibit both channels will require twice the logical "0" or logical "1" current required by a single strobe.

Unused Common Strobe. For optimum enabling and inhibiting delays the unused common strobe should be tied to a positive-voltage source of 2.4 to 5.5 V. It is also advisable to use a limiting resistor as described in the input-output section.

18.3 LINE-RECEIVER-CIRCUIT DESCRIPTION

High-speed voltage-discriminator circuits, such as the Texas Instruments SN75107, are designed to be used in many applications, such as line receivers (balanced, unbalanced, party-line, and general-use receivers) or comparators on data-processing equipment, process-control computers, radar interface systems, and telephone switching systems.

The monolithic dual line receiver shown in Figure 18.7 has two independent channels (except for the common current source, supply voltages, and ground). Each line receiver consists of a differential input stage that provides a high-input impedance, followed by a level-shifting stage and a second differential amplifier that enhances the common-mode rejection ratio and drives a TTL gate output.

A strobe or gating input may be used on the output stage of either channel to hold the output at a logical "1" regardless of the input signal applied to the corresponding channel. A common strobe is also available for both channels.

Input Differential Stage. Basically the input differential stage (see Figure 18.8) operates as a switch. If V_{IN1} is greater than V_{IN2}, Q_1 is on and Q_2 is off; therefore

$$V_{OUT(A)} = V_{CC1} - RI_S = 3.9 \text{ V},$$

$$V_{OUT(B)} = V_{CC1} = 5.0 \text{ V}.$$

$$(18.9)$$

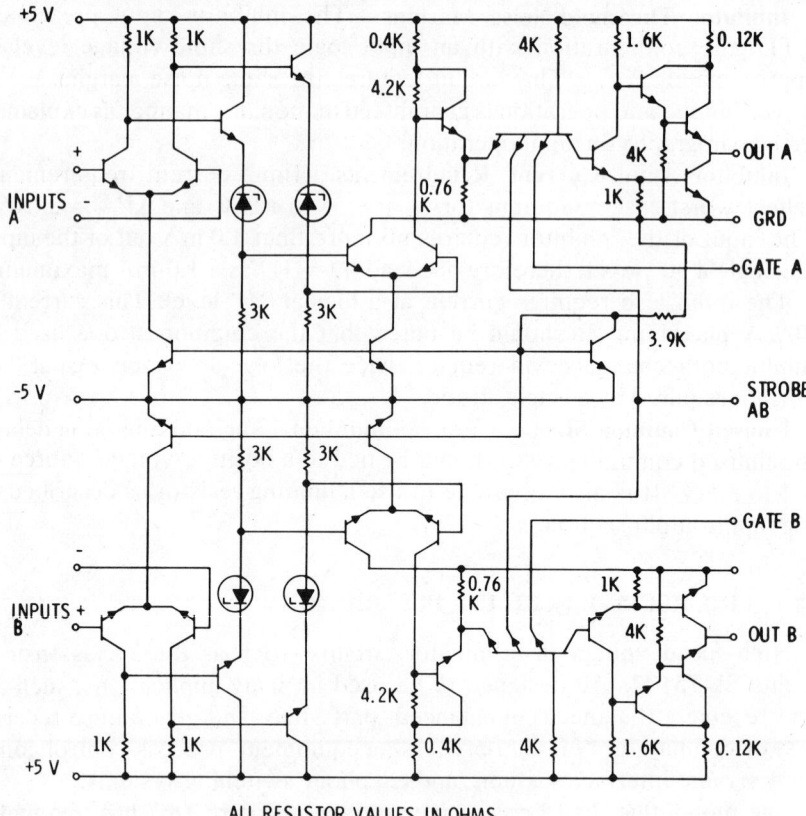

Figure 18.7.   SN75109 circuit schematic.

This reverse situation occurs when V_{IN1} is less than V_{IN2}.

It appears that either of the inputs could withstand about $+3.9$ V common-mode voltage (in nominal conditions) before Q_1 or Q_2 starts saturating and affecting the speed of the overall system.

In the same manner point C is 1 V_{BE} above V_{CC2} (i.e., nominally -4.2 V). Either V_{IN1} or V_{IN2} could go almost as low as -4.2 V before the current source Q_3 starts saturating.

To cover worst-case conditions recommended operating common-mode voltage range is ± 3 V. The input bias current is nominally 30 nA when $I_B = I_S (Q_1$ or $Q_2)$. The logic input impedance is then high. This receiver will therefore provide very little loading to the transmission line, making it very useful in party-line data-transmission systems where cable and installation costs are minimized.

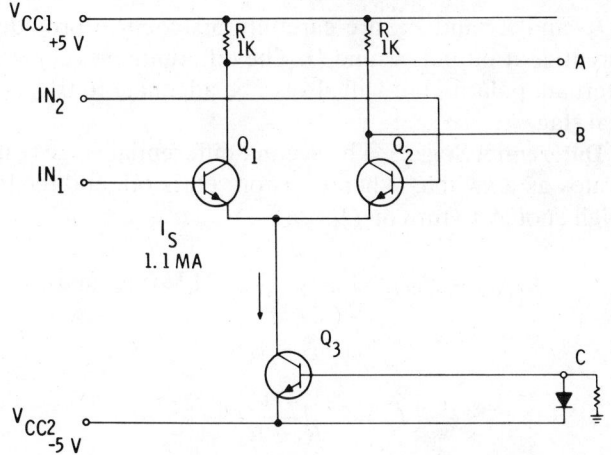

Figure 18.8. Driver input stage.

Level-Shifting Stage. (See Figure 18.9.) If we refer back to the preceding section, $V_{OUT(A)}$ and $-V_{OUT(B)}$ can be more exactly expressed as

$$-V_{OUT(A)} = V_{CC1} - R(I_S + I_B),\qquad(18.10)$$

$$-V_{OUT(B)} = V_{CC1} - R_{1b}\qquad(18.11)$$

when V_{IN1} is greater than V_{IN2}, these levels are shifted down through Q_3 and Z_1, or Q_4 and Z_2, to

$$-V_{OUT(C)} = V_{CC1} - R(I_S + I_B) - V_{BE} - V_Z,\qquad(18.12)$$

$$-V_{OUT(D)} = V_{CC1} - R(0 + I_B) - V_{BE} - V_Z.\qquad(18.13)$$

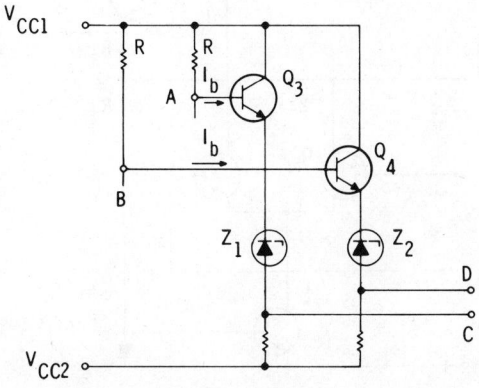

Figure 18.9. Driver level-shifting stage.

Q_3 and Q_4, and Z_1 and Z_2, are carefully matched to provide nominally 1-V differential at outputs C and D. The differential level between C and D will alternate polarity but will always be adequate to trigger the second differential stage.

Second Differential Stage.   The second differential stage (Figure 18.10) also operates as a switch. When Q_5 is on, Q_6 is off, and the base voltage of Q_7 is high enough to turn on Q_7.

$$V_{CE\ Q7} = R_2 I_B + V_{BE\ Q7}, V_{CE} = 1 \text{ V (nominal)}, \tag{18.14}$$

$$V_{OUT(E)} = I_E R_3, \tag{18.15}$$

where

$$I_E = \frac{V_{CC1} - V_{CEQ7}}{R_1 + R_3}.$$

This results in

$$V_{OUT(E)} \text{ (logical ``1'')} = V_{CC1} - (R_2 I_B + V_{BE\ Q7})\frac{R_3}{R_1 + R_3} \tag{18.16}$$

and is approximately 2.5 V. With 2.5 V at point E no current will pass through the base-emitter diode of Q_8. This constitutes a logical "1" level for the output gate.

When Q_5 is off and Q_6 sinks I_S (1 mA), the base of Q_7 is at a voltage level of $V_{CC1} - (R_1 + R_2)I_S$ (0 V nominal). This is low enough to turn off Q_7.

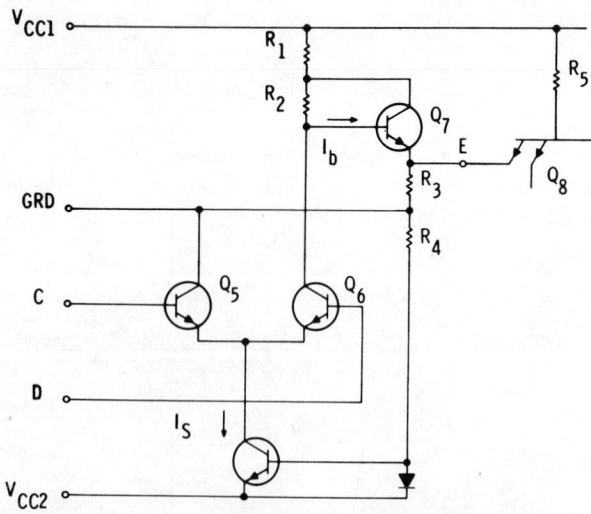

Figure 18.10.   Driver output stage.

The resulting low voltage at point E will allow current to flow through the base-emitter junction and R_3 and R_5 to act as a divider, resulting in

$$V_{OUT(E)} \text{ (logical ``0'')} = (V_{CC1} - V_{BE\,Q8})\frac{R_3}{R_3 + R_5} = 0.6 \text{ V (nominal)}, \quad (18.17)$$

$$V_{CC1} - V_{BE\,QS} = 4.2 \text{ V (nominal)}. \quad (18.18)$$

This constitutes the logical "0" level for the output gate. Values and layout of R_1, R_2, R_3, R_4, and R_5 have been carefully arrived at to achieve convenient logical "0" and logical "1" levels for temperatures between -55 and $125°C$ under supply-voltage variations of $\pm 10\%$.

Output Gate.   The output gate uses a standard series 54 TTL gate with a nominal $-V_{OUT0} = 240$ mV at 20 mA and $V_{OUT1} = 3.35$ V at -0.5 mA. Two strobes have been provided at the input of each gate. The receiver function will be enabled or inhibited, respectively, when a logical "1" level is applied to both strobes or a logical "0" level to either strobe.

18.4   RECEIVER-INPUT CONSIDERATIONS

The input sensitivity is defined as the differential dc voltage required at the inputs of the receiver to force the output to the logic-gate threshold-voltage level. The input sensitivity of the SN75107 is nominally ≤ 3 mV. This feature is particularly important when data are transmitted down a long line and the pulse deteriorates because of cable losses.

Common-Mode Voltage Range.   The common-mode voltage range (CMVR) is defined as the voltage which is applied simultaneously to both input terminals and which, if exceeded, will not allow normal operation of the receiver.

Recommended operating CMVR is ± 3 V. However, in some particularly noisy environments common-mode voltage could easily reach ± 10 to ± 15 V if precautions are not taken to reduce problems of ground noise, power-supply noise, and crosstalk. When the receiver is to operate under such conditions, input attenuators should be used to decrease the voltage seen by the differential inputs. Differential noise will also be reduced by the same ratio.

These attenuators have been intentionally omitted from the receiver input terminals so that the designer may select resistors that will be compatible with his particular application or environment. Furthermore the use of attenuators will adversely affect input sensitivity, propagation time, power dissipation, and in some cases input impedance (depending on the selected resistor values) and versatility of the receiver.

Input Termination Resistors.   To prevent reflections the transmission line should be terminated in its characteristic impedance. Matched termination resistances normally in the range of 25 to 200 Ω are required not only to terminate the transmission line in a desired impedance but also to provide a necessary dc path for the receiver input bias.

If careful matching of the resistor pairs is not observed, the effective common-mode rejection ratio will be reduced.

Reference Voltage. The receiver can be used as a single-ended line receiver or comparator by referencing one input. The operating threshold-voltage level is established by, and is approximately equal to, the applied reference input voltage V_{REF} (selected within the operating range).

A simple method of generating the reference voltage is the use of a resistor voltage divider from either the positive V_{CC1} or negative V_{CC2} voltage supplies.

The reference could also be obtained by a diode or a reference supply or just ground. Bias current required at the reference input is low (nominally $30\,\mu A$). Therefore voltage dividers of this type may normally be operated with very low current requirements and may be used also to supply a number of paralleled reference inputs.

In noisy environments the use of a filter capacitor may be helpful.

18.5   DUAL DIFFERENTIAL COMPARATOR

Connected as a differential comparator, the SN75107 may be used to compare the noninverting input terminal with the inverting input, so that a digital "1" or "0" is experienced at the output resulting from one input being greater than the other (see Figure 18.11).

There are many applications for differential comparators, such as voltage comparison, threshold detection, controlled Schmitt trigger, and pulse-width control.

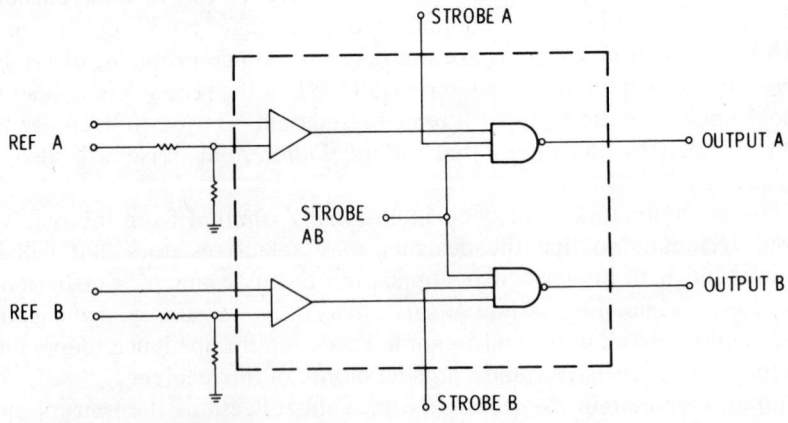

Figure 18.11.   Line receiver as a differential comparator.

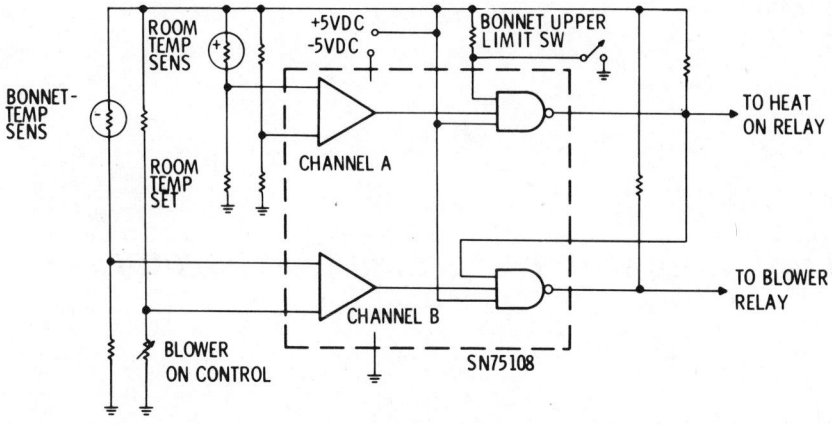

Figure 18.12. Line receiver as a furnace control.

The strobe inputs allow for additional control over the circuit, permitting either output or both to be inhibited.

18.6 FURNACE CONTROL

The SN75108 is identical to the SN75107 except that it features an open-collector output. The circuit in Figure 18.12 is given as an example of a possible use for the IC in areas other than what would normally be considered electronic systems.

Basically, where the room temperature is below the desired level, channel A input will be above (more positive than) the reference level set on the input differential amplifier. This will in turn cause a high output to operate, the heat-on relay turning on the heat. The output is tied to one of the strobes of channel B.

When channel A is on, channel B can be turned on. The channel B input will be turned on when the bonnet temperature of the furnace reaches the desired level. Normally the furnace will be shut down when the room temperature reaches the desired level and channel A is turned off. There is also a safety switch in the bonnet that will shut down the furnace if the temperature at this point exceeds desired limitations. The types will be determined by the particular operating conditions.

19

Designing with Integrated Comparators

by Alfredo Gomez

Computer Components, Palm Beach Gardens, Florida

In a memory application a sense amplifier extracts information contained in a memory array and conditions it so that it can be further processed by other logic elements in the computer. A typical three-dimensional ferrite core memory system is shown in Figure 19.1. Acting on an external command, the memory address register selects the proper X- and Y-lines. In each memory plane a given pair of X- and Y-lines has only one core in common; this core is in the particular word being read. The number of bits per word equals the number of planes, and all of the cores in one plane are connected to a common sense winding. It follows that there is one sense amplifier per plane.

The sense amplifier detects and conditions the "1" signal and rejects the "0" signal contained in each bit and places the information in the memory data register (MDR). This information is then used by the control and arithmetic units. The amount of time taken to extract the information from the cores to the MDR is called access time.

In destructive-type memories the information must be written back into the cores through a write cycle. The sum of read plus write time is the memory cycle time.

If a sense amplifier is to do its job, it must terminate the sense line in its proper impedance (which is usually low). It must provide sufficient gain with stability and high common-mode rejection. Its frequency response should be adequate for the input-signal waveform, and it should be able to recover quickly from differential and common-mode signals. Its

288

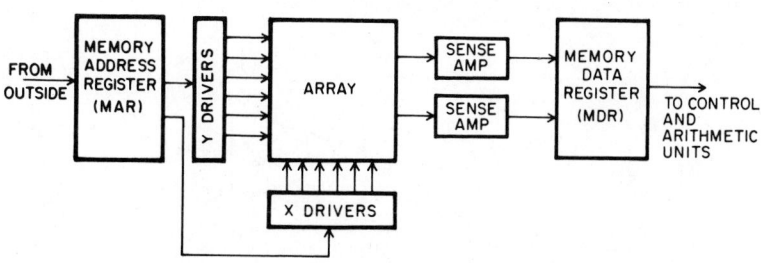

Figure 19.1.   A typical core-memory system. Sense amplifier detects and conditions a one signal or rejects a zero signal; then it places the information in the memory data register.

signal-propagation time should be short for improved memory cycle time, and its input threshold should be stable.

Typically the engineer will first design a working model of the sense-amplifier system; then, simulating a source and load impedance, he will make a complete worst-case evaluation. From this start he will have a pretty good idea of the comparator needed for his application. Suppose it looks as though he can take advantage of the price benefits offered by resorting to the popular old standard, the 711.

The specifications developed by this engineer must include the actual circuit in which the 711 is to perform; in addition the specifications should not be overly conservative as far as noncritical parameters are concerned.

Now let us take a closer look at some of these specifications.

19.1   INPUT THRESHOLD

The threshold for the IC is determined externally by means of a resistor divider. Parameters that affect the value of the threshold are (a) tolerance of the threshold resistors and (b) the input offset voltage change of the IC with temperature and power supply.

A general expression for the total threshold variation is

$$\Delta V_T = \frac{\delta V_T}{\delta R_B}\Delta R_B + \frac{\delta V_T}{\delta V^-}\Delta V^- + \frac{\delta V_T}{\delta V^+}\Delta V^+ + \frac{\delta V_T}{\delta T}\Delta T. \qquad (19.1)$$

A common connection used for a sense amplifier is shown in Figure 19.2. The threshold in this case is determined by the voltage across R_3 and R_4. The specification being evolved by the engineer should include maximum and minimum threshold. The minimum threshold at which the 711 can be operated is determined by its offset voltage. The offset voltage also determines the threshold uncertainty. In commercial versions of the 711 this voltage is 5 mV.

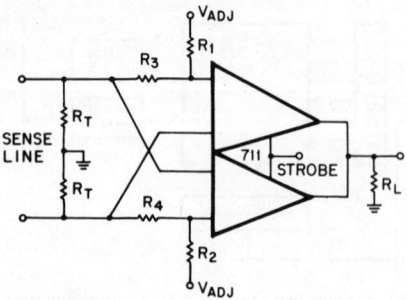

Figure 19.2.   The 711 in a typical sense-amplifier application.

With input signals of less than 15 mV amplification is needed, as indicated in Figure 19.3. The preamplifier to be used must have the necessary frequency response to reproduce the input signals and must either use a tightly controlled matched pair or ac coupling.

19.2 THRESHOLD VARIATIONS WITH POWER SUPPLIES

Power-supply variations affect the input offset voltage and consequently the input threshold. Therefore a specification covering the maximum change in threshold for variation in power-supply voltage should be included.

In a typical setup, such as the one shown in Figure 19.2, the variation with power supply should be under 500 μV/V; the variation with a negative supply should be very linear and under 4 mV/V. Of course this variation is determined by the degree of matching of the input resistors.

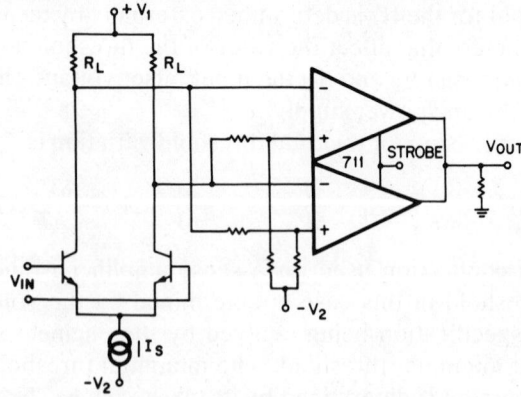

Figure 19.3.   For low-level signals a circuit such as the one shown is needed to reproduce the input signal.

19.3 THRESHOLD VARIATIONS WITH TEMPERATURE

This characteristic is determined by the temperature coefficient of the input offset voltage and the temperature coefficient of the resistors used in the input. The 711C specifies a typical temperature coefficient of input offset voltage of 5 μV/°C. Assuming that the resistors do not contribute significantly, a specification of 10 μV/°C can be met very easily by the IC.

19.4 SIGNAL PROPAGATION AND OUTPUT RISE TIME

Propagation time is the time that elapses between the application of the "1" signal and the appearance of the output. This characteristic is strongly dependent on the amount of overdrive; how it is to be measured should be carefully specified. (For example, it can be measured from the peak of the "1" signal to 50% of the output or from 50% of the "1" signal to 50% of the output). The output rise time is not a strong function of the overdrive, but signal propagation, as shown in Figure 19.4, is very sensitive to overdrive. In this figure the propagation delay measured from 50% of the "1" signal to 10% of the output is plotted against the input signal in millivolts. For this example the input signal has a constant base-line width of 45 ns and input rise and fall times of 20 ns. As can be seen, the propagation delay varies linearly from 5 to 15 ns as the input signal is varied from 80 to 30 mV. In Figure 19.5 the same parameter is plotted, but this time the input signal has rise and fall times of 5 ns. In this case the variation is not linear, the propagation delay varying from 8 to 13 ns as the input is changed from 80 to 30 mV.

Note that the circuit previously discussed was slower for a narrow input of low amplitude. The shape of the input signal in general is not available to the designer since it is determined by the core used in the memory. Figure 19.6 shows oscilloscope traces for this circuit.

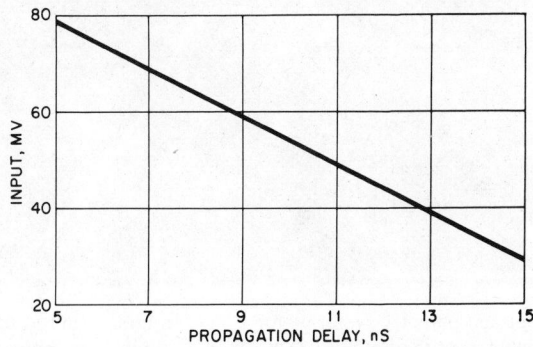

Figure 19.4. Signal propagation versus overdrive for a 711 with rise and fall times of 20 ns.

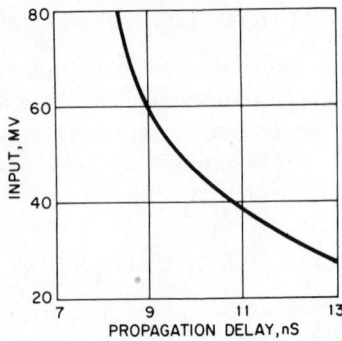

Figure 19.5. Signal propagation versus overdrive for a 711 with rise and fall times of 5 ns.

Differential recovery time is the delay after the decay of the differential noise before the strobe pulse can be applied and the signal read out. The best way to see if a 711 can meet this requirement is to look at the trailing edge of the noise pulse and the leading edge of the strobe waveshape with the allowed time lapse specified. A specification should be determined for the maximum output voltage allowed. Obviously the output should be small enough not to turn a transistor on. A good value is 400 mV. Figure 19.7 shows how this specification can be written. The noise fall time,

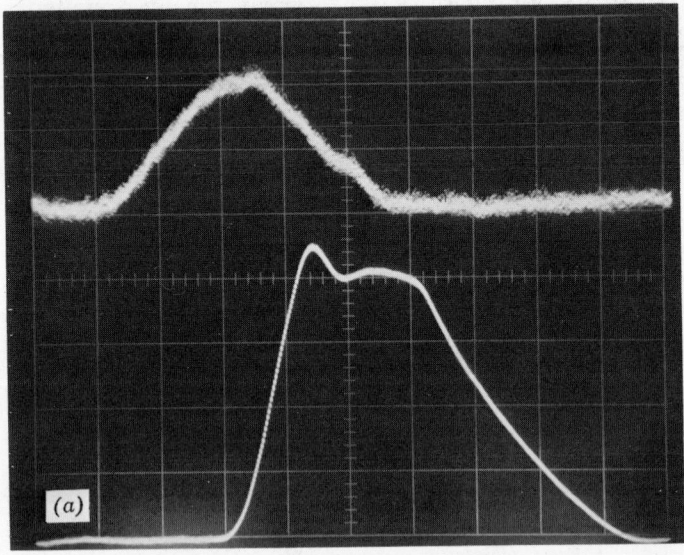

Figure 19.6. Input and output waveforms for a 711. In both *A* and *B*, the top waveform is a 20-mv div. input, and the bottom waveform is a 500-mV/div. output. Time (*X*-axis) scale is 10 ns/div.

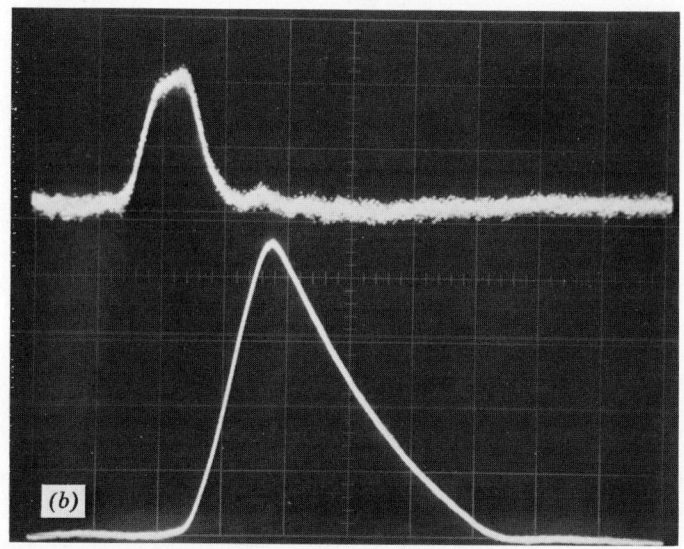

Figure 19.6. (Contd.)

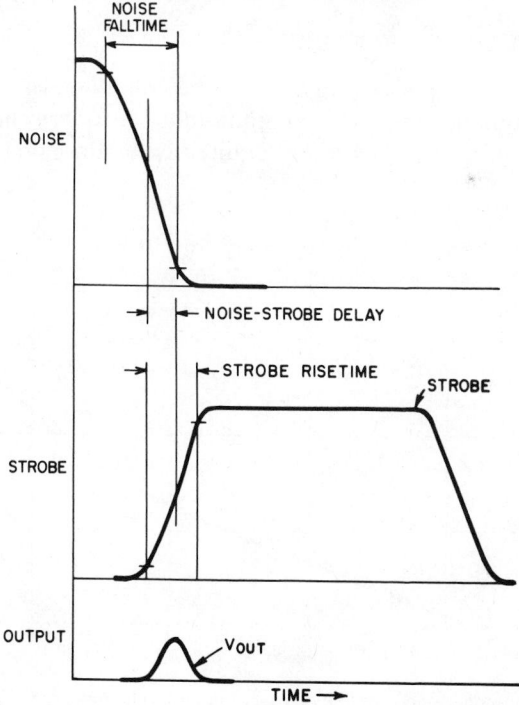

Figure 19.7. Waveforms illustrating specification of 711 differential recovery.

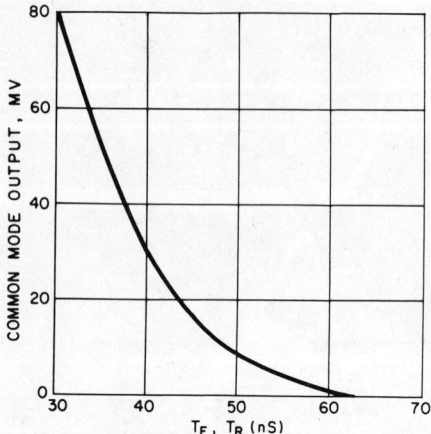

Figure 19.8. Common-mode output versus input rise time for a 711 with $V_{CM(ON)} = 2$ V.

strobe rise time and voltage level, as well as the time from noise to strobe, should be specified.

19.5   COMMON-MODE RECOVERY

Common-mode output is a function of the amplitude rise and fall times of the common-mode input. The common-mode recovery should be specified as a maximum output with the required common-mode input voltage applied.

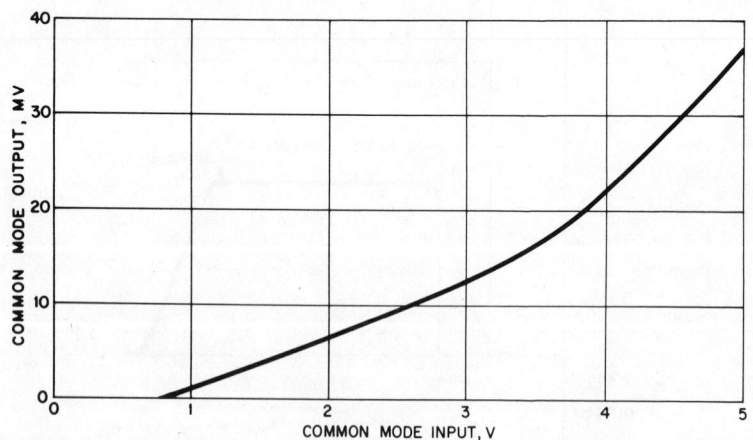

Figure 19.9. Common-mode output versus common-mode input for a 711 with rise and fall times of 40 ns.

The matching or allowable tolerance of the threshold resistors, as well as the rise time and times of the common-mode pulse, should be specified. The output voltage to a 400-mV common-mode noise pulse versus its rise and fall times is given in Figure 19.8. With a 60-ns rise and fall times the common-mode output is practically unmeasurable. If the output is increased to 80 mV, the rise and fall times are reduced to 30 ns. Figure 19.9 shows that common-mode output versus common-mode input keeps a constant rise time and fall time of 40 ns. Practically no common-mode output is observed with a 1-V input. The common-mode output increases to around 40 mV with a 5-V common-mode input.

Of course this is typical performance, and the specification must be written so that the maximum common-mode output does not turn a transistor on (it should be kept less than 40 mV).

20

Practical Considerations in the Design of Systems Using Linear Integrated Circuits

by A. C. Markkula, Jr.

Fairchild Semiconductor, Mountain View, California

After the first practical linear ICs were offered to the marketplace in 1964, the industry grew from an annual volume of approximately 100,000 units to something in the area of 25,000,000 units in 5 years.

Most engineers have assumed that the reason for this growth and the current interest in using these devices is their improved electrical performance. This is only partly true. The real reason for the success of linear circuits is the significant advantage they provide when overall cost/performance of a system is considered.

The linear IC today offers a two-to-one savings in component cost when compared with a discrete-component design of equivalent performance. In addition to the savings in actual component cost, the use of an IC offers cost savings in (a) assembly, (b) inventory, (c) incoming inspection, (d) engineering, and (e) maintenance. Today's engineer can turn his talents to the complex and challenging problems of the total system, rather than designing "another amplifier."

In the practical world the successful sale of an electronic system is accomplished when the system offers the best overall performance for the lowest price. Overall performance includes (a) electrical performance, (b) mechanical environment performance, and (c) reliability performance.

Each of these factors must be considered with respect to a system's requirements.

Certainly, many tradeoffs exist in the search for an optimal approach to the design of a system. Should you use discrete components, ICs, or hybrids? Even if ICs clearly appear to be the right approach, there still remains the job of choosing the right IC.

For example, consider a unity-gain voltage follower. Voltage followers are used in systems in which it is desired to buffer between a high-impedance source and a low-impedance load. If the application is in an instrumentation system, the accuracy must be very high; if it is used in a high-repetition-rate display, the frequency response becomes most important. An excellent way to assess the relative merits of discrete components versus IC is to make a table like Table 20.1. Table 20.1 and Figures 20.1 through 20.5 can be completed with little more than a few data sheets and an hour's time. A simple, easy-to-make table such as this one can be compared with the required system performance to provide practical guidelines for finding the best cost/performance solution to the design problem.

It is easy to see that for general-purpose applications a good solution is found with the μA741 because of its excellent electrical performance, high reliability, immunity to short-circuit conditions, and general ease of use. However, for systems requiring tight input specifications, such as a transducer amplifier, the μA727/μA741 combination offers a still better solution, but costs nearly four times as much.

Where high reliability and low maintenance are system requirements, the μA741 offers 2.75 times the reliability of the discrete approach (almost one-third the maintenance required).

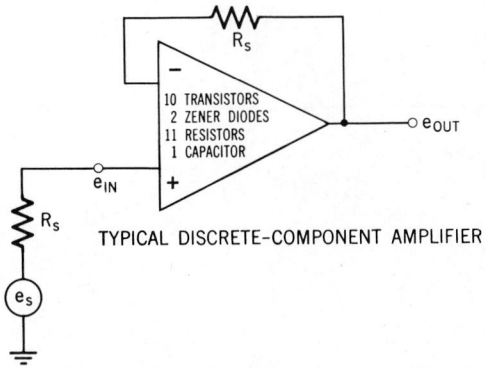

Figure 20.1. Discrete voltage follower.

The relative cost-comparison figures include assembly, testing, inventory, and component costs. These figures will vary from company to company, and of course the component cost will depend on the volume.

TABLE 20.1 Comparison of Typical Performance of Five Voltage Followers

Parameter	Discrete Voltage Follower	μA702 Voltage Follower	μA709 Voltage Follower	μA741 Voltage Follower	μA727/μA741 Voltage Follower	Units
Offset voltage	5	0.5	1.0	1.0	2.0	mV
Offset adjust	Yes	No	No	Yes	Yes	–
Offset current	100	180	50	30	2.5	nA
Offset-voltage drift	15	2.5	3.0	4.5	0.6	$\mu V/°C$
Offset-current drift (+25 to +125°C)	10	1.0	3.0	2.0	0.002	$nA/°C$
Bias current	1000	2000	200	200	12	nA
Input resistance without feedback	0.5	0.04	0.4	1.0	300	$M\Omega$
Input-voltage range	±8	+0.5,−4.0	±10	±13	±13	V
Noise $\frac{BW = 10\,kHz}{optimum\ R_s}$	3.0	2.0	2.5	3.0	3.0	μV rms
Open-loop voltage gain	10,000	3600	45,000	400,000	40,000,000	–
Closed-loop gain accuracy	0.005	0.028	0.0022	0.00025	0.0000025	%
Common-mode rejection	60	95	90	90	100	dB
Power-supply rejection	100	75	25	30	80	$\mu V/V$
Power consumption	400	90	80	50	500	mW
Latch-up proof	No	No	No	Yes	Yes	–
Bandwidth (unity-gain frequency)	3	18	1	1	0.001	MHz
Output-voltage swing	±10	±5.3	±14	±14	±14	V
Short-circuit proof	No	No	No	Yes	Yes	–
Slew rate	5	35	0.15	0.50	0.50	$V/\mu s$
Total components	24	5	6	2	5	–
Circuit design time	?	1	1	1	1	–
Relative MTBF	1	2.37	2.27	2.75	1.36	–
Relative cost	1	0.57	0.60	0.43	3.75	–
Performance rating[a] for:						
General purpose	5	2	9	10	2	–
High speed	7	9	3	4	2	–
High accuracy	3	1	4	8	10	–
High reliability	5	7	7	9	6	–

[a]10 = Excellent; 1 = poor.

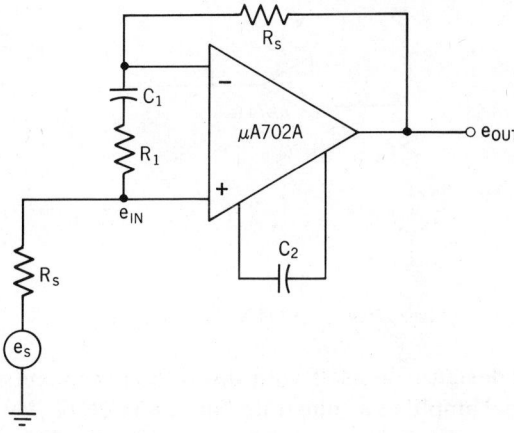

Figure 20.2. μA702A Voltage follower.

20.1 VOLTAGE REGULATORS

Next to the operational amplifier, the voltage regulator is the most common circuit building block. Since the "glow bottles" of the old days, the regulator has progressed to today's sophisticated but low-cost circuits. Because of the extremely competitive nature of the electronics industry, the design engineer must give close attention to the cost/performance ratio in his circuit design in order to remain competitive in tomorrow's market. This is true even in military electronics. The engineer who must decide to buy or build a power supply is faced with several choices. He may buy complete power supplies or build a supply using commercially available modules, hybrids, or monolithic voltage regulators. He may

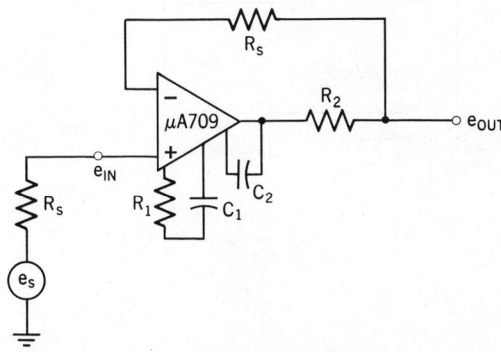

Figure 20.3. μA709 Voltage follower.

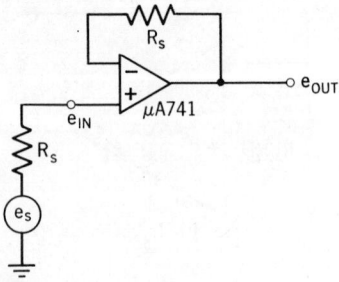

Figure 20.4. μA741 Voltage follower.

even decide to design it himself with discrete components and an integrated operational amplifier as illustrated in Figure 20.6.

A better, lower cost approach is to use the μA723, a monolithic precision voltage regulator. Illustrated in Figure 20.7, the circuit consists of a temperature-compensated reference amplifier, error amplifier, power series-pass transistor, and current-limit circuitry. The circuit will operate with either positive or negative supplies and as a series, shunt, switching, or floating voltage regulator. Examples of the use of this circuit are given in Figures 20.7 through 20.14.

The μA723 may be used with *npn* or *pnp* external pass elements when output currents higher than 150 mA are required. Provisions are made for adjustable current limiting with or without foldback and for remote shutdown. The IC employs compatible *N*-channel junction FETs, MOS capacitors, and pinch resistors as well as well-matched *npn* and *pnp* transistors. It is useful in a wide variety of applications, including local board regulators, laboratory power supplies, isolation regulators for

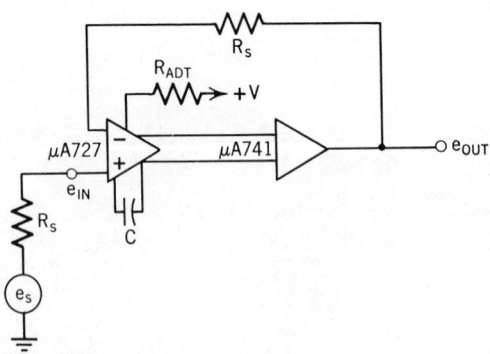

Figure 20.5. μA727/μA741 Voltage follower.

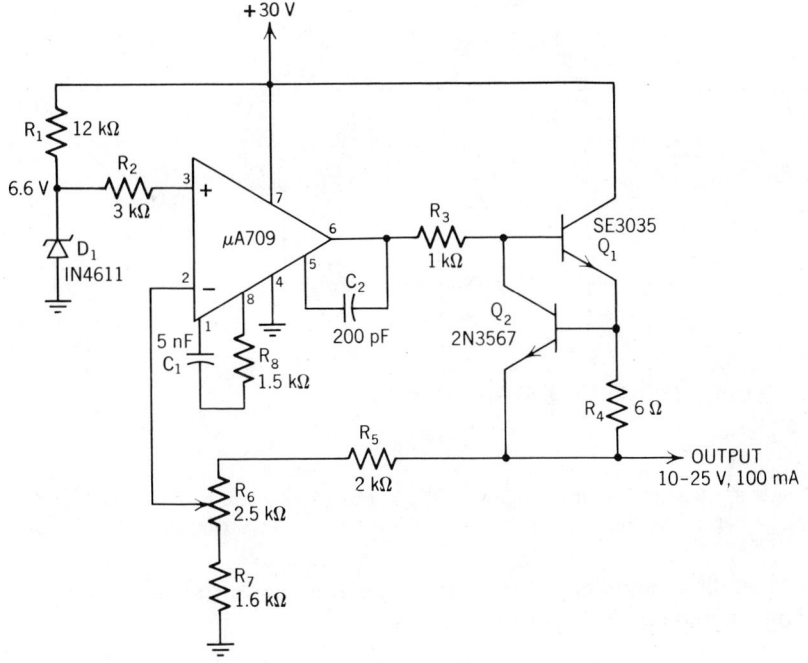

Figure 20.6. Power supply built with 709.

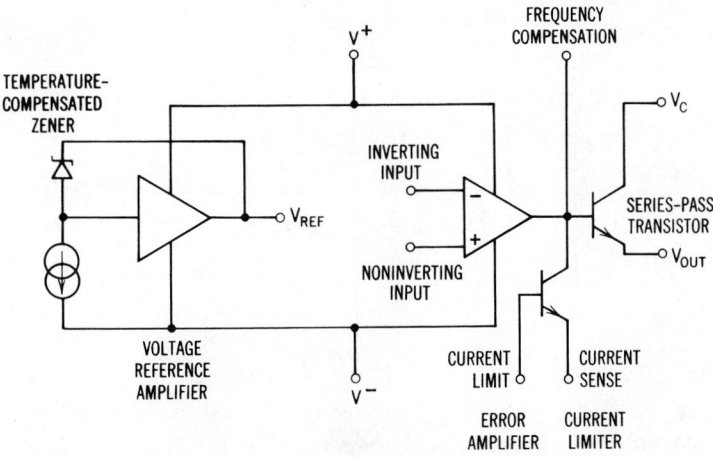

Figure 20.7. Equivalent circuit.

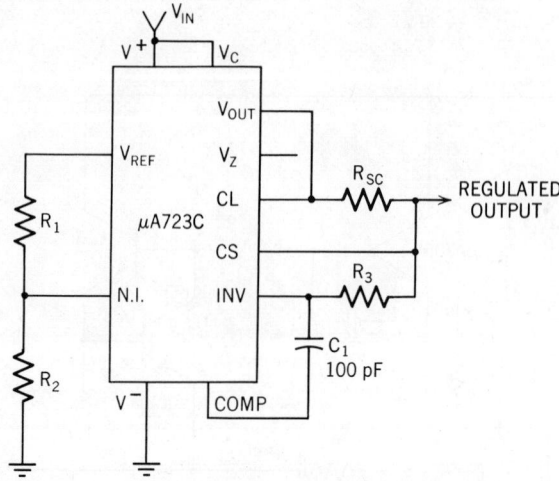

Figure 20.8. Basic low-voltage regulator, $V_{out} = 2$ to 7 V. Typical performance: regulated output voltage, 5 V; line regulation ($\Delta V_{in} = 3$ V), 0.5 mV; load regulation ($\Delta I_L = 50$ mA), 1·5 mV.

low-level data amplifiers, logic board regulators, airborne power supplies, and digital and linear IC power supplies.

20.2 OPERATIONAL AMPLIFIERS

The operational amplifier is one of the most versatile devices available to the electronics industry today. In addition to performing the traditional

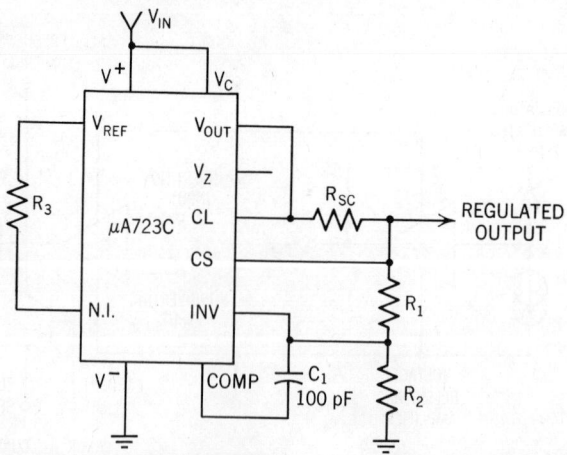

Figure 20.9. Basic high-voltage regulator, $V_{out} = 3$ to 37 V. Typical performance: regulated output voltage 15 V; line regulation ($\Delta V_{in} = 3$ V), 1.5 mV; load regulation ($\Delta I_L = 50$ mA), 4.5 mV.

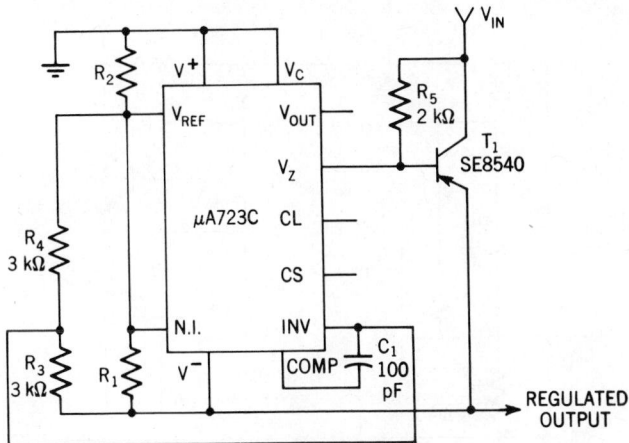

Figure 20.10.   Negative voltage regulator. Typical performance: regulated output voltage, -15 V; line regulation ($\Delta V_{in} = 3$ V), 1 mV; load regulation ($\Delta I_L = 100$ mA), 2 mV.

computing functions of addition, subtraction, integration, and differentiation, it is widely used in such diverse applications as signal conditioning, analog instrumentation, active filters, servo systems, process control, nonlinear function generators, regulators, and many other routine functions.

The versatility of the operational amplifier results from the use of a large amount of negative feedback around the device. The characteristics

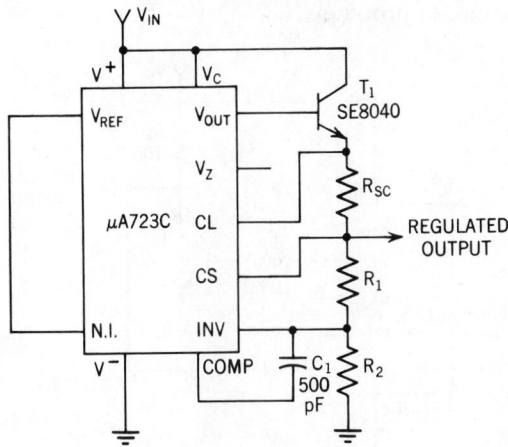

Figure 20.11.   Positive voltage regulator (external *npn* pass transistor) Typical performance: regulated output voltage, $+15$ V; line regulation ($\Delta V_{in} = 3$ V), 1.5 mV; load regulation ($\Delta I_L = 1$ A), 15 mV.

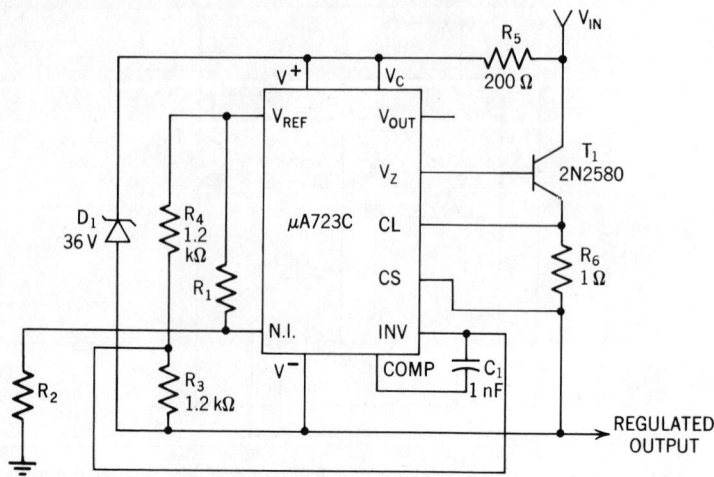

Figure 20.12. Positive floating regulator. Typical performance: regulated output voltage, + 100 V; line regulation (ΔV_{in} = 20 V), 15 mV; load regulation (ΔI_L = 50 mA), 20 mV.

of the amplifier in a given application with feedback are determined by the external feedback elements alone, over which the designer can exercise the degree of control required by his application. He can therefore use a single amplifier in many different functional circuits.

Now that high-performance operational amplifiers have become available, more and more engineers will find it economical to use these devices to solve circuit problems.

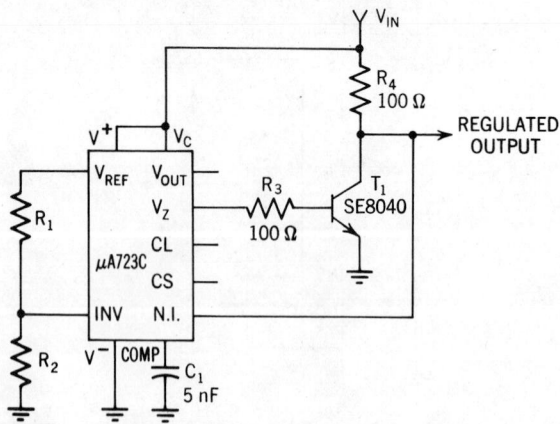

Figure 20.13. Shunt regulator. Typical performance: regulated output voltage, (+ 5 mV; line regulation (ΔV_{in} = 10 V), 2 mV; load regulation (ΔI_L = 100 mA), 5 mV.

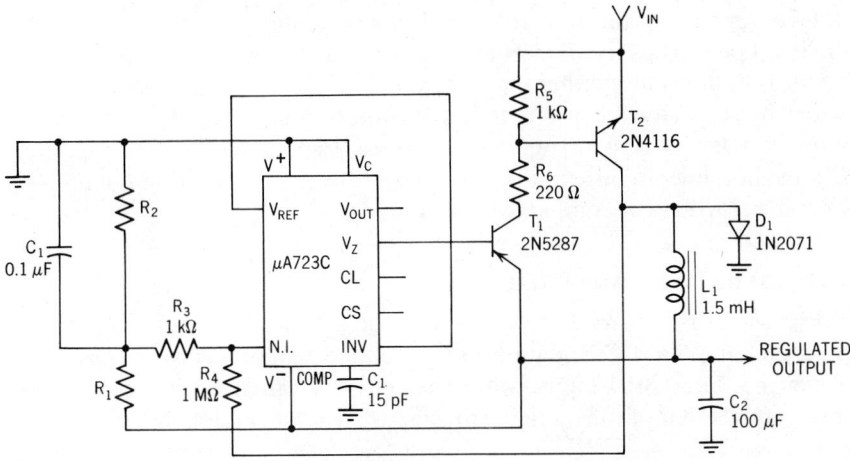

Figure 20.14. Negative switching regulator. Typical performance: regulated output voltage, -15 V; line regulation ($\Delta V_{\text{in}} = 20$ V), 8 mV; load regulation ($\Delta I_L = 2$ A), 6 mV.

20.3 THE IDEAL OPERATIONAL AMPLIFIER

The most versatile operational amplifier has a differential input and a single-ended output (Figure 20.15). The circuit amplifies the difference between the voltages applied to its two input terminals; a positive voltage at the inverting input (or "summing point") produces a negative output, while one at the noninverting input produces a positive output.

The ideal operational amplifier is characterized by

1. Infinite voltage gain.
2. Infinite input resistance.
3. Zero output resistance.
4. Infinite bandwidth.
5. Zero offset.

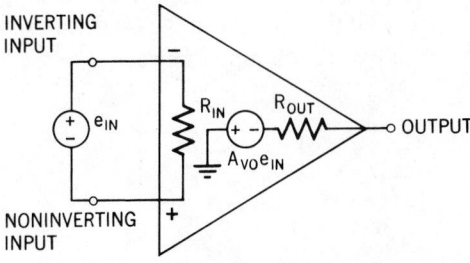

Figure 20.15. Equivalent circuit for basic operational amplifier. Ideal amplifier has $R_{in} = \infty$, $A_{VO} = \infty$, $R_{\text{out}} = 0$.

Two very powerful tools for circuit analysis and design are implied by the ideal properties listed above: (a) as a result of infinite input resistance, no current flows into either input terminal; (b) because of the infinite gain, when negative feedback is applied around the amplifier, the differential input voltage is zero. Proper use of these two simple, basic properties makes possible rapid, first-order analysis of any operational-amplifier circuit, regardless of complexity.

20.4 INVERTING AMPLIFIER

Figure 20.16 shows the connection for a basic feedback circuit, the inverting amplifier. Calculation of the voltage gain proceeds very simply. Since the differential input voltage is zero, the potential at the inverting input equals that of the noninverting input (ground), and therefore the two currents are

$$I_1 = \frac{E_{IN}}{R_s}, \tag{20.1}$$

$$I_2 = \frac{E_{OUT}}{R_f}. \tag{20.2}$$

Since no current flows into the amplifier, $I_1 = I_2$, and thus the voltage gain is

$$\frac{E_{OUT}}{E_{IN}} = \frac{R_f}{R_s} \tag{20.3}$$

The input impedance is R_s, the output impedance is zero, and any value of gain can be obtained by proper choice of the feedback elements.

Because of the virtual ground at the summing point, any number of input voltages may be applied to the amplifier and summed at the output without interaction between the sources. Each input sees its respective resistor as the input resistance, and the current in the feedback resistor is the algebraic sum of the current from each input source.

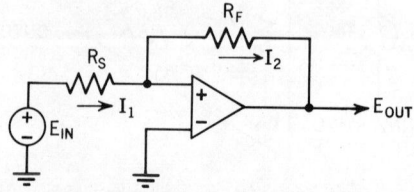

Figure 20.16.   Inverting amplifier.

The operational amplifier may also be used as a current source. This is accomplished by putting the load in the feedback loop (i.e., $R_L = R_f$). The current through the load is given by (20.1) and is completely independent of the load impedance.

20.5 NONINVERTING AMPLIFIER

Another basic feedback circuit is given in Figure 20.17; this is the non-inverting amplifier, or potentiometric connection. Since no current flows into the amplifier, inputs R_f and R_s form a simple voltage divider and the voltage at the inverting input is equal to

$$E_{IN} = \frac{R_s}{R_f + R_s} E_{OUT}.$$ (20.4)

This voltage must be equal to the input voltage because of the infinite voltage gain, and therefore

$$\frac{E_{OUT}}{E_{IN}} = 1 + \frac{R_f}{R_s}.$$ (20.5)

In this case the input impedance is infinite, the output impedance is zero, and only voltage gains above unity are possible.

A unity-gain buffer, or voltage follower, results when the source resistor (R_s) is removed; any value of R_f can be used in the ideal case since no current flows in the feedback path.

20.6 DIFFERENTIAL AMPLIFIER

Figure 20.18 shows a circuit that uses both inputs to the operational amplifier. Operation is best seen by considering each input separately. The output voltage due to the signal on the inverting input is

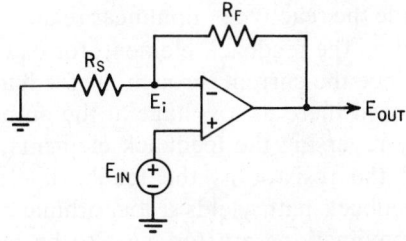

Figure 20.17.   Noninverting amplifier.

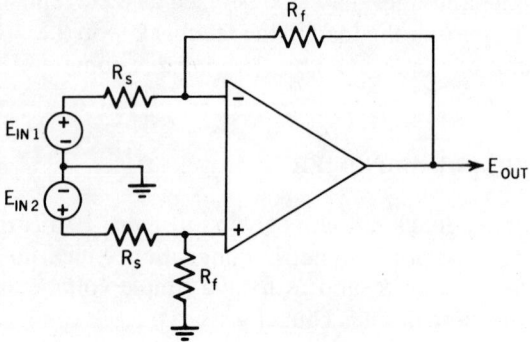

Figure 20.18.   Differential amplifier.

$$E_{\text{OUT 1}} = -\frac{R_f}{R_s} E_{\text{IN 1}},$$ (20.6)

and the output from the noninverting input is

$$E_{\text{OUT 2}} = 1 + \frac{R_f}{R_s} \frac{R_f}{R_f + R_s} E_{\text{IN 2}}.$$ (20.7)

The voltage divider at the noninverting input has been included to make the overall gains from both signals equal, so the total output voltage will be

$$E_{\text{OUT}} = \frac{R_f}{R_s} (E_{\text{IN 2}} - E_{\text{IN 1}}).$$ (20.8)

20.7   FEEDBACK ELEMENTS

Resistance feedback elements have been shown so far, but in general, any form of complex or nonlinear feedback may be used. The overall transfer function may be derived similarly, with appropriate changes being made to include the reactive or nonlinear relationships.

A capacitor used as the feedback element, for example, will integrate the input voltage, since the current through the feedback loop charges the capacitor and is stored there as a voltage at the output. A differentiator can be obtained by reversing the feedback elements, with the capacitor as the source and the resistor as the feedback element. A diode or transistor in the feedback path yields a logarithmic output. The various possibilities and combinations are too vast to be mentioned here, but several practical examples are given in the chapter on applications.

20.8 SOURCES OF ERROR

Unfortunately no manufacturer has yet produced an ideal operational amplifier. In this section the imperfections that cause practical amplifiers to depart from the ideal are considered, along with their effect on circuit performance.

Offset. The most significant limitation affecting accuracy in dc amplifiers is offset and its variations with temperature, time, supply voltage, and common-mode voltage. Although the ideal operational amplifier has exactly zero output for zero input, this is never quite achieved in practice because of the small, unavoidable mismatch that exists between components in a practical circuit. The output therefore will have a dc offset when there is no input signal. Offset is generally referred to the input and, being independent of the amplifier gain, can be directly compared with the input signal.

Figure 20.19 gives an equivalent circuit for the operational amplifier showing the principal sources of offset. The input offset voltage (V_{OS}) is defined as the voltage that must be applied between the input terminals to obtain zero output. Input bias current is the average of the two currents $[(I_{B1}+I_{B2})/2]$ that flow into the inputs when the output is nulled, and input offset current (I_{OS}) is the difference of the two input currents under the same conditions. Both voltage and current offset (which have random and independent polarities), together with the impedance levels of the external components, must be considered when predicting the performance of an operational amplifier circuit.

The total output offset voltage developed by the general circuit of Figure 20.19 is

$$\Delta V_{OUT} = \left(1+\frac{R_f}{R_s}\right)V_{OS}+I_{B_1}R_f-I_{B_2}R_{eq}\left(1+\frac{R_f}{R_s}\right). \qquad (20.9)$$

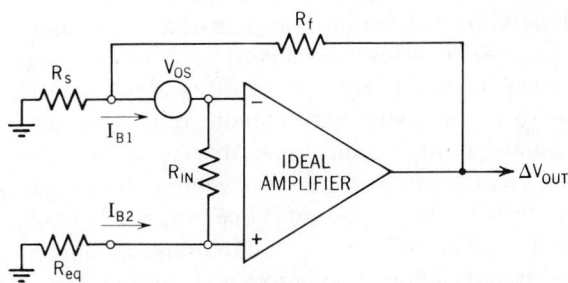

Figure 20.19. Equivalent circuit showing sources of offset, for minimum offset $I_{OS}=I_{B1}-I_{B2}$, $R_{eq}=R_sR_f/(R_s+R_f)$.

Since the two bias currents in a well-matched differential amplifier are approximately equal, their effect on offset can be canceled by making the impedance to ground equal at both inputs. Thus,

$$R_{eq} = \frac{R_s R_f}{R_s + R_f},$$

the output offset becomes

(20.10)

$$\Delta V_{OUT} = \left(1 + \frac{R_f}{R_s}\right) V_{OS} + R_f I_{OS}.$$

It is assumed in the following discussions that the resistances have been equalized; however, in those applications where it is not possible to do this, the contribution of the input bias currents must be considered, as shown in (20.9).

It should be noted [from (20.10)] that the offset produced at the output is independent of whether the amplifier is being operated in the inverting or noninverting connection. Referred to the input signal, this means that the offset error will be different for the two configurations, even though the voltage gains are equal. For the inverting amplifier the input-referred offset is

$$\Delta V_{IN} = \left(1 + \frac{R_s}{R_f}\right) V_{OS} + R_s I_{OS}, \tag{20.11}$$

whereas for the noninverting amplifier it becomes

$$\Delta V_{IN} = V_{OS} + I_{OS}\left(\frac{R_s R_f}{R_f + R_s}\right). \tag{20.12}$$

A fixed input offset is not usually a great problem because biasing circuits can be added to cancel it out in critical applications. However, drift of offset with temperature, time, and so on, introduces a basic input error because this change cannot be distinguished from the input signal. Drift with temperature is generally specified as an average over a specified temperature range. This is done because a fairly large change in temperature is necessary to make accurate drift readings, and because it is uneconomical to record data and compute drifts at a large number of temperature points. Drift specifications, therefore, should be interpreted as a maximum change in offset over the temperature range, and do not imply that the temperature coefficient is linear over this range.

By virtue of their differential design, operational amplifiers are relatively unaffected by power-supply regulation and ripple. The ability of the amplifier to discriminate against supply variations is termed the supply-voltage rejection ratio, and is defined as the ratio of the change in input offset voltage to the change in supply voltage. It is usually specified as microvolts per volt or microvolts per percent. This factor must be considered in critical applications in which the supplies may not be well regulated.

A basic property of the differential amplifier is its ability to amplify signals applied between its input terminals, while rejecting those common to both inputs. When the gains from the inputs are not exactly equal, an output will be produced for a common-mode input voltage. The ratio of the common-mode voltage to this error (which is referred to the input as a change in offset) is the common-mode rejection ratio and is generally specified in decibels. The input-voltage range specification defines the maximum amplitude of common-mode voltage that may be applied to the amplifier without exceeding the common-mode rejection-ratio figure. Rejection ratios on the order of 70 to 100 dB are commonly obtained with practical amplifiers. In the circuit of Figure 20.18, it is necessary that the R_s and R_f resistors at each input be very closely matched if the inherent rejection capability of the amplifier is to be used. If the resistors are balanced to a fraction (δ) of nominal value, and it is assumed that the worst-case combination of mismatch exists between the resistors, the output error caused by a common-mode input (V_{CM}) is given by

$$\Delta V_{\text{OUT}} = V_{CM} \frac{4\delta}{[1 + (R_s/R_f)]},\tag{20.13}$$

where R_s and R_f are nominal values, and $\delta \ll 1$. Therefore, for a given change of input offset (V_{OS}) the resistors must be matched to an accuracy of

$$\delta = \frac{V_{OS}}{V_{CM}}\left[\frac{1 + (R_f/R_s)}{4}\right].\tag{20.14}$$

If the ratio $V_{CM}/\Delta V_{OS}$ is equal to or larger than the minimum common-mode rejection-ratio specification of the amplifier, the maximum possible untrimmed rejection ratio will be obtained. Note that slightly unbalancing either of the R_s or R_f resistors can cancel the dc common-mode error resulting from the amplifier and give an effective rejection ratio of infinity. The resultant common-mode error then consists only of distortion components developed in the amplifier as the inputs are swung over the common-mode range.

It should be remembered that common-mode errors are present only when a voltage is applied to the noninverting input and effectively disappear whenever either input voltage becomes zero.

Another source of input offset, which is sometimes overlooked, is the rectification of high-frequency signals. These signals may be coupled into the input of the amplifier by capacitive or inductive coupling, or they may even be present in the input signal itself. The specification for the maximum frequency at which full output can be obtained from the amplifier is usually regarded as a limitation on the output-slewing-rate capabilities of the amplifier. However, another reason for this specification is that offsets may be generated when the input signal contains high-frequency components that exceed the full output response specification.

Noise. Any spurious signal at the output of an amplifier that is not present in the input signal can be considered as noise. For ac amplifiers random noise generated within the amplifier limits the smallest signal that can be distinguished at the input, whereas in dc applications offset voltage and offset drift are the dominant factors. Like offset and drift, random noise can be characterized by a series noise-voltage generator and a parallel noise-current generator at the amplifier inputs, as shown in Figure 20.20.

The generators $\overline{e_n^2}$ and $\overline{i_n^2}$ represent the mean-square value of voltage and current assumed to be responsible for the noise generated within the amplifier, and are usually defined in terms of power per unit bandwidth. In general the amplifier noise generators are not statistically independent; for high-gain transistors operated at low collector currents, however, the correlation coefficient is quite small and may be neglected.

The noise current is found from the noise voltage produced when the amplifier is operated with very high source resistances, and the noise voltage is found from the noise developed with the inputs shorted. With these generators placed in front of the amplifier as inputs, it is possible to calculate the noise performance of the amplifier for any source resistance and bandwidth.

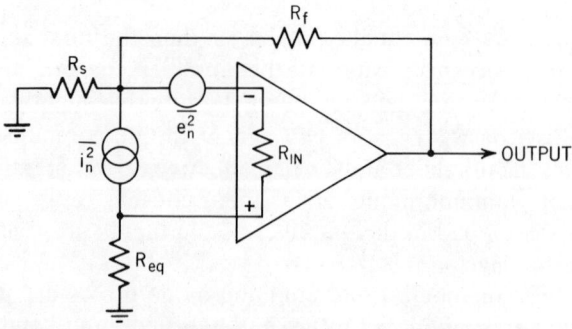

Figure 20.20.   General feedback circuit with noise sources.

Narrowband Noise. The input-referred noise of an amplifier connected in the general feedback circuit of Figure 20.20 is given by

$$\overline{e_t^2} = 4kTR_t + \overline{i_n^2}R_T^2 + \overline{e_n^2}, \tag{20.15}$$

where $R_T = R_{eq} + R_s R_f/(R_s + R_f)$ is the total resistance seen by the input terminals. The first term of (20.15) is the thermal noise generated in the source and feedback resistors and is the noise that would be obtained if the amplifier contributed no noise. The second term is the noise voltage produced by the input noise current flowing through the input resistors, and the third term is the contribution from the input noise-voltage generator. It should be noted that the total input noise is independent of the amplifier input resistance, and of any feedback except insofar as these parameters influence the closed-loop gain.

Noise figure is perhaps the most widely used parameter for indicating amplifier noise performance. It is a measure of the degradation in signal-to-noise ratio suffered by a signal passing through the amplifier. Noise figure (F) may be defined as the ratio of the total input noise power to the noise power from the signal source alone and is commonly expressed in decibels. Thus

$$F = \frac{\overline{e_t^2}}{\overline{e_g^2}}, \tag{20.16}$$

where $e_g^2 = 4kTR_g$ is the thermal noise generated by the output resistance of the signal source. In Figure 20.20, R_g can be represented by either R_s or R_{eq}, depending on whether the inverting or noninverting connection is used. The other resistors in R_t must be chosen so that their effect is small compared with that of R_g to keep from degrading the noise figure.

The noise figure will have a minimum value F_m when the source resistance has the optimum value R_{gm}, where

$$R_{gm} = \left(\frac{\overline{e_n^2}}{\overline{i_n^2}}\right)^{1/2} \tag{20.17}$$

and

$$F_m = 1 + \frac{\overline{e_n^2}}{2kTR_{gm}}. \tag{20.18}$$

It is not always possible to connect a matching network between signal source and amplifier to obtain the optimum noise figure. It can be seen from (20.15) that the noise figure for low source resistances is determined primarily by the value of the noise-voltage generator, and for high source resistances by the noise-current generator. Both of these generators are usually functions of frequency, with a noise-power spectrum that is constant at high frequencies and inversely proportional to frequency at low frequencies. Hence the spot-noise figure will vary with frequency as well as with source resistance.

The source resistance used in calculating noise figure must be that resistance seen looking directly into the output terminals of the signal source and should not include external resistors added between source and amplifier. External resistors can only increase the noise figure and thus should be made small compared with R_g. The noise figure will also be degraded by a frequency-compensation network connected across the input terminals, as is sometimes used to achieve a high slew rate. This is because the compensation network increases the high-frequency gain seen by the amplifier noise-voltage generator and hence causes a severe increase in high-frequency noise output.

Wideband Noise.   In general the noise figure measured over a wide bandwidth will differ from the spot-noise figure because of $1/f$ noise. The total wideband input noise can be found by integrating (20.15), including the frequency dependence of the noise generators and the frequency response of the amplifier. Thus the mean-square wideband noise is

$$\overline{E_t^2} = \int_0^\infty \overline{e_t(f)^2} A(f)\, df, \tag{20.19}$$

where $A(f)$ is the relative frequency response of the circuit.

Equation 20.19 is difficult to solve explicitly by using exact expressions for noise voltage and gain response. A close approximation can be made, however, by using asymptotes to represent the frequency-dependent characteristics and then integrating by parts. The noise spectrum can be represented as shown in Figure 20.21a, where e_{tot}^2 is the total high-frequency spot noise and f_N is the $1/f$ break frequency. Thus

$$\overline{e_t(f)^2} = \overline{e_{\text{tot}}^2} \quad \text{for} \quad f_N \leqslant f \leqslant \infty \tag{20.20}$$

and

$$\overline{e_t(f)^2} = \overline{e_{\text{tot}}^2}\left(\frac{f_N}{f}\right) \quad \text{for} \quad 0 \leqslant f \leqslant f_N. \tag{20.21}$$

A typical amplifier frequency response is given in Figure 20.21b; it rolls off at low frequencies at a rate of r_1 dB/octave beginning at f_L and at high frequencies at r_2 dB/octave beginning at f_H. Other amplifier frequency characteristics can be approximated in the same manner. Hence for this example $A(f)$ is given by

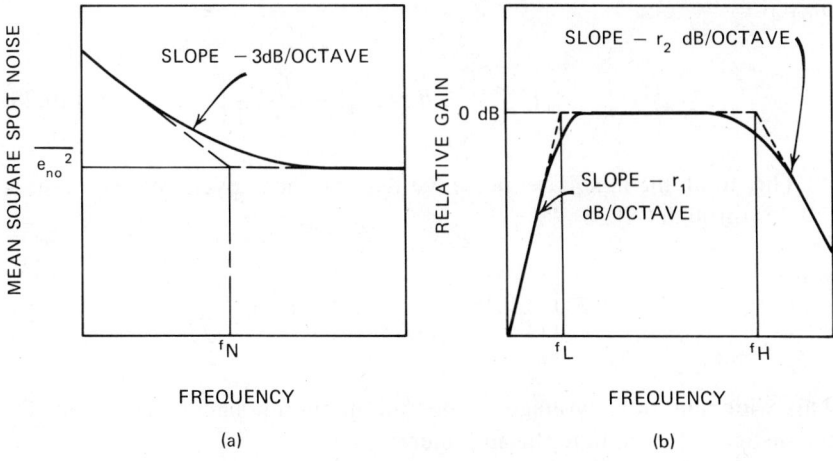

Figure 20.21. Approximate frequency characteristics for finding wideband noise: (*a*) noise spectrum approximation; (*b*) amplifier frequency-response approximation.

$$A(f) = \left(\frac{f}{f_L}\right)^{r_1/3} \quad \text{for} \quad 0 \leq f \leq f_L, \tag{20.22}$$

$$A(f) = 1 \qquad \text{for} \quad f_L \leq f \leq f_H, \tag{20.23}$$

$$A(f) = \left(\frac{f_H}{f}\right)^{r_2/3} \quad \text{for} \quad f_H \leq f \leq \infty. \tag{20.24}$$

Assuming that the $1/f$ break frequency of the noise voltage falls within the amplifier passband ($f_L < f_N < f_H$), the integral of (20.19) can be broken into four parts, as follows:

Part 1: $0 \leq f \leq f_L$

$$\overline{e_1^2} = \int_0^{f_L} \overline{e_{\text{tot}}^2} \left(\frac{f_N}{f}\right)\left(\frac{f}{f_L}\right)^{r_1/3} df = \overline{e_{\text{tot}}^2}\left(\frac{3f_N}{r_1}\right). \tag{20.25}$$

Part 2: $f_L \leq f \leq f_N$

$$\overline{e_2^2} = \left(\frac{f_N}{f}\right) df = \overline{e_{\text{tot}}^2} \ \ln\left(\frac{f_N}{f_L}\right). \tag{20.26}$$

Part 3: $f_N \leq f \leq f_H$

$$\overline{e_3^2} = \int_{f_N}^{f_H} \overline{e_{\text{tot}}^2} \ df = \overline{e_{\text{tot}}^2} \ (f_H - f_N). \tag{20.27}$$

Part 4: $f_H \leqslant f \leqslant \infty$

$$\overline{e_4{}^2} = \int_{f_H}^{\infty} e_{\text{tot}}^2 \left(\frac{f_H}{f}\right)^{r_2/3} df = \overline{e_{\text{tot}}^2}\left[\frac{f_H}{(r_2/3)-1}\right]. \tag{20.28}$$

The total mean-square noise voltage is then given by the sum of (20.25) through (20.28).

$$\overline{E_t{}^2} = \overline{e_{\text{tot}}^2}\left\{\frac{f_H}{[1-(3/r_2)]} + f_N\left(\frac{3}{r_1} - 1 + \ln\frac{f_N}{f_L}\right)\right\}. \tag{20.29}$$

This wideband noise voltage defines the minimum signal that can be distinguished at the input to the amplifier.

The wideband noise from the signal source alone is found by integrating over the bandwidth:

$$\overline{E_g{}^2} = \int_0^{\infty} \overline{e_g{}^2} A(f)\, df = \overline{e_g{}^2}\left\{\frac{f_H}{[1-(3/r_2)]} - \frac{f_L}{[1+(3/r_1)]}\right\} \tag{20.30}$$

Assuming that the bandwidth is reasonably wide ($f_H \gg f_L$), the overall noise figure is

$$F = \frac{\overline{E_t{}^2}}{\overline{E_g{}^2}} = \frac{\overline{e_{\text{tot}}^2}}{4kTR_g}\left[1 + \frac{f_N}{f_H}\left(1 - \frac{3}{r_2}\right)\left(\frac{3}{r_1} - 1 + \ln\frac{f_N}{f_L}\right)\right]. \tag{20.31}$$

In some instances it is necessary to know the peak-to-peak value of the wideband noise voltage rather than the rms value given by (20.29). If the bandwidth is wide enough for the effect of $1/f$ noise to be neglected, the distribution of the peak amplitude of the noise can be represented by a normal distribution with a standard deviation equal to the rms value. By defining the peak-to-peak amplitude as the voltage that is exceeded less than 1% of the time, the peak-to-peak noise voltage will be equal to 2.6 times the rms voltage.

20.9   OPEN-LOOP GAIN

A factor that contributes error in every application employing operational amplifiers is that the amplifier gain is not infinite. Because it is not, ideal transfer characteristics cannot be obtained exactly and can only be approached, but with an accuracy that is usually limited by the accuracy of the passive components in the circuit.

The general gain relationship for closed-loop circuits where the amplifier has a finite open-loop gain, A_{VO}, is

$$A = \text{(ideal gain)} \left[\frac{1}{1 + (1/\beta A_{VO})} \right], \tag{20.32}$$

where

$$\frac{1}{\beta} = \left(1 + \frac{R_f}{R_s} \right) \left\{ 1 + \frac{R_{\text{eq}} + [R_s R_f / (R_s + R_f)]}{R_{\text{IN}}} \right\} \tag{20.33}$$

and R_s, R_f, R_{eq}, R_{IN} are as shown in Figure 20.19.

The term βA_{VO} is defined as the "loop gain" and is the factor that determines how close to the ideal a given amplifier circuit will be. Note that the expression for loop gain is independent of the particular configuration used. This means that an inverting amplifier will have less loop gain for a given closed-loop gain than a noninverting amplifier. Note also from (20.33) that the feedback elements must be small compared with the finite amplifier input resistance if the loop gain is not to be degraded.

From (20.32) the percentage error resulting from finite gain is approximately

$$E(\%) = \frac{100}{\beta A_{VO}}. \tag{20.34}$$

The gain error given above is not, in itself, particularly important because the feedback resistor ratio can always be trimmed to compensate for this error. However, the stability of the closed-loop gain is an important consideration in most circumstances. Gain stability is found by differentiation of (20.32):

$$\frac{\Delta A}{A} = \frac{\Delta A_{VO}/A_{VO}}{1 + \beta A_{VO}}. \tag{20.35}$$

This shows that any variation in open-loop gain is reduced by the loop gain. In general output impedance, input impedance, linearity, distortion, and gain stability are all improved by the loop-gain factor.

Frequency Response. Like all amplifying devices, operational amplifiers have the ability and inclination for oscillation under appropriate feedback conditions. Inspection of (20.32) reveals that, if the loop gain equals unity and its sign is negative (positive feedback), the circuit will oscillate. Therefore it is necessary to ensure that the loop gain be reduced to less than unity before the loop phase shift reaches 180°. This is accomplished by designing the open-loop gain to have a uniform rolloff with frequency, at a rate of about 6 dB/octave, beginning at a relatively low frequency and continuing until it passes through unity. Since the phase shift associated with such a rolloff (Figure 20.22) is 90°, the circuit cannot become unstable.

Discrete-component operational amplifiers usually have this frequency compensation built in, but IC versions do not because of the impracticality of integrating the large-value capacitors normally required. The user must therefore supply his own frequency compensation, external to the microcircuit itself. This has both advantages and disadvantages: it means the user must understand the principles of frequency compensation and be able to apply them to the circuit at hand; but it also means the usefulness and versatility of the amplifier are considerably increased because optimum high-frequency bandwidth and loop gain can be obtained for any value of closed-loop gain. For example, 40-dB amplifier with fixed compensation would have a closed-loop bandwidth of only 10 kHz (Figure 20.23), whereas variable compensation gives a full 1-MHz bandwidth.

It should be remembered that all parameters that depend on loop gain (gain stability, input and output impedance, phase shift, linearity, and so on) are degraded at high frequencies because of the necessary rolloff in loop gain.

The closed-loop response of an operational amplifier to a pulse or step-function input depends on the amplitude of the signal. For small signals the output will be an exponential with a time constant inversely proportional to the closed-loop bandwidth. The closed-loop bandwidth, as seen

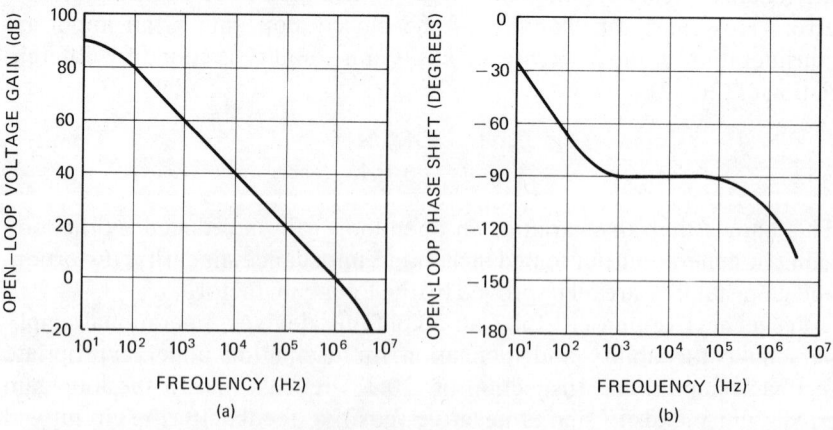

Figure 20.22.   Typical open-loop gain and phase-frequency response.

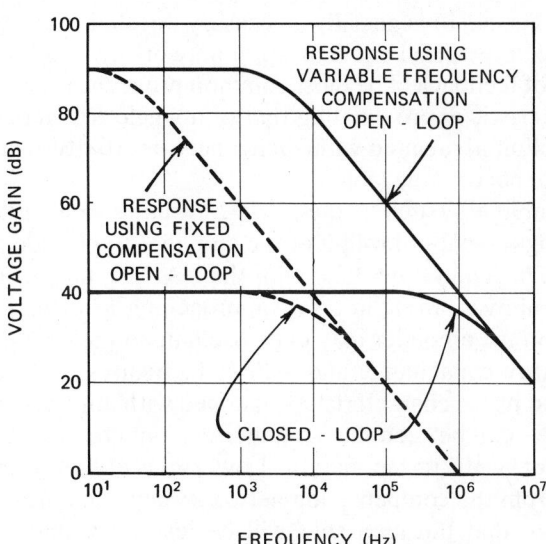

Figure 20.23.   Performance with adjustable frequency compensation.

above, can be maximized for any particular gain and does not necessarily have to be inversely proportional to the closed-loop gain, as with discrete amplifiers.

Apart from bandwidth, operational amplifiers have limitations on the maximum rate of change that the output can follow for large input signals. This is a result of the finite current available to charge the internal capacitances at various nodes within the amplifier. The maximum rate of change, or slew rate, also defines the maximum frequency at which full sine-wave output swing can be obtained from the amplifier. The slew rate (p) is related to the peak sine-wave signal (A_p) at a given frequency (ω) by the equation

$$p = A_p\omega. \tag{20.36}$$

Driving an amplifier beyond its slewing limit results in a triangular output that decreases with increasing frequency. It can also disturb the dc conditions within the amplifier and cause an effective change in the offset voltage, as already mentioned.

20.10 FREQUENCY COMPENSATION FOR THE μA709

According to feedback theory, an amplifier will be unstable if the high-frequency loop gain is greater than or equal to unity when the phase shift reaches 180°. Since the natural response of the amplifier is limited by internal capacitances, it is usually necessary to shape the gain-phase characteristics with external compensation networks to achieve stability for any amount of feedback. The most common procedure is to synthesize a rolloff characteristic approximating that of a single *RC* network; since the maximum rolloff associated with such a network (6 dB/octave) is 90°; the circuit cannot become unstable.

With some amplifiers (such as the μA702A), large bandwidths can be obtained by using the natural rolloff of the amplifier to provide part of the compensation. This cannot be done with the μA 709, however, because its gain falls off above 2 MHz at a rate approaching 18 dB/octave. Without compensation the amplifier may even oscillate in the open-loop mode as a result of stray capacitance and high gain. Figures 20.24 and 20.25 show the gain and phase characteristics obtained with minimum frequency compensation. As can be seen, the amplifier can only be closed down to a gain of 50 dB for a 30° phase margin. Lower closed-loop gains require that the rolloff from the compensation networks begin at a frequency low enough to ensure that the loop gain will be less than unity before the amplifier introduces additional phase shift.

20.11   COMPENSATION

Two sets of frequency-compensation points have been provided for the μA709 since it is usually difficult to obtain compensation of more than

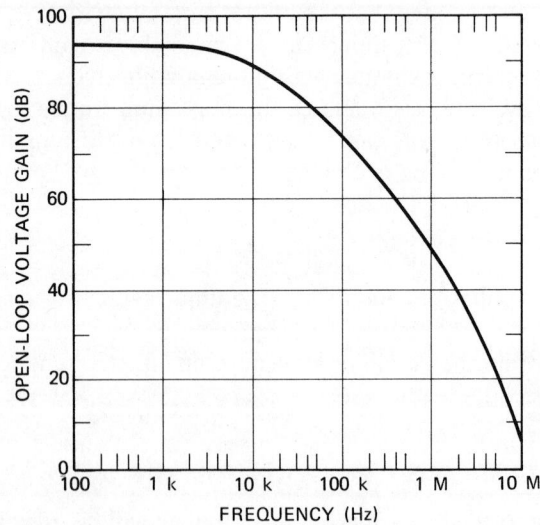

Figure 20.24. Open-loop frequency response with minimum compensation $C_1 = 10 \, \text{pF}$, $C_2 = 3 \, \text{pF}, V_s = \pm 15 \, \text{V}, T_A = 25°\text{C}$.

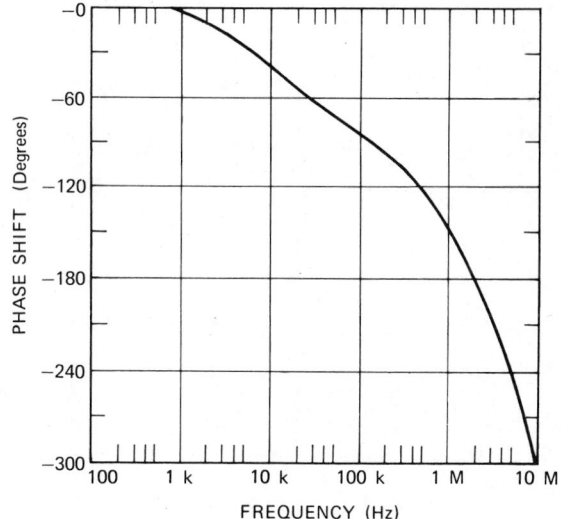

Figure 20.25.   Open-loop phase shift with minimum compensation, $C_1 = 10\,\text{pF}$, $C_2 = 3\,\text{pF}$, $V_s = \pm 15\,\text{V}$, $T_A = 25°\text{C}$.

60 dB at one point. The points chosen (see circuit diagram of Figure 20.19) have quite high transfer resistances so that the amplifier can be fully compensated with small external capacitors. Figure 20.26 shows the general compensation networks required to stabilize the amplifier. Collector-to-base feedback around the second stage via R_1 and C_1 provides the first 60 dB of rolloff, and another feedback loop around the output stage gives the remaining compensation. The transfer resistance of the input-compensation terminals varies from 1 to 2 mΩ and is typically 1.4 MΩ; it varies for the output compensation from 10 to 80 kΩ and typically is 36 kΩ. Relative changes with temperature and supply voltage are given in Figures 20.27 and 20.28. The output-compensation feedback loop has a dominant pole as a result of parasitic capacitance. When the

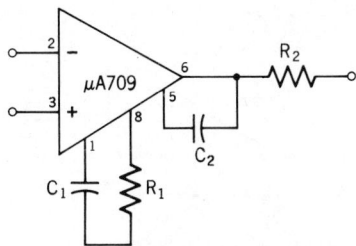

Figure 20.26.   Frequency compensation networks.

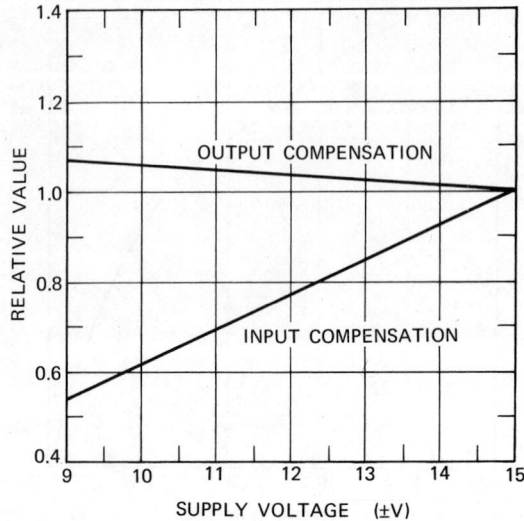

Figure 20.27. Compensation terminal impedance as a function of supply voltage, $T_A = 25°C$.

amplifier is operated with capacitive loading, the second pole introduced at the emitter of the *npn* output transistor may cause instability. A degeneration resistor was included in the μA709 to make the circuit less sensitive to this problem, but it does not cure the oscillation for all combinations of resistive and capacitive loading. For capacitive loading,

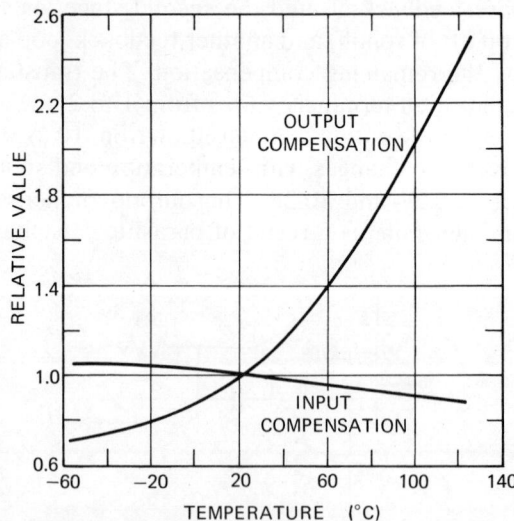

Figure 20.28. Compensation terminal impedance as a function of ambient temperature.

therefore, series compensation resistor R_2 should be used to isolate the output compensation from the load; the output-voltage swing is not significantly affected by this resistor since its value is only 50 Ω.

20.12 RECOMMENDED NETWORKS

The frequency-compensation networks used in a given application must provide stability for any μA709 selected from the full production distribution. The unit-to-unit variation of transfer resistance, open-loop voltage gain, and high-frequency phase shift must be taken into account, as well as the effects of temperature and power supply voltage. A design based on worst-case limits for each of these parameters, however, would be unnecessarily conservative since they are correlated to some degree in an integrated circuit. The change of gain with supply voltage, for example, is partially compensated for by a change in transfer resistance, and thus the closed-loop bandwidth is only slightly affected. Therefore, rather than having separate limits for each of these factors, it is better to consider the amplifier as a whole and specify the complete networks to be used to guarantee stability for the full distribution of units.

Figure 20.29 gives the networks recommended for frequency compensation of noninverting amplifiers with closed-loop gains of 0, 20, 40, and 60 dB, along with the frequency responses obtained using these networks; values for intermediate gains can be found by interpolation. For inverting

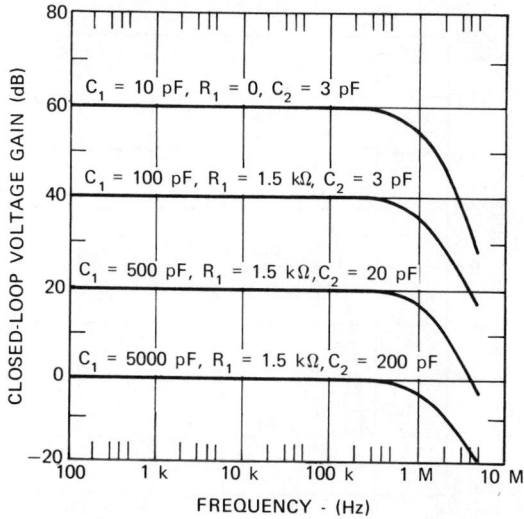

Figure 20.29. Closed-loop response using recommended compensation networks, $V_s = \pm 15$ V, $T_A = 25°$C.

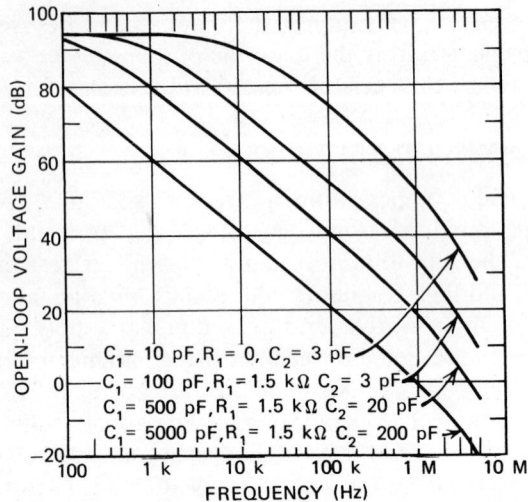

Figure 20.30. Open-loop response using recommended compensation networks, $V_s = \pm 15$ V, $T_A = 25°C$.

amplifiers the capacitor values should be divided by the factor $(1 + Rs/Rf)$ to obtain the same bandwidths. The bandwidth can be expected to vary from 0.4 to 1.8 MHz with less than 1 dB of peaking, depending on the particular unit. Figure 20.30 shows the corresponding open-loop frequency responses.

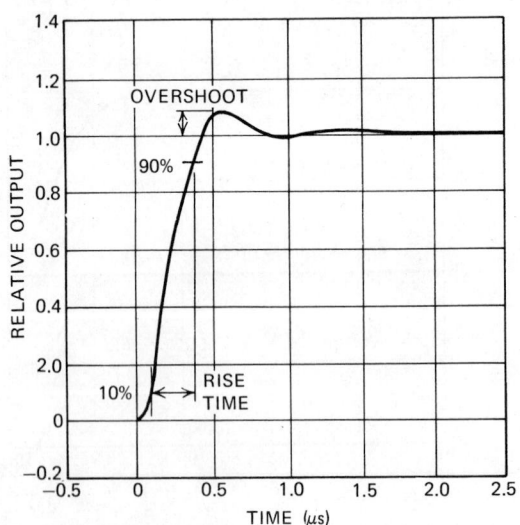

Figure 20.31. Transient response; $V_s = \pm 15$ V, $T_A = 25°C$.

A simple test that indicates both closed-loop bandwidth and stability of a circuit using the recommended compensation networks is the small-signal step-function response. The rise-time of the output step (Figure 20.31) is related to the bandwidth by the approximate formula:

$$\tau_r = \frac{0.35}{\text{BW}}, \tag{21.37}$$

and the overshoot is a measure of the stability. The effect of capacitive loading can also be included in the measurement. The significant advantage of transient-response testing is that the combined effect of all factors on stability is indicated by one easily made test, including any correlation between the parameters. Rise times for production units can range from 0.2 to 1.0 μs for closed-loop gains of 60 dB or less, and the overshoot will be less than 30% with 100-pF capacitive loading.

20.13 RATE LIMITING

The response of an operational amplifier to large changes in input signal is not as fast as might be expected from the small-signal bandwidth. This is due to the early rolloff in open-loop gain caused by the compensation networks. A large step change in signal forces the feedback to overdrive the input stage as it attempts to correct for the slow rise time of the frequency-compensated stages. The clipped signal is integrated by the

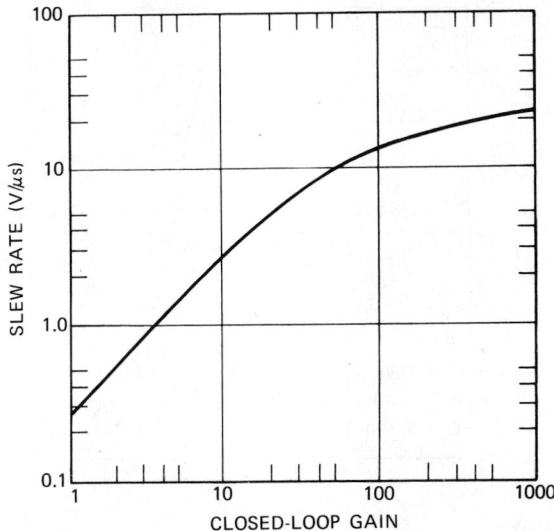

Figure 20.32. Slew rate as a function of closed-loop gain using recommended compensation networks; $V_s = \pm 15$ V, $T_A = 25°$C.

compensation capacitors, resulting in an output voltage that rises at a fixed rate. This rate limit, or slew rate, determines the speed with which the amplifier can respond to large signals. Figure 20.32 gives the slew rate of the μA709 as a function of closed-loop gain with the recommended compensation networks.

The maximum sine-wave output that can be handled at high frequencies is also limited by slewing. When the rate of change of voltage required from the amplifier exceeds the slew rate, the output amplitude begins to fall off, and the waveform becomes triangular. The peak undistorted sine-wave output that can be obtained at a given frequency is given by

$$V_p = \frac{\rho}{2\pi f} \tag{20.38}$$

where ρ is the slew rate in volts per microsecond and f is the frequency in megahertz. Curves of output-voltage swing as a function of frequency are shown in Figure 20.33 for various compensation networks.

20.14 SUPPLY VOLTAGE AND TEMPERATURE EFFECTS

All of the open-loop characteristics are functions of power-supply voltage and temperature. The correlation between the various parameters, however, is such that the closed-loop performance is not affected as much

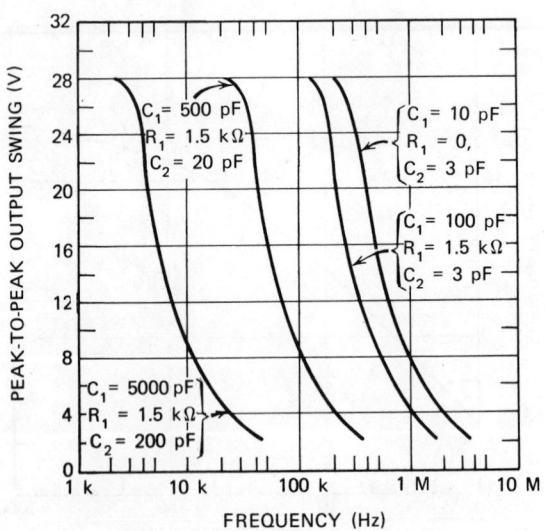

Figure 20.33. Output-voltage swing as a function of frequency for various compensation networks; $V_s = \pm 15$ V, $T_A = 25°C$, $R_L = 10$ kΩ.

as might be expected from the worst-case changes in individual open-loop parameters.

The relative change in closed-loop characteristics with supply voltage is shown in Figure 20.34. The decrease in open-loop voltage gain as the voltage goes from ±15 to ±9V is partially compensated by a corresponding decrease in input-compensation transfer resistance; as a result the closed-loop bandwidth changes less than 25%. The output-compensation transfer resistance is not appreciably affected by supply voltage.

The change in gain with temperature is also compensated for by the input transfer resistance, and so the closed-loop bandwidth varies only as the output transfer resistance. At −55°C the bandwidth is about 37% higher than its room-temperature value and decreases to 55% at +125°C, as shown in Figure 20.35 (both Figure 20.34 and 20.35 apply for closed-loop gains of 60 dB or less).

20.15 BASIC COMPARATOR APPLICATION

The basic circuit for using the μA710 comparator is shown in Figure 20.36*a*. A reference voltage between ±5 V is inserted on one input, and the signal is inserted on the other. When the input exceeds the reference voltage, the output switches either positive or negative, depending on how the inputs are connected. Figure 20.36*b* shows the general input-output characteristic.

The circuit has a variety of uses. It can be employed as a voltage comparator in analog-to-digital converters, in which one input is driven by the analog input signal and the other by a ladder network. It also has use as a tape or drum memory sense amplifier and threshold detector.

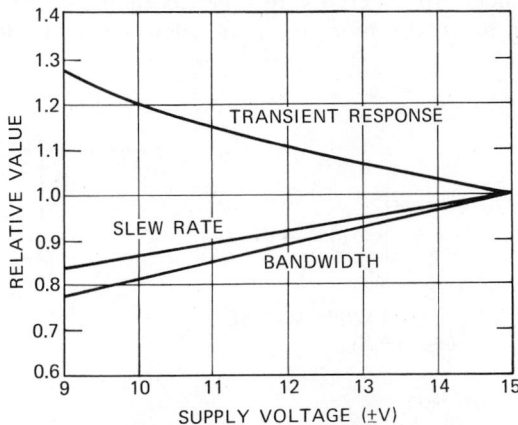

Figure 20.34.   Change of characteristics with supply voltage; $T_A = 25$°C.

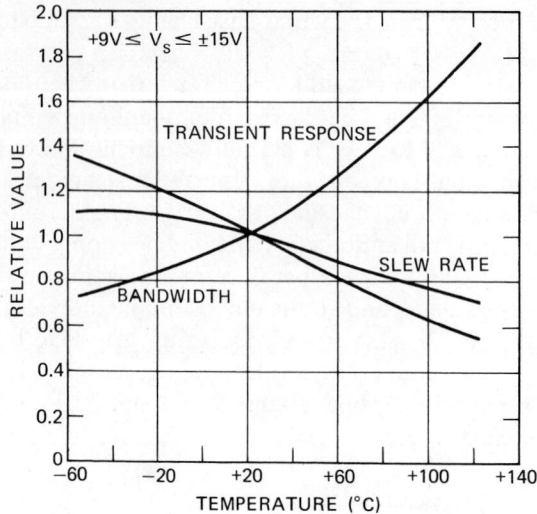

Figure 20.35. Change of characteristics with ambient temperature; $\pm 9\,\text{V} \leq V_s \leq \pm 15\,\text{V}$.

Other applications include a high-noise-immunity buffer for going from high-level logic into low-level integrated circuits or a pulse-shape restorer in digital circuits.

In order to achieve maximum accuracy in the circuit of Figure 20.36 the dc resistance of the signal source (R_s) should equal the source resistance of the reference voltage (R_1). When this is done, the bias currents of the two inputs produce nearly equal drops across these source resistances, which should be made as low as possible, preferably less than 200 Ω, for best performance. Any increase in offset is then due only to the offset current, which is usually more than an order of magnitude less than the bias current.

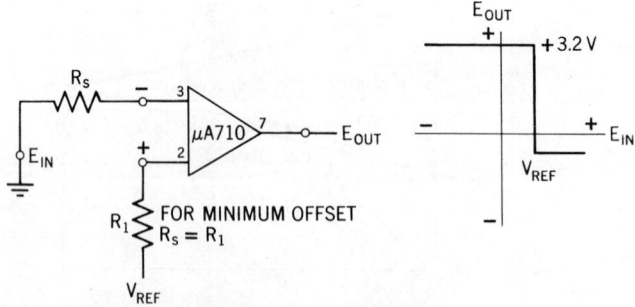

Figure 20.36. Basic level detector circuit and its transfer function.

Although the input-voltage range of the μA710 is ± 5 V, the maximum voltage between the inputs is also ± 5 V. If one of the inputs is at $+5$ V, for example, the other can only be driven as low as ground potential without exceeding the differential input-voltage limit. It is important to observe this maximum rating since exceeding the differential input-voltage limit and drawing excessive current in breaking down the emitter-base junctions of the input transistors could cause gross degradation in the input offset current and input bias current.

Exceeding the absolute maximum positive-input-voltage limit of the device ($+7$ V) will saturate the input transistor and possibly cause damage through excessive current. However, even if the current is limited to a reasonable value so that the device is not damaged, erratic operation can result. When the transistor on the inverting input saturates, for example, it no longer functions as an inverting amplifier stage; instead, it makes a direct connection between the input and the base of the second-stage transistor, so that the inverting input becomes a noninverting input. The negative limit of the input-voltage range is specified at -5 V, but it is necessary to increase the negative supply voltage to -7 V to ensure that the input-stage current source does not saturate at $-55°$C, causing improper operation.

Some attention to power-supply bypassing is required with the μA710. This device is a multistage amplifier with gain to several hundred megahertz. Long unbypassed supply leads or sloppy layouts can therefore cause oscillation problems. Bypassing with electrolytic or tubular paper capacitors is ineffective. What is recommended is that both the positive and negative supplies be bypassed to ground by using low-inductance, disk-ceramic capacitors (0.01 μF) located as close as practical to the device. A neat physical layout, keeping the input away from the output, is also important.

20.16 DOUBLE-ENDED LIMIT DETECTOR

The design of test equipment frequently calls for a circuit that will indicate when a voltage goes outside some present tolerance limits. The circuit in Figure 20.37, using a μA711 dual comparator, will accomplish this function. A lower limit voltage (V_{LT}) and an upper limit voltage (V_{UT}) are supplied to the dual comparator. When the input voltage exceeds the upper limit or drops below the lower limit, the output of the comparator swings positive and turns on the lamp driver. A feature of the circuit is that the limit detector can be disabled, when it is not being used, by grounding the strobe terminals. In addition, up to eight dual comparators can be wired with common outputs and used to feed a single lamp driver.

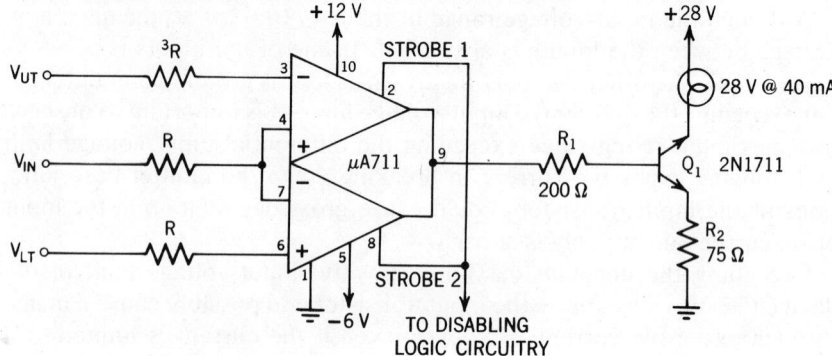

Figure 20.37.   Double-ended limit detector for automatic go/no-go test equipment.

The peak output current of the lamp driver is limited by R_2 while the bulb is turning on and the filament resistance is low; R_1 limits the output current of the comparator after the lamp driver saturates. To make the accuracy dependent on offset currents rather than bias currents the relative values of the source resistances for the signal and reference voltages should be as indicated on the schematic, and should be as low as possible.

BIBLIOGRAPHY

Operational Amplifiers, Parts I–IV, Analog Devices, Cambridge, Mass.

Handbook of Operational Amplifier Applications, Burr-Brown Research Corporation, Tucson, Ariz.

Handbook of Operational Amplifier Active RC Networks, Burr-Brown Research Corporation. Tucson, Ariz.

Review of Operational Amplifier Principles, Fairchild Instrumentation, Mountain View, Calif.

Applications Manual for Computing Amplifiers, Philbrick Researches, Inc., Dedham, Mass. Second Edition, Second Printing. (This publication also has an extensive bibliography on operational amplifiers.)

Nexus Notes, Nexus Research Laboratories, Inc. Canton, Mass.

Index